Accession no.
36183288

The Routledge Handbook of Events

The Routledge Handbook of Events explores and critically evaluates the debates and controversies associated with this rapidly expanding discipline. It brings together leading specialists from a range of disciplinary backgrounds and geographical regions, to provide state-of-the-art theoretical reflection and empirical research on the evolution of the subject. It is the first major study to examine what events is as a discipline in the twenty-first century, its significance in contemporary society and growth as a mainstream subject area.

The book is divided into five interrelated sections. Section 1 evaluates the evolution of events as a discipline and defines what Events Studies is. Section 2 critically reviews the relationship between events and other disciplines such as Tourism and Sport. Section 3 focuses on the management of events, Section 4 evaluates the impacts of events from varying political, social and environmental perspectives and Section 5 examines the future direction of growth in event-related education and research.

It offers the reader a comprehensive synthesis of this field, conveying the latest thinking and research. The text will provide an invaluable resource for all those with an interest in Events Studies, encouraging dialogue across disciplinary boundaries and areas of study.

Stephen J. Page formerly, Senior Professor of Sustainable Tourism Management at London Metropolitan University and now Professor of Tourism at Bournemouth University

Joanne Connell is a Lecturer in Tourism Management at Exeter University Business School.

The Routledge Handbook of Events

Edited by
Stephen J. Page and Joanne Connell

LIS LIBRARY

Date	Fund
6/7/15	bs-Che

Order No.	
2638228	

University of Chester	

Routledge
Taylor & Francis Group

LONDON AND NEW YORK

First published in paperback 2015
First published 2012
by Routledge
2 Park Square, Milton Park, Abingdon, Oxon OX14 4RN

And by Routledge
711 Third Avenue, New York, NY 10017

Routledge is an imprint of the Taylor & Francis Group, an informa business

© 2015 and 2012 Editorial matter and selection: Stephen J. Page and Joanne Connell;
individual chapters: the contributors.

The right of Stephen J. Page and Joanne Connell to be identified as the author of the editorial
material, and of the authors for their individual chapters, has been asserted in accordance with
sections 77 and 78 of the Copyright, Designs and Patents Act 1988.

All rights reserved. No part of this book may be reprinted or reproduced or utilised in any
form or by any electronic, mechanical, or other means, now known or hereafter invented,
including photocopying and recording, or in any information storage or retrieval system,
without permission in writing from the publishers.

Trademark notice: Product or corporate names may be trademarks or registered trademarks, and
are used only for identification and explanation without intent to infringe.

British Library Cataloguing in Publication Data
A catalogue record for this book is available from the British Library

Library of Congress Cataloging in Publication Data
Page, Stephen J.
  The Routledge handbook of events / Stephen J. Page and Joanne Connell.
    pages cm
  Includes bibliographical references and index.
  GT3405.P35 2014
  394.2–dc23

                                       2014025927

ISBN: 978-0-415-58334-3 (hbk)
ISBN: 978-1-138-83281-7 (pbk)
ISBN: 978-0-203-80393-6 (ebk)

Typeset in Bembo
by Taylor & Francis Books

MIX
Paper from
responsible sources
FSC® C013604
www.fsc.org

Printed and bound by CPI Group (UK) Ltd, Croydon, CR0 4YY

Contents

Contents

Contents

Illustrations

Tables

Figures

Plates

Acknowledgements

The editors' thanks are also extended to Emma Travis and Faye Leerink at Routledge for their help in the administration and production of the Handbook. We would also like to thank the Thomas Cook archive for the images reproduced in Chapter 1.

List of contributors

Paul Barron, Reader in Hospitality in the School of Marketing, Tourism and Languages at Edinburgh Napier University.

Pierre Benckendorff, Senior Lecturer, School of Tourism, University of Queensland, Queensland 4072, Australia.

Graham Berridge, Senior Lecturer, University of West London, London, UK.

Andrew Bradley, Course Leader for Event Management, University of Gloucestershire, Cheltenham, UK.

Robert Case, Associate Lecturer, Southampton Solent University, UK.

Joanne Connell, Lecturer in Tourism Management at Exeter University Business School.

Marg Deery, Professor, Tourism Research Cluster, School of Management, Curtin Business School, Curtin University, Perth Australia.

Larry Dwyer, Professor of Tourism, University of New South Wales, Australia.

Deborah Edwards, Senior Research Fellow, Leisure, Sport and Tourism, University of Technology, Sydney.

Graeme Evans, Director of the Cities Institute, London Metropolitan Business School, London, UK., and Professor of Culture and Urban Development, University of Maastricht.

Nicole Ferdinand, Senior Lecturer and Programme Director of the Events Management postgraduate programmes at London Metropolitan Business School, London, UK.

Warwick Frost, Course Director of the Bachelor of Business (Events Management) at La Trobe University, Melbourne, Australia.

Sean Gammon, Senior Lecturer, School of Sport, Tourism and the Outdoors, University of Central Lancashire, UK.

Donald Getz, School of Tourism, The University of Queensland, Brisbane, Australia and Norwegian School of Hotel Management, University of Stavanger; Visiting Professor at Mid-Sweden University, Bournemouth University, England, and Northwestern University, South Africa; Professor Emeritus at the University of Calgary; Adjunct Professor at the Haskayne School of Business, University of Calgary, Canada.

John R. Gold, Professor of Urban Historical Geography, Oxford Brookes University, Oxford, UK.

Margaret M. Gold, Senior Lecturer in Arts and Heritage Management, London Metropolitan Business School, London, UK.

C. Michael Hall, Professor in the Department of Management, University of Canterbury, New Zealand and School of Tourism and Hospitality Management, Southern Cross University, Australia; Docent, Department of Geography, University of Oulu, Finland; and Visiting Professor, Linneaus University, Kalmar, Sweden and Sheffield Business School, Sheffield Hallam University, UK.

Clare Hanlon, Senior Lecturer, Institute of Sport, Exercise and Active Living, Victoria University, Melbourne, Australia.

Leo Jago, Professor, University of Nottingham, UK.

Robert J. Johnston, Director, The George Perkins Marsh Institute and Professor, Department of Economics, Clark University, Worcester, MA, USA.

Anna Leask, Reader in Tourism in the School of Marketing, Tourism and Languages at Edinburgh Napier University.

Tom Lunt, Principal Lecturer in Learning and Teachnig, London Metropolitan Business School, London, UK.

Diane O'Sullivan, Senior Lecturer, University of Glamorgan, Pontypridd, Wales, UK.

Michael Pacione, Chair of Geography, University of Strathclyde, Glasgow, UK.

Stephen J. Page formerly, Senior Professor of Sustainable Tourism Management at London Metropolitan University and now Professor of Tourism at Bournemouth University

Philip L. Pearce, Foundation Professor of Tourism and Chair in Tourism, School of Business, James Cook University, Townsville, Queensland 4811, Australia.

J.R. Brent Ritchie, Chair, World Tourism Education & Research Centre; Professorship in Tourism Management, University of Calgary, Calgary, Alberta, Canada.

Martin Robertson, Lecturer in the School of International Business, Victoria University, Melbourne Australia.

Chris Ryan, Professor of Tourism, University of Waikato, New Zealand.

Katie Schlenker, Lecturer in the School of Leisure, Sport and Tourism at the University of Technology, Sydney.

Richard Sharpley, Professor of Tourism and Development, School of Sport, Tourism and the Outdoors, University of Central Lancashire, Preston, UK.

Stephen J. Shaw, Reader in Regeneration and City Management at the Cities Institute, London Metropolitan Business School University, London, UK.

Richard Shipway, Senior Lecturer, University of Bournemouth, UK.

Karen Smith, Senior Lecturer, Victoria Management School, Victoria University of Wellington, Wellington, New Zealand.

Robyn Stokes, Management Consultant and Principal of Stokes Strategy and Research, Alderley, Queensland, 4051, Australia.

Philip R. Stone, Senior Lecturer, School of Sport, Tourism and the Outdoors, University of Central Lancashire, UK.

Julia Tum, University Teacher Fellow, Leeds Metropolitan University, UK.

Timothy J. Tyrrell, Professor, School of Community Resources and Development, Arizona State University, Phoenix, Arizona, USA.

Kenneth Wardrop, Tourism and Brand Management Consultant and Visiting Research Fellow in the School of Marketing, Tourism and Languages, Edinburgh Napier University, UK.

Stephen Wearing, Associate Professor at the University of Technology, Sydney, Australia.

Mike Weed, Professor, Centre for Sport, Physical Education and Activity Research (SPEAR), Canterbury Christ Church University, UK.

Linda Wilks, Senior Lecturer in Event Management at the University of Hertfordshire, UK.

Nigel Williams, Senior Lecturer in Project Management in the Business Systems Department at the University of Bedfordshire, UK.

Allison Wylde, Director of the Security Industry Observatory, Course Leader MSc Project Management/Senior Lecturer in Business Analysis, London Metropolitan Business School, London, UK.

Ian Yeoman, Associate Professor, Victoria Management School, Victoria University of Wellington, Wellington, New Zealand.

Foreword

J. R. Brent Ritchie

I am delighted to have been asked to prepare this Foreword. However, I fear that both my interest and my expertise in relation to the topic of Event Studies is rather focused to have been accorded this honour. In brief, I have had an interest in the related areas of mega-event and hallmark events, dating from the beginning of my career – when my first major study was an attempt to evaluate the economic impact of the Quebec City Winter Carnival/Carnaval de Québec. Indeed, I was mildly astounded at the attention garnered by this study – and the fact that I immediately became an 'expert' in Tourism Studies – if only in my own mind. I insert this disclaimer since this initial foray into event research was also a most humbling experience. In particular, I learned a lot about the design of a data collection instrument intended for use in a major winter 'carnival' setting. More specifically, I learned that sophisticated questionnaire design (beautiful graphics and careful wording) have little effect on response rates when the instrument is to be completed by half-frozen liquor-fuelled respondents who have just returned to their hotel rooms after an evening of carnival revelling. In brief, I fail to comprehend why I was so surprised and disappointed in a 0.05 per cent response rate. All this to say that despite, or perhaps because of, this experience I owe a great debt to the field of Event Studies for launching me into a career in Tourism Studies/tourism management – a career which has, to date, spanned more than thirty years, and one which will, I hope, continue.

While the Quebec Winter Carnival study served as my launching pad into the world of tourism, it was a longitudinal study of the impact of the 1988 Olympic Winter Games on the international level of awareness and the image of the host city of Calgary, Alberta, Canada, that represents what I believe to be my most significant single contribution to the field of Event Studies. If I may be permitted, this study, which monitored the awareness/image impacts of the Games over nearly a ten-year period (from the day the Games were accorded to Calgary, in 1981, to over one year following the event, in 1989) was an exercise in dedication. Not only do I view this study (which has been termed 'pioneering' by the organisers of the 2010 Olympic Winter Games which were held in Vancouver) as my most significant contribution to the field of Event Studies – to the point where I am hopeful that it may even become a 'classic' – that is, a study that, while frequently referenced, is unlikely to be repeated. I make this statement not because of any particularly unique methodology, but rather because of the generous support I received from colleagues in over ten cities in Europe and ten cities in the United States. This generous and unstinting support was accorded over nearly a decade, in order to gather the data used to assess the impact of this mega-event and to measure the level of awareness of the host city over the duration of the study, as well as its image in each of the twenty cities. I can only imagine what the cost would be to replicate this study if data were to be collected using commercial research houses, given the nature and the significance of the results from this widely published series of 'OLYMPULSE' studies, which found that resident support for hosting the event remained steady at 90 per cent, and that awareness of the host city increased by over 400 per cent compared with the 'control' city of Edmonton, Alberta, located some 300 km to the north. In effect, then, the hosting of this one mega-event provided residents with a highly memorable once-in-a-lifetime experience, and in so doing raised their city from almost total obscurity, providing it with international legitimacy relative to its more mature 'sister city' to the north. This example of the extent to which one event can literally transform the stature of a city from a 'relatively unknown' to a recognised member of an elite international club of 'Olympic citie' is but one indication of the major role which events can play in enhancing the reputation of a destination – and, in so doing, contribute to the tourism appeal of the destination, thus helping to improve the long-term well-being of its residents. In summary, events are a proven vehicle for tourism development, for economic development and for community development. It follows that systematic study of the manner by which these different forms of development can be optimised to the benefit of destination residents is a logical means of seeking to better understand how best to design, develop, and deliver such events in order to derive the maximum benefits.

While mega-events certainly have the potential for creating the greatest economic and tourism impact, they also possess the greatest risk of failure – with the result that the host destination may see its reputation negatively rather than positively affected. In addition, although the organisers of certain mega-events wisely choose to involve volunteers, thus enhancing the social and cultural value of the mega-event, it is the many small events and festivals sponsored by large and small communities and destinations throughout the world that represent the true fabric of the events sector. These many local festivals and events reflect the underlying values and culture of the local residents of a destination – and, as such, significantly enhance the value and long-term impact of any mega-event that a destination may choose to develop and deliver.

It is with the foregoing background experience in mega-events clearly in mind that I am especially pleased to provide these few opening words of welcome to readers of this *Routledge Handbook of Events* – which I firmly believe will greatly strengthen and complement the existing literature on events. I refer most especially to such flagship contributions on the topic as those authored by my most respected scholar and friend, Dr Donald Getz (*Event Management and Event Tourism* (1997); and *Event Studies: Theory, Research and Policy for Planned Events* (2007)), as well as those by my colleague Dr Joseph Goldblatt (*Special Events: Global Event Management in the 21st Century* (2002)) and Dr C. Michael Hall (*Hallmark Tourist Events: Impacts, Management and Planning* (1992)).

While the foregoing textbooks on events have provided the most traditional perspectives on the field, the present work provides the field of Event Studies with yet another recognised approach to understanding a topic or field. I refer to the concept of the 'handbook' – a compendium of contributions to a field from a broad range of respected authors, each possessing expertise in given area. I have identified over sixty such handbooks of which some twenty pertain to tourism or one of its sub-fields of study. In this regard, allow me to selectively identify certain of these tourism handbooks as follows:

1 *The Sage Handbook of Tourism Studies* (Jamal and Robinson 2009)
2 *Handbook of Travel* (Allen 1918)

3 *Stats to Go: A Handbook for Hospitality, Leisure and Tourism Studies* (Buglear 2000)
4 *Oceania: A Tourism Handbook* (Cooper and Hall 2005)
5 *International Handbook on the Economics of Tourism* (Dyer and Forsyth 2006)
6 *The ATTT Tourism Education Handbook* (The Tourism Society 1997)
7 *The 2002 Travel and Leisure Market Research Handbook* (Miller and Associates 2002)
8 *Regional Tourism Handbooks* (Hall and Cooper 2000)
9 *The Tourism Development Handbook* (Godfrey and Clarke 2000)
10 *North America: A Tourism Handbook* (Fennel 2006)
11 *Handbook on Tourism Destination Branding* (ETC-UNWTO 2009)
12 *Successful Event Management: A Practical Handbook* (Shone and Parry 2001)
13 *The 2002 Hotel and Lodging Market Research Handbook* (Walter Consulting 2002)
14 *Handbook for Distance Learning in Tourism* (Williams 2005)
15 *Tourism Marketing and Management Handbook* (Witt and Moutinho 1989)
16 *Tourism at World Heritage Cultural Site: The Site Manager's Handbook* (UNWTO 1993)
17 *Shining in the Media Spotlight: A Communications Handbook for Tourism Professionals* (UNWTO 1995)
18 *Handbook on Natural Disaster Reduction in Tourist Areas* (UNWTO 1998)
19 *Tourism Signs and Symbols: A Status Report and Handbook* (UNWTO 2001)
20 *Handbook on Tourism Congestion Management at Natural and Cultural Sites* (UNWTO 2003)

A final example of such works is my *Handbook of Travel, Tourism and Hospitality Research* (Ritchie and Goeldner 1994). Because such handbooks provide both academics and practitioners with a carefully developed collection of materials focused on a range of subjects designed to provide both a comprehensive overview of the field and an in-depth examination of topics judged to be a critical component of the total knowledge in the field addressed by the handbook in question, they often become one of the most highly valued references in the field. The current *Routledge Handbook of Events* (RHE) demonstrates once more the value of the handbook concept. As an examination of the table of contents of this Handbook will reveal, the thirty-three chapters which have been contributed to the RHE represent the best thinking of well-established tourism scholars as well as some of the newer ideas springing from the minds of what may be termed 'emerging' scholars. True to the tradition of existing handbooks, the content of the present RHE covers definitional, disciplinary, conceptual, methodological, managerial and future-oriented topics. The end product is a reference document which I believe will very quickly become the initial source of guidance for both researchers and practitioners in the field of events management as they seek to better understand the field and to improve their effectiveness in event management. Having prepared a handbook myself, I am aware of the tremendous effort involved in providing such a key reference document. As such, all of us owe a great debt of gratitude to Stephen Page and Joanne Connell. This said, and while I know they will do so, I would ask all who have the opportunity to benefit from this Handbook to convey their appreciation to Stephen and Joanne.

Preface

Stephen J. Page and Joanne Connell

According to Getz (2008: 403), the growth of Events Studies in recent years has been 'spectacular', as destinations realise the potential of events to raise their profile in an ever-increasing competitive global tourism industry. The volume and range of events and festivals around the world at any one time has reached overwhelming levels. In any one year, a number of large-scale events of international significance take place, attracting large numbers of participants and spectators, along with their associated entourages – one only has to think of peripatetic mass sporting events (such as Olympic Games, Commonwealth Games and World Cup events), one-off celebratory events (such as the Queen's Golden Jubilee held in London in 2003) and annual sporting, artistic, cultural or other events (such as Wimbledon tennis championships, European City of Culture or Glastonbury Music Festival). Particularly marked is the growth in niche events, such as local festivals and themed festivals, often initiated at the community level and sometimes with the support of the public sector in an attempt to pump-prime such activity, leveraging it as a potential economic development tool. Subsequently, by far the most numerous types of events are those which operate at this smaller scale and reflect local or regional interests and identities, and there are undoubtedly tens of thousands of these kinds of events in any one year. The remarkable growth in activity, the increasing investments witnessed in the mega-events sector, the expansion of the events industry and the implications of this multifaceted phenomenon have become a topic of major and increasing interest for academic study.

There has been a massive explosion in taught undergraduate, postgraduate and PhD students since the late 1980s worldwide focusing on event themes. In the UK, there are over sixty single honours degree courses in event management alone, with an expanding provision at postgraduate level in institutions across the UK. Most of these courses have been established in the last seven years, indicating the rapid growth and high demand for such courses. For example, many 'old' and 'new' universities have seen this as a new key growth area following on from the boom in Sports Studies, which has now plateaued. This subject specialism has emerged as a hybrid replacement, blending Sport, Tourism and Leisure Studies. In the USA and Australia the supply of university-level Events courses is abundant. In addition to this most courses in Tourism or Sport have a module or specialism in Events Tourism, and this does not include those non-Tourism programmes that also focus on this from a business or management perspective.

The recent growth of interest in events has led to an increased demand for textbooks and other reference works for both students and experts. But to date, there is no reference work which maps out the current status and future direction for Events Studies as a mainstream subject.

The *Routledge Handbook of Events* aims to explore and critically evaluate the debates and controversies inherent to Events Studies. It brings together commissioned essays from leading specialists aiming to provide critical reviews and appraisals of the current state of the art in the field. All the contributors are active researchers or teachers in the field and so bring together a wide range of knowledge and experience which informs this collection of essays on events. It will offer the reader an overview of this field, conveying the latest thinking and research in an accessible way. The text will provide an invaluable resource for all those with an interest in Events Studies, encouraging dialogue across disciplinary boundaries and areas of study.

Rationale and aims

This book builds upon the editors' recent successful development of *Event Tourism*, Routledge Major Works series (Connell and Page 2010), which was the first major reference work in the field of Event Studies. It also builds upon the growth during the 1990s of the publication of a number of seminal books (e.g. Hall 1992; Getz 1997) and papers in the top peer-reviewed social science journals which raised the profile and developed a burgeoning research agenda. The advancement of understanding has, as Getz (2008) argues, a long way to go. This is reflected in the fact that a wide range of niche texts have been published on these themes, but there have been virtually no reference works (excluding Connell and Page 2010) that have mapped out the evolution of the subject. It is therefore pertinent for the research community in events research to examine a defined market niche for a Handbook that is able to provide that retrospective synthesis and look forward by creating a review of the research agendas pertinent to this fast-expanding subject within social science and business and management studies.

Aims for the Handbook

The Handbook is designed to achieve a number of specific aims:

- To encourage a greater multidisciplinary debate among leading scholars in the field of Event Studies and to synthesise these diverse debates in a rational and logical framework which advances understanding and knowledge of the subject area.
- To engage with the diverse range of subject specialists that are now working in the broad domain of Event Studies so as to help map out the academic landscape, further exploring the interconnections of social science with event research.
- To disseminate the current and future development of the subject area to a wider audience than is currently occurring in a number of specialist journals and texts.
- To fill the gap in the market for a major synthesis of the subject which can be used in teaching and research.

To facilitate these aims the book has assembled a specific international editorial board who have reviewed the chapters and treated them as peer review essays seeking to contribute to the critical debates on the subject area. The international editorial board consisted of the following individuals who have made a major contribution to helping shape this innovative publication:

Dr Joanne Connell, Exeter University Business School, UK
Professor Alan Fyall, Bournemouth University, Bournemouth, UK

Ms Nicole Ferdinand, London Metropolitan University, London, UK
Professor Donald Getz, University of Calgary, Canada
Professor C. Michael Hall, University of Canterbury, Christchurch, New Zealand
Professor Tom Hinch, University of Alberta, Canada
Professor Stephen J. Page, London Metropolitan University, London, UK
Professor J. Brent Ritchie, University of Calgary, Canada
Dr Steve Shaw, London Metropolitan University, London, UK
Professor Rhodri Thomas, Leeds Metropolitan University, Leeds, UK
Professor Mustaffer Uysal, Virginia Tech, Blacksburg, Virginia, USA

We would like to show our appreciation to each of the aforementioned people who have been very generous in the time they have devoted to providing very detailed feedback alongside the editorial work, as this has acted not only as a quality control but also as a critique of the work to ensure it is informed by current debates and thinking in the field. The balance of essays in the collection reflects the very diverse scope of the subject area and the editors' desire to allow authors greater scope to pursue issues in depth, rather than limit the contributions to very short pieces that are typical of edited books.

We hope you will enjoy using and reading this book and that it helps stimulate thinking and debates on the subject area.

Stephen J. Page and Joanne Connell
January 2011

References

Connell, J. and Page, S.J. (eds) (2010) *Event Tourism: Critical Concepts in Tourism*, four-volume collection, London: Routledge.
Getz, D. (1997) *Event Management and Event Tourism*, New York: Cognizant.
——(2008) 'Event tourism: definition, evolution, and research', *Tourism Management* 29(3): 403–28.
Hall, C.M. (1992) *Hallmark Tourist Events: Impacts, Management and Planning*, London: Belhaven.

1

Introduction

Stephen J. Page and Joanne Connell

Introduction to events

Events have been an important part of society since time immemorial. However, over the last few decades, the volume, range, meaning and significance of events and festivals around the world has grown particularly rapidly. Every year, a number of large-scale events of international significance take place, attracting large numbers of participants and spectators, along with their associated entourages, huge media interest and 'armchair' spectators: one only has to think of roving mass sporting events (such as the Olympic and Commonwealth Games, the World Cup); one-off celebratory events (such as Millennium Night across the world (1999/2000) and the Queen's Golden Jubilee (2002) held in London); and annual sporting, artistic, musical, cultural or other events (such as the Tour de France, European City of Culture and the Edinburgh Military Tattoo). Such events are designed to be of great importance to the destinations within which they take place, and the competitive bidding processes that governments enter into in order to secure a global event for their nation clearly indicates the growing credence attached to hosting events on the international stage. In parallel to these events of global significance has been a marked growth in niche events, such as local and/or themed festivals, often initiated at the community level and sometimes with the support of the public sector in an attempt to pump-prime such activity, leveraging it as a potential economic development tool. This array of event phenomena makes its study and analysis fascinating, relevant and a marker of not just changing political and economic agendas but also a changing consumer society.

Accordingly, research on events has been embraced by social science and developed into a distinct, multifarious and innovative area of intellectual inquiry. The emergence and expansion of academic interests in event-related themes, in part, reflects the transformations occurring across global society and the relationship, role and meaning of events within the processes of social, cultural, political and economic development and change. The various rationales developed for global, large or 'mega' events are multi-faceted, often complex and frequently controversial, creating openings for applied and academic research activity to assist the understanding of processes, relationships and impacts. What is also frequently overlooked is that events are not a new phenomenon in society, since their development for mass audiences and to achieve different political and social objectives is evident from mega-events such as the Great Exhibition of 1851 and the hosting of the Olympic Games in the late nineteenth century (see Plates 1.1 and 1.2) Therefore, while events research is comparatively recent, the interest and development of events is far from a new phenomenon. The burgeoning events research agenda has grown in relation to the emphasis placed on global processes that continue to stimulate interests in event bidding, development, hosting and staging. At local levels, concerns about conserving and celebrating traditions, culture and customs, and developing sustainable forms of tourism and leisure, are strong features in both developing competitive destinations and strengthening community relations, all of which are key areas for those engaged in the social sciences. Clearly, events have become a major theme within Tourism, Sport, Leisure and Hospitality research

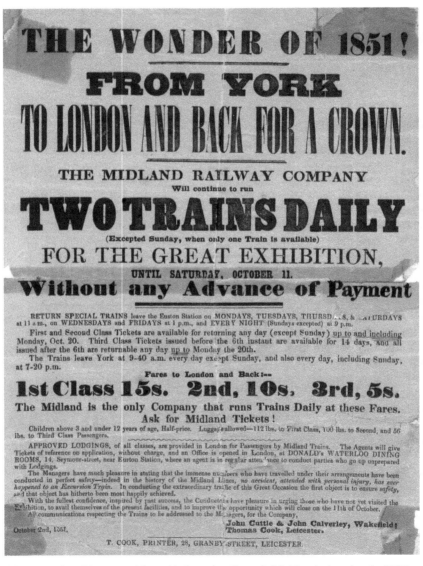

Plate 1.1 Poster advertising travel from York to the Great Exhibition in London in 1851

OLYMPIC GAMES AT ATHENS.

5th—15th of April, 1896 (24th March—3rd April, Greek Calendar).

Under the Presidency of H.R.H. the CROWN PRINCE OF GREECE.

The International Committee for the Re-union of Olympic Games at Athens in 1896 having placed in our hands all the necessary official arrangements, not only in respect of the journey from different countries of Europe to Athens, but as regards the accommodation of visitors in Athens, we take this opportunity of publishing the following Itineraries of Routes.

ROUTE.	SINGLE JOURNEY.		RETURN.	
	1st Class.	2nd Class.	1st Class.	2nd Class.
LONDON AND PARIS TO ATHENS.	£ s. d.	£ s. d.	£ s. d.	£ s. d.
*London, Dover, Calais, Paris, Marseilles, Messageries Maritimes, "Syrian" Line steamers to Athens	15 0 3	10 10 0	18 9 6	12 16 6
*London, Dieppe, Paris, as above	13 17 9	9 15 9	16 18 6	11 12 9
*London, Southampton, Paris, as above	13 17 0	9 15 0	16 11 6	11 7 3
Paris, etc., as above	12 3 0	8 10 3	13 14 6	9 6 6

*If from Marseilles by "Constantinople" steamer: 1st Class Single, £3 1s. 8d. ; 1st Class Return, £1 12s. less than above.

ROUTE.	1st Class.	2nd Class.	1st Class.	2nd Class.
London, Dover, Calais, Laon, Bale, St. Gothard, Milan, Bologna, Foggia, Brindisi steamer to Patras, rail to Athens	15 5 0	10 14 0	23 5 0	16 10 0
London, Dover, Calais, Paris, Turin, Genoa, Naples, as above	16 3 0	11 4 3	24 0 6	17 1 9
London, Dieppe, Paris, as above	15 0 6	10 10 3	22 9 0	15 18 0
London, Southampton, Paris, as above	14 19 9	10 9 6	22 2 0	15 12 3
Paris, etc., as above	13 6 0	9 4 9	19 5 3	13 11 6
London, Dover, Ostend, Bale, St. Gothard, Milan, Bologna, Foggia, Brindisi, as above	15 0 0	10 15 6	22 8 6	16 0 0
London, Queenboro', Flushing, as above	15 1 0	10 12 0	22 15 9	16 1 0
Paris, Bale, and as above	12 8 0	8 12 6	18 14 9	13 4 6
London, Harwich, Antwerp, Brussels, Luxemburg, Bale, St. Gothard, Milan, as above	14 12 6	10 6 6	22 11 6	15 19 9

We have also arranged Itineraries and Fares from a large number of British and Continental Cities, full particulars of which will be found in the Special Programme we have issued, and which can be obtained at any of our Offices.

SPECIAL CONDUCTED

TOUR TO ATHENS,

Leaving LONDON, Tuesday, March 24th, 1896.

26 Days' Tour - Fare 30 Guineas (2nd Class).

For full particulars of this Tour and also of Independent Tickets see Special Programmes, to be obtained at any of our Offices.

Chief Office—LUDGATE CIRCUS, LONDON.

Plate 1.2 Extract from the Thomas Cook Excursionist monthly brochure advertising travel to the 1896 Olympic Games in Athens

literature, and as an area of curriculum and programme development for universities and other education providers globally, with a burgeoning cohort of graduates, post-graduates and event professionals with event-specific qualifications.

The purpose of this introductory chapter is threefold: first, to set out the role of *The Handbook of Events* and to outline its contribution to the understanding of events in an academic research perspective; second, to establish the broad context for academic research in the events field, particularly in relation to understanding the role, diversity, role and significance of events in contemporary society; and third, to outline the chapters that form the basis of the Handbook, highlighting the subjects covered and the significance of each to academic research and progression of Event Studies. So, first, a brief explanation of what this new Handbook seeks to achieve now follows.

A rationale for *The Routledge Handbook of Events*

The diversity of research in this field (including the journal literature) makes a collection timely, in so far as the major subject areas in social science have contributed to its development and growth as outlined by Getz (2008) and in considerably more depth by Connell and Page's (2010) collection of influential studies in the field. A Handbook is a very useful tool in any subject area to reflect on progress in the subject, particularly in key themes, to assess how far it has come and what type of journey it may follow in the future. It is a key tool to identify debates, methods of analysis and the way the academy of researchers is approaching a specific research agenda.

The thematic scope of the events research agenda has not been mapped in any great detail to date, and the absence of an interdisciplinary synthesis means that a range of approaches, theories, concepts, themes and research agendas exist in a fragmented vacuum. No textbooks can adequately address these themes as many are written from a disciplinary perspective (e.g. geography, planning, management, economics, sociology and political science) and are aimed at undergraduate audiences primarily. The literature is also quite fragmented across a wide range of subject-specific and interdisciplinary journals and books. While much research on events is published within the broad Tourism, Hospitality, Sport and Leisure subject area, significant research interests exist outside this arena, as Connell and Page (2010) highlight. Further, and in common with other emerging research subjects, a problem that events research has suffered is that all too often, as the chapters within this book will show, the notion of 'events' has been conveniently pigeon-holed into different sub-areas of expanding subjects such as Leisure, Tourism and Sports Studies. As such, much of this literature is disparate and scattered across different subject areas. *The Routledge Handbook of Events* seeks to bring together much of this interdisciplinary knowledge in one place for the first time. For this reason, the scope and scale of the Handbook at twice to three times the normal length of a textbook embraces the interdisciplinarity associated with the development of Event Studies and the associated event management focus. However, some researchers have argued that events now exists as a defined area of study in its own right, reflecting its growth and evolution (see Chapter 2 by Getz for more discussion).

Accordingly, *The Routledge Handbook of Events* is an attempt to produce a state-of-the-art review of the field of events research. It aims to document current progress in research, seeking to provide a debate around the key concepts, themes, approaches and paradigms now firmly established within the field of study. At this crucial juncture in the development of events as an academic subject, the role of this Handbook is to present a synthesis of the research activity at a more conceptual and theoretical level, where issues of methodology, new approaches and established research areas are reviewed by researchers working in the field. Priorities, influences, debates and challenges are evaluated, analysed and discussed, clearly depicting the status of event research and its future directions, by experts in the field.

The Handbook is unlikely to be a comprehensive compendium of all the possible dimensions and issues within the domain of events management and studies, given the wide-ranging practitioner focus occurring alongside the academic analysis of events. The Handbook does not set out to be a 'check-list' style text: the leading textbooks in the subject currently perform this function well (e.g. Bowdin *et al.* 2010). Further, this Handbook does not seek to follow the operational issues dealt with in many manuals and texts now appearing to guide the event manager (e.g. Conway 2009) and thematic studies of specific issues such as risk (e.g. Silvers 2007) and more overarching studies of operational issues (e.g. Tum *et al.* 2005). Within these studies it is evident that event managers have wide-ranging briefs that can cover the development of the event and issues such as the site, budgeting and finance, procurement, the supply chain and technical issues alongside legal and safety issues (e.g. see Health and Safety Executive 1999). At the event many technical issues associated with logistics, the staging of the event and its organisation are also within the remit of event management (see Matthews 2008a, 2008b). Specific issues within the wider management remit that have not been developed in the Handbook but that are dealt with elsewhere include visitor management, crowd management and the role of queuing, managing the transport provision and infrastructure. Instead, this Handbook seeks to understand the macro processes underlying and propelling events in a global context.

Macro processes and the growth of event research

The evolution of Event Studies closely parallels the debates in social science about how society has evolved from an industrial to post-industrial stage and the associated discourse. Events reflects a range of established and emergent social, economic, political and cultural transformations. One of the most profound social changes affecting tourism and leisure (including its worldwide commodification and analysis as a form of consumption under the aegis of events), is the process of *globalisation* (see Table 1.1 for a summary of the main changes and impacts). Globalisation has created a world stage for events through the growth of event destinations and internationalisation of events via enhanced media and digital forms of transmission, sometimes resulting in audiences (actual and virtual) of millions. In fact, Plate 1.3 is an example of one of the early globalised events – the Coronation of Queen Elizabeth II in 1953, which was not only a major event in London, attracting dignitaries from all across the world, but was a televised event that extended the reach of the event to many unable to attend the event in person. Therefore, some of the very early elements of globalisation and the impact of the media in televising major events can be seen in this one example. Yet, as Table 1.1 also suggests, a number of processes occurring within the umbrella term 'globalisation', and outcomes of this international growth, impact upon the way events are created, perceived and consumed.

Progressive increases in education levels, affluence and living standards have proven to be significant influences on the idea of leisure and tourism consumption, stimulating knowledge and interest in a wider range of opportunities and placing greater demands for leisure and tourism experiences. As Page and Connell (2010) argue, events have been a major focus of these consuming experiences since they reflect a shift and growth in the range of leisure preferences as a consequence of macro processes of change which have (re)shaped the way we view and consume leisure in contemporary society.

As Table 1.1 indicates, globalisation has produced a series of international processes transforming our lives, especially in how we use our leisure time and in what we choose to do outside of the home (Page and Connell 2010). Consequently it is not surprising that globalisation is accepted as one of the most important contributors to the global rise of events as a form

Table 1.1 Major impacts upon leisure as a result of globalisation

	Impact	Effects
1	Globalisation of the economy	Goods, services, labour and capital investment now move around the world more freely in a 'borderless world'. Leisure goods are available on a global rather than regional basis.
2	Dematerialisation and digitisation of the economy	In material terms, goods are produced in low-cost locations to be sold globally (e.g. Nike sportswear). Companies produce for global markets and innovation/cost reduction and distribution chains distribute leisure goods globally. The rise of 'entertainment' or an 'experience' economy has arisen in leisure, where time, experiences and the value added in the experience consumed is key, epitomised by events.
3	Transnational corporations dominate leisure production	Large corporations operating globally (e.g. BSkyB, Disney and McDonald's) now have a major impact on our consumption of leisure time.
4	Global organisations such as the UN, World Trade Organization and EU policies have a major impact on the nation-state	Many nation-states have lost control over the direction of development of their leisure economies and now compete with each other to attract global capital investment to develop leisure industries.
5	Time–space compression in our daily lives	The rise of the virtual and non-virtual 24-hour society, cheap transport (low-cost carriers) and expansion of the internet has meant everything is readily available or easily accessible via transport and personal forms of mobility.
6	The rise of a network society	Our lives are now more connected than ever before with global events, through media, work, better education and technology. A defining feature of leisure consumption is the amassing of 'cultural capital' (i.e. the cultural value we derive from social and leisure experiences) which are now highly individualised.
7	Labour (work) and leisure have become blurred and de-differentiated	The rise of 'serious leisure', the blurring of holiday-making with work and working at home have eroded the distinction between work and leisure.
8	An abundance of 'leisure choices'	Our participation in a 'connected world' opens up boundless opportunities for leisure which are limited by our ability to fit them into our lives. Daily life is not a simple concept, with defined roles in a household and traditional distinctions. Instead, accommodating leisure choices is a complex process for many households, especially those who perceive they are time-poor but cash-rich.

Source: Developed from van der Poel (2006: 99–101) in Page and Connell (2010: 86).

of leisure consumption. Debates over globalisation, such as the recent review by Ashworth and Page (2011), illustrate how the wide-ranging globalisation processes have led places to position themselves to display their distinctive attributes at a local level to create a competitive appeal to visitors through events and festivals. Not surprisingly, the corresponding growth in event tourism, as Getz (2008: 403) argues, has been nothing short of 'spectacular', as destinations realise

Plate 1.3 Brochure advertising global travel to London during the Coronation Year, 1953

the potential of events to raise their profile in an ever-increasing competitive global tourism industry. To achieve such growth, organisations in the public and private sector have pursued organisational and place-based event strategies to achieve event development.

Event strategies

The development of event strategies by the public sector with the aim of 'attracting non-residents to the community with the expectation that their spending will contribute significantly to the local economy' (Long and Perdue 1990: 10) is a core principle in strategic event development. Thus, extensive public sector investment in many locations worldwide is justified on the premise that event-based development, particularly large-scale events of international significance, provides diverse benefits to the host area ranging from tangible elements like inward investment to more subjective outcomes such as improving civic pride. For organisations charged with economic development, the draw of events as a means of promoting destinations is based on the potential benefits to be derived from successful event strategies, namely to: develop and expand visitor markets; encourage repeat visits stimulated by a first-time visit to an event; increase off-peak appeal and reduce the problems of seasonality for the tourism industry; create new products and attractions, thereby expanding the destination portfolio; encourage visitors to spend more time and more money in a destination; and create an image and brand a destination, thus providing a stimulus for development in an embryonic tourism destination (or repositioning and re-imaging to fuel rejuvenation in a more mature market). Getz (1997) adds to this the importance of bringing a destination to life through events (described as 'animating it'), with the aim of connecting the attractions and tourism capacity to promote better utilisation. Essentially, the idea of building awareness and interest in a destination, adding value, generating economic benefits and improving the visitor experience are core elements of interest for all destination marketing organisations and subsequently, events have become of prime importance for those charged with developing tourism. Event development also supports and justifies public sector spend on destination infrastructure, environmental regeneration and social initiatives (Page and Connell 2009), which can assist in post-event local and community development.

In reality, and perhaps rather controversially, critics of the lead role and funding provided by the public sector have questioned the premise that events and festivals generate increased levels of tourism, or indeed meet stated wider objectives. In many cases, tourism is used as one justi-fication of a significant event proposal (alongside leisure capacity and improving cultural attractions) but there are several problems linked with this supposition. It is very difficult to measure the numbers of visitors to some events, unless there is a strict ticketing rule applied to entrance. As academic research and consultancy studies frequently show, evaluating the actual impacts of an event is a challenge, especially in circumstances where incomplete data and/or limited access to information that would help to corroborate the results of sample surveys and track visitor numbers and activity limits accurate assessment. For those seeking to assess the impact of an event in generating visits to a specific destination (e.g. one year city-based festi-vals), to suggest with any precision how many people had decided to visit as a direct result of an event is fraught with difficulties, given that some methodologies used to evaluate levels of visits and activity are decidedly problematic, e.g. number of hits on a promotional website, media coverage and hotel occupancy. The level of displacement of existing levels of tourism needs to be taken into consideration, as does the long-term effect on tourism, where in some cases a one- to two-year timeframe is as much as a destination might expect in terms of increased tourism numbers. Further, there are very few examples of large-scale events that have created profit, and in most cases a significant loss is generated which must be met by public sector funds (see Crompton 2006). Public bodies justify these costs given their perception of desirable returns across a wide spectrum and, as Gold and Gold (2005) argue, city-based mega-event objectives are easily moulded to political, social and economic agendas of host destinations. Underlying objectives and goals to develop the event capacity and attributes of the place (i.e. its culture) as a differentiating feature given the global competition for visitors have undoubtedly become a key area of interest for political and economic stakeholders, as discussed in the next section. One of the principal features used in the process of event development by destinations, especially cities, has been the way in which culture has been harnessed as a basis for event development.

Culture, event development and the eventful city

A recent synthesis by Richards and Palmer (2010) of the role of culture and creativity has examined its use as means of adding meaning to cultural events and the event experience in cities. Richards and Palmer (2010) identify three models that have influenced the way urban places have used culture and events to develop a competitive edge in the post-industrial society. These models examined *the entrepreneurial city*, *the creative city* and *the intercultural city* as explanations of how events have been embraced as a tool to revitalise and develop an event portfolio that has helped to transform the place's unique appeal to complement the existing tourism and cultural infrastructure. As Richards and Palmer (2010) suggest, globalisation processes have created cities as places of cultural globalisation and so events perform a vital role as an intangible element of the culture of cities through the differentiated experiences available to visitors and residents. The first approach, characterised by urban managerialism and entrepreneurialism (the entrepreneurial city) has traditionally linked the public funding of events to cultural outputs such as European City of Culture. The state has been a key stakeholder and facilitator of the event development process to fund the initiatives with other partners to deliver a defined event strategy. This has been a clear element of the cultural strategies that cities have pursued in this model to give places symbolic culture. The second model, defined as the creative city, has moved on from the entrepreneurial model to embrace a wider range of attributes around events so that design, the expanding cultural industries and cultural amenities contribute to a wider concept of liveable cities. These ideas are embodied in key studies such as Landry's (2000) *creative city* and other landmark studies such as Florida's (2002) *creative class*, where lifestyle features alongside urban entertainment and cultural infrastructure to attract the creative class. In this model, intra-urban competition for visitors and the creative class moves us from a simple commercialisation of the city assets, such as its heritage. The creative class, it is argued, alongside the clustering of the cultural industries, gives the city its competitive edge and ability to attract the high-profile cultural events. The last model, the intercultural city, offers a comparatively new approach to event development based on the notion of a growing global diaspora associated with processes of globalisation. It results from a diversity of ethnic groups now living in major cities across the globe and creates an extensive range of cultural resources which event organisers can draw upon in seeking to portray the intercultural appeal of specific places. In fact, the analysis by Richards and Palmer (2010) demonstrates that events are far more than 'indispensable product alternatives for many destinations' (Dimanche 2008: 173) adding to the attractiveness of the destination: they are a more profound element of the destination's rationale if one engages with the theoretical debates which Richards and Palmer (2010) outline. This growing theorisation of events in post-modern society also provides a strong case for a Handbook that is able to elevate the level of critical academic debate and analysis. This is important given the predominance of the case study approach and descriptive level of much events research published in academic journals in its early and expansive phases as well as in many other professional outlets. As a benchmark, it might be argued that event research area is almost twenty years behind the state of mainstream Tourism or Sport research in terms of the methodological, theoretical and conceptual development. Interestingly, this Handbook has a series of case studies in every chapter at the insistence of the publisher, reflecting the dominance of this mode of analysis in Event Studies as a basis to provide in-depth examples of specific themes. Despite this publisher requirement (not the editors' preference), the authors maintain their criticisms that event research is typically a descriptive subject area which is a function of its early evolution and reliance upon case studies as a basis for such discussion, perpetuated by the tension between a practical focus and the pursuit of intellectual development by academic researchers.

Table 1.2 A city with events versus the eventful city

A city with events	The eventful city
Sectoral	Holistic
Tactical	Strategic
Reactive	Proactive
A container of events	A generator of events
Ad hoc	Coordinated
Competition	Cooperation
Pandering to audiences	Provoking publics
Left-brain thinking	Right-brain thinking
Event policy	Events as a policy tool
Market-led	Market leader
City marketing	City-making
Spectacle	Involvement

Source: Richards and Palmer (2010: 43).

Table 1.3 Event development strategies

Generic strategies	Specific strategies
Growing events	Organic growth
	Harnessing the creative 'life force' of a city
Creating events	Creating new events
	Commissioning artworks as events
Rejuvenation	Rejuvenating existing events
	Rejuvenating tradition
Bidding for events	Footloose recurrent events
	Enticing events from other cities
Emulation and copying	Franchising existing events
Meeting political objectives	Determined by political interests

Source: Richards and Palmer (2010: 54).

Debates and arguments over how events have been used at a strategic level to leverage economic development goals reflect the shift which Richards and Palmer (2010) described from a city with events to one which was an eventful city, as depicted in Table 1.2. Here, the whole issue of events assumes a more integrated and holistic position in the way cities approach the event–city relationship that revolves around the development of an effective stakeholder network, the development of a strategic vision for events and the creation of a programme of events and the effective marketing of events to a variety of publics and audiences (i.e. visitors) alongside effective monitoring and evaluation of the outcomes and a greater focus on sustainability (Richards and Palmer 2010). This requires the public sector as principal drivers of event development to shift from more generic to more event-led strategies to develop their event potential (Table 1.3), where many strategies may be deployed concurrently in the eventful city. One ambition of the eventful city is its strategic goal to extend the tourist season, thereby addressing issues of seasonality in its visitor economy, marking the shift towards what Richards and Palmer (2010) call *the festivalisation of places* such as Edinburgh with an all-year-round events programme (see also Prentice and Andersen 2003). This is also part of a much more fundamental shift in the economy of many post-industrial cities, with the economic realignment from a productive economy to one based on consumption and a greater development of spaces in the city for performative uses. Indeed, the pursuit of highly developed festival and event economies sitting alongside the growth in its night-time economy with a dominant focus on entertainment and leisure consumption epitomises the eventful city. The implementation of eventful strategies also requires a clear understanding of the leadership, resources and spaces within cities to create these event experiences, which need the creative use of the resources, culture and place to develop meaning and value in the experience which people now seek from events in a 24-hour society.

Yet by far the most numerous types of events are those which operate at the smaller scale and reflect local or regional interests and identities, and there are undoubtedly tens of thousands of these kinds of events in any one year. These are less visible than the globalised mega-event but nevertheless important at a local scale. With this dichotomy to the fore, it is a valuable point in the chapter to consider what events actually are and how they might be defined, conceptualised and understood.

Events: what are they and why are they important?

Events and event-based tourism are not new ideas, as an historical appreciation shows that the celebration of special occasions, and the idea of travelling to a place away from home to engage in festivities, is a practice common since ancient times, remaining deeply embedded within social, cultural and religious beliefs and customs, as well as economic and community tasks and activities. Further to this, Bergmann (1999) argues that societies and individuals define themselves through spectacle, a concept which underpins the whole concept of festivals and events. In the context of events, the notion of spectacle can be conceptualised as:

> any form of public display put on for the entertainment and benefit of a large crowd of spectators. It is created by consciously manipulating space, landscape or objects to produce displays that draw a powerful emotional response from an audience ... in the open air, in an enclosed auditorium, or some mixture of the two. It may appeal to several senses, but remains predominantly visual.
>
> *(Gold and Gold 2005: 15)*

Spectacle, of course, may have multiple audiences (i.e. the resident, commuter, day visitor and tourist) who view, enjoy and understand what they experience in different ways.

The concept of spectacle is one of the enduring themes that assist in enhancing or even creating the atmosphere, ambience and interest in a place, thereby transforming a static and lifeless environment to a dynamic, enlivened and meaningful experience. This process is clearly at the core of developing events that have meaning, significance and practical value. Events not only add to and contribute meaning to the experience of a place but may constitute the entire 'experience' when visitors visit a location for the primary purpose of attending an event or festival, namely in the case of hallmark events like the Rio Carnival, the New Orleans Mardi Gras and the Commonwealth Games, and the opening ceremonies of mega-events such as the Olympic Games.

The inherent difficulty in conceptualising the complex phenomenon of the world of events (see Getz 1997; Hall 1992) has spawned a number of academic definitions, debates and disciplinary perspectives. From a general review of the literature on the nature and scope of events, it is evident that an event is a temporary experience based on a unique combination of timing, location, theme, design and ambience created and complemented by participants, spectators and organisers. The connotation here is that it is the distinctiveness and special qualities allied with an event experience that create interest, appeal and motivation to participate compared with those motivations generally associated with everyday leisure and tourism activities. Accordingly, the role of events in creating or stimulating emotional and sensual responses to an activity, place, society or environment creates a heightened sense of interest and activity which has dramatic tourism destination marketing potential. Important in this is that the specialness of events does not necessarily 'just happen' and, as Goldblatt (1990: 1) states, special events are 'always planned, always arouse expectations, and always motivate by providing a reason for celebration'.

As the chapters in this Handbook will show, the term 'event' covers a broad spectrum, from significant international events requiring huge capital investment which attract an enormous number of people and global media attention (known as *mega-events*) and *hallmark events* used to literally 'hallmark' or define and distinguish a destination such as the Rio Carnival or Munich Oktoberfest, characterised by a high level of media exposure, positive imagery and perceived value in gaining competitive destination advantage. In this instance, the place becomes synonymous with the event. While the term 'hallmark event' is often used interchangeably to embrace special or mega-events, Hall (1992) argues that the true identification of a hallmark event is differentiated by the scale of its impact. The most recognised and universally acceptable definition is that of Ritchie (1984: 2), where a hallmark event is a

> major one-time or recurring events of limited duration, developed primarily to enhance the awareness, appeal and profitability of a tourism destination in the short and/or long term. Such events rely for their success on their uniqueness, status, or timely significance to create interest and attract attention.

Festivals are events which are designed for public participation; they may be either traditional or contemporary in form and celebrate a range of themes. From a community perspective, festivals can help to maintain values through increasing a sense of social identity and/or celebrating local culture. Traditional themed celebrations focus on particular facets of local life with a combination of historical, modern, cultural and social associations, while sporting, arts, music, entertainment and fun might form the key focal point. Festivals based on political and educational interests are widespread, which, while they may have a leisure focus, aim to convey specific values, meanings and interests (Sharpe 2008).

As Connell and Page (2010) show, the idea of a public celebration is key in much of the event literature, although it does not constitute the total sum of interest. A significant proportion of the business tourism market impinges on the events market, with the acknowledgement of the growing international market for conferences, conventions, seminars, meetings, trade fairs, expositions and exhibitions. Conference business is a major growth sector and many regions aspire to nurture this lucrative part of the events industry. Over 100 countries are active in marketing their facilities to the conventions industry, while in the UK alone there are about 5,000 conference venues (Rogers 2003). Similarly, events that sit firmly within the private/individual/family sphere (such as weddings) are worthy of mention, as they create a significant demand for tourism services and facilities, and contribute to the tourism economy. Wedding tourism has become a significant part of the private events industry in many destinations worldwide, from traditional destinations such as Paris and Las Vegas to more exotic environments offering wedding packages to foreigners in the Caribbean and India. Wedding tourism in New Zealand has increased dramatically in recent years and is estimated to contribute about 30 million dollars per year to the country's economy. In 2003, 1,000 couples travelled to New Zealand to marry, and a further 1,200 couples in 2004 (Johnston 2006). For many destinations, the development of an events industry, whether it be niche, specific, hallmark or more generic, and an understanding of how event activity impacts on the local economy, society and other areas of local, regional and national interest will be important.

The impacts of events

While the premise of developing successful events is believed to assist destinations in growing their visitor economy, such actions have not been without impacts and criticisms. The very basis of holding an impact at an abstract level is about seeking to create an impact of some type and magnitude (social, psychological, economic and environmental), and so it is a natural corollary that impacts will occur whenever an event is staged, and such impacts will inevitably comprise a combination of positive, negative and sometimes contentious outcomes. Several event studies point to the social and cultural effects felt by local residents and host cultures, where tourists engage in festivities that have real meaning for the destination and its people, but little meaning to the tourist. Such incidents are marked in the developing world, but also occur within Western society: a great example of cultural expropriation through events is evident in Venice, where the incongruities between celebrating Venetian culture through traditional events and using such events to draw in tourists are sharply contested (Davis and Marvin (2004). As Getz (2008) argues, there is a need for event organisers to be stakeholders in tourism destination planning and to engage and work effectively with communities. There are many examples where this has been a success from a community perspective and it is clear that collaboration and partnerships prove a solid foundation for generating events with multiple benefits for a range of stakeholders. Much research has focused on destination competitiveness, and how to win bids and create effective events, as well as economic considerations such as impact evaluation, return on investment and financial sustainability. However, less consideration has been given to environmental, social and cultural impacts. For this reason, a contemporary example of the Commonwealth Games hosted in India is used to depict one often-neglected dimension of hosting a mega-event, that of the social and cultural impact.

The social and cultural impact of the 2010 Commonwealth Games, Delhi, India

In October 2010, Delhi in India hosted the Commonwealth Games (CWG) amidst a public focus on the poor state of the preparations of the infrastructure prior to hosting the event. A very insightful and detailed report by the organisation Equations (2010) published in the lead-up to the CWG identified the history of the Games approval process and the public policy environment associated with the event. It highlighted the major public subsidies which the event has required as costs spiralled out of control, and media reports suggest it rose over £3.8 billion (or may even rise higher, as some estimates suggest), which is 114 times the original cost budgeted for in 2002. This is a huge cost for a country which has extremes of wealth and poverty. The Beijing Olympics were reported to have cost US$40 billion to host, illustrating the huge costs associated with mega-events. The 2010 CWG will rate as one of the most expensive held to date, although the problems of costs are not very different from the experience of the London Olympics, where costs have risen sharply though not at the same magnitude as the Delhi example

---

suggests. But what makes the Delhi Games and the Equations report interesting reading from a research perspective is that the forecasting and assessment of impacts has lacked methodological sophistication. Land costs have also risen sharply in the city as result of the projected effect of the Games. For example, Equations (2010) point to the cost of building hotels where globally land costs comprise about 15–20 per cent of total costs. In Delhi, the Games effect had seen these land costs rise to 70–75 per cent of the project costs for some hotels. Yet the report rightly criticises the employment impacts heralded as being a positive feature of the Games, since it suggests these are no more than transitory. What is more worrying is the social and cultural impact of hosting the Games on the local population. Up to 2007, Equations (2010) pointed to 300,000 people evicted and displaced to create the space for the Games, while it was predicted that demand for prostitution during the event would rise. The government restricted the number of street vendor licences available in 2010 to try and reduce the visual impact of street traders for visitors. Equations (2010) pointed to comparative data for other mega-events, where 720,000 people were forcibly evicted to make way for the 1988 Seoul Olympics, 1.25 million in Beijing and 30,000 in Atlanta due to the process of gentrification. Equations (2010) argued that the development of Games infrastructure and projects did not follow established environmental-impact assessment guidelines, noting the huge impacts on natural resources of hosting the Games (i.e. in terms of demand for water and power, sewage discharge and solid waste management). What the CWG example shows is that issues of sustainability from a social/cultural and environmental perspective are downplayed in pursuit of economic objectives that may not even be achieved in the final analysis of hosting a mega-event. The ultimate political objectives of place-building and showcasing a destination on the world stage may also not be realised in the case of the Delhi Games, due to the public relations problems just prior to the Games commencing. There may be a growing public sector realism now emerging in some developed countries that recognises the wider costs and benefits of hosting mega-events to the extent that some countries have chosen not to continue or enter the bidding process because of the long-term debt they may incur, which does not justify the expected benefits.

The case of the 2010 CWG raises serious concerns about the extent to which event development can embrace issues of sustainability, bearing in mind the relative paucity of research in the events/sustainability field. A study by Behr and Cierjacks (2010: 1) suggests 'as the paradigm of sustainable development becomes more widespread among the general public, event managers increasingly have to respond to public scrutiny over the sustainability performance of their events'. Their research focused on benchmarking and argued that 'Benchmarking in event management, and particularly sustainability benchmarking, is rarely carried out' (Behr and Cierjacks 2010: 2), given the inability to transfer the approaches used in other areas of industry. However, the study is innovative as it outlines examples of the types of indicators and data-collection tools required to implement sustainability benchmarking approaches in events. Mega-events have become part of a global culture associated with modernisation, illustrated by the pursuit of large events by developing countries (Roche 1992), and many nations have striven to change others' perceptions of them through hosting events on an international stage, such as South Korea (FIFA World Cup, hosted 2002) and China (Olympic Games, held in 2008). Undoubtedly, the emergence of a modern event sector and its associated infrastructure has changed the way in which many events are perceived, created and staged.

The development of event-related research

The extent and coverage of the Handbook illustrate how far the subject area has progressed since many of the embryonic yet seminal event research studies of the 1970s. Despite a recent comment suggesting that 'the study of events in the tourism literature started with the pioneering work of Getz in the 1980s' (Dimanche 2008: 173), Connell and Page (2010) demonstrate, to the contrary, that Event Studies has much deeper roots and intellectual origins, with notable contributions in recognised Tourism literature from the early 1970s, while articles across the disciplines dating back to the early twentieth century clearly chart interests in events as an area of interest and investigation. Even prior to this, shorter intellectual pieces relating to specific events are identifiable (e.g. the Great Exhibition and World Fairs).

Whether event research has evolved sufficiently to be accepted as a distinct area of study or a specialist niche within other more established subjects such as Sport, Leisure and Tourism might remain a moot point for some but, whatever perspective is adopted, the evidence of a considerable body of knowledge surrounding events is indisputable. Substantiation of this is Connell and Page's (2010) timely four-volume collection, which reproduces many of the classic studies in the field and outlines the evolution and development of the subject, and its analysis, across different areas of social science. Other studies which review the literature (e.g. Getz 2007, 2008) highlight the growing quantum of research activity. One example is a conference paper by Mair (2010), which marks this rise in research effort within one specialist area of events research – business events (meetings, incentives, conventions and exhibitions) for the period 2000–9. Mair argued that the review of the field by Yoo and Weber (2005) identified 115 articles published in fourteen academic journals for the period up to 2003. In a similar vein, a review by Lee and Back (2005) for the period 1990–2003 found that 137 conventions articles had been published, which illustrates a growing interest in sub-themes within the broader domain of Event Studies, but at this point certainly not a massive expansion compared with other topics in Tourism, Sport and Leisure. In contrast, Mair found that 144 were published for the period 2000–9, mainly in Tourism, Hospitality and Marketing journals though predominantly in specialist journals (i.e. *Journal of Convention and Event Tourism*, *Journal of Convention and Exhibition Management*, *Tourism Management*, *Event Management*, *Journal of Travel Research* as well as smaller numbers in other journals). The analysis of themes and sub-themes in the research published also highlighted significant gaps in the research literature such as the environmental and social and cultural impacts of events, a feature which we will return to later in this introductory chapter.

Within the contemporary research literature, several approaches to the study of events are identifiable, which clearly illustrate the extent, dimensions and disciplinary foci of the academic study of events. Within the realms of business and management research (much of which now encompasses tourism interests), research on events tends towards one of two forms: first, the strategic role of events in developing and sustaining local economies or in meeting other longer-term political, economic or socio-cultural objectives, and the tangible and intangible benefits and costs of events; second is the more applied and narrowly focused event management stream that includes the practical and operational aspects of designing, producing and staging events. Since the late 1980s, a plethora of research-based papers within the latter category have been published, with a large proportion of studies based on specific destinations and case study material, and including the lessons learned from planning, hosting and evaluating the impacts of a range of events, from small localised community festivals to mega-events on an international scale. Many of these studies refer to sporting events almost certainly because their high public profile and guaranteed audience makes them the most prolific events sought by tourism destinations and event units within national and local government (see Hall 1992). As Page and Connell (2009) argued, research on individual events or specific types of events tends to measure the economic impacts rather than the more holistic and complex impacts of the event. While much of this research provides very useful information at the micro level on this narrow element of Event Studies, there is a dearth of research at the macro level, indicating that the subject is still in its infancy. Having said that, a number of key research papers aim to move the field on in terms of conceptualisation and application (Getz 2008), and a range of papers recognise the dangers of relying on events as a panacea in relation to social and economic problems (Crompton 2006; Horne 2007). This Handbook marks a step forward in developing the existing knowledge and concepts, with a view to progressing a more holistic understanding of events, how they have come to play such an important role in contemporary society and the role of academic research in understanding the key attributes of the phenomenon.

The Routledge Handbook of Events: an outline of the contributions

Trying to blend together some of the academic (as opposed to practitioner) themes is a major challenge for the Editors, but we have sought to try and integrate the academy of event researchers together in a holistic manner in this first major research-oriented Handbook. As some of the discussion in this introductory chapter indicates, a great deal of detective work is required to root out the extent of progress across specific themes. An area which is noticeably absent in this collection is the state of research in non-Western contexts, especially regional reviews of Latin America, Africa and the non-English research literature. Interestingly a recent text produced by McCartney (2010) in part addresses the absence of Asian perspectives but it also draws extensively on Western principles of events management in its discussion. Indeed, the macro perspectives offered in many of the contributions are widely applicable. Nonetheless, a brief précis of the dimensions of the Handbook now follows.

The contributions

It is fitting that the first of the contributions (Chapter 2) is by Donald Getz, one of the most widely published researchers in the field of Event Studies, who has been extremely influential in shaping the ongoing research agenda (not least through the early formation of an academic journal dedicated to the subject – *Event Management* – and several books on the subject). Getz's wide-ranging chapter sets out the debates on the subject and what exactly we mean by Event Studies. This is an important basis upon which many of the subsequent chapters will build. Expanding upon one of the themes developed in Getz's chapter is a philosophical discussion of the development of typologies of events in the subsequent chapter by Tom Lunt. Lunt's discussion critically reviews some of the different ways of examining event typologies, with an emphasis on theoretical and conceptual issues. Chapter 4 by Mike Weed on new research agendas and interdisciplinary developments within Sport, Tourism and Leisure and Event Studies seeks to look across the common areas which encompass the study of events (Sport, Tourism and Leisure and the relationship with events) to evaluate how events are viewed and analysed. This provides a much needed interdisciplinary perspective and basis upon which the next section of the book is based – disciplinary studies and events: theory, concepts and methods of analysis. It seeks to introduce the concepts, approaches and methodologies used by different disciplines in the social sciences to show how they approach the study of events. What is particularly interesting about the event tourism domain is that, even more so than Tourism Studies, the study of festivals and events is multidisciplinary, with a diversity of subjects making important contributions: for example, Music, Film and Theatre, Anthropology, Ethnology, Sociology, Psychology, Cultural and Urban Studies, Geography, History, Economics, Politics, Planning, Sports Studies, Religious Studies. The focus of this section of the book is also to draw attention to the rich social science traditions that provide the foundations for the development of knowledge and further research in the evolving subject domain of events. The first contribution in this section on tourism by Warwick Frost provides a very wide-ranging analysis of the relationship between tourism and Event Studies and the relationship often cited between events as a basis to grow tourism. This provides an insight into the relationship that is poorly understood by many policy-makers and planners, who seek to host events and fail to understand the complexity of the markets and people who they wish to attract. Visitors are not a uniform or homogenous group, and the next chapter by Diane O'Sullivan illustrates that leisure is another part of the jigsaw puzzle in understanding the visitor market and use of events as a tool used by the public sector for different community-oriented reasons. These arguments, as debated in Page and Connell (2010) pose wider debates on who is the visitor at events. What type of audiences can be developed, what are their diverse needs and are these being met by the cultural industries' strategies increasingly being implemented in the public sector? This theme is picked up in the next chapter by Sean Gammon in relation to sport and events. Gammon examines some of the themes debated by Lunt concerning sport events and the role in developing sport audiences such as fans, as well as critical issues associated with space and place (a theme we will pick up again in a later chapter by Michael Hall and Stephen Page in the contribution geography has made to the study of events).

Having reviewed the different approaches to events from the Tourism, Leisure and Sport domain, attention now turns to the contribution of history to the study of events with a contribution from Margaret and John Gold. Over time, a number of historical appreciations of events and event development have added depth to current understanding, and show today's audiences that events are nothing new, but their conceptualisation has undergone a process of change in the way we frame, contextualise and theorise about their status, meaning and impact in society.

In contrast to the wide-ranging debates in the historical analysis of events and their value in understanding continuity and change in the way events have been developed, staged and used in society, the economists have developed a very specialist knowledge that is often used to assess whether events should be staged. The economist's perspective has not been without its critics, since it is not an exact science but, as the chapter by Larry Dwyer and Leo Jago shows, there is a tradition of economic appraisal and analysis that has evolved through time. Their tools and techniques (a theme also picked up later in the book) have often underpinned the decision by the public and private sector to nurture, develop and invest in events. Assessing the impact remains a key challenge for the events researcher, often working with a paucity of reliable data that can mean local evaluations are required pre- and post-event to try and gauge how successful an event was and to decide on its continuation, further development or perhaps closure. Some of these themes are debated further in the next chapter by Michael Hall and Stephen Page, who develop some of the key themes which the geographer's long history of event study has brought to the expansion of research in this area. They argue that while events are a shared experience, their hosting raises significant issues associated with the combination of time, place and space. Their analysis suggests that event visitors are transient communities (as opposed to much of the analysis in mainstream geography that has developed models of phenomena fixed in time and space with a permanent spatial fixity). Events are about what Richards and Palmer (2010) argue is celebration in time and space, and event managers need to create event spaces which are safe and trusted to enable a flow of activities (building on the recreation literature on adventure, excitement and flow of activities). As Amin and Thrift (2002) suggest, events produce a flow of activities that give life and rhythm to a city or place. This is why events are a major social spatial and experiential activity that has the potential to enrich one's sense of place and enjoyment, albeit a transient one. Events thereby add animation to places and colour the participant's perception of space while allowing people and events to come together. This stimulates the visitor's senses through excitement, exhilaration and sometimes through a visual display that is memorable. What the geographer's contribution to events highlights is the need for an appreciation of the psychologist's approach to events as represented in the next chapter by Pierre Benckendorff and Phil Pearce. This chapter on the psychology of events examines the theories, methods and type of analysis used to study events. One of the underlying themes they address is to try and explain why people are involved with event phenomenon as spectators, attendees, performers and as participants. They deal with concepts such as motivation, personality, the experience of the event and attitudes.

The next chapter by Michael Hall develops an often neglected theme – the political analysis and political economy of events as illustrated earlier in this chapter in the case of the Commonwealth Games in Delhi 2010. Understanding why decisions are taken, the political basis of the decisions and how they relate to the staging and development of events sometimes helps to understand why illogical and incomprehensible decisions are taken by a small group of decision-makers that can commit a region or nation to huge debts associated with the staging of mega-events. This sometimes occurs where research that contradicts the prevailing political doctrine is downplayed and a boosterist mentality pursues idiosyncratic goals that are relatively unachievable. Interestingly, it also deflects attention away from other areas of government policy that may be problematic. Once these decisions have been taken at different geographical scales, it is over to the event planners and managers to grapple with the huge management teams to implement the event concept and design, develop and then manage the event. This is the theme of the next chapter by Julia Tum, building on her work in establishing the operational context of events (Tum *et al.* 2005) from the discipline of management and sub-disciplines such as operations management. This provides a conclusion to the section on how different disciplines approach events.

The next section, on policy, planning and management, commences with a chapter by Robyn Stokes which is a major contribution to the debate on how the private sector approaches events and the challenges they face, with a focus on managing individual events and strategic leverage. This is an important context for the next chapter by Nicole Ferdinand and Nigel Williams on staging an event and the wide-ranging issues associated with staging. What Ferdinand and Williams highlight is the critical role of staging as the way an event is organised and the wider issues of how the venue needs to be managed alongside issues such as logistics and the visitor experience. The chapter also points to new directions in expanding areas of event research such as animation and virtual technology, green events and cultural events (as highlighted earlier in relation to the debates in Richards and Palmer 2010). This aligns much of the discussion throughout the book on the experience economy, a theme we then turn to, given the wider platform which Ferdinand and Williams provide for the next three chapters. Chris Ryan looks at events consumption and experience from an ethnographic perspective and from an insider's perspective, and Linda Wilks addresses a neglected theme of social capital as a theoretical construct that has great salience for events and festivals articulated through an analysis of a music festival experience. Graham Berridge's chapter on designing events experiences is an important move on, since it focuses on the key issue of the experience economy. The chapter engages with the key debates over the experience of events for the visitor and issues associated with designing, managing, planning and developing the visitor experience. This in part reflects the growing debate from the literature on the experience economy and the expanding focus on the design

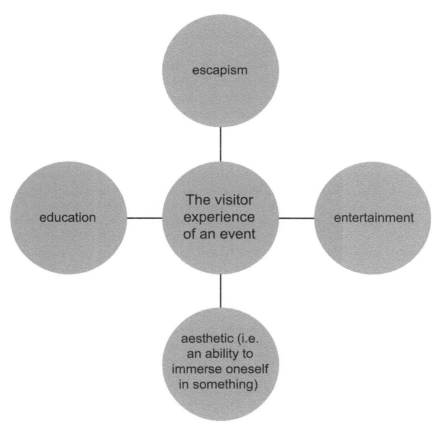

Figure 1.1 The dimensions of an event experience to develop

of experiences (Haahti and Komppula 2006), as well as the debates on the experience economy raised initially by Pine and Gilmore (1999) which posited that this represented the next stage in the evolution of society from a service economy. The logic of such arguments is that events, for example, will need to create a sensation and build a relationship with the consumer. In relation to the development of experiences, their focus was on four distinct areas, as shown in Figure 1.1.

This argument is embodied in Berridge's chapter and illustrates the shift in thinking which event managers need to make in adding value to experiences. This closely links to other debates occurring in the way services are produced and consumed in terms of the notion of service-dominant logic (see Vargo and Lusch 2004, 2008). Berridge's chapter also provides an important framework in which the two preceding chapters can be situated. For any destination, there is a great deal of value to be added to visitor experiences through a coherent programme of events and this requires a clear understanding of the media and events. This is the focus of the next chapter by Andrew Bradley, since the competition between places to host events (and the problem of emulation and copying) means a clearly thought-out media strategy is required to attract the right audience. Yet alongside having the right media strategy is the need to have the right people in the right jobs to develop, lead and manage the event process. This is the focus of the chapter by Clare Hanlon and Leo Jago, entitled 'Staffing for successful events: Having the right skills in the right place at the right time', which is aptly named and describes the challenge of events. The following chapter builds on this proposition, illustrating the reliance upon volunteers to run events. Chapter 21, by Katie Schlenker, Deborah Edwards and Stephen Wearing, illustrates the key role which volunteers can play at events alongside the challenge of managing this diverse group of individuals epitomised by the London Olympics seeking to recruit 70,000 Games Makers in October 2010. The chapter makes many important observations about the episodic nature of event organisation, with its pulsating nature that requires the formation of a large body of temporary staff (often accompanied by volunteers) alongside the challenge of motivating, managing and retaining such people across events.

Section 4, on the impacts of events, treads the well-worn path of the three distinct areas of sustainability: the economic, social and cultural and environmental dimensions of events. In this section we address each theme separately with a chapter by Timothy Tyrrell and Robert Johnson. Their chapter on the spatial extension to a framework designed to assess the economic impacts of events highlights the very complex issues that economic modellers face combined with many of the spatial issues: that of assessing a dispersed event across multiple locations. Tyrell and Johnson also emphasise many of the issues germane to geographical analysis, particularly the integration of space in economic analysis. The next chapter by Richard Sharpley and Philip Stone examines the social and cultural impacts of events. Their arguments highlight the diversity of audiences for events (participants, local residents and visitors) and the problem of simply ascribing cause and effect to impacts. Sharpley and Stone examine two different perspectives on the analysis of such impacts: unidimensional and multidimensional approaches. In Chapter 24, Robert Case picks up the less developed area of research on event impacts, namely the environmental effects and the broader issue of sustainability which we broached earlier in the discussion. What is apparent from such research is that the debates over sustainability are now moving higher up the events agenda with the International Olympics Committee (IOC) now paying greater attention to such issues in bids to host the Games, as is the case with the Sydney Games and attempts to develop more sustainable venues. Part of the argument put forward by organisations like the IOC and national governments is that events can be harnessed as a tool to drive forward urban regeneration, which is the theme developed in this and subsequent chapters.

An urban focus in this section of the Handbook is warranted given the fact that many larger cities are the sites of mega-events as well as being environments in a stage of transition from industrial to post-industrial states in the Western world, and so events have been seen as one way of providing a new economic rationale and basis for economic activity based upon event consumption. Chapter 25 by Michael Pacione on urban regeneration and events examines the conceptual basis of such strategies for urban redevelopment and the logic of harnessing events, highlighting some notable successes. It is a theme which is far more sophisticated and complex than many policy-makers realise, as some notable failures of state intervention to develop major tourist attractions have sought to drive visitor audiences by developing events programmes to try and offset over-optimistic forecasts of visitor numbers and to animate attraction sites. Even many non-urban visitor attractions are using events (e.g. the Eden Project in Cornwall) to expand their visitor markets and revenue from periods when the attraction is either under-utilised or unused (e.g. evenings in the summer) with pop and music concerts. Remaining with the theme of urban areas, Steve Shaw examines the growing interest (discussed earlier in relation to the rise of the intercultural event city) in the diverse ethnic population and heritage of cities and the attraction for event development in Chapter 26, entitled 'Faces, spaces and places: social and cultural impacts of street festivals in cosmopolitan cities'. Taking the urban theme a stage further and with a focus on a new and emerging research agenda in Urban Studies, Graeme Evans provides an insightful chapter on the development of late-night events and the rise of the twenty-four-hour entertainment city, entitled 'Events, cities and the night-time economy'. The Olympic Games are naturally a major focus of much of the research efforts

Plate 1.4 Poster advertising travel to the 1976 Montreal Olympics

on events (see Plate 1.4) given their scale and global reach, and therefore it is appropriate that the next chapter blends together some of the conventional interest in mega-events alongside the growing concerns of safety and security at these events. Chapter 28, the last chapter in this section, by Allison Wylde and Stephen J. Page draws together the themes associated with the safety and security of urban events from the perspectives of event staging and event participants.

The chapter highlights the growing research agenda associated with safety and security at events, focusing on the case of the London Olympics 2012.

These different perspectives of urban events and event development highlight the need for a framework and tools to evaluate events, and the next chapter by Richard Shipway, Leo Jago and Marg Deery examines 'Quantitative and qualitative research tools in events' as a summary review of the different approaches being developed to address the need for events research. This is a natural conclusion to the section, as it is able to draw upon many of the perspectives, offered from different chapters, we have seen so far in the book and to provide a reflective overview of the directions future research methodologies may need to take. A comparative review of quantitative and qualitative research is an important chapter to synthesis many of the different research tools and techniques used in event research.

Section 5 of the book concludes with a focus on issues related to the future of events, commencing with a chapter by Paul Barron and Anna Leask on events education which has seen a major growth worldwide running parallel with the growth of the subject area. The next chapter by Martin Robertson and Ken Wardrop sets out a distinctive view from two authors (one of whom was and one who still is) employed in the public sector and so provides a government perspective on events. The next chapter by Ian Yeoman, Martin Robertson and Karen Smith, entitled 'A futurist's view of the future of events', adopts a scenario planning approach, reviewing drivers of change and a number of scenarios of the future change that may occur in events in the case of New Zealand. The book concludes with a review chapter by the editors, which is both retrospective and an assessment of the prospects for events in the near future.

References

Amin, A. and Thrift, N. (2002) *Cities: Reimaging the Urban*, Cambridge: Polity.

Ashworth, G. and Page, S.J. (2011) 'Urban tourism research: recent progress and current paradoxes', *Tourism Management*, 32(1): 1–15.

Behr, F. and Cierjacks, A. (2010) 'Benchmarking in event management – a sustainability approach', conference paper presented at the Global Events Congress IV, Festival and Events Research: State of the Art, Leeds Metropolitan University, 14–16 July; www.eventsandfestivalresearch.com

Bergmann, B. (1999) 'Introduction: The art of ancient spectacle', in B. Bergmann and C. Kondoleon (eds) *The Art of Ancient Spectacle*, Washington, DC: National Gallery of Art, pp. 8–35.

Boorstin, D. (1973) *The Image: A Guide to Pseudo-Events in America*, New York: Athaneum.

Bowdin, G., Allen, J., O'Toole, W., Harris, R. and McDonnell, I. (2010) *Events Management*, Oxford: Elsevier.

Connell, J. and Page, S.J. (2010) 'Introduction: Progress and prospects – an introduction to event tourism', in J. Connell and S.J. Page (eds) *Event Tourism. Critical Concepts in Tourism*, four-volume collection, London: Routledge.

Conway, D. (2009) *The Event Manager's Bible: The Complete Guide to Planning and Organising a Voluntary or Public Event*, London: How to Books, third edition.

Crompton, J.L. (2006) 'Economic Impact Studies: instruments for political shenanigans?', *Journal of Travel Research* 45: 67–82.

Davis, R.C. and Marvin, G. (2004) *Venice, the Tourist Maze: A Cultural Critique of the World's Most Touristed City*, Berkeley: University of California Press.

Dimanche, F. (2008) 'From attractions to experiential marketing: the contributions of events to "new" tourism', in C. Kronenberg, S. Mueller, M. Peters and K. Wieiermaier (eds) *Change Management in Tourism*, Berlin: Erich Schmidt Verlag, pp. 173–84.

Equations (2010) *Humanity–Equality–Destiny? Implicating Tourism in the Commonwealth Games 2010*, Bengaluru: Equations; available at www.equitabletourism.org (accessed 5 October 2010).

Florida, R. (2002) *The Rise of the Creative Class and How It's Transforming Work, Leisure, Community and Everyday Life*, New York: Basic Books.

Getz, D (1989) 'Special events: defining the product', *Tourism Management* 10(2): 125–37.

——(1997) *Event Management and Event Tourism*, New York: Cognizant.

——(2002) 'Event Studies and Event Management: on becoming an academic discipline', *Journal of Hospitality and Tourism Management* 9(1): 12–23.

——(2007) *Event Studies: Theory, Research and Policy for Planned Events*, Oxford: Butterworth-Heinemann.

——(2008) 'Event Tourism: definition, evolution, and research', *Tourism Management* 29(3): 403–28.

Gold, J.R. and Gold, M.M. (2005) *Cities of Culture: Staging International Festivals and the Urban Agenda, 1851–2000*, Aldershot: Ashgate.

Goldblatt, J. (1990) *Special Events*, New York: Wiley.

Greenwood, D.J. (1972) 'Tourism as an agent of change: a Spanish Basque case', *Ethnology* 11(1): 80–91.

Haahti, A. and Komppula, R. (2006) 'Experience design in tourism', in D. Buhalis and C. Costa (eds) *Tourism Business Frontiers*, Oxford: Elsevier, pp. 101–10.

Hall, C.M. (1992) *Hallmark Tourist Events: Impacts, Management and Planning*, London: Belhaven.

Health and Safety Executive (1999) *The Event Safety Guide: A Guide to Health, Safety and Welfare at Music and Similar Events* (Guidance Booklets) London: Health and Safety Executive.

Horne, J. (2007) 'The four "knowns" of sports mega-events', *Leisure Studies* 26(1): 81–96.

Johnston, L. (2006) '"I do down-under": naturalizing landscapes and love through wedding tourism in New Zealand', *ACME: An International e-Journal for Critical Geographies* 5(2): 191–208.

Landry, C. (2000) *The Creative City. A Toolkit for Urban Planners*, London: Earthscan.

Lee, M.J. and Back, K.-J. (2005) 'A review of convention and meeting management research 1990–2003 – identification of statistical methods and subject areas', *Journal of Convention and Event Tourism* 7(2): 1–20.

Long, P.T. and Perdue, P.R. (1990) 'The economic impact of rural festivals and special events: assessing the spatial distribution of expenditures', *Journal of Travel Research* 28(4): 10–14.

MacCannell, D. (1971) 'Staged authenticity: arrangements of social space in tourist settings', *American Journal of Sociology* 79(3): 589–603.

McCartney, G. (2010) *Events Management: The Asian Perspective*, Singapore: McGraw Hill Education Asia.

Mair, J. (2010) 'A review of business events literature 2000–2009', conference paper presented at the Global Events Congress IV, Festival and Events Research: State of the Art, Leeds Metropolitan University, 14–16 July; www.eventsandfestivalresearch.com

Matthews, D. (2008a) *Special Event Production: The Resources*, Oxford: Elsevier.

——(2008b) *Special Event Production: The Process*, Oxford: Elsevier.

Page, S.J. and Connell, J. (2009) *Tourism: A Modern Synthesis*, London: Cengage, third edition.

Page, S.J. and Connell, J. (2010) *Leisure: An Introduction*, Harlow: Pearson.

Philips, D. (2004) 'Stately pleasure domes – nationhood, monarchy and industry: the celebration exhibition in Britain', *Leisure Studies* 23(2): 95–108.

Pine, B. and Gilmore, J. (1999) *The Experience Economy*, Boston: Harvard University Business School Press.

Prentice, R. and Andersen, V. (2003) 'Festival as creative destination', *Annals of Tourism Research* 30(1): 7–30.

Richards, G. and Palmer, R. (2010) *Eventful Cities: Cultural Management and Urban Revitalisation*, Oxford: Elsevier.

Ritchie, J.R.B. (1984) 'Assessing the impact of hallmark events: conceptual and research issues', *Journal of Travel Research* 23(1): 2–11.

Ritchie, J.R.B. and Beliveau, D. (1974) 'Hallmark events: an evaluation of a strategic response to seasonality in the travel market', *Journal of Travel Research* 13(1): 14–20.

Roche, M. (1992) 'Mega-events and micro-modernization: on the sociology of the new urban tourism', *British Journal of Sociology* 43(4): 563–600.

Rogers, T. (2003) *Conferences and Conventions: A Global Industry*, Oxford: Butterworth-Heinemann.

Sharpe, E.K. (2008) 'Festivals and social change: intersections of pleasure and politics at a community music festival', *Leisure Sciences* 30(3): 217–34.

Silvers, J. (2007) *Risk Management for Meetings and Events*, Oxford: Elsevier.

Tum, J., Norton, P. and Wright, J. (2005) *Management of Event Operations*, Oxford: Elsevier.

Vargo, S.L. and Lusch, R.F. (2004) 'The four service marketing myths: remnants of a goods-based, manufacturing model', *Journal of Service Research* 6(4): 324–35.

——(2008) 'From goods to service(s): divergences and convergences of logics', *Industrial Marketing Management* 37: 254–59.

Yoo, J.J.E. and Weber, K. (2005) 'Progress in convention tourism research', *Journal of Hospitality and Tourism Research* 29(2): 194.

Section 1
Defining Events Studies

2

Event studies

Donald Getz

Introduction

Planned events, from the smallest meeting or private party to the grandest festival or world championship, are an essential part of human civilization. They have been with us throughout recorded history. Events help define cultures and sub-cultures, give identity to places and individuals, and bind communities together. Events facilitate commerce and trade, they entertain us, and shape our competitive and playful spirits. A civil society without the full array of events is not imaginable.

Until fairly recently most events were organic, springing from the needs and aspirations of communities, and they were informal – people helped out because it was expected and necessary. However, events planned to meet specific goals or reflect particular values have always been popular, and increasingly they are planned to meet public policy and strategic corporate or industry objectives.

Although many events are periodic, and some even become permanent institutions in their host communities, they are often held only once. But as a population, planned events are institutionalized – that is, they are expected to perform important social, cultural and economic roles, and so they receive the support of powerful stakeholders as well as their resident communities. The population of events in any place says a great deal about how that society functions, the degree to which it shares and cooperates, and how it is managed. While any one event can be replaced or substituted, every place needs a healthy population of events.

Definitions and typologies

An event is an occurrence that is discrete in both time and place. If you miss it, that event is gone forever – it cannot be completely re-created. Something in the mix of setting, people-to-people interactions, or situational forces (including management) will ensure that it is different in some important respect. And even if a person goes to the 'same' event repeatedly, their experience will always be different – in part because they have changing knowledge and expectations about that event.

A useful typology, based on the distinct form of events, consists of the following: festivals and other cultural celebrations: arts and entertainment; religious, including pilgrimages; fairs and exhibitions (or expositions, including trade and consumer shows); meetings and conferences (or congresses, conventions); sports and other athletic competitions/games; recreational; private events (or 'functions' for the hospitality industry); state and political, and educational/scientific events.

> 'Planned events' are created to achieve specific outcomes, including those related to the economy, culture, society and environment. Event planning involves the design and implementation of themes, settings, consumables, services and programmes that suggest, facilitate or constrain experiences for participants, guests, spectators and other stakeholders. Every event-goer's experience is personal and unique, arising from the interactions of setting, programme and people, but event experiences also have broader social and cultural meanings.

These commonly recognized planned event types are in some respects social constructs, having different meanings in different cultures and among specific groups. This is particularly true of festivals and other cultural celebrations that reflect the values and beliefs of particular groups. Social constructs do change over time, and in response to globalization forces there is very widespread understanding of what constitutes sport, entertainment, a convention or exhibition.

A clear trend is towards the blurring of event types. Many events are packaged as a mixed group of smaller events, so that community festivals include sports, exhibitions, parades and entertainment, while sport events are augmented in length and appeal by being promoted as festivals. The programming of events is now more like employing a recipe book, with various 'elements of style' (i.e. unique ways of doing things) that can be blended to create the experiences that event designers want to achieve. In this way, celebration is not only a discrete type of event, but also an important element in sports and political/religious events.

All planned events occur at various scales and degrees of organization or professionalism. They range from small and informal to those requiring major new facilities and large-scale investment in organization. They also range from the intimacy of a dinner party to the global significance of Millennium celebrations. A number of variables can be employed to examine the differences between planned and unplanned, large and small events. To differentiate events, ask these basic questions: is a professional or a formal organization responsible and accountable for the event? does it have a purpose and identifiable goals? is the event managed and controlled? is there a formal programme and schedule? is it open to the public?

Another consideration is that of frequency, which can range from a regularly scheduled programme of events (including theatre performances and sport meets), through periodic events (typically annual festivals) all the way to rare, one-time-only events that either move around (e.g. world championships, the Olympics, world fairs) and those that only come along once in a lifetime, such as the Millennium celebrations of 2000. Frequency is not an issue when it comes to event management or the study of planned events, but it does affect how people and organizations perceive events.

The term 'special event' is often used, but it is rather ambiguous. Getz (2005) listed a number of variables that help make events more special in the eyes of guests or consumers, the most important being their perceived uniqueness, and provided a definition that pertains to both consumers and organizers. This approach makes it clear that 'special' is a relative term, subject to various perspectives:

1 A special event is a one-time or infrequently occurring event outside the normal programme or activities of the sponsoring or organizing body.
2 To the customer or guest, a special event is an opportunity for an experience outside the normal range of choices or beyond everyday experience.

Rather than focus on the form of events, or what we normally expect to be the differences in programme and setting between, say, festivals and sports, we can categorize them by their purpose or function. In this typology, planned events are instruments for policy and strategy. For example, in the tourism literature the terms 'mega-event' and 'hallmark event' are widely used. A mega-event (defined in relative terms) is the biggest or most important that a place can host in terms of attracting tourists and generating economic impacts, or through positive image-creation. We normally think of the Olympics, or a World's Fair, but for any given place a conference or festival can be a mega-event. A 'hallmark event' is typically periodic and co-branded with the destination, yielding a positive image. By contrast, local events have little in the way of tourist impact, and regional events can potentially be grown into hallmark events.

Other events are employed for purposes of social marketing, to make people more aware of, and to support, a particular policy initiative such as smoking cessation. Some are specifically intended to raise money for worthwhile causes, others to promote a corporate marketing scheme. 'Media events' are those created specifically for media broadcast, to reach target audiences, and might have few spectators or participants – but any event can have image-making value through media exposure. Events that facilitate economic exchange are somewhat distinct, and usually they are defined as fairs, markets, exhibitions and shows. However, business (sales and marketing) can be done at any event. It is also possible to suggest whole categories of events (of any type) that help groups and communities develop their identity and bind people together in a civil society. Again, it is the purpose, not the form, that distinguishes events in this typology.

Categorization of events according to experiences is much more difficult, in both theoretical and practical terms. While event designers want their guests or participants to have enjoyable and memorable experiences, this can never be guaranteed because it is a consequence of personal experiences. As well, a particular event might be designed as amusing and entertaining, but certain customers might find it to be predictable and boring. And, depending on one's expectations, situation and mood, any event can stimulate a full range of personal experiences as defined by the three dimensions of experience: one's actions/behaviour (the conative dimension); cognitive processes (i.e. thinking) and one's emotions (the affective dimension).

At the margins of event management, from a professional point of view, are a whole range of assemblies such as 'flash mobs', 'gorilla gigs', protests and riots that have elements of spontaneity and informal planning. Not all of these are socially acceptable or condoned by authorities, yet all can be considered some kind of celebration, or at least a form of ritualistic, cultural expression. At the grand scale, nobody actually coordinates the diverse celebrations that occur around the world on New Year or other special dates. Mass media enable everyone to participate, albeit merely as spectacle and entertainment.

Business events can also be viewed in a continuum reflecting scale and organization, starting with very small and informal meetings (maybe at the golf course or around the water cooler) all the way up to major political/economic forums that bring together world leaders, huge numbers of media, and inevitably, the protesters. Assemblies held by societies, associations and numerous social worlds (constructed around any community of interest) are typically organized hierarchically, from local to global. Sport is always organized hierarchically, from local to global competitions, but at the margins are spontaneous recreational events and the entertainment put on by organizers, host communities and fans themselves.

The study of planned events

Event studies is the academic field devoted to creating knowledge and theory about planned events. The core phenomenon includes the experience of planned events, and meanings attached to them. Event studies draws mainly from the social sciences, management, the arts, humanities and a number of closely related professional fields.

In the academic world, most courses and degree programmes are actually called 'event management'. This is a very recent development, with university degrees arising only since the early 1990s. But event management is also taught within sports, leisure, hospitality and other closely related fields, and within tourism schools we also find event management specializations and specific courses on 'event tourism'. None of these would exist without a well-established 'industry', a range of professional associations, and of course a demand by employers for event management graduates.

Most academics teaching event management and event tourism are also compelled to do research and get published in peer-reviewed journals, thereby contributing to knowledge and theory development. To a large degree they can publish within established disciplines and fields, but more and more they want to form a community of scholars with similar interests, and this has led to the establishment of several event-specific journals, commencing with *Event Management* (formerly *Festival Management and Event Tourism*) in 1993.

It is clear from reviewing the event-related literature that 'event tourism' and 'event management' are separate but sometimes overlapping 'discourses' in which the focus is on either the function of events in serving tourism goals, or the improvement of event management in the context of professionalism or business success. These are the instrumentalist discourses. But the study of planned events within social and cultural contexts is much older, and well established within the cultural anthropology and sociology disciplines. This can be called the classical discourse, devoted to improved understanding of the roles, importance and impacts of events in society and culture. Integration of all three discourses is essential to the field of event studies, and the ensuing framework has been developed to show the various elements and their interdependencies.

A framework for understanding and creating knowledge about planned events

The framework in Figure 2.1 can be a starting point for exploring the literature, conducting research and developing interdisciplinary theory applied to events. There is no particular beginning or end, as it is an integrative system. But there is a core which defines the field of event studies, and that should be discussed first.

Core phenomenon

At one level, the core phenomenon is simply the planned event (or all events). This is logical, since no other field is devoted to events exclusively or in their full range. In contrast, theatre studies covers only one type of event, as does sport management, while leisure studies is interested only in the leisure dimensions of certain events. Within hospitality and tourism events are not at the core, but they are important as attractions or profit-centres.

Of greater interest to academics, and of considerable relevance to everyone interested in what events can accomplish as instruments of policy or strategy, are event experiences and the meanings attached to them. The essence of the planned event is that of an experience that has been designed (or at least the experience is facilitated) and would not otherwise occur. There are many styles of planned events, produced for many purposes, but in every case there is intent to create, or at least shape, the individual and collective experiences of the audience or participants. New forms are always being created, and this in itself is of considerable interest.

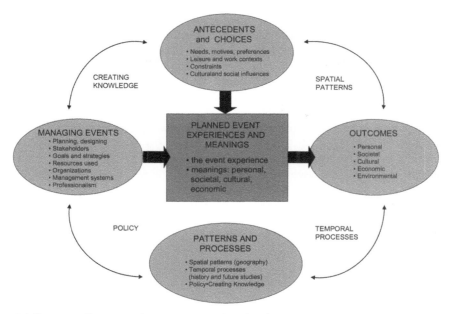

Figure 2.1 Event studies: core phenomenon and major themes

Multiple perspectives on experiences and meaning have to be included. Obviously there are paying customers or invited guests at planned events, but also the organizers including staff, sponsors and other facilitators (providing resources and support), regulators (e.g. city officials), co-producers, participants (as in athletics events), exhibitors and suppliers. Let's not forget volunteers, as numerous events cannot exist without them. What motivates all these stakeholders and what different experiences do they have? How do all these stakeholders react to the designed experience?

We are also concerned about how meanings are attached to planned events. For example, is the event perceived to be a shared cultural experience or personally self-fulfilling? And we also have to examine meanings from different perspectives. Each stakeholder in the process wants, expects and receives potentially different experiences and attaches potentially different meanings to the event. Do they have the experiences that were planned for them?

Nevertheless, it is reasonable to suggest that there are typical event experiences realized by guests and participants, depending on circumstances. These range from the highly personal (spirituality, relaxation and healthy renewal, learning, aesthetic appreciation, self-development through skill development and meeting a challenge) to the social. Especially important is Turner's (1974) notion of 'communitas', which can be described as a feeling of belonging and sharing among equals that particularly marks rituals and celebrations, but can also be felt at conventions and sport events.

Whether or not event experiences can be transforming (that is, a permanent change in religiosity, spirituality, personality or character) is an open question theoretically, but transformation will depend upon both personal antecedents (what the guest brings to the event) and meanings attached to the event experience. The meanings attached to personal event experiences can include any of the following, derived in part from the work of Diller *et al.* (2006: 320).

- communitas (as a result of belonging and sharing, from reaffirmation of roots or of connections and values)

31

- esteem: validation of oneself in the opinions of others; self-worth; prestige and reputation (such as may be realized through competitive or intellectual accomplishments)
- learning or enlightenment (for example, from new cultural experiences or a connoisseur's appreciation of food, art, or music
- self-discovery, self-actualization, understanding, wonder
- redemption and atonement (from failure or sins)
- mastery (from skills, physical triumph)
- accomplishment or success (from business, trade, commerce, networking, creativity, artistic expression)
- creativity or innovation (making a lasting contribution)
- fulfilment of responsibility (professionalism, or as a dedicated sport fan, or from getting involved as a volunteer)
- health and wellbeing (through physical activity, learning)
- security (living without fear)
- duty (military or civic) fulfilled; patriotism and loyalty to a cause
- truth, honesty, integrity (a meaning given to relationships and to one's own behaviour)
- beauty or aesthetic appreciation
- freedom (acting without constraint; intrinsically rewarding pursuits)
- harmony (with nature or others) and oneness (belonging, unity)
- justice (fairness and equality; democratic expression).

It should be possible for a person to assign any or all of these meanings to an experience without it being considered a transforming experience. In any event, how do we know when we have been fundamentally changed?

Theory on the nature of event experience and meanings

A considerable amount of pertinent theory can be drawn from leisure studies where 'experiential sampling' has been pioneered to more fully understand what constitutes leisure. Csikszentimi-halyi's theory suggests that people seek 'optimal arousal', leading to 'flow' – which can be characterized by deep involvement, intense concentration, lack of self-consciousness, and transcendence of self. These are intrinsically rewarding experiences. To the extent that designers can facilitate 'flow', event-goers can be expected to report exhilaration (from fantasizing or total immersion in music or activity), a sense of accomplishment (athletic achievement, mastery of a skill, intellectual stimulation) or transformation (through an intense emotional or spiritual process). How to foster a high level of engagement is the real challenge, and events that provide mere entertainment will find this illusive.

Borrowing from cultural anthropology and sociology, Getz (2007) constructed a model of the event experience as occurring in a special liminal/liminoid time (from Turner 1974) and a special place, incorporating Falassi's (1987) notion of 'valorization' through ritual. Although much of the event experience stems from personal antecedents and levels of involvement or engagement, the designer or producer seeks to influence, and through theming and program-ming suggest, the desired experiences. Outcomes may be memorable, even transforming, which shape expectations for subsequent event experiences. Meaning is conveyed through opening ceremonies, symbolism such as banners or logos, and the theme. Some event experiences can be called 'sacred' (religious, spiritual) and others 'profane' (fun, escapist). However, it should always be a 'time out of time', to use Falassi's terminology – that is, it should be perceived to be outside the normal, beyond routine, unique.

To the extent possible, all those involved with the event should experience the b⌄⌄ and sharing that defines 'communitas'. Research supports the existence and importance of 'communitas' at events. Hannam and Halewood (2006) in a study of participants in Viking festivals, concluded that group identity was fostered, even to the point of establishing a 'neo-tribal' community. Green and Chalip's (1998) study of women athletes determined that the event was a celebration of sub-cultural values.

It is easy to think of this special place as an event venue, like an arena, theatre or convention centre. But it can also be a temporary event space, or a whole community. The question of scale is important, because as we move from venue to large public space to entire community, we have a much more complex and difficult job of design and programming. Nevertheless, many communities manage to make themselves festive throughout, or at least at important entrances and meeting places, during the time of special events.

Antecedents and choices

What are the antecedents to attending events, and how are choices and decisions made about events and related travel? Both theoretical and marketing implications arise, so a lot of the contributing theory has been adapted from consumer behaviour researchers in leisure and travel. We have to consider the personal dimension including personality, needs and motives, personal and interpersonal factors, expectations and event careers. Both 'intrinsic' (related to free choice and leisure) and 'extrinsic' (related to work and obligation) motives are important.

Barriers and constraints must be examined (e.g. Funk et al. 2009), drawing from leisure constraints theory. There are structural, personal and interpersonal constraints acting against our desires to participate in or attend events. The decision-making process starts with how people negotiate through constraints, as some people manage better than others to realize their personal goals. Attention has to be given to information searching and use (Chen and Wu 2010), event attractiveness (the pull factors), substitution, loyalty and novelty seeking.

A considerable amount of research has been done on festival and event motivation, and indeed this is one of the most developed lines of research in event studies. Early papers were published by Mohr et al. 1993; Uysal et al. 1993; and Saleh and Ryan 1993 and the work continues (e.g. Wamwara-Mbugua and Cornwell 2010). A number of review papers are available (Gibson 2004; Li and Petrick 2006), all of which tends to confirm that generic seeking and escaping motives apply (especially novelty seeking and socializing), but that there are usually a mix of generic as well as specific motives for customers or participants at any given event.

Following from event experiences we have to consider satisfaction (partly with reference to expectations), the meanings attached to experiences, and the possibility of personal transformation. These factors, plus ongoing recollection (if indeed the experience was memorable), shape future intentions. Identifying and catering to the 'highly involved' is of particular interest to event designers and marketers. Recent research on Stebbins' (1982) concept of serious leisure (e.g. Mackellar 2009), involvement (Chen and Wu 2010) and social worlds (Shipway and Jones 2007) helps explain why people establish event travel careers, as hypothesized by Getz (2008).

A recent trend (e.g. Lee et al. 2009; Hall et al. 2010; Kim et al. 2010) has been to apply consumer behaviour theory and structural equation modelling to examine the interrelationships between antecedents, event quality, satisfaction and various outcomes such as loyalty or word of mouth recommendations. The danger in this line of research is in treating events as substitutable consumer products, like toothpaste, and ignoring the fundamental social and cultural factors shaping event preferences and behaviour.

Planning, design and management of events

Planned events happen by conscious human design, created by organizations with many stakeholders, with specific goals in mind. This is largely the event management or business domain, focusing as it does on mobilizing resources, transforming processes, management systems and professionalism. Because events are means towards an end (e.g. profit, celebration, branding, political benefits, place marketing), we always must carefully assess goals and take a multi-stakeholder approach to answering the 'why' question. This is also the realm of event tourism, wherein events have specific roles to play in attracting tourists, fostering a positive destination image, acting as animators and catalysts.

Design is a combination of creativity and technical problem solving, specifically to design and produce an event that meets the organizer's (and other stakeholders') goals. Because personal experiences cannot be designed, they largely occur internally and consist of cognitive and affective processes, plus overt behaviour. The event designer has to be content with designing and implementing parts of the setting, programme and management that will either restrict or suggest and enhance the visitors' or participants' experiences. In this way, event designers consider the interactive effects of setting (location, decoration, crowd control, etc.), consumables (food, beverages, gifts, merchandise), service quality (staff and volunteers interacting with guests) and the theme and programme (what actually happens).

In the book *Event Design*, Berridge (2006) discussed the field of 'experience design' at length, saying it is in its infancy. Unfortunately, the term is being used to describe the design of everything from websites (digital media) to storytelling, theme parks and corporate 'brand events'. He argued that the purpose is to create desired perceptions, cognition and behaviour. Building and maintaining relationships is at the core, and stimulating emotional connections through engagement is the vehicle.

There are now many books available on the planning and management of events, and while the first such books were general overviews, now each specific management function is being treated separately, in line with the needs of event management degree programmes. Some of these are mentioned later.

Outcomes

'Outcomes' appears to follow logically from the other themes, but can also be a starting point. Many events are created or assisted by authorities and sponsors with intended outcomes clearly expressed. Tourism organizations work backwards from the goals of putting customers in seats or beds, then decide what events to bid on, create or market. Sponsors determine which target segments to build relationships with, or to sell to, then decide on their event marketing strategies.

Government agencies routinely formulate social and cultural policies, then assist the event sector in implementing those policies. Impacts can also be unintended and unmeasured, giving rise to evaluation and accountability problems. In a comprehensive approach, we must equally consider personal, social, cultural, economic and environmental outcomes. For each of these outcomes, research and theory are needed to answer the question: how do events cause specific impacts?

Most of the research literature has been devoted to economic impact assessments, followed by social impacts (see Chapter 5, 'Events and tourism', for details). Least understood are the ways in which events cause environmental and cultural impacts. The sustainable development paradigm has certainly influenced event studies, with a number of scholars advocating specific ways to introduce a triple-bottom-line approach to the evaluation of both event worth and outcomes.

Two books represent the current acceptance of the sustainability paradigm: *Event Management and Sustainability* by Raj and Musgrave (2009) and *Sustainable Event Management* by Jones (2010). More and more research articles are appearing with a sustainable events theme (e.g. Collins and Flynn 2008; Dickson and Arcodia 2010; Laing and Frost 2010; Mair and Jago 2010) or sustainable event tourism theme (Park and Boo 2010). The triple-bottom-line approach to evaluation has been explicitly utilized by a number of authors (e.g. Hede 2007).

Patterns and processes

The theme 'patterns and processes' represents the broader environmental influences and the dynamic aspects of our event studies 'system'. The three disciplines of history, human geography and future studies together help us answer questions like 'Where do events come from and how do they evolve over time? How are they distributed in time and space, and why? What cultural and political, technological and economic forces shape events?'

Policy is a force that both reacts to and shapes the planned event system. Events are increasingly influenced by formal government policy, including funding and regulations. Numerous events are created and marketed for strategic policy reasons, usually economics, but also cultural and social. And as events become larger and generate more substantial impacts, they cannot be ignored by policy-makers and political parties. Specific attention has to be given to what event-related policy should consist of, in an integrated approach, and how it should be formulated. All too often, policy affecting events is uncoordinated and haphazard (see a policy discussion by Getz 2009).

The largely geographical work of Janiskee (1980, 1994, 1996) is important in assessing the temporal and spatial patterns of festivals in America, including connections to resources, population and the seasons. Historical analysis has lagged, but includes published work by Sofield and Li (1998), Knox (2008), and Brewster *et al.* (2009). Future studies as a discipline has not been applied to the study of events in any systematic way, but deserves attention. What, for example, will happen to planned events if people are forced to stop travelling? Mostly this aspect of event studies has consisted of speculation about the impacts of virtual reality on the need or desire to meet in person, but the evidence strongly suggests that in-person meetings are always going to be preferred, regardless of the ease of communications.

Creating knowledge about events is also an important process. The more research, theory and management knowledge that is generated, the better we will be at creating meaningful experiences, formulating effective policy, achieving goals, marketing events or managing outcomes. To accomplish this requires knowledge about knowledge creation! What is the nature of knowledge and theory, what are the appropriate methodologies and techniques we can use, and how should events-related research be done? This leads us directly to the ensuing discussion.

Three discourses on planned events

A thorough review and analysis of the event-related literature provides evidence for this discussion of what we know (or claim to know) about planned events and the epistemological basis for these claims (as derived from the core tenets and methodologies of various foundation disciplines). It is clear that there are three predominant discourses concerning planned events. While they tend to go in separate directions, it is essential for event studies to integrate them more fully. They are: (a) a classical discourse, rooted in anthropology and sociology, that considers the roles, importance and effects of planned events in society and culture; (b) event tourism, which is focused on how events can contribute to economic development and place marketing, and (c) event management, which concentrates on how to produce and manage events and their organizations.

Although it makes perfect sense to start with foundation disciplines and what they have contributed to event studies, it is simpler and more instructive to examine the three main discourses on event studies and then look at their evolution and foundations. This is also a good approach because no institution has yet established event studies as a distinct field, and its affiliations are clearly related to quite distinct academic homes in tourism, event management programmes (sometimes in tourism/hospitality, sometimes separate), and the social and behavioural sciences. These 'homes', and the fact that various research journals cater to them, provide legitimacy, but also institutionalize divisiveness.

Discourse

'Discourse' can be narrowly defined as a conversation, or in a more formalized way as a rule-based dialogue among parties. An event can be interpreted as a discourse. Crespi-Vallbona and Richards (2007: 103) viewed festivals as 'arenas of discourse enabling people to express their views on wider cultural, social and political issues'. But we are here more concerned with academic discourses pertaining to festivals and other events.

Foucault (1972 [1969]) saw discourse as a system of ideas or knowledge, with its own vocabulary; this can result in the power to monopolize communications and debate, and to enforce particular points of view. My preference is to follow along the lines of Foucault, viewing a discourse as a system, or structured line of reasoning, ideas and approaches to knowledge creation, including theory development and practical applications. Meaning is assigned within a discourse, based on researchers' values, so that the language and concepts define and delimit what is legitimate or expected of those contributing to it; as well, some understandings are marginalized or ignored completely.

For example, Tribe (2004: 57) argued that 'the business discourse' in tourism has 'some coherence and structure, and a framework of theories and concepts (borrowed from the field of business studies)', and that tourism studies tends to crystallize around this interdisciplinary approach. Translated into the subject of this chapter, the business discourse becomes 'event/ festival tourism' and is also applicable to the profession of 'festival/event management'. Tribe also argued that the other main area of knowledge creation in tourism studies, undertaken by researchers not interested in the business approach, draws from specific disciplines and leads to interdisciplinarity.

If it is simply asked, 'What is being researched pertaining to planned events?' then the answer is found in an extensive and systematic literature review identifying the terminology and concepts employed by researchers. From just such a review, conducted by the author, three discourses were identified, encompassing both the concepts and research themes within event studies and related debate and argument, including contested meanings and the appropriateness of applying particular theories and methodologies. The matter of research and theory-building paradigms comes into question, although individual scholars might never question where they stand on such philosophical issues.

To illustrate, consider that the knowledge domain of event tourism includes considerable attention to economic impact assessment and related issues such as the 'attribution problem' (i.e. what criteria and evidence are necessary to attribute impacts to a particular event?). This is part of the study of event tourism but is neither theoretical nor debated; it simply has to be understood and applied. However, the concept of 'authenticity' is often hotly debated, such as through claims that tourism commodifies festivals and renders them culturally inauthentic.

As will be seen, the classical discourse is rooted in social sciences and seems to naturally foster debate and philosophizing, whereas festival tourism and management is much more applied, and less critical. Scholars seeking greater interdisciplinarity are generally responsible for bringing challenging concepts and theoretical/philosophical debate into the tourism and management discourses.

The classical discourse

An extensive literature review has identified the following classical themes within this discourse: myth, ritual and symbolism; ceremony and celebration; spectacle; communitas; host–guest interactions (and the role of the stranger); liminality, the carnivalesque and festivity; authenticity and commodification; pilgrimage; and a considerable amount of political debate over impacts and meanings. There are landmark works by van Gennep (1960 [1909]), Victor Turner (1969, 1974, 1982, 1983, 1987; Turner and Turner 1978), Abrahams (1982, 1987), Falassi (1987) and Manning (1983). Numerous contemporary studies of specific cultural celebrations have been published in literature outside events and tourism (e.g. Cavalcanti 2001). Two recent books make explicit connections between tourism and the cultural dimensions of festivals: Long and Robinson (2004) and Picard and Robinson (2006).

It is highly relevant to note that Eric Cohen's (1988a) article entitled 'Traditions in the qualitative sociology of tourism' identified three principal traditions that all have importance for the study of festivals and events, namely those associated with the seminal works of Boorstin, MacCannell and Turner. Boorstin (1961), a historian, invented the term 'pseudo-event' to describe contrived attractions that create a self-perpetuating system of illusions that are sought out by gullible and unsophisticated mass tourists. Cohen described him as the first in a long line of socio-critical authors in America and Europe. Much more influential was MacCannell's (1973, 1976) sociological thesis on the tourist, which mainstreamed the ongoing discussion of authenticity and the notion that it is sought out because of the inauthenticity of modern life. His term 'staged authenticity' gained enduring popularity, and his work directly stimulated early articles on 'spurious' festivals (Papson 1981), as well as Buck's (1977) notion of using events for 'boundary maintenance' between tourists and sensitive cultural groups.

Victor Turner's work on pilgrimage (Turner 1979; Turner and Turner 1978), liminality and communitas (1974) (which draw from van Gennep's 1909 work on rites de passage) have had tremendous influence on tourism and event studies, including direct incorporation into a recent (Getz 2007) model of the planned-event experience. Whereas 'liminal' experiences are associated with ritual and the 'sacred', 'liminoid' are part of the 'profane' everyday life, including festivity and carnivalesque, revelry and role inversions.

Duvignaud's (1976) conceptual article on the sociology of festivals and festivity provides documentation of the ways in which these phenomenon have been 'explained', including the dialectic between those, like Durkheim (1978), who viewed festivity as an 'intensification of the collective being' and those who see them as being inherently subversive. Duvignaud also discussed festivity as play and commemoration, concluding there was no one correct interpretation.

Within the tourism literature commodification and authenticity have been important, festival-related themes. Greenwood (1972, 1989) first suggested that tourism commoditized culture, and particularly a festival, leading to the event's loss of meaning among residents. E. Cohen (1988) defined commoditization as a process by which things become valued in monetary terms, or exchange value. Cohen's concept of 'emergent authenticity' applies to festivals; Cohen described how a re-created, tourist-oriented festival could become accepted as being authentic, over time. Thus, commoditization might lead to a festival acquiring new meanings for both tourists and residents.

Recently, scholars within and outside tourism and the traditional foundation disciplines have been examining events with regard to an increasing variety of issues and employing different theoretical perspectives. Mixed methods are increasingly the norm, as, for example, Holloway *et al.* (2010) have outlined the use of ethnography in events research.

One of the growing themes concerns place identity, with results often challenging long-standing notions of the negative effects of festival tourism on culture and communities. De Bres and Davis (2001) concluded that the Rollin' Down the River festival in communities along the Kansas River in the USA, despite being characterized as an example of tourist commodification, did lead to a positive self-identification for the local community. They used mixed methods, with considerable weight given to interviews with community festival organizers. Jeong and Santos (2004) examined the Kangnung Dano festival in Korea from the perspective of cultural politics and promotional products, involving conflicts between globalization, tradition and place identity. The researchers proposed that regional identity has been dynamically constructed and is reconstructing due to contested meanings of place.

Contested place identities surrounding creation of the Parkes Elvis Revival Festival in small-town Australia were studied (through interviews with residents) by Brennan-Horley *et al.* (2007). Here, a superimposed, tourism-oriented event with no connection to the local culture has become a local tradition, put the town on the tourist map, and generated economic benefits – but not without tensions. Winchester and Rofe (2005) researched the annual Festival of Lights in a small South Australian village, Lobethal. It originated in the 1940s and now attracts over 250,000 visitors. The Festival builds upon existing traditions and religious and rural discourses permeate it. The researchers believe the event provides a significant local place identity.

Discourse on event tourism

'Event tourism' as a separate discourse takes an instrumentalist approach in which the dominant themes are the production and marketing of festivals for tourism and other forms of development, with a heavy methodological emphasis on marketing and economic impact assessment. A thorough review of this discourse has been published by Getz (2008), is the subject of a separate chapter in this book (Chapter 5), and is summarized through a major collection of articles on event tourism, compiled in four volumes by Connell and Page (2009).

The roles of events in tourism include attracting tourists (to specific places, and to overcome seasonality), contributing to place marketing (including image formation and destination branding), animating attractions and places, and acting as catalysts for other forms of development. Dominating this discourse has been the assessment of economic impacts of events and event tourism, planning and marketing event tourism at the destination level, and studies of event-tourism motivation and various segmentation approaches. The study of negative impacts of events and event tourism is a more recent line of research.

'Festival tourism' is an important element in 'event tourism', so much so that the term 'festivalization' has been coined to suggest an over-commodification of festivals exploited by tourism and place marketers (see, for example, Quinn (2006) and Richards (2006)). Indeed, a marked trend towards treating festivals as commodities has emerged. In this approach, drawing heavily upon consumer behaviour and other marketing concepts, motivations for attending festivals have been studied at length, and more recently the links between quality, satisfaction, and behaviour or future intentions have been modelled.

Note that theory development in event tourism borrows heavily from economics and consumer behaviour. Much of the knowledge base of this discourse is, however, purely 'factual' (what you need to know in order to develop event tourism) and of the problem-solving kind (how to attract tourists). Looking for event-specific theory, we need to refine the concept of 'attractiveness' as it applies to various events (that is, their drawing power for specific segments) and in the context of combating seasonality of demand and the over-concentration of tourism. This relates to the notion of an event travel career trajectory for people who become more and more involved in serious-leisure pursuits.

Discourse on event management

This is the most recent discourse or sub-field to develop in the research literature, even though professional practice of event management has a much longer history. From an academic perspective, there had to be a clear demand for graduates, and support from professionals and policy-makers, before event management could become established as a field of study. The first major textbook on this subject was Goldblatt's *Special Events: The Art and Science of Celebration* (published in 1990), and Goldblatt has remained at the forefront of event management studies and professional development through multiple books. This was followed closely by Getz (1991) with the book *Festivals, Special Events and Tourism*, and a year later came C.M. Hall's book *Hallmark Tourist Events*.

Reviewing the literature, it is clear that an explosion of educational programmes, books and research articles on event management has occurred in the two ensuing decades. If we can draw inferences from the life cycles of closely related fields, especially leisure and tourism studies which became established in the 1970s and 1980s, then event management will likely continue to grow and spread globally for at least another decade before peaking. This constitutes a diffusion curve that inevitably results in maturity and decline in numbers, though not disappearance or irrelevance. Those event management university departments wanting to remain healthy will have to pursue an evolution to event studies, based on sound research and theory development, otherwise declining student numbers will cause many to shrink or disappear.

Numerous introductory texts have now been published, as well as more practical books from the event practitioners' point of view, and the trend is to publish texts on specific elements of event management including: human resources (Van der Wagen 2006); risk (Tarlow 2002; Silvers 2007); project management and logistics (O'Toole and Mikolaitis 2002); sponsorship (Skinner and Rukavina 2003); coordination (Silvers 2004); operations (Tum *et al.* 2006); marketing (Hoyle 2002), and communications (Masterman and Wood 2005). As well, the management of specific types of events has been addressed in books: on arts and cultural festivals (Yeoman *et al.* 2004); Hall and Sharples (2008) on international food and wine festivals); sports (Graham *et al.* 1995; Solomon 2002; Masterman 2004; Supovitz and Goldblatt 2004); on meetings and conventions (Rogers 2003; Fenich 2005; Allen 2008); and on exhibitions (Morrow 1997).

EMBOK, the event management body of knowledge (Silvers *et al.* 2006), has been created by practitioners and academics to codify the skills and knowledge required by professional event managers. There are five main knowledge domains: administration; design; marketing; operations; and risk, each with numerous sub-divisions. Much of this knowledge base has to come from business or managerial literature. For example, 'marketing mix' and 'stakeholder management' are generic. The managerial and problem-solving skills needed by professionals are stressed, whereas theory is not addressed. EMBOK also has implications for licensing and cross-border job mobility. It tells academics what a full degree programme in event management should cover, but the means of acquiring all the pertinent skills and knowledge has to include on-the-job experience.

A full 'ontology' of event management has yet to be constructed. It should pinpoint and interrelate the key terms and concepts that are unique and/or essential to this professional field. For example, what does 'social entrepreneurship' mean in the not-for-profit festivals sector? It has not been addressed. Or, how are event 'stakeholders' typically organized (see Getz *et al.* 2007), and is the stakeholder management process different for festivals or major sport events (see Parent and Seguin 2007; Andersson and Getz 2008)? The research literature is growing and diversifying at a fast pace, facilitated by a growing number of event-specific journals, making ontological mapping more difficult.

Interdisciplinary theory development for event studies

It is difficult to imagine one grand, unifying theory of planned events, but the field of event studies does need its own theoretical constructs, and they will certainly be derived from inter-disciplinary theory-building. A number of overarching questions require advances on the theoretical plane:

- Why are planned events found in all societies, as they have been throughout history? (their *raison d'être*; values to various societies and cultures)
- Do all societies institutionalize generic types of events, and are their functions identical? Are the functions enduring or constantly evolving?
- What are the basic functions they perform, or the goals they meet (from multiple stakeholder perspectives)?
- Why do people want, or need, to attend events, and how do they select them? (not merely a marketing issue, as we need to explain how various events are perceived and attitudes shaped towards them, in different cultures and settings)
- How do individuals and groups experience different events, and how are these experiences affected by management and other variables?
- How are people changed (if at all) by event experiences?
- In what ways are planned events evolving (through policy, strategy, social and individual action)?
- What is the future of planned events (and related professions)? Can virtual events replace in-person experiences?

Theory on the forms and functions of planned events

There is an existing, multidimensional construct, called exchange theory, which answers many fundamental questions about planned events. A common theme in all planned events is exchange, because they are all social experiences with a purpose – whether economic, social, cultural or familial in scope. Even planned virtual events fulfil these roles to some degree.

The 'rational choice' version of exchange theory would see planned events as cooperation mechanisms to facilitate necessary exchanges, primarily economic in nature. This especially applies to markets, fairs and exhibitions, but also covers many meetings, conventions, corporate and political events. Social order arises, unplanned, from the necessity and the social conventions associated with these events.

However, 'anthropological exchange theory' takes an alternative view, with social order and the pursuit of individual advantages arising from underlying ritual and the symbolic nature of exchanges between people – often obligatory in nature. When exchange processes break down, social disorder or conflict results. According to Marshall (1998), this anthropological approach draws on Durkheim's claim that not everything in the contract is contractual, that is, rational (business) exchange cannot itself be the source of settled, morally regulated social order, but instead presupposes it. Social sentiments must be embodied in symbols (or collective representation) of society's obligatory rules and commands which define the scope remaining for the pursuit of individual interest.

Festivals and other cultural celebrations appear to conform more to the anthropological approach to exchange theory, as they clearly embody ritual and symbolism, but these elements are found in many events. In Figure 2.2 four dimensions are shown, based on the premise that any event can potentially embody both economic and social exchanges, and possess symbolic and ritualistic value. As well, many event experiences are highly personal in nature, pertaining to entertainment at one end and self-development at the other. Planned events both arise from social order and help define and maintain it. Increasingly, we look to planned events as institutionalized forms of business, means of personal or group expression, social order and celebration.

At the innermost zone of convergence, major festivals and events of all forms can possess high value on social, economic, personal and symbolic dimensions. This reflects, in part, their scale and related attractiveness to residents, tourists and the media – they generate substantial economic exchanges even if that is not their goal. Individuals will find ample scope for meeting their self-development needs through volunteering and direct participation. These events – often called mega, iconic, hallmark or signature – are symbols for their host communities/ nations and foster pride, identity and cohesion. By their nature, permanent events in this zone tend to become institutions, supported by powerful stakeholders because they perform all these necessary functions. As well, they tend to converge in terms of form, with a high degree of blending of all the elements of style.

At the outermost range of the economic exchange dimension are events, like attending a market to shop or a consumer show to look around and learn, that are low in social exchange

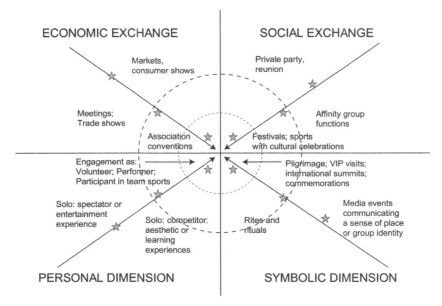

Figure 2.2 Types and functions of planned events: four dimensions and zones of convergence

(individuals or small groups attend and group experiences are not facilitated), symbolic value and personal development. But a trade show, while ostensibly all about business for particular industry groups, does also embody social and symbolic dimensions. Although meetings and conventions are often conducted for business reasons, they can also be positioned (alternatively or equally) in the social exchange dimension for purposes of group identity-building and cohesion. Those attending events for specific groups generally experience a sense of communitas.

The social exchange dimension emphasizes the importance of events as both reflections and facilitators of essential social exchanges, the kinds that form and reinforce group identity – from the level of friends and family, through all kinds of affinity groups and sub-cultures, all the way to place and national identity. Private parties are at the outer range, while public festivals/celebrations are within the inner zone. The largest and most public events also generate economic activity by attracting sponsors, grants and tourists; they are typically high in symbolic value, with the event being iconic within some group and important to places, as in hallmark events. These planned events typically combine elements, such as sports with festivals and exhibitions, or conventions with gala banquets and tours. And they offer many opportunities for personal engagement and growth.

Along the continuum representing the personal dimension, the individual displays a range of levels of involvement or engagement, beginning with being a solo spectator at a sport competition or concert in which entertainment/spectacle prevails. Solo experiences in social events are frequent, such as running in a race or going to an event as a learning or aesthetic opportunity (e.g. art exhibitions). Within the inner zone the individual experiences a high level of engagement (or involvement), such as in team sports, as a volunteer or performer, and these experiences are associated with both personal development (or self-actualization) and socializing.

All events can hold symbolic value to persons and groups, but many fall primarily within this dimension. Events broadcast to the community or world are often intended to foster a positive image, community pride and group identity; they may be any type of event, or expressly produced as media events with small numbers of direct participants or guests. A panoply of rites and rituals exist that are more social in nature, clearly engaging individuals and groups in symbolic activities: from birthdays and anniversaries to bar mitzvahs and religious processions. Parades, read as social texts, can easily fit into this category. Within the inner zone of convergence are large-scale social events that also have economic significance, such as pilgrimages, VIP visits, international summits and heritage commemorations. Individuals can experience these events as being spiritually, culturally or intellectually rewarding, and even transforming.

Closing words

However the professional practice of event management progresses, and the field of event studies evolves in the academic world, there will remain two constants. Planned events will continue to occupy essential, institutional roles in society, culture and the economy. And people will continue to study them. Although there is no real need for formalizing event studies as a separate branch of academia, there is certainly a need to continue interdisciplinary research, both to build theory and to support policy and professional practice.

References

Abrahams, R. (1982) 'The language of festivals: celebrating the economy', in V. Turner (ed.) *Celebration: Studies in Festivity and Ritual*, Washington, DC: Smithsonian Institution Press, pp. 160–77.
——(1987) 'An American vocabulary of celebrations', in A. Falassi (ed.) *Time out of Time, Essays on the Festival*, Albuquerque: University of New Mexico Press, pp. 173–83.

Allen, J. (2008) *Event Planning: The Ultimate Guide to Successful Meetings, Corporate Events, Fundraising Galas, Conferences and Conventions, Incentives and Other Special Events*, Mississauga: Wiley Canada.

Andersson, T. and Getz, D. (2008) 'Stakeholder management strategies of festivals', *Journal of Convention and Event Tourism* 9(3): 199–220.

Becher, T. and Trowler, P. (2001) *Academic Tribes and Territories: Intellectual Enquiry and the Cultures of Discipline*, Buckingham: Open University Press.

Belhassen, Y. and Caton, K. (2006) 'Authenticity matters', *Annals of Tourism Research* 33(3): 872–75.

——(2009) 'Advancing understandings: a linguistic approach to tourism epistemology', *Annals of Tourism Research* 36(2): 335–52.

Berridge, G. (2006) *Event Design*, Oxford: Butterworth-Heinemann.

Boorstin, D. (1961) *The Image: A Guide to Pseudo-Events in America*, New York: Harper and Row.

Brennan-Horley, C., Connell, J. and Gibson, C. (2007) 'The Parkes Elvis Revival Festival: economic development and contested place identities in rural Australia', *Geographical Research* 45(1): 71–84.

Brewster, M., Connell, J. and Page, S. (2009) 'The Scottish Highland Games: evolution, development and role as a community event', *Current Issues in Tourism* 12(3): 271–93.

Buck, R. (1977) 'Making good business better: a second look at staged tourist attractions', *Journal of Travel Research* 15(3): 30–1.

Cavalcanti, M. (2001) 'The Amazonian Ox Dance Festival: an anthropological account', *Cultural Analysis* 2: 69–105.

Chen, A. and Wu, R. (2010) 'Understanding visitors' involvement profile and information search: the case of Neimen Song Jiang Battle Array Festival', *Event Management* 13(4): 205–22.

Cohen, E. (1988a) 'Traditions in the qualitative sociology of tourism', *Annals of Tourism Research* 15: 29–46.

——(1988b) 'Authenticity and commoditization in tourism', *Annals of Tourism Research* 15: 371–86.

Collins, A. and Flynn, A. (2008) 'Measuring the environmental sustainability of a major sporting event: a case study of the FA Cup Final', *Tourism Economics* 14(4): 751–68.

Connell, J. and Page, S.J. (eds) (2009) *Event Tourism*, London: Routledge.

Crespi-Vallbona, M. and Richards, G. (2007) 'The meaning of cultural festivals: stakeholder perspectives in Catalunya', *International Journal of Cultural Policy* 13(1): 103–22.

Csikszentimihalyi, M. (1990) *Flow: The Psychology of Optimal Experience*, New York: Harper Perennial.

De Bres, K. and Davis, J. (2001) 'Celebrating group and place identity: a case study of a new regional festival', *Tourism Geographies* 3(3): 326–37.

Dickson, C. and Arcodia, C. (2010) 'Promoting sustainable event practice: the role of professional associations', *International Journal of Hospitality Management* 29(2): 236–44.

Diller, S., Shedroff, N. and Rhea, D. (2006) *Making Meaning*, Upper Saddle River, NJ: Pearson.

Durkheim, E. (1978) 'Sociology and the social sciences', in M. Traugott (ed.) *Emile Durkheim on Institutional Analysis*, Chicago: University of Chicago Press.

Duvignaud, J. (1976) 'Festivals: a sociological approach', *Cultures* 3: 13–28.

Falassi, A. (ed.) (1987) *Time Out of Time: Essays on the Festival*, Albuquerque: University of New Mexico Press.

Fenich, G. (2005) *Meetings, Expositions, Events, and Conventions: An Introduction to the Industry*, Upper Saddle River, NJ: Pearson.

Foucault, M. (1972 [1969]) *The Archaeology of Knowledge*, London: Tavistock Publications. Originally published in French as *L'Archéologie du Savoir*.

Funk, D., Alexandris, K. and Ping, Y. (2009) 'To go or stay home and watch: exploring the balance between motives and perceived constraints for major events: a case study of the 2008 Beijing Olympic Games', *International Journal of Tourism Research* 11(1): 41–53.

Getz, D. (1991) *Festivals, Special Events, and Tourism*, New York: Van Nostrand Reinhold.

——(2005) *Event Management and Event Tourism*, New York: Cognizant, second edition.

——(2007) *Event Studies: Theory, Research and Policy for Planned Events*, Oxford: Elsevier.

——(2008) 'Event tourism: definition, evolution, and research', *Tourism Management*, 29(3): 403–28.

——(2009) 'Policy for sustainable and responsible festivals and events: institutionalization of a new paradigm', *Journal of Policy Research in Tourism, Leisure and Events* 1(1): 61–78.

Getz, D., Andersson, T. and Larson, M. (2007) 'Festival stakeholder roles: concepts and case studies', *Event Management* 10(2/3): 103–22.

Gibson, H.J. (2004) 'Moving beyond the "what is and who" of sport tourism to understanding "why"', *Journal of Sport and Tourism* 9(3): 247–65.

Goldblatt, J. (1990) *Special Events: The Art and Science of Celebration*, New York: Van Nostrand Reinhold.

Graham, S., Goldblatt, J. and Delpy, L. (1995) *The Ultimate Guide to Sport Event Management and Marketing*, Chicago: Irwin.

Green, B. and Chalip, L. (1998) 'Sport tourism as the celebration of subculture', *Annals of Tourism Research* 25(2): 275–91.

Greenwood, D. (1972) 'Tourism as an agent of change: a Spanish Basque case study', *Ethnology* 11: 80–91.

——(1989) 'Culture by the pound: an anthropological perspective on tourism as cultural commodification', in V. Smith (ed.) *Hosts and Guests: The Anthropology of Tourism*, Philadelphia: University of Pennsylvania Press, second edition, pp. 171–85.

Hall, J., Basarin, V. and, Lockstone-Binney, L. (2010) 'An empirical analysis of attendance at a commemorative event: Anzac Day at Gallipoli', *International Journal of Hospitality Management* 29(2): 245–53.

Hall, M. (1992) *Hallmark Tourist Events: Impacts, Management and Planning*, London: Belhaven.

Hall, M. and Sharples, L. (2008) *Food and Wine Festivals and Events Around the World*, Oxford: Butterworth-Heinemann.

Hannam, K. and Halewood, C. (2006) 'European Viking themed festivals: an expression of identity', *Journal of Heritage Tourism* 1(1): 17–31.

Hede, A. (2007) 'Managing special events in the new era of the triple bottom line', *Event Management* 11 (1/2): 13–22.

Holloway, I., Brown, L. and Shipway, R. (2010) 'Meaning not measurement: using ethnography to bring a deeper understanding to the participant experience of festivals and events', *International Journal of Event and Festival Management* 1(1): 74–85.

Hoyle, L. (2002) *Event Marketing*, New York: Wiley.

Janiskee, R. (1980) 'South Carolina's harvest festivals: rural delights for day tripping urbanites', *Journal of Geography* 1: 96–104.

——(1994) 'Some macroscale growth trends in America's community festival industry', *Festival Management and Event Tourism* 2(1): 10–14.

——(1996) 'The temporal distribution of America's community festivals', *Festival Management and Event Tourism* 3(3): 129–37.

Jeong, S. and Santos, C. (2004) 'Cultural politics and contested place identity', *Annals of Tourism Research* 31(3): 640–56.

Jones, M. (2010) *Sustainable Event Management: A Practical Guide*, London: Earthscan.

Kim, Y.H., Kim, M., Ruetzler, T. and Taylor, J. (2010) 'An examination of festival attendees' behaviour using SEM', *Journal of Event and Festival Management* 1(1): 86–95.

Knox, D. (2008) 'Spectacular tradition Scottish folksong and authenticity', *Annals of Tourism Research* 35(1): 255–73.

Laing, J. and Frost, W.(2010) 'How green was my festival: exploring challenges and opportunities associated with staging green events', *International Journal of Hospitality Management* 29(2): 261–67.

Lee, J.S., Lee, C.K. and Yoon, Y. (2009) 'Investigating differences in antecedents to value between first-time and repeat festival-goers', *Journal of Travel and Tourism Marketing* 26(7): 688–702.

Li, R. and Petrick, J. (2006) 'A review of festival and event motivation studies', *Event Management* 9(4): 239–45.

Long, P. and Robinson, M. (eds)(2004) *Festivals and Tourism: Marketing, Management and Evaluation*, Sunderland, UK: Business Education Publishers.

MacCannell, D. (1973) 'Staged authenticity: arrangements of social space in tourism settings', *American Journal of Sociology* 79(3): 589–603.

——(1976) *The Tourist: A New Theory of the Leisure Class*, New York: Schocken Books.

Mackellar, J. (2009) 'An examination of serious participants at the Australian Wintersun Festival', *Leisure Studies* 28(1): 85–104.

Mair, J. and Jago, L. (2010) 'The development of a conceptual model of greening in the business events tourism sector', *Journal of Sustainable Tourism* 18(1): 77–94.

Manning, F. (ed.) (1983) *The Celebration of Society: Perspectives on Contemporary Cultural Performance*, Bowling Green, OH: Bowling Green University Popular Press.

Marshall, G. (1998) 'Exchange theory', in *A Dictionary of Sociology*, Encyclopedia.com. Available at: www.encyclopedia.com/doc/1O88-exchangetheory.html (accessed 24 December 2009).

Masterman, G. (2004) *Strategic Sports Event Management*, Oxford: Butterworth-Heinemann.

Masterman, G. and Wood, E. (2006) *Innovative Marketing Communications: Strategies for the Events Industry*, Oxford: Butterworth-Heinemann.

Mohr, K., Backman, K., Gahan, L. and Backman, S. (1993) 'An investigation of festival motivations and event satisfaction by visitor type', *Festival Management and Event Tourism* 1(3): 89–97.

Morrow, S. (1997) *The Art of the Show: An Introduction to the Study of Exhibition Management*, Dallas: International Association for Exhibition Management.

Nash, D. and Smith, V. (1991) 'Anthropology and tourism', *Annals of Tourism Research* 18: 12–25.

O'Toole, W. and Mikolaitis, P. (2002) *Corporate Event Project Management*, New York: Wiley.

Papson, S. (1981) 'Spuriousness and tourism: politics of two Canadian provincial governments', *Annals of Tourism Research* 8(2): 503–7.

Parent, M. and Seguin, B. (2007) 'Factors that led to the drowning of a world championship organizing committee: a stakeholder approach', *European Sport Management Quarterly* 7(2): 187–212.

Park, E. and Boo, S. (2010) 'An assessment of convention tourism's potential contribution to environmentally sustainable growth', *Journal of Sustainable Tourism* 18(1): 95–113.

Picard, D. and Robinson, M. (eds) (2006) *Festivals, Tourism and Social Change: Remaking Worlds*, Clevedon: Channel View.

Quinn, B. (2006) 'Problematising "festival tourism": arts festivals and sustainable development in Ireland', *Journal of Sustainable Tourism* 14(3): 288–306.

Raj, R. and Musgrave, J. (2009) *Event Management and Sustainability*, Wallingford, UK: CABI.

Rice, E. (1983) *The Grand Procession of Ptolemy Philadelphus*, Oxford: Oxford University Press.

Richards, G. (ed.) (2006) *Cultural Tourism: Global and Local Perspectives*, New York: Haworth.

Rogers, T. (2003) *Conferences and Conventions: A Global Industry*, Oxford: Butterworth-Heinemann.

Saleh, F. and Ryan, C. (1993) 'Jazz and knitwear: factors that attract tourists to festivals', *Tourism Management* 14(4): 289–97.

Shipway, R. and Jones, I. (2007) 'Running away from home: understanding visitor experiences and behaviour at sport tourism events', *International Journal of Tourism Research* 9(5): 373–83.

Silvers, J. (2004) *Professional Event Coordination*, Hoboken, NJ: Wiley.

——(2007) *Risk Management for Meetings and Events*, Oxford: Butterworth-Heinemann.

Silvers, J., Bowdin, G., O'Toole, W. and Nelson, K. (2006) 'Towards an international event management body of knowledge (EMBOK)', *Event Management* 9(4): 185–98.

Skinner, B. and Rukavina, V. (2003) *Event Sponsorship*. Hoboken, NJ: Wiley.

Sofield, T. and Li, F. (1998) 'Historical methodology and sustainability: an 800-year-old festival from China', *Journal of Sustainable Tourism* 6(4): 267–92.

Solomon, J. (2002) *An Insider's Guide to Managing Sporting Events*, Champaign, IL: Human Kinetics.

Stebbins, R. (1982) 'Serious leisure: a conceptual statement', *Pacific Sociological Review* 25(2): 251–72.

Supovitz, F. and Goldblatt, J. (2004) *The Sports Event Management and Marketing Handbook*, New York: Wiley.

Tarlow, P. (2002) *Event Risk Management and Safety*, New York: Wiley.

Tribe, J. (2004) 'Knowing about tourism – epistemological issues', in L. Goodson and J. Phillimore (eds) *Qualitative Research in Tourism: Ontologies, Epistemologies and Methodologies*, London: Routledge, pp. 46–62.

Tum, J., Norton, P. and Wright, J. (2006) *Management of Event Operations*, Oxford: Butterworth-Heinemann.

Turner, V. (1969) *The Ritual Process: Structure and Anti-Structure*, New York: Aldine de Gruyter.

——(1974) 'Liminal to liminoid, in play, flow and ritual: an essay in comparative symbology', in E. Norbeck (ed.) *The Anthropological Study of Human Play*. Rice University Studies 60: 53–92.

——(1979) *Process, Performance, and Pilgrimage: A Study in Comparative Symbology*, New York: Concept.

——(ed.) (1982) *Celebration: Studies in Festivity and Ritual*, Washington, DC: Smithsonian Institution Press.

——(1983) 'Carnival in Rio: Dionysian drama in an industrializing society', in F. Manning (ed.) *The Celebration of Society: Perspectives on Contemporary Cultural Performance*, Bowling Green, OH: Bowling Green University Popular Press, pp. 103–24.

——(1987) *The Anthropology of Performance*, New York: PAJ Publications.

Turner, V. and Turner, E. (1978) *Image and Pilgrimage in Christian Culture*, New York: Columbia University Press.

Uysal, M., Gahan, L. and Martin, B. (1993) 'An examination of event motivations: a case study', *Festival Management and Event Tourism* 1(1): 5–10.

van der Wagen, L. (2006) *Human Resource Management for Events: Managing the Event Workforce*, Oxford: Butterworth-Heinemann.

van Gennep, A. (1960 [1909]) *The Rites of Passage*, trans. M. Vizedom and G. Coffee, London: Routledge and Kegan Paul.

LIBRARY, UNIVERSITY OF CHESTER

Wamwara-Mbugua, L. and Cornwell, T. (2010) 'Visitor motivation to attending international festivals', *Event Management* 13(4): 277–86.

Winchester, H. and Rofe, M. (2005) 'Christmas in the "Valley of Praise": intersections of the rural idyll, heritage and community in Lobethal, South Australia', *Journal of Rural Studies* 21: 265–79.

Yeoman, I., Robertson, M. and Ali-Knight, J. (2004) *Festival and Events Management: An International Arts and Culture Perspective*, Oxford: Butterworth-Heinemann.

3

Typologies and Event Studies

Tom Lunt

As we saw in Chapter 1, the development of Event Studies has generated a great deal of debate over how we understand events. One of the key themes of the debate relates to the categorisation of events and the construction of event typologies. This chapter seeks to explore this theme and begins by asking, 'What is a typology and why are they constructed?' The term 'typology' is examined through several definitions, offered from the domains of sociology, marketing, management and events. An analysis of existing event typologies will be offered along with a case study which will be used to suggest an alternative approach to developing a typological framework for the reader to consider so as:

- to understand the general purpose and methods behind the construction of typologies;
- to critically evaluate current event typology frameworks;
- to develop their own typological frameworks in the event domain.

What do we mean by the term 'typology'? Lewin and Somekh (2005: 349) suggest it is 'the term used for a list or table which organises phenomena into categories and hierarchies. Typologies are often used as an organising framework in research, or the development of a typology may be an outcome of the research.'

This, it would seem, is not controversial. Indeed, Winch (1947: 68) suggests typologies are created, 'to perceive order in the "infinite complexity" of the universe ... for the purpose of discovering systems'. Furthermore, Winch contends that typologies may be classified as either heuristic or empirical,[1] suggesting that a heuristic typology has the following characteristics:

(a) Insofar as it is distinguishable from theory, it is deduced from theory.
(b) It is constructed for the purpose of enhancing the vision of the research, i.e. by facilitating the statement of hypotheses, the conception of testing situations, the ordering of observations.
(c) It represents the voluntary distortion of empirical phenomenon by positing the extreme forms of relevant characteristics.
(d) In the logical order of things it stands between theory and the test of theory.

An empirical typology, as its name suggests, is one that is derived primarily from data rather than theory. The aim is to summarise observations rather than enhance vision or identify essences.

Logically, empirically derived theory stands between observation and the reformulation of theory, being anchored in a logical positivist paradigm.

The link with empiricism is continued by Capecchi (1968: 9), who defines typology thus,

> A typology therefore, is the reduction of a property space, in other words *the selection of a certain number of combinations of groups or variables.* This selection may be more or less explicit, more or less valid, more or less based on the data afforded by empirical research.

An alternative perspective is offered by Cohen (1979), who develops a phenomenological typology of tourist experiences. In the context of this chapter, Cohen's paper is interesting for two reasons; first because it is a useful example of the development of a typology on which to base empirical research, and second because it deals with the subject of experience which has gained increasing prominence in the events domain. This is a subject which we will revisit throughout the book, as outlined in the Introductory chapter and those that follow which focus on experiential issues (e.g. Chapter 11, 'The psychology of events'). Getz (2007) questions the use of experience as one form of criteria through which to develop event typologies because of the multiplicity of experiential possibilities that may be found at any given event. He does, however, endorse the possibility of using phenomenology to better understand event experiences, citing Chen (2006). Another example of a phenomenological approach within the event management research is Derrett (2009), who takes up qualitative methods to explore how events emerge as cultural products from the communities in which they take place.

In contrast, Doty and Glick (1994) highlight, in the context of organisational structures and in particular the work of Mintzberg (1979), differing conceptions of what typologies are and strongly criticise the simplistic understanding of typologies as purely systems of categorisation. 'Typologies are differentiated from classification systems, shown to meet several important criteria of theories, and shown to contain multiple levels of theory' (Doty and Glick 1994: 231). Their argument is based on three assertions: typologies are distinct from classification systems; typologies meet key criteria for being theories; and typologies are complex, containing several levels of theory. As part of their critiques, Doty and Glick (1994) offer five guidelines for developing a typology:

1 In offering a typology the researcher should make clear the grand theoretical assertions that are driving it. For Mintzberg (1979) the grand theory related to organisational 'fit' to his typology would lead to greater effectiveness. This will enable others to test the typology.
2 A typology should define the complete set of ideal types. Doty and Glick (1994) show how Mintzberg (1979) offers five ideal types of organisation but then introduces hybrids or combinations of the ideal types. It is important that all hybrids allowed by the theory are included or that the pattern for their creation is explained.
3 A typology should describe each ideal type using a consistent set of dimensions. It is often the case, and Mintzberg's work is no exception, that rich descriptions are used which should use a consistent set of constructs.
4 Typological theories should state clearly the assumptions about the theoretical importance of each construct used to describe the ideal types.
5 Typological theories should be tested with conceptual and analytical models that are consistent with the theory.

In the light of these claims to the purpose and nature of typologies we turn to review their use in the extant literature on Event Studies.

As Getz has shown in Chapter 2, much of the early literature on events research concerned itself with the definition and categorisation of events. As this has been discussed in some detail in the preceding chapter it is not necessary to dwell on definitions in great detail here. However, it is worth looking at the assumptions that have driven definitions of events and typologies.

Goldblatt (1997) describes how, in 1955, Disney's Head of Public Relations Robert Jani created parades at the theme parks to prolong customer visit times into the evening. The parades were described by Jani as special events, 'that which is different from an normal day of living' (Goldblatt 1997: 2). Clearly Jani's use of the word 'normal' is problematic. In the same way as Getz highlights the difficulty of using experience as a foundation for a typology due to their variability from individual to individual, so too will a 'normal' day of living vary widely between individuals. While this is a key point and will be returned to later in this chapter, it is the motivation behind Jani's development of the parades at Disney which is instructive here. Essentially, the parades were created to increase the amount of time that the visitors spent at the theme park. This issue of the motivation to put on events is taken up by Hall (1992: 10), who suggests, 'Perhaps the most fundamental question which needs to be asked in the examination of hallmark events is that of for what and for who are the events being held?'

In the Disney example it is clear that the answer to 'for what?' is commercial profit and therefore 'for who?' is contingent. One could argue that the parade was put on for the visitors to enjoy, but there is the commercial imperative, the increased profit, derived from prolonging the length of visits to the theme park. Given this, it is perhaps unsurprising that early event literature focused on impacts, and in particular economic impacts, for example the work of Shaw (1985), Getz (1991) and Ritchie and Yangzhou (1987) which focused on hallmark, special and mega-events. An alternative lens has been employed recently by Xiao and Smith (2003), who used a grounded theory approach to analyse responses to an open question in a survey of residents. From this they developed a typology of event participant roles, namely the supporters, the complaint makers, the mild opponents and the radical opponents.

The question of event purpose or goal has been categorised by Goldblatt (2002: 8) as 'celebration, education, marketing, and reunion'.

Matthews (2008: 3) develops Goldblatt's categories and gives 'the primary reasons for holding special events [as] religious, political, social, educational and commercial', going on to suggest (2008: 5), 'the primary reason for holding special events has now become almost completely commercial'.

Matthew's typology of event purposes is valid; however, his confinement of modern-day special events to a commercial imperative may be questioned. Does an analysis that finds commerce as the primary driver of events imply an essentialising approach? Lavenda (1980), in a fascinating paper, looks at the purpose of the Caracas Carnival in Venezuela from what Matthews (2008) might term a political perspective. In charting the rise of a new elite within Venezuelan society, Lavenda (1980) shows how the carnival was developed to assert their position and, moreover, to engender the formation of a modern Venezuelan state based on the European model. Of particular interest is his analysis of a newspaper article from the time which described the new European-style carnival:

> Through the use of the language of battle, language which only a short time before had been used to describe the real battles in real wars among the Venezuelans, the editor contrives to paint a charming, amused picture of civilized diversion, clearly harmless and without threat. Here, too, the threatening chaos of the old Carnival was brought under control.
>
> *(Lavenda 1980: 470)*

Lavenda argues that the event was used to curb the agency of the lower classes who had taken part in the old Carnival. The analysis of the language is instructive in that it relates to what Getz alludes to in Chapter 2, when he introduces the idea of Foucauldian discourse analysis and, in particular, a classical discourse.

Perhaps in employing discourse analysis to events an alternative approach to the development of typologies may be conceived. A discourse analysis of a given event would include not only the literature of an event but, for example, the promotional materials and the voices of those who took part, the organisers, actors and onlookers. It could go further, as Jaworski and Coupland (2005: 6) observe, 'It is worth noticing that discourse reaches out further than language itself in the forms as well as the meanings that can be the focus of analysis.' In the case study of the Lewes Passion Plays 2010 which follows, the text of the programme for the plays is reproduced, along with parts of the website, the voices of some of those who took part and the authors' observations of the feedback evening that took place a month after the plays on 5 May.

The Lewes Passion Plays are organised at Easter every ten years by churches in the Lewes town area. The 2010 project, involving approximately 100 people, was driven entirely by volunteers and cost £6,000 to stage. Fifteen months of planning led to an event consisting of four outdoor acts or plays in different parts of the town which were watched by audiences of between 300 and 600 people and were featured on the BBC news. The following, taken from the programme for the events, gives an overview of what took place.

The cover of the programme states,

> Lewes Passion Play 2010. A Holy Week Experience. Sunday March 28th, Thursday April 1st, Friday April 2nd, Sunday April 4th.
>
> To enable the churches of Lewes, together with the community, to share in the telling of the story of Christ's passion.
>
> **2 p.m. 28 March. Palm Sunday. Entry into Jerusalem; Miracles**. Procession leaves from St Anne's church (opposite Pelham Arms) down the High Street to Cliffe Precinct [the main shopping area].
>
> The Prologue: Luke [writer of the third Gospel] will introduce the events to come in Holy Week; a crowd cheers and follows as Jesus travels with a donkey to be welcomed into Jerusalem by the people who have heard of his miracles and teaching. The crowd sees him as King and Liberator, who will set them free from the Romans. But Jesus makes clear that his kingdom is of a different nature.

In Cliffe Precinct:

> A crowd gathers to welcome Jesus. Jesus establishes his identity as healer and demonstrates his authority. A blind beggar is healed. The procession will move off along Friars' Walk to the Grange Gardens where further amazing events will occur. Please walk with us.
>
> **3 p.m. Grange Gardens.** Women are weeping beside the body of Lazarus. Jesus has been asked to come and heal Lazarus when he fell ill, but had not done so. Here he is now though, with amazing results …
>
> Jesus then moves to the Temple courtyard and makes plain how he feels about the moneylenders and the traders dealing there.
>
> Much of what Jesus did during his lifetime challenged the authorities of his day. They also felt threatened by his popularity and were determined to bring him to trial – using false allegations if necessary.

Figure 3.1 Judas wrestles with himself – should he betray his friend Jesus?

8.30 p.m. 1 April. Maundy Thursday; Last Supper, Arrest, Trial. Venue – Grange Gardens. This play takes place on and around a temporary stage. In atmospheric surroundings of the Grange Gardens and in gathering darkness key moments of the passion are enacted culminating in Judas' betrayal of Jesus and the subsequent trial at the house of the High Priest Caiaphas.

We meet Judas as he struggles with his disappointment that Jesus has not rushed in and displaced the Romans but is spreading a message of love and forgiveness (see Figure 3.1).

12.30 p.m. 2 April. Good Friday; Trail Venue – Cliffe Precinct

Jesus is brought to trial before Pilate who sees no real case for execution but is weak before the insistence of the Priests and Pharisees. He tries to evade matters by sending Jesus to Herod, Tetrarch of Galilee. Jesus does not answer Herod's questioning so is returned to Pilate for him to deal with. Evading the decision once more Pilate gives the people a choice: one prisoner is traditionally released at Passover – it can be Jesus or Barabbas. Stirred up by the leaders the crowd call for Barabbas to be released. Pilate then sentences Jesus to be flogged and crucified. Soldiers take him off. His kingship is reflected in their mockery. Process with us, following Jesus, to the Mount.

The audience walk with Jesus as he carries his cross piece to the Mount where he is nailed to the cross and left to die a slow, agonising death.

The programme for the play states,

Brutal and cruel as his death is, it offers each of us a chance to start again. 'Father forgive them,' he calls out, 'for they know not what they do.' The prayer of forgiveness is ours for

51

the taking and extends to the way in which we daily turn our back on God and give in to what we know is wrong.

3 p.m. 4 April. Easter Sunday; Resurrection. Venue – Grange Gardens.

The women find the tomb empty and their distress turns to amazement and awe when, in seeking help, they encounter the living Jesus. In this and other revelations of himself after the resurrection Jesus stresses his real presence – in breaking of bread, teaching and commissioning his followers to go and spread the message of God's love and salvation for all who hear and believe.

The message of forgiveness and salvation is demonstrated in the final scenes of the play when Judas and Jesus come face to face and embrace.

Message from the director: we have grown together as a community in our faith as we have worked on this very special project. We hope you have benefited from sharing with us our Holy Week Experience and it has helped you understand the Passion of Christ. It has been a privilege to be part of a wonderful team of volunteer scriptwriters, actors, singers, musicians, seamstresses, technicians, and prayer groups and my heartfelt thanks goes out to everyone who has made this community venture possible.

The author attended a feedback event for those who had produced the play to observe and conduct informal but focused discussions. Peter Shears, one of the scriptwriters, when asked about the decision to use authentic costumes rather than a more contemporary wardrobe, said, 'We wanted to move people out of their everyday reality.'

Those involved in the play also found it a moving experience that impacted on their lives. The director of music, Stella Hull, spoke of a 'divine jigsaw' referring to the way the music and musicians had come together to perform. Serena Smith, the director of the plays, described how her acceptance of the role of director had been a life-changing moment. She and others spoke of the strong emotions they had felt. Some comments from those involved included, 'Thank you for letting me join such a deep and moving set of events, never so overwhelmed and mesmerised by a group of people', and 'I'm not a Christian but now I'm really thinking about my beliefs.'

Both the programme and the conversations at the feedback meeting convey messages that relate to community and inclusivity. Peter Shears commented, 'We wanted to tell the story of the Gospel in a way that was accessible to all.' And Serena talked about how the script had been amended to involve women more; in particular, a scene was introduced in which Mary, mother of Jesus, talks to her son. Further, the text of the programme invites the audience to participate: for example, 'Please walk with us' and, 'We meet Judas as he struggles … ' These instructions were reinforced by the action of the plays when actors mingled with the audience during certain scenes.

The previous Passion Play in 2000 had been organised differently, with individual churches putting on different acts autonomously. The new approach, in which the churches of Lewes collaborated to produce the plays, represented a major departure and this is reflected in the message on the programme from the director, who states that 'We have grown together as a community … '

So what are the implications of this case study for the construction of event typologies? The approach to categorisation offered by Allen *et al.* (2008: 14) would suggest that this is a community event: 'Most communities produce a host of festivals and events that are targeted mainly at local audiences and are staged primarily for their social, fun and entertainment value.' Equally, one could apply Matthews' (2008: 7) category, celebrations, ceremonies and spectacles: 'Public events: these include such events as parades, festivals, sporting events, concerts and one-off theatrical presentations.' So one could categorise the Lewes Passion Play as a public community event. However, is this approach to categorisation adequate? Goldblatt (2002: 10) acknowledges that his subfield categorisation of the event management profession is 'not scientifically categorized – there are many linkages between them'. Further, Matthews (2008: 8) suggests that there is 'often much cross-pollenization among the categories, in spite of the different primary reasons for events'. For this reason the next section will suggest an approach to categorisation and ultimately typology development through the study of the discourse generated by event organisers, participants and the texts and other symbols they generate.

In suggesting an alternative route to the development of typologies, it is the author's contention that discourse and discourse analysis could be used to develop an event typology. In Chapter 2 Getz introduced discourses on events and tourism, using the term 'discourse' after the tradition of Foucault (1972). In *The Archaeology of Knowledge* Foucault states his intention,

> to show that discourse is not a slender surface of contact, or confrontation, between a reality and a language (*langue*), the intrication of a lexicon and an experience; I would like to show with precise examples that in analysing discourses themselves, one sees the loosening of the embrace, apparently so tight, of words and things, and the emergence of a group of rules proper to discursive practice ... A task that consists of not – of no longer – treating discourses as groups of signs (signifying elements referring to contents or representations) but as practices that systematically form the objects of which they speak. Of course discourses are composed of signs; but what they do is more than use these signs to designate things.
>
> *(Foucault 1972: 48–9)*

Foucault's work focused on the idea that within given social cultural and historical periods are particular ways of seeing, analysing and acting in the world that distributes power so that people (subjects) live within the discipline of that period's discourse. For the purposes of this discussion I will use the term 'discourse' as suggested by Potter and Weatherall (1987: 7) as covering 'all forms of spoken interaction, formal and informal, and written texts of all kinds'.

Earlier in this chapter, the problem of what constitutes a normal day was raised in relation to defining an event. What an individual considers to be normal will relate to his or her conception of reality. Before going any further it is necessary to consider briefly two theoretical areas that are important to discourse analysis, the nature of reality and the construction of self.

Macnaghten (1993) acknowledges that it is difficult to summarise the ontological[2] position of discourse analysis in relation to reality. However, Macnaghten (1993: 53) suggests that many approaches to discourse analysis would agree that 'all knowledge is irretrievably connected to a reality – produced, bounded and sustained by human meanings and constructions'. In essence this can be seen as a post-structuralist, socially constructed epistemological position.

The methodology of membership category analysis (Sacks 2006) suggests that the way category descriptions are sequenced in conversation enables people to make sense and derive meaning. Sacks' approach to discourse is different from that of Foucault in that he uses an ethnomethodological, conversation analysis-based technique. In particular, Sachs analyses the sequences of talk. These categories will, whether they are imposed by others or by ourselves, impact on our individual identity, and discourse analysts are particularly interested in this process or what may be called the construction of self.

If we take the comment by one of those who took part, 'I'm not a Christian but now I'm really thinking about my beliefs', we can see how this individual links the word 'Christian' with belief. The individual wishes to make clear that s/he is not a Christian but does have belief. This discourse ties in well with Giddens' (1991) description how old faith-based systems of belief have been eroded by secularisation to uncover a multitude of ideologies from which we can choose. Thus identity may change over time and is not fixed, and this links closely to the social constructionist position mentioned above. Furthermore, the fact that this individual's statement was read out at the feedback evening speaks to the way in which the organisers of the event wished to position it as an event which shared the Christian message. This statement was an instance of the event disturbing an individual so that s/he re-examined what s/he believed.

Considering the text and voices presented in the case study it may be possible to develop a typology following a pattern similar to that of Holt (1995), who observed baseball spectators at games to develop a typology of consumption. However, rather than develop an analytic approach to data generated predominately through observation, the proposed approach is based on an analysis of the language used by those who organise and participate in the event. For example, the programme for the event contains the following two extracts,

1   To enable the churches of Lewes, together with the community, to share in the telling of the story of Christ's passion.
2   Message from the director: we have grown together as a community and in our faith as we have worked on this very special project.

The word 'community' has two meanings in the text: on the one hand, it refers to the churches as a community of faith (Christians) and on the other to the wider community of Lewes who are invited to share in the Passion Play. Extract 1 refers to both of these groups while Extract 2 refers only to the community of faith, which, while it included non-Christians, was predominantly made up of individuals who would describe themselves as Christian. Referring back to Allen *et al.* (2008) one could categorise this event as a community event. However, using discourse analysis to identify how the event organisers construct their identity and then relating identity to the fundamental question of the event's purpose (i.e. Hall 1992) one may be able to develop an alternative approach to event typology which recognises that, like the identities of those who take part in the event, the result may change over time.

Returning to Extract 1 above, given in the programme, and the event's website (Extract 3) a clearer indication of the event's purpose may be given

3   Please continue to pray for all those who saw it, and whose hearts may be moved to want to learn more.

The text of the programme and the website indicates that the purpose was to enable the churches of Lewes to share the story of the Passion in the hope that those from the wider community of Lewes and beyond would also share in it and want to know more. As mentioned above, the text of the programme often invites the reader to 'walk with us' or 'process with us', and in the Good Friday section,

> 'Father forgive them,' he [Jesus] calls out, 'for they know not what they do.' The prayer for forgiveness is ours for the taking and extends to the way in which we daily turn our back on God and give in to what we know is wrong.

There is a strong message from the Christian community through the Passion Play to the wider community to share in the Christian message and believe in it. But it seems that the primary purpose is for the church communities, Anglican, Catholic, Methodist and other denominations, to share the story of the Passion. In this way, the event could be described as a religious community-building event.

The discussion of typology in the event domain given in this chapter has aimed to develop the discussion and understanding of how typology methodology may be employed within the event domain. The discussion has drawn from other subject areas to demonstrate the functions of typologies and given alternative perspectives on their nature and use. Furthermore, in employing the methodology of discourse analysis to a case study an alternative approach to event typology is offered.

It is hoped that the introduction of a social constructivist approach, employing discourse analytical methodology, will provide a greater understanding of the relationship between individuals and events and their role. From a more practical perspective the intention is to give the event organiser and marketer additional resources with which to develop their objectives and therefore evaluate the success of their events.

For the organisers of the Lewes Passion Play, the fact that all the churches in the town contributed to the production and the comments made at the feedback evening by individuals from the wider community who were involved attest to the event's success. Clearly if some churches had not been included this would have been a failure in terms of the objective set by the organisers.

The approach to typology employed in this chapter has not focused on quantitative aspects of events such as size and economic impact. This is in part because of the prevalence of this type of analysis in the event literature. Further research, employing a discourse analysis approach, should be conducted on a range of events, and this methodology be combined with existing quantitative approaches. Such approaches will be well suited to demystifying the role events play in forming individual and community identities. Furthermore, the role events play in terms of knowledge production and therefore of power relations can also be approached by researchers who take up discourse analysis. Some of these themes have been taken up, for example in relation to commodification of events (Foley *et al.* 2009) and instrumentalisation of cultural policy (Glow and Johanson 2009). Such investigations will provide a rich new perspective for students of Event Studies.

Notes

1 The distinction between heuristic and empirical relates to informed judgement and insight grounded in experience (heuristic) rather than judgement based on systematic analysis of data (empirical). Heuristic discovery/problem solving may draw on empirical data, but it goes beyond the data to deeper insights.
2 By ontological position I mean a view of the nature of being or existence. Discourse analysis takes many forms and therefore it is difficult to label them as taking a particular ontological position. For a useful discussion of different approaches to discourse analysis see Maclure (2003).

References

Allen, J., O'Toole, W., Harris, R. and McDonnell, I. (2008) *Festival and Special Event Management*, Milton, Australia: Wiley.

Capecchi, V. (1968) 'On the definition of typology and classification in sociology', *Quality and Quantity* 2(1): 9–30.

Chen, P. (2006) 'The attributes, consequences, and values associated with event sport tourists' behavior: a means end chain approach', *Event Management* 10(1): 1–22.

Cohen, E. (1979) 'A phenomenology of tourist experiences', *Sociology* 13(2): 179–201.

Derrit, R. (2009) 'How festivals nurture resilience in regional communities', in A.-K.E. Al (ed.) *International Perspectives of Festivals and Events: Paradigms of Analysis*, San Diego, CA: Elsevier.

Doty, D.H. and Glick, W.H. (1994) 'Typologies as a unique form of theory building: toward improved understanding and modelling', *Academy of Management Review* 19(2): 230–51.

Foley, M., McPherson, G. and McGillivray, D. (2009) 'International perspectives of festivals and events: paradigms of analysis', in J. Ali-Knight, M. Robertson, A. Fyall and A. Ladkin (eds) *International Perspectives of Festivals and Events: Paradigms of Analysis*, San Diego, CA: Elsivier.

Foucault, M. (1972) *The Archeology of Knowledge*, London: Tavistock Publications.

Getz, D. (1991) *Festival, Special Events, and Tourism*, New York: Van Nostrand Reinhold.

——(2007) *Event Studies : Theory, Research and Policy for Planned Events*, London: Elsevier Butterworth-Heinemann.

Giddens, A. (1991) *Modernity and Self-identity: Self and Identity in the Late Modern Age*, Cambridge: Polity Press.

Glow, H. and Johanson, K. (2009) 'Instrumentalism and the "helping" discourse: Australian Indigenous performing arts and policy', *International Journal of Cultural Policy* 15(3): 315–28.

Goldblatt, J. (1997) *Special Events Best Practices in Modern Event Management*, New York: John Wiley.

——(2002) *Special Events: Twenty-First Century Global Event Management*, New York: Wiley.

Hall, C. (1992) *Hallmark Tourist Events Impacts, Management and Planning*. London: Belhaven.

Holt, D.B. (1995) 'How consumers consume: a typology of consumption', *Journal of Consumer Research* 22(1): 1–16.

Jaworski, A. and Coupland, N. (2005) 'Introduction', in A. Jaworski and N. Coupland, *The Discourse Reader*, London: Routledge, second edition.

Lavenda, R.H. (1980) 'The festival of progress: the globalizing world-system and the transportation of the Caracas carnival', *Journal of Popular Culture* 14(3): 465–75.

Lewin, C. and Somekh, B. (2005) *Research Methods in the Social Sciences*, London: Sage.

Maclure, M. (2003) *Discourse in Educational and Social Research*, Oxford: Oxford University Press.

Macnaghten, P. (1993) 'Discourses of nature: argumentation and power', in E. Burman and I. Parker (eds) *Discourse Analytic Research*, New York: Routledge.

Matthews, D. (2008) *Special Event Production: The Process*, Oxford: Butterworth-Heinemann.

Mintzberg, H.T. (1979) *The Structuring of Organisations*, Englewood Cliffs, NJ: Prentice Hall.

Potter, J. and Weatherall, M. (1987) *Discourse and Social Psychology*. London: Sage.

Ritchie, J. and Yangzhou, H. (1987) 'The role and impact of mega-events and attractions on national and regional tourism: a conceptual and methodological overview', paper presented at the Thirty-seventh Annual Congress of the International Association of Scientific Experts in Tourism AIEST, Calgary, Alta.

Sacks, H. (2006) 'The baby cried. The mommy picked it up', in A. Jaworski and N. Coupland (eds) *The Discourse Reader*, London: Routledge.

Shaw, B. (1985) 'Fremantle and the America's Cup … the spectre of development?', *Urban Policy and Research* 3: 38–40.

Winch, R.F. (1947) 'Heuristic and empirical typologies: a job for factor analysis', *American Sociological Review* 12(1): 68–75.

Xiao, H. and Smith, S. (2003) 'Residents' perceptions of Kitchener-Waterloo Oktoberfest: an inductive analysis', *Event Management* 8: 151–60.

4

Towards an interdisciplinary events research agenda across sport, tourism, leisure and health

Mike Weed

1 Introduction

Events have been addressed by academics from a range of subjects and disciplines. As chapters elsewhere in this handbook demonstrate, events are studied within the subjects of tourism, leisure and sport, and from the disciplinary perspectives of history, economics, geography, psychology, politics and management. To these lists we might also reasonably add culture and health, two areas which tend to be important ambitions of Olympic and Paralympic hosts (Weed *et al.* 2009; McCartney *et al.* 2010). Events have also stimulated a wide range of policy and strategy research, and also research on their impacts and how such impacts should be evaluated (Chalip 2004, 2006; Weed 2010). This provides a rich tapestry of subjects, disciplines, topics and issues for event researchers to draw on. However, this chapter will attempt to draw together the key higher-level themes across events research to move towards an interdisciplinary events research agenda.

The boundaries of what Getz (2008) calls events studies are indistinct. Tom Lunt has discussed event typologies in the previous chapter (Chapter 3). However, Getz (2005) suggests a list of events under eight categories which attempts to provide comprehensive coverage of the 'planned events' sector. Table 4.1 adds two higher-level dimensions[1] to Getz's (2005) list of event categories.

Table 4.1 suggests that events might be considered public or private. Private events such as weddings, parties and other private gatherings tend to be on a relatively small scale, with few broader policy implications, and as such they will not be part of the discussion in this chapter. Events may also involve discretionary engagement (i.e. participants or viewers may choose to engage with the events, either corporeally or virtually), or engagement may be required as a consequence of work, education or position. Because issues surrounding events with which engagement is required are largely concerned with the details of managing these events and, in some cases, their resulting media coverage, the focus of this chapter will be on public events with which engagement is discretionary, for which there is a much broader range of research issues. Therefore, throughout the remainder of this chapter, the use of the word 'events' is to refer to public events with which engagement is discretionary.

Table 4.1 Dimensions and categories of events

Public events		Private events
Required engagement	*Discretionary engagement*	
Business and trade	Arts and entertainment	Private events
(e.g. meetings, conventions, trade shows)	(e.g. concerts, award ceremonies)	(e.g. weddings,
Educational and scientific	Cultural celebrations	parties, private
(e.g. conferences, seminars, clinics)	(e.g. festivals, carnivals,	social gatherings)
Political and state	commemorations, religious events)	
(e.g. summits, royal occasions,	Recreational	
political events, VIP visits)	(sport or games for fun)	
	Sport competition	
	(amateur or professional,	
	spectator or participant)	

2 Towards an aim for an interdisciplinary events research agenda

The nature of interdisciplinarity is the integration of perspectives and practices from different disciplines towards a common research agenda (Salter and Hearn 1997; Sehr and Weingart 2000). As such, the first step towards an interdisciplinary events research agenda would seem to be the establishment of an aim for such an agenda that can engage the wide-ranging and varying perspectives and subjects involved in the study of events. In short, what overarching research question or problem should an interdisciplinary research agenda seek to answer?

The first step towards such a question might be to consider the nature of events. One thing that is clear from the events listed in Table 4.1 is that events are utilitarian. That is, they are organised towards some purpose including, *inter alia*, economic development, social celebration, visitor attraction, community engagement, and product, service or area promotion. Unlike some of the arguments that are often made in relation to, for example, the value of sport for its own sake (see Green 2004), it is hard to conceive of convincing arguments for the intrinsic value of events. Events are universally a means to some other end. As such, it would appear that one part of an overarching question for an event research agenda should relate to the outcomes that are sought from events.

Of course, if outcomes are to be sought from events, then some insight as to how to achieve those outcomes is necessary. In recent years, several authors (e.g. O'Brien 2006, 2007; Weed 2009a), led by Laurence Chalip (2004, 2006), have suggested that there is a need to move beyond research which emphasises impacts to approaches that emphasise leveraging:

> Unlike impact assessments, the study of leverage has a strategic and tactical focus. The objective is to identify strategies and tactics that can be implemented prior to and during an event in order to generate particular outcomes. Consequently, leveraging implies a much more pro-active approach to capitalising on opportunities, rather than impacts research which simply measures outcomes.
>
> *(Chalip 2004)*

The increasing emphasis on the concept of leveraging would seem to suggest that as well as considering what outcomes are sought from events, an overarching events research question might also include a consideration of processes: that is, of how such outcomes are leveraged.

Work in tourism has long examined the relationship between hosts and guests (e.g. Doxey 1975; Fredline 2005). For events, rather than hosts and guests there is a relationship between hosts and audiences. Audiences for events may be those who attend to actively take part or to view, and those who engage with events remotely and virtually through various media. Of course, in many cases hosts and audiences may be one and the same, and in the case of more local events there is unlikely to be an audience for events that extends beyond those who might also be considered hosts. The key issue that tends to determine the nature of the relationship between hosts and audiences is: who are the intended beneficiaries of event outcomes? Obviously, events are intended to engage audiences who are *de facto* beneficiaries of events, although there remains a question about which audiences are sought. However, the extent to which events are perceived by hosts to deliver benefits for them is a key factor (Fredline 2005; Cragg Ross Dawson 2007; Weed *et al.* 2009). Such benefits may be direct, in terms of hosts also being audiences for the event, but also may be more indirect in terms of economic, social, cultural or health benefits. What this suggests for an overarching question for events research is that the question of for whom outcomes are sought should be considered.

Finally, because events are utilitarian, they clearly do not exist in isolation from broader social policy goals, nor from networks of power relations with entrenched interests. Work on major sports events has critiqued boosterist approaches to hosting such events (Hiller 2000; Mooney 2004), because hosting events to serve often vague boosterist goals relating to civic profile has been seen as serving the interests of local political elites at the expense of local populations. This issue is also linked to the relationship between hosts and audiences, as local populations' interests can be overlooked in the face of the needs and interests of a range of audiences, including some powerful economic interests such as event sponsors (Mooney 2004). As such, the final aspect of an overarching question for event research should be a consideration of whose interests are served by the outcomes sought from events.

The above discussions, therefore, suggest that an interdisciplinary events research agenda might be guided by an overarching research question that might be expressed as follows:

What outcomes are sought from events, how, for whom, and to serve what interests?

As an overarching question for an interdisciplinary events research agenda, the first role of the above is to generate a wide range of further, more specific questions that might be addressed within a range of subjects areas utilising a range of disciplines. As such, the remainder of this chapter will seek to examine in detail what further research questions might be generated as part of an interdisciplinary events research agenda, and therefore build a picture of what such an agenda might comprise. Following these discussions, and in conclusion, the chapter will present a more detailed framework for such an interdisciplinary events research agenda.

3 Towards an interdisciplinary events research agenda across sport, tourism, leisure and health

3.1 What outcomes are sought from events?

There are a wide range of outcomes that event providers seek; however, they can perhaps be grouped into five broad areas. First, outcomes might be sought relating to the development of participation or interest in whatever activity is the focus of the event. This might be sport, dance, theatre, music or a whole range of other cultural, sporting and recreational activities (cf. Weed *et al.* 2009). The interest sought may be that of active participants, of live audiences, and/or of virtual or mediated audiences. A second set of outcomes sought may relate to community and social development. This may be in terms of providing interesting cultural activities for local populations, in developing community cohesion and pride, and/or to contribute directly or indirectly to public health (cf. McCartney *et al.* 2010). A third group of outcomes might relate to the protection or revitalisation of the environment. Events in urban locations are often used as a catalyst to upgrade public spaces, contributing to the liveability (Baade and Sanderson 1997; Mason *et al.* 2005) of local areas. In some cases, however, sought outcomes may be to minimise the impact of an event on the environment, particularly in more fragile rural areas. A fourth set of outcomes relates to a positive impact on local, regional or national economies (cf. Preuss 2007). Certainly, this is the outcome most often sought from events, particularly larger events, and the nature and extent of economic outcomes are the most debated in the event literature. Of course, in some cases the economic motive will be that of a private event hosting or management company seeking to generate a profit. Finally, an event might be hosted to secure media coverage for an area, either to promote the area for inward investment, trade and business links, or to promote tourism (cf. Green *et al.* 2003).

Larger events, such as the Olympic and Paralympic Games, the Edinburgh Festival or Paris Fashion Week, are likely to be hosted with the aim of seeking multiple outcomes across sectors, while smaller events such as local fun runs, open-air theatre seasons or carnival weeks are likely to be more focused on only one or two types of outcomes. The key issues for an inter-disciplinary events research agenda is what outcomes have been achieved, or are likely to be achievable, by different events, and what the cumulative impact may be of the different types of outcome. These would appear to be relatively straightforward research questions to answer, but while there are a significant number of published studies attempting to assess the outcomes of a range of different events, a coherent and reliable picture of the nature and extent of such outcomes has not emerged from the literature (Weed 2006, 2009a).

Take as an example the area of large-scale sports events. As a result of the work of, *inter alia*: Barker *et al.* (2003) on the 2000 America's Cup in Auckland; Dermody *et al.* (2003) on NFL games; Horne and Manzenreiter (2004) on the 2002 Football World Cup in Korea and Japan; Jones (2001) on the 1999 Rugby World Cup in Wales; Madden (2002) on the Sydney Olympic Games in 2000; Preuss (2004) on the Olympic Games; Ritchie and Lyons (1990) on the 1988 Calgary Winter Olympic Games; Roche (1994) on mega-events generally; and Tyrrell *et al.* (2004) on the Vancouver 2012 Winter Olympic Games; there is wide-ranging evidence that hosting large-scale sport events has economic implications. However, there have been a number of authors who have critiqued economic impact studies. Crompton (2004, 2006), Hudson (2001), Kasimati (2003) and Preuss (2005, 2007) each suggest that there is both meth-odological incompetence and deliberate obfuscation as a result of political pressures in many economic impact studies, with a further clear suggestion that, at best, these studies are not directly comparable and, at worst, they are political window dressing.

A further critique of the existing literature in this area is that it has been dominated by economic perspectives at the expense of social and environmental issues. In particular, Gibson (2003) and Weed and Jackson (2008) highlight the concerns of a range of authors that social and environmental impacts are not entirely positive. Key examples include: COHRE's (2007) studies of the forced displacement of local communities to facilitate Olympic development for the 1992 Games in Barcelona and the 2008 Games in Beijing; Dovey's (1989) work high-lighting the use of the America's Cup in Fremantle to manipulate the planning process for new development in Perth; Hall and Hodges' (1996) work highlighting the disproportionate burden placed on the lowest-income residents for the Sydney 2000 Olympic Games; Roche's (1994: 1) critique of 'short term events with long term consequences'; and Weed's (2002) work on football hooligans as undesirable sports tourists. These critiques have led some authors (e.g. Higham 1999; Gibson *et al.* 2003) to suggest that a focus on regular and often small-scale events may provide communities with greater benefits and fewer burdens than large-scale events, something that aspects of the literature (e.g. Garnham 1996; Irwin and Sandler 1998; Hinch and Higham 2001) appear to support.

A key issue here is that asking a question relating to the outcomes sought from events implies that the only outcomes considered are those that are positive – after all, what provider would seek negative outcomes? One of the failings of event research has been a tendency to assume that 'outcomes' and 'positive outcomes' are the same thing, particularly in relation to larger events where the discourse centres on 'legacy' rather than outcomes or impacts (Weed *et al.* 2009). Preuss (2007) notes that outcomes from events may be planned or unplanned, positive or negative (or, indeed, neutral) and tangible or intangible; however, event evaluations and strategies only tend to consider those outcomes that are planned, positive and tangible. As such, if an overarching research question for an interdisciplinary events research agenda is going to lead with the question 'What outcomes are sought from events?' then this question must consider whether providers are seeking to reduce both potential unplanned negative outcomes and potential negative 'side-effects' from planned outcomes. The question should also consider the extent to which providers are seeking to capture and manage planned and unplanned positive and negative intangible outcomes.

In summary, an interdisciplinary events research agenda must seek to extend the quality and breadth of current event impacts research. There is a need to ensure that non-economic event outcomes are more regularly considered, as well as those outcomes that may be unplanned, negative or intangible. There is also a need to understand more about the potential of smaller events to generate outcomes. Higher-quality event impacts research across the broad range of potential outcomes provides foundational understanding for the next part of the overarching question for an interdisciplinary events research agenda: how can outcomes sought from events be achieved?

3.2 How can outcomes sought from events be achieved?

A recurring theme in the events literature in recent years (e.g. Chalip 2001; O'Brien 2007; Weed 2009a) has been that there is a need to shift the focus of research relating to the outcomes of events from an impacts to a leverage approach. As noted earlier, Laurence Chalip (2001, 2004, 2006) has been the leading voice in this area, with Weed (2008) drawing on his work to suggest that an events research framework that considers only impacts may now be outmoded. Undoubtedly, Chalip's (2001) argument that positive benefits and legacies are not an inherent feature of events, but must be leveraged, is one that has been developed further, both by Chalip himself (e.g. Chalip 2004, 2006; Chalip and Leyns 2002) and by other authors (e.g. O'Brien 2006, 2007; Weed 2008). However, as the discussions above have noted, what has often been missing is a recognition that, in addition to leveraging positive impacts, steps should be taken to mitigate potential negative consequences. If the leveraging concept can be applied to mitigation as well as leverage, then it can form the basis for an interdisciplinary events research agenda that seeks to identify how both the maximisation of positive outcomes and the minimisation of negative outcomes can be sought from events. Weed (2009a) suggested that Chalip's (2004) exposition of leveraging might be modified to explicitly include mitigation alongside leverage:

> Unlike impact assessments, the study of leverage and mitigation has a strategic and tactical focus. The objective is to identify strategies and tactics that can be implemented prior to and during an event in order to generate or moderate particular outcomes. Consequently, leveraging and mitigation implies a much more pro-active approach to capitalising on

opportunities and ameliorating undesirable consequences, rather than impacts research which simply measures outcomes.

The move to a leveraging and mitigation approach requires a move from an input/output or dose/response model of event research (in which the provision of an event is seen as an input or dose, and the outcomes, impacts or legacies are seen as an output or response) to an events research framework that focuses on *processes of change*. An exploration of processes of change focuses on the ways in which event-related leveraging or mitigation strategies can effect change, be that in individual behaviours, in societies and communities, in the environment, in economies, or in media coverage and perceptions. Unlike an impacts framework, which demonstrates what outcomes a particular event in a particular place at a particular point in time has achieved, a leveraging and mitigation framework exploring processes of change can make a much clearer contribution to an events research body of knowledge, because it demonstrates *how* changes have been effected, and therefore can contribute to the development of theories of change on which to build leveraging and mitigation strategies for future events (Chalip 2004, 2006; Weed 2010).

The world's biggest event, the Olympic and Paralympic Games, provides a useful example of the difficulties of input/output models of event research. Following the award of the 2012 Olympic and Paralympic Games to London in 2005, there was some criticism that a sport and physical activity participation legacy from London 2012 was unlikely because no previous Games had increased sport participation (Weed *et al.* 2009). However, this view had come about through two things: the lack of good available evidence, and the lack of any previous attempt to leverage a sport and physical activity participation legacy. Previous evidence of participation legacies had been derived from studies which had simply looked at sport participation statistics *ex post*. That is, drawing on a medical model, they had used data collected for other purposes to see if the Olympic and Paralympic Games as a 'dose' had elicited a sport participation response. Such studies showed little evidence of an effect, and where there was an effect it was short term and/or it was impossible to attribute participation as a response to the Games as a dose (Weed *et al.* 2009; McCartney *et al.* 2010). This is not surprising, as there had been no attempt to leverage a sport and physical activity legacy from previous Games, so any effect from previous Games would have been the result of an inherent effect of the Olympic and Paralympic Games on participation, rather than, as is now assumed, there being a potential effect that must be leveraged (Weed *et al.* 2009). London 2012, as the first Games that has attempted to leverage a sport and physical activity participation legacy, provides a significant opportunity for event researchers to seek to examine processes of change in this legacy area.

In the last quarter century, the Olympic and Paralympic Games have developed beyond simply being two-week sport competitions into four-year festivals, with a range of supporting events in arts, culture, education and popular engagement, brought together under the label of a 'Cultural Olympiad' (Shipway and Brown 2007; Kennell and MacLeod 2009). This is perhaps the highest-profile example of the use of a series of interconnected events, of varying scale, to extend opportunities to leverage outcomes. Another example is the extension of the impact of the Edinburgh Festival through the incorporation of the 'alternative' Fringe, which adds an additional week at the start of the Festival. While the Olympic and Paralympic Games and the Edinburgh Festival provide examples of leveraging large-scale events through developing a series of related events, an increasing trend has been for locations to seek to develop strategies for an ongoing event provision to achieve development outcomes for the local community and economy (Richards and Palmer 2010). However, the development of such approaches, whether linked to a large-scale event or as an ongoing strategy, tends to be based on intuition or anecdote, as the utility of the available evidence-base is limited by the failure to consider opportunity cost.

Opportunity cost is a concept embedded at the heart of economics and, simply put, is the idea that the true cost of anything is the alternative that is given up (Mincer 1963; Preuss 2007). Therefore, although event impact studies will list a range of outcomes that have been generated by a particular event, the key question that needs to be asked is 'compared to what?' (Crompton 2006: 75). What outcomes could have been achieved by investing the resources absorbed by a particular event in other types of events, or in other public policy initiatives, and how do the outcomes from the event in question compare to the likely outcomes of these other events or initiatives (Weed 2010)? Put simply, this is a cost-effectiveness question: how cost-effective is a particular event in comparison to other events or other public policy initiatives in achieving desired outcomes?

Research on the cost-effectiveness of events in achieving outcomes is an essential part of an interdisciplinary events research agenda, as it can provide event providers with the answer to the question: 'How, if at all, can events best achieve the outcomes we are seeking?' For example, a series of open-air theatre events targeting families during the school summer holidays might be promoted to encourage engagement with the arts among young people. However, the outcomes of such an initiative should be compared with the outcomes of investing in other alternatives, either other events such as a street dance festival, or other initiatives such as a drama programme in schools. The open-air theatre programme may cost £100,000 and generate 125 extra arts group memberships. In comparison, a local drama initiative in schools might cost the same but generate 150 new arts group memberships, while a street dance festival might generate 100 new memberships for the same cost. If the sought outcome of the event is engagement with any form of the arts, then open-air theatre would be more cost-effective than a street dance festival, but the opportunity cost of a drama education programme in schools is higher than the outcomes either of these events might generate. Of course, the events might have a range of additional desirable outcomes that a drama programme in schools would not deliver, and these should also be part of any cost-effectiveness evaluation.

In summary, in asking how outcomes sought from events might be achieved, an interdisciplinary events research agenda should focus on processes of change, using a framework that explores the ways in which event-related leveraging or mitigation strategies can effect change, be that in individual behaviours, in societies and communities, in the environment, in economies, or in media coverage and perceptions. There is also a need for an events research agenda to consider opportunity costs in seeking to establish not only 'how' sought outcomes might be achieved but, through cost-effectiveness research, 'how best' such sought outcomes can be achieved.

3.3 For whom are outcomes from events sought?

For many smaller events, the beneficiaries are quite simply the audience for the event, and the benefit is the contribution the event makes to their enjoyment of the activity. So the main beneficiaries of a local 10 km running event will be runners in the region who take part. The same might be said of local theatre productions, carnivals or concerts. While there may be an economic benefit, the primary reason for hosting these events is for the benefit of the event audiences, and this is a perfectly reasonable and legitimate reason for doing so (Hill *et al.* 1995).

Small local events are usually hosted for local audiences; however, host and audience are rarely completely coterminous, as it would be a rare event indeed that appealed to all parts of a local community. As such, while local events are hosted for the benefit of local audiences, there is still a need to ensure that those sectors of the local population that do not wish to engage with, for example, carnivals are not inconvenienced by the need for road closures or by excessive noise. Therefore, even at the very local level there is a need for research to establish the most appropriate leveraging and mitigation approaches to ensure not only that the benefits of events are maximised for their audiences, but also that negative consequences are minimised for those parts of the local population that do not wish to engage with them (Small 2008).

The issues relating to smaller events, where the intended beneficiaries are local audiences for the event, are largely concerned with how the event can be most effectively managed. However, as events increase in size the audience tends to expand to include both visitors from outside the local community and mediated audiences through media coverage (Weed and Bull 2009). At this stage, because events are most often funded by resources within the host community (e.g. host area taxation, volunteers and business interests), claims are made that there are 'structural' benefits for local, regional or even national economies and communities (Preuss 2007; Smith and Fox 2007). Such structural benefits might include: increased participation, engagement or opportunities in culture, sport and recreation; increased community pride; improvements in public health and the environments in which people live and work; and benefits to the local economy as a result of inward investment, tourism and/or improved perceived image (EdComs 2007; Weed et al. 2009; McCartney 2010). For medium-sized events, such as those held as part of the UK city of Liverpool's year as the European Capital of Culture, these structural outcomes would be largely claimed for the city's economy and population (Sapsford and Southern 2007), but for larger events such as the Football World Cup or the Olympic and Paralympic Games, while outcomes are still claimed for local populations, some structural outcomes are claimed for the country as a whole (Horne and Manzenreiter 2004; Cragg Ross Dawson 2007).

When the beneficiaries of events are intended to be entire economies or populations, there is increasing pressure to conduct 'supra-evaluations' in which there is some assessment of the overall outcome of an event or series of events for the city, region or country (Weed 2010). One suggestion to facilitate this has been to develop a 'triple-bottom-line' approach, in which indicators for economic, socio-cultural and environmental impacts are collected and compared (Sherwood et al. 2004, 2005). Fredline et al. (2005) suggest the use of a concept they have termed 'event footprint' to plot scores from key indicators across the three triple-bottom-line dimensions. However, Weed and Jackson (2008) argue that analyses that set economic considerations against environmental and socio-cultural impacts rarely lead to an agreed bottom line, and thus suggest that triple-bottom-line evaluations may struggle to reach holistic conclusions. This may be the reason why Sherwood (2007), in his analysis of eighty-five event impact studies in Australia, found that only one study employed a triple-bottom-line approach. Weed (2009a) has suggested that if, as outlined earlier in this chapter, the leveraging concept can be applied to mitigation of negative consequences as well as to leveraging positive outcomes, then it may offer a more effective and efficient route to assessing holistic outcomes for communities and economies than 'triple-bottom-line' evaluations, which are simply a multi-dimensional form of event impact assessment.

More recently, an Economic and Social Research Council (ESRC) funded study in the UK, which examined how the social, cultural and health impacts of the London 2012 Olympic and Paralympic Games might be assessed in regions outside the host city, suggested that there may be some potential to develop an approach that focuses on the 'human impact' of events (Weed 2009b). This study noted that one of the problems of attempting to integrate outcome measures from a range of dimensions (e.g. socio-cultural, health, environmental and economic) is that there is an inevitable pressure to convert these dimensions into a single measure. Almost universally, such single measures are economic: so health impacts are measured by the cost saving in health care, or social impacts are measured by the productivity increases that might derive from more cohesive communities, and so on. There are two problems with such an approach: first, the empirical foundation for the assumptions that underpin the use of such economic measures to evaluate these aspects of people is not as strong as is often assumed (cf. Pezzey and Toman 2002); but, second and perhaps more importantly, representing the social or health value of an event by economic measures of cost savings or productivity increases can seem some distance from the lives of the people such events are supposed to benefit. Consequently, although value can be demonstrated quantitatively in economic terms, people cannot necessarily see or feel how an event has affected their lives.

As a result, the ESRC-funded study suggested that an approach focusing on human impact could take as its starting point the impact that large-scale events have on the lives of the individuals, groups, communities and societies that they are intended to reach (Weed 2009b). The focus would be both on how macro-economic and broad societal forces, and on how more immediate local economic, political, social and environmental changes, are felt collectively by individuals, groups, communities and societies. Put simply, the focus would be on how changes attributable to the event(s) in question across a range of dimensions collectively affect people's lives. Exploring legacy in this way presents impacts that are more immediate to the lives of those the events are intended to benefit. As such, as well as increasing the relevance of large-scale events to the communities that they are intended to benefit, a human impact approach would also provide clearer information to inform both policy goals and leveraging and mitigation strategies.

However, a focus on such human impact clearly presents considerable methodological challenges, and would demand an interdisciplinary approach drawing on, *inter alia*, macro-economic analysis, social policy analysis, community sociology and development, environmental impact assessment and detailed qualitative research techniques. Such an approach would be far more challenging than single-dimension studies, or than multi-disciplinary and multi-dimensional studies drawing on multiple indicators across sectors. However, if an agenda for events research is to be truly interdisciplinary, then such methodological challenges should be embraced and welcomed.

In summary, research needs in relation to the question of for whom outcomes for events are sought can often depend on the size of the event. For smaller local events, research needs to focus on leveraging and mitigation strategies to maximise audience benefits, while minimising community disruption. However, at a larger scale, when event outcomes are sought and claimed for entire economies or communities, there is a clear need for a truly interdisciplinary research approach that can provide a comprehensive and holistic evaluation of the impact of events. Such an approach should be integrative rather than simply comparative. That is, it should seek to reach an integrated assessment of the impact of the range of outcomes on people's lives, rather than merely comparing the impacts across different dimensions.

3.4 What interests do outcomes sought from events serve?

On the surface, those for whom outcomes are sought from events would appear to be those whose interests are served by generating such outcomes. Certainly early literature on the concept of 'boosterism' (Whitson and Macintosh 1993) suggested that the joining together of local political and business leaders to develop events as a 'corporate civic project' to boost their city (Critcher 1991) is a positive thing that benefits the whole community.

However, despite claims of benefits, the outcomes sought from events are not always in the interests of those who are claimed to be the beneficiaries. While benefits for local communities in terms of living standards and improved infrastructure are often claimed for events, this is not always beneficial to all. For example, the Barcelona Olympic and Paralympic Games of 1992 are often held up as the best example of positive event legacies, with developments including a new ring road, new airport and an upgraded waterfront area (Sanahuja 2002). However, according to the Centre on Housing Rights and Evictions (COHRE 2007), this was at the cost of the displacement of 624 families (approximately 2,500 people). Yet this was a mere drop in the ocean against COHRE's estimations, in 2007, that almost 1.25 million people had been displaced to make way for the preparations for the Beijing Olympic and Paralympic Games of 2008, and that this figure was set to rise to 1.5 million by the time the Games had commenced (COHRE 2007).

Consequently, more recently critics have argued that boosterist approaches are best understood as serving the interests of the governing elites that advocate them. Hiller (2000: 440), for example, criticises 'governments ... [that link events] ... to its own objectives of aggrandizement ... [and] ... the power and vast resources of the created coalition of elite who become bid advocates'. Hiller (2000) suggests that boosterism symbolically constructs consensus but favours the economic and political interests of the dominant class. Mooney's (2004) critique of the long-term impacts of the Glasgow City of Culture initiative in 1990 provides a useful illustration of this perspective. Mooney's (2004) analysis suggests that while the 'official' story is one of economic success, such impacts have not necessarily benefited the local population. Although Glasgow City Council, backed by Scottish Enterprise Glasgow (2001) and the Glasgow Economic Forum (2003), claim an economic renaissance for Glasgow, Mooney (2004) notes that there is increasing evidence of deep-rooted unemployment. Furthermore, aspects of the local population had long opposed the City of Culture initiative. Mooney (2004: 331) cites a pamphlet produced by a community opposition group, Workers' City, in 1990:

> the Year of Culture has more to do with power politics than culture. It has more to do with millionaire developers than art ... With Saatchi and Saatchi's expert help they revamp the image and leave reality behind. They propagate an image which is false. There is deprivation and dereliction of the housing schemes ... there is chronic unemployment and widespread DSS poverty with the usual concomitants – drug abuse and the manifold forms of community violence. This is not the Merchant City, but this is the real Glasgow.
>
> *(Workers' City 1990: 87)*

The presentation of this more negative perspective is not to suggest that events universally lead to the interests of local communities being systematically cast aside to serve the interests of dominant political and economic elites. In fact, there is much research that the social benefits of events for local populations can be significant, and that they can be leveraged (Chalip 2006). However, Dimeo (2008: 603) suggests that research in this area can suffer from too great a focus on management perspectives, derived from 'the desire to draw from and please user organisations'. Consequently, Dimeo's (2008) perspective suggests there is a need for an interdisciplinary events research agenda to include a body of work seeking to interrogate and critique foundational management ideas that assume events can be positive as long as they incorporate efficient strategies and management practices based on a clear understanding of contributing and affected groups. Such research might seek to develop an evidence base to argue that the use of events as a social or economic policy tool should be limited, or even prohibited.

In summary, an interdisciplinary research agenda for events must include a consideration of the interests that are served by the outcomes sought from events. Furthermore, such a consideration must interrogate the extent to which the interests of those who are claimed to be the beneficiaries of event outcomes are truly being served by the political and social elites that are most often the drivers of event management and strategy.

Conclusion: a framework for an interdisciplinary events research agenda

The above discussions have highlighted the issues that an interdisciplinary events research agenda across the subject areas of sport, tourism, leisure and health might address. The discussions focused on unpacking the overarching question suggested for an events research agenda: what outcomes are sought from events, how, for whom, and to serve what interests? In particular, the specific issues that might be addressed in each part of this question have been highlighted. In attempting to summarise these discussions, and by way of conclusion, a framework for an interdisciplinary events research agenda across sport, tourism, leisure and health is proposed, and this is illustrated in Figure 4.1.

At the left of Figure 4.1, the five types of outcomes that might be sought from events are listed: culture, sport and recreation; social and community; environmental; economic; and media and promotion. These potential outcome types were discussed in Section 3.1, together

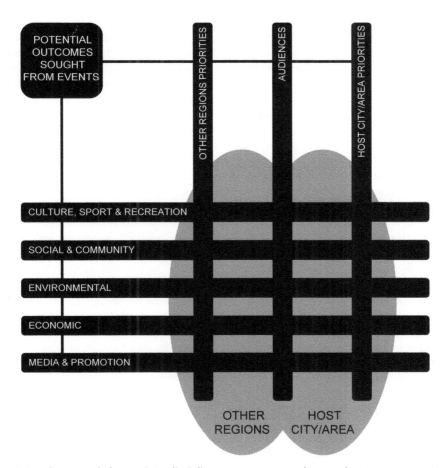

Figure 4.1 A framework for an interdisciplinary events research agenda across sport, tourism, leisure and health

with the need to improve the quality of research across all of these areas. Section 3.1 also noted that as well as investigating positive outcomes sought, research should focus on the extent to which providers have sought to ameliorate negative consequences, and to consider potential intangible and unplanned outcomes. In addition, as discussed in Section 3.2, research should also consider the processes of change that leveraging and mitigation strategies have employed to effect outcomes in individual behaviours, in societies and communities, in the environment, in economies, or in media coverage and perceptions (the five areas included on the left of Figure 4.1). Furthermore, through employing the concept of opportunity cost and developing cost-effectiveness approaches, research should explore not only how, but how best, outcomes can be achieved.

Section 3.3 considered the question of for whom outcomes from events are sought. Across the top of Figure 4.1, potential outcomes for three groups are highlighted. First, the host city or area will have a range of policy priorities that it might seek to address through events, and these will intersect with the five outcome areas included on the left of Figure 4.1 to varying extents depending on the event(s) in question. Similarly, other regions outside of the host city or area will also have social policy priorities which may, for different event(s), intersect with the five outcome areas. Finally, drawn from both the host city or area and from other regions, audiences, either corporeal or virtual, will benefit in varying ways from event(s). Of course, for smaller events, such as a local open-air theatre season, the relevant intersections will be small, perhaps simply research on the intersection of host city or area priorities and audiences with cultural, sport and recreation outcomes. However, for larger events such as the Olympic and Paralympic Games, where a wide range of outcomes and legacies are sought across a wide range of policy areas, all intersections in the framework are likely to be relevant for event researchers. Where multiple intersections are relevant, there are significant interdisciplinary challenges in developing an integrated approach to comprehensively assessing the holistic human impact of events across sectors. It is in reaching an integrated assessment of the impact of the full range of outcomes on people's lives, rather than simply comparing impacts across dimensions, that an events research agenda must be truly interdisciplinary.

Finally, Section 3.4 discussed the interests that are served by the outcomes that are sought from events, and noted that the event policy priorities developed by political and economic elites do not always serve the interests of all parts of the population. This is illustrated in Figure 4.1 by the two ellipses that represent the host city or area and other regions. Events research must focus on all parts of the populations in these areas, not just the stated priorities for them, and interrogate the extent to which stated priorities are in the interests of the populations for whom they are claimed, not just the interests of the political and economic elites that are claiming them.

The intention of this chapter has been to move towards an interdisciplinary events research agenda across sport, tourism, leisure and health. As such, it is intended as a discussion starter for researchers in the field, not as a comprehensive prescription. However, the chapter has attempted to highlight key considerations for events research, both in terms of substantive issues and in enhancing methodological quality. Ultimately, the aims have been to move towards an events research agenda that might assist in increasing the utility and relevance of events research, and also to set a context for the far more detailed chapters that follow.

Note

1 The higher-level dimensions are not absolute. There may, for example, be some discretionary attendees at royal occasions, and some required attendance at sport competitions. Similarly, there may be an element of implied requirement in attending private family events. As such, the location of particular

events as examples within each of these dimensions is intended as an illustration of the broader concept of public/private events and discretionary/required engagement rather than as set of detailed and absolute boundaries.

References

Baade, R.A. and Sanderson, A.R. (1997) 'Minor league teams and communities', in R.G. Noll and A. Zimbalist (eds) *Sports, Jobs, and Taxes: The Economic Impact of Sports Teams and Stadiums*, Washington, DC: Brookings Institution Press.

Barker, M., Page, S.J. and Meyer, D. (2003) 'Urban visitor perceptions of safety during a special event', *Journal of Travel Research* 41(4): 355–61.

Chalip, L. (2001) 'Sport and tourism: capitalising on the linkage', in D. Kluka and G. Schilling (eds) *The Business of Sport*, Oxford, UK: Meyer & Meyer.

——(2004) 'Beyond impact: a general model for sport event leverage', in B.W. Ritchie and D. Adair (eds) *Sport Tourism: Interrelationships, Impacts and Issues*, Clevedon, UK: Channel View Publications, pp. 226–52.

——(2006) 'Towards social leverage of sport events', *Journal of Sport and Tourism* 11(2): 109–27.

Chalip, L. and Leyns, A. (2002) 'Local business leveraging of a sport event: managing an event for economic benefit', *Journal of Sport Management* 16(2): 132–58.

COHRE (Centre on Housing Rights and Evictions) (2007) *Fair Play for Housing Rights: Mega-Events, Olympic Games and Housing Rights*, Geneva: COHRE.

Cragg Ross Dawson (2007) *Before, During and After: Making the Most of the London 2012 Games*, London: DCMS.

Critcher, C. (1991) 'Sporting civic pride: Sheffield and the World Student Games of 1991', in C. Knox and J. Sugden (eds) *Leisure in the 1990s: Rolling back the Welfare State*, Brighton: Leisure Studies Association.

Crompton, J. (2004) 'Beyond economic impact: an alternative rationale for the public subsidy of major league sports facilities', *Journal of Sport Management* 18(1): 40–58.

——(2006) 'Economic impact studies: instruments for political shenanigans', *Journal of Travel Research* 45 (1): 67–82.

Dermody, M.B., Taylor, S.L. and Lomanno, M.V. (2003) 'The impact of NFL games on lodging industry revenue', *Journal of Travel and Tourism Marketing* 14(1): 21–36.

Dimeo, P. (2008) 'Review of "Sports Tourism: Participants, Policy and Providers" by Mike Weed and Chris Bull', *Tourism Management* 29: 603.

Dovey, K. (1989) 'Old scabs/new scares: the hallmark event and the everyday environment', in G.J. Syme, B.J. Shaw, D.M. Fenton and W.S. Mueller (eds) *The Planning and Evaluation of Hallmark Events*, Aldershot: Avebury.

Doxey, G.V. (1975) 'A causation theory of visitor–resident irritants: methodology and research inferences', *Proceedings of the 6th Annual Conference of the Travel and Tourism Research Association* 1: 195–8.

EdComs (2007) *London 2012 Legacy Research: Final Report*, London: COI/DCMS.

Fredline, E. (2005) 'Host and guest relations and sport tourism', *Sport in Society* 8(2): 263–79.

Fredline, E., Raybould, M., Jago, L. and Deery, M. (2005) 'Triple bottom line event evaluation: a proposed framework for jolistic event evaluation', paper presented at the third international event management research conference, University of Technology, Sydney.

Garnham, B. (1996) 'Ranfurly Shield Rugby: an investigation into the impacts of a sporting event on a provincial city, the case of New Plymouth, Taranaki, New Zealand', *Festival Management and Event Tourism* 4: 145–9.

Getz, D. (2005) *Event Management and Event Tourism*, New York: Cognizant, second edition.

——(2008) 'Event tourism: definition, evolution and research', *Tourism Management* 29(3): 403–28.

Gibson, H.J. (2003) 'Sport tourism', in J.B. Parks and J. Quarterman (eds) *Contemporary Sport Management*, Champaign, IL: Human Kinetics.

Gibson, H.J., Willming, C. and Holdnak, A. (2003) 'Small-scale event sport tourism: fans as tourists', *Tourism Management* 24(2): 181–90.

Glasgow Economic Forum (2003) *Glasgow's Continuing Prosperity*, Glasgow: GEF.

Green, B.C., Costa, C. and Chalip, L. (2003) 'Marketing the host city: analysing the exposure generated by a sport event', *International Journal of Sport Marketing and Sponsorship*, December/January: 335–53.

Green, M. (2004) 'Changing policy priorities for sport in England: the emergence of elite sport development as a key policy concern', *Leisure Studies* 23(4): 365–85.

Hall, C.M. and Hodges, J. (1996) 'The party's great, but what about the hangover? The housing and social impacts of mega-events with special reference to the 2000 Sydney Olympics', *Festival Management and Event Tourism* 4: 13–20.

Higham, J. (1999) 'Commentary – sport as an avenue of tourism development: an analysis of the positive and negative impacts of sport tourism', *Current Issues in Tourism* 2(1): 82–90.

Hill, E., O'Sullivan, T. and O'Sullivan, C. (1995) *Creative Arts Marketing*, Oxford: Butterworth-Heinemann.

Hiller, H.H. (2000) 'Mega-events, urban boosterism and growth strategies: an analysis of the objectives and legitimations of the Cape Town 2004 Olympic bid', *International Journal of Urban and Regional Research* 24(2): 439–58.

Hinch, T. and Higham, J. (2001) 'Sport tourism: a framework for research', *International Journal of Tourism Research* 3(1): 45–58.

Horne, J.D. and Manzenreiter, W. (2004) 'Accounting for mega-events: forecast and actual impacts of the 2002 Football World Cup Finals on the host countries Japan/Korea', *International Review for the Sociology of Sport* 39(2): 187–203.

Hudson, I. (2001) 'The use and misuse of economic impact analysis', *Journal of Sport and Social Issues* 25(1): 20–39.

Irwin, R.L. and Sandler, M.A. (1998) 'An analysis of travel behaviour and event-induced expenditures among American collegiate championship patron groups', *Journal of Vacation Marketing* 4(1): 78–90.

Jones, C. (2001) 'Mega-events and host region impacts: determining the true worth of the 1999 Rugby World Cup', *International Journal of Tourism Research* 3(3): 241–51.

Kasimati, E. (2003) 'Economic aspects and the Summer Olympics: a review of related research', *International Journal of Tourism Research* 5(6): 433–44.

Kennell, J. and MacLeod, N. (2009) 'A grey literature review of the Cultural Olympiad', *Cultural Trends* 18(1): 83–8.

McCartney, G., Thomas, S., Thomson, H., Hamilton, V., Hanlon, P., Morrison, D.S. and Bond, L. (2010) 'The health and socio-economic impacts of major multi-sport events: systematic review (1978–2008)', *British Medical Journal* 340: c2369.

Madden, J.R. (2002) 'The economic consequences of the Sydney Olympics: the CREA/Arthur Andersen Study', *Current Issues in Tourism* 5(1): 7–21.

Mason, D.S., Duquette, G.H. and Scherer, J. (2005) 'Heritage, sport tourism and Canadian junior hockey: nostalgia for social experience or sport place?', *Journal of Sport Tourism* 10(4): 253–71.

Mincer, J. (1963) 'Market prices, opportunity costs and income effects', in C.F. Christ (ed.) *Measurement in Economics*, Stanford: Stanford University Press.

Mooney, G. (2004) 'Cultural policy as urban transformation? Critical reflections on Glasgow, European City of Culture 1990', *Local Economy* 19(4): 327–40.

O'Brien, D. (2006) 'Event business leveraging: the Sydney 2000 Olympic Games', *Annals of Tourism Research* 33: 240–61.

——(2007) 'Points of leverage: maximizing host community benefit from a regional surfing festival', *European Sport Management Quarterly* 7(2): 141–65.

Pezzey, J.C.V. and Toman, M.A. (2002) *The Economics of Sustainability: A Review of Journal Articles*, Washington, DC: Resources for the Future.

Preuss, H. (2004) *The Economics of Staging the Olympics: A Comparison of the Games 1972–2008*, Cheltenham: Edward Elgar.

——(2005) 'The economic impact of visitors at major multi-sport events', *European Sport Management Quarterly* 5(3): 283–303.

——(2007) 'The conceptualisation and measurement of mega sport event legacies', *Journal of Sport and Tourism* 12(3–4): 207–27.

Richards, G. and Palmer, R. (2010) *Eventful Cities: Cultural Management and Urban Revitalisation*, Oxford: Butterworth-Heinemann.

Ritchie, J.R.B. and Lyons, M. (1990) 'Olympulse VI: a post-event assessment of resident reaction to the XV Olympic Winter Games', *Journal of Travel Research* 28(3): 14–23.

Roche, M. (1994) 'Mega-events and urban policy', *Annals of Tourism Research* 21(1): 1–19.

Salter, L. and Hearn, A.M.V. (1997) *Outside the Lines: Issues in Interdisciplinary Research*, Quebec: McGill-Queens University Press.

Sanahuja, R. (2002) 'Olympic City – the city strategy 10 years after the Olympic Games in 1992', paper to the International Conference on Sports Events and Economic Impact, Copenhagen, Denmark, April.

Sapsford, D. and Southern, A. (2007) *Measuring the Economic Impacts of Liverpool European Capital of Culture. Baseline Economic Indicators and the Merseyside Business Base*, Liverpool: Impacts 08.

Scottish Enterprise Glasgow (2001) *Upbeat Glasgow*, Glasgow: SEG.

Sehr, N. and Weingart, P. (2000) *Practising Interdisciplinarity*, Toronto: University of Toronto Press.

Sherwood, P. (2007) 'A triple bottom line evaluation of the impact of special events: the development of indicators', unpublished doctoral dissertation, Victoria University, Melbourne.

Shipway, R. and Brown, L. (2007) 'Challenges for a regional cultural programme of the 2012 Games', *Culture @ the Olympics* 9(5): 21–35.

Sherwood, P., Jago, L. and Deery, M. (2004) 'Sustainability reporting: an application for the evaluation of special events', in C. Cooper (ed.) *Proceedings of the Annual Conference of the Council for Australian University Tourism and Hospitality Education*, Brisbane: University of Queensland.

——(2005) 'Unlocking the triple bottom line of special event evaluations: What are the key impacts?', in J. Allen (ed.) *Proceedings of the Third International Event Management Research Conference, Sydney*, Sydney: University of Technology.

Small, K. (2008) 'Social dimensions of community festivals: an application of factor analysis in the development of the social impact perception (SIP) scale', *Event Management* 11(1/2): 45–55.

Smith, A. and Fox, T. (2007) 'From "event-led" to "event-themed" regeneration: the 2002 Commonwealth Games legacy programme', *Urban Studies* 44(5/6): 1125–43.

Tyrrell, T.J., Williams, P.W. and Johnston, R.J. (2004) 'RESEARCH NOTE – Estimating sport tourism visitor volumes: the case of Vancouver's 2010 Olympic Games', *Tourism Recreation Research* 29(1): 75–81.

Weed, M. (2002) 'Football hooligans as undesirable sports tourists: some meta analytical speculations', in S. Gammon and J. Kurtzman (eds) *Sport Tourism: Principles and Practice*, Eastbourne: LSA.

——(2006) 'Sports tourism research 2000–2004: a systematic review of knowledge and a meta-evaluation of method', *Journal of Sport and Tourism* 11(1): 5–30.

——(2008) 'Editor's introduction: Impacts of sport and tourism', in M. Weed (ed.) *Sport and Tourism: A Reader*, London: Routledge.

——(2009a) 'Progress in sports tourism research? A meta-review and exploration of futures', *Tourism Management* 30: 615–28.

——(2009b) 'Leveraging social, cultural and health benefits from London 2012: conclusion report', ESRC Grant No. RES-451-26-0403.

——(2010) 'How will we know if the London 2012 Olympics and Paralympics benefit health?', *British Medical Journal* 340: c2202.

Weed, M. and Bull, C. (2009) *Sports Tourism: Participants, Policy and Providers*, Oxford: Elsevier, second edition.

Weed, M. and Jackson, G.A.M. (2008) 'The relationship between sport and tourism', in B. Houlihan (ed.) *Sport and Society*, London: Sage.

Weed, M., Coren, E., Fiore, J., Chatziefstathiou, D., Mansfield, L., Wellard, I. and Dowse, S. (2009) *A Systematic Review of the Evidence Base for Developing a Physical Activity and Health Legacy from the London 2012 Olympic and Paralympic Games*, London: DoH.

Whitson, D. and Macintosh, D. (1993) 'The hosting of international games in Canada: ecological and ideological ambitions', Loughborough. Unpublished.

Workers' City (1990) *The Reckoning*, Glasgow: Workers' City.

Section 2
Disciplinary studies and events: theory, concepts and methods of analysis

5

Events and tourism

Warwick Frost

Introduction

Tourism is consistently seen as one of the key objectives of events, providing broad economic benefits and justifying stakeholder involvement and funding. This chapter considers how a wide range of tourism destinations are increasingly utilizing events as an integral part of their strategic planning. It is important to begin with two important qualifications regarding how we see events. The first is that the term 'events' covers a wide range of activities and occurrences. This is recognized in the common typologies, which are based on scale (for example mega, hallmark, small, community) or subject (for example sporting, business, commemorative, cultural, exhibition). With such a complexity, we must be careful not to over-generalize. Instead, it is important to recognize that the tourism dimension of events may vary quite widely from case to case.

The second qualification is that in focusing on tourism we should not forget that this is only one reason for staging events. Tourism may only be one of a number of objectives and it may not be the main one. For some events, social objectives – such as building national or community identity or communicating persuasive messages – are more important. A good example of this is London's Notting Hill Carnival. Though it attracts a very large audience, including many tourists, it started as (and remains) primarily a celebration of the identity of the West Indian diaspora (Burr 2006). For some commercial events, such as exhibitions, selling participants' wares may be the first priority. Indeed, there are some events (for example religious or local) in which tourism is irrelevant.

Events and destinations

Bearing those qualifications in mind, we can construct a common 'model' or pattern of tourism and events. Commercial tourism and hospitality operators (the 'Tourism Industry') tend to see events as one of their 'products' which can be 'leveraged off' to attract tourists and revenue for their businesses. Utilizing a destination-based focus, private operators co-operate with each other and government agencies. This combination of competing and co-operating ('co-opition') and government–industry 'partnerships' are features of the common Destination Marketing

Organization (DMO) approach. For DMOs, events are an increasingly attractive tool for achieving their primary objectives of promoting tourism. DMOs may seek to build a suite of attractive events through partnering with existing event organizers, networking with other stakeholders, providing assistance with marketing, funding, bidding processes and working as an 'advocate' of specific events through liaison with governments (Stokes 2007; Getz 2008). These relationships may become quite formal, with key tourism representatives joining event organizing committees. In some cases DMOs may take the lead in creating new events specifically to target specific market segments or attract tourists during traditional low seasons.

In taking this approach to events, DMOs occupy a different position to their conventional role. Usually DMOs simply co-operatively market the attractions and services of their constituent members. However, with events they often take a far more active role in product development, even arguably becoming the providers of the event product (Getz 2008). Certainly this is often the case in the competitive bidding for events.

Mega events

There are many examples of destination cities which have benefited from events tourism. The primary emphasis has often been on mega events, particularly sporting ones and this is reflected in the events literature. Mega events are characterized as 'typically global in their orientation and require a competitive bid to "win" them as a one-time event for a particular place' (Getz 2008: 408). Standing out are the Olympic Games and Soccer World Cups – true mega events involving large numbers of countries and attracting global media audiences. Both are held every four years in different cities and entail stiff competition as cities bid to host them. Bidding success requires co-operation between city and national governments, DMOs and major tourism operators. The pursuit of mega events harbours risks: a great deal of resources might be invested in an unsuccessful bid and some cities are serial losers. Furthermore, as mega events are one-time occurrences, the risk is that if they are not successful, there is no second chance for a destination to get them right.

The appeal of mega events is in the large numbers of international tourists who may be attracted to the destination and who would not otherwise come. Consider the example of the 2010 Soccer World Cup in South Africa. There were 2.8 million seats on sale, of which about a half were sold to international tourists. These were mainly from high-income Western countries, the first three in ticket sales being the USA, Great Britain and Australia. Many of these came on package sports tours. All accommodation in the venue cities was sold out, with one tour company being forced to construct a tent 'city' in a stadium for its clients. In addition to tickets to matches, these tours included visits to other South African tourism attractions, particularly wildlife tours of game reserves and national parks (publicity brochures for the 2010 World Cup featured charismatic animals such as elephants).

Staging these mega sporting events requires huge infrastructure investment, such as new stadia and improved public transport systems. Much of this funding comes from national governments and they view increased tourism revenue flowing to the private sector as the economic justification for that public expenditure (for the tourism benefits of the World Cup see Florek *et al.* 2008 and Byeon *et al.* 2008).

Just below the Olympics and Soccer World Cups are a range of international sporting competitions which might arguably be classified as mega events. These include the Cricket and Rugby World Cups, the Commonwealth Games, Formula 1 Grand Prix and various soccer tournaments. Again these require large investment, primarily from governments, and are justified primarily in terms of tourism (Higham 1999; Carlsen and Taylor 2003; Smith 2005; Custodio and Gouveia 2007; Weed and Bull 2009; Henderson *et al.* 2010). For example, the Singaporean government provided 60 per cent of the funding for the Formula 1 Grand Prix and in return budgeted for an increase in international tourism of 40,000 visits (Henderson *et al.* 2010).

Hallmark events

Distinct from sporting events which destinations bid for are those which have evolved within the city and are held regularly. These are a form of hallmark event, where the event and destination 'become inextricably linked' and cannot be separated (Getz 2008: 407, see also Hall 1992). As they have evolved over a long time period, hallmark events have a tradition and a sense of place and this gives the destination a strong competitive advantage. Their regularity allows DMOs to gradually build them into the destination's brand. Examples include the Indianapolis 500 car race, Mardi Gras in Rio de Janeiro and the tennis at Wimbledon in London.

Another strategy is to develop hallmark events based on culture. These may be traditional events repackaged for tourists or specifically invented to capture this market. As many of these events are based on the distinct cultural attributes of a city or region, they are effective means for distinguishing the destination in the competitive marketplace. In this sense, they contrast sharply with sporting and business events, which could really take place anywhere. European cities, in particular, have focused their resources on cultural events (see, for example, Formica and Uysal 1998; Gold and Gold 2005; Peters and Pikkemaat 2005; Richards and Palmer 2010).

In contrast, other cities have followed the path of popular rather than classical culture. This had led to an eclectic mix of carnivals, pop festivals, dance parties and other performances. Such an approach stresses the modernity of these destinations, even their 'edginess' and 'hipness' (Florida 2005; Burr 2006; Reid 2006; Cohen 2007; Frost 2008; Stone 2008).

Historic anniversaries used to be marked by events directed mainly at local communities. However, these are increasingly being developed as tourism events (see, for example, Frost 2001 and Liburd 2008). This is an area which requires much more research, though it seems that tourists are being sought for both their economic return and their role in validating local or national identity as of interest to the broader world.

Business tourism: conventions and exhibitions

Business and trade exhibitions (or Expos) may be either mega or hallmark events. Like sporting events, they are seen as the opportunity to generate tourist arrivals which would not otherwise have come. The template is the 1851 Great Exhibition held at the Crystal Palace in London. While this exhibition claimed to display and celebrate the achievements of all nations, in reality it showcased both the new technology and the economic power of the British Empire. Its venue, setting the scene for many later events, was an audacious, seemingly impossible construction of glass and steel. In an effort to maximize visitation, its organizers contracted with Thomas Cook to bring trainloads of tourists from the industrial north of England. Attracting 6 million visitors, its profits were sufficient to construct permanent attractions including the Victoria and Albert Museum and the Natural History Museum.

Later great exhibitions strove to duplicate this success. The 1876 Centennial International Exhibition in Philadelphia commemorated the 100th anniversary of the Declaration of Independence and attracted 10 million visitors. The 1889 Exposition Universelle in Paris commemorated the French Revolution and provided an enduring tourism legacy through the Eiffel Tower. This tradition of World Expos continues today. A variation in the USA were the World's Fairs. Held in various cities and primarily appealing to domestic tourists, their legacies include the inspiration for Disneyland (Chicago 1893 and 1934), the popularization of the hot dog, peanut butter and the ice cream cone (St Louis 1904) and iconic permanent structures such as Seattle's 1962 Space Needle (Rydell 1993).

Apart from major exhibitions, a wide range of conventions, trade shows, fashion weeks and specialist exhibitions come under the umbrella of business tourism. Cities aim to strategically build a calendar of such events, investing in convention and exhibition centres and associated tourism facilities (see, for example, MacLaurin and Leong 2000). The appeal of such events for DMOs and governments is that they attract high-spending tourists whose economic impact is greatest on high-end hotels, restaurants and shops.

The market for conventions is becoming increasingly competitive. In the 1950s and 1960s US cities pioneered this field, investing heavily in convention centres, often as the lynchpin of large tourism/events/entertainment precincts. These centres prospered thanks to the massive size of the American business market, post-war economic growth and cheap domestic airfares. Since the 1990s, globalization and a shift in the world's economic centre of power to Asia has stimulated the growth of competitors. Singapore and Hong Kong, for example, have developed as key destinations for conventions, particularly tapping into their positions as transport hubs within East Asia (MacLaurin and Leong 2000). In addition, European cities have also increasingly striven to attract business events, trading on their location, relative stability and safety and distinctive cultural attributes.

Destination event strategies

In attempting to attract tourists, cities are using two main event strategies (often as an integrated part of their tourism strategy). The first is to bid for mega events, hoping for one dominating event which will propel them into the international spotlight. The second is to develop a range (or calendar) of events. None of these series of events necessarily dominate, but in combination they project an image to tourists of this as being an exciting, dynamic 'Eventful City' (Richards and Palmer 2010). This second strategy is becoming increasingly popular with governments and DMOs, for while it may not be as spectacular as hosting a mega event, it entails less commercial risk and is cheaper to implement.

The strategy of a range of events is particularly popular with 'second-tier' cities. Such cities, lacking the 'place luck' of iconic buildings or strong and appealing destination images, need to engage in strategic planning to 'remake' or 're-imagine' themselves in order to compete (Fainstein and Judd 1999). Accordingly these cities look to events, particularly sporting, business and cultural, for this reinvention. In Asia, this strategic event planning has been a major feature of destination development for cities such as Singapore and Dubai (MacLaurin and Leong 2000; Foley et al. 2008; Henderson et al. 2010; Richards and Palmer 2010). In Britain, sporting events have been strategically utilized to reinvigorate declining post-industrial cities (Carlsen and Taylor 2003; Smith 2005). In Europe, European Union funding, particularly the European Cities of Culture programme, has been used to promote destinations through events (Richards and Palmer 2010).

Tourism Victoria's sporting and cultural events strategy

The city of Melbourne has long been seen as secondary in tourism appeal to Sydney. However, in 2008 there was quite a media and industry stir when tourism statistics showed that Melbourne had exceeded Sydney in the all-important expenditure by international tourists. The industry body Tourism and Transport Forum Australia identified Melbourne's events strategy as a key factor in its success, noting, 'Melbourne has things to do, not just things to look at – that's its strategic advantage' (quoted in Topsfield 2008: 3).

Melbourne is a good example of a second-tier city which has re-created (or re-imagined) itself as a tourist destination through events. Its has adopted a strategic approach with industry and government agencies working together to plan how they will use events as an integral and ongoing part of tourism. This contrasts with an *ad hoc* approach of opportunistically bidding for mega events. This is partly a reaction to the disappointment of a failed Olympics bid in the 1990s.

Tourism Victoria has developed a series of five-year plans. How they utilize events is best illustrated by the 2002–6 plan which focused on sporting and cultural events (Tourism Victoria 2002). This emphasis on promoting tourism through events has continued in later plans, though it has not been detailed to the same extent.

The 2002–6 plan promoted a vision of Melbourne as an 'Events Capital'. This was to be achieved through five key objectives:

1 Ensure Victoria's events leverage significant economic impact and media exposure for the State.
2 Further develop the considerable range of existing events to maximize the social and economic benefits as well as individual destination profiles.
3 Build the geographic and seasonal dispersal of event activity with a particular emphasis on regional events.
4 Enhance communication among event-related organizations and agencies within Victoria.
5 Establish a brand leverage strategy for Melbourne and Victoria to maximize exposure through signage, media partnerships and corporate sponsorship alliances.

Central to the strategy is the development of a suite of hallmark events. These are mainly annual events and offer the opportunity to promote Melbourne to domestic and international tourists. The State Government of Victoria provides some sponsorship and Tourism Victoria highlights them in its destination marketing. The events are staggered throughout the year to spread the impact across the seasons.

Melbourne's sporting hallmark events are:

- Australian Open Tennis Championships
- Formula 1 Grand Prix
- Australian Motorcycle Grand Prix
- Australian Football League Grand Final
- Bells Beach Surfing Classic
- Spring Horse Racing Carnival (including the Melbourne Cup)
- Cricket Test Match (held on Boxing Day, the day after Christmas).

Most of these events are staged at permanent venues in central Melbourne. The two exceptions are the motorcycle and surfing competitions which are held at coastal areas approximately two hours' drive from the city. While the emphasis is on annual championships, the Victorian Government also bids for lesser mega events, staging, for example, the Commonwealth Games and World Swimming Championships. However, these are opportunistic and supplementary; the core of the strategy are the annual hallmark events.

Melbourne's cultural hallmark events are:

- Australian International Airshow
- The Melbourne Food and Wine Festival

- Melbourne International Comedy Festival
- The Melbourne International Flower and Garden Show
- Melbourne International Festival of the Arts
- Wangaratta Festival of Jazz
- Equitana Asia Pacific (a horse-themed exhibition).

With the exception of the Wangaratta Jazz Festival, these are all staged in Melbourne. While generally grouped as cultural, a number of them (such as the Airshow, Food and Wine Festival and Equitana) also have objectives of promoting local industries. All of the cultural events may be characterized as festivals, packaging together a series of events at multiple venues. Melbourne also has a strong programme of concerts, art exhibitions, plays and performances, and though some of these are tourist drawcards they are not given much prominence in the strategy.

Failures and limitations

While events may commonly be viewed as the deliverer of tourism benefits, this is not always the case. Some events do not draw the promised tourists, typically due to the organizers over-estimating predicted visitor numbers. Two examples illustrate this problem. In 2009 Yokohama in Japan staged ExpoY 150, as part of the commemoration of the 150th anniversary of the port being opened to Western traders. The five-month exhibition was budgeted with an attendance of 5 million visitors. Instead it received only 1.24 million. As recriminations started, the event organizers began legal action against three travel companies for failing to deliver contracted numbers of tourists (Takebe 2010).

Wishful thinking was also in evidence in the case of the Millennium Dome Exhibition staged in London in 2000. Its business plan was based on 12 million visitors over the year, essentially just above its break-even point. However, that projection had been agreed upon before the organizers had decided on ticket prices, the contents of the exhibition, a marketing plan or transport logistics. The final numbers were only 4.5 million paying customers (National Audit Office 2000).

Another difficulty may be where the event theme is attractive to tourists but does not fit with the marketing strategy of the DMO or the aspirations of key stakeholders. The Sydney Gay and Lesbian Mardi Gras, for example, generates international tourists, but for some conservative political leaders these are the wrong type of visitors. Liverpool is renowned as the home of the Beatles and hosts a number of events associated with the band. However, the authorities are more interested in pursuing other avenues of promoting the destination (Cohen 2007). Further dissonance occurs where stakeholders argue that city funding of events is only of benefit to an elite few (Reid 2006).

Faced with such contested views of what a destination's image should be and how events should support that, many cities opt for sporting events. Sports, the argument seems to be, are so widely appealing that they cause no dissonance, encouraging tourism without raising any unfortunate issues or offending stakeholders. However, here there are still potential pitfalls. If most cities are focusing on sporting events, how do they distinguish themselves? The paradox for competing cities is that, 'whereas the appeal of tourism is the opportunity to see something different, cities that are remade to attract tourists seem more and more alike' (Fainstein and Judd 1999: 12–13). Some potentially attractive market segments may be discouraged by mass tourism events. Consider the example of the Creative Class segment – the sort of professional, high-income, trendsetting people that cities dream of attracting. However, event-led attractions, particularly sporting stadia and entertainment precincts, are 'irrelevant, insufficient, or actually unattractive to many Creative Class people' (Florida 2005: 35–6).

Economic impact studies

The emphasis on the tourism benefits of events demands measures to demonstrate these benefits. Economic impact studies are intended to show the net benefit to a destination of spending money in staging an event. Tourism is the key, for organizers, DMOs and other stakeholders want to prove that the money spent (especially if it was public money) was well spent and resulted in money flowing into the regional economy. That local people attended is irrelevant, for they have only shifted their expenditure options within the economy. Only tourists count, their money is new money which the destination would not have gained without the event. This tourism dimension can make events an attractive export industry.

However, the ubiquitous economic impact study comes in for regular criticism. While purporting to be empirical and objective, the assumptions which underlie economic impact studies may be highly subjective. There is a long-running debate over the validity and reliability of these studies. Nor is this debate confined to academics – a wide range of stakeholders, including funding providers, sponsors, the media, politicians and local communities, may question the monetary value of events.

The range of criticism of economic impact studies are well summarized in Crompton (2006). One common problem worth noting is counting all visitors as being generated by an event (and therefore assigning their expenditure to the economic impact of the event). This effect is well illustrated by considering package tours to China during the 2010 Shanghai World Expo. Most standard tours spend a few days in Shanghai. During the course of the World Expo, tour operators made one of these days a visit to the event. On paper this seemingly generated large numbers of international tourists visiting for the World Expo, yet the reality was that they were coming anyway and there was no net benefit to the destination. There is also a problem in that most conventional tourism statistical collections find it difficult to identify tourists attending events.

Longer-term benefits

There is an increasing realization that events have longer-term tourism benefits. This is particularly the case with mega events, which through their global media exposure provide the opportunity to implant and develop attractive destination attributes and images. A viewer watching the Olympics or World Cup on television might be influenced to visit the host destination. The television coverage might include short snippets ('postcards') of tourist attractions and experiences, shown during breaks in play. These inserts have often been produced by DMOs and provided to the broadcaster. There may also be extensive destination marketing campaigns tied in with the event, as with the use of the 2000 Sydney Olympics by the Australian Tourism Commission (Brown *et al.* 2002).

The aim of this marketing is not to attract the viewer to the event – it is too late for that. Rather, it is to encourage them to plan a holiday in the *future*. A successful marketing campaign linked to a mega event should result in an increase in tourism over the next one to two years. Indeed, the tourism legacy might stretch out for as much as five years.

Hallmark events also aim to attract tourists in the longer term through promoting a particular destination image. Cultural events, for example, may project an image of a city as cultured, sophisticated and 'cool', worth visiting at any time. In this sense the effect is similar to those of mega events. However, hallmark events also work in the longer term in two different ways. Effective destination marketing associated with a hallmark event might first draw in tourists for a future year's event and, second, encourage repeat visitation.

Another long-term benefit is the legacy of infrastructure. How will the stadia, convention centres or performance venues be used in the future? It may encourage the destination to stage more events to pay off the cost, perhaps even dominating future strategies. Destinations may develop regular hallmark events primarily to effectively use the facilities they have already paid for. This again raises the issue of destination sameness – with many cities striving to offer the same range of events in similar types of venues.

Events and tourist attractions

The discussion of the tourism benefits of events is usually couched in terms of destinations, but we should also consider individual attractions. The operators of attractions are increasingly relying on events to generate added visitation and broaden market appeal. For many attractions, events become a regular part of their offerings to visitors, utilizing their built facilities and the ambiance of the location. This is an area which requires much more research, but some examples are worth considering. Historic buildings stage open days and historic re-enactments. Zoos have popular music programmes, usually weekly on summer evenings. Wineries also stage musical performances, for example Opera in the Vines. Even national parks are now starting to develop event programmes.

Rural events

Much of the focus on events is in the context of large cities. This is not surprising given their scale and the tourism flows they generate. However, events are also important in rural towns and districts. Indeed, it might be argued that they are proportionately more important to small rural destinations, for their resources are limited. Many small towns are unable to generate the funding for developing effective tourism attractions and marketing campaigns. Faced with these limitations, they turns to events as the most effective way to marshal their scarce resources to capture the attention of the tourist market (Frost 2001, 2009; Penaloza 2001; Paradis 2002; Lade and Jackson 2004; Moscardo 2007).

Rural events differ from those of major cities in three main ways. First, events in country towns are more likely to be about building and celebrating local identity, with tourism of secondary importance. With some rural events there is a strong disconnection between their organizers and local tourism operators, with the latter opting out as they see little benefit in being involved. Second, rural events lack resources. They struggle to access national funding and major sponsors. Many rely heavily on volunteers – indeed, they are often characterized by a high level of volunteerism in their planning and management. Third, the reach of rural events is primarily local and any tourism generated is domestic rather than international.

Balancing these negativities are some positives. Rural events may appeal to tourists because they are local, celebrating a sense of place and community that is perceived as no longer available in crowded and alienated cities. Strong social capacity and identity may be reflected in these local events, with some more innovative and 'green' than their city counterparts (Lade and Jackson 2004; Laing and Frost 2009). In essence, rural events appeal to concepts of authenticity and nostalgia. This is illustrated in how events involving livestock, particularly rodeos and agricultural shows, generate domestic tourism from cities. These urban visitors are great consumers of the paraphernalia of the frontier or cowboy myth, including boots, hats and Western clothing (Penaloza 2001). In addition, as with city events, tourists to a rural event may stay longer in the region.

The greatest difficulty for a rural event is standing out in a crowded marketplace. Many rural events are very similar in theming and content. For example, in California's Central Valley, many small towns base their tourism image and events on local agricultural produce. There are annual festivals celebrating almonds (Oakley), artichokes (Castroville), asparagus (Stockton), avocadoes (Carpinteria, Fallbrook), carrots (Bakersfield), garlic (Gilroy), mushrooms (Morgan Hill), mustard (St Helena), peaches (Marysville), strawberries (Roseville, Watsonville and Wheatlands) and tomatoes (Yuba City) (Frost 2009).

To break out of this mould, some small towns have developed themes relying on popular culture. Examples include Metropolis (Illinois) which has an annual 'Superman Celebration', Riverside (Iowa) which claims to be the 'Future Birthplace of Captain James T. Kirk' and holds a 'Trek Fest' promoted as 'the small town fair with a Sci-Fi flair', and Roswell (New Mexico) which stages the 'Roswell UFO Festival' (Paradis 2002; Frost 2009). While attractive to tourists, these wild themes may be alienating to some local people. As Paradis (2002) found in his study of Roswell, there was a great deal of opposition to an event built around something that many saw as having no real connection to the town.

The Lone Pine Film Festival in California

This is an annual festival in a small town, which has successfully focused tourism into a particular week and provided profits which have been used to establish a heritage museum.

Lone Pine is a small town halfway between Death Valley and the Sierra Nevada Mountains. Since the 1920s Hollywood has been attracted to the area by its arid and rocky landscapes. Over 350 movies have been made at Lone Pine, the most recent being *Rocket Man* (2008). The Lone Pine Film Festival began in 1990. The initial idea was to screen a number of films and then conduct tours to the exact sites where they were shot. This quickly expanded to include a parade, a number of concerts and dinners, and panel sessions with experts talking about the films. While a wide variety of films have been made at Lone Pine, the festival is dominated by interest in Westerns. Each year is given a theme. In 2004 it was the stuntmen and in 2006 it was horses.

The film festival has been successful in drawing in tourists to the town. Its role in shaping its destination image is demonstrated in how the festival details are now the main part of the town's entry in tourist guidebooks for California. Furthermore, profits from the festival have been used in developing a permanent Lone Pine Film History Museum. Opened in 2006, this is a purpose-built museum modelled on a 1930s art-deco cinema.

The Lone Pine Film Festival appeals to a wide range of tourists interested in film history and the Wild West. Its strength is its authenticity: this is a remote town in which films were made and with close associations with a range of movie stars. Festival attendees can watch films and the next day visit where they were shot. A range of guest speakers and panels give them a 'behind the scenes' insight into film-making and its history. There is a communitas in interacting with kindred spirits with the same passions and interests.

Lone Pine is an instructive example of how a small country town may successfully build its tourism strategy on an event. Isolated and lacking resources, it had little ability to attract tourists. However, in using its quirky history and connections to Hollywood as a theme, it developed an event that set it apart from its competitors.

Conclusion

For the tourism industry, events are a major tool in attracting tourists. Many destinations take a strategic approach in which the expense of events is justified through the increased tourism revenue they generate. Such events strategies tend to focus on either mega or hallmark events. Mega events have the advantage of promoting a destination to a global audience, though they also have disadvantages in essentially being one-off opportunities and being costly to bid for. Hallmark events are closely linked to a specific place. Despite having less potential for global reach, they help develop a destination's brand and their regularity ensures a steady flow of tourists.

Events are particularly attractive for second-tier cities which lack iconic attractions or a strong recognized image. Developing tourism through an events strategy allows these cities to compete in a crowded marketplace. Similarly, rural towns look to events as the opportunity to develop their destination image and attract tourists.

While events seem an ideal solution for the problem of encouraging tourism, there may be limitations. Many destinations may be involved in competing for the same tourists and they may be using identical strategies. Bidding for mega events is costly, with no guarantee of ultimate success. A tendency to overestimate visitor numbers and their economic impact has led to some spectacular failures. Rural towns struggle to find resources to effectively compete. Despite such possible shortcomings, more and more destinations are becoming committed to events as a tool to promote tourism.

Further reading

Brown, G., Chalip, L., Jago, L. and Mules, T. (2002) 'The Sydney Olympics and Brand Australia', in N. Morgan, A. Pritchard and R. Pride (eds) *Destination Branding: Creating the Unique Destination Proposition*, Oxford: Butterworth-Heinemann, pp. 163–85. (Case study of how a mega-event is used within a destination marketing campaign.)

Crompton, J.L. (2006) 'Economic impact studies: instruments for political shenanigans?', *Journal of Travel Research* 45: 67–82. (A provocative critique of economic impact studies.)

Frost, W. (2009) 'Projecting an image: film-induced festivals in the American West', *Event Management* 12(2): 95–104. (Case studies of two US towns using film-related festivals to develop their image.)

Getz, D. (2008) 'Event tourism: definition, evolution, and research', *Tourism Management* 29: 403–28. (Comprehensive literature and conceptual review.)

Hall, C.M. (1992) *Hallmark Tourist Events: Impacts, Management and Planning*, London: Belhaven. (Pioneering study of events and tourism.)

Paradis, T.W. (2002) 'The political economy of theme development in small urban places: the case of Roswell, New Mexico', *Tourism Geographies* 4(1): 22–43. (Case study of contested community views on an event.)

Richards, G. and Palmer, R. (2010) *Eventful Cities: Cultural Management and Urban Revitalisation*, Oxford and Burlington: Butterworth-Heinemann. (Extended coverage of cities developing events strategies.)

Weed, M. and Bull, C. (2009) *Sports Tourism: Participants, Policy and Providers*, Amsterdam: Butterworth-Heinemann, second edition. (Good coverage of growing area.)

References

Brown, G., Chalip, L., Jago, L. and Mules, T. (2002) 'The Sydney Olympics and Brand Australia', in N. Morgan, A. Pritchard and R. Pride (eds) *Destination Branding: Creating the Unique Destination Proposition*, Oxford: Butterworth-Heinemann, pp. 163–85.

Burr, A. (2006) 'The freedom of slaves to walk the streets: celebration, spontaneity and revelry versus logistics at the Notting Hill Carnival', in D. Picard and M. Robinson (eds) *Festivals, Tourism and Social Change: Remaking Worlds*, Clevedon: Channel View, pp. 84–98.

Byeon, M., Carr, N. and Hall, C.M. (2008) 'The South Korean hotel sector's perspective on the "pre" and "post-event" impacts of the 2002 Football World Cup', in J. Ali-Knight, M. Robertson, A. Fyall and A. Ladkin (eds) *International Perspectives on Festivals and Events: Paradigms of Analysis*, London: Academic, pp. 65–93.

Carlsen, J. and Taylor, A. (2003) 'Mega-events and urban renewal: the case of the Manchester 2002 Commonwealth Games', *Event Management* 8(1): 15–22.

Cohen, S. (2007) *Decline, Renewal and the City in Popular Music Culture: Beyond the Beatles*, Aldershot: Ashgate.

Crompton, J.L. (2006) 'Economic impact studies: instruments for political shenanigans?', *Journal of Travel Research* 45: 67–82.

Custodio, M. and Gouveia, P. (2007) 'Evaluation of the cognitive image of a country destination by the media during the coverage of mega-events: the case of UEFA EURO 2004 in Portugal', *International Journal of Tourism Research* 9: 285–96.

Fainstein, S.S. and Judd, D.R. (1999) 'Global forces, local strategies and urban tourism', in D.R. Judd and S.S. Fainstein (eds) *The Tourist City*, New Haven: Yale University Press, pp. 1–17.

Florek, M., Breitbarth, T. and Conejo, F. (2008) 'Mega sports events and host country image: the case of the 2006 FIFA World Cup', *Journal of Sports and Tourism* 13(3): 80–8.

Florida, R. (2005) *Cities and the Creative Class*, London and New York: Routledge.

Foley, M., McPherson, G. and McGillvray, D. (2008) 'Establishing Singapore as the events and entertainment capital of Asia: strategic brand diversification', in J. Ali-Knight, M. Robertson, A. Fyall and A. Ladkin (eds) *International Perspectives on Festivals and Events: Paradigms of Analysis*, London: Academic, pp. 53–64.

Formica, S. and Uysal, M. (1998) 'Market segmentation of an international cultural–historical event in Italy', *Journal of Travel Research* 36(4): 16–24.

Frost, W. (2001) 'Golden anniversaries: festival tourism and the 150th anniversary of the gold rushes in California and Victoria', *Pacific Tourism Review* 5(3/4): 149–58.

——(2008) 'Popular culture as a different type of heritage: the making of AC/DC Lane', *Journal of Heritage Tourism* 3(3): 176–84.

——(2009) 'Projecting an image: film-induced festivals in the American West', *Event Management* 12(2): 95–104.

Getz, D. (2008) 'Event tourism: definition, evolution, and research', *Tourism Management* 29: 403–28.

Gold, J.R. and Gold, M.M. (2005) *Cities of Culture: Staging International Festivals and the Urban Agenda*, Aldershot: Ashgate.

Hall, C.M. (1992) *Hallmark Tourist Events: Impacts, Management and Planning*, London: Belhaven.

Henderson, J.C., Foo, K., Lim, H. and Yip, S. (2010) 'Sports events and tourism: Singapore Formula One Grand Prix', *International Journal of Event and Festival Management* 1(1): 60–73.

Higham, J. (1999) 'Sport as an avenue of tourism development', *Current Issues in Tourism* 2(1): 82–90.

Jayswal, T. (2008) 'Event tourism: potential to build a destination', *Tourism Marketing and Promotion* 4(1): 53–61.

Lade, C. and Jackson, J. (2004) 'Key success factors in regional festivals: some Australian experiences', *Event Management* 9(1/2): 1–11.

Laing, J. and Frost, W. (2009) 'How green was my festival: exploring challenges and opportunities associated with staging green events', *International Journal of Hospitality Management* 29(2): 261–7.

Lee, C.-K. and Taylor, T. (2005) 'Critical reflections on the economic impact assessment of a mega-event: the case of the 2002 FIFA World Cup', *Tourism Management* 26: 595–603.

Liburd, J.L. (2008) 'Tourism and the Hans Christian Andersen bicentenary event in Denmark', in J. Ali-Knight, M. Robertson, A. Fyall and A. Ladkin (eds) *International Perspectives on Festivals and Events: Paradigms of Analysis*, London: Academic, pp. 41–52.

MacLaurin, D. and Leong, K. (2000) 'Strategies for success: how Singapore attracts and retains the convention and trade show industry', *Event Management* 6(2): 93–104.

Moscardo, G. (2007) 'Analyzing the role of festivals and events in regional development', *Event Management* 11(1): 23–32.

National Audit Office (2000) *The Millennium Dome*, London: The Stationery Office.

Paradis, T.W. (2002) 'The political economy of theme development in small urban places: the case of Roswell, New Mexico', *Tourism Geographies* 4(1): 22–43.

Penaloza, L. (2001) 'Consuming the American West: animating cultural meaning and memory at a stock show and rodeo', *Journal of Consumer Research* 28: 369–98.

Peters, M. and Pikkemaat, B. (2005) 'The management of city events: the case of Bergsilvester in Innsbruck, Austria', *Event Management* 9(3): 147–53.

Reid, G. (2006) 'The politics of city imaging: a case study of the MTV Europe Music Awards Edinburgh 03', *Event Management* 10(1): 35–46.

Richards, G. and Palmer, R. (2010) *Eventful Cities: Cultural Management and Urban Revitalisation*, Oxford and Burlington: Butterworth-Heinemann.

Rydell, R.W. (1993) *World of Fairs: the Century-of-Progress Expositions*, Chicago: University of Illinois Press.

Smith, A. (2005) 'Reimaging the city: the value of sports initiatives', *Annals of Tourism Research* 32(1): 217–36.

Stokes, R. (2007) 'Relationships and networks for shaping events tourism: an Australian study', *Event Management* 10: 145–58.

Stone, C. (2008) 'The British pop music festival phenomenon', in J. Ali-Knight, M. Robertson, A. Fyall and A. Ladkin (eds) *International Perspectives on Festivals and Events: Paradigms of Analysis*, London: Academic, pp. 205–26.

Takebe, Y. (2010) 'Yokohama's anniversary snafu sparks suits over losses', *The Japan Times Online*, 14 May. Available at: www.searchjapantimes.co.jp/cgi-bin/nn20100514b1.html (accessed 4 June 2010).

Topsfield, J. (2008) 'A country in pursuit of the vanishing tourist', *The Melbourne Age*, news section, 4 June: 3.

Tourism Victoria (2002) *Advantage Victoria: Tourism Victoria's Strategic Plan 2002–6*, Melbourne: Tourism Victoria.

Weed, M. and Bull, C. (2009) *Sports Tourism: Participants, Policy and Providers*, Amsterdam: Butterworth-Heinemann, second edition.

6

Public events, personal leisure

Diane O'Sullivan

Introduction

Events as a subject area spans a variety of interdisciplinary areas as we saw in Chapter 4 by Mike Weed. One of the less well-known and debated areas in the research literature is the relationship between leisure and events, particularly the events–public leisure nexus. Any attempt to understand the role of leisure in society must be prepared for a 'moveable feast'. As society shifts and alters, so leisure demand, provision and consumption inevitably change in response. This is also relevant for the leisure–event nexus. However, it is at least conceivable that this debate on leisure and society is not all one way and that changing leisure, in turn, has the capacity to change society. For this reason, if no other, the relationships between society and public leisure events are worthy of consideration given the growing significance of events as a dimension of the cultural industries of cities and other places and their contribution to public leisure, as reflected in leisure strategies.

Discussions about leisure often begin with its role and meaning in people's lives (where we live, what we do, our tastes, who we choose to spend time with) and the way in which it influences, and is influenced by, society. Sociologists use the concept of *lifestyles* to explain 'self-concept' (DeCrop 2006: 11): that is, how we explain to ourselves, and to others, who we are. The growing consumption of leisure events – sporting, cultural, visual arts, music, festivals, heritage, etc. – has resonance with contemporary tourists being described as accumulators of 'social and cultural capital' (Shaw and Williams 2004: 132). Given the relatively well-developed literature around the leisure phenomenon, it is certainly possible that leisure studies has something useful to contribute to explaining the motivations, experiences and behaviours of event attendees (Getz 2007). And indeed, this has been the case (see, for example, Jackson 2005 and Li and Petrick 2006) but there may be a further question to be explored: does leisure theory have something to contribute to event effectiveness and event evaluation?

A significant and stubborn difficulty around public sector event provision has been the measurement of anticipated benefits. Initially, considerable attention was given to establishing the economic benefits of individual events (Getz 1989; Long and Perdue 1990; Crompton and McKay 2001; Tyrrell and Johnston 2001) though there was little agreement that such approaches were reliable, cost-effective, accurate or comparable (Dwyer *et al.* 2000; Jura Consultants and Gardiner & Theobold 2001; Craig 2006; Jones 2008; Bowdin *et al.* 2011). More recently there have been attempts to capture frequently lauded social and environmental benefits from events (Arts Council Wales 2007) such as the 'the triple bottom line' (a term coined by John Elkington in 1994 to mean that business should consider 'people, planet, profit') and other potentials, such as social capital and entrepreneurship (O'Sullivan *et al.* 2008). However, a report to the Scottish Cultural Commission (Ruiz 2004) claimed that, despite the almost universal agreement for the need for a better system of evaluation, the complexity and nuances of the task mean that it remains, at best, problematic.

Despite the challenge of measuring outputs, contemporary cities have recently been described as demonstrating a 'desire for eventfulness' and as moving towards a state of 'festivalisation', with texts promising to reveal how to 'develop and manage an eventful city' in order to optimise contributions to 'economic and social prosperity' (Richards and Palmer 2010: 2). However, evaluating public event outcomes is now widely recognised as a complex task fraught with multiple potential pitfalls, any of which could either singly, or in combination, undermine a reliable understanding of what objectives have been set or achieved (O'Sullivan *et al.* 2009). Consequently, with the measurement of public event outcomes so notoriously challenging, there is a danger that public policy decision-making on events might be less *evidence-based*, more *wishful thinking*.

This chapter has two key purposes. First, it seeks to explore some of the benefits of leisure with particular reference to public sector leisure events. Second, it considers whether leisure theory might have something to offer the understanding of what outcomes public sector leisure events can reasonably be expected to deliver, and consequently, how these might be more effectively assessed and understood.

Understanding leisure in a social context

Much contemporary Western thinking on leisure stems from an understanding of leisure as it occurred in the ancient civilisations of Greece and Rome. Continuing this historical perspective changes in leisure activity through the Middle Ages, the Renaissance, the Reformation, and the Industrial Revolution are generally covered to provide the context for contemporary ideas (see Haywood *et. al.* 1995; Torkildsen 2005 [1999]). At first, attempts to define leisure at the conceptual level, of which there are many, tended to address the role of play (Ellis 1973) and its contribution to human development (physical and mental) and then to explore leisure in relation to time (free time), activity (freely chosen) and state of mind (the motive of the participant) (Bull *et al.* 2003).

A common theme of the work of sociologists on leisure has been the comparisons to be drawn with its relationship to work and then expanding that relationship further to cover leisure/work and politics; leisure/work and class; leisure/work and gender; and, leisure/work and economics (Critcher *et al.* 1995; Haywood *et al.* 1995; Veal and Haworth 2004; Critcher 2006; Roberts 2006). The 1960s saw the field of urban studies raising early concerns over a perceived decline in a sense of community and a move towards individualism (Mumford 1961) which could be evidenced by changes in structures for leisure. Social psychology has a long history of interest in leisure, seeking to understand 'why people need social relationships and how these are expressed in terms of leisure behaviour, attitudes and activities' (Page and Connell 2010: 154). The work of Argyle (1996) offers an overview of leisure as a form of social integration which provides positive opportunities for social advantage, identity and improved self-esteem and governments commonly seek strategies to support society by addressing social exclusion (and, more positively, promoting social inclusion) via the removal of barriers to leisure participation for disadvantaged social groups (Page and Connell 2010: 154). Such concerns may also be evidenced by increased interest in the notion of social capital, which deals with the reciprocal relationships to be gained by individuals working together, via the activities that occur in leisure time, to achieve shared objectives (Putnam 1993). Leisure's link to social capital has been investigated in a variety of ways (Warde *et al.* 2005) and events are no exception. For example, O'Sullivan *et al.* (2008) considered the role of festivals and events in rural areas of Wales, concluding that they make a significant contribution to local communities by providing opportunities for supporting and encouraging social capital and entrepreneurship, often filling a vacuum caused by a lack of support from local authorities.

As the nature and structure of society shift, so too does the nature and structure of leisure. An early modern focus of leisure was, arguably, within the home, centred upon listening to the radio and reading; later the watching of television, computer games and accessing the internet (Kynaston 2007: 295). However, Roberts (1999: 41) argues that in the second half of the twentieth century leisure outside the home has also flourished as evidenced by the growth of tourism, involvement in sport and physical activity, and other recreational activities, such as those offered by the entertainment sector including visits to public houses and high-tech cinemas. Though it may at first seem counterfactual, events can – and do – fall into both home-based and out-of-home typologies of leisure.

One of the key contemporary aspects of events as leisure is the notion of events as 'experience' and of successful events being built upon 'predictably satisfying experiences' (Mannell and Kleiber 1997: 11). The idea of controlling and replicating such experiences absorbs an increasing amount of time and effort for those involved in the design and management of 'live' events (Berridge 2006). This concept stems from a focus on the customer experience as a natural extension of the provision and marketing of products and services, where the engagement of and with customers is achieved in a 'personal, memorable way' (Pine and Gilmore 1999: 3). In the seminal text *The Experience Economy*, Pine and Gilmore offer advice on how to create positive experiences and, though their experiences focus mainly on retail exchanges, the concepts are frequently discussed by advisors on event management (Getz 2007: 173; Shone and Parry 2010; Bowdin *et al.* 2011). The concept proposes a theatrical approach covering the experience theme (including scripting a story); surprise (staging the unexpected); the production team (the sum of roles required to produce and event); and, finally, a process of 'transformation' which positively changes the individual (Pine and Gilmore 1999: 165). The 'wow factor', where live event attendees are 'dazzled' (Citrine 1995), has become increasingly sought after but increasingly difficult to achieve in a 'safe and guaranteed' experience (Getz 2007). However, planned events are not always designed solely for the spatially 'live' audience.

Events created primarily to be packaged and broadcast via television and the World Wide Web have the potential to reach a truly global audience and are now commonplace. The broadcasting of live events such as the Olympic Games and golf's Ryder Cup, like the actual events themselves, is said to offer intangible benefits such as community pride, cultural renewal, increased tourist interest and investment in the host community or destination (Getz 2007). Traditional home-based leisure pursuits, particularly listening to the radio or watching television, were viewed as passive forms of leisure but increasingly live broadcasts transcend that description. Work undertaken by Lincoln (2005) on youth culture and music suggest that music, both live and recorded, is one of the ways in which young people develop 'socially, politically and culturally' … determining their 'attitudes, appearance and friendships' (cited in Page and Connell 2010: 104). The marriage of Prince William, son of the Prince of Wales in April 2011, was an event celebrated by the designation of a public holiday in the UK; local community parties and celebrations were planned, increased international tourism was anticipated and media coverage accessible around the globe (BBC News UK 2010). Such celebratory events offer an opportunity for home-based and out-of-home leisure; individual and community leisure; personal and public leisure; local and visitor leisure; and live and broadcast leisure. This event serves to demonstrate that leisure and events are inextricably linked in both theory and practice.

Understanding leisure in a public policy context

Early thinking about post-industrial societies centred round American academics who, in the 1960s, argued that advances in technology, productivity and economic growth would lead to social structures and lifestyles dominated by leisure (Critcher and Bramham 2004: 34). Meanwhile, in the UK, increased public spending on leisure and the arts culminated in the creation of large departments for leisure in local authorities, supported by huge increases in spending under the banner of 'community welfare' (Veal 1993). However, by the economic crisis of 1976, which necessitated the government approaching the International Monetary Fund for a loan, public spending on leisure began to be 'targeted' in order to achieve specific economic, social and public order goals (ibid.). In this way public sector support for leisure moved from a policy of 'leisure for all' to a policy of targeting 'hard-to-reach groups' (including women, the poor) and geographical areas (such as the inner cities).

During the Margaret Thatcher governments of the 1980s spending on leisure was increasingly squeezed, forcing provision to become more *market-facing* (for example, by the introduction of Compulsory Competitive Tendering for local public leisure provision) and *economically justified* in terms of outcomes produced (Bull *et al.* 2003). However, by 1990 a newly elected party leader took a different view of leisure, and in creating a new Department of National Heritage the John Major government sought a return to the view that culture (sport, tourism, the arts, heritage and broadcasting) offered benefits for society as a whole, rather than being just a tool for dealing with isolated problems. By the late 1990s the New Labour government inherited leisure policies they were ideologically able to retain, many of which were made possible by the introduction of the National Lottery in 1994. Despite the original intention that the Lottery should provide additional funding, over and above that which previously existed, that goal was 'all but abandoned', with more of the original funding being directed at social policies (Bull *et al.* 2003).

By the 1990s the notion of the *creative industries* had replaced the earlier focus on culture with its – potentially negative – connotations of cultural consumption and increasing consumerism (Page and Connell 2010: 350). It is argued that a move from tangible elements of culture (buildings, museums, monuments, etc.) to the intangible elements (image, identity, lifestyle, etc.) indicates a shift to a symbolic economy (Richards and Wilson 2007). This shift culminated in a strategy for the creative industries designed to make the UK a focus for the sector across the world (DCMS 2008), while the latest estimates claim that the creative industries contributed 6.2 per cent of the UK's Gross Value Added in 2007 and made up 4.5 per cent of all goods and services exported (www.culture.gov.uk).

With a new Conservative/Liberal Democrat coalition government being elected in 2010 and the promise of severe spending cuts being discussed for the new government's budget, it appears that the public sector will 'bear the brunt of paying of the [budget] deficit' (*Guardian* 2010). What this will mean for leisure provision, particularly given its fragmentation and lack of cohesive political identity (Bull *et al.* 2003) is, at present, uncertain.

Why are events significant for the public sector?

Perhaps the place to start with this question is to ask why governments get involved in anything at all. First, where involvement is a function of governance, they have no choice. Examples here would include education, public health and national security. However, there are areas of activity where government involvement is not mandatory and where choices may be made. In these cases governments' particular political ideologies come into play, but in general terms their involvement in supporting events tends to be driven by the concept of the 'public good'. Getz (2007: 330) suggests that the benefits of public events might include:

- contributions to social equity with regard to, for example, leisure access or health;
- redressing market failures or inadequacies, such as stimulating business and encouraging enterprise and job creation;
- generating income via profits to be made from public events;
- intangible benefits, such as contributions to culture including for non-users;
- sustaining and protecting public resources, including the physical environment.

Other writers highlight the benefit of public leisure events as being their role in national and local economic development strategies (Hughes 1999; Harcup 2000; Hall and Rusher 2004; Whitford 2004; Bowdin et al. 2011). Observers of contemporary city development highlight the value of events to the restructuring of 'post-industrial cities' such as Glasgow, Manchester and Dublin (Miles and Miles 2004) and to the 'entrepreneurial city' (Hannigan 1998; Judd 1999) where development partnerships between the public and private sectors become the dominant development model. Additional claims for the value of public events include their contribution to 'creative cities' (Landry 2000) which focus on attracting businesses and people who fit into Richard Florida's (2002) definition of the 'creative class' and where cultural capital is used to attract 'innovative businesses and services' (Zukin 2004: 13). This is extended even further to the notion of the 'intercultural city' which is said to be able to utilise complex internal cultural resources, demonstrated by diverse cultural events and festivals (Wood et al. 2006), to adapt to changing external circumstances and so 'extend their competence base' (Lambooy, cited in Richards and Palmer 2005). Consequently, public sector involvement in leisure events has become one way in which places seek to attract visitors, labour, businesses and investment capital.

Understanding public leisure events

It has been suggested that the study of events might usefully receive contributions from at least fourteen foundation disciplines and eleven closely linked professional fields (Getz 2007). Before 2000 much of the writing and research on events was scattered through wider fields of study, notably 'tourism and hospitality, business and economics' (Bowdin et al. 2011: 449). Academics and practitioners in Australia set a new agenda in 2000 at the first international event management research conference, and since that time specific event research, journals and programmes of education have proliferated around the globe (Getz 2007). Discussions arising from such events conferences in Australia led to the claim that academics and practitioners were not communicating very well (Harris and Jago 2000) and it was as recently as 2006 that an Event Management Body of Knowledge (EMBOK; www.embok.com) was published. Establishing how and when a field of study is 'born' is contentious, but it is said to have occurred when it becomes generally accepted that practitioners need an understanding of the variety of theoretical foundations and research methodologies that underpin their professional activities (Tribe 2006). Arguments against disciplinary status for fields of study such as events suggest that by their very nature they are too complex and that such a move would limit further development. The longer established field of study around tourism is still said to lack the cohesion required to claim the status (Echtner and Jamal 1997: 875; Tribe 2004, 2006).

Though the relationship between events and public policy has received limited analysis (Gratton and Henry 2001; Hall and Rusher 2004) their inclusion in local and regional development strategies suggest they may be of considerable significance (Roche 2000; Hinch and Higham 2004; Pugh and Wood 2004; Whitford 2004). However, this lack of analysis in no way indicates a lack of event activity. Public sector involvement in events at the regional level has become more visible with the creation of dedicated events departments or events units. Visit Britain, the British Tourist Authority, created eventBritain (www.visitbritain.com/en/campaigns/eventbritain) which claims to offer an extensive range of benefits to help achieve its core objective of working with UK industry partners to support bids for major business, cultural and sporting events. EventScotland has a similar objective (www.eventscotland.org) with a budget of around £5 million, and the Welsh Assembly developed its own Major Events Unit in 2009. In one of the few texts yet to emerge which attempts to deal with events as a concept, Getz (2007: 329–49) argues that events offer government a potential for economic, social, cultural and environmental benefits on the condition that they are planned and managed effectively.

It has been suggested that, in the UK, the public sector is responsible for much of the existing event activity and that local authorities have 'substantial and varied events programmes' (Pugh and Wood 2004). Research undertaken in Wales in 2006–7 revealed that, at a conservative estimate, all twenty-two local authorities were involved with events in some way and that the vast majority were targeted mainly at local audiences and 'staged primarily for socio-cultural reasons linked to basic social-capital building activity' (O'Sullivan *et al.* 2009: 26).

In summary, it is clear that while leisure studies is generally viewed as a more established discipline, the much younger study of events is still limited by a focus on managing practice rather than developing theory and exploring meaning. Differences between leisure and events are notable in that while public sector involvement in leisure provision in the UK is well recorded and comparatively well understood, the history of involvement in events appears significant but less easy to disentangle from involvement with tourism, sport and the arts more generally.

Leisure benefits and public sector events

It has been suggested that there are (at least) five benefits of leisure which might have significance for events and that these are fitness and health, social benefit, community benefit, self-actualisation and environmental benefit (Figure 6.1) (Getz 2007). Here these benefits are used as a framework for exploring ways in which public sector events might be linked to notions of leisure. However, it should be remembered that, in reality, such factors are not easily separated and remain complex and interrelated.

To avoid the temptation to view benefits as compartmentalised it may be more appropriate to view them as a continuum moving from the personal, to the individual, to the community, to society and finally, at the broadest level, to the physical environment which supports all human activity. What follows is an attempt to consider how our understanding of leisure might usefully contribute to an improved understanding of public sector event activity.

Figure 6.1 Understanding the potential for benefit from leisure

Public sector leisure and the potential for self-actualisation

The need for self-actualisation is said to be the pinnacle of a human *hierarchy of needs* (as conceived by Abraham Maslow in 1954) and despite its critics (see, for example, Cooper *et al.* 2008) the concept is often quoted in attempts to understand the role of leisure in people's lives. Maslow theorises that once the physiological needs of life are satisfied (hunger, rest, thirst, shelter) human beings move along a hierarchy of needs to include safety and security, belonging and love, esteem and finally, at the pinnacle of the triangle, self-actualisation or personal self-fulfilment. In a similar vein, a key concept in understanding the role of leisure in modern life may be the notion of 'serious leisure', which is defined as:

> the serious pursuit of an amateur, hobbyist or volunteer activity that participants find so substantial and interesting that, in the typical case, they launch themselves on a career centred on acquiring and expressing its special skills, knowledge and experience.
>
> *(Stebbins 2004: 200)*

Serious leisure is contrasted with casual leisure, characterised as an 'immediately intrinsically rewarding, relatively short-lived pleasurable activity requiring little or no special training to enjoy it' (Stebbins 2004: 201).

Serious leisure, a concept developed by Robert Stebbins, is defined as amateurism, hobbyist activities and career volunteering. The amateur pursuit of activities in art, sport, science and entertainment are contrasted to professional pursuit, defined by employment for financial reward. Hobbyists are not simply non-professionals and can be collectors, makers, followers of non-competitive rule-based pursuits (such as mountain climbing) or sports and games in competitive activities where there is no professional equivalent (such as hockey) and can be enthusiasts of liberal arts hobbies pursuing knowledge for its own sake (such as literature) (Stebbins 2004). Volunteering is defined as 'voluntary individual or group action oriented toward helping oneself or others or both' (ibid.: 201). Stebbins offers a taxonomy of sixteen forms of organisational volunteering and coins the term 'career volunteering' (in education, science, civic life, religion, politics, economic development, safety, the physical environment, etc.) where there is 'continuous and substantial helping' rather than single donations or acts (Stebbins 2004: 202).

Serious leisure is said to be further defined by seven personal and three social rewards:

Personal:

1 Personal enrichment – cherished experiences
2 Self-actualisation – development of skills, abilities, knowledge
3 Self-expression – expressing skills, abilities and knowledge developed
4 Self-image – identification as a participant
5 Self-gratification – superficial enjoyment and deep satisfaction
6 Recreation – leisure after a day's work
7 Financial return – from a serious leisure activity

Social:

8 Social attraction – engagement with others in a social world
9 Group achievement – a sense of helping, being needed, altruism
10 Contribution to the group – helping, being needed, altruism.

Stebbins (2004: 204)

It appears that finding satisfaction from serious leisure provides a mix of personal rewards and social rewards which are satisfying in themselves but far outweigh the inevitable tensions and disappointments to be encountered along the way.

Much has been made of the value of social capital and the third-sector activity (voluntary, not-for-profit) in recent years, with parties of different political persuasions both claiming them for their own ideologies (*Economist* 2005). More recently a newly elected government led by Conservative David Cameron has launched the concept of the 'Big Society' in which there is a power shift from politicians to people. This is to be achieved by, among other things, a volunteering programme for sixteen-year-olds; public service delivery by social enterprises; charities and voluntary groups; and, the launch of a Big Society Day to encourage more people to take part in social action (www.theconservatives.com). Critics might claim that this policy is simply a way to achieve the right-wing ideal of reducing the size of the state 'by the back door', yet regardless of the ideology the implications for the public sector and the third sector are significant.

Public sector events designed to encourage volunteering or community engagement could use the literature on career volunteering as *serious leisure* to inform their approach and also to measure effectiveness. Such events might be designed to focus primarily on the personal advantages to be gained which far outnumber the social ones. They might usefully highlight the fun and satisfaction to be gained, the sense of involvement and belonging, the recreational benefit and respect to be gained from one's community. Volunteering traditionally implies selflessness and service, but the literature on volunteering as *serious leisure* suggests that benefits are overwhelmingly personal rather than social. Involvement in career volunteering as characterised by Stebbins' notion of serious leisure suggest a focus on the *personal* benefits to be gained might be a useful way of getting over the problem of volunteering being negatively perceived as no more than low-cost labour subsidising publicly funded service provision.

Public sector leisure and individual benefit

Social scientists tend to disagree about whether the amount of working time has declined or increased since the 1980s (Zuzanek 2004). The traditional view on work and leisure time suggested that by the 1980s leisure time would overtake the time spent on work; however, by the 1990s a 'vicious work-and-spend' cycle was said to have resulted in 'time squeeze' for both men and women (Schor 1991: 1). Though this view is contested (Robinson and Godbey 1997; Gershuny 2000: 74) there remains support for research reporting that people feel 'always rushed' (Robinson 1993) or that they 'never have enough time' (Bond *et al.* 1998) or that they perceive themselves to have 'less time than they did five years ago' (Zuzanek and Smale 1997). While this may be a psychological response to the general 'speeding up of modern life' (Robinson and Godbey 1997: 25) the fact remains that contemporary Western-style societies report feeling 'time crunched'. Despite the controversy over the interpretation of the research, statistical data is available to support the claim that paid and unpaid workloads appear to have increased hours worked and that that there is, to a lesser extent, a 'speeding up' of non-work activities such as voluntary work or social leisure. Nevertheless, it appears that it is time spent on personal needs and continuing education, rather than leisure, that has been reduced to accommodate the change (Zuzanek 2004: 125).

It has been claimed that if good health behaviour (good nutrition, exercise, non-smoking and moderate alcohol intake) were widely practised, average life expectancy would rise by seven years, but that if all types of cancer were eliminated the gain would be only two years (Ornstein and Erlich 1989). With much of what is controllable in individuals' lifestyles being leisure-related, why is it that so few of us engage in active leisure or only do so reactively (for example, in response to a heart attack) despite the benefits of physical activity being widely promoted? One theory is that home entertainment provides 'the path of least resistance', saving us money, time and effort. A second is that trends in modern living (concerns for family togetherness and stress caused by work, commuting and financial pressures) combine to push us towards the passive and reactive lifestyle (Iso Ahola and Mannell 2004).

So what motivates us to engage in leisure? Iso Ahola and St Clair (2000) argue for three factors:

1   that we can be biologically predisposed and socialised into leisure;
2   that knowledge and values/attitudes can play a part;
3   that constraints and facilitators affecting our ability to engage with leisure combine to determine our motivation.

Further, it is argued that engagement in physically active leisure has to be self-determined and intrinsically rewarding, and that engagement of this nature is characterised by fun, enjoyment, excitement and enthusiasm (Iso Ahola and Mannell 2004).

A scan of any UK local authority's event activity is likely to reveal involvement in those which seek to encourage physical activity and to raise awareness of the role of exercise in health, such as heart health and healthy eating. Yet engagement levels remain lamentably low, and even where successful are only temporarily so. Perhaps this explains why estimates suggest that 50 per cent of people will leave an exercise programme within six months of starting it (Iso-Ahola 1999). So, does an understanding of leisure theory offer anything which might improve the effectiveness of public sector leisure events which seek to encourage individual health and fitness?

This short tour of the literature suggests that public sector events could usefully emphasise the following aspects of an individual's engagement with active leisure programmes:

1   Value for money – relative to home entertainment options
2   Time investment – relative to the busy 'time squeezed' lifestyle
3   Effort – easy to access and physically achievable
4   Family togetherness – activities that can be enjoyed by family groups
5   De-stressing – a sense of personal autonomy and friendship
6   Intrinsic rewards – fun, enjoyment, excitement, enthusiasm.

While not all programmes might be able to offer all these benefits to all individuals all of the time, if the purpose of an event is to encourage engagement in physical activity, perception of these factors as barriers to engagement is likely to work against that goal. It is possible that public sector events created to encourage physical activity could be made more effective by successfully addressing these issues in the minds of the target audience.

Public sector leisure and community benefit

The concept of community in leisure studies has changed markedly in recent years. It has moved from traditional sociological approaches (breaking it down to the sum of its parts – geography, interests, common union – while at the same time accepting that it is more than these) to a contemporary view of community as something much less tangible (Blackshaw and Crawford 2009). It is argued that community has overwhelmingly positive connotations and is viewed as 'warm and friendly' (Bauman 2001: 1) but also that it is (over) used 'indiscriminately' and 'emptily' (Hobsbawm 1995: 428).

In considering the link between community and leisure, it has been suggested that the concept of *community practice* is viewed as an alternative to, and a critique of, traditional approaches to public sector policy and service provision (Butcher 1994). Butcher lists a variety of occupations and services that have sought to apply the community practice approach, including community care, community education, community development, community business, community radio and community leisure (1994: 3). He also notes the critical perspective which suggests that community is used as a '"spray-on word", deployed to lend legitimacy and positive feelings to a variety of otherwise very diverse and maybe, in the end, not particularly new and innovative practices and approaches' (1994: 4).

Community practice then may be defined an approach to public sector service delivery which:

- views service users and the public as co-participants in the determining what should be provided and how;
- takes a collective approach to problems and decision-making;
- recognises the value of indigenous community resources in the promotion and delivery of services designed to meet community needs;
- is aware of cultural diversity with regard to community needs, taking a cultural sensitive and responsive approach to service delivery;
- is committed to prioritising the needs of disadvantaged people and groups.

(Butcher 1994: 5)

Despite criticism of the concept, community practice in public service delivery, including community leisure, has been promoted since the early 1990s. The move towards this type of public service delivery can be evidenced, not least by the proliferation of community development officer-type posts and projects in the local government arena and, more recently, by the growth in programmes designed to educate for effective community facilitation. Of course, the notion of community practice approaches requires a community willing and able to be involved, and this resonates with the notions of the engaged individual and career volunteering (discussed earlier). David Cameron's Big Society ideas will depend on the availability of a society willing and able to rise to the challenges and responsibilities on offer, and perhaps individuals able to see the personal benefits to be gained, as opposed to viewing involvement as purely selfless public service.

In the framework developed from Getz (2007) at the start of this chapter it was suggested that public leisure events might provide community benefit, and in this section I have introduced the notion of community practice. It is relatively easy to see how community-based events would be generally positive for their community. Indeed, work undertaken on events across the principality of Wales has suggested that of over 1,000 events with public sector involvement, support is justified primarily for socio-cultural reasons, community development and social-capital building outcomes (O'Sullivan *et al.* 2009). But can community leisure practice offer public sector events any practical lessons?

It does appear that public sector events which seek to benefit their community might usefully focus upon issues such as:

- communities of interest and disadvantaged groups;
- involving service users in determining what should be done and devolving responsibility to them where possible;
- attempting to engender a sense of belonging and community spirit;
- linking events with other service provision such as education and training for socially excluded young people or hard-to-reach ethnic groups;

- considering methods of service delivery by taking

  - a facilitating and enabling management style
  - a partnership focus
  - user-led approaches
  - capacity building for community groups
  - viewing the community as a resource.

If you are thinking that these approaches sound familiar with regard to public sector event delivery, I would not be surprised. There is some evidence to support the claim that these approaches are already happening within arts, sport, recreation and leisure events supported by the public sector. Indeed, it may be one of the factors contributing to the growth of interest in event management and provision generally (Bowdin *et al.* 2011). However, I suggest that what the leisure literature might still have to contribute is support for a change to the way in which such events are evaluated. If the value of events were understood and discussed from the perspective of their contribution to community practice (as described above), and evaluated on the same basis, this might help to address the seemingly intractable problems currently surrounding approaches to event evaluation discussed earlier (O'Sullivan *et al.* 2009).

Public sector leisure and social benefit

The study of groups of people and how they are organised has contributed much to the contemporary understanding of leisure and the field of leisure studies. While it is not possible, or desirable, to explore all social science contributions to leisure here, it is claimed that there is no 'defined tradition of leisure theory' and that leisure remains largely 'under-theorised' (Haywood *et al.* 1995). Reasons put forward for this omission are that other social institutions, such as work, politics, and family, have taken precedence and that leisure is often studied in relation to these 'big' social issues. It is also suggested that leisure, conceptualised as 'free-time', is a relatively recent construction and rarely has a clear history of its own. It may also be the case that conceptualising and even classifying leisure is a particularly complex task, making theory development 'problematic' (ibid.).

In broad terms there have been two key approaches in understanding leisure in the context of society (for an overview see Roberts 2006; Page and Connell 2010). The view preferred by the 'leisure studies' tradition focuses upon the individual's freedom to choose, to control their own actions and express themselves in a huge variety of freely chosen leisure forms, where supporting football and playing football are equally valid. The second approach takes a structuralist perspective which views leisure as a function of society, with society conceptualised as a system made up of institutions (family, work, politics and culture) that combine to maintain social order. This approach can be sub-divided into a view of the social order as a broad consensus, where structures of society help integrate individuals into acceptable types of behaviours, and one of conflict, where structures are controlling, with dominant and subordinate groups playing out power struggles. Here the Marxist view sees capitalism as dominant over the interest of the majority of people (the working classes or the proletariat), while feminist writers have viewed social structures as designed to benefit white middle-class males. Critical theorists, led by the Frankfurt School of sociologists, take the view that freedom in leisure is an illusion, with human needs suppressed and leisure commodified for the promotion of false needs and desires which combine to support and maintain capitalism.

These perspectives, leisure as freedom and leisure as control, are presented as polarised but much of the writing on society, and the role of leisure within it, is not necessarily constrained simply in this way. Instead, thinking on leisure and society may be more fully understood by reference to the complex sociological traditions from which it has emerged, including feminist analysis, cultural studies and postmodernism. So, what might the thinking on society and leisure offer the thinking on public sector events?

Academic studies of the role of public sector events as leisure in society can be undertaken from a variety of perspectives, such as economics, financial management, marketing and geography, to name but a few. However, as discussed earlier, work on events has been disparate and, until recently, significantly under-represented. Within sociology a variety of perspectives might be taken to public sector events, and undertaking research from specific sociological perspectives may facilitate a way through the complexity of the subject matter. Below is a list of suggested titles for research on public sector leisure events undertaken from an individual action or specific sociological perspective:

- Community arts events: opportunity for individual self-expression?
- Examining the role of the Olympic Games in maintaining societal cohesion within the host nation.
- Public sector leisure events as 'bread and circuses': a Marxist analysis.
- Community-led events: more leisure for men, more work for women?
- Public sector events and economic development: evidencing the commodification of leisure and the debasement of culture?

With leisure viewed as under-theorised in comparison to issues such as work, politics and culture (Haywood *et al.* 1995), and events only just emerging as a field of study in its own right (Getz 2007), the complexity of leisure still appears to daunt researchers. However, there is a view that this complexity must be celebrated and incorporated into approaches which examine both the individual leisure experience and the structures within which it operates (Bull *et al.* 2003). It is possible that closer sociological analysis of public sector events as leisure will inform the understanding of the purposes and outcomes they seek to achieve and, consequently, ways in which they can more effectively be evaluated.

Public sector leisure and the environmental benefit

The concern about human impact on the environment is also often discussed from two opposing perspectives. In the *anthropocentric* view the human race is dominant and nature is harnessed for human gain, while the *ecocentric* view argues that the quality of the natural environment is more important than the human race. While concern over the direction of human development can be identified in the 1960s, it was in 1984 that the United Nations appointed a World Commission on Environment and Development. From this work the now famous document *Our Common Future* (1987) (often referred to as *The Brundtland Report* after its lead author) was produced. The report contained what must be the most widely quoted definition of sustainable development as 'development which meets the needs of the present without compromising the ability of future generations to meet their own needs'. From the Rio Earth Summit in 1992 the *Agenda 21* international blueprint for development was produced and 182 heads of state agreed to implement its principles. Although *Agenda 21* did not mention leisure specifically, regional and local governments in the UK attempted to apply its principles across their operational and development activity.

Concern about the ways in which leisure exploits the environment centre around pollution (ground, water, air, noise) and, more broadly, the degradation and resource depletion mass leisure can cause (Blackshaw and Crawford 2009). Leisure travel and tourism have been a key focus of concern, and one response has been to encourage environmentally conscientious travellers to make 'off-setting' payments equal to the carbon emitted by their trip (see, for example, www.responsibletravelpartnership.org). However, lack of consensus on principles, definitions and the measurement of damage caused by human activity mean that despite attempts to assess environmental impacts, to establish maximum capacities for development and to put limits on how much development is acceptable, progress is criticised as slow and inadequate.

Sociological notions of consumption and consumerism are also relevant in relation to the physical environment. It is argued that during the 1950s spending became increasingly central in people's lives throughout the Western world (Cross 1993) and that, over time, more and more goods and services are produced and purchased by more and more people. Rising standards of living for many create governments elected on promises of maintaining, or improving, society's ability to purchase non-essential, often leisure-based, goods including electronic equipment and holidays, leading to a 'self-sealing circle' (Roberts 1999: 170). As all types of experiences (including events) become commoditised or available to buy, so the more people really feel that what they need is spending power with which to buy more consumables. Sociologists have linked this to notions of identity and lifestyle and suggest that it is driven by a media culture of marketing, promotion and leisure shopping experiences (Cashmore 1994). It is here that the leisure literature has been focused, and though much of the work has concentrated on public sector leisure with an anti-commercial bias (Taylor 1992), the future dominance of consumerism is not uncontested (Cross 1993) nor without its defenders. Commercial leisure provision has expanded leisure choice and been a liberating force for many people. A positive view of the expansion of commercialised leisure points to the rise in the skilled consumer, who is active rather than passive in structuring their leisure choices and engaged in a 'pick and mix' approach to leisure lifestyles (Gratton 1992). Much of the concern around the direction of human development has been its impact on the physical, socio-cultural and economic environments of a world driven by consumption and consumerism. Products and services draw upon fragile and ultimately finite resources and it is in this that leisure, largely viewed as non-essential or as a 'created need', comes under fire. So how do organisations square the unlimited leisure demand circle and its potential for degradation across the planet?

Increasingly, organisations have developed strategies, policies and initiatives to demonstrate their commitment to the principle of sustainable development, and the event sector is no exception. Despite their long history the number of newly created festivals and events has grown significantly since the 1960s (Picard and Robinson 2006) but it is only recently that a standard for sustainable events has been attempted. British Standard 8091 Specification for a Sustainability Management System for Events is a management standard designed to help organisations in the events industry to improve the sustainability of their business. Launched in November 2007 and revised in 2009, BS 8901 has three significant differences from many other guides that exist for the events industry. First, rather than relying on a 'checklist', BS 8901 prescribes the management system elements that an organisation has to have in place in order to enable it to improve the sustainability of its operations. Second, BS 8901 does not apply to specific events, rather to the management system that an organisation uses, so it is the organisation that is certified and not the event. Third, BS 8901 is about sustainability – not just of the physical environment but strategies which seek to ensure long-term business success, to drive social prosperity and progress, and to reduce environmental degradation (SEC.com).

One of the potential benefits of a development strategy based on events is that their temporary nature facilitates permanent impacts on the physical environment being limited. Efforts to minimise or balance impacts on the physical environment are common in local government as many of the issues, for example waste management, are controlled by departments increasingly familiar with their own environmental agendas. However, for larger events the legacy of permanent physical regeneration may be a desirable key outcome. One objective of the London Olympic Games (LOG) 2012 is to physically transform an area of East London. The LOG 2012 website claims that sustainability was embedded in the bid for the Games and committed the team to:

- use venues already existing in the UK where possible;
- only make permanent structures that will have a long-term use;
- build only temporary structures for everything else.

The Games seek to encourage people to make immediate behavioural changes with regard to their impact on the environment but also to educate them towards sustainability for life (www.london2012.com). The stated objectives listed above will be relatively easy to review at the end of the event. It will be easy enough to know whether structures are temporary or permanent. However, what would also be necessary is a willingness to deal with consequences of non-compliance. Though not impossible, this would be much more difficult to deal with both politically and organisationally.

How does it all add up?

This chapter began by examining the thinking around the role of leisure in people's lives and suggesting that the relatively well-developed literature on leisure might have something to contribute to the emergent understanding of where events might fit within this mix. After the setting out of a context for reasons why, and how, events have been employed by the public sector in the UK, the benefits of leisure more generally were linked to the potential for benefit from public sector leisure events. Potential benefits of leisure were conveniently grouped under five headings (self-actualisation, individual benefit, community benefit, social benefit and environmental benefit) providing a framework for study. The issues were then explored in turn and, in each case, the difficulty of measuring the outcomes of events was considered.

- Public sector events could offer an opportunity for serious leisure and volunteerism but would need to acknowledge that it is personal self-fulfilment which truly engages people in the long term. At the personal level research suggests that many of us *feel time-crunched* and *always rushed*. These issues would need to be considered.
- The health of individuals is an area where public sector interventions are common and there are many public sector events which seek to encourage, for example, good nutrition and exercise. Such events might usefully consider the leisure literature findings on barriers to such engagement and aim to address these to improve outcomes and their evaluation.
- While community is a difficult concept to pin down, the leisure literature has provided some useful ideas about engaging communities at the local level, and these have been widely applied by the public sector in the area of arts, sport and recreation. What has thus far been less successful is a willingness to accept that objectives such as target group engagement, involving service users in decision-making and engendering a sense of belonging, are valid criteria in measuring programme success.
- Sociologists have conflicting views about understanding society from a variety of perspectives, including Marxism, critical theory and feminism. Others argue that the study of leisure should focus upon individual freedom to choose and human self-expression. This controversy serves

to offer a variety of ways in which public sector leisure events could be researched, with the potential for new insights for practice and evaluation to emerge.

• While the environment can be viewed from an anthropocentric or an ecocentric standpoint, notions of societies becoming defined by their ability (or lack of ability) to consume ever increasing amounts of products and services are now well established. Organisations are developing ways of persuading increasingly environmentally sensitive customers that their activity is sustainable. A UK standard has been established for event management, making the achievement of these objectives within event activity, to some degree, assessable. What remains to be addressed is what should happen if standards are breached.

Public sector leisure events do appear to have the potential to contribute to wider objectives including self-actualisation, to benefit the individual, community and society and even to play a more positive role in environmental protection, but only if managed and assessed appropriately. As with most deceptively simple-sounding aims, these objectives will be difficult to achieve – in the current economic, social and environmental climate, even more so.

References

Argyle, M. (1996) *The Social Psychology of Leisure*, London: Penguin.

Arts Council Wales (2007) Website at: www.artswales.org.uk/page.asp?id=158 (accessed 30 April 2007).

Bauman, Z. (2001) *Community: Seeking Safety in an Insecure World*, Cambridge: Polity.

BBC News UK (2010) Website at: www.bbc.co.uk/news/uk-11818049 (accessed 24 November 2010).

Berridge, G. (2006) 'Analysing event experiences', paper presented at AEME conference, Bournemouth.

Blackshaw, T. and Crawford, G. (2009) *The Sage Dictionary of Leisure Studies*, London: Sage.

Bond, J., Galinksy, E. and Swanberg, J. (1998) *The 1997 National Study of the Changing Workforce*, New York: Families and Work Institute.

Bowdin, G., McDonnell, I., Allen, J. and O'Toole, W. (2011) *Events Management*, Oxford: Butterworth-Heinemann, third edition.

Bull, C., Hoose, J. and Weed, M. (2003) *An Introduction to Leisure Studies*, Harlow, UK: Prentice Hall.

Butcher, H. (1994) 'The concept of community practice', in L. Haywood (ed.) *Community Leisure and Recreation*, Oxford: Butterworth-Heinemann.

Cashmore, E. (1994) *And There was Television*, London: Routledge.

Citrine, K. (1995) 'Site planning for events', in *Event Operations*, Port Angeles, WA: International Festivals and Events Association, pp. 17–19.

Cooper, C., Fletcher, J., Fyall, A., Gilbert, D. and Wanhill, S. (eds) (2008) *Tourism: Principles and Practice*, Harlow, UK: Prentice Hall, fourth edition.

Craig, S. (2006) *The Urban Cultural Programme: Final Evaluation Report*, London: Leisure Futures.

Critcher, C. (2006) 'A touch of class', in C. Rojek, S. Shaw and A. Veal (eds) *A Handbook of Leisure Studies*, Basingstoke, UK: Palgrave.

Critcher, C. and Bramham, P. (2004) 'The devil still makes work', in J.T. Haworth and A.J. Veal (eds) *Work and Leisure*, London: Routledge, pp. 34–50.

Critcher, C., Bramham, P. and Tomlinson, A. (1995) *Sociology of Leisure: A Reader*, London: E. and F.N. Spon.

Crompton, J. and McKay, S. (1994) 'Measuring the impact of festivals and events: some myths, misapplications and ethical dilemmas', *Festival Management and Event Tourism* 3(2): 33–43.

Cross, G. (1993) *Time and Money: The Making of Consumer Culture*, London: Routledge.

DCMS (2008) *Before, During and After: Making the Most of the Olympic Games – A Consultation*, London: Department for Culture Media and Sport.

Decrop, A. (2006) *Vacation Decision Making*, Wallingford, UK: CABI.

Dwyer, L., Mellor, R., Mistillis, N. and Mules, T. (2000) 'A framework for assessing "tangible" and "intangible" impacts of events and conventions', *Events Management* 6: 175.

Echtner, C.M. and Jamal, T.B. (1997) 'The disciplinary dilemma of tourism studies', *Annals of Tourism Research* 24(4): 868–83.

Economist (2005) 'Good for me, good for my party', *The Economist* 377(8454): 71–2.

Ellis, M. (1973) *Why People Play*, New York: Prentice Hall.

Florida, R. (2002) *The Rise of the Creative Class and How its Transforming Work, Leisure, Community and Everyday Life*, New York: Basic Books.

Gershuny, J. (2000) *Changing Times*, New York: Oxford University Press.

Getz, D. (1989) 'Special events: defining the project', *Tourism Management* 10(2): 125–37.

——(2007) *Event Studies: Theory, Research and Policy for Planned Events*, Oxford: Butterworth-Heinemann.

Gratton, C. (1992) 'A Perspective on European Leisure Markets', paper presented at the conference on Internationalisation and Leisure Research, Tilburg.

Gratton, C. and Henry, I. (eds) (2001) *Sport in the City: The Role of Sport in Economic and Social Regeneration*, London: Routledge.

Guardian (2010) Website at: www.guardian.co.uk/society/2010/mar/31/public-sector-managers-alleviate-anxiety-recession

Hall, C. and Rusher, K. (2004) 'Politics, public policy and the destination', in I. Yeoman, M. Robertson, J. Ali-Knight, S. Drummond and U. McMahon-Beattie (eds) *Festival and Events Management: An Arts and Culture Perspective*, Oxford: Elsevier.

Hannigan, J. (1998) *Fantasy City: Pleasure and Profit in the Postmodern Metropolis*, London: Routledge.

Harcup, T. (2000) 'Reimaging a post-industrial city: the Leeds St Valentine's Fair as a civic spectacle', *City* 4(2): 215–31.

Harris, R. and Jago, L. (2000) 'Event management education and training Australia: industry needs, programs and outcomes', in L.K. Jago and L.J. Veal (eds) *Events Beyond 2000: Setting the Agenda*, Sydney: Australian Centre for Event Management.

Haworth, J. and Veal., A. (eds) (2004) *Work and Leisure*, London and New York: Routledge.

Haywood, L., Kew, F., Bramham, P., Spink, J., Capenerhurst, J. and Henry, I. (1995) *Understanding Leisure*, Cheltenham: Stanley Thornes, second edition.

Hinch, T. and Higham, J. (2004) *Sport Tourism Development*, Clevedon: Channel View Publications.

Hobsbawm, E. (1995) *Age of Extremes: The Short Twentieth Century 1914–1991*, London: Abacus.

Hughes, G. (1999) 'Urban revitalisation: the use of festive time strategies', *Leisure Studies* 18: 119–35.

Iso-Ahola, S. (1999) 'Motivational foundations of leisure', in E. Jackson and T. Burton (eds) *Leisure Studies: Prospects for the Twenty-First Century*, State College, PA: Venture.

Iso-Ahola, S and Mannell, R. (2004) 'Leisure and health', in J Haworth and A. Veal (eds) *Work and Leisure*, London: Routledge.

Iso-Ahola, S. and St Clair, B. (2000) 'Toward a theory of exercise motivation', *Quest* 52: 131–71.

Jackson, E. (ed.) (2005) *Constraints on Leisure*, State College, PA: Venture.

Jones, C. (2008) *BBC Wales News*, 27 May. Available at: http://news.bbc.co.uk/1/hi/wales/mid/7422323.stm (accessed 8 June 2008).

Judd, D. (1999) 'Constructing the Tourist Bubble', in D.R. Judd and S.S. Fainstein (eds) *The Tourist City*, New Haven, NJ: Yale University Press, pp. 35–53.

Jura Consultants and Gardiner & Theobold (2001) 'Millennium Festival Impact Study', Vol. 1, pp. 1–68. Report, Edinburgh.

Kynaston, D. (2007) *Austerity Britain 1945–1948: Smoke in the Valley*, London: Bloomsbury.

Landry, C. (2000) *The Creative City: A Toolkit for Urban Planners*, London: Earthscan.

Li, X. and Petrick, J. (2006) 'Research note: A review of festival and event motivation studies', *Event Management* 9(4): 239–45.

Lincoln, S. (2005) 'Feeling of noise: teenagers, bedrooms and music', *Leisure Studies* 4: 399–440.

Long, P. and Perdue, R. (1990) 'The economic impact of rural festivals and special events: assessing the spatial distribution of expenditures', *Journal of Travel Research* 28(4): 10–14.

Mannell, R. and Kleiber, D. (1997) *A Social Psychology of Leisure*, State College, PA: Venture.

Miles, S. and Miles, M (2004) *Consuming Cities*, Basingstoke, UK: Palgrave Macmillan.

Mumford, L. (1961) *The City in History*, New York: Harcourt, Brace and World.

Ornstein, R. and Erlich, P. (1989) *New World–New Mind: Moving toward Conscious Evolution*, New York: Doubleday.

O'Sullivan, D., Pickernell, D., Senyard, J. and Keast, R. (2008) 'The roles of festivals and special events in rural areas: the Welsh experience', *Journal of Rural Enterprise and Management* 4(2): 44–61.

O'Sullivan, D., Pickernell, D. and Senyard, J. (2009) 'Public sector evaluation of festivals and special events', *Journal of Policy Research in Tourism, Leisure and Events* 1 (March): 19–36.

Page, S.J. and Connell, J. (2010) *Leisure: An Introduction*, Harlow, UK: Prentice Hall.

Picard, D. and Robinson, M. (2006) *Festivals, Tourism and Social Change*, Clevedon: Channel View Publications.

Pine, B. and Gilmore, J. (1999) *The Experience Economy*, Boston: Harvard University Business School Press.

Pugh, C. and Wood, E. (2004) 'The strategic use of events within local government: a study of London Borough Councils', *Event Management Journal* 9(1): 61–71.

Putnam, R. (1993) *Making Democracy Work*, Princeton, NJ: Princeton University Press.

Richards, G. and Palmer, R. (2010) *Eventful Cities*, Oxford: Butterworth-Heinemann.

Roberts, K. (1999) *Leisure in Contemporary Society*, Wallingford, UK: CABI.

——(2006) *Leisure in Contemporary Society* Wallingford, UK: CABI, second edition.

Robinson, J. (1993) 'Your money or your time', *American Demographics,* November 22–26.

Robinson, J. and Godbey, G. (1997) *Time for Life: The Surprising Ways Americans Use their Time*, Pennsylvania: Pennsylvania State University Press.

Roche, M. (2000) *Mega-events and Modernity*, London: Routledge.

Ruiz, J. (2004) *A Review of the Literature on the Impacts of Arts, Sport and Culture*, Scottish Office research paper. Available at: www.scotland.gov.uk/Publications/2004/08/19784/41507

Schor, J. (1991) *The Overworked American: The Unexpected Decline of Leisure*, New York: Basic Books.

SEC Sustainable Event Certification (1990) BS 8091. Available at: www.sustainableeventcertification.com (accessed 22 July 2010).

Shaw, G. and Williams, A. (2004) *Tourism and Tourism Spaces*, London: Sage.

Shone, A. and Parry, B. (2010) *Successful Event Management*, London: Cengage, third edition.

Stebbins, R. (2004) 'Serious leisure, volunteerism and quality of life', in J. Haworth and A. Veal (eds) *Work and Leisure*, London: Routledge.

Taylor, P. (1992) 'Commercial leisure: exploiting consumer preference', in J. Sugden and C. Knox (eds) *Leisure in the 1990s*, Eastbourne: Leisure Studies Association.

Torkildsen, G. (2005 [1999]) *Leisure and Recreation Management*, London and New York: E. and F. Spon, fifth edition.

Tribe, J. (2004) 'Editorial: Business as usual', *Journal of Hospitality, Leisure, Sport and Tourism Education* 3(2): 1–4.

——(2006) 'The truth about tourism', *Annals of Tourism Research* 33(2): 360–81.

Tyrrell, T. and Johnston, R. (2001) 'A framework for assessing direct economic impacts of tourist events: distinguishing origins, destinations, and causes of expenditure', *Journal of Travel Research* 40: 94–100.

UN-Habitat (n.d.) Website at: www.unhabitat.org/downloads/docs/3070_67594_K0471966%20WUF2–2.pdf (accessed 21 July 2010).

Veal, A. (1993) 'The concept of lifestyle: a review', *Leisure Studies* 12(4): 233–52.

Veal, A. and Haworth, J. (2004) *Work and Leisure*, London: Routledge.

Warde, A., Tampubolon, G. and Savage, M. (2005) 'Recreation, informal social networks and social capital', *Journal of Leisure Research* 37(4): 402–25.

Whitford, M. (2004) 'Regional development through domestic and tourist event policies: Gold Coast and Brisbane, 1974–2003', *Journal of Hospitality, Tourism and Leisure Science* 1: 1–24 (HTL Science Library of Congress).

Wood, P., Landry, C. and Bloomfield, J. (2006) *Cultural Diversity in Britain: A Toolkit for Cross-cultural Co-operation*, York: Joseph Rowntree Foundation.

Zukin, S. (2004) 'Dialogue on urban cultures: globalisation and culture in an urbanising world', paper presented at the World Urban Forum, Barcelona, 13–17 September.

Zuzanek, J. (2004) 'Work, leisure, time-pressure and stress', in J. Haworth and A. Veal (eds) *Work and Leisure*, London: Routledge.

Zuzanek, J. and Smale, B. (1997) 'More work – less leisure? Changing allocations of time in Canada 1981–92', *Society and Leisure* 20(1): 73–106.

7

Sports events

Typologies, people and place

Sean Gammon

Introduction

Outside the high-profile mega types, the ubiquity and breadth of sports events can paradoxically make them less obvious choices for research. In addition, the overwhelming studies in sports events tend to involve economic impact analyses and consequently miss the many issues and additional impacts that such events engender. In reviewing the literature related to the study of sport events it became apparent that there has been a notable lack of critical commentary exploring the problems associated with applying traditional event categories to sport events. Moreover there is a deficiency of information concerning particular event types such as those associated with smaller events, along with those connected to parades and festivals. Therefore the aims of this chapter are twofold: first to introduce and evaluate current sport event typologies, and second to present an argument for sports events to be treated separately because of their complexity and nature.

It will be contended that there are two elements of distinction – a taxonomical distinction related to the specific criteria adopted for sport events, as well as an innate distinctiveness that aims to illustrate the special nature of sport events. For the sake of simplicity and clarity these two themes will be explored separately though it is acknowledged there will be some obvious overlaps.

Exploring the sport event landscape

Given sport's irrefutable importance and significance in the field of event studies it is perhaps surprising that there still remains no definitional conformity to the many different types of events that take place. In fact there appears no unified definition of what constitutes a sports event, probably because it is felt that there is no need as it is patently obvious what it is and consequently needs no further description. Nonetheless, the sport event landscape is a complex one, incorporating not only competitive events but also parades, celebrations and exhibitions, etc. To date sport event typologies have been situated within broader event types which in many cases overlap, primarily because they have been formatted using differing criteria such as form, size, function and experience (Getz 2007). The confusion is made worse through typologies having varying definitions depending upon the author or the studies in which they are based. Consequently we are left with a situation in which an event such as the Olympic Games can be described as mega, hallmark, special, prestigious and festival all at the same time. This is not to suggest that such typologies are not useful or have little merit as they often help in distinguishing specific features of events, though clearly readers should be aware of their limitations and potential repetitiveness. The following sections aim to shed light on some of the problems with current event categorisations while at the same time introducing often neglected sports event types linked to celebration and commemoration.

Special sport events

Unsurprisingly numerous sports events have been situated within the special event category (which is a term often used as an umbrella term for all planned events) as sport, for many, imbues loyalty, engagement, identity investment, belonging, and so will be perceived as – 'special'. Of course, as Getz (2007) points out, such events may be special – but special to whom? For example according to Badmin *et al.* (1992: 109), 'a special event can most simply be described as something that happens which is outside the normal routine of an organisation'. In this case the specialness is linked to the organisation rather than the perception of the participant or spectator, whereas other authors tend to concentrate on how positively the event is perceived by attendees and potential attendees. To what degree any sport event will be taken to be special is purely subjective and can incorporate a diverse and enormous range of events. Work undertaken by Jago and Shaw (1999) has helped to identify key characteristics of special events by first outlining the attributes highlighted in the literature of what constitutes this type of event, and comparing it with how such events are perceived by the public (Table 7.1).

The attributes listed in Table 7.1 certainly help in tying down some of the key ingredients which make up special events, though some attributes are more commonly linked to other event types such as mega-events (e.g. international attention and large economic impact, etc.) and hallmark events (e.g. raising awareness and tourism development). The significance of the problems and inconsistencies associated with event attributes are not lost on Jago and Shaw (1999: 22) who argue that current event definitional disparity sends out confusing messages:

> Terms are used to simplify communication but if there is not a general consensus as to the meaning of terms, such communication can be greatly impeded. If a widely accepted definitional framework cannot be adopted voluntarily by the industry, there is then the possibility that government would impose one in order to overcome the frustrations caused by incorrect communication.

Table 7.1 The attributes of events

Event attributes from literature	Event attributes as perceived by the public
Attracting tourists or tourism development	Number of attendees
Being of limited duration	International attention
Being a one-off or infrequent occurrence	Improvement to image and pride of the host region
Raising awareness, image or profile of a region	An exciting experience
Attracting media attention	
Having a large economic impact	
Being out of the ordinary or unique	

Source: Adapted from Jago and Shaw (1999).

The concerns outlined by Jago and Shaw (1999) are well made and encompass broader issues related to the general event landscape rather than just sport – though the current incongruity feeds down to all event forms.

Mega sport events

Some of the more high-profile sports events are those associated with mega-events, obvious examples being the Olympic and Paralympic Games and the Football World Cup. But when does an event become 'mega' and what features should it display before being described as such? Similarly to special events, definitions range in the criteria adopted and in whether they focus upon general attributes and characteristics, or specific quantitative features. For example Rooney (1988) believes that mega-events display distinctive characteristics linked to tradition, international media coverage, myth-making, history, and the ability to trigger off additional events such as parades and festivals (particularly pertinent to this is the relatively new phenomenon of fan zones). Rooney (1988) also goes on to note that mega-sports events can occur irregularly or regularly in different places such as the Football World Cup and the Olympic Games; can occur in one of a limited choice of sites such as the British and American Open Golf Championships (Hall 1997); or can take place at one particular site which over time attains a hallmark status (see following section). Roche (2000), on the other hand, outlines the global appeal of mega-events, and notes that the organisation and management of such events would normally involve national and international bodies. Others such as Marris (1987) propose a more quantitative approach, suggesting that visitor numbers and event costs should be taken into consideration, though this would be largely dependent upon to what extent new stadia and venues would be needed and where the event took place, especially in terms of accessibility. However, the most widely used criteria adopted in the literature are related to the various impacts that such events engender. In very simple terms they revolve around the significance of the economic impacts coupled with irregularity and mass appeal (Gratton et al. 2001). Arguably the most succinct definition is offered by Getz (2007: 25):

> Mega events, by way of their size of significance, are those that yield extraordinary high levels of tourism, prestige, or economic impact for the host community, venue or organisation.

It is worth pointing out here that, much like special events, the extent to which an event is defined as 'mega' is dependent upon to whom and to what it is directed. Getz (2007) points out that even a relatively modest event can still have a huge impact on a small community. Furthermore the perceived size and importance of any given event will vary between individuals and cultures depending upon their previous experiences and interests. Also an often neglected feature of mega-sports events is that they are often a collection of events rather than a single event, each of which is likely to generate varying degrees of interest and media coverage. This multi-event feature is common among all event types, including those that achieve 'hallmark' status.

Hallmark sport events

The term 'hallmark event' is commonly used to describe an event that becomes synonymous with the location in which it takes place (Getz 1992; Hall 1997; McDonnell et al. 1999). Consequently, it is less about the operational features and more about the outcomes that the event generates over time, particularly with regard to tourism. Usually, hallmark events display a distinctiveness that makes them stand out from the event landscape; they have been defined by Ritchie (1984: 2) as:

> Major one-time or recurring events of limited duration, developed primarily to enhance the awareness, appeal and profitability of a tourism destination in the short and/or long term. Such events rely for their success on uniqueness, status, or timely significance to create interest and attract attention.

Because of the nature of many sports (i.e. being locationally fixed), it is unsurprising that many sports events have taken on the mantle of hallmark status. Examples of prominent sports hallmark events are the Wimbledon Tennis Championships; the Indianapolis 500; the Augusta Masters and the London Marathon. However, Ritchie (1984) maintains that hallmark events can be major one-off events, whose impacts are so significant and memorable that they build an association with a location that far outlives the duration of the event itself. These types of events such as the Olympic Games and various European championships differ from the events outlined above in that their 'hallmarkness' will often wane over time as new cities host future events. However, cities such as Barcelona have maintained and built upon their hosting of the Games, and continue to benefit from it in tourism receipts alone, primarily owing to re-imaging strategies and urban renewal (Gold and Gold 2006; Weed 2008).

An additional example of how sport helps in the promotion of places can be seen when sports teams assume a hallmark status with the town and cities in which they compete. Clubs such as Manchester United, Liverpool FC and the Baltimore Orioles regularly attract thousands of visitors, some of whom may stay for more than one night (Hinch and Higham 2001, 2004; Stevens 2001). Furthermore, the global media interest that such clubs generate firmly establishes recognition of where the matches take place and so fuels the synonymy between place and event. But to what extent a region, town or city is able to establish strong associations with the event is to some extent reliant on the knowledge and passion of the individual. For those who follow horseracing or snooker, the fact that the Grand National takes place at Aintree (Liverpool) or that the World Snooker Championship is held at the Crucible in Sheffield is well known. This is unlikely to be the case for those people who have little or no interest in these events.

Sports heritage, parades and festivals

Although the above examples represent the more commonly adopted and adapted categories found in sport events, there are others that have largely been neglected in the literature. For example, there are those events which are linked to celebration, heritage and festivals. Indeed, the term 'festival' is often confusingly used in a number of different contexts and situations. First, it can be found when organisers or the media (for a variety of reasons) wish to underplay the competitive features of an event, ranging from mega-events such as the Olympic Games through to smaller youth-based events. Second, a sports event may be referred to as a festival when spectator and fan involvement is a clear signature of the event profile. An illustration of this is the Isle of Man TT motor cycle event, which promotes the recreational features of the event as well as the races themselves. In addition there are a number of peripheral events which take place during the two-week event, least of which is the opportunity for spectators to ride on the circuit themselves (worryingly known as 'Mad Sunday'). Third, and more obviously, when teams or individuals return after sporting success, many fans will line the streets in order to celebrate and pay respects to the victor or victors. The parade by the successful Spanish team through the streets of Madrid after their Football World Cup win illustrates this type of sports festival well. Also, parades linked with the celebration of new inductees to sport halls of fame (primarily taking place in North America) can generate significant spectator interest and economic impact (see Pro-Football Enshrinement Festival 2010) and demonstrates well the heritage components of sports events (Gammon and Ramshaw 2007). Last, impromptu celebrations can occur after particularly important victories. Such celebrations often take place in and around the event itself or anywhere else where particular fans and/or nationalities may congregate or live.

Small-scale/community sports events

Smaller-scale sports events have tended to take a less prevalent place in the literature and suffer similarly to the other categories with definitional inconsistency. Size as always is in the eye of the perceiver, whether it be from the perspective of the customer or the organiser. For example, Higham (1999: 87), when referring to sporting occasions of a more modest scale, describes them as:

> regular season sporting competitions (ice hockey, basketball, soccer, rugby leagues), international sporting fixtures, domestic competitions, Masters or disabled sports and the like.

It may first appear that Higham's (1999) description hardly indicates small-scale events, though it must be taken on board that the examples given were framed around those events likely to generate tourism. Other contributors have focused upon the community element of smaller events, in that local community involvement at both organisational as well as participant levels can generate powerful social ties and various other positive externalities (Watt 1998; Shone and Parry 2004; Page and Connell 2010). Therefore these types of events are more local or at best regional, and do not require the same levels of cost, risk and expertise that other larger-scale events call for. Examples of smaller-scale, community-based events could range from local school sports days through to regional competitions. The impact of these events can contribute in social terms to the local community through identity building, civic pride and improvements to health, though – similar to its much larger counterparts – the advantages of these types of events are often exaggerated and/or ephemeral (Coalter 2007). This is not to suggest that smaller-scale sports events generate little impact locally, only that in some cases the broader values of sports participation are optimistically adopted and used by organisers in order to justify the event – a custom arguably practised by those responsible for larger events.

Sport event categorisations: the way ahead

At present, sport event definitions and categorisations are influenced by an event's function, its form, the experiences it provokes or a combination of all three. Although it is important to consider the key features of all sports events, care must be taken to ensure that any criterion used neither conflicts nor overlaps with any other. As mentioned at the beginning of the chapter, current event types can generate confusion as many sports events will, to a greater or lesser extent, fit into more than one event type. The present situation is analogous to distinguishing foods using random criteria such as those that could be considered flavoursome, green in colour, fruit or apples. Such terms, while being superficially helpful, are in practice taxonomically pointless.

Getz (2007: 43), identifies sport events as an event form, and outlines that sport events represent an enormous category. He offers a broad classification which could be referred to as a starting point:

- Professional or amateur
- Indoor or outdoor (and other differences in their need for special venues)

- Regularly scheduled (league play, plus play-offs or championships or one-time exhibition or friendly matches)
- Local, regional, national or international in scope
- For participants, for spectators, or both
- Sport festivals (a celebration of sport, often youth, involving many sports) single or multi-sport events.

While the above classification outlines some of the many differing characteristics that sport events generate, it still separates features which overlap, such as for example a regional amateur indoor competition. Many may question the need for any detailed sport event classification, but if the study of sport events is to progress academically and operationally then a system which details clearly defined sport event types is urgently required.

The primary problem with any sport event classification is that each sport can produce very specific issues related to planning, impacts and complexity. It is beyond the scope of this chapter to map out a more detailed classification index, though future studies may wish to look first at sports-specific events (such as those associated with football, basketball, tennis) before establishing more general categorisations. Work undertaken by Gratton *et al.* (2000) that established a typology for major sports events, largely based upon economic impact, media interest and the extent the event is spectator-/competitor-driven, offers a possible solution. Although their typology is limited to major events and lists only four basic types, ranging from Type A (mega, international events, such as the Olympic Games) through to Type D (major competitor events such as national championships), its strength lies in that each event type is less likely to be open to interpretation. Of course, the typology would have to be extended to incorporate the full range of sport events (e.g. A1, A2, A3, B1, etc.) and perhaps incorporate some of the features outlined earlier (see Table 7.2).

It is worth noting that Table 7.2 acts only as an illustrative example of how future typologies may progress and hopefully will act as a starting point for future research.

Table 7.2 Event typology example

Event type	Economic activity	Local, regional, national, international	Single or multi event	Media interest	Regular, irregular	Spectator, competitive	Tourism potential	Sport development opportunity
A1 Olympics	High	International	Multi	High	Irregular	Both	High	High
B1 FA Cup Final	High/med	National	Single	High	Regular	Spectator	Med	Med
C1 National athletics champs	Med/low	National	Multi	Med	Regular	Both	Low	Med
D1 Regional swimming champs	Low	Regional	Multi	Low	Regular	Comp	Low	Med

These taxonomical distinctions illustrate the specific sport event features which collectively indicate the need for these event types to be treated separately in the event literature. This is not to suggest that the traditional categories outlined earlier should be totally discounted as they highlight some important event characteristics. The problem lies in the generality of these characteristics, in that they are ineffective in delineating clear specific sport event types. To add to the confusion it is common for certain sport events to be offered as 'typical' examples of one particular traditional category, ignoring the possibility of them fitting into others. The sports event landscape is a complex one, incorporating many event types that are not effectively addressed in the present categorisations. But it is not just the breadth and intricacy of sports events that distinguishes them from other events; it is also their unique innate qualities that make them worthy of special attention. Such qualities can be framed around how sport is followed and supported, the authenticity of the action and spectacle, and the singular virtues that the places and venues of where the events take place evoke. The following section will explore these qualities further.

Sport event specific attributes

The manner in which sport events are delivered and consumed has changed considerably over the last thirty years. There has been a notable movement towards a more customer-orientated approach that no longer believes that the competition alone warrants the price of the ticket. Improvements in hospitality, along with technological advances, have meant that spectators can sit in relative comfort while reliving the key moments through large plasma screens which repeatedly replay the action in slow motion. Music will often be played to celebrate success during the game or will be played live during intervals along with other forms of entertainment. Owing to these changes, there have been suggestions that rather than being different or distinct from other events, sport events are beginning to resemble non-sporting events linked to entertainment and the arts. The introduction of more entertainment elements (beyond the sport itself) is to be expected, given the increased competition in leisure-related opportunities (Crawford 2004), as well as the desire to be entertained being one of the key motives for supporters to attend live sport events (Wann 1995; Wann et al. 2001). Nevertheless, sport events display and generate quite specific attributes that differ from other event types. Many of these attributes can be framed around how sport is consumed and experienced, and can be explained in terms of fan and spectator behaviour, authenticity and the power of place. Before exploring these elements further it is important to mention that it is dangerous to generalise sports and sports spectators, as each sport is not only delivered differently but is also followed and supported by individuals and groups as diverse as the many sports on offer. The behaviour of a highly identified football fan will differ greatly from that of a golf fan, as will the structure and delivery of the events. However, there will be some similarities which should be constant across all sport events.

The sports fan

Literature relating to studies of sports fandom are considerable and far beyond the scope of this chapter to cover in any detail (for further details see Wann et al. 2001; Crawford 2004; Brown 2007). However, it is important to state that large-scale sports events will often attract the full spectrum of spectator, from the highly identified fanatic through to the impartial spectator. Some may be followers of a team or individual, while others may simply have an interest in the sport. Precisely what criteria constitutes the many types of sports spectator has been debated often in the literature, with no one classification adhered to. Terms such as 'connoisseur', 'aficionado', 'die-hard', 'glory hunter' and 'casual observer' have all been used to describe the behaviour and motives of different types of supporter or fan. But the question to ask is: to what extent do sport fans differ from other fans found in other interest domains? To gain a better insight it is worth focusing upon that part of the fan spectrum which denotes some form of commitment.

Work undertaken by Hunt *et al.* (1999: 440) identifies five broad fan types, based upon basking in reflected glory, information processing, and attachment as it relates to the self. First they describe the 'temporary fan' as being one whose interest and enthusiasm is ephemeral. The temporary fan's support may occur over the period of high-profile and/or irregular events such as the Football World Cup, Olympic Games or Masters Golf, or may stem from an unexpected success by a team or individual which has gained significant media interest. Alternatively, an attraction to a team may be centred around a particular player; consequently, when the player leaves the interest in the team diminishes. According to Hunt *et al.* (1999) this type of fan behaviour and motive can be explained by referring to a study by Cialdini *et al.* (1976), which found that less committed fans tended to BIRG (bask in reflective glory) after their team won and CORF (cut off reflected failure) when they lost. This may manifest itself by wearing team colours, shirts and scarves after a win, or displaying dissociative behaviour and distance after a loss. Second, the 'local fan' is drawn in to support through identification with a geographic area. Any affiliations are solely based on them residing in and around where a team and/or player competes. According to Hunt *et al.* (1999), once an individual moves from a particular area it is likely that any identification with the 'local' team will decrease. Not so for the 'devoted fan', whose loyalty is unaffected by such moves, primarily through an emotional attachment with a team and/or player which in turn forms an important part of their self-concept. Their attachment is impervious to defeat, and so they are unlikely to BIRG or CORF as their allegiance supersedes any negative outcome and results. One step up from this is the 'fanatical fan', whose identification with a team and/or player is very close to the centre of the self, though not in preference to other significant life aspects such as family, work and religion. Hunt *et al.* (1999: 446) add further details which help distinguish the fanatical fan from the devoted fan:

> The fanatical fan engages in behavior that is beyond the normal devoted fan, yet the behavior is accepted by significant others (family, friends, and other fans) because it is considered supportive of the target – sport, team, or player. The devoted fan may go to games. The fanatical fan will go to the game and paint their body the colors of the team, go in costume, or in some way exhibit behaviour different from the devoted fan.

In contrast, the 'dysfunctional fan', the last in the categories proposed by Hunt *et al.* (1999), describes fans whose fanaticism is of core importance to their self-identification. In other words, being a fan is the most important thing in their lives, as is winning. In some cases (though not always) dysfunctional fan conduct will manifest itself in anti-social behaviour such that exhibited in soccer hooliganism. Such is the total identity investment upon the team or player that it is common that other life facets (family, work, etc.) are neglected and consequently negatively affected.

It could be argued that the fan types listed above display characteristics that could be found in other event contexts such as those associated with music, entertainment and the arts. However, the passion, coupled with the persistent emotional and financial investment that is common among sports fans, irrespective of how disappointing the spectacle may be, is rare. Furthermore, that such passion could in some cases lead to maladaptive behaviour and violence is unusual in other non-sporting events. For the sports event organiser, the notion that customers are in some cases willing to pay for a season ticket for experiences that may be disappointing could indicate that little should be invested in other features aimed at improving the overall event experience. But it must be taken on board that sport events attract the full spectrum of visitors, many of which would expect some level of comfort and additional entertainment. Furthermore, investment in a range of hospitality facilities, along with improved audio-visual facilities, goes some way to justify the ticket price. Indeed, some commentators suggest that sports event organisers should attempt to influence the event experience holistically (i.e. before, during and after the event) and in doing so improve sociability and crowd harmony (Chalip 2006).

Authenticity

One of the salient features of sport competitions is that the outcome is unknown. No result is predetermined before the competition, irrespective of whether one player or team is perceived as far superior to another (Jennings 1996; Coakley 2009). Therefore the eternal attraction of attending a sport event can be found in the uncertainty of the result(s). What of course this means is that there is a good chance that a significant proportion of the spectators will leave the event dissatisfied. But unlike spectators and audiences of other event forms who go through negative experiences, the ardent sports fan will return time and again in the hope of rectifying any previous disappointments. The uncertainty of the result has meant that the draw of some sports is an economic one, fuelled by both legitimate and unlawful gambling industries. Recently, the influence that such darker sides of the industry may have on sports results (such as international cricket matches) has called into question the validity of both the result and the action that takes place during matches. Time will tell the extent to which such practices are widespread across all sports, and whether it will affect attendance figures and spectator enjoyment.

The wish to attend a live event is not solely driven by curiosity concerning the result, as fan and spectator motives are complex and can incorporate purposes linked to psychological, social and economic factors (Wann *et al.* 2001). Nevertheless, the prospect of experiencing the atmosphere of a sports event as well as being part of it is particularly important for all spectators (Gaffney and Bale 2004). Related to this is the opportunity to behave (especially for local fans) in ways that celebrate and sustain the many traditions and rituals of the past, and in doing so to channel authentic feelings of community and belonging (Zillman *et al.* 1989; Robson 2000). This interaction between spectacle and spectator can be summed up by Crawford (2004: 85), who notes that:

> It is the delight of watching the crowd and experiencing the atmosphere which attracts many supporters to the 'live' venue. However, it is the supporters themselves, through their performance (for instance, as part of a 'Mexican wave', chanting or singing, displaying flags, banners or using musical instruments), who play a crucial role in generating the spectacle and atmosphere within the venue. Moreover, participation within the crowd can help cement their feelings of belonging and membership of this supporter 'community'.

Also, high-profile, irregular sports events such as world championships will draw a range of spectators whose desire is to be part of a global spectacle that 'may deliver defining moments in history' (Higham and Hinch 2009: 106). Furthermore, it has been argued that sports events represent opportunities for visitors to experience a nation or community at play, and in doing so gain a deeper insight into the cultural nuances and traditions that take place there (Nauright 1996; Jarvie 2006; Higham and Hinch 2009; Gammon 2010). As a result sport events are becoming significant features of many tourists' itineraries as they arguably quench the desire for authentic experiences of both a place and a people.

The phenomenon of fan zones, recently made popular through the last two Football World Cups in Germany and South Africa, should be mentioned here. Fan zones essentially are areas specifically designed for fans to assemble and watch a live match on huge video screens. They are often set up near to where the live event takes place and will thus cater for those who have been unable to obtain tickets but still wish to soak up the atmosphere of the event. Recently the term 'fan zone' has been adopted to describe areas for fans to congregate before a game in order to promote stronger ties with the fans and local community as well as encouraging the social features of the event experience discussed earlier. The City Square development outside the stadium at Manchester City FC is a good example of this, where large media screens stream edited and live video information while the club's community arm provides match-day activities for children (Place North West 2010). This initiative may be the first of many, and represents an example of how the event experience can be managed more holistically, as discussed earlier.

It is worth noting that peripheral events can take place anywhere and, in the case of European or international football competitions, are sometimes assembled in the 'home' stadia for fans who are unable to travel to the event. There has been scant research concerning the motives and experiences associated with fan zones but they pose, and will undoubtedly generate, some fascinating debates relating to atmosphere authenticity and place.

Sports events and place

It is perhaps easy and understandable to sideline or ignore the places in which sports events take place, for the action in front of the spectator will often render the structure that houses events at best peripheral or at worst unimportant. But for highly identified fans as well as less passionate spectators, the places and structures in which sports events take place are important, a point raised by Gammon (2010: 124):

> It must not be forgotten that stadia are the vessels that house these experiences and, therefore, have important social and cultural meanings in their own right. To ignore or dismiss them is equivalent to solely focussing on the wine whilst neglecting the significance of the container in which it is drunk.

Obviously, the relationships between person and place will vary depending upon geographical and community ties as well as fan motivation discussed earlier. For the less passionate spectator, sports stadia represent symbolic reminders of the event(s) that have taken and continue to take place there. These large and often imposing structures have, like many other traditional tourist attractions, become famous for being famous (MacCannell 1999). Recently, modern designs of major sports stadia have changed from the rather bland utilitarian structures of the past to stadia which have distinctive architectural signatures, and so clearly help in the marketing of place. The Bird's Nest stadium in Beijing is a case in point, with its distinctive iconic design and its ability to attract an astounding 30,000 visitors daily after the Olympic and Paralympic Games had ended (Reuters 2009). For the more devoted fan the sites in which regular or one-off events take place transcend their functional purpose and become powerful symbols of place and of home. Such deep connections are not just the preserve of the locals, but also of the travelling fans who develop strong associations with their 'home' ground (Higham and Hinch 2009).

It was John Bale (1982, 1993, 1994, 1996), who first explored the connections between sport, people and place by adopting and adapting work by Tuan (1974). Tuan uses the term 'topophilia' (possibly coined by the poet W.H. Auden) to describe in very simple terms a love of place. According to Bale (1993) sports fans can often endow meaning to sport places through a quasi-religious allegiance that elevates these often modest structures into sites more akin to modern-day shrines. Moreover, where sports sites are bestowed positions of heritage, such as the spiritual home of a sport or team (e.g. Lord's Cricket Ground, St Andrew's golf course) it is not uncommon for visitors to take a form of secular pilgrimage in order to pay their respects (Gammon 2004; Gammon and Ramshaw 2007). In fact, most major sports stadia incorporate visitor tours which feed off the desires for individuals to gain a deeper connection with a famous site, as well as to the sport and/or the team that compete there.

Of course, it is not just sports events that generate such powerful ties with the places in which they take place. Many festivals, carnivals and music sites (such as the Bayreuth Festspiel- haus for Wagner fans) generate strong ties with place. But the global appeal and interest that sport stadia generate often cross the boundaries of fandom to the less attached visitor, who acknowledges the cultural significance of the events that have taken place there. Undoubtedly, the massive media coverage of sports events helps fuel the interest in the sites where the action takes place, and may indicate why the Camp Nou (the home ground of FC Barcelona) is the number one visitor attraction in Barcelona.

Six Nations rugby tournament: Twickenham

Event outline

The Rugby Union Six Nations tournament is an annual international sporting event that is contested by England, Wales, Scotland, Ireland, France and Italy. In its present format the competition has been in existence for ten years, the first game taking place in 2000. Prior to this it was known as the Five Nations, but was changed when Italy joined the event in 2000.

The origins of the tournament go back to 1883 when the championship comprised of the four home nations, but it was later extended to include France in 1910 which led to the event being known as the Five Nations. The competition format is straightforward, with each team playing the other teams once, with home advantage alternating each year. A win is worth two points, a draw one point and there are no points for a loss. The team with the most points are declared the winners. Achieving victory in every game is the pinnacle of every team's ambition and is known as the 'Grand Slam'. England hold the record for the number of Grand Slams with twelve, followed by Wales with ten, France with eight, Scotland with three and Ireland with two. Within the competition there are a number of additional trophies associated with competitions between specific teams, such as the Calcutta Cup (England vs Scotland), the Millennium Trophy (England vs Ireland) and the Giuseppe Garibaldi Trophy (France vs Italy). In addition there is the Triple Crown, which is awarded to the home nation team which has successfully beaten the other three home nation teams.

The competition takes place usually over the months of January and March and is attended by over 980,000 spectators. The competition generates significant media coverage, with key matches boasting up to 10 million viewers. Each match could be considered a hallmark event, as the stadia are firmly linked to both location and tournament and include Twickenham (London, England), the Millennium Stadium (Cardiff, Wales), Murrayfield (Edinburgh, Scotland), Croke Park (Dublin, Ireland), Stade de France (Paris, France) and the Stadio Flamino (Rome, Italy). However, the tournament as a whole could be considered as 'mega' owing to its international media coverage and collective atten- dance figures. Furthermore the championship has confusingly been described by the media as a festival of rugby, which illustrates the limitations of current event typologies. The impacts generated by each contest will of course differ and be dependent upon where they take place, between whom, and at what stage of the competition. Consequently, it is possible that event types will vary with each match, though it is likely that most would reside within the B category outlined in Table 7.2.

Twickenham Stadium

Positioned on the west of London, Twickenham Stadium is the home venue for all English games in the Six Nations. It is owned and operated by the Rugby Football Union, who are the governing body of rugby union in England, and is often affectionately referred to by the English fans as HQ. It has a long heritage; hosting its first rugby international in 1919. Since that time it has gone through many transformations and designs, culminating in the present state-of-the-art stadium that boasts seating for 82,000, making it the biggest designated stadium for rugby union in the world and the second largest stadium in the UK. However, the stadium hosts many other sporting and non-sporting events, such as domestic rugby events and rock concerts. Because of its historical significance and the many important events taking place there, the stadium not only markets itself as the home of English rugby but also as the spiritual home of rugby (Ramshaw and Gammon 2010). Consequently it runs a popular stadium tour and houses the World Rugby Museum, which contains a plethora of important rugby ephemera.

Fans

Fan profiles for attending international rugby union events are internationally diverse, though studies have suggested that home fans tend to derive from higher socio-economic groups. With the exception of the dysfunctional fan (as violence and anti-social behaviour are rare at these events), spectators represent the full spectrum of fan types (Ritchie 2004) with many devoted fans willing to travel to all fixtures. The attached Marriott Hotel at Twickenham offers the opportunity for visitors to extend their stay and so caters for a growing sport tourist market. However, the majority of the fan base will mostly comprise a mixture of devoted and casual fans. The attendance of less identified fans will undoubtedly be drawn as much by the spectacle as by the match.

Because of the international nature of the event, the presence of local fans would not be as significant as it would be in local team fixtures, although it is worth noting that as part of the RFU community relations programme local residents living close to Twickenham Stadium are invited to enter a ballot for 400 free tickets.

Authenticity

In recent years the championship has become more competitive, with no one team sustaining a winning streak year on year. This has undeniably added interest to the contests and has created increased attention from a wider scope of fans, as well as from the media. Organisations selling packages to watch the games are also keen to promote the special and unique qualities of the fixtures. They not only 'sell' the deep rivalries held between the teams but also promise spectators the opportunity to soak up the atmosphere of a special sporting occasion.

Sean Gammon

Conclusion

Without doubt sport-related events represent a significant segment of the event industry, yet their inclusion in the literature, not including studies relating to mega-events, is relatively small. However, it is encouraging to see that sport-specific texts are emerging now, supported by research studies that go beyond the many economic impact analyses of the past. Given the growth in these recent publications it is surprising that a more detailed and agreed sports event typology has not been proposed, one that goes beyond the more general event types adopted in much of the event literature. Current typologies fail to both distinguish and convey the extent and complexity of a market that has great importance in cultural, social and personal terms. The economic contribution of sports events, when managed and forecast realistically, can act positively for communities, cities and regions in which they take place.

Sports events are like no other events in that they offer an authentic insight of a people at play, as well as generating levels of passion and emotional investment rarely seen in other event forms. They generate mass media interest and so are able to assist in place-marketing initiatives as well as a number of other positive outcomes related to health, regeneration and community cohesion. In some cases the stadia in which the events take place become attractions in their own right and can generate additional income for the organisations responsible for them. There are, of course, the darker and less positive sides to sports events associated with dysfunctional fan behaviour and the over-optimistic estimates that promote them as the panacea to failing local economies and social deprivation. Nevertheless it is all these features that distinguish the sports event as a significant event form that in turn warrants its status as a separate focus of study.

Further reading

Bale, J. (1994) *Landscapes of Modern Sport*, London: Leicester University Press. An interesting discussion on sports event structures and their impacts.
Crawford, G. (2004) *Consuming Sport: Fans, Sport and Culture*, London: Routledge. An in-depth and enlightening evaluation of how sport is consumed.
Gammon, S. and Ramshaw, G. (eds) (2007) *Heritage, Sport and Tourism: Sporting Pasts – Tourist Futures*, London: Routledge. Examples and discussion on the heritage components of sports events.
Gold, J. and Gold, M. (eds) (2006) *Olympic Cities: City Agendas, Planning and the World's Games, 1896–2012*, London: Routledge. Helpful analysis of the key issues and impacts relating to past Olympic Games.
Gratton, C., Dobson, S. and Shibli, S. (2001) 'The role of major sports events in the economic regeneration of cities: lessons for six World or European Championships', in C. Gratton and I.P. Henry (eds) *Sport in the City: The Role of Sport in Economic and Social Regeneration*, London: Routledge, pp. 35–45. An alternative approach to categorising mega and major events.
Higham, J. and Hinch, T. (2009) *Sport and Tourism: Globalization, Mobility and Identity*, Oxford: Butterworth-Heinemann. Includes important discussion relating to the authenticity of sport.
Masterman, G. (2004) *Strategic Sports Event Management: An International Approach*, Oxford: Elsevier Butterworth-Heinemann. A beginner's guide to the key issues in sport event operations.
Wann, D.L., Melnick, M.J., Russell, G.W. and Pease, D.G. (2001) *Sports Fans: The Psychology and Social Impact of Spectators*, New York: Routledge. An overview of sport fans' motives and behaviour.

References

Allen, J., O'Toole, W., McDonnell, I. and Harris, R. (2002) *Festival and Special Event Management*, Melton: John Wiley.
Badmin, P., Coombes, M. and Rayner, G. (1992) *Leisure Operational Management Volume 1: Facilities*, London: ILAM/Longman.
Bale, J. (1982) *Sport and Place: A Geography of Sport in England, Scotland and Wales*, London: Hurts.
——(1993) *Sport, Space and the City*, London: Routledge.

——(1994) *Landscapes of Modern Sport*, London: Leicester University Press.

——(1996) 'Space, place and body culture: Yi-Fu Tuan and geography of sport', *Geografiska Annaler* 78B(3): 163–71.

Berridge, G. (2007) *Events Design and Experience*, Oxford: Butterworth-Heinemann.

Brown, S. (2007) 'Fleet feet: the USSF and the peculiarities of soccer fandom in America', *Soccer in Society* 8(2–3): 366–80.

Chalip, L. (2006) 'Towards social leverage of sport events', *Journal of Sport and Tourism* 11(2): 109–27.

Cialdini, R.B., Borden, R.J., Thorne, A., Walker, M.R., Freeman, S. and Cloan, L.R. (1976) 'Basking in reflected glory: three (football) field studies', *Journal of Personality and Social Psychology* 34: 366–75.

Coakley, J. (2009) *Sports in Society*, New York: McGraw-Hill.

Coalter, F. (2007) *A Wider Social Role for Sport. Who's Keeping the Score?* London: Routledge.

Crawford, G. (2004) *Consuming Sport: Fans, Sport and Culture*, London: Routledge.

Gaffney, C. and Bale, J. (2004) 'Sensing the stadium', in P. Vertinsky and J. Bale (eds) *Sites of Sport. Space, Place, Experience*, London: Routledge, pp. 25–39.

Gammon, S. (2004) 'Secular pilgrimage and sport tourism', in B. Ritchie and D. Adair (eds) *Sport Tourism: Interrelationships, Impacts and Issues*, Clevedon: Channel View Publications, pp. 1–28.

——(2010) '"Sporting" new attractions? The commodification of the sleeping stadium, in R. Sharpley and P. Stone (eds) *Tourism Experiences: Contemporary Perspectives*, London: Routledge, pp. 115–26.

Gammon, S. and Ramshaw, G. (eds) (2007) *Heritage, Sport and Tourism: Sporting Pasts – Tourist Futures*, London: Routledge.

Getz, D. (1992) *Event Management and Event Tourism*, New York: Cognizant.

——(2007) *Event Studies: Theory, Research and Policy for Planned Events*, Oxford: Butterworth-Heinemann.

Gold, J. and Gold, M. (eds) (2006) *Olympic Cities: City Agendas, Planning and the World's Games, 1896–2012*, London: Routledge.

Gratton, C., Dobson, S. and Shibli, S. (2000) 'The economic importance of major sports events', *Managing Leisure* 5(1, January): 17–28.

——(2001) 'The role of major sports events in the economic regeneration of cities: lessons for six World or European Championships', in C. Gratton and I.P. Henry (eds) *Sport in the City: The Role of Sport in Economic and Social Regeneration*, London: Routledge, pp. 35–45.

Hall, C.M. (1997) *Hallmark Tourist Events: Issues, Management and Planning*, Chichester: Wiley.

Higham, J. (1999) 'Commentary – sport as an avenue of tourism development: an analysis of the positive and negative impacts of sport tourism', *Current Issues in Tourism* 2(1): 82–90.

——(ed.) (2005) *Sport Tourism Destinations: Issues, Opportunities and Analysis*, Oxford: Elsevier Butterworth-Heinemann.

Higham, J. and Hinch, T. (2009) *Sport and Tourism: Globalization, Mobility and Identity*, Oxford: Butterworth-Heinemann.

Hinch, T.D. and Higham, J.E.S. (2001) 'Sport tourism: a framework for research', *International Journal of Tourism Research* 3(1): 45–58.

——(2004) *Sport Tourism Development*. Clevedon: Channel View Publications

Hunt, K.A., Bristol, T. and Bashaw, R.E. (1999) 'A conceptual approach to classifying sports fans', *Journal of Services Marketing* 13(6): 439–52.

Jago, L.K. and Shaw, R.N. (1999) 'Consumer perceptions of special events: a multi-stimulus validation', *Journal of Travel and Tourism Marketing* 8(4): 1–21.

Jarvie, G. (2006) *Sport, Culture and Society: An Introduction*, London: Routledge.

Jennings, A. (1996) *The New Lords of the Rings: Olympic Corruption and How to Buy Gold Medals*. London: Simon and Schuster.

MacCannell, D. (1999) *The Tourist: A New Theory of the Leisure Class*, London: University of California Press.

McDonnell, I., Allen, J. and O'Toole, W. (1999) *Festival and Special Event Management*, Chichester: John Wiley and Sons.

Marris, T. (1987) 'The role and impact of mega-events and attractions on regional and national tourism development: resolutions', *Revue de Tourisme* 4: 3–10.

Masterman, G. (2004) *Strategic Sports Event Management: An International Approach*, Oxford: Elsevier Butterworth-Heinemann.

Nauright, J. (1996) '"A besieged tribe"? Nostalgia, white cultural identity and the role of rugby in a changing South Africa', *International Review for the Sociology of Sport,* 31(1): 69–85.

Page, S.J. and Connell, J. (2010) *Leisure: An Introduction*, Harlow, UK: Pearson Education.

Place North West (2010) Website at: www.placenorthwest.co.uk/news/archive/6854-man-city-unveils-fan-zone-plans.html (accessed 11 August 2010).

Pro-Football Enshrinement Festival (2010) Website at: www.profootballhofef.com/ (accessed 6 July 2010).

Ramshaw, G. and Gammon, S. (2010) 'On home ground? Twickenham stadium tours and the construction of sport heritage', *Journal of Heritage Tourism* 5(2): 87–102.

Reuters (2009) Website at: www.reuters.com/article/idUSPEK20331620090316 (accessed 5 July 2009).

Ritchie, B.W. (2004) 'Exploring small-scale sport event tourism: the case of rugby and the Super 12 competition', in B.W. Ritchie and D. Adair (eds) *Sport Tourism. Interrelationships, Impacts and Issues*, Clevedon: Channel View Publications, pp. 135–54.

Ritchie, J.R.B. (1984) 'Assessing the impact of hallmark events: conceptual and research issues', *Journal of Travel Research* 23(1): 2–11.

Robson, G. (2000) *No One Likes U, We Don't Care: The Myth and Reality of Millwall Fandom*, Oxford: Berg.

Roche, M. (2000) *Mega-events and Modernity: Olympic and Expos in the growth of global Culture*, London: Routledge.

Rooney, J.F. (1988) 'Mega-sports events as tourist attractions: a geographical analysis', Proceedings, *Tourism Research: Expanding Boundaries, Travel and Tourism Research Association*, 19th Annual Conference, Montreal: Travel and Tourism Research Association, pp. 93–9.

Shone, A. and Parry, B. (2004) *Successful Event Management. A Practical Handbook*, London: Thompson.

Stevens, T. (2001) 'Stadia and tourism-related facilities', *Travel and Tourism Analyst* 2: 59–73.

Tuan, Y. (1974) *Topophilia: A Study of Environmental Perception, Attitudes and* Values, Englewood Cliffs, NJ: Prentice Hall.

Wann, D.L. (1995) 'Preliminary validation of the sport fan motivational scale', *Journal of Sport and Social Issues* 19(4): 377–96.

Wann, D.L., Melnick, M.J., Russell, G.W. and Pease, D.G. (2001) *Sports Fans: The Psychology and Social Impact of Spectators*, New York: Routledge.

Watt, D.C. (1998) *Event Management in Leisure and Tourism*, New York: Addison Wesley Longman.

Weed, M. (2008) *Olympic Tourism*, Oxford: Butterworth-Heinemann.

Zillman, D, Bryant, J. and Sapolsky, N. (1989) 'Enjoyment from sports spectatorship', in J. Goldstein (ed.) *Sport, Games and Play*, Hillsdale, NJ: Lawrence Erlbaum, pp. 241–78.

8

The history of events

ideology and historiography

John R. Gold and Margaret M. Gold

Introduction

The words 'history' and 'events' are closely associated. Two of the key entries provided by the *Oxford English Dictionary*, for example, define 'history' as that 'branch of knowledge which deals with past events, as recorded in writings or otherwise ascertained' and as a 'series of events (of which the story is or may be told)'. Yet if the notion of history as interpreting flows of events is largely taken for granted – at least, in popular conceptions of the nature and purpose of historical study – the practice of studying the history *of* events, defined as specially organised and non-routine temporary gatherings, has seldom received close scrutiny.

This, of course, is not to say that scholars have ignored the provenance of specific types of events or have failed to recognise their wider historical context (e.g. see Shone and Parry 2001: 8–16; Berridge 2007: 5). For example, there are considerable literatures on events such as World's Fairs, circuses and arena spectacle, princely pageants, celebrations of political revolution, public executions and sporting mega-events (Gold and Gold 2005). Moreover, given that many events are defined by occurrences such as anniversaries, it is rare for accounts of their development to lack a historical dimension. Even recently founded events attract narratives that seek to situate them deep in local, regional or national tradition owing, at least in part, to reasons that mirror the benefits (including economic) that close association with the past is felt to confer (Lowenthal 1985: xxiii). Nevertheless, most researchers have treated the crafting of event histories *per se* as being largely unproblematic. Certainly, there have been relatively few attempts to connect them with the growing scrutiny of what Burrow (2009: xvi) recognises as 'the plurality of "histories" and the interests embodied in them'.

Against that background, this chapter examines the contribution that explicit analysis of historical writings can make to the study of events. In particular, it explores two related propositions. The first concerns 'narrative', understood here as a structured account, rendered in textual form, of a sequence of events that occurred in the past. We argue that the history of events *per se,* like other forms of history, puts forward narratives that are shaped by their authors and by the contexts in which those authors are situated, rather than offering value-free and 'objective' accounts of reality. This point is substantiated in the next section by reference to histories that derive as much from the world of practice as from the writings of academic historians, culminating in a case study that shows how ideologies have influenced the narratives put forward over time in official histories of a specific event: namely, the Festivals held annually at Salzburg in Austria since 1920. The second proposition concerns 'narration', or the way in which the story is told (Munslow 2007: 4). Here, we argue that understanding of the history of events would benefit from more explicit recognition of the ways in which that history has been, and could be, written. To develop that point, the latter half of this chapter draws examples from the history of the modern Olympic Games both to identify the prevalence of a dominant discourse and to indicate the insights available from alternative historical approaches.

Ideology

The idea that histories are shaped by interests embodied in them (see above) is readily apparent when dealing with a subject such as events. From the Age of Antiquity, for example, accounts of the staging of Roman triumphs – civic and religious ceremonies staged to honour the achievements of military commanders – conventionally reported proceedings in light of the prevailing regimes' interpretations of moral lessons (Versnel 1970). In Medieval Europe, where administration of justice turned public executions into spectacular events that drew large audiences, court records preserved for prosperity the accounts of the trials overlain with the theology of Good and Evil (Merback 1999; Turning 2009). In more recent times, the written histories of events such as festivals or exhibitions were frequently written either by their organisers or by scholars who supported their endeavours (e.g. Cole 1853; Hitchcock and Johnson 1932).

These and many other potential examples (see Gold and Gold 2005: 23–48) point to a degree of agency that means that it is impossible to treat historical texts as unadulterated factual sources. Rather, the history of events, like any other brand of history, is a form of discourse that represents an authored narrative (or collection of such narratives), with the impossibility of removing the 'author-historian' and his or her value-set from the equation (Munslow 2007: 3). On that basis, rejection of the idea that historians can produce 'objective' descriptions of flows of events, uncontaminated by their own attitudes and values (Burke 1999: 396), has emphasised the need to understand, in the context of their own times, 'the material and/or ideological situatedness' of the historians who shape and structure the past through their writings (Munslow 2000: 143).

The question of 'ideological situatedness' is worth pursuing further, notwithstanding the notoriously wide-ranging nature of a term encompassing a 'family of concepts' that includes ideas, beliefs, political philosophies, *Weltanschauungen* and moral justifications (Plamenatz 1970: 27). In Marxist discourse, the word 'ideology' had pejorative overtones, referring to a 'limited material practice which generates ideas that misrepresent social contradictions in the interest of the ruling class' (Larrain 1983: 27–8). From this standpoint, ideologies are justifications which can mask specific sets of interests (Bell 2000: 414). Another definition – and one that is used here – takes ideology to be a pervasive set of ideas, beliefs and images that a group employs to make the world more intelligible to itself, a meaning that leaves untouched the question of whether or not the representation is false or oppressive (Mitchell 1986: 4). Ideology is sometimes conceived as being part of a conscious process of manipulation, but equally can operate by being a frame, embedded in commonsense wisdom, which helps to make sense of experience. The following case study illustrates this point, by reference to the changing histories written about a specific event in relation to their underlying ideologies.

The Festspiele, held annually at the central Austrian city of Salzburg from late July through August, is one of Europe's oldest and most prestigious arts gatherings. Now possessing three component Festivals (Opera, Drama and Concerts), the 2010 Festspiele attracted just under 250,000 paying visitors from seventy-two nations. The festival's original rationale derived substantially from an allegiance of local interests that sought to strengthen the city's cultural standing. This had roots in the 1870s with attempts to establish a music festival to build upon historic connections with Wolfgang Amadeus Mozart – conveniently overlooking the fact that the composer, who was born in the city in 1756, was only too keen to leave its 'stifling provincialism' for 'glittering' Vienna in 1781 (Gallup 1987: 2). These failed to gain significant local support, but a more sustained campaign began in 1903 with suggestions for a theatre festival. While this and sub-sequent initiatives failed to produce a festival before 1914, the Festspiele finally came to fruition in August 1920 in the very different conditions that prevailed in the aftermath of the First World War.

The literature produced by those who had supported the creation of the Festspiele embraced two different readings of history that co-existed in uneasy alliance. One reflec-ted collective recoil from war, centring on Enlightenment principles that 'only art could bring the people [of Europe] together again' and, for reasons primarily linked to local boosterism, deemed that Salzburg was 'the perfect place for it' (SFS 2007: 2). The other shifted the emphasis in favour of a nationalist project intended 'to support the creation of a new Austrian identity' after the First World War, based on 'tradition and cultural restoration' (Lasinger 2010). Salzburg could act as a new symbol for that identity and, given the demise of the Austro-Hungarian Empire, could serve to reassert Austria's prominence on the European cultural scene. Noticeably, those who supported this view particularly favoured locating the new Festival venues in the park where, in the seventeenth century, the first opera to be performed in a German-speaking country was staged – an event deemed crucial 'in Salzburg history-mythology' (Steinberg 2000: xii and 55).

The ideology of pan-Germanism simmered as an influence on writings about the history of the Festival throughout the interwar period, with allusions back to a golden age of German Enlightenment and to the work of early romantic thinkers (Steinberg 2000: 84) existing alongside the overt statements supporting the ideology of European artistic cosmopolitanism. The former ideology, however, would eclipse the supposedly 'deca-dent' ideology of cosmopolitanism after Germany's annexation of Austria in 1938 through the imposed *Anschluss* or 'union'. For the next six years, the Festival became overtly part of the propaganda apparatus of the Nazis, responding to Goering's dictum that it should be 'a festival of the "German soul"' (Gallup 1987: 108). It was now pre-sented as a symbol of the convergence of Germany and Austria and as a forum for Aryan culture. As such, the Festival's history as well as its programme was rewritten to reflect the cultural theories of National Socialism (Kriechbaumer 2009).

After the Second World War, efforts were quickly made to remove explicit Nazi ideology from the history of the event. This reopened both the programme and its supporting historical interpretations to the ideological agendas typical of the years from 1920 to 1938. With that development, the ambiguity between cosmopolitanism and nationalism re-emerged, especially with propagation of the new, postwar definitions of Austrian national identity (Lasinger 2010). Over time, further challenges appeared that the Festival's historians needed to take on board, such as the new context of closer European integration (with Austria having joined the European Union in 1995). Yet, even here, the tendency was to return to established narratives and ambiguities. The 2007 Festival Society's President, for example, quoted with approval the view offered by Hugo von Hofmannsthal, one of the founders of the modern Festspiele, that Salzburg lay at 'the heart of the heart of Europe' (SFS 2007: 2). His intention was to point to the continuing relevance of the Festival's unchanging purpose, but he unwittingly also evoked the older and continuing ideological debate. More than nine decades after its establishment, an event that appeared to be a culturally cosmopolitan festival could still be regarded equally as a culturally nationalist festival in disguise (Steinberg 2000: xiii). Moreover, what appeared to be a seemingly benign comment about 'the heart of Europe' extracted from the history of an event could actually prove to mask pervasive ideological conflict.

Historiography and Olympic histories

The recognition of ideological shaping of historical texts shown by this and other European arts and cultural festivals (Gold and Gold 2012) offers one lens on the construction of event histories. Closer attention to historiography – defined as the academic study of the way that 'history has been and is written' (Furay and Salevouris 2010: 223) – offers another. Although the discipline of historiography has ancient roots (see Breisach 2006 [1983]), it has gained considerable popularity over the last forty years with the growth of a more reflexive view amongst historians about the purpose and limitations of historical knowledge. This has contributed to a more critical reading of traditional approaches and, in turn, underpinned the growth of alternatives. It has also emphasised the importance of understanding that the activity of history-writing is embedded in the intellectual climate of the times. While the implications of these points have as yet impacted lightly on the history of events, there are grounds for suggesting that closer engagement with the main lines of historiographic debate would bring benefits, particularly when interrogating the origins and continuing meaning of events such as arts, sports and cultural festivals. This contention is admirably exemplified by considering historical writings about the foundation of the modern Olympics.

Some background on the Olympics-as-event, however, is necessary first to gain an understanding of the intricate dialectical relationship between tradition and modernity in historical narratives about the Games. Despite the last classical Games having been held in AD 393, knowledge about them and their significance for the classical world had never faded from the European consciousness. The idea of appropriating the title 'Olympic' had appealed to organisers of sporting events from the seventeenth century onwards in England, Scandinavia, North America and, significantly, Greece (Gold and Gold 2011: 21–2). The key developments, however, occurred in the 1890s under the leadership of Baron Pierre de Coubertin, who campaigned successfully for the revival of the Olympics as a way of addressing the 'democratic and international' dimension of sport. An international Sports Congress that he organised in 1894 supported the re-establishment of the Games and laid down key principles for a festival open to competition by amateur sportsmen, with its founding ideals enshrined in a Charter of 'fundamental principles, rules and by-laws', now normally known as the Olympic Charter, and underpinned by a humanist philosophy known as 'Olympism' (see below). A new organisation known as the International Olympic Committee (IOC) would be responsible for controlling the Olympic movement and selecting host cities for the Games (ibid.: 23–4). In essence, they perceived their task as resuscitating an event that represented the quintessence of ancient cultural achievement to which Western civilisation in general, rather than the late nineteenth-century Greek state, was heir. They enthusiastically organised the event around a romanticised notion of the Games as a *panegyris* – a festive assembly in which the entire people came together to participate in religious rites, sporting competitions and artistic performance. At the same time, they studiously rejected the idea that the *panegyris* itself should have a permanent home, which inevitably would have been in Greece. That outlook, which had ideological overtones in terms of maintaining the IOC's control over the events, effectively imbued the modern Olympics with an internationalist stance, able continually to move to new host cities without loss of purpose (Gold and Gold 2011: 23).

In the ensuing years, the IOC would play a key role in nurturing the historical record of the Olympic movement. Besides meticulously compiling written records of the proceedings of its own assemblies and committees and playing a general role as the guardian of Olympic traditions, the IOC has encouraged the process of writing the history of the Olympics in a variety of ways. *Inter alia*, these include maintaining the movement's archives at Lausanne, sponsoring symposia and other gatherings and, perhaps more directly, by requiring the Organising Committees of host cities to compile Official Reports for each Games – documents that have landmark status not just for scholarship about the Olympic festivals but also more generally for the understanding of sporting mega-events.

Whig history

Not surprisingly given their leading role in the revival of the Olympics, the IOC and Coubertin have always taken central place in the history of the Games. For the first few decades, the official history of the Games followed a style of historicising known as the 'Whig interpretation'. In general terms, this was the title that Butterfield (1931), in a polemic essay, first applied to an approach that 'purveyed a conception of progress as the central theme of English history, dividing historical agents into canonized forefathers and mere obstacles' (Burrow 2009: 473). *Sensu stricto*, he applied the expression to the thinking of a specific group of nineteenth-century historians, flippantly referred to as 'Whigs', who saw the condition of Victorian England as the outcome of a Grand Narrative in which progressives had vanquished reactionaries to bring about the 'superior' state of the modern world (Bentley 2005: 5–6). More generally, though, Whig history came to stand for historical narratives that selectively viewed the past in terms of the march towards ever greater achievement and enlightenment, replete with heroic figures who advanced the cause and villains who sought to hinder its inescapable triumph.

Given the timing of the revival of the modern Games, it was always likely that Whig interpretations would influence the history of the Olympic movement in the same way that they did in many other areas of historical scholarship at the turn of the twentieth century. For the Olympics, these histories particularly centre on the foundation of the IOC and the 'visionary' role played by Pierre de Coubertin. When writing about Coubertin's role in early sports promotion in France, for example, Eugen Weber (1970: 15–16) commented that

> Sport played an important part in what Coubertin described in a fencing term as possible *parades* against the industrial civilisation that he disliked and feared. Industrial civilisation stood for the four Sancho Panzas of the Apocalypse: greater comfort, specialisation, exaggerated nationalism, and the triumph of democracy. Sport and education could provide remedies to all these evils and counter them to foster a human progress which Coubertin conceived as the unlimited development of individual capacities.

In 1920, Coubertin provided an overview of the history of the early Games (Müller 2000: 476–7). His survey looked at progress made from Athens 1896 to Antwerp 1920, where:

John R. Gold and Margaret M. Gold

At long last, the primordial nature of these festivals was understood – festivals that are above all, at a time of dangerous specialization and regrettable 'compartmentalization', festivals of human unity ... [Antwerp 1920] has shown the universe, in radiant relief, the educational, moral and social dynamism that restored and modernized Olympism harbours.

(Ibid.: 477)

Coubertin's views, however, were always more complex than those of many of his supporters. For example, his support of the modernising element present in Whig history was never con-flated with modernism's more iconoclastic rupture with the past (Bentley 2005) and his belief that nationality was the 'indispensable core of individual identity' meant that his 'inter-nationalism was never cosmopolitan' (Guttmann 2002: 2). By contrast, his supporters were less inhibited, often prone to making triumphalist claims that projected the path of the Olympic movement towards idealistic, even utopian goals. In that manner, for instance, the Reverend Robert Courcy-Laffan, a British member of the IOC from 1897 to 1927, urged his audience at the closing banquet for London 1908 not to forget that:

[the] Olympic Games in London are only an episode in a great Movement and a great life. The first revival took place at Athens in 1896. What is 12 years in the life of a Movement that sets out before it those great ideals: of perfect physical development, of a new humanity, the spreading out all over the world of that spirit of sport which is the spirit of the truest chivalry, and the drawing together of all the nations of the Earth in bonds of peace and mutual amity?

(Miller 2008: 57)

Challenging orthodoxy, mapping alternatives

These and countless similar statements to be found in official documentation laid down the lines of a pervasive Whig historical narrative that for many years provided the dominant discourse for the Olympic movement. The past was interpreted from the point of view of the present. The narrative seamlessly linked together a set of hallowed but largely imagined origins (see Hobsbawm 1983: 1), applauded the struggle and vision of the pioneers (especially Coubertin) in re-establishing the Games, celebrated progress made up to the present and looked ahead to the completion of a historic project. The adverse experiences associated with particular festivals (Lenskyj 2000; Yarborough 2000; Barney *et al.* 2004) have eroded Whig optimism, but the spirit of that interpretation has retained sufficient vitality to provide a powerful orthodoxy that later historians have contested.

The nature of the resulting contestation has taken many forms: some fully articulated, others still primarily exploratory. One source of reappraisal has come from the work of critics whose writings broadly fits into the framework of the history of ideas, the sub-discipline that focuses on 'the historical investigation of the textual and cultural remains of human thought processes' (Kelley 1990: 3). Brownell (2005), for example, dissected the triadic relationship between nineteenth-century Western classicism, the modern nation-state of Greece and the revival of the Olympic Games, arguing for the importance of reasserting the importance of the Greek state in the Games' revival (also Koulouri 2005). Loland (1995) showed that the concept of 'Olympism' – described as 'a philosophy of life, exalting and combining in a balanced whole the qualities of body, will and mind' (IOC 2007: 11) – has functioned effectively primarily because it possessed an important but permissive vagueness (see also MacAloon 1981). Segrave and

Chatziefstathiou (2008: 31) provided another perspective on Olympism in a discussion of the way that it was influenced by Coubertin's distinctive notions of beauty, which they argue tended towards 'exclusivity, elitism and the atomization of self'. It is possible to speculate that these values contributed to the failure to develop a satisfactory cultural programme at Olympic events that could match the sports programme. Schantz (2008) argued that the universality allegedly present in Olympism founders in the face of a 'civilizing mission' that still promotes 'Western or westernized sports exclusively'.

Another, more radical source of critical reappraisal has come from historians influenced by the 'cultural turn' in the arts and humanities. Booth and Tatz (2000: xv; quoted in Bale and Christensen 2004: 3) made the textually subversive suggestion that the capital letter should be removed from the word 'Olympism'. Their argument was that the original Games merited upper case because they were named after Olympia, but that the notion of Olympism no more deserved a capital than 'liberalism, humanitarianism, fascism or utopianism'. To use upper case tended 'to deny its status as an ideology and instead, to hypostatize it, to present it as something substantial or unchanging' (ibid.). Booth (2004), in a related analysis of post-Olympian historiography, categorised the various styles of writing about Olympic events with a seven-point spectrum ranging from traditional narrative to deconstructionist history, which holds that past events are explained and acquire their meaning as much by their representation as by their 'knowable actuality' (Munslow 2007: 14). As yet few studies have attempted such analysis, but two exceptions are studies by Brown (2001), who applied Foucauldian discourse analysis to early editions of the *Revue Olympique*, the IOC's official journal, and Møller (2004) who studied the transgressive qualities of doping at Olympic events.

Historians have also applied textual analysis to the way that media constructions have influenced understanding of past Olympic events. Dyreson (1998: 26–7) commented on the way that the organisers of the Winter Games at Salt Lake City 2002 used Native-American iconography to sell the arguable contention that the United States had no racial barriers in sport. Lennartz (2008) used examples of the first three modern Games, with particular reference to the staging of the marathon competitions, to show how erroneous media reporting has been taken as fact by later writers who have never bothered with verification. Finally, Hughson (2010) examined official film footage and associated archive materials from the 1956 Summer Games at Melbourne to reveal the tensions between two different tropes of 'Australian-ness', namely, imagined cultural diversity and neo-liberal multiculturalism.

Conclusion

In drawing this chapter to a close, we perforce recognise the limitations of the foregoing analysis. Given the lack of any consolidated body of comparative scholarship on the history of events, we have sketched some directions that such a history might follow, using examples principally relating to festivals and the Olympic Games. Naturally, the extent of the lessons that can be drawn for other forms of events will vary, among other things according to the scale, frequency, duration, spatial extent and perceived importance of the events concerned. Nevertheless, many of the basic principles may be said to enjoy a broad applicability. These include: the idea that historical accounts of events are invariably ideologically constructed rather than 'objective' and 'value free'; acknowledgment that histories can be written in many different ways; and recognition that harnessing contrasting approaches to historical knowledge can provide very different perspectives on the same event. Building on these points, if the guiding aim of historiography is to further understanding by bringing about 'an informed reading of texts' (Spalding and Parker 2007: 148), then the goal of a historiography of events would logically be to assemble and synthesise the knowledge about events that comes from analysis informed by conscious reflection on the nature of historical approaches, methods and sources. At its best, it is an analysis that will not just say something about the origins of events, but will also supply insight into their continuing purpose.

Further reading

On issues concerned with ideology, see

Boudon, R. (1989) *The Analysis of Ideology*, Chicago: University of Chicago Press.
Freeden, M. (2003) *Ideology*, Oxford: Oxford University Press.
van Dijk, T.A. (1998) *Ideology: A Multidisciplinary Approach*, London: Sage.

For more on historiography, the reader might consult:

Budd, A. (2008) *The Modern Historiography Reader*, Abingdon: Taylor and Francis.
Tucker, A. (2010) *A Companion to the Philosophy of History and Historiography*, Chichester: John Wiley.

For relevant commentary on the historiography of types of events not considered in detail here, see:

Geppert, A.C.T. (2010) *Fleeting Cities: Imperial Expositions in Fin-de-Siecle Europe*, Basingstoke: Palgrave Macmillan.
Gold, J.R. (2011) 'Carnival redux: Hurricane Katrina, Mardi Gras and contemporary United States experience of an enduring festival form', in O. Kaltmeier (ed.) *Selling EthniCity: Urban Cultural Politics in the Americas*, Farnham, UK: Ashgate, pp. 27–40.
Gold, J.R. and Gold, M.M. (2012) *Festival Cities: Culture, Planning and Urban Life since 1918*, London: Routledge.

References

Bale, J. and Christensen, M.K. (2004) 'Introduction: Post-Olympism?', in J. Bale and M.K. Christensen (eds) *Post-Olympism?* Oxford: Berg, pp. 1–12.
Barney, R.K., Wenn, S.R. and Martyn, S.G. (2004) *Selling the Five Rings: The International Olympic Committee and the Rise of Olympic Commercialism*, Salt Lake City: University of Utah Press, revised edition.
Bell, D. (2000) 'Ideology', in A. Bullock and S. Trombley (eds) *The New Fontana Dictionary of Modern Thought*, London: HarperCollins, third edition, p. 414.
Bentley, M.J. (2005) *Modernizing England's Past: English Historiography in the Age of Modernism, 1870–1970*, Cambridge: Cambridge University Press.
Berridge, G. (2007) *Events Design and Experience*, Oxford: Butterworth-Heinemann.
Booth, D. (2004) 'Post-[O]lympism? Questioning [O]lympic historiography', in J. Bale and M.K. Christensen (eds) *Post-Olympism?* Oxford: Berg, pp. 201–10.
Booth, D. and Tatz, C. (2000) *One-Eyed: A View of Australian Sport*, Sydney: George Allen and Unwin.
Breisach, E. (2006) *Historiography: Ancient, Medieval, and Modern*, Chicago: University of Chicago Press, third edition.
Brown, D. (2001) 'Modern sport, modernism and the cultural manifesto: de Coubertin's *Revue Olympique*', *International Journal of the History of Sport* 18: 78–109.
Brownell, S. (2005) 'The view from Greece: questioning Eurocentrism in the history of the Olympic Games', *Journal of Sport History* 32: 203–16.
Burke, P. (1999) 'Historiography', in A. Bullock and S. Trombley (eds) *The New Fontana Dictionary of Modern Thought*, London: HarperCollins, third edition, p. 396.
Burrow, J. (2009) *A History of Histories*, Harmondsworth: Penguin.
Butterfield, H. (1931) *The Whig Interpretation of History*, London: George Bell and Sons.

Cole, H. (1853) 'On the international results of the exhibition of 1851', in *Lectures on the Results of the Great Exhibition of 1851, delivered before the Society of Arts, Manufactures and Commerce, at the Suggestion of H.R.H. Prince Albert, President of the Society*, second series, London: David Bogue, pp. 419–51.

Dyreson, M. (1998) 'Olympic Games and historical imagination: notes from the faultline of tradition and modernity', *Olympika: The International Journal of Olympic Studies* 7: 25–42.

Furay, C. and Salevouris, M.J. (2010) *The Methods and Skills of History: A Practical Guide*, Wheeling, IL: Harlan Davidson, third edition.

Gallup, S. (1987) *A History of the Salzburg Festival*, London: Weidenfeld and Nicolson.

Gold, J.R. and Gold, M.M. (2005) *Cities of Culture: Staging International Festivals and the Urban Agenda, 1851–2000*, Aldershot: Ashgate Press.

——(eds) (2011) *Olympic Cities: City Agendas, Planning, and the World's Games, 1896–2016*, London: Routledge, second edition.

——(2012) *Festival Cities: Culture, Planning and Urban Life since 1918*, London: Routledge.

Guttmann, A. (2002) *The Olympics: A History of the Modern Games*, Champaign: University of Illinois Press.

Hitchcock, H.-R. and Johnson, P.C. (1932) *The International Style: Architecture since 1922*, New York: W.W. Norton.

Hobsbawm, E. (1983) 'Introduction: inventing tradition', in E. Hobsbawm and T. Ranger (eds) *The Invention of Tradition*, Cambridge: Cambridge University Press, pp. 1–14.

Hughson, J. (2010) 'The Friendly Games – the "official" IOC film of the 1956 Melbourne Olympics as historical record', *Historical Journal of Film, Radio and Television* 30: 529–42.

IOC (2007) *The Olympic Charter*, Lausanne: International Olympic Committee.

Kelley, D.R. (1990) 'What is happening to the history of ideas?', *Journal of the History of Ideas* 51: 3–25.

Koulouri, C. (2005) 'The inside view of an outsider: Greek scholarship on the history of the Olympic Games', *Journal of Sport History* 32: 217–28.

Kriechbaumer, R. (2009) Salzburger Festspiele: Ihre Geschichte von 1960 bis 1989: Die Ära Karajan, Salzburg: Jung und Jung.

Larrain, J. (1983) *Marxism and Ideology*, London: Macmillan.

Lasinger, M. (2010) 'The history of the Salzburg Festival', available at: www.salzburgerfestspiele.at/DIEINSTITUTION/GESCHICHTE/DieFestspielIdee (accessed 28 December 2010).

Lennartz, K. (2008) 'Some case studies on how media construct Olympic legends', in R.K. Barney, M.K. Heine, K.B. Wamsley and G.H. Macdonald (eds) *Pathways: Critiques and Dialogues in Olympic Research*, Beijing: Capital University of Physical Education, pp. 241–6.

Lenskyj, H.J. (2000) *Inside the Olympic Industry: Power, Politics and Activism*, Albany, NY: State University of New York Press.

Loland, S. (1995) 'Coubertin's ideology of Olympism from the perspective of the history of ideas', *Olympika* 4: 49–78

Lowenthal, D. (1985) *The Past is a Foreign Country*, Cambridge: Cambridge University Press.

MacAloon, J.J. (1981) *This Great Symbol: Pierre de Coubertin and the Origins of the Modern Olympic Games*, Chicago: University of Chicago Press.

Merback, M.B. (1999) *The Thief, the Cross and the Wheel: Pain and the Spectacle of Punishment in Medieval and Renaissance Europe*, London: Reaktion Books.

Miller, D. (2008) *The Official History of the Olympic Games and the IOC: Athens to Beijing, 1894–2008*, Edinburgh: Mainstream Publishing.

Mitchell, W.J.T. (1986) *Iconology: Image, Text, Ideology*, Chicago: University of Chicago Press.

Møller, V. (2004) 'Doping and the Olympic Games from an aesthetic perspective', in J. Bale and M.K. Christensen (eds) *Post-Olympism?* Oxford: Berg, pp. 201–10

Müller, N. (ed.) (2000) *Pierre de Coubertin, 1893–1937: Olympism, Selected Writings*, Lausanne: International Olympic Committee.

Munslow, A. (2000) 'Historiography', in A. Munslow, *The Routledge Companion to Historical Studies*, London: Routledge, pp. 142–4.

——(2007) *Narrative and History*, Basingstoke: Palgrave Macmillan.

Plamenatz, J.P. (1970) *Ideology*, London: Pall Mall Press.

Schantz, O.J. (2008) 'Pierre de Coubertin's "Civilizing Mission"', in R.K. Barney, M.K. Heine, K.B. Wamsley and G.H. Macdonald (eds) *Pathways: Critiques and Dialogues in Olympic Research*, Beijing: Capital University of Physical Education, pp. 53–62.

Segrave, J.O. and Chatziefstathiou, D. (2008) 'Pierre de Coubertin's ideology of beauty from the perspective of the history of ideas', in R.K. Barney, M.K. Heine, K.B. Wamsley and G.H. Macdonald (eds) *Pathways: Critiques and Dialogues in Olympic Research*, Beijing: Capital University of Physical Education, pp. 31–41.

SFS (Salzburg Festival Society) (2007) 'Letter from Dr Helga Rabl-Stadler', in SFS (ed.) *Salzburg Festival 2007*, New York: Salzburg Festival Society.

Shone, A. and Parry, B. (2001) *Successful Event Management: A Practical Handbook*, London: Continuum.

Spalding, R. and Parker, C. (2007) *Historiography: An Introduction*, Manchester: Manchester University Press.

Steinberg, M.P. (2000) *Austria as Theatre and Ideology: The Meaning of the Salzburg Festival*, Ithaca, NY: Cornell University Press.

Turning, P. (2009) '"With teeth clenched and an angry face": vengeance, visitors and judicial power in fourteenth-century France', in A. Classen (ed.) *Urban Space in the Middle Ages and Early Modern Age*, Berlin: Walter de Gruyter, pp. 353–71.

Versnel, H.S. (1970) *Triumphus: Inquiry into the Origin, Development and Meaning of the Roman Triumph*, Leiden: E.J. Brill.

Weber, E. (1970) 'Pierre de Coubertin and the introduction of organised sport in France', *Journal of Contemporary History* 5: 3–26.

Yarborough, C.R. (2000) *And They Call Them Games: An Inside View of the 1996 Olympics*, Macon: Mercer University Press.

9

The economic contribution of special events

Larry Dwyer and Leo Jago

Introduction

Special events provide important recreational opportunities for local communities. In many destinations, they form a fundamental component of the destination's tourism development strategy. There are many types of special events and it is quite difficult to find an all-embracing definition. For present purposes, special events are defined as 'one-time or infrequently occurring events of limited duration that provide consumers with leisure and social opportunities beyond their everyday experience' (Jago and Shaw 1998: 29).

Special events of one kind or another have played an important role in the economic and social development of communities internationally for many years. In recent years there has been a substantial increase in the number and type of special events (Getz 2005, 2008). This growth is due largely to the emphasis being placed on regional economic development and destination marketing by many governments and tourism marketing organisations (Cornelissen and Swart 2006; Cornelissen 2007). Special events increase the opportunities for new expenditure within a host region by attracting visitors to the region (Dickinson *et al.* 2007). They are acknowledged to potentially stimulate business activity, creating income and jobs in the short term and generating increased visitation and related investment in the longer term.

For the purpose of this paper we take the 'economic contribution' of an event to refer either to its 'economic impact' or its 'net economic benefits'. While event researchers and commentators often take these concepts to be the same, we shall argue that they are quite different, requiring different approaches to their measurement.

Governments are often asked to provide financial support for special events including the allocation of substantial funds to provide or upgrade the facilities required to stage the event. As a consequence, governments will generally require credible forecasts of the event impacts and comprehensive evaluations after the event. The theoretical basis of economic impact assessment of special events is to be found in the pioneering work of Burns *et al.* (1986) in their study of the Adelaide Grand Prix. Since then, refinements have been made by several authors including Getz (1987), Crompton and McKay (1994), Crompton (1995), Dwyer and Forsyth (1997), Delpy and Li (1998), Mules (1999), Dwyer *et al.* (2000, 2004, 2005, 2006a, 2006b).

In recent years, a growing number of researchers have been critical of the approach taken to assessing the economic contribution of special events. Three main types of criticism have been advanced:

1   Some argue that the economic contributions of events are often exaggerated. Many of the problems in event assessment arise due to exaggeration of event participant numbers and/or their expenditure (Crompton and McKay 1994; Delpy and Li 1998). Only that proportion of expenditure which represents an injection of 'new money' into a destination is relevant to the calculation of the economic impacts. A number of critics (e.g. Porter 1999; Dwyer *et al.* 2000; Matheson 2002; Matheson and Baade 2003; Crompton 2006) have highlighted inappropriate practices in event assessment (for example, inclusion of residents' expenditure as 'new money', exaggerating visitor numbers and expenditure, abuse of multipliers, inclusion of time switchers and casuals), as well as the tendency to ignore the various costs associated with special events such as opportunity costs borne by the local community, and displacement costs.
2   Other researchers have argued that the standard model used in event assessment needs a re-examination. Economic impact analysis involves estimating the additional expenditure generated by the event, and then using some form of economic model to estimate how this expenditure translates into increased income and employment in the destination. At issue is the relevance of input–output (I–O) modelling which until recently has been the standard technique for converting event expenditure data into economic impacts. These critics argue that the economic assessment models used for estimating the economic impacts of major events should reflect contemporary developments in economic analysis, particularly regarding the use of Computable General Equilibrium (CGE) modelling. They argue that, in most cases, I–O modelling does not provide an accurate picture of the economic impacts of events and is thus incapable of informing event funding agencies or governments of the 'return on investment' estimated from event funding (Dwyer *et al.* 2005, 2006a, 2006b; Blake 2005; Madden 2006).
3   A third group of researchers argues that event assessment which focuses only on economic impacts is too narrow in scope to provide sufficient information to policy makers and government funding agencies and that, where practical, a more comprehensive approach should be employed to embrace the importance of social and environmental impacts in addition to economic impacts. These critics highlight the potential importance of cost benefit analysis (CBA) in event evaluation (Fleischer and Felsenstein 2002; Shaffer *et al.* 2003; Mules and Dwyer 2005; Jago and Dwyer 2006; Victoria Auditor General 2007; Dwyer and Forsyth 2009).

Economic impact analysis of an event

The 'new' expenditure that occurs as a result of an event is used as the input to an economic model to determine the economic impacts of the event in the destination. The economic model identifies and quantifies the linkages between different sectors of the local economy and linkages with other regions. As displayed in Figure 9.1, the injected expenditure of visitors and organisers/sponsors stimulates economic activity and creates additional business turnover, employment, value added, household income and government revenue in the host community.

The relationship between expenditure and output, income, value added and employment (direct, indirect or induced) can be described by multipliers. The size of the multipliers will depend upon the type of model used to estimate the impacts. Unfortunately, it is in the area of event assessment that multipliers are often employed in a most uncritical way. A major reason for this has been the use of I–O models to estimate the economic impacts of special events. Thus, Dobson *et al.* (1997) examined the economic impact of the Euro 1996 Football

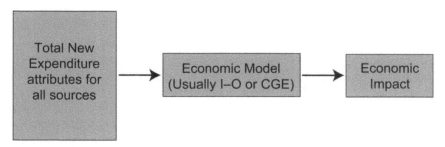

Figure 9.1 The economic impact of an event

Championship using an I–O model. Ahlert (2001) employed I–O modelling to estimate the economic effects of the Soccer World Cup 2006 in Germany, while Mabugu and Mohamed (2008) estimated the economic impacts of government financing of the 2010 FIFA World Cup using a fiscal social accounting matrix model. Each of these approaches assumes fixed prices and thus fail to capture the industry interactive effects that would be revealed in the use of a more sophisticated model for economic impact assessment.

Shaffer *et al.* (2003) have criticised what they argue to be the exaggerated projections of economic impacts of the Vancouver 2010 Winter Olympics estimated by government-commissioned consultants using an I–O model. The model employed assumed no capacity constraints and consequently no impact on wages or prices. Shaffer *et al.* offer two main types of criticisms of the government-commissioned economic impact study of the event.

First, they point out how uncertain the economic effects are when the event destination already has high demand. Unemployment rates in the cities of Whistler and Vancouver are relatively low compared to other areas in the Province of British Columbia (BC) and it is unlikely that a large percentage of the local workers hired as a result of the Games would otherwise be un- or under-employed. The more likely effect will be that the Olympic Games will lead to wage increases that will attract local workers from other activities, or possibly un- and under-employed people from other regions within BC and from elsewhere in Canada. Thus, even if unemployment exists in a host region, an event will not reduce unemployment by much because labour will flow from other states to take up the jobs.

Second, Whistler tourism facilities are not under-utilised in peak periods. Expanding capacity for a relatively short impact period, however, is not generally financially worthwhile. Unless capacity were to expand to meet the increased demand for goods and service, prices would likely rise, given the limited supply. Therefore, some increase in prices (including, for example, reductions or the elimination of promotional rates) is likely to occur.

As this example makes clear, many of the failures of 'good practice' event assessment and the confusions of many analysts are due to their thinking within the restrictive box of I–O modelling. It is unrealistic to use models to estimate the economic impacts of events which assume no capacity constraints and consequently no impact of the event on wages or prices. The assumption of constant prices alone makes these models unsuitable for event assessment, particularly for larger scale events.

In recent years, the literature on event assessment has moved away from the use of I–O models to provide the multiplier effects of the new expenditure, and towards the use of CGE models (Industry Commission 1996; Blake 2005; Dwyer *et al.* 2005, 2006a, 2006b; Madden 2006; Victoria Auditor General 2007). Actual economies comprise a complex pattern of feedback effects and resource constraints which are captured by CGE analysis. The advantages of CGE models for event economic impact assessment are set out in Box 9.1.

Box 9.1 Advantage of CGE models for event economic impact assessment

- The events sector will need to expand output to meet additional demand by employing additional land, labour, capital plant and equipment. CGE models can allow for the resource constraints on land, labour and capital that generally are present in an economy and that can limit changes in economic activity through an event-related increase in the final demand for goods and services. The constraints are perhaps most evident in the case of labour which has some skills component and may be in limited supply, for example, particular labour skills or workers for particular shifts or locations.
- CGE models include more general specifications of the behaviour of consumers, producers and investors, than those allowed for in I–O models, thus permitting specific models to be calibrated to actual conditions for a particular event in a particular economy.
- CGE models recognise that relative prices of land, labour and capital may change because of an event causing businesses to change the composition of their inputs. When there are capacity constraints, the prices of inputs and wages will increase in the face of an increase in demand. These price rises, including (for some destinations) any upward pressure on the exchange rate due to increased foreign expenditure associated with an event, will limit the extent of economic expansion associated with the event, and may even lead to contractions in economic activity in some sectors.
- CGE models recognise the behaviour of the government budget sector as relevant to the estimated economic impacts of a special event. For example, if additional infrastructure spending by government is required to support a special event, such as expenditure on stadia, roads and airport landing facilities, there will be a positive effect on spending but it must be financed. This may moderate the growth in private consumption associated with the event, leading to downward pressure on the output of consumption-oriented industries.
- CGE models can recognise that the net impact on economic activity within the state, in the rest of the economy, and the national economy will differ according to the source of the additional spending.
- The distributional impact of a special event is often ignored. CGE models provide information as to who gains and who loses, both within and outside the event location. To make informed decisions about events policy, governments need to know the answers to questions such as: how much will the event add to economic activity and jobs after accounting for inter-industry effects? to what extent do the benefits of the event in the host region come at a cost to other regions? CGE modelling can address such questions.
- The assumptions of a CGE model can be varied and the sensitivity to them tested to assess the economic impacts of an event. These include assumptions about factor constraints, workings of the labour market, changes in real wage rates and prices, and government taxing and spending policies. The fact that CGE simulations can be undertaken using different assumptions, the realism of which can be discussed and debated, provides a transparency to the event assessment process that rarely exists in I–O modelling. This can provide very useful information in predicting the economic impacts of particular types of events in different macroeconomic contexts.

Source: adapted from Dwyer *et al.* (2010: Chapter 11)

In a study of the economic impacts of the Sydney Olympics 2000, Madden (2006) employed a multiregional CGE model to examine the effects on economic and financial variables within a single analytical framework. Simulations were conducted for three phases over a twelve-year period. Careful attention was paid to the presence of constraints on labour supply and capital and on the sources of savings funding Olympic investments. The simulations assumed that no effects from the Games remain on the debt position of Australian governments or the nation's external debt five years after the Sydney Games. The results indicate that, provided there is not too large a financial loss on the Games, inclusive of construction costs, a modest positive impact on the state hosting the Games can occur. The degree to which this positive impact comes at the expense of other states depends crucially on assumed labour-market conditions.

Recognising the limitations of the standard I–O modelling technique for events assessment, Bohlmann and van Heerden (2008) used a CGE model to simulate the impacts of the 2010 FIFA World Cup. They examined the impact of the pre-event phase expenditure attributed to the hosting of the event on the South African economy. Simulating an increase in government expenditure on construction, they found a positive impact of the event on most macroeconomic variables, including GDP and employment. These gains were found to be driven mainly by unskilled unemployed resources that were drawn into economic activity by the demand injection.

In the study by Blake (2005) of the London Olympics 2012 using a CGE model, it is forecast that the impact of the Games will vary significantly across different sectors of the UK economy. Sectors that expand include construction, passenger land transport, business services, hotels and restaurants. Sectors that are not directly related to the Games may contract in size indirectly as a result of hosting the Games. These include manufacturing, agriculture, fishing and other services. However, these results are relative to the 'No Games' scenario in which a substantial amount of growth takes place in all sectors of the economy. Thus, while no sector is predicted to contract in the time span modelled, some will grow less because of the impact of hosting the Olympics. The simulations indicate that any changes to the UK economy associated with the Olympics 2012 will be comparatively small. Even in the Olympic year, the total economy-wide effect for the UK is only 0.066 per cent of total UK GDP at 2004 prices (Blake 2005).

The results of the studies by Madden (2006), Bohlmann and van Heerden (2008), and Blake (2005) could not have been forthcoming using an I–O model. That the type of model used to estimate the economic impacts of special events has a substantial effect on the assessment results became evident in a study by Dwyer et al. (2005) which compared the results of using CGE and I–O modelling to estimate the economic impacts of a special event held in Australia, namely, the Qantas Formula 1 Grand Prix. Both a CGE and an I–O model were used to estimate the results. The expenditure data fed into the I–O and CGE models included the total injected amount of expenditure associated with visitation and administration of the event from interstate and overseas sources (A\$51.25 million). Expenditure injected from interstate sources was A\$28.55 million, while expenditure injected from overseas was A\$22.7 million. The same as for visitor expenditure, injected organiser expenditure was allocated to the main industry sectors prior to the modelling exercise. The comparison revealed substantial differences between the techniques with respect to estimates of the economic impacts on real output, real Gross State Product/ Gross Domestic Product and employment.

Differences in real output, GSP and employment

Table 9.1 contains estimated impacts of a major event that injects A\$51.25 million into the New South Wales (NSW) economy. The impacts are distinguished according to the model used (I–O, CGE) and the impact on the host state (NSW), the rest of Australia (RoA) and the nation as a whole (Aus).

Table 9.1 I–O and CGE output, GSP and employment multipliers for NSW and RoA, for a large event

Macroeconomic variables	I–O model			CGE model		
	NSW	RoA	Aust.	NSW	RoA	Aust.
Change in real output ($million)	112.00	8.1	120.1	56.70	−32.24	24.46
Output multiplier	2.2	0.16	2.3	1.1	−0.3	0.5
Change in real GSP/ GDP ($million)	38.90	4.4	43.3	19.41	−10.61	8.80
GSP/GDP (or value-added multiplier)	0.8	0.09	0.8	0.4	−0.2	0.2
Change in employment (number of jobs)	521	71	592	318	−189	129
Employment multiplier (jobs created per million dollars injected expenditure)	10.2	1.4	11.6	6.2	-3.7	2.5

Source: Adapted from Dwyer *et al.* (2005).
Note: Shock = $51.25 million AUD; NSW = State of New South Wales; RoA = Rest of Australia; Aust = Australia.

The differences in the projected impacts of the event on real output are substantial. The simulations reveal that I–O modelling projects a much greater impact on real output for both New South Wales and Australia (A$112.0 million and A$120.1 million), as compared to CGE modelling (A$56.70 million and A$24.46 million).The percentage by which the I–O model overestimates the impact on real output, compared to CGE, is 80 per cent for New South Wales and 491 per cent for Australia. The output multiplier for New South Wales is 2.185 using the I–O model but only 1.106 using the CGE model. For Australia as a whole, the I–O model yields an output multiplier of 2.343 whereas the CGE model yields a substantially smaller output multiplier of 0.477.

The absolute differences in GSP/value added yielded by the two methods are smaller but the percentage differences are even greater than the percentage differences in real output. On the I–O model, the projected change in GSP/GDP due to the event is A$38.9 million for New South Wales and A$43.3 million for Australia, a difference of −11 per cent. In contrast, the CGE model projects a change in GSP/GDP of A$19.41 million for the state and A$8.80 million for Australia, a difference of −55 per cent.

The value-added multiplier using I–O modelling is 0.759 and 0.844 for New South Wales and Australia, respectively, as compared to value-added multipliers of 0.432 and 0.267 using CGE analysis.

The two models give different employment projections also. The projected increase in employment using an I–O model is 521 (full-time equivalent) jobs in NSW and 592 jobs throughout Australia. Using a CGE model the projected employment effects are 318 jobs and 129 jobs, respectively. The CGE employment projections are 61 and 22 per cent of the I–O employment projections. Once again the I–O model projects increased employment in RoA whereas the CGE model projects relatively large job losses in RoA. The I–O employment multiplier is 10.169 for New South Wales and 11.548 for Australia, while the CGE employment multipliers are 6.2 and 2.5, respectively.

Industry differences

I–O modelling projects a positive change in output and employment in all industries in New South Wales except oil, natural gas and brown coal, where no change is projected. In contrast, the CGE model projects reduced output and employment in several industries in New South Wales, including some mining sectors and transport services.

Irrespective of the model used in event impact assessment, there are several issues that have been unfortunately neglected in estimation of the economic impacts of a special event. Four of the more important of these issues will now be discussed. These refer to the relevance of the labour market, relevance of the scope of assessment, the treatment of construction expenditure, and the treatment of taxes and event subsidies. We discuss each in turn.

Relevance of the labour market

The workings of the labour market are particularly relevant to event economic impact assessment. Particular caution needs to be exercised in use of employment multipliers in event impact assessment, since they tend to exaggerate the amount of employment generated by an event (Dwyer et al. 2006a, 2006b). In many firms, staffing levels may be relatively insensitive to changes in turnover, while other firms may better utilise their current staff (for example, provision of overtime, weekend work). Volunteers provide services for many events. The relatively short duration of events means that any employment effects, if they occur at all, may be small and are likely to be brief.

If the demand for labour increases and there is unemployment in the economy, the real wage stays constant, unemployment will be reduced, and economic activity will increase significantly. On the other hand, if the response to an increase in demand for labour is a wage increase (which can take place even though there is considerable unemployment), the impact on unemployment will be much less, as will be the impact on overall economic activity. In Madden's study of the Sydney Olympics 2000 (Madden 2006), simulations were undertaken under three alternative scenarios. Under one of these scenarios, a tighter labour market is assumed. This has the effect of generating a slightly negative overall impact on national real household consumption from the Olympics.

The outcome depends importantly on whether (1) there exists a separate local or regional labour market, or else a wider national labour market, and (2) whether there is unemployment in the event region.

1   In an integrated national economy, as a consequence of an event, labour will flow to the region that is experiencing increased demand for resources. If a national labour market exists, labour will flow from other states to meet this demand. Interstate differences in wages and in unemployment rates will be eliminated. Thus, if resource markets are highly integrated, the event will lead to greater impact on economic activity in the host state or region than if they are not.

2   On the other hand, if a region operates as a moderately separate economy, the economic impact of an event taking place within its borders will be smaller than if the state is part of a seamlessly integrated national economy. With statewide labour markets, an increase in labour demand that comes about because of an event will lead to some combination of

reduction in unemployment within the state and increase in wage rates in the state. The increased prices and wages choke off some of the potential increase in economic activity.

How well integrated are the state or regional labour markets in any destination is an empirical matter. The degree of integration, particularly in the short run, will depend on how far separated the states are and on cultural factors such as the willingness of workers to move out of their home state to seek employment. The long-term persistence of regional unemployment in many industrial countries of Europe and in Australia suggests that labour markets are often far from perfectly integrated.

Relevance of the jurisdiction

The role of government has been unduly neglected in special event assessment. To make informed decisions about events policy, governments may need to know the answers to questions such as: how much will the event add to economic activity and jobs after accounting for inter-industry effects? is the event likely to produce net economic benefits, and if so, how much is it worth subsidising? to what extent do the benefits of the event in the host region come at a cost to other regions? (Dwyer *et al.* 2006a, 2006b.).

The sizes of the value-added and employment multipliers associated with a particular event will vary according to the region under study and will reflect the different economic structures of different regions. Multiplier values for a smaller region within a destination, given greater leakages of expenditure, will be lower than those for the destination economy as a whole.

A local council might undertake an economic impact study to determine whether to support a festival in the town. If the perspective of the local government is taken, it is only the local effects of the event that are relevant.

A state or federal government contemplating financial support for an event will be interested not just in the impact in the local area, but also the impacts on the state and/or nation. Local impact studies will not provide public sector decision-makers with sufficient guidance as to whether they should support local events financially, since they will also need to know the overall state-wide impacts. An event may increase economic activity substantially within a local area but its net impact on the economic activity within the state will normally be much less, and conceivably negative. The impact on national output will be even less again. Blake's results for the London Olympics show that while London gains from the 2012 Olympics, it implies reduced GDP and employment for the rest of the UK (Blake 2005). Reasons for this include: spending in London by UK residents from outside London visiting the Games; movement of workers, whether migrants, commuter or temporary migrants, into London because of higher wages in the capital; and the provision of Lottery funding, which in effect transfers money to London.

For these reasons, the perspectives on evaluation of an event from the local, state and national levels will be quite different. An event may be highly attractive to a rural city, though only of marginal or negative benefit to a state. Even so, a state or national government may be prepared to subsidise the event, even though it is basically shifting, rather than creating, economic activity and jobs. This could be so if a region is depressed, and the central government wishes to provide a stimulus for the local economy. For this to be worthwhile, the event must be assessed in comparison with other forms of stimulus – there may be ways in which the same funds could generate a greater impact on local economic activity, or a similar impact without as large a negative impact on other parts of the economy. If so, it would be more effective to subsidise these alternatives rather than the event. Such decisions should be taken in full awareness of who will be the winners and losers within the state, in both regional and industry terms. The losers might well be other depressed regions, or industries, within the wider economy.

Treatment of construction expenditure

Special events, particularly those scheduled for a dedicated venue, often generate investment in direct infrastructure (e.g. facilities for the event) and indirect infrastructure (e.g. roadways, increased sewage facilities). Following the event, expenditure may be required to re-adapt or to dismantle facilities. Additional investment in tourism/recreation infrastructure can increase the attractions available in an area for use by locals as well as visitors. The Sydney Olympics generated around A$5 billion worth of stadia and sporting infrastructure, as well as investment in road, rail and transport interchange systems, all of which benefit residents of, and visitors to, Sydney into the future. The main stadium for the Sydney 2000 Olympics has subsequently hosted large crowds at football matches of various codes, including the Rugby World Cup in 2003, but still does not return a financial profit. Meanwhile, many of the stadia constructed for the Athens Olympics continue to lie in a disused state years after the event.

Facility construction associated with events can be a source of economic and urban development, and bid documents for cities wishing to host an Olympic Games emphasise this (Pillay and Bass 2009; Rogerson 2009). While the investment generated by events, privately or publicly sourced, has multiplier effects on income, value added and employment, so also would alternative forms of investment that it replaces. For purposes of assessing the economic impacts of special events, it is only investment that would not have been generated except for the special event, and which represents the injection of 'new money' into the destination, that is relevant. If the construction would have proceeded with or without the event, then it does not count as associated with the event and thus is not counted in economic impact assessment. The question must be asked: was the money redirected from another project (public capital switching) and, if so, was that project within the impact area or outside? If a central government reallocated funds originally earmarked for hospital construction in one region to build an event facility in another, this switching would be a net gain to the second region and a net loss to the first. The issues here are not straightforward since they involve hypothetical issues of what would have occurred had the particular type of investment not taken place (Matheson 2008).

In the case of public sector investment, taxation revenue used to fund facilities' construction reduces the net disposable income of residents and hence their consumption of goods and services and thus does not represent a net gain of expenditure within the destination. Funding may well have been allocated to other infrastructure projects had it not been allocated to support an event. In this case the expenditure can be regarded as 'switched' from one type of investment to another. An important exception to this is where the investment expenditure is based on a special grant from an external source, for example a federal government grant to a state, or an internationally sourced grant to a developing country for a specific purpose. In the case of new investment from the private sector, there are two alternatives – no new investment would have been undertaken, or else it would have been investment of another type. Only in the first case will the investment be considered to have economic impacts resulting from the injection of new money into the destination. For the second case, the issue arises as to the opportunity cost of the investment alternative foregone.

Analysts, using I–O modelling to generate event impact multipliers, sometimes mistakenly regard construction expenditures as always having a positive effect on the economy. However, the economic resources required to stage the event are correctly modelled as a cost (Blake 2005; Madden 2006). From a national or state government perspective, investment expenditure on event facilities must be funded by a reduction in some other component of domestic demand (domestic savings) or an increase in external liabilities (foreign savings). CGE models require income-expenditure conditions to be met, implying that the construction spending must be paid for. Since government spending on construction is usually financed from taxation, the net effect of the construction projects may be negative. Researchers have examined the relationship between building new facilities and economic growth in urban areas. Siegfried and Zimbalist (2000) and Matheson (2002) point out that independent work on the economic impact of stadia and arenas has found that, taking opportunity costs into account, there is no statistically significant positive correlation between sports facility construction and economic development.

A dynamic CGE model that takes into account the time dimension can also include the effects of the availability of infrastructure following the event. This is to recognise that capital stocks should increase in the relevant industries, with income from this infrastructure accruing to whoever owns the capital (for example, the government that financed the construction), which might lease out the built infrastructure or receive income from its sale. If the value of constructed capital exactly meets the construction costs, there may be an initial net zero effect on GDP. As Blake (2005) emphasises, certain distortions may be introduced into the economy by the holding of the event since investors would not have chosen the same industry in which to put their investments; construction costs may be increased during the construction phase because of the increased demand for construction services; and the value of the capital may fall because of increased supply of capital in the relevant sector. For these reasons, the net effects of construction projects are therefore likely to be small, and also negative (Blake 2005: 13).

Treatment of taxes and subsidies

Special events affect government revenues and outlays in the destination. Possible revenue sources for the state or national government include: taxes or fees imposed on visitor expenditure, taxes on business expenditure; income taxes; and ticket sales on state-owned public transport and admission fees to publicly owned attractions.

Changes in the patterns of expenditure brought about by an event give rise to increases and decreases in tax revenues from different sectors because different aspects of economic activity are taxed differently. While tourism-related industries may gain from the special event, other industries may experience reduced output and sales revenues and thus pay less taxation. The net effect on government tax revenue cannot be known prior to the modelling exercise (Gooroochurn and Sinclair 2005). Furthermore, changes in tax revenues lead to changes in government spending and tax rates that in turn influence economic activity. I–O models cannot be used to estimate the net effects of the event on tax revenue since they do not estimate the negative impacts on expenditure and activity. These effects are captured in CGE models (Dwyer *et al.* 2004). CGE models also pose the question of what the government does if increased economic activity leads to increased tax receipts. The government could add the tax receipts to its budget surplus (or subtract them from its deficit), or it could increase spending or lower taxes. The different options will have different effects on economic activity.

Governments often subsidise events. In addition to direct subsidisation, including tax concessions, this can take various indirect forms, for example public expenditure on construction of facilities and supporting infrastructure such as road works, provision of additional police, ambulance officers and so on. These subsidies must be financed from government revenue or reductions in other government spending, with consequent effects on economic activity.

A special event that stimulates economic activity generates an increase in tax receipts for the host destination. In a federal system, some of these will accrue to the host-region government and some to the national government. When the event increases economic activity, the net cost to the government will be less than the subsidy to the event. Indeed, it is possible that an event that receives only a limited subsidy relative to the revenue effects could be revenue positive for the government. Where there is a net cost to the government, however, this cost must be funded. The government has several funding options. It could cut expenditure in other areas, leading to reduced economic activity. Alternatively, it may increase taxes. For example, it might raise taxes on doing business in the destination. This could have a significant negative impact on economic activity in the region because it would make the region less competitive and economic activity would shift to other regions.

Whichever way subsidies are funded, they can be incorporated into a CGE model, and the negative impacts on the host region from expenditure cuts or tax increases can be estimated. These will reduce the overall impact of the event on economic activity. It is possible that the overall net impact on economic activity of an event that relies very heavily on subsidies could be negative. Mules and Faulkner (1996) point out that, as most large sporting events run at a loss with taxpayer revenues failing to cover taxpayer contributions, it is difficult to avoid the conclusion that the taxpayer is generally the loser in hosting major sporting events.

Using a CGE model, the researcher can set up model simulations, in which governments neutralise the effects of the event on their own budgetary positions and, in the case of a national government, on the country's external debt. As Blake (2005) notes, this feature is particularly important in weighing up negative fiscal effects in relation to an estimated stimulus to economic activity. Welfare losses caused by distortionary taxation can be very large, both on average and at the margin (Ballard *et al.* 1985).

The issues highlighted above are unfortunately often ignored in event assessment. This indicates that considerable caution must be employed before the results of any economic impact assessment of an event may be accepted. The issues addressed certainly need to be better understood by the research community, but importantly they need to be better understood by industry stakeholders since it is their hired consultants who often flaunt 'best practice' in their objective to provide the client with large numbers and optimistic economic impact assessments of events.

There are three problems with using estimated economic impacts as the sole basis for policy formulation. One problem is that it may not always be practical to employ an economic model for this purpose. Another problem is that economic impacts are not net benefits and so have limited policy significance. A third problem is that economic impact analysis does not take account of the wider costs and benefits that are often associated with larger events. We discuss these three issues in turn.

The injected expenditure approach

Of course, it may not always be practical to employ a CGE model. CGE models are not generally available for regions below state or province level. In some event evaluations, the budget available to undertake the assessment may not be sufficient to cover the cost of constructing or purchasing a CGE model. Despite this, however, there is increasingly the expectation that some form of economic assessment should be undertaken. On the other hand, as has been noted, there has been substantial abuse of multipliers in the past that has led to the gross overstatement of economic impact. As a practical response to the situation where economic models are unavailable, it has been recommended that *new expenditure* be used as the basis to measure economic performance of the event to the host region (Jago and Dwyer 2006). In similar vein, Porter (1999) and Matheson and Baade (2003) employ the concept of taxable sales as a proxy for economic impacts. Whilst this approach does not measure the actual economic impact of the event it has some advantages:

- New expenditure measures the level of new funds that are attracted to the region as a result of the event, and which provide the injection for subsequent flow-on impacts in the local economy.
- New expenditure can be used to compare quite simply the economic performance of one event with another and thus underpin government decisions as to which events to support as higher priorities.
- A further benefit of this approach is that economic impact analysis can be done subsequently if required, given that a new expenditure figure is the fundamental starting point for any economic impact study irrespective of which economic impact model is used.
- As long as it is understood to be *indicative* of the economic significance of the event, the new expenditure estimate can be a very informative key performance measure.

Destination managers allocate budgets to support the development of special events. Once a decision is made to provide a pool of funds to the event sector, the key issue is then to decide which particular events to support and to what level. This is where new expenditure can be used to compare quite simply the economic performance of one event with that of another and thus underpin government decisions as to which events to support as higher priorities. When the economic impacts of events are compared, it is often more a function of a comparison between the workings of the host economies rather than of the events themselves. Using new expenditure as the basis to compare events overcomes this problem. The limitations of this approach must be explicitly acknowledged, however.

Economic impacts are not benefits

Contrary to what might be implied in much of the economic impacts literature, estimates of the economic impacts of special events provide, in themselves, an imperfect basis for decisions about resource allocation. The problem with the usual outputs of most economic impact models is that they are in gross terms, and this limits their use in policy making. The fact that a particular change has a positive impact, in terms of increased economic activity, does not necessarily mean that it is a desirable change – it all depends on what are the costs of achieving this extra activity (Mules and Dwyer 2005; Dwyer and Forsyth 2009).

The problem arises from a failure to distinguish clearly between the *impacts* and the (net) *benefits* of an event-related demand shock. Economists know that prices do not always reflect full benefits from consumption or full costs of production. Since changes in output resulting from the holding of an event reflect unadjusted market prices, the estimated economic impacts are an inaccurate measure of the real net benefits accruing to the destination. Impacts on economic activity are measured by changes in Gross Domestic (Regional) Product or similar measures, as discussed above. The change in GDP/GRP is a measure of the value of the additional economic activity which occurs as a result of the injection of new money, but this measure does not allow for the costs of achieving this extra activity. The provision of goods and services to satisfy the needs of event goers requires the use of scarce resources in their production and these resources must be paid for. To enable the addition to GRP/GDP, inputs are needed – additional labour must be hired, additional capital must be made available, more land will be alienated and more natural resources will be used up. As a result of an event, destination output may increase by $50 m, but if $45 m of additional factors are used up to meet the extra demand, the benefit to the destination is only $5 m. Thus, the change in GSP/GDP attributed to an event exaggerates how much better off are residents of the destination.

In contrast to impacts, 'net benefits' are a measure of the value of the gain in economic activity less the cost needed to enable this extra activity. Net benefits are a measure of how much better off, in economic terms, members of the community are in aggregate given some change. A measure of the net benefit to the community as a whole can be obtained by adding up the monetary evaluation of the gains and losses experienced by all in the community. As a result of a change, individual firms, consumers, and/or workers may be better or worse off, as a result of changes in their own consumption, income and level of effort, as well as through how they are affected by government consumption. Firms can gain if profits are increased, consumers gain from price reductions or quality improvements, and workers can gain from additional wages less any costs of additional effort. Governments may gain from a change, through increased tax receipts at existing tax rates, and they will pass these gains on to the community in a number of ways – through tax cuts, or additional expenditures which benefit the community; or they may save their gains and pass them on to future generations.

Some CGE models are explicitly designed to measure changes in welfare. In his study of the economic impacts of the London Olympics 2012, Blake (2005) includes a measure of resident welfare. Consistent with economic theory, Blake's model measures a change in welfare by Equivalent Variation (EV), which indicates how much the change in welfare is worth to the economy at the pre-simulation set of prices. Blake takes the Equivalent Variation (the nominal income the consumer needs at one set of prices in order to be as well off at an alternative set of prices) as a measure of economic welfare. He employs this as a monetary measure of the welfare effects of different policy scenarios. Compared to the estimated discounted value of all future GDP of £1,559, the value of all the future changes attributable to the hosting of the Games in 2012 is £736 million. This is the change in welfare, measured in terms of the equivalent amount of money that could be given to the UK in 2005 that would have the same benefit as hosting the Games. This measure takes the results from what may be quite complex effects of a simulation on a household and produces a single value to describe how much better (or worse) off the economy is as a result of such effects. The credibility of such estimates depends upon how robust they are to alternative specifications of the utility functions, production functions, ability of factors to move from jurisdiction to jurisdiction, and many other assumptions inherent in the CGE model.

With information about the net economic benefits from the event, the government or agency is in a better position to make an informed decision about the extent to which it is prepared to support any event. Even so, the analysis omits wider costs and benefits that are crucial inputs to policy. To take these wider effects into account a cost–benefit analysis is required.

Cost–benefit analysis

The success or contribution of a particular event should not be measured only by its economic impact. It is recognised that there may be other perceived benefits from events, such as enhancing the image of a city or region, facilitating business networking and civic pride. Events can also result in associated social and cultural benefits to a destination, providing forums for continuing education and training, facilitating technology transfer and the like. Sponsorship by governments of special events, even when they are run at a financial loss, is often justified by the claim that the events produce economic benefits for the region, and country, in which they are hosted

(Crompton 2006). Event organisers may emphasise the developmental benefits of targeted infrastructural investments in deprived areas and the long-term 'legacy' benefits that the increased exposure to the international media brings through increased tourist arrivals and tourism receipts in the years after (and before) a special event (O'Brien 2006). The Olympic Games and World Cup Football are probably the best current examples of events with expected large flow-on benefits (Matheson 2008). Others such as ethnic festivals or events for disadvantaged groups may help to address social/cultural issues in the community (Pillay and Bass 2008, 2009). On the other hand, events are recognised to generate adverse environmental impacts such as various forms of pollution and adverse social impacts such as disruption to local business and community backlash (Matheson and Baade 2003).

While economic impact assessments of events emphasise the injected expenditure associated with events as the basis for estimating its significance, a cost–benefit analysis (CBA) recognises that the consumer surpluses of residents are essential to event evaluation. While the expenditures of residents is regarded as transferred expenditure for economic impact assessment purposes, the consumer surpluses they receive through the holding of the event is a primary component of benefit assessment in a CBA. In a CBA, 'value' or 'benefit' is measured by willingness to pay – what people are willing to pay (or give up) to get what a project provides. Economic costs are measured by 'opportunity cost' – what people or a society give up by investing capital and employing workers in one project or activity as opposed to any other. The relevant question is: what are the implications to a region of holding an event as compared to what could be expected without it, and what costs and benefits do they entail?

CBA estimates the sum of welfare effects of an event for a particular community. These welfare effects include benefits and costs experienced by (a) household consumer surpluses from direct enjoyment of the event (attendees), (b) household consumer surpluses of attendees of off-site events/activities; (c) household benefits from indirect enjoyment of the event (non-attendees); (d) surpluses to destination businesses (returns to destination-owned capital above opportunity costs); and (e) benefits to destination labour (above opportunity costs) (Victoria Auditor General 2007). Event related costs can include those incurred by state government agencies such as road and traffic authority, police, ambulance, fire brigade, and destination emergency services. Also included would be social and environmental costs such as disruption to business and resident lifestyles, traffic congestion, road accidents, crime, litter, noise, crowds, property damage, environmental degradation, vandalism congestion, noise, pollution, carbon footprint.

CBA can be applied in a straightforward manner to special events. Unfortunately there are not many such applications. The ACT Auditor General (2002) concluded that the V8 supercar races created net costs for the ACT in both 2000 and 2001. This was despite the estimation of positive economic impacts on the region using traditional I–O analysis. Fleischer and Felsenstein (2002) conducted a cost–benefit analysis to ascertain the social justification for the Eurovision Song Contest. This was undertaken from the perspective of Israel focusing on the benefits accruing to the Israeli population from the public spending that accompanies staging such an event, while acknowledging the opportunity cost of diverting public resources from other areas. On the assumptions made the event is estimated to have yielded a positive but relatively low net gain to Israel. Shaffer *et al.* (2003) forecast that the Vancouver Winter Olympics 2010 would entail a significant net cost to BC taxpayers. Meanwhile a CBA study commissioned by the Victoria Auditor General (2007) concluded that the Formula 1 Grand Prix held in Melbourne in 2005 had negative net benefits (that is, net costs) to the state of Victoria. Thornton (2003, 2007, quoted by Mabugu and Mohamed 2008) undertook a cost–benefit analysis for South Africa hosting the 2010 FIFA World Cup. The 2003 study found that the staging of the

2010 FIFA World Cup would create significant direct and indirect economic benefits for the country's economy, with minimal tangible and intangible costs.

On the basis of a CBA, it is possible for the decision-maker to make a judgement of whether the economic benefits of the event are greater than the costs, and to also judge whether the event would represent the best use of the funds, when funds are limited and alternative calls on funds exist. The aggregate result of a CBA indicates whether the estimated gains exceed the costs to the community as a whole. If the estimated net social benefit of an event is positive (the total benefit exceeds the total cost) then the event is said to be an efficient use of society's economic resources. The main problem, of course, involves identifying and valuing the event associated costs and benefits as accurately as is feasible. The comprehensiveness of the CBA may depend on event size and the potential social benefits and costs that may be generated.

Some outcomes of an event on a destination are not sufficiently well accepted or measurable to be included in a CBA. These are often referred to as 'intangible' outcomes. They include such items as increased business confidence, increased trade and business development and enhancement of skills and induced tourism to the destination after the event. Costs include the perception that events cause the destination to be crowded, with inflated prices, causing a loss of tourism and business to the host destination. For many of these effects there are no observable financial transactions that could be used to measure their magnitude. In any case, they are likely to vary greatly from one event to another, depending upon size and type. These effects, economic as well as non-economic, are often ignored unless a particular effort is made to include them in a comprehensive event assessment. They represent, nonetheless, very real effects of events on a destination and need to be recognised in the overall assessment of the costs and benefits of special events to the host destination. Given measurement difficulties, these so-called 'intangible' costs and benefits are typically discussed as an addendum to a CBA.

On the basis of a CBA, it is possible for the decision-maker to make a judgement of whether the economic benefits of the event are greater than the costs, and to also judge whether the event would represent the best use of the funds, when funds are limited and alternative calls on funds exist. In the case of the Vancouver Winter Olympics 2010, a pre-event CBA forecast that the event would generate net costs to the Province of British Columbia of $1.2 billion. This is despite an economic impact study commissioned by the government of British Columbia that concluded that the event would generate over $10 billion in provincial GDP and more than 200,000 jobs (Shaffer *et al.* 2003). Coates and Humphreys (2003: 347) conclude that the evidence for mega sporting events generating positive economic benefits 'should be considered weak at best'. More studies of events using CBA would be welcome, given the paucity of research using this technique. This raises the question: what technique should be used in event assessment?

Economic modelling or CBA?

While a CBA addresses the extent of net social benefit to the host destination from the event itself, it cannot measure the level of economic activity generated from the event or the wider flow-on effects. On the other hand, while economic impact analysis measures the level of economic activity associated with the event it cannot address the issue of whether the event should receive government support. A CBA picks up a whole range of benefits and costs which would not be picked up in an economic impact model. This includes non-priced effects which do not get included in the markets which are modelled – noise from an event, the consumers' surplus of home patrons, loss of park amenity and traffic congestion associated with the event and so on. The economic impact analysis, in contrast, picks up the increased income to households resulting from the event.

Because CBA and economic impact analysis are quite different in their purpose, method and application, in the area of event assessment at least their results appear to be regarded as not directly comparable with one another. However, some researchers (Mules and Dwyer 2005; Dwyer and Forsyth 2009) have claimed that arguments about the relative merits of economic impact analysis and CBA rest to some extent on a false dilemma. These researchers argue that a CBA would measure benefits and costs, such as consumers' surplus, which would not be picked up in a CGE study, while the CGE study would pick up general equilibrium effects which the partial CBA is not capable of detecting. Thus, in response to the question of which technique should be used for event assessment, these researchers say that the answer is *both*. Since neither technique is completely comprehensive, both have a role in a comprehensive evaluation of event. A method of integrating the two approaches is discussed in Dwyer and Forsyth (2009).

Conclusions

Special events play an important role in the economic and social development of communities internationally. They have the potential to attract visitors, stimulate business activity, generate income and job opportunities in the short term, and garner investment in the longer term. The success or contribution of a particular event should not be measured only by its direct financial contribution. There may be other perceived benefits from events, such as enhancing the image of a city or region, facilitating business networking and civic pride. Events can also result in associated social and cultural benefits to a destination, providing forums for continuing education and training, facilitating technology transfer and so on. On the other hand, all events have a carbon footprint and generate various other forms of pollution and adverse social impacts such as disruption to local business and.community harmony.

The total new expenditure associated with an event is used as the input to an economic model to determine the economic impacts on the destination. Estimates of impacts such as contribution to GDP, value added and employment will depend both on the type of model used and on the particular assumptions that underlie that model. As the discussion makes clear, there are a number of key factors (labour market conditions, potential to improve the terms of trade, and degree of public subsidisation) that are likely to be major determinants of the size and sign of the impacts of larger events. CGE models are well equipped to highlight these determining factors and to enable scenario analysis.

Although CGE modelling is the preferred approach to assessing the economic impact of special events, it will not always be practical to employ a CGE model for every event needing assessment. As a practical response to the situation where economic models are unavailable, it has been recommended that new injected *expenditure* be used as the basis to measure economic performance of the event to the host region. As long as it is understood to be *indicative* of the economic significance of the event, the new expenditure estimate can be an informative key performance measure.

The economic impacts of an event are not the same thing as the economic benefits which arise. Economic impact studies can only estimate the effect on economic variables such as GDP, employment and the like. The impact on GDP is a *gross* measure of the change in value of output as a result of an event. This addition to output normally requires additional inputs, of land, labour and capital, to enable it to be produced. These inputs have a cost, and this cost must be deducted from the change in value of gross output if a measure of the net economic gain is to be made.

Given that governments have alternative uses for funds, it should be expected that any request for government support would need to demonstrate the nature and extent of the benefits to justify the request for funds. There are many potential effects of events that are often not accounted for in a standard economic impact analysis. Event assessments need to be broadened to take, where practicable, a more comprehensive approach embracing not only economic but social and environmental factors. The standard tool of measurement of such effects in order to undertake a holistic or comprehensive evaluation of an event is cost–benefit analysis. On the basis of a CBA, it is possible for the decision-maker to judge whether the economic benefits of the event are greater than the costs, and to also judge whether the event would represent the best use of the funds, when funds are limited and alternative calls on funds exist.

There is common ground between CBA and economic impact analysis of special events, since the two techniques focus on different aspects of the evaluation problem. CBA is the established technique for assessing the wider benefits and costs of a project and, as such, it is an appropriate framework for classification and measurement of the projected outcomes of an event. While CBA would emphasise consumer surplus as a primary source of gains from an event, in the case of larger special events, however, their outcomes are not aimed specifically at providing benefits to local consumers, but rather at attracting tourists and their expenditure from outside the region, requiring economic impact analysis to identify the effects. It would seem then that economic impact analysis can provide important information on what is essentially a major source of benefit of a special event.

References

ACT Auditor General (2002) *ACT Auditor General's Office Performance Audit Report V8 Car Races in Canberra – Costs and Benefits*, Canberra: ACT.

Ahlert, G. (2001) 'The economic effects of the Soccer World Cup 2006 in Germany with regard to different financing', *Economic Systems Research* 13(1, March): 109–27.

Ballard, Charles L., Shoven, John B. and Whalley, John (1985) 'The welfare cost of distortions in the United States tax system: a general equilibrium approach' (June), NBER Working Paper Series, Vol. w1043.

Blake, A. (2005) 'The economic impact of the London 2012 Olympics', research report 2005/5, Christel DeHaan Tourism and Travel Research Institute, Nottingham University.

Bohlmann, H.R. and van Heerden, J.H. (2008) 'Predicting the impact of the 2010 World Cup on South Africa', *International Journal of Sport Management and Marketing* 3(4): 383–96.

Coates, D. and Humphreys, B.R. (2003) 'Professional sports facilities, franchises and urban economic development', *Public Finance and Management* 3(3): 335–57.

Cornelissen, S. (2007) 'Crafting legacies: the changing political economy of global sport and the 2010 FIFA World Cup', *Politikon* 34: 241–59.

Cornelissen, S. and Swart, K. (2006) 'The 2010 Football World Cup as a political construct: the challenge of making good on an African promise', *Sociological Review* 54: 108–23.

Crompton, J.L. (1995) 'Economic impact of sports facilities and events: eleven sources of misapplication', *Journal of Sport Management* 9(1): 14–35.

——(2006) 'Economic impact studies: instruments for political shenanigans?', *Journal of Travel Research* 45: 67–82.

Crompton, J.L. and McKay, S.L. (1994) 'Measuring the economic impact of festivals and events: some myths, misapplications and ethical dilemmas', *Festival Management and Event Tourism* 2(1): 33–43.

Delpy, L. and Li, M. (1998) 'The art and science of conducting economic impact studies', *Journal of Vacation Marketing* 4(3): 230–54.

Dickinson, J., Jones, I. and Leask, A. (2007) 'Event tourism: enhancing destinations and the visitor economy', *International Journal of Tourism Research* 9: 301–2.

Dobson, N., Gratton, C. and Holliday, S. (1997) *Football Came Home: The Economic Impact of Euro 96*, Sheffield: Leisure Industries Research Centre.

Dwyer, L. and Forsyth, P. (1997) 'Measuring the benefits and yield from foreign tourism', *International Journal of Social Economics* 24(1/2/3): 223–36.

——(2009) 'Public sector support for special events', *Eastern Economic Journal* 35(4, Fall): 481–99.

Dwyer, L., Mellor, R., Mistilis, N. and Mules, T. (2000) 'A framework for assessing "tangible" and "intangible" impacts of events and conventions', *Event Management* 6(3): 175–91.

Dwyer, L., Forsyth, P. and Spurr, R. (2004) 'Evaluating tourism's economic effects: new and old approaches', *Tourism Management* 25: 307–17.

——(2005) 'Estimating the impacts of special events on the economy', *Journal of Travel Research* 43: 351–9.

——(2006a) 'Assessing the economic impacts of events: a computable general equilibrium approach', *Journal of Travel Research* 45: 59–66.

——(2006b) 'Assessing the economic impacts of special events', in L. Dwyer and P. Forsyth (eds) *International Handbook of Tourism Economics*, Cheltenham: Edward Elgar.

Dwyer, L., Forsyth, P. and Dwyer, W. (2010) *Tourism Economics and Policy*, Clevedon: Channel View Publications.

Fleischer, A. and Felsenstein, D. (2002) 'Cost–benefit analysis using economic surpluses: a case study of a televised event', *Journal of Cultural Economics* 26(2, May): 139–56.

Getz, D. (1987) 'Events tourism: evaluating the impacts', in J.R.B. Ritchie and C.R. Goeldner (eds) *Travel, Tourism and Hospitality Research: A Handbook for Managers and Researchers*, New York: John Wiley and Sons.

——(2005) *Event Management and Event Tourism*, Elmsford, NY: Cognizant, second edition.

——(2008) 'Event tourism: definition, evolution and research', *Tourism Management* 29(3): 403–28.

Gooroochurn, N. and Sinclair, T. (2005) 'The economics of tourism taxation: evidence from Mauritius', *Annals of Tourism Research* 32(2): 478–98.

Industry Commission (1996) *State and Local Government Assistance to Industry: Report 55*, Canberra: Australian Government Publishing Service.

Jago, L. and Dwyer, L. (2006) *Economic Evaluation of Special Events: A Practitioner's Guide*, Altona, Australia: Common Ground Publishing.

Jago, L. and Shaw, R. (1998) 'Special events: a conceptual and definitional framework', *Festival Management and Event Tourism* 5(1/2): 21–32.

Mabugu, R. and Mohamed, A. (2008) 'The economic impacts of government financing of the 2010 FIFA World Cup', Stellenbosch Economic Working Papers: 08/08.

Madden, J. (2006) 'Economic and fiscal impacts of mega sporting events: a general equilibrium assessment', *Public Finance and Management* 6(3): 346–94.

Matheson, V. (2002) 'Upon further review: an examination of sporting event economic impact studies', *The Sport Journal* 5(1): 1–3.

——(2008) 'Mega-events: the effect of the world's biggest sporting events on local, regional, and national economies', in Dennis Howard and Brad Humphreys (eds) *The Business of Sports, Vol. 1*, Westport, CT: Praeger Publishers, pp. 81–99.

Matheson, V. and Baade, R. (2003) 'Bidding for the Olympics: fool's gold?', in C. Barros, M. Ibrahim and S. Szymanski (eds) *Transatlantic Sport*, London: Edward Elgar.

Mules, T. (1999) 'Estimating the economic impact of an event on a local government area, region, state or territory', *Valuing Tourism Methods and Techniques*, Occasional Paper no. 28, Canberra: Bureau of Tourism Research.

Mules, T. and Dwyer, L. (2005) 'Public sector support for sport tourism events: the role of cost–benefit analysis', *Sport in Society* 8(2, June): 338–55.

Mules, T. and Faulkner, B. (1996) 'An economic perspective on special events', *Tourism Economics* 2(2): 314–29.

O'Brien, D. (2006) 'Event business leveraging: the Sydney 2000 Olympic Games', *Annals of Tourism Research* 33(1): 240–61.

Pillay, U. and Bass, O. (2008) 'Mega-events as a response to poverty reduction: the 2010 FIFA World Cup and its urban development implications', *Urban Forum* 19: 329–46.

——(2009) *Mega-events as a Response to Poverty Reduction: The 2010 World Cup and Urban Development. Development and Dreams: The Urban Legacy of the 2010 Football World Cup*, Cape Town: HSRC Press, pp. 76–95.

Porter, P. (1999) 'Mega-sports events as municipal investments: a critique of impact analysis', in J.L. Fizel, E. Gustafson and L. Hadley (eds) *Sports Economics: Current Research*, New York: Praeger Press.

Rogerson, Christian M.(2009) 'Mega-events and small enterprise development: the 2010 FIFA World Cup opportunities and challenges', *Development Southern Africa* 26(3): 337–52.

Shaffer, M., Greer, A. and Mauboules, C. (2003) 'Olympic costs and benefits', Canadian Centre for Policy Alternatives Publication, February.

Siegfried, J. and Zimbalist, A. (2000) 'The economics of sport teams and their communities', *Journal of Economic Perspectives* 14(3): 95–114.

Thornton, G. (2003) *SA 2010 Soccer World Cup Bid Executive Summary*. Available at www.polity.org.za

——(2007) '2010 Soccer World Cup facts you should know', report by Grant Thornton's Tourism, Hospitality and Leisure consulting group.

Victoria Auditor General (2007) *State Investment in Major Events*, Victoria: Victorian Government Printer, May.

10

Geography and the study of events

C. Michael Hall and Stephen J. Page

Introduction

One of the criticisms sometimes levelled at relatively young subject areas such as Event Studies is that they suffer from a lack of theory which in turn limits their ability to make major contributions to the development of knowledge. This criticism has been particularly strong with respect to the management of large-scale hallmark or mega-events (Grün 2004), where the perceived lack of theory is similar to that which surrounds the management of many large projects. Furthermore, there is a significant 'performance paradox' with many events that may have substantial long-term effects on regional and national economies given the sheer economic size of mega-events (Hall 2010):

> At the same time as many more and much larger infrastructure projects are being proposed and built around the world, it is becoming clear that many such projects have strikingly poor performance records in terms of economy, environment and public support.
>
> *(Flybjerg et al. 2003: 3)*

As Grün (2004) notes, the relative lack of theory is related to, but cannot be sufficiently explained by, the relatively recent beginnings of systematic research and lack of comprehensive empirical data. Therefore, two additional factors were suggested. The first is the 'success syndrome', the second is the dominance of descriptive and normative aspects in event management and Event Studies. In the context of events, the 'success syndrome' addresses the fact that some events have been very successfully run over the short period of hosting the event, although their broader and long-term success remains a moot point. Therefore, the theoretical basis of event project management is sufficient for the term-period of the event, although it is likely to be deficient for addressing the economic, social and environmental concerns that underlie a long-term perspective on events (Grün 2004). The dominance of descriptive and normative aspects that focus on project planning and control techniques, structures and procedures, and behavioural dimensions again means that research are focused on the short term with a relative lack of attention to the implications for the broader environment.

These criticisms are partly focused on the seeming inability of Event Studies to achieve a substantial shift in the thinking associated with the area to move it from an empiricist–rational tradition to one that also adopts a more critical and social constructionist stance in the analysis of event-related phenomenon. However, such criticisms may not be as relevant as they seem at a superficial level because when researchers begin to look at the historiography of different disciplines such as geography and their contribution to the analysis of event-related phenomenon, there is in fact a rich theoretical and empirical tradition that has created a series of studies on events. Many of these studies are not necessarily connected or synthesised into an overall framework, yet they make a valuable contribution to our understandings of events. While there are a limited number of studies produced by geographers that have sought to synthesise these contributions (e.g. Hall 1992; Di Méo 2001, 2005; Waitt 2008) they do not provide a comprehensive account of the more recent forays of geographical inquiry into this fast-expanding area of academic and practitioner research. For this reason, this chapter seeks to outline some of the principal issues, debates and themes within geography that provide a distinctive and often unique contribution to the analysis of events.

But first what do we mean by the term 'geography' and what particular approaches, tools and skills do geographers bring to the study of event-related phenomenon?

What does the geographer study?

The study of geography has a long and rich history in the social sciences (Johnston and Sidaway 2004) and its hallmark features are its concern with place, space and the environment (Hall and Page 2006). Its distinctive contribution to these three elements (and geography of course does not have a monopoly on their analysis) is the way in which the synergies are examined, focusing on how the spatial elements (i.e. locational issues of where, why and, more importantly, who and what) exist in relation to human and physical phenomenon. More recently, human geography has also seen major transformations in the approaches and methods that drive the subject, particularly the issue of social and cultural themes in geographical analysis. For some researchers, this has been termed a 'cultural turn' (Crang 1997; Wilson 2011) or the 'new economic geography' (Lee and Wills 1997), reflecting wider debates in the social sciences that have informed and caused human geography to rethink the theories and epistemologies at the heart of the subject (Barnes 2001). There is also evidence that human geography has begun to move into the traditional remit of management with the development of geographies of management as part of economic geography (Jones 2007). Such repositioning has also reinforced the long critical traditions that exist in geography (Harvey 2002, 2006; Berg 2004; Smith 2005; Blomley 2006; Kwan and Schwanen 2009). Interestingly, critical approaches in geography and the geography of tourism (Britton 1991; Hall 1994; Mullins 1994) predate the adoption of many of these newfound agendas in Tourism Studies (Gibson 2009). The focus on consumption (as well as the production) of event-related phenomena as a critical issue was already well established in the geographical analysis of tourism by the 1980s, especially with respect to the role of mega-events as spectacles of consumption (Ley and Olds 1988). Indeed, calls for the geographical study of consumption were already well established by the mid-1990s (Glennie and Thrift 1992; Crewe and Lowe 1995; Pred 1996).

In view of the synergies between the study of tourism and events (with many geographers studying event tourism as a phenomenon) it is important to identify what types of contribution the geographer can make to the study of events and the synergy with tourism. According to Mitchell (1979: 237), in his discussion of the contributions that geography can make to the investigation of tourism:

The geographer's point-of-view is a trilogy of biases pertaining to place, environment and relationships ... In a conceptual vein the geographer has traditionally claimed the spatial and chorographic aspects as his realm ... The geographer, therefore, is concerned about earth space in general and about place and places in particular. The description, appreciation, and understanding of places is paramount to his thinking although two other perspectives (i.e. environment and relationships) modify and extend the primary bias of place.

This is particularly salient for a number of reasons, not least because events have a spatial context (i.e. they occur at a set point in time and space) and their temporary nature has implications for the way in which this phenomena and its impact on people and the environment is approached. As a transitory phenomenon, there has been less interest within human geography of issues such as events that are not a permanent feature of the landscape, although where events are related to urban re-imaging and regeneration then, as discussed below, researchers have addressed these issues in substantially more depth. Nevertheless, there is also a long-standing and substantial body of applied geographical literature that seeks to identify the economic (Murphy and Carmichael 1991; Borgonovi 2004; Connell and Page 2005), social (Hall and Hodges 1996; Olds 1988, 1989; Barker *et al.* 2002), and environmental impact (Chalkley and Essex 1999a; Hall 1997) of events at various scales (Hall 1992), as well as the spatial pattern of event-related activity (Zelinsky 1994; Oppermann 1996). However, rather than focus on the more applied dimensions of geographical analysis, much of which is detailed elsewhere in the volume, the chapter focuses on some of the more distinctive geographical contributions to the study of events.

Theoretical approaches to the geographical study of events

Event Studies has been characterised by a comparative neglect of the way in which events and festivals transform places and spaces from what are everyday environments 'into temporary environments that contribute to the production, processing and consumption of culture, concentrated in time and space' (Waterman 1998: 54). It is this critical transformation that alters both the place and the landscape in which tourism and leisure-related phenomena such as events occur (Ley and Olds 1988). Whilst Waterman's (1998) study raises many of these issues, it is rather focused on one type of event – the arts festival – and the way it can lead to culture being contested as well as a source of tension where specific groups seek to promote and preserve their culture. Whilst this review is not explicitly focused on the issues of culture one cannot ignore Waterman's (1998: 55) important association between culture and events where culture has become an agent of change 'no longer solely a reflection of material civilisation but rather an active force manipulating images not only into saleable commodities but also to form the basis of tourist and real-estate markets and to inform visions of collective identity' (Waterman 1998: 55). Waterman's comments point to the way in which the study of arts events (and we would argue events *per se*) epitomise many of the contemporary debates in human geography with respect to issues of political economy and radical geography (see Chapter 12 by Hall) as well as the 'cultural turn' in human geography (Gibson and Kong 2005; Gotham 2005a, 2005b; Evans 2007; Bianchi 2009). Here, the distinction has blurred between the conventional notion of social and cultural geography as new themes such as tourism and events have become focal points for research, reflecting a shift towards the study of the interplay between consumption and production in a spatially contingent context (Gibson and Connell 2007, 2011; Grundy and Boudreau 2008). This is especially the case in spatial settings where events characterise the out-of-home forms of leisure (as opposed to the in-home forms except for where they are televised and consumed within the home – see Page and Connell 2010 for more detail on this conventional distinction of leisure consumption). What characterises the event and its significance is the way it transforms everyday living and also serves as a means to reinterpret and represent locality and identity (Guan 2001; Lee 2001; Teather 2001; Corr 2003; Pettersson 2003; Schnell 2003; Holloway 2004; Greene 2005; Morris and Cant 2006).

As Waterman (1998: 56) aptly argues

> a conventional approach to festivals in human geography in which the arts festival was little more than a transient cultural event with a measurable impact on the landscape, environment and economy might simply have been mapped or modelled ... But festivals are cultural artefacts which are not simply bought and consumed but which are also accorded meaning through their active incorporation into people's lives ... They epitomise the representation of contemporary accumulation through spectacle.

This quotation embodies an important transformation from description and analysis to more in-depth interpretation and a critical reasoning associated with theoretical developments in postmodernism and urban theory (Warren 1996), which have only slowly permeated research in tourism (Ashworth and Page 2011). In addition, this marks a recognition of the importance of different forms of consumption under postmodernity and the significant place of the spectacle of events and their meaning and place in leisure activities of modern-day consumers (Ley and Olds 1988).

Whilst researchers may well seek to differentiate events in terms of their elite or popular cultural forms, a defining characteristic of events of all types is that they are ephemeral in time but may have distinct spatial forms in the urban landscape (Hall and Page 2006). If one begins to interpret the role of events and festivals in particular, research in human geography has suggested that popular festivals may have a manipulative role to neutralise conflict in the urban environment. For example, Jackson's (1992) study argues that the Notting Hill Carnival in London acts as a vehicle for expression of underlying political tensions as one of Europe's largest street festivals. These types of festivals have deep roots that can be dated to the Caribbean, where carnival was steeped in Afro-Caribbean history, slavery and celebration (De Oliveira 2008).

Carnival has been a long-standing theme in geographical research on events both in its more traditional religious forms and as a modern secular event (Spencer 2003). The inversion of normality that is part of carnival has arguably been an important connection with the interest of geographers in the role of events in confirming and representing ethnic (Burnley 2010; McCleary 2010), sexual and other identities, including queer theory and the development of queer geography (Jones 2010), as well as the role of events as a form of political opposition (Bogad 2010). Nevertheless, over time what was once an event of opposition may become an event of promotion (Markwell 2002).

Such issues highlight the critical relationship between events, place and identity in much contemporary geographical analysis of events (Brettell and Nibbs 2009). However, they perform different roles in relation to the places which host them, reflecting the motivations, traditions and political differences they evoke (Comeaux 2010; Eisinger 2000). However, in theoretical terms, Waterman (1998: 60) connected the growing interest by geographers in place and the way events have been used to drive place promotion, as

> the cultural facets of festivals cannot be divorced from the commercial interests of tourism, regional and local economy and place promotion. Selling the place to the wider world or selling the festival as an inseparable part of the place rapidly becomes a significant facet of most festivals.

151

In simple terms, events have been used as a facet of boosterism to raise the place image (Boyle 1997; Waitt 2001). However, increasingly, identity and culture are being highly commodified for urban re-imaging and regeneration purposes and are inextricably related to the hosting of events at various scales, with notable examples of geographical research including the European Capital of Culture (Clohessy 1994; Jones and Wilks-Heeg 2004; Richards and Wilson 2004); García 2004a, 2004b, 2005; Deffner and Labrianidis 2005; Griffiths 2006; Herrero *et al.* 2006; Boland 2007, 2008, 2010a, 2010b; Connelly 2007; Paskaleva *et al.* 2009; Quinn 2009; World Fairs and Expositions (Ley and Olds 1988; Gold and Gold 2005; Jansson and Lagerkvist 2009; Gotham 2011), Olympic Games (Hall 1996, 2001; Chalkley and Essex 1999a, 1999b; Waitt 1999, 2001; Whitelegg 2000; Shoval 2002; Tufts 2004; García 2004b; McCallum *et al.* 2005; Smith and Himmelfarb 2007) or other hallmark events (Hall 1998, 2006; Gotham 2005b; Smith and Fox 2007; Coaffee 2008; Hall and Sharples 2008; Matheson 2010; Gibson and Connell 2011). Indeed, even the rights to host events such as the Eurovision Song Contest can lead to substantial place competition (Andersson and Niedomysl 2010).

Events, globalisation and the new international economic geography of competitiveness

The analysis of globalisation by geographers has seen a focus on economic, technological and political processes and how these have led to economic restructuring in mature capitalist countries and the increased mobility of global capital. For example, this is manifest in the relocation of industries from western countries to low cost-of-production economies (e.g. South and South East Asia), where capital seeks to maximise profitability by reducing costs. The corollary for the urban industrial centres of the developed world has been a major transformation of the economic structure of the main centres of production and a shift to new economic forms such as services and the leisure, tourism and event economy.

An important part of this process has been the development of a discourse of competitiveness for countries, cities and places of all kinds (Connelly 2007; Hall 2007). The focus on competitiveness has emerged out of the belief that globalisation has created a world of intense place competition. As Bristow (2005: 285) observes, 'Competitiveness is portrayed as the means by which regional economies are externally validated in an era of globalization, such that there can be no principled objection to policies and strategies deemed to be competitiveness enhancing, whatever their indirect consequences.' For example, according to Kotler *et al.* (1993: 346) one of the leading texts of place competition, 'In a borderless economy, [places] will emerge as the new actors on the world scene.' According to Kotler *et al.* (1993), we are living in a time of 'place wars' in which places are competing for their economic survival with other places and regions not only in their own country but throughout the world.

> All places are in trouble now, or will be in the near future. The globalization of the world's economy and the accelerating pace of technological changes are two forces that require all places to learn how to compete. Places must learn how to think more like businesses, developing products, markets, and customers.
>
> *(Kotler* et al. *1993: 346)*

Nevertheless, while all this is being done there is still substantial confusion 'as to what the concept actually means and how it can be effectively operationalised ... policy acceptance of the existence of regional competitiveness and its measurement appears to have run ahead of a number of fundamental theoretical and empirical questions' (Bristow 2005: 286).

One of the major issues facing places that engage in competitive strategies is, of course, that not everyone can be a winner. There are, therefore, both benefits and problems inherent in such place competition, within which hallmark events are clearly embedded. However, it is significant that within the regional development literature, events are primarily seen as part of an imitative 'low-road' policy in contrast to a 'high-road' knowledge-based development strategy. It is apparent that events are perceived as providing a quick return on investment for funders of event development as a means of economic development where funding is based on short-term measurable gains. Where the events are large mega-events then the critical debate hinges upon the legacy benefits or costs to the locality and state. The problem with these event-related gains is that they are transient and highly questionable in terms of the measures used to calculate employment gains and long-run economic growth: the theory behind calculating such gains may indicate that full-time employment was required to meet the needs of an event, but this would normally only be for the duration of the staging and running of the event. Such employment is not normally converted into full-time employment unless there are clear legacy outcomes and an ongoing commitment to develop the event capacity and capability. Even so, this has not negated against economic development agencies and local authorities supporting events for their perceived economic benefits with evaluation studies claiming these economic wins. Yet all too often this is based on incomplete knowledge of the place-benefits and very naive models of economic impacts with small sample surveys undertaken to justify the initial pump-priming investment. Such evaluations also lack any spatial component to understand the winners and losers at different spatial scales. This is part of the 'win' culture and competitiveness of places that occurs at different scales from the international scale down to the local level, with town pitted against town in seeking to attract visitor spending through event activity to revitalise its image as a lively and dynamic place in which to live and invest.

Malecki (2004: 1103) argues 'The disadvantages of competition mainly concern the perils that low-road strategies build so that no strengths can prevail over the long-term, which presents particular difficulties for regions trying to catch up in the context of territorial competition based on knowledge.' Low-road strategies are regarded as being focused on 'traditional' location factors such as land, labour, capital, infrastructure and location; more intangible factors, such as intellectual capital and institutional capacity are secondary. Such low-road strategies of regional competitiveness are bound up with the property-oriented growth machines that focus on the packaging of the place product, re-imaging strategies and the gaining of media attention (Hall 2007). With respect to urban place competition, for example, investment in infrastructure is 'similar from city to city' with respect to meetings and conventions, and sporting and cultural events, because they are aimed at the same markets with few cities being able to 'forgo competition in each of these sectors' (Judd 2003: 14). Such a situation was described by Harvey (1989) as being indicative of 'urban entrepreneurialism', a concept which has proven influential in theorising of utilisation of events by urban growth coalitions (Boyle 1994; MacLeod 2002; Owen 2002):

> Many of the innovations and investments designed to make particular cities more attractive as cultural and consumer centers have quickly been imitated elsewhere, thus rendering any competitive advantage within a system of cities ephemeral ... Local coalitions have no option, given the coercive laws of competition, except to keep ahead of the game thus engendering leap-frogging innovations in lifestyles, cultural forms, products and service mixes, even institutional and political forms if they are to survive.
>
> (Harvey 1989: 12)

153

From the late 1990s the fusion of urban entrepreneurialism with the neo-liberal political agenda provided the ideological justification for place competitive re-imaging and regeneration strategies including the hosting of mega-events (Hall and Hubbard 1996; Hubbard 1996; Peck and Tickell 2002). Nevertheless, the sustainability of place competitive strategies that utilise high-profile events, let alone their real economic benefits, is increasingly questionable (Lowes 2004; Whitson and Horne 2006). For example, Swyngedouw (1992) noted that the 'frenzied' and 'unbridled' competition for cultural capital, such as through cultural events and the cultural economy, results in over-accumulation and the threat of devaluation. Even Kotler *et al.* (1993), who provided the standard case text for place marketing, acknowledged that 'the escalating competition … for business attraction has the marks of a zero-sum game or worse, a negative-sum game, in that the winner ultimately becomes the loser' (1993: 15). The desire to host events and the requirements of having to constantly develop new or upgrade existing sports and visitor infrastructure has meant that cities 'face the possibility of being caught in a vicious cycle of have to provide larger subsidies to finance projects that deliver even fewer public benefits' (Leitner and Garner 1993: 72). Yet the remarkable thing is that, some thirty years on from the first wave of geographical critique of the low long-term value of events as a means of place competitiveness, many cities continue to bid for them and seek to utilise them as a response to the problems of economic restructuring and the mobility of capital (Waitt 2008; Hall and Wilson 2011).

The use of events as a response to the negative effects of globalisation on places has, even despite the substantial number of criticisms of the use of events as an economic development strategy (Gotham 2011), created a global market for the event industry as a perceived substitute for lost employment. This situation also illustrates the shift to consumer services and the link between globalisation and new consumption and production practices. Events, and associated infrastructure and real estate development, provide a visible transformation of many cities with the creation of new fixed infrastructure such as stadia, event and convention centres, and associated accommodation, cultural and leisure facilities to 'compete' for and host the increasingly mobile capital of visitors, businesses and residents. Therefore, place competition and promotion via the bidding for and hosting of events has a very real physical effect on the urban landscape as well as on visual consumption and place experience, both of which are significant recent themes in human geography (Davidson and Milligan 2004; Thrift 2004; Thien 2005; Tolia-Kelly 2006). Moreover, events are deliberately integrated into strategic processes of place branding in which the physical spaces and the accompanying experience that people have of them is seen as the physical evidence of the place brand. Although some more critical authors regard such a process as part of the geography of spectacle (Pinder 2000; Gold and Gold 2005; Butcher 2010), for others it is an essential part of the need for cities and places to brand and market themselves in order to become (or remain) competitive (Kotler and Gertner 2002; Page and Hall 2003). Nevertheless, the attempted creation of a 'unique selling proposition' for a location via the use of events and an associated regeneration strategy is not unproblematic, with there being at least four differences between branding a product and branding a city through the use of events and flagship developments (Hall 2008; Jensen 2005):

- There is a difference in the number of stakeholders and their related interests; branding a city or a place includes a complex web of preferences.
- It is a hard task to negotiate a legitimate local value base with local participation. This is almost never an issue when branding a product.
- Branding a city or a place usually has to follow the paths of existing notions or historical identities of a place. Most products do not have the same depth of history or associations to consider.

- The consumers of an urban brand are often more diverse than the consumers of a normal product since urban branding has to serve diverse groups of potential investors, residents and tourists.

The development of urban brand identities via place marketing and promotional strategies and tactics, such as media campaigns and the use of events to gain increased media attention, is part of the 'software' by which brands are developed (Evans 2003) and expressed aesthetically (Julier 2005). However, while often expressed in terms of symbols and values, brands ultimately also need to be connected with some tangible dimension in order to be 'believable'. In the case of place brands this is the physical manifestation of place in terms of architecture, design and the lived experience of a location, including event-related infrastructure and associated regeneration projects. In essence, this is the 'hardware' of place brands (Hall 2008).

The word 'scape' refers to a view or a scene as well as to realist and abstract representations of a view (Hall 2008). For example, Highmore (2005) uses the notion of a cityscape to emphasise both the material and the symbolic dimensions of the contemporary city. In marketing and related literature, the notion of a scape has been utilised to refer to the physical environment that a consumer experiences and which is, often, deliberately produced so as to encourage consumption, provide a specific set of experiences or at least satisfy a consumer's desires (e.g. Julier 2005). Sherry (1998: 112) uses the term 'brandscape' to refer to the 'material and symbolic environment that consumers build with marketplace products, images, and messages, that they invest with local meaning, and whose totemic significance largely shapes the adaptation consumers make to the modern world'. Brandscapes are utilised by companies such as Disney and Starbucks to provide a symbolic retail space that is familiar to consumers no matter where they are in the world and that also enables them to physically inhabit and experience brandspace (Thompson and Arsel 2004).

At a broader urban scale it is possible to conceive of a 'consumptionscape' (Guliz and Belk 1996) or an 'experiencescape' (O'Dell 2005) to refer to the creation of new planned experiential environments in urban areas as a way to generate new spaces of material and visual consumption and reinforce place brands. Indeed, such elements are integral to the visitor experiential strategies that focus on the creation of new relational spaces that accompany mega-events such as International Expositions, Olympic Games and other large-scale events (Wainwright and Ansell 2008; Weller 2008). Similarly, although from more of a cultural event perspective, Julier (2005) uses the term 'urban designscapes' to explore the use of the regeneration of areas within cities to create a place-identity. Urban designscapes are defined as 'the pervasive and multilevel use of the symbolic capital of design in identifying and differentiating urban agglomerations' (Julier 2005: 874) with reference not only to brand design, architecture, events and urban planning but also the productive processes of design promotion, organisation and policy-making. Although, as Hall (2008) notes, the numerous scapes of the city may be somewhat confusing, they do highlight the way in which the physical environment is consciously designed and manipulated in order to enhance atmospherics for consumers, not just in retail environments but in the very fabric of urban space itself and the aesthetic experiences and social interactions that occur within it.

The focus on creating positive visitor experiences in event strategies is also significant for the design of events (see Chapter 18 by Berridge on event design) and the infrastructure they directly occupy. For example, with respect to sports events 'there has been a quantum shift in marketing strategies over the past few decades, with teams and franchises moving from a product orientation focused on providing quality sport, to a service orientation focused on providing a quality entertainment experience' within the context of the sportscape (Hill and Green

2000: 146). Given that the consumer entertainment experience has become the focus of sporting events (Wakefield *et al.* 1996), the role of the sportscape is to shape the customer experience through facilitating activities, enticing entry, encouraging lengthy stays and ultimately contributing to the satisfaction of consumers (Pine and Gilmore 1999). By encouraging a positive atmosphere and interactions between customers, well-designed sportscapes have the potential to increase customer satisfaction and the likelihood of attendance at future events (Hill and Green 2000). Nevertheless, while eventscapes may have an immediate novelty effect, the potential effect of consumer arousal provided from the existence of new event facilities may diminish over time (John and Sheard 2000). Interestingly, in contrast some events may exist for a substantial period of time utilising the same space, and it is to some of these types of events that we will now turn.

The historical geography and analysis of events

Events are not a new phenomenon despite their comparatively recent discovery in social science and geography, although Allix's (1922) study highlighted the overriding significance of fairs as places which attracted gatherings of people. In Europe many such fairs can be dated to at least the thirteenth century, and in mediaeval England they were authorised by royal grant (Royal Charter) where they have been studied in relation to their association with markets (Hall and Sharples 2008). In their basic forms, fairs and markets were an early form of event as they attracted people to gather and transact business on a peripatetic basis. Even where ancient and mediaeval fairs existed, the relationship to events as community-based affairs, focused on trade, markets of entertainment or a combination of each produced distinctive historical geographies across Europe.

Many of the established historical geography texts identify the motivation and scale of such events along with their impact as regular or scheduled events as part of the yearly calendar. In the UK, mediaeval fairs such as the Barnstaple, Cambridge, Hull and Loughborough Fairs had traditions (along with many other local examples), of combining urban and rural economic activities. These combined entertainment typified in their nineteenth-century characterisation in the novels of Thomas Hardy that often include a fair. The provision of popular entertainment, which predates many of the commercialised later forms of entertainment, such as the theatre and sporting events, contributed to the heritage and culture of individual places (Yli-Jokipii 1999). The hosting of fairs dramatically transformed the locations in a temporary manner in much the same way as modern-day events do (Royo 1999). As with many methodologies used in historical geography, their application to the study of events and fairs, in particular, illustrate two distinct features: *continuity* in terms of the maintenance and ongoing hosting of fairs, most notably the Nottingham Goose Fair, which have seen a degree of resurgence, and some degree of *change* based on traditional sites. Such historical analyses also point to the importance of looking to the past as a basis to begin to understand the way in which place and space featured in the transformational effect of events in past and present times and the growing recognition of how such traditions can be harnessed for cultural event development (Johnson 1999; Bærenholdt and Haldrup 2006; Ray *et al.* 2006; Hall and Sharples 2008). As Richards and Palmer (2010) suggest, some cities as sites for event development have given rise to what they term 'eventful cities'. One good example of this is the European Cities of Culture programme over the last twenty years, which has drawn upon past and present cultural forms, and where competing bids between cities are based on their ability to be eventful.

As fairs, markets, civic ceremonies and religious festivals were a source of local pride and activity to attract visitors and traders at a more local and regional scale in mediaeval and subsequent times (Royo 1999), the same type of process of using events now sees places at a city level competing to be eventful as part of the globalised competition for people, investment, trade and an enhanced image and economy (see Ashworth and Page 2011 for more detail). In some respects, eventfulness is the natural corollary of the local-scale event and place-making, where a Royal Charter bestowed the opportunity to host a regular event. Winning a City of Culture competition and being a venue for event development has a similar role in a more complex postmodern society where consumption and urban development can be leveraged to grow the local economy. But as the critics of event- and tourism-related development suggest, seeking eventful approaches may be a last-ditch attempt for many cities and places that now believe they have few alternative economic development options. It is rarely framed in this respect, with place image development seen as a major benefit but often at a huge public cost, and not always with the intended social and economic benefits, as noted in the introduction. Such a situation may highlight the importance of understanding the relationships between power and interests in hosting events (see Chapter 12) that point to the prevailing hegemony associated with those controlling and directing the development process of eventfulness and the political objectives (Hall 2006).

So where does this leave us in the theorising of events and their historical corollaries? In one respect, these debates mirror the debates on the history of leisure and the debates on the way historical analysis and narratives suggest distinct eras and epochs, each of which has distinct forms of leisure associated with specific forms of events. From the pre-industrial to industrial/ modern and postmodern eras, events have persisted as a form of expression of the vitality of places and communities albeit adapting to and evolving in the different historical eras depending upon the effect of different processes (e.g. regulation in the Victorian period) where sponta- neous and working-class events were seen as being distracting and diversionary to the main purpose of the Christian work ethic – productive labour and output. The pre-industrial to industrial society transition saw a decline in traditional community-based events epitomised by Billinge's (1996) paper, 'A time and place for everything', where the regulation of events to allocate them to their correct place and banning of certain street events created the notion of events we are familiar with today – their provision in a more regulated and organised setting. This process was accelerated by the commercialisation of sports events by different forms of capital to meet the working-class demand for events in their leisure time, reflecting the twin processes of continuity and change albeit as the location and venues of events saw a transition from the street to stadia and formal settings. Therefore, what we can establish from the existing theoretical analyses of events by geographers and social historians is that they perform a crucial role in the social life of urban and rural communities, with many based on cultural traditions. What is different and of interest in theoretical terms in current-day events is the manner in which place and space have been transposed, so that the event is now a new temporary form of space that has different forms and shapes in the postmodern environment: the landscapes, signs and symbols of the event have assumed a new meaning, as the era of mass marketing from the 1920s and 1930s has been revitalised (although see Hagen 2008). These forms of marketing have been globalised and refined using branding and the concept of uniqueness and experience to realign events to a special quality that is place- and space-specific but primarily-event focused in both a real-time world setting and increasingly in a media-transmitted form.

Conclusion

This chapter has highlighted how some of the main approaches in human geography can inform theorisation and empirical analysis of the hosting of events. The role of physical geography and the environmental–sustainability debate has remained virtually absent from our analysis, owing to the limited number of perspectives they have offered. Although the more applied dimensions of geographical research have long informed Event Studies (Hall 1992), it is notable that much of the more critical geographical discourse has been of only marginal interest. Yet, as this chapter has demonstrated, geographical literature clearly provides a rich resource for better understanding both the context within which events are held and their effects on the space around them. The fact that events temporarily transform everyday spaces utilising a unique and celebratory or entertainment function should be a key research agenda for human geography, especially when the temporality of events is considered (see Chapter 27 by Evans on the night-time city). In addition, the development of designed environments in association with the hosting of events may also shed light on the nature of the visitor experience as well as their transformation of areas within cities (see Chapter 26 by Shaw).

Significantly, much geographical research on events, particularly with respect to place marketing, regeneration and the urban experience, has also been developed with little reference to the contemporary Event Studies literature. This is a major weakness that has clearly not assisted in a greater theorisation of the area. Instead, there is a clearly well-developed set of events literature that is theorised in terms of wider social science concerns such as globalisation, consumption and the construction of identity, rather than a narrow managerialism. It is also important to note that as such the geographical contribution to the understanding of events with respect to such fields as urban planning and regional studies, and particularly the role of events in regeneration, is therefore substantial and is arguably becoming even more important at a time of continued place competition. Event research has a great deal of synergy with the contribution which the geographer has and may make to event-related research, not least because of the concern with place, space and environment as articulated by Hall and Page (2006) in relation to tourism: this can be applied to the event domain. In fact, we argue that geographical perspectives of events may even become pivotal for the future justification of events – where events are developed on the premise of benefiting the economy of an area or upon regeneration objectives. All too often, economic evaluation studies point to an overall figure/revenue to a destination. However, what is questionable is *where* and *how* that revenue has filtered into a local economy. Spatial understanding of events and economic impacts is crucial in identifying whether events can create wealth where it is needed (particularly if public sector funds have been used to fund events). Or is it the case that events merely boost income to already established multi-national corporations and large business interests and in thriving tourism areas at the expense of SMEs, to the detriment of areas that need regeneration? To even begin to answer these fundamental questions, we need to embrace the skill set of geographers (Hall and Page 2009) to look behind broad-brush economic studies so that a greater degree of fine-tuning occurs to identify impacts and spatial analysis of these impacts. This is particularly the case in a period of austerity in many western countries where events are seeking to attract a diminishing pot of public funds. All too often the public sector is unable to view such issues in a spatial manner, which is why some assistance from geographers is invaluable in policy analysis and evaluation of event impacts so that the benefits get targeted where they are needed.

Further reading

Andersson, I. and Niedomysl, T. (2010) 'Clamour for glamour? City competition for hosting the Swedish tryouts to the Eurovision Song Contest', *Tijdschrift voor Economische en Sociale Geografie* 101(2): 111–25. (Good study of the link between events and competitiveness.)

Connell, J. and Page, S.J. (2005) 'Evaluating the economic and spatial effects of an event: the case of the World Medical and Health Games', *Tourism Geographies* 7: 63–85. (Provides a good overview of a more spatial approach to event analysis.)

Gold, J.R. and Gold, M.M. (2005) *Cities of Culture: Staging International Festivals and the Urban Agenda, 1851–2000*, Aldershot: Ashgate. (Good overview of some of the issues associated with the use of large events for urban regeneration and promotion.)

Gotham, K.F. (2005) 'Theorizing urban spectacles', *City: Analysis of Urban Trends, Culture, Theory, Policy, Action* 9: 225–46. (Excellent discussion of urban theory in relation to events.)

Hall, C.M. (2006) 'Urban entrepreneurship, corporate interests and sports mega-events: the thin policies of competitiveness within the hard outcomes of neoliberalism', *The Sociological Review*, 54(Issue Supplement s2): 59–70. (Relates hosting of events to urban entrepreneurialism and neoliberal discourse.)

Hall, C.M. and Sharples, L. (eds) (2008) *Food and Wine Festivals and Events Around the World: Development, Management and Markets*, Oxford: Butterworth-Heinemann. (Provides examples of a range of different geographical approaches to the study of events.)

Ley, D. and Olds, K. (1987) 'Landscape as spectacle: World's Fairs and the culture of heroic consumption', *Environment and Planning D: Society and Space* 6: 191–212. (Classic study that also indicates the long interest of geographers in the relationship between events and consumption.)

Olds, K. (1988) 'Urban mega-events, evictions and housing rights: the Canadian case', *Current Issues in Tourism* 1: 2–46. (A benchmark examination of the impacts of mega-events on housing that remains relevant to the present day.)

Smith, A. and Fox, T. (2007) 'From "event-led" to "event-themed" regeneration: the 2002 Commonwealth Games legacy programme', *Urban Studies* 44(5–6): 1125–43. (Very good discussion of how the notion of an event legacy is linked to regeneration.)

Waitt, G. (2008) 'Urban festivals: geographies of hype, helplessness and hope', *Geography Compass* 2(2): 513–37. (A useful review of the hosting of urban festivals and their roles.)

References

Allix, A. (1922) 'The geography of fairs: illustrated by old-world examples', *Geographical Review* 12(4): 532–69.

Andersson, I. and Niedomysl, T. (2010) 'Clamour for glamour? City competition for hosting the Swedish tryouts to the Eurovision Song Contest', *Tijdschrift voor Economische en Sociale Geografie* 101(2): 111–25.

Ashworth, G. and Page, S.J. (2011) 'Progress in tourism management: urban tourism research: recent progress and current paradoxes', *Tourism Management* 32(1): 1–15.

Bærenholdt, J.O. and Haldrup, M. (2006) 'Mobile networks and place making in cultural tourism. Staging Viking ships and rock music in Roskilde', *European Urban and Regional Studies* 13(3): 209–24.

Balsas, C.J.L. (2004) 'City centre regeneration in the context of the 2001 European Capital of Culture in Porto, Portugal', *Local Economy* 19(4): 396–410.

Barker, M., Page, S.J. and Meyer, D. (2002) 'Modeling tourism crime: the 2000 America's Cup,' *Annals of Tourism Research* 29: 762–82.

Barnes, T.J. (2001) 'Retheorizing economic geography: from the quantitative revolution to the "cultural turn"', *Annals of the Association of American Geographers* 91: 546–65.

Berg, L. (2004) 'Scaling knowledge: towards a critical geography of critical geographies', *Geoforum* 35: 553–8.

Bianchi, R. (2009) 'The "cultural turn" in tourism studies: a radical critique', *Tourism Geographies* 11: 484–504.

Billinge, M. (1996) 'A time and place for everything: an essay on recreation, re-creation and the Victorians', *Journal of Historical Geography* 22(4): 443–59.

Blomley, N. (2006) 'Uncritical critical geography?', *Progress in Human Geography* 30: 87–94.

Bogad, L.M. (2010) 'Carnivals against capital: radical clowning and the global justice movement', *Social Identities* 16: 537–57.

Boland, P. (2007) 'Unpacking the theory–policy interface of local economic development: an analysis of Cardiff and Liverpool', *Urban Studies* 44: 1019–39.

——(2008) 'The construction of images of people and place: labelling Liverpool and stereotyping Scousers', *Cities* 25(6): 355–69.

——(2010a) '"Capital of culture – you must be having a laugh!" Challenging the official rhetoric of Liverpool as the 2008 European cultural capital', *Social and Cultural Geography* 11(7): 627–45.

——(2010b) 'Sonic geography, place and race in the formation of local identity: Liverpool and Scousers', *Geografiska Annaler, Series B: Human Geography* 92(1): 1–22.

Borgonovi, F. (2004) 'Performing arts attendance: an economic approach', *Applied Economics* 36: 1871–85.

Boyle, M. (1994) 'The politics of urban entrepreneurialism in Glasgow', *Political Geography* 25: 453–70.
——(1997) 'Civic boosterism in the politics of local economic development – "institutional positions" and "strategic orientations" in the consumption of hallmark events', *Environment and Planning A* 29: 1975–97.
Brettell, C.B. and Nibbs, F. (2009) 'Lived hybridity: second-generation identity construction through college festival', *Identities* 16: 1547–3384.
Bristow, G. (2005) 'Everyone's a "winner": problematising the discourse of regional competitiveness', *Journal of Economic Geography* 5: 285–304.
Britton, S. (1991) 'Tourism, capital, and place: towards a critical geography of tourism', *Environment and Planning D: Society and Space* 9: 451–78.
Burnley, I. (2010) 'Submergence, persistence and identity: generations of German origin in the Barossa and Adelaide Hills, South Australia', *Geographical Research* 48: 427–39.
Butcher, M. (2010) 'Navigating "New" Delhi: moving between difference and belonging in a globalising city', *Journal of Intercultural Studies* 31: 507–24.
Chalkley, B. and Essex, S. (1999a) 'Sydney 2000: The "Green Games"?', *Geography* 84(365): 299–307.
——(1999b) 'Urban development through hosting international events: a history of the Olympic Games', *Planning Perspectives* 14(4): 369–94.
Clohessy, L. (1994) 'Culture and urban tourism: Dublin 1991 – European City of Culture', in U. Kockel (ed.) *Culture, Tourism and Development: The Case of Ireland*, Liverpool: Liverpool University Press, pp. 189–96.
Coaffee, J. (2008) 'Sport, culture and the modern state: emerging themes in stimulating urban regeneration in the UK', *International Journal of Cultural Policy* 14(4): 377–97.
Comeaux, M. (2010) 'Photojournal: the Cajun Mardi Gras in southwest Louisiana', *Focus on Geography* 53(1): 14–23.
Connell, J. and Page, S.J. (2005) 'Evaluating the economic and spatial effects of an event: the case of the World Medical and Health Games', *Tourism Geographies* 7: 63–85.
Connelly, G. (2007) 'Testing governance – a research agenda for exploring urban tourism competitiveness policy: the case of Liverpool 1980–2000', *Tourism Geographies* 9: 84–114.
Corr, R. (2003) 'Ritual, knowledge, and the politics of identity in Andean festivities', *Ethnology* 42: 39–54.
Crang, P. (1997) 'Cultural turns and the (re)constitution of economic geography: Introduction to section one', in R. Lee and J. Wills (eds) *Geographies of Economies*, London: Arnold, pp. 3–15.
Crewe, L. and Lowe, M. (1995) 'Gap on the map? Towards a geography of consumption and identity', *Environment and Planning A* 27: 1877–98.
Davidson, J. and Milligan, C. (2004) 'Embodying emotion sensing space: introducing emotional geographies', *Social and Cultural Geography* 5(4): 523–32.
Deffner, A.M. and Labrianidis, L. (2005) 'Planning culture and time in a mega-event: Thessaloniki as the European City of Culture in 1997', *International Planning Studies* 10(3–4): 241–64.
De Oliveira, C.D.M. (2008) 'Carnivalization and touristic complexity: construction of rituals landscapes in events in the State of Ceará [Carnavalização e complexidade turística: formação de paisagens rituais em eventos no estado do ceará]', *RA'E GA – O Espaco Geografico em Analise* 12(16): 37–46.
Di Méo, G. (2001) 'The geographical meaning of festivities [Le sens géographique des fêtes]', *Annales de Geographie* 622: 624–46.
——(2005) 'The geographical implications of festival renewals [Le renouvellement des fêtes et des festivals, ses implications géographiques]', *Annales de Geographie* 643: 227–43.
Eisinger, P. (2000) 'The politics of bread and circuses: building the city for the visitor class', *Urban Affairs Review* 35: 316–33.
Evans, G. (2003) 'Hard-branding the cultural city – from Prado to Prada', *International Journal of Urban and Regional Research* 27: 417–41.
Evans, O. (2007) 'Border exchanges: the role of the European Film Festival', *Journal of Contemporary European Studies* 15: 23–33.
Flybjerg, B., Bruzelius, B. and Rothengatter, W. (2003) *Megaprojects and Risk: An Anatomy of Ambition*, Cambridge: Cambridge University Press.
García, B. (2004a) 'Cultural policy and urban regeneration in western European cities: lessons from experience, prospects for the future', *Local Economy* 19(4): 312–26.
——(2004b) 'Urban regeneration, arts programming and major events: Glasgow 1990, Sydney 2000 and Barcelona 2004,' *International Journal of Cultural Policy* 10: 103–18.
——(2005) 'Deconstructing the city of culture: the long-term cultural legacies of Glasgow 1990', *Urban Studies* 42: 841–68.

Gibson, C. (2009) 'Geographies of tourism: critical research on capitalism and local livelihoods', *Progress in Human Geography* 33: 527–34.

Gibson, C. and Connell, J. (2007) 'Music, tourism and the transformation of Memphis', *Tourism Geographies* 9: 160–90.

——(eds) (2011) *Festival Places: Revitalising Rural Australia*, Bristol: Channel View Publications.

Gibson, C. and Kong, L. (2005) 'Cultural economy: a critical review', *Progress in Human Geography* 29: 541–61.

Glennie, P.D. and Thrift, N.J. (1992) 'Modernity, urbanism, and modern consumption', *Environment and Planning D: Society and Space* 10: 423–43.

Gold, J.R. and Gold, M.M. (2005) *Cities of Culture: Staging International Festivals and the Urban Agenda, 1851–2000*, Aldershot: Ashgate.

Gotham, K.F. (2005a) 'Theorizing urban spectacles', *City: Analysis of Urban Trends, Culture, Theory, Policy, Action* 9: 225–46.

——(2005b) 'Marketing Mardi Gras: commodification, spectacle and the political economy of tourism in New Orleans', *Urban Studies* 39: 1735–56.

——(2011) 'Resisting urban spectacle: the 1984 Louisiana World Exposition and the contradictions of mega events', *Urban Studies* 48: 197–214.

Greene, V. (2005) 'Dealing with diversity: Milwaukee's multiethnic festivals and urban identity, 1840–1940', *Journal of Urban History* 31: 820–49.

Griffiths, R. (2006) 'City/culture discourses: evidence from the competition to select the European Capital of Culture', *European Planning Studies* 14: 415–30.

Grün, O. (2004) *Taming Giant Projects: Management of Multi-organization Enterprises*, Berlin: Springer-Verlag.

Grundy, J. and Boudreau, J.-A. (2008) '"Living with culture": creative citizenship practices in Toronto', *Citizenship Studies* 12(4): 347–63.

Guan, Y.S. (2001) 'Producing locality: space, houses and public culture in a Hindu festival in Malaysia', *Contributions to Indian Sociology* 35(1): 33–64.

Guliz, G. and Belk, R.W. (1996) 'I'd like to buy the world a Coke: consumptionscapes in the less affluent world', *Journal of Consumer Policy* 19: 271–304.

Hagen, J. (2008) 'Parades, public space, and propaganda: the Nazi culture parades in Munich', *Geografiska Annaler, Series B: Human Geography* 90: 349–67.

Hall, C.M. (1992) *Hallmark Tourist Events*, Chichester: John Wiley.

——(1994) *Tourism and Politics: Policy, Power and Place*, Chichester: John Wiley and Sons.

——(1996) 'Hallmark events and urban reimaging strategies: coercion, community and the Sydney 2000 Olympics', in L.C. Harrison and W. Husbands (eds) *Practicing Responsible Tourism: International Case Studies in Planning, Policy and Development*, New York: John Wiley and Sons.

——(1997) 'Mega-events and their legacies', in P. Murphy (ed.) *Quality Management in Urban Tourism*, New York: John Wiley and Sons, pp. 77–89.

——(1998) 'The politics of decision making and top-down planning: Darling Harbour, Sydney', in D. Tyler, M. Robertson and Y. Guerrier (eds) *Tourism Management in Cities: Policy, Process and Practice*, Chichester: John Wiley and Sons.

——(2001) 'Imaging, tourism and sports event fever: the Sydney Olympics and the need for a social charter for mega-events', in C. Gratton and I.P. Henry (eds) *Sport in the City: The Role of Sport in Economic and Social Regeneration*, London: Routledge.

——(2006) 'Urban entrepreneurship, corporate interests and sports mega-events: the thin policies of competitiveness within the hard outcomes of neoliberalism', *The Sociological Review* 54 (Issue Supplement s2): 59–70.

——(2007) 'Tourism and regional competitiveness', in J. Tribe and D. Airey (eds) *Advances in Tourism Research, Tourism Research, New Directions, Challenges and Applications*, Oxford: Elsevier.

——(2008) 'Servicescapes, designscapes, branding, and the creation of place-identity: south of Litchfield, Christchurch', *Journal of Travel and Tourism Marketing* 25(3–4): 233–50.

——(2010) 'Crisis events in tourism: subjects of crisis in tourism', *Current Issues in Tourism* 13: 401–17.

Hall, C.M. and Hodges, J. (1996) 'The party's great, but what about the hangover? The housing and social impacts of mega-events with special reference to the Sydney 2000 Olympics', *Festival Management and Event Tourism* 4(1/2): 13–20.

Hall, C.M. and Page, S.J. (2006) *The Geography of Tourism and Recreation: Environment, Place, and Space*, London: Routledge, third edition.

——(2009) 'Progress in tourism management: from the geography of tourism to geographies of tourism – a review', *Tourism Management* 30(1): 3–16.

Hall, C.M. and Sharples, L. (ed) (2008) *Food and Wine Festivals and Events Around the World: Development, Management and Markets*, Oxford: Butterworth-Heinemann.

Hall, C.M. and Wilson, S. (2011) 'Neoliberal urban entrepreneurial agendas, Dunedin Stadium and the Rugby World Cup: or "If you don't have a stadium, you don't have a future"', in D. Dredge and J. Jenkins (eds) *Stories of Practice: Tourism Policy and Planning*, Farnham: Ashgate, pp. 133–152.

Hall, T. and Hubbard, P. (1996) 'The entrepreneurial city: new urban politics, new urban geographies?', *Progress in Human Geography* 20(2): 153–74.

Harvey, D. (1989) 'From managerialism to entrepreneurialism: the transformation in urban governance in late capitalism', *Geografiska Annaler* 71B: 3–17.

——(2002) *Spaces of Capital: Towards a Critical Geography*, New York: Routledge.

——(2006) 'Editorial: the geographies of critical geography', *Transactions – Institute of British Geographers* 31: 409–12.

Herrero, L.C., Sanz, J.Á., Devesa, M., Bedate, A. and del Barrio, M.J. (2006) 'The economic impact of cultural events: a case-study of Salamanca 2002, European Capital of Culture', *European Urban and Regional Studies* 13(1): 41–57.

Highmore, B. (2005) *Cityscapes: Cultural Readings in the Material and Symbolic City*, London: Palgrave Macmillan.

Hill, B. and Green, C.B. (2000) 'Repeat attendance as a function of involvement, loyalty, and the sportscape across three football contexts', *Sport Management Review* 3: 145–62.

Holloway, S.L. (2004) 'Rural roots, rural routes: discourses of rural self and travelling other in debates about the future of Appleby New Fair, 1945–69', *Journal of Rural Studies* 20(2): 143–56.

Hubbard, P. (1996) 'Urban design and city regeneration: social representations of entrepreneurial landscapes', *Urban Studies* 33: 1441–61.

Jackson, P. (1992) 'The politics of the streets: a geography of Caribana', *Political Geography* 11(2): 130–51.

Jansson, A. and Lagerkvist, A. (2009) 'The future gaze: city panoramas as politico-emotive geographies', *Journal of Visual Culture* 8(1): 25–53.

Jensen, O.B. (2005) 'Branding the contemporary city – urban branding as regional growth agenda?', plenary paper for Regional Studies Association Conference 'Regional Growth Agendas', Aalborg, Denmark, 28–31 May.

John, G. and Sheard, R. (2000) *Stadia: A Design and Development Guide*, Oxford: Architectural Press, third edition.

Johnson, N.C. (1999) 'Framing the past: time, space and the politics of heritage tourism in Ireland', *Political Geography* 18: 187–207.

Johnston, R.J. and Sidaway, J.D. (2004) *Geography and Geographers: Anglo-American Human Geography since 1945*, London: Hodder Education, sixth edition.

Jones, A.M. (2007) '"More than managing across borders?" The complex role of face-to-face interaction in globalizing law firms', *Journal of Economic Geography* (7): 223–4.

Jones, C.C. (2010) 'Playing at the queer edges', *Leisure Studies* 29: 269–87.

Jones, P. and Wilks-Heeg, S. (2004) 'Capitalising culture: Liverpool 2008', *Local Economy* 19: 341–60.

Judd, D.R. (2003) 'Building the tourist city: editor's introduction', in D.R. Judd (ed.) *The Infrastructure of Play: Building the Tourist City*, Armonk: M.E. Sharpe, pp. 3–16.

Julier, G. (2005) 'Urban designscapes and the production of aesthetic consent', *Urban Studies* 42: 869–87.

Kotler, P. and Gertner, D. (2002) 'Country as brand, product, and beyond: a place marketing and brand management perspective', *Journal of Brand Management* 9: 249–61.

Kotler, P., Haider, D.H. and Rein, I. (1993) *Marketing Places: Attracting Investment, Industry, and Tourism to Cities, States, and Nations*, New York: Free Press.

Kwan, M.-P. and Schwanen, T. (2009) 'Quantitative revolution 2: the critical (re)turn', *The Professional Geographer* 61: 283–91.

Lee, L.H. (2001) 'Cultural performance, subjectivity and space: Osaka's Korean festival', *Geographical Review of Japan, Series B* 73(4): 78–91.

Lee, R. and Wills, J. (eds) (1997) *Geographies of Economies*, London: Arnold.

Leitner, H. and Garner, M. (1993) 'The limits of local initiatives: a reassessment of urban entrepreneurialism for urban development', *Urban Geography* 14: 57–77.

Ley, D. and Olds, K. (1988) 'Landscape as spectacle: World's Fairs and the culture of heroic consumption', *Environment and Planning D: Society and Space* 6: 191–212.

Lowes, M. (2004) 'Neoliberal power politics and the controversial siting of the Australian Grand Prix motorsport event in an urban park', *Society and Leisure* 27(1): 69–88.

McCallum, K., Spencer, A. and Wyly, E. (2005) 'The city as an image-creation machine: a critical analysis of Vancouver's Olympic bid', *Association of Pacific Coast Geographers Yearbook* 67: 24–46.

McCleary, K. (2010) 'Ethnic identity and elite idyll: a comparison of carnival in Buenos Aires, Argentina and Montevideo, Uruguay, 1900–920', *Social Identities* 16: 497–517.

MacLeod, G. (2002) 'From urban entrepreneurialism to a "revanchist city"? On the spatial injustices of Glasgow's renaissance', *Antipode* 34: 602–24.

Malecki, E.J. (2004) 'Jockeying for position: what it means and why it matters to regional development policy when places compete', *Regional Studies* 38(9): 1101–20.

Markwell, K. (2002) 'Mardi Gras tourism and the construction of Sydney as an international gay and lesbian city', *GLQ: A Journal of Lesbian and Gay Studies* 8(1–2): 81–99.

Matheson, C.M. (2010) 'Legacy planning, regeneration and events: the Glasgow 2014 Commonwealth Games', *Local Economy* 25(1): 10–23.

Mitchell, L.S. (1979) 'The geography of tourism: an introduction', *Annals of Tourism Research* 9(3): 235–44.

Morris, N.J. and Cant, S.G. (2006) 'Engaging with place: artist, site-specificity and the Hebden Bridge Sculpture Trail', *Social and Cultural Geography* 7: 863–88.

Mullins, P. (1994) 'Class relations and tourism urbanization: the regeneration of the petite bourgeoisie and the emergence of a new urban form,' *International Journal of Urban and Regional Research* 18: 591–608.

Murphy, P.E. and Carmichael, B. (1991) 'Assessing the tourism benefits of an open access sports tournament: The 1989 BC Winter games', *Journal of Travel Research* 29(3): 32–36.

O'Dell, T. (2005) 'Experiencescapes: blurring borders and testing connections', in T. O'Dell and P. Billing (eds) *Experiencescapes: Tourism, Culture and Economy*, Copenhagen: Copenhagen Business School Press, pp. 11–33.

Olds, K. (1988) 'Urban mega-events, evictions and housing rights: the Canadian case', *Current Issues in Tourism* 1: 2–46.

——(1989) 'Mass evictions in Vancouver: The human toll of Expo '86', *Canadian Housing* 6(1): 49–53.

Oppermann, M. (1996) 'Convention cities – images and changing fortunes', *Journal of Tourism Studies* 7: 10–19.

Owen, K.A. (2002) 'The Sydney 2000 Olympics and urban entrepreneurialism: local variations in urban governance', *Australian Geographical Studies* 40: 323–36.

Page, S.J. and Connell, J. (2010) *Leisure: An Introduction*, Pearson: Harlow.

Page, S.J. and Hall, C.M. (2003) *Managing Urban Tourism*, Harlow: Prentice Hall.

Paskaleva, K., Besson, E. and Sutherland, M. (2009) 'Tourism and European capitals of culture: the role of destination competitiveness governance', *International Journal of Tourism Policy* 2: 107–23.

Peck, J. and Tickell, A. (2002) 'Neoliberalizing space', *Antipode* 34: 380–403.

Pettersson, R. (2003) 'Indigenous cultural events: the development of a Sami winter festival in northern Sweden', *Tourism* 51(3): 319–32.

Pinder, D. (2000) '"Old Paris is no more": geographies of spectacle and anti-spectacle', *Antipode* 32: 357–86.

Pine, B.J. and Gilmore, J.H. (1999) *The Experience Economy: Work is Theatre and Every Business a Stage*, Boston: Harvard Business School Press.

Power, M. and Sidaway, J.D. (2005) 'Deconstructing twinned towers: Lisbon's Expo '98 and the occluded geographies of discovery', *Social and Cultural Geography* 6: 865–83.

Pred, A. (1996) 'Interfusions: consumption, identity and the practices and power relations of everyday life', *Environment and Planning A* 28(1): 11–24.

Quinn, B. (2009) 'The European capital culture initiative and cultural legacy: an analysis of the cultural sector in the aftermath of Cork 2005', *Event Management* 13(4): 249–64.

Ray, N.M., McCain, G., Davis, D. and Melin, T.L. (2006) 'Lewis and Clark and the corps of discovery: re-enactment event tourism as authentic heritage travel', *Leisure Studies* 25: 437–54.

Richards, G. and Palmer, R. (2010) *Eventful Cities: Cultural Management and Urban Revitalisation*, Oxford: Butterworth-Heinemann.

Richards, G. and Wilson, J. (2004) 'The impact of cultural events on city image: Rotterdam, Cultural Capital of Europe 2001', *Urban Studies* 41: 1931–51.

Royo, J.A.M. (1999) 'All the town is a stage: civic ceremonies and religious festivities in Spain during the golden age', *Urban History* 26(2): 165–89.

Schnell, S.M. (2003) 'Creating narratives of place and identity in "Little Sweden, USA"', *Geographical Review* 93: 1–29.

Sherry, J.F., Jr (1998) 'The soul of the company store: Nike Town Chicago and the emplaced brandscape', in J.F. Sherry, Jr (ed.) *Servicescapes: The Concept of Place in Contemporary Markets*, Lincolnwood, IL: Nike Town Chicago Business Books, pp. 109–50.

Shoval, N. (2002) 'A new phase in the competition for the Olympic Gold: the London and New York bids for the 2012 Games', *Journal of Urban Affairs* 24: 583–99.

Smith, A. and Fox, T. (2007) 'From "event-led" to "event-themed" regeneration: the 2002 Commonwealth Games legacy programme', *Urban Studies* 44(5–6): 1125–43.

Smith, J. and Himmelfarb, K.M.G. (2007) 'Restructuring Beijing's social space: observations on the Olympic Games in 2008', *Eurasian Geography and Economics* 48: 543–54.

Smith, N. (2005) 'Neo-critical geography, or, the flat pluralist world of business class', *Antipode* 37: 887–99.

Spencer, E.G. (2003) 'Adapting festive practices: carnival in Cologne and Mainz, 1871–1914', *Urban History* 29: 637–56.

Swyngedouw, E.A. (1992) 'The mammon quest. "Glocalisation", interspatial competition and the new monetary order: the construction of new scales', in M. Dunford and G. Kaflakas (eds) *Cities and Regions in the New Europe*, London: Belhaven.

Teather, E.K. (2001) 'Time out and worlds apart: tradition and modernity meet in the time-space of the gravesweeping festivals of Hong Kong', *Singapore Journal of Tropical Geography* 22: 156–72.

Thien, D. (2005) 'After or beyond feeling? A consideration of affect and emotion in geography', *Area* 37: 450–4.

Thompson, C.J. and Arsel, Z. (2004) 'The Starbucks brandscape and consumers (anticorporate) experiences of glocalization', *Journal of Consumer Research* 31: 631–42.

Thrift, N. (2004) 'Intensities of feeling: towards a spatial politics of affect', *Geografiska Annaler, Series B: Human Geography* 86: 57–78.

Tolia-Kelly, D.P. (2006) 'Affect – an ethnocentric encounter? Exploring the "universalist" imperative of emotional/affectual geographies', *Area* 38: 213–17.

Tufts, S. (2004) 'Building the "competitive city": Labour and Toronto's bid to host the Olympic Games', *Geoforum* 35: 47–58.

Wainwright, E. and Ansell, N. (2008) 'Geographies of sports development: the role of space and place', in V. Girginov (ed.) *Management of Sports Development*, Oxford: Butterworth-Heinemann, pp. 183–200.

Waitt, G. (1999) 'Playing games with Sydney: marketing Sydney for the 2000 Olympics', *Urban Studies* 36: 1055–77.

——(2001) 'The Olympic spirit and civic boosterism: the Sydney 2000 Olympics', *Tourism Geographies* 3: 249–78.

——(2008) 'Urban festivals: geographies of hype, helplessness and hope', *Geography Compass* 2(2): 513–37.

Wakefield, K.L., Blodgett, J.G. and Sloan, H.J. (1996) 'Measurement and management of the sportscape', *Journal of Sport Management* 10(1): 15–31.

Warren, S. (1996) 'Popular cultural practices in the "postmodern city"', *Urban Geography* 17(6): 545–67.

Waterman, S. (1998) 'Carnivals for elites? The cultural politics of arts festivals', *Progress in Human Geography* 22: 54–74.

Weller, S. (2008) 'Beyond "global production networks": Australian Fashion Week's trans-sectoral synergies', *Growth and Change* 39: 104–22.

Whitelegg, D. (2000) 'Going for gold: Atlanta's bid for fame', *International Journal of Urban and Regional Research* 24: 801–17.

Whitson, D. and Horne, J. (2006) 'Underestimated costs and overestimated benefits? Comparing the outcomes of sports mega-events in Canada and Japan', *The Sociological Review* 54 (Issue Supplement s2): 71–89.

Wilson, J. (ed.) (2011) *New Perspectives in Tourism Geographies*, London: Routledge.

Yli-Jokipii, P. (1999) 'The cultural geography of the summer dance pavilions of Ostrobothnia, Finland', *Journal of Cultural Geography* 18(2): 109–32.

Zelinsky, W. (1994) 'Conventionland USA: the geography of a latterday phenomenon,' *Annals of the Association of American Geographers* 84: 68–86.

11

The psychology of events

Pierre Benckendorff and Philip L. Pearce

Introduction

The discipline of psychology consists of a sprawling array of theories, methods and levels of analysis as its researchers attempt to forge a scientific approach to the analysis of people's behaviour and experience. From its foundation period through to its most contemporary summaries, the discipline has been characterised by highly abstract areas of inquiry as well as substantial fields of applied expertise (Boring 1950; Furnham 2008). The present consideration of psychology and its contribution to the study of events draws on select insights from both the theoretical area and the applied fields. The specialised area of social psychology, which can be succinctly defined as how other people influence behaviour, is particularly relevant to the management of events as leisure activities. The initial section of this chapter briefly documents the main psychological concepts and applications which will be used to frame the present analysis of people's involvement in events. These considerations include a discussion of motivation and personality, role theory, identity and liminality, experience analysis, and post-event attitudes. The emotional, aesthetic and performative labour which describes the world of event participants will also be reviewed. Additionally, the concepts of flow and mindfulness will be noted to help understand elite performance. The key sections which then follow these introductory remarks are the psychology of event spectators and attendees, the psychology of event performers and active participants, and then, briefly, the psychology of elite event participants. An organising diagram illustrating these links and approaches is provided in Figure 11.1.

A framework of psychology ideas

What kinds of people seek to involve themselves in events and what motivates them to do so? These are questions which are at the heart of event studies (Getz 2007: 9–12). The research in psychology which can assist in answering these questions derives from a combination of applied expertise in personality assessment and the study of social motivation. Personality assessment is an activity which profiles individuals according to suggested consistencies in their behaviour across situations. It produces well-known profiles along such dimensions as extraversion, neuroticism and psychoticism (Martin *et al.* 2007). Two further dimensions which make up what is sometimes

	Pre-experience	On-site experience	Post-experience
Spectators and Attendees	Personality, motivation and involvement	+ Role theory, identity, liminality, experience analysis	→ Satisfaction, loyalty
Performers and Participants	Personality, motivation and involvement	+ Role theory, identity, liminality, experience analysis	Satisfaction, self-actualisation → personal development quality
Elite Participants	Personality and motivation	+ Flow, mindfulness, emotional and performative labour	→ Superior performance

Figure 11.1 Applying psychological ideas to event participation

called the big five in personality profiling are conscientiousness and agreeableness (Soldz and Vaillant 1999). The profiling of sports players in particular is often used as a part of the selection of players since the ability to handle stress in contemporary competitive sport may be important in justifying money spent on player recruitment and development (Hoye *et al.* 2009). Subsequent sections of this chapter consider further the personality profiles of event spectators, participants and performers.

Many applied psychologists and practitioners have expressed concern about the generic power of personality profiling and prefer to understand how participants perceive and approach specific contexts. This perspective, stemming from the original situational or interactionist approach to understanding behaviour developed by Mischel (1968, 1984), stimulates researchers to ask more focused questions about the specific contexts of interest. In particular, the interactionist perspective directs researchers to the topic of social motivation and values where the needs of individuals are examined and represented as common factors. In this approach the reasons for spectating at a sports event, for example, may be less about being an extravert and much more about need to belong to a group, the desire to develop family relationships and the anticipated pleasure of feeling a sense of achievement. It is important to note that motives may be forward-looking or teleological (a desire to experience a future state) as well as restoring diminished or reduced states (Harre *et al.* 1985). The studies considered in subsequent sections about spectator and participant involvement in events build heavily on social motivation and values assessments. In particular the classification of those who attend or participate in events as specialists or generalists or alternatively as engaging in casual or serious leisure is built precisely on motivational and values approaches (Bryan 1977; Gursoy and Gavcar 2003; Stebbins 2004).

A framework known as role theory which is derived from social psychology provides a third organising topic informing the discussion of people and events. The field of social psychology emphasises the influence of actors on one another and encompasses a diversity of topics including role theory, social motivation and the influence of others on our attitudes. Role theory, in particular, has links to micro-sociology in terms of the desire to seek front or back-stage experiences (Goffman 1959; MacCannell 1976) as well as to the anthropological terms of liminality and thresholds (cf. Turner and Turner 1978; Ryan 2002). In common with the interactionist perspective, role theory suggests that people display varied behaviours as their socially defined position changes (Pearce 2005: 21). Key concepts include role conflict (a disquiet over clashes among multiple roles), role ambiguity (an uncertainty about how to behave), role distance (a desire to reject core elements of a particular role) and altercasting (being forced into a role by others and accepting the position with reluctance). These concepts pave the way for the treatment of the different behaviour of attendees at an event compared to the selves they display at home or work; the ideas of role theory can help researchers consider whether or not participants are seeking to occupy front or backstage roles in their event participation and the role-based concepts can help analysts understand the enthusiasm with which people embrace experiences.

Additional conceptual schemes to be deployed in the treatment of people and the events in which they engage include the analysis of people's experience and the use of post-experience attitude and evaluation frameworks. These ideas apply most directly to people's reactions to events as leisure activities. Attitude studies and the analysis of immediate experience have long roots in psychology's history, but the recent efforts in the field of positive psychology have added to this rich past with experiential sampling methods and an emphasis on reporting emotional states and subjective wellbeing (Diener and Biswas-Diener 2008). The deep involvement of participants in leisure experiences can be understood in terms of a focused level of concentration referred to as the concept of flow (Csikszentmihalyi 1990), supported by the notion of mindfulness which defines the mental state of processing new information with full attention (Langer 1989). The final guiding concepts to be applied in this chapter are the self-perceptions accompanying work and its stresses. The terms 'emotional', 'performative' and 'aesthetic' labour arise out of studies in both psychology and human resource management, and they offer insights into the lives of the performers wherever and however they entertain event audiences (Bryman 2004; Pearce 2008).

Psychology of event spectators and attendees

It is useful to clarify at the outset that a variety of labels are used to describe passive consumers of events. Depending on the context and setting, consumers are variously referred to as spectators, audience members, attendees, delegates and patrons. For convenience the term 'attendees' will be used in this section to refer to passive event consumers. The focus is therefore on the passive consumption of 'performances' that are witnessed by attendees either directly or indirectly and which rely on the abilities of the actors or players delivering the performance (Deighton 1992). Although the passive consumption of events requires few skills, consumers can often be further delineated based on their level of involvement and specialisation. For example, 'fans' are a specialist group in the case of sport and celebrity events. These initial distinctions provide some boundaries for the present discussion and imply that the psychological elements that underpin the behaviours of attendees vary enormously according to the setting and the level of involvement or specialisation. The following discussion will examine the role of personality, motives and involvement before considering how identity and roles contribute to an understanding of the on-site behaviour of individuals and crowds. The discussion will conclude with a brief review of the literature on attendee satisfaction.

The study of motives has received considerable scientific attention in both the psychology and events management literature (Getz 2007). The motivation to visit events is a special subset of the wider interest area of human motivation which in its broad sense can be defined as the total network of biological and cultural forces which give value and direction to travel choice, behaviour and experience (Pearce et al. 1998). The key implication for all those considering and event issues in motivation is that it is this force which energises and generates people's behaviour (Mansfeld 1992; Hsu and Huang 2008).

In order to tackle this topic a key preliminary perspective is needed. A professional view of motivation requires the analyst to be mindful that other event attendees may not be driven by the same social, cultural and biological needs as the observer. An enduring challenge for students, professionals and academics researching motivation is to allow the possibility that other people may see the world in other ways, their needs may be different and their approach to the destinations, attractions and events they visit may be unconventional. This issue emphasises the importance of taking an emic perspective, which amounts to seeing and researching the world from the insider and participant's point of view (Pike 1966; Cohen 1979).

Three classic motivation theories dominate most studies of leisure, sport and tourism: Murray's (1938) Needs Theory of Personality, Maslow's (1943) Hierarchy of Needs, and Berlyne's (1960) concept of optimal level of stimulation. Iso-Ahola (1980: 230) describes a motive as 'an internal factor that arouses, directs, and integrates a person's behaviour'. An understanding of event motives can be useful when designing offerings for event attendees, monitoring satisfaction and trying to understand attendees' decision-making processes (Crompton and McKay 1997). However, motives also provide insights into on-site behaviours and are a useful lens for understanding outcomes such as repeat visitation and loyalty.

A number of integrative frameworks have been used to understand attendees' motives for attending events in a range of different contexts. Li and Petrick (2006), in their review of festival and event motivation research, observe that a majority of motivation studies have adapted theoretical frameworks from tourism and leisure research. A number of studies have been conceptually grounded in Iso-Ahola's (1982) escape-seeking dichotomy or the push–pull travel motivation models initially developed by Dann (1977, 1981) and Crompton (1979). However, these observations are limited largely to festivals, cultural and special events and there is also a second, substantial body of literature examining the motives of spectators at sports events (Wann et al. 2008).

The work that emerges from the travel and leisure area has been extended and adapted to events, and a large body of literature has developed in the last decade. While some researchers have sought to develop a unified theory of event motivation, others have recognised that the diversity of event settings and multiplicity of motives make this an ambitious goal. There are, however, some consistent patterns that are evident in many studies (Li and Petrick 2006). It is clear that many attendees seek events as an opportunity for escape from their daily routine. However, other motives are also consistently identified, including a need of excitement, family or group togetherness, affiliation and socialisation. Following a broad review of the literature, Morgan (2009) groups the internal motives associated with events into three categories: (1) the personal benefits of hedonic enjoyment (e.g. novelty, escape) and achievement (e.g. growth through overcoming challenges); (2) social interaction with family, staff and other visitors; and (3) wider symbolic meanings derived from personal narratives and shared cultural values. A number of studies report that event novelty is a particularly important motive, but this motive is often linked with pull factors or characteristics that relate to the uniqueness of individual events (Nicholson and Pearce 2001). In the case of business events, it has been reported that networking and learning are major motives but that these motives vary according to the type of meeting (Oppermann and Chon 1997; Severt et al. 2007).

One further tourist motivation approach which has considerable potential to be cast as a source of ideas and research planning for event studies is that of the travel career pattern (TCP) (Pearce and Lee 2005). It essentially provides a patterned description of motives and then asserts that event participants will have different configurations of needs due to previous event and travel experience as well as difference due to their life stages (Hsu and Huang 2008). Fourteen core factors are used to describe travel motivation and these factors were identified from a rich array of previous studies and empirically confirmed across large international studies (Pearce 2005). The defining forces were (in order of importance) novelty, escape/relax, relationship strengthening, autonomy, seeking nature, self-development through involvement with hosts or the site, stimulation, self-development of a personal kind, relationship security (enjoying being with similar others), self-actualisation (getting a new life perspective), isolation, nostalgia, romance and recognition (prestige of travelling). These motive categories reflected many of the forces described in previous studies and together provide one of the more complete motivation inventories undertaken in the tourism and event field. The key feature of the travel career pattern approach was then to use the levels of previous experience and the stages of the individual's life cycle to formulate a three-part model which described the relationships among the fourteen motives and the key career factors.

The varied importance of the motives suggested that a pattern could be imposed on the data such that for all travellers there was a core layer of motives which were very important. These motives were to escape and relax, to experience novelty and to build relationships. These motives were relatively unaffected by how much travelling the participants had experienced or where they were located in the life cycle. These findings were in close accord with the early studies in the field, especially the work of Crompton (1979). There were further motives which were structured into a middle and outer layer of importance. For the most experienced travellers, the middle layer of motives was more important than the outer layer. By way of contrast, those with limited travel experience tended to see all motives as quite important. It was noted further that for the middle and outer levels of the pattern the phases or stages of the travellers' life cycle were also linked to the travellers' motive patterns. For western contexts later stages of the life cycle also tended to be linked to more travel experience and middle layer motives, while younger respondents differentiated less among the travel motives and their importance. There is the possibility that the common career patterns we find empirically amongst groups with different levels of participation and varied interests in set activities may reproduce patterns of motivation similar to those described by Cohen, Crompton, Morgan and others in qualitative category schemes. The potential power of this approach is to offer guidelines for event researchers and practitioners concerning how we might predict event motivation to change with continuing participation and according to social circumstances. Its direct use in event studies is likely to modify some detail for the patterns derived from tourism-generated context but the core principles of a shifting motivational career tapestry offer structure to the field.

The sports literature provides further insights about event motives by adding several additional extrinsic and intrinsic dimensions. Sloan (1989) proposed that most motives for attending sporting events fall under one of several theories: the salubrious effects theory, stress and stimulation theories, catharsis and aggression theories, entertainment theory, or achievement-seeking theories. A variety of frameworks have subsequently been developed and tested to understand the motives of sport spectators and these are summarised in Table 11.1.

Funk et al. (2004) suggest that the frameworks which have received the most attention in the literature can be classified under four general categories: (a) stress and stimulation seeking, (b) entertainment, (c) achievement seeking and (d) social interaction. It is clear when examining the various sport motivation models that many of the motives identified for other types of events are present. However these frameworks also extend the core set of motives identified by other authors. Several of the frameworks include the notion of eustress or drama, which refers to the excitement associated with a close game versus a one-sided game and the element of

Table 11.1 Motives of sport spectators

Authors	Framework	Motives
Wann (1995)	Sports Fan Motivation Scale (SFMS)	Eustress, self-esteem, escape, entertainment, economic (gambling), aesthetic, group affiliation, family
Milne and McDonald (1999)	Motivation of Sport Consumers (MSC)	Risk-taking, stress reduction, aggression, affiliation, social facilitation, self-esteem, competition, achievement, skill mastery, aesthetics, value development and self-actualisation
Trail and James (2001)	Motivation Scale for Sport Consumption (MSSC)	Achievement, acquisition of knowledge, aesthetics, drama, escape, family, physical attraction, physical skills of players, social interaction
Funk *et al.* (2001, 2002, 2003)	Sport Interest Inventory (SII)	Family bonding, friends bonding, drama, entertainment value, escape, excitement, player interest, role model, socialisation, team interest, vicarious achievement
James and Ross (2004)	—	Entertainment, skill, drama, team effort, achievement, social interaction, family, team affiliation, empathy
Mehus (2005)	Entertainment Sport Motivation Scale	Social, excitement
Koo and Hardin (2008)	—	Vicarious achievement, team performance, escape, family, eustress, aesthetics, entertainment value, social opportunities

uncertainty about the outcome of the game (Funk *et al.* 2001). This motive appears to be particularly important in competitive team sports. The motive of vicarious achievement, whereby an attendee experiences a heightened sense of personal or collective esteem based on the performance and psychological association with the team, is also an interesting extension of a broader need for achievement (Funk *et al.* 2001). 'Basking in the reflected glory' of a successful team allows spectators to enhance their own self-esteem and satisfy achievement needs (Cialdini *et al.* 1976). For some sports the need to appreciate the excellence, beauty, creativity of athletic performance and style of play (aesthetics) is also an important motive (Wann 1995). Wann, Schrader, and Wilson (1999) found that intrinsic motives such as aesthetics, excitement and entertainment were more important than extrinsic motives such as self-esteem, escape and family time. There is also some evidence that motives vary enormously based on whether sports are team-based, aggressive or stylistic (Wann *et al.* 2008).

A related psychological concept that is frequently discussed as an antecedent of behaviour is the level of involvement or specialisation in events. Rothschild (1984) describes involvement as a state of motivation, arousal, or interest with regard to a product, an activity or an object. In the consumer behaviour field, involvement is regarded as one of the most important influences on behaviour and decision-making.

Kapferer and Laurent's (1985) Consumer Involvement Profile (CIP) framework and Zaichkowsky's (1985) one-dimensional Product Involvement Inventory (PII) have both informed more specific frameworks developed to understand involvement in the context of recreation and leisure. The application of Kapferer and Laurent's CIP framework has tended to result in a three- or four-dimensional construct in tourism and leisure settings. For example, Gursoy and Gavcar (2003) identified a three-dimensional construct consisting of pleasure/interest, risk probability and risk importance, while Brown *et al.* (2007) developed a Wine Involvement

Scale (WIS) consisting of enjoyment, expertise and symbolic centrality. Kyle and Chick (2002), drawing on the work of McIntyre and Pigram (1992), observe that there is strong support in the leisure literature for three dimensions consisting of:

1 Attraction: the perceived importance or interest in an activity or a product, and the pleasure or hedonic value derived from participation or use.
2 Sign: the unspoken statements that purchase or participation conveys about the person (e.g. identification as a fan of the team).
3 Centrality to lifestyle: encompassing interaction with friends and family, and the central role of the activity in the context of an individual's life.

The involvement construct is useful because it has been suggested that more involved attendees, such as fanatics, have a different motivational profile from less involved, casual attendees. As a result, a number of authors have differentiated between event attendees based on their level of involvement. For example, Gross and Brown (2006) examined the importance of food involvement in tourism experiences, while Ritchie et al. (2000) identified three types of fans in their work on sports tourism: the avid spectator/fan, the frequent spectator/fan, and the casual spectator/fan. Other authors distinguish between spectators and fans (cf. Wann 1995; Gibson et al. 2002; Robinson and Trail 2005). Fans are identified as a unique group of individuals to study because they are highly involved and have an emotional attachment to sport (Shank and Beasley 1998). These distinctions are analogous to the constructs of serious vs casual leisure (Stebbins 1982, 1997) and specialists vs generalists (McIntyre and Pigram 1992; Pearce 2005) discussed by other authors in the leisure and tourism literature. These ideas have been developed further by Getz (2007) who, drawing on the work of Pearce (1988), proposes that serious participants follow an event careers trajectory. According to Getz, these event participants specialise by seeking out similar types of events to satisfy the need for stimulation and personal development. Essentially varying degrees of engrossment, passion and commitment are at the core of all of these frameworks. This involvement or commitment to an activity is often underpinned by different motives and results in different participation and behavioural patterns. While psychological involvement is a useful concept for understanding pre-visit behaviour, it is also important for understanding how attendees experience events and subsequent post-event outcomes such as satisfaction and loyalty.

An understanding of identity and role theories further extend the inquiry into the psychology of events. Attendee involvement and motives such as affiliation, vicarious achievement and togetherness can be linked with identity. It has been argued that motives such as the need for vicarious achievement are antecedents to identification; however, the relationships between motives, involvement and identity are more complex because identity may in turn intensify associated motives and involvement (Laverie and Arnett 2000; Gwinner and Swanson 2003; Snelgrove et al. 2008). Social psychology offers two dominant theories of identity: social identity theory and identity theory.

Social identity theory is derived from Festinger's (1954) social comparison theory, and focuses on the ways in which individuals perceive and categorise themselves, based on their social and personal identities. Social identity theory argues that identities are shaped by group membership and that identity is a function of attachment to a particular group (Tajfel 1982; Hogg et al. 1995). An individual's evaluation of who they are is affected by the social groups that they belong to, and how they believe others see them as a group member. Social identity theory is useful for understanding how membership of a particular group influences behaviour. In an events context, social identity theory has been applied to the understanding of crowd behaviour

(Reicher 1984, 1996). Reicher's work suggests that members of a crowd act in terms of shared social identity that determines both the normative limits of action (what people do) and the extent of participation (who joins in). In the case of sports events collective identities define borders between 'in groups' (us) and 'out groups' (them), thereby creating both opponents and solidarities which reinforce social norms (Snow and Oliver 1995; Wann, Carlson, and Schrader 1999).

In-group identification at events offers social benefits such as feelings of camaraderie, community and solidarity, as well as enhanced social prestige and self-esteem (Zillmann et al. 1979). Interaction with other attendees can foster shared norms and values and instil a transient sense of closeness or 'communitas' (Turner 1974; Arnould and Price 1993; Getz 2007; Morgan 2009). Attendee identification reinforces a number of positive collective behaviours but may also result in aggression, crowd violence and hooliganism. These concepts are particularly relevant in the context of sports events and riots. Several authors have reported that the degree of fan identification is a major predictor of spectator violence at sports events (Branscombe and Wann 1992; Simons and Taylor 1992). Research also indicates that level of team identification is a significant predictor of positive and negative post-attendance reflection (Wann et al. 1994; Madrigal 2003) and that identification can change significantly throughout a season (Wann 1996). As a result of the importance of identification to sports events, several researchers have attempted to develop valid and reliable measures of attendee identification; however, the most widely used instrument is the Sport Spectator Identification Scale (SSIS) (Wann and Branscombe 1993).

Identity theory, on the other hand, is based on McCall and Simmons' (1966) role-identity theory, which suggests that individuals will base their actions on how they like to see themselves and how they like to be seen by others. According to Stryker and Burke (2000) individuals live their lives through roles that support their participation in relatively small and specialised networks of social relationships. These roles are external because they are linked to social positions, whereas identity is viewed as internal and consisting of internalised meanings and expectations associated with a role. Role-identity therefore has two components: the role itself and the identity associated with that role. Identity theory emphasises role behaviours rather than group processes and inter-group relations. However, the interactions and juxtapositions of the different roles played by attendees in event settings can lead to a better understanding of collective behaviours. According to Edensor (2000) people use roles to convey particular meanings and values in front-stage social settings while dropping their façade when they reach the domestic safety of backstage regions. In the events context, it is useful to consider the extent to which attendees redefine their identity by adopting roles that are specific to the event setting.

Identity theory suggests that event attendees define themselves by attending events that carry symbolic significance. For example, attending cultural events and acquiring unique artifacts enables attendees to express their cultural identity (Hannam and Halewood 2006; Wamwara-Mbugua and Cornwell 2009). Ritzer (1999) argues that the rationalisation of society by economic and market forces deprives human activities of their symbolic significance and that extravaganzas and simulations are ways of re-enchanting human life by staging symbolically charged events. Bankston and Henry (2000) demonstrate that commodified ethnic events provide a 'vicarious sense of primordial identity' even for attendees who do not have ethnic ties with the event. This view is certainly supported by the growing role of events as symbolic representations and sources of individual identity and group membership.

Concepts within role theory and the linked notions of liminality also describe the disjunction for individuals between everyday behaviour and intense attendee involvement at sports events. A link can be made here to the colloquial concept of 'white line fever', which is applied to players and refers to heightened aggression and personality changes when the event is in play. In an analogous fashion, liminal or crossing the threshold behaviour and the assumption of a new role (from regular citizen to committed fan) allows attendees to engage in behaviours (shouting, chanting, jeering) which would be socially unacceptable outside of the spectator role (Mann and Pearce 1978).

The application of social psychology to leisure studies provides particularly fertile ground for understanding the dimensions of event experiences. Events are essentially leisure experiences and Holbrook and Hirschman (1982) suggest that, in contrast to ordinary consumer behaviour, the consumption of experiences is characterised by emotion, play, pleasure, aesthetic appreciation and symbolism. The consumption of event experiences involves absorbing the symbolic meanings associated with more subjective characteristics (Madrigal 1995). Madrigal (1995) draws on a number of the concepts already discussed to develop a set of parsimonious scales that measure the underlying dimensions of sports event consumption. These scales are referred to collectively as the FANDIM model of sport event consumption. In contrast to a motive-based model intended to satisfy specific needs, the FANDIM model considers the dimensions along which sporting events are consumed. Drawing heavily on the work of Csikszentmihalyi (1975, 1990) and Holt (1995), Madrigal proposes that the consumption of event experiences can be analysed in terms of two higher-order factors that are each comprised of three uni-dimensional factors:

- *Autotelism:* focuses on immersion in the performance based on (a) flow, intense absorption, loss of self-consciousness, and an altered sense of time; (b) fantasy, a sense of playfulness typified by feelings of escape, pleasure, and relaxation; and (c) evaluation and value judgments about the quality of the performance and the actions and skills of the performers.
- *Appreciation:* emphasises the consumption of the artistry and personal characteristics of those involved in delivering the performance based on (a) aesthetics and appreciation for the grace and beauty of the performance itself; (b) a voyeuristic appreciation of the physical attractiveness of performers; and (c) an appreciation of the performers' personalities, especially when focusing attention on specific performers, usually those possessing the greatest prominence or notoriety.

While this framework has been applied specifically to sports events, it is more sophisticated than the conceptualisations that have been developed in the broader events literature and provides a useful model for considering a wide range of performative events. However, it is important when considering event experiences to differentiate between 'skill performances' and 'show performances' (Deighton 1992). Skill performances (e.g. sporting events) are staged displays of competence occurring in settings that emphasise the event's realism. This differs from show performances (e.g. theatre), which are contrived for the audience's benefit, occur in an artificial setting and involve elements of fantasy. While the outcomes of show performances are usually predictable or ritualistic, skill performances are characterised by tension and suspense about the eventual outcome.

From a psychological perspective, event experiences are influenced by motives and levels of involvement and can be described in terms of conative, cognitive and affective responses to the stimulation provided by the event (Getz 2007; Pettersson and Getz 2009). The conative dimension of experience describes the actual behaviour and activities of attendees. The cognitive dimension of experience refers to how attendees add meaning to their experiences through awareness, interpretation, learning and understanding. The affective dimension of experience is concerned with the feelings and emotions of attendees. These psychological responses are critical to a better understanding of the design, staging and evaluation of memorable event experiences.

Another perspective concerning the design of event experiences involves the application of environmental psychology to understand how event settings influence attendee behaviour.

Specific considerations relevant to events include social interaction, capacity and crowding, personal space, signs, physical features, sound, lighting, colour, temperature and airflow (Getz 2007). In this interpretation, frameworks such as Bitner's servicescapes model are very useful for understanding the elements of event settings (Bitner 1992; Wakefield and Blodgett 1994). However, congruent with Pine and Gilmore's (1999) argument of the transition from service economies to experience economies, it would seem more appropriate to examine event settings in terms of 'experiencescapes'. Experiencescapes are co-created through staging and the direct participation of attendees (Mossberg 2007). O'Dell (2005) describes these experiencescapes as fluid spaces in which diverse groups with competing and overlapping interests and ideologies stage and consume experiences. The design of experiencescapes includes not only the setting but also the sensory, symbolic, temporal and meaningful aspects of experiences (Diller *et al.* 2006). An understanding of event experiencescapes therefore needs to consider cognitive, conative and affective responses to the setting, theme, programming, personal interactions and provision of services and tangible goods such as food, beverages and merchandise. The design of event experiences and experiencescapes provides ample opportunities for further research using innovative experiential sampling approaches. The psychological dimensions mentioned here and in other chapters by Ferdinand and Williams, Berridge and Ryan (Chapters 15, 16 and 18) are a useful starting point for considering the links between experiencescapes and behaviour.

Psychology also provides a useful lens for understanding post-event experiences; however, Morgan (2009) observes that the complexity of event experiences is problematic for research into post-event responses. Hover and van Mierlo (2006) argue that there are three levels of experience with varying degrees of influence on post-experience behaviour. The first level is concerned with 'basal' experiences which represent reactions to external stimuli but which are not committed to memory and therefore do not influence post-experience behaviour. At the next level participants may report memorable experiences but this recall does not alter behaviour or attitudes. The third level is concerned with transformative experiences which have sufficient impact to change the attitudes and behaviour of participants. Surprisingly little research attention has been paid to attitude change, customer satisfaction, loyalty or other post-consumption outcomes of transformative event experiences.

The small number of studies examining event satisfaction have tended to focus on overall satisfaction, attribute performance or expectancy disconfirmation approaches focused on service quality (cf. Thrane 2002; Lee and Beeler 2007). The Expectancy Disconfirmation Paradigm (EDP), also known as the Disconfirmation of Expectations Model (DEM), is based on the premise that attendees have expectations about the quality of an event which are used as a basis for a post-event evaluation of performance. Satisfaction therefore results from expectations being met or exceeded. While this model has been successfully used to explain customer satisfaction with goods and has some appeal, many authors in the tourism, leisure and events fields have been highly critical of this approach (Arnould and Price 1993; van Leeuwen *et al.* 2002; Pearce 2005). The diverse, intangible and variable nature of event experiences suggest that attendees may at best have vague expectations of affective outcomes such as enjoyment, absorption and 'having a good time' (Arnould and Price 1993). It is possible that an attendee may indicate a high level of satisfaction with an event without the experience being memorable (Cole and Chancellor 2009). Furthermore, these expectations are likely to be altered by the experience itself and traditional approaches to measuring satisfaction during or after the event are therefore problematic. The expectations associated with events may also be multi-faceted. Miller (1977), for example, suggested that customers might hold several different types of expectations including ideal (can be) expectations, expected (will be) expectations, minimum tolerable (must be) expectations and deserved (should be) expectations.

The expectancy disconfirmation approach also implies that satisfaction is derived from cognitive evaluations rather than affective responses to the overall experience (Buttle 1996). Models that include both cognitive and affective determinants of satisfaction may provide a more accurate measure of attendee evaluations. Madrigal (1995) developed a model of the determinants of spectator satisfaction with sport events which included three cognitive determinants (disconfirmation of expectations, team identification and quality of opponent) and two affective determinants (enjoyment and 'basking in reflected glory'). Similarly, the Sport Spectator Satisfaction Model (SSSM) developed by van Leeuwen et al. (2002) extends the DEM by including identification and win/lose outcomes as influences on the satisfaction of spectators.

Another approach to measuring satisfaction is to conceptualise it as a complex multi-dimensional construct influenced by both the psychological characteristics of attendees as well as the external tangible and intangible aspects of the event itself. Fournier and Mick (1999: 5) suggest a more holistic, context-dependent approach to understanding satisfaction which includes 'a multi-model, multi-modal blend of motivations, cognitions, emotions, and meanings, embedded in sociocultural settings, which transforms during progressive and regressive consumer-product interactions'. Morgan (2009) adopts this approach to develop a framework for exploring the nature of an extraordinary event experience using netnographic analysis. His 'prism' model brings together the six external and internal elements of the festival experience: design and programming, physical organisation, social interaction, personal benefits, symbolic meanings and cultural communication.

Psychology of event performers and participants

A number of authors have distinguished between active event participants and passive attendees (Standevan and De Knop 1999; Pettersson and Getz 2009). This distinction is noteworthy, because active participants are likely to have different motives and higher levels of involvement. Here the concern is not with paid or professional performers and elite participants, but with participants and performers who actively participate in the event to co-create the experience. There are a range of sports, business and cultural events where the opportunity to become actively involved is a key attraction of the event. Examples of performers and participants might include amateur sports athletes such as marathon runners, mountain bikers, surfers and skiers; conference delegates, presenters and exhibitors; trivia buffs; food and wine enthusiasts; collectors; plant/animal breeders and primary producers; rioters; talent quest entrants and karaoke singers. In some cases the line between passive and active participation can be rather blurred, as is the case when passive sports fans can turn into active and intimidating crowds. The categorisation of attendees and participants is therefore not intended to be discrete but there is a tipping point at which passive behaviour becomes active. Despite the distinction between active and passive participation and the prevalence of active participants in a range of events, very little research has focused explicitly on this group (McGehee et al. 2003).

It is important to note that the frameworks and concepts discussed in the previous section provide useful starting points for understanding the behaviour of active event participants and performers. Although many active participants would personify Stebbins' notion of serious leisure, different levels of involvement can be identified for event participants. McGehee et al. (2003) found that participants' level of involvement in recreational running events impacted on both travel behaviour and expenditure. The discussion of motives also continues to be relevant but active participants exhibit a different pattern of motives. Motives such as the need for self-development and socialisation are likely to be more influential. When examining participation in extreme sports events such as BASE jumping, Allman et al. (2009), reported that participants were motivated by the opportunity for self-development, self-actualisation and the need for transformative experiences that would contribute to their quality of life.

The concept of edgework is particularly helpful in helping to understand motives for participation in some types of events. While there are some similarities with the concept of flow, Laurendeau (2006: 584) describes edgework as 'exploring the limits of one's ability and/or the technology one is using while maintaining enough control to successfully negotiate the edge'. The concept has been applied particularly to risk-taking activities such as skydiving and BASE jumping (Lyng and Snow 1986; Lyng 1990; Allman *et al.* 2009), but it is argued here that the concept is equally relevant to amateur sports participants and performers who participate in events as a means of moving beyond their comfort zone and testing their endurance, fitness or skill level. An organised event provides a safety net in which participants can move closer to the edge to negotiate the boundaries of their abilities. Sometimes edgework also occurs in the context of competing with or against other participants, but participants are primarily competing against themselves (Kurtzman and Zauhar 1998). In the case of more intellectual events, such as research conferences, it could be argued that some participants may be motivated to push the boundaries of knowledge. Self-actualisation is seen as a core motive for driving edgework behaviour, but motives such as enjoyment, a sense of accomplishment and a sense of belonging have also been reported (Allman *et al.* 2009).

The importance of identity has also been discussed in the literature on active event participants. Shipway and Jones (2007, 2008) used the concepts of serious leisure and social identification to explore the experiences of active participants taking part in a marathon. They reported that there was a clear subculture amongst runners that was reinforced by the unique ethos, language and behaviours of participants. This subculture resulted in homogeneity of dress, behaviour and values amongst the group. Such subcultures can be identified across a range of events that involve the gathering of enthusiasts and specialists, including non-professional sports events, rallies, swap meets and conferences. Shipway and Jones (2008) argue that 'serious leisure', such as competing in a sporting event, has significant potential to provide social identity while 'casual leisure' is unlikely to do so.

While identity is a useful lens for understanding event participation, psychology provides a number of other useful conceptual frames for understanding event experiences. Events play a role in creating opportunities for ludic and liminal experiences, a time of pleasure and play and a 'time out of time' (Turner 1969; Falassi 1987; Pettersson and Getz 2009). Morgan (2009: 83) observes that event experiences occur

> outside normal productive life in a time and space set aside for a special purpose ... objects (props and sets) and people (actors, audience) are assigned symbolic values and roles, and all attending observe rules and conventions that are different from those of everyday life.

The extraordinary nature of event experiences therefore has both ritualistic and performative elements (Arnould and Price 1993; Morgan 2009).

Aho (2001) presents a seven-stage process model of the tourism experience which consists of orientation, attachment and visiting, and four post-consumption aspects of experience: evaluation, storing, reflection and enrichment. While the post-consumption aspects have not been heavily studied, they represent further opportunities to apply psychology to the understanding of event participants. Most of the research has focused on evaluative outcomes such as attendee satisfaction, repeat visitation, enjoyment, value for money and willingness to recommend, but there are also opportunities to examine Aho's four aspects of post-event consumption experiences in more detail. This would include the use of psychological frameworks to understand the meaning of events, their impact on individual and group identity and the contribution of events to self-development, wellbeing and quality of life.

Psychology of elite performers

Many events depend heavily on the impressive, emotion-stirring performances of key individuals. The elite performers may be individual sports celebrities, the stars of the music world or well-known figures from public life who are capable of drawing crowds to speeches, rallies or celebrated causes (Moss 2009). There are two key contributions of applied psychology studies to the roles of these elite personnel; the first influence is on the development and enhancement of their skills and the second application lies in the management of the wellbeing of the performer.

The application of cognitive psychology in particular to the development of performers' skills has been one of the specialist core contributions of sports psychologists (Milne and Common 1998). In this approach athletes and others are encouraged to mentally rehearse their performances by developing clear images of when, how and what they should do in the phases of the game or event. This approach has several benefits since the mental rehearsal both simulates diverse situations which could not be replicated through direct training experiences and reduces fatigue and strain on the participants' bodies. It has become common practice for coaches and psychologists to work in tandem to develop these mental training routines for performers. The outcomes are visible for many spectators when watching athletes prior to their participation in such Olympic events as high jump, pole vault and 100-metre sprint. Similar cognitive and affective processes are at work in the case of performing arts events. Classical forms of acting require performers to simulate thoughts and emotions while techniques such as method acting require performers to draw upon their own emotions and memories.

The psychology of managing and supporting elite performers can be further understood by considering the concepts of emotional, aesthetic and performative labour (Bryman 2004; Harris 2005). These terms refer, in turn, to presenting the right kinds of emotion while participating, of looking the part while performing and finally being effective in the role. These requirements create considerable stress on individuals since at so many events there are literally thousands of people reviewing the performance, thus generating considerable evaluation anxiety. Making mistakes while performing at a key event may reduce future involvement in desirable events and tarnish the image of individuals. Some globally well-known examples of athletes and performers failing to respond within the constraints of these emotional, performative and aesthetic demands include the French soccer player Zidane head butting an opposition player in the final of the 2006 World Cup, the tennis star Serena Williams swearing at a referee in the 2009 US Open and the singer Justin Timberlake exposing Janet Jackson's breast while performing at the US Super Bowl. Even for the most experienced event performers, the manufacture of a positive environment to create the emotional stage for their work may be necessary. Harris (pers. comm.) reports that the global music star Elton John required a complete makeover of the change rooms of a local sporting stadium as well as the option to choose among fifty pairs of sunglasses to make him psychologically ready for his concert performance in regional Australia.

Amongst elite performers there is the intriguing phenomenon of producing truly superior instances of their work. Such performances can be witnessed not only in the sports arena but also in popular music and comedy concerts as well as in classical music, opera and live theatre. Audiences and spectators often respond enthusiastically to such occasions with standing applause, repeated ovations and even a certain rapturous adulation. The psychological underpinnings of such truly elite performances appear to lie in the timely conjunction of exacting physical and mental preparation which produces a focused state of task concentration. The post-event interviews with key performers produces such phrases as being 'in the zone' or having an altered sense of power and time control or 'floating'. Csikszentmihalyi (1990) has developed an understanding of these kinds of psychological states which include the key notions of:

1 A balance between the challenge of the task and the skill to do it.
2 The merging of action and awareness (deep involvement leads to an awareness of the self as integrated with the actions one is performing; this is also referred to as a loss of self-consciousness).
3 Clear goals (there is a strong sense of what is to be done).
4 Unambiguous feedback (clear and immediate feedback that the person is doing the activity well and is succeeding).
5 Total concentration on the task at hand.
6 A sense of exercising control without actively trying to be in control.
7 Time transformation (time disorientation or a loss of time awareness).
8 Deep enjoyment of the experience, referred to as Autotelic experience, involving intrinsically satisfying performance.

Additionally, the superior execution of these high-level performances can be linked to the concept of mindfulness where this concept describes the performer's acute awareness of the possibilities in the situation (Langer 2009). Mindfulness as a concept is having an increasingly widespread application in tourism and event studies because it identifies differences in the way tourists and event participants pay attention to and process the world around them (Moscardo 2009). The puzzle for psychologists, directors and performance managers in this area of interest is how to assist performers achieve these desirable mindful and flow states.

The application of psychology to assisting performers extends beyond the event stage or the field. Psychological research underpins the work of applied psychologists and counsellors who act as advisers to elite performers. They frequently provide rational emotive therapy and guidance to help individuals deal with success and failure (Ellis 1973; Haaga and Davison 1989). In this approach participants are encouraged to change their opinions and perspectives on how they view the world, as the underlying theory argues that human experience is modifiable through conscious control of thought patterns. In this approach a tennis player, for example, who loses a match may be encouraged not to think specifically about the outcome but to focus on the improving percentage of winning shots they have been practising. In this way success is possible even in defeat.

Additionally psychologists to the 'celebrities' are sometimes involved in further specialist counselling and advice programmes dealing with such areas of concern as drug and alcohol use, anger management and sexual indulgence. These applications of psychology have recently been given a new label, that of positive health (Seligman 2008) and represent efforts by psychology practitioners to develop agendas and support individuals to build character strengths. It is perhaps not an exaggeration to suggest that the industry of events depends in part on the industry of caretaking the psychological wellbeing of its key performers.

The hybrid nature of events: building a fan base for the North Queensland Fury A-League football club

The commercial world of professional sport witnesses the occasional creation of new teams joining ongoing competitions. Such developments arise from the intentions of sporting associations to spread the appeal and success of their code (Hoye *et al.* 2009). These kinds of initiatives can also reflect the changing demographics of regions and cities. The globally dominant sport of football with its international profile in terms of the FIFA World Cup and its powerful European and South American competitions has not been a dominant sport in Australia. Three other football codes (Australian Rules, rugby union and rugby league) have stronger support. In Australia, football is quite often referred to locally as soccer to distinguish it from the other forms of football. In 2009 the A-League, the Australian national competition for football, offered a franchise for a team to be developed in the rapidly expanding regional city of Townsville, North Queensland (population 175,000). The North Queensland Fury football team was somewhat hastily put together and became a part of a ten-team competition. The national competition actually includes one New Zealand team.

The initiative provided an interesting opportunity to research the hybrid nature of contemporary events. Bryman (2004) amongst others has noted that many twenty-first-century consumption settings demonstrate the conjunction of activities which were once separate and distinct. Ritzer (1999) notes that several sports stadia now have restaurants and sophisticated bars as well as amusement park attractions and special promotions of a range of business services. In the case study being considered here, while the core purpose for many to attend the football event was undoubtedly to watch the game, a number of associated activities were designed to broaden the appeal of the event and to involve those less devoted to the sporting contest. In particular the North Queensland Fury club was very keen to attract families and new attendees to the events. As a consequence facilities were provided in an open space at the rear of one of the grandstands for children's games and activities. These were the kinds of diversionary amusements more commonly associated with a local fair or children's party. Additionally entertainers were employed to add to the appeal of the sporting event. The additions to the event included some nationally recognised music performers and a group of drummers. There were also several competitions involving celebrities or spectators where prizes were offered. Other physical participatory opportunities were also included for children, with quite young players (mostly less than ten years old) being given an opportunity to have very brief matches of football on the ground during the half-time interval. There is some innovation in these activities as this kind of public involvement in football matches is very uncommon in the major leagues of world football.

An evaluation of the new sporting event in the city and its associated hybrid activities was conducted by asking spectators at five home games to complete an online survey. Over 900 respondents completed the online questions. In addition to exploring the loyalty to the team an evaluation of the atmosphere of the event and the ancillary activities was conducted. The motivation and interest in attending games was rated on four social sets of factors; entertainment, bonding with friends, bonding with family and socialising with other general crowd members. The entertainment component of the event, taken as a whole, was rated as the most important of the reasons to attend the game. The family facilities and the entertainment provided were both rated very positively by the survey participants. Nearly a quarter of the respondents purchased some Fury merchandise at the game, confirming the value of the hybrid shopping element at the games.

From the evaluation of the game-day experience, which as a whole was seen as very positive, a strong theme emerged in the study that attending this kind of well-managed sporting event with its ancillary activities offered safe, family-oriented entertainment. The hybrid consumption model supported the other findings in the study that the team was well received because it reflected local community pride and a different way of presenting competitive sport. Over 97 per cent of spectators said they would come to more games and there was a high level of optimism (6.1 on a 7-point scale) that the team would be more successful in the next season. Some 60 per cent of the spectators had purchased a Fury shirt with its predominantly bright green colours. The choice of colours arguably boosts the regional identification with a team based in the tropics and playing most of their games in the wet season. In a generic sense this case study suggested that a positive response to the hybrid nature of consumption was supporting the success of the event.

Conclusion

The review of psychology perspectives and concepts in the previous sections effectively transects the phases of people's involvement in events. At the outset, approaches to assessing the motives for participation and attendance were considered. Some event-specific motivational typologies were identified and approaches from tourism studies such as the travel career pattern approach were included in the discussion. This review of motivation was supplemented by key ideas drawn from social identity and identity theory and supported by the application of role theory. Actually being at, or participating in, an event was the next phase of the full event landscape to be considered. Here, it was suggested that emerging studies in experiencescapes have much to offer researchers intent on classifying and investigating what happens during on-site phases of the event panorama. Attendees' and participants' post-event evaluations were considered as a final set of research efforts and topics. The challenge to the expectancy disconfirmation paradigm approach was noted and richer affect-laden multi-faceted evaluations were highlighted. These phases of the event panorama were considered predominantly for event attendees with some additional variations noted for actual event participants and elite performers.

A methods-based contribution to event studies from psychology can also be suggested. While surveys of attendees and the use of structured scales are valuable tools for research in this field, both older and more recent techniques from psychology research practice can be considered for adoption. Experimental and quasi-experimental techniques can easily be overlooked when planning event studies. There are, however, many opportunities to assess attendees' and participants' reactions to planned and systematically manipulated features of settings. The events arenas are large laboratories, and sometimes difficult ones in which to work, but the logic of assessing human reactions to altered conditions, particularly changes in experiencescapes, offers a pathway for study. Emerging experiential sampling approaches offer many opportunities for understanding how the various components of events influence visitor behaviour. Comparative studies too should not be ignored, as researchers may be able to provide new insights from naturally occurring variations in event management practice and presentation. In the more recent array of research techniques deriving from developments in positive psychology there are ways of asking questions and conducting interviews which have a ready applicability to event studies. By using written response formats as well as employing mobile recording devices and cameras, event attendees and participants can be asked to focus on the ideal as well as the required qualities of event production. Some of the novel components of these techniques involve researchers coding contemporary social communication channels and asking respondents to contribute their observations on events to such web tools. It is also possible to use the positive psychology ideas to develop studies of the character strengths and personal growth of those who participate in richly fulfilling activities. Through its methods and in its conceptual schemes contemporary psychology can potentially enrich event studies and support the evolution of event phenomena.

References

Aho, S.K. (2001) 'Towards a general theory of touristic experiences: modelling experience process in tourism', *Tourism Review* 56(3/4): 33–7.

Allman, T., Mittelstaedt, R., Martin, B. and Goldenberg, M. (2009) 'Exploring the motivations of BASE jumpers: extreme sport enthusiasts', *Journal of Sport and Tourism* 14(4): 229–47.

Arnould, E.J. and Price, L.L. (1993) 'River magic: extraordinary experience and the extended service encounter', *Journal of Consumer Research* 20: 24–35.

Bankston, C. and Henry, J. (2000) 'Spectacles of ethnicity: festivals and the commodification of ethnic culture among Louisiana Cajuns', *Sociological Spectrum* 20(4): 377–407.

Berlyne, D. (1960) *Conflict, Arousal and Curiosity*, New York, NY: McGraw-Hill.

Bitner, M. (1992) 'Servicescapes: the impact of physical surroundings on customers and employees', *The Journal of Marketing* 56(2): 57–71.

Boring, E.G. (1950) *A History of Experimental Psychology*, New York: Appleton-Century-Crofts, second edition.

Branscombe, N.R. and Wann, D.L. (1992) 'Role of identification with a group, arousal, categorization processes, and self-esteem in sport spectator aggression', *Human Relations* 45: 1013–33.

Brown, G.P., Havitz, M.E. and Getz, D. (2007) 'Relationship between wine involvement and wine-related travel', *Journal of Travel and Tourism Marketing* 21(1): 31–46.

Bryan, H. (1977) 'Leisure value systems and recreational specialization: the case of trout fishermen', *Journal of Leisure Research* 9: 174–87.

Bryman, A. (2004) *The Disneyization of Society*, London: Sage.

Buttle, F. (1996) 'SERVQUAL: review, critique, research agenda', *European Journal of Marketing* 30: 8–32.

Cialdini, R.B., Borden, R.J., Thorne, A., Walker, M.R., Freeman, S. and Sloan, L.R. (1976) 'Basking in reflected glory: three (football) field studies', *Journal of Personality and Social Psychology* 34: 366–75.

Cohen, E. (1979) 'Rethinking the sociology of tourism', *Annals of Tourism Research* 6 (1): 18–35.

Cole, S. and Chancellor, H. (2009) 'Examining the festival attributes that impact visitor experience, satisfaction and re-visit intention', *Journal of Vacation Marketing* 15(4): 323.

Crompton, J. (1979) 'Motivations for pleasure vacation', *Annals of Tourism Research* 6(4): 408–24.

Crompton, J. and McKay, S. (1997) 'Motives of visitors attending festival events', *Annals of Tourism Research* 24(2): 425–39.

Csikszentmihalyi, M. (1975) *Beyond Boredom and Anxiety*, San Francisco: Jossey-Bass.

——(1990) *Flow: The Psychology of Optimal Experience*, New York: Harper and Row.

Dann, G. (1977) 'Anomie, ego-involvement and tourism', *Annals of Tourism Research* 4: 184–94.

——(1981) 'Tourist motivation: an appraisal', *Annals of Tourism Research* 8(2): 187–219.

Deighton, J. (1992) 'The consumption of performance', *Journal of Consumer Research* 19: 362–72.

Diener, E. and Biswas-Diener, R. (2008) *Happiness: Unlocking the Mysteries of Psychological Wealth*, Oxford: Blackwell.

Diller, S., Shedroff, N. and Rhea, D. (2006) *Making Meaning: How Successful Businesses Deliver Meaningful Customer Experiences*, Upper Saddle River, NJ: New Riders.

Edensor, T. (2000) 'Staging tourism: tourists as performers', *Annals of Tourism Research* 27(2): 322–44.

Ellis, A. (1973) 'Rational-emotive therapy', in R. Corsini (ed.) *Current Psychotherapies*, Itasaca, IL: Peacock.

Falassi, A. (1987) *Time out of Time: Essays on the Festival*, Albuquerque: University of New Mexico Press.

Festinger, L. (1954) 'A theory of social comparison processes', *Human Relations* 7: 117–40.

Fournier, S. and Mick, D.G. (1999) 'Rediscovering satisfaction', *Journal of Marketing* 63: 5–23.

Funk, D.C., Mahony, D.F., Nakazawa, M. and Hirakawa, S. (2001) 'Development of the Sports Interest Inventory (SII): implications for measuring unique consumer motives at sporting events', *International Journal of Sports Marketing and Sponsorship* 3: 291–316.

Funk, D.C., Mahony, D.F. and Ridinger, L. (2002) 'Characterizing consumer motivation as individual difference factors: augmenting the Sport Interest Inventory (SII) to explain level of spectator support', *Sport Marketing Quarterly* 11: 33–43.

Funk, D.C., Ridinger, L.L. and Moorman, A.M. (2003) 'Understanding consumer support: extending the Sport Interest Inventory (SII) to examine individual differences among women's professional sport consumers', *Sport Management Review* 6(1): 1–31.

——(2004) 'Exploring origins of involvement: understanding the relationship between consumer motives and involvement with professional sport teams', *Leisure Sciences* 26(1): 35–61.

Furnham, A. (2008) *50 Psychology Ideas You Really Need to Know*, London: Quercus.

Getz, D. (2007) *Event Studies Theory, Research and Policy for Planned Events*, Amsterdam: Elsevier.

Gibson, H., Willming, C. and Holdnak, A. (2002) '"We're Gators … not just Gator fans": serious leisure and University of Florida football', *Journal of Leisure Research* 34(4): 397–426.

Goffman, E. (1959) *The Presentation of Self in Everyday Life*, New York: Doubleday.

Gross, M. and Brown, G. (2006) 'Tourism experiences in lifestyle destination setting: the roles of involvement and place attachment', *Journal of Business Research* 59(6): 696–700.

Gursoy, D. and Gavcar, E. (2003) 'International leisure tourists' involvement profile', *Annals of Tourism Research* 30(4): 906–26.

Gwinner, K. and Swanson, S.R. (2003) 'A model of fan identification: antecedents and sponsorship outcomes', *Journal of Services Marketing* 17: 275–94.

Haaga, D.A. and Davison, G.C. (1989) 'Cognitive change methods', in A.P. Goldstein and F.H. Kanfer (eds) *Helping People Change*, New York: Pergamon Press, third edition.

Hannam, K. and Halewood, C. (2006) 'European Viking themed festivals: an expression of identity', *Journal of Heritage Tourism* 1(1): 17–31.

Harre, R., Clarke, D. and De Carlo, N. (1985) *Motives and Mechanisms*, London: Methuen.

Harris, D. (2005) *Key Concepts in Leisure Studies*, London: Sage.

Harris, T. (pers. comm.) 'Lecture on sports stadium management', Townsville, James Cook University, 10 April 2010.

Hogg, M., Terry, D. and White, K. (1995) 'A tale of two theories: a critical comparison of identity theory with social identity theory', *Social Psychology Quarterly* 58: 255–69.

Holbrook, M. and Hirschman, E. (1982) 'The experiential aspects of consumption: consumer fantasies, feelings and fun', *Journal of Consumer Research* 9: 132–40.

Holt, D.B. (1995) 'How consumers consume: a typology of consumption practices', *Journal of Consumer Research* 22: 1–16.

Hover, M. and van Mierlo, J. (2006) 'Imagine your event: imagineering for the event industry', unpublished manuscript, Breda University of Applied Sciences and NHTV Expertise, Netherlands, Event Management Centre.

Hoye, R., Smith, A., Nicholson, M., Stewart, B. and Westerbeek, H. (2009) *Sport Management*, Amsterdam: Elsevier.

Hsu, C.H.C. and Huang, S. (2008) 'Travel motivation: a critical review of the concept's development', in A. Woodside and D. Martin (eds) *Tourism Management Analysis, Behaviour and Strategy*, Wallingford, UK: CABI, pp. 14–27.

Iso-Ahola, S.E. (1980) *The Social Psychology of Leisure and Recreation*, Dubuque: William C. Brown.

——(1982) 'Toward a social psychological theory of tourism motivation: a rejoinder', *Annals of Tourism Research* 9(2): 256–62.

James, J.D. and Ross, S.D. (2004) 'Comparing sport consumer motivations across multiple sports', *Sport Marketing Quarterly* 13(1): 17–25.

Kapferer, J. and Laurent, G. (1985) 'Consumer involvement profiles: a new practical approach to consumer involvement', *Journal of Advertising Research* 25(6): 48–56.

Koo, G. and Hardin, R. (2008) 'Difference in interrelationship between spectators' motives and behavioral intentions based on emotional attachment', *Sport Marketing Quarterly* 17(1): 30.

Kurtzman, J. and Zauhar, J. (1998) 'Sport tourism: a business inherency or an innate compulsion? *Visions in Leisure and Business* 17(2): 21–30.

Kyle, G. and Chick, G. (2002) 'The social nature of leisure involvement', *Journal of Leisure Research* 34(4): 426–49.

Langer, E.J. (1989) *Mindfulness*, Reading, MA: Addison-Wesley.

——(2009) *Counterclockwise: Mindful Health and the Power of Possibility*, New York: Ballantine Books.

Laurendeau, J. (2006) '"He didn't go in doing a skydive": sustaining the illusion of control in an edgework activity', *Sociological Perspectives* 49(4): 583–605.

Laverie, D. and Arnett, D. (2000) 'Factors affecting fan attendance: the influence of identity salience and satisfaction', *Journal of Leisure Research* 32(2): 225–46.

Lee, J. and Beeler, C. (2007) 'The relationships among quality, satisfaction, and future intention for first-time and repeat visitors in a festival setting', *Event Management* 10(4): 197–208.

Li, X. and Petrick, J. (2006) 'A review of festival and event motivation studies', *Event Management* 9(4): 239–45.

Lyng, S. (1990) 'Edgework: a social psychological analysis of voluntary risk taking', *American Journal of Sociology* 95(4): 851–86.

Lyng, S. and Snow, D.A. (1986) 'Vocabularies of motive and high-risk behavior: the case of skydiving', *Advances in Group Processes* 3: 157–79.

McCall, G.J. and Simmons, J.L. (1966) *Identities and Interactions*, New York: Free Press.

MacCannell, D. (1976) '*The Tourist: A New Theory of the Leisure Class*, New York: Schocken Books.

McGehee, N., Yoon, Y. and Cardenas, D. (2003) 'Involvement and travel for recreational runners in North Carolina', *Journal of Sport Management* 17(3): 305–24.

McIntyre, N. and Pigram, J.J. (1992) 'Recreation specialization reexamined: the case of vehicle-based campers', *Leisure Research* 14: 3–15.

Madrigal, R. (1995) 'Cognitive and affective determinants of fan satisfaction with sporting event attendance', *Journal of Leisure Research* 27(3): 205–27.

——(2003) 'Investigating an evolving leisure experience: antecedents and consequences of spectator affect during a live sporting event', *Journal of Leisure Research* 35: 23–48.

Mann, L. and Pearce, P.L. (1978) 'The social psychology of the sports spectator', in D. Glencross (ed.) *Sport in Australia*, Sydney: Macmillan, 173–201.

Mansfeld, Y. (1992) 'From motivation to actual travel', *Annals of Tourism Research* 19: 399–419.

Martin, G.N., Carlson, N.R. and Buskit, W. (2007) *Psychology*, Harlow, UK: Pearson, third edition.

Maslow, A. (1943) 'A theory of human motivation', *Psychological Review* 50: 370–96.

Mehus, I. (2005) 'Sociability and excitement motives of spectators attending entertainment sport events: spectators of soccer and ski-jumping', *Journal of Sport Behavior (JSB)* 28(4): 333–50.

Miller, J.A. (1977) 'Studying satisfaction, modifying models, eliciting expectations, posing problems, and making meaningful measurements', in H.K. Hunt (ed.) *Conceptualization and Measurement of Consumer Satisfaction and Dissatisfaction. Conference Conducted by Marketing Science Institute with Support of National Science Foundation*, Cambridge, MA: Marketing Science Institute, pp. 72–91.

Milne, D. and Common, A. (1998) 'Delivering and evaluating psychological skills training for athletes and coaches', in H. Steinberg, I. Cockerill and A. Dewey (eds) *What Do Sports Psychologists Do?* Leicester: British Psychological Society.

Milne, G.R. and McDonald, M.A. (1999) *Sport Marketing: Managing the Exchange Process*, Sudbury, MA: Jones & Bartlett.

Mischel, W. (1968) *Personality and Assessment*, New York: Wiley.

——(1984) 'Convergences and challenges in the search for consistency', *American Psychologist* 34: 740–54.

Morgan, M. (2009) 'What makes a good festival? Understanding the event experience', *Event Management* 12(2): 81–93.

Moscardo, G. (2009) 'Exploring mindfulness and stories in tourist experiences', paper presented to the 6th CPTHL Symposium, Vienna, Austria: MODUL University Vienna, 1–3 June.

Moss, S. (2009) *The Entertainment Industry. An Introduction*, Wallingford, UK: CABI.

Mossberg, L. (2007) 'A marketing approach to the tourist experience', *Scandinavian Journal of Hospitality and Tourism* 7(1): 59–74.

Murray, H. (1938) *Exploration and Personality*, New York: Oxford University Press.

Nicholson, R. and Pearce, D. (2001) 'Why do people attend events? A comparative analysis of visitor motivations at four South Island events', *Journal of Travel Research* 39(4): 449.

O'Dell, T. (2005) 'Experiencescapes: blurring borders and testing connections', in T. O'Dell and P. Billing (eds) *Experiencescapes – Tourism, Culture and Economy*, Copenhagen: Copenhagen Business School Press.

Oppermann, M. and Chon, K. (1997) 'Convention participation decision-making process', *Annals of Tourism Research* 24(1): 178–91.

Pearce, P.L. (1988) *The Ulysses Factor: Evaluating Visitors in Tourist Settings*, New York: Springer–Verlag.

——(2005) *Tourist Behaviour: Themes and Conceptual Schemes*, Clevedon: Channel View Publications.

——(2008) 'Studying tourism entertainment through micro-cases', *Tourism Recreation Research* 33(2): 151–63.

Pearce, P.L. and Lee, U. (2005) 'Developing the travel career approach to tourist motivation', *Journal of Travel Research* 43: 226–37.

Pearce, P.L., Morrison, A. and Rutledge, J. (1998) *Tourism: Bridges across Continents*, Sydney: McGraw-Hill.

Pettersson, R. and Getz, D. (2009) 'Event experiences in time and space: a study of visitors to the 2007 World Alpine Ski Championships in Åre, Sweden', *Scandinavian Journal of Hospitality and Tourism* 9(2): 308–26.

Pike, K.L. (1966) *Language in Relation to a Unified Theory of the Structure of Human Behaviour*, The Hague: Mouton.

Pine, B.J. and Gilmore, J.H. (1999) *The Experience Economy*, Boston: Harvard Business School Press.

Reicher, S.D. (1984) 'The St Paul's "riot": an explanation of the limits of crowd action in terms of the social identity model', *European Journal of Social Psychology* 14: 1–21.

——(1996) ' "The Battle of Westminster": developing the social identity model of crowd conflict', *European Journal of Social Psychology* 26: 115–34.

Ritchie, B., Mosedale, L. and King, J. (2000) 'Profiling sport tourists: the case of Super 12 rugby union in Canberra', in B. Ritchie and D. Adair (eds) *Sports Generated Tourism: Exploring the Nexus. Proceedings of the First Australian Sports Tourism Symposium, 5–7 October 2000, Canberra, Australia*, Canberra: CRC for Sustainable Tourism, pp. 57–67.

Ritzer, G. (1999) *Enchanting a Disenchanted World: Revolutionizing the Means of Consumption*, Thousand Oaks, CA: Pine Forge Press.

Robinson, M.J. and Trail, G.T. (2005) 'Relationships among spectator gender, motives, points of attachment, and sport preference', *Journal of Sport Management* 19(1): 58–80.

Rothschild, M.L. (1984) 'Perspectives on involvement: current problems and future directions', *Advances in Consumer Research* 11: 216–17.

Ryan, C. (ed.) (2002) *The Tourist Experience*, London: Continuum, second edition.

Seligman, M. (2008) 'Positive health', *Applied Psychology* 57: 3–18.

Severt, D., Wang, Y., Chen, P. and Breiter, D. (2007) 'Examining the motivation, perceived performance, and behavioral intentions of convention attendees: evidence from a regional conference', *Tourism Management* 28(2): 399–408.

Shank, M.D. and Beasley, F.M. (1998) 'Fan or fanatic: refining a measure of sports involvement', *Journal of Sport Behavior* 21(4): 436–50.

Shipway, R. and Jones, I. (2007) 'Running away from home: understanding visitor experiences and behaviour at sport tourism events', *International Journal of Tourism Research* 9(5): 373–83.

——(2008) 'The great suburban Everest: an "insider's" perspective on experiences at the 2007 Flora London Marathon', *Journal of Sport and Tourism* 13(1): 61–77.

Simons, Y. and Taylor, J. (1992) 'A psychosocial model of fan violence', *International Journal of Sport Psychology* 23: 207–26.

Sloan, L.R. (1989) 'The motives of sports fans', in J.H. Goldstein (ed.) *Sports Games and Play: Social and Psychological Viewpoints*, Hillsdale, NJ: Lawrence Erlbaum Associates, second edition.

Snelgrove, R., Taks, M., Chalip, L. and Green, B.C. (2008) 'How visitors and locals at a sport event differ in motives and identity', *Journal of Sport and Tourism* 13(3): 165–80.

Snow, D. and Oliver, P. (1995) 'Social movements and collective behavior: social psychological dimensions and considerations', in K. Cook, G. Fine and J. House (eds) *Social Psychology: Sociological Perspectives*, Boston, MA: Allyn and Bacon, pp. 571–600.

Soldz, S. and Vaillant, G.E. (1999) 'The big five personality traits and the life course: a 45-year longitudinal study', *Journal of Research in Personality* 33: 208–32.

Standevan, J. and De Knop, P. (1999) *Sport Tourism*, Champaign: Human Kinetics.

Stebbins, R. (1982) 'Serious leisure: a conceptual statement', *Pacific Sociological Review* 25(2): 251–72.

——(1997) 'Casual leisure: a conceptual statement', *Leisure Studies* 16(1): 17–25.

——(2004) 'Fun, enjoyable, satisfying, fulfilling: describing positive leisure experience', *LSA Newsletter* 69: 8–11.

Stryker, S. and Burke, P. (2000) 'The past, present, and future of an identity theory', *Social Psychology Quarterly* 63: 284–97.

Tajfel, H. (1982) *Social Identity and Intergroup Relations*, Cambridge: Cambridge University Press.

Thrane, C. (2002) 'Music quality, satisfaction, and behavioral intentions within a jazz festival context', *Event Management* 7(3): 143–50.

Trail, G.T. and James, J.D. (2001) 'The Motivation Scale for Sport Consumption: assessment of the scale's sychometric properties', *Journal of Sport Behavior* 24(1): 108–27.

Turner, U. and Turner, E. (1978) *Image and Pilgrimage in Christian Culture*, New York: Columbia University Press.

Turner, V. (1969) *The Ritual Process: Structure and Anti-Structure*, New York: Aldine de Gruyter.

——(1974) *Social drama and ritual metaphors*, Ithaca, NY: Cornell University Press.

van Leeuwen, L., Quick, S. and Daniel, K. (2002) 'The sport spectator satisfaction model: a conceptual framework for understanding the satisfaction of spectators', *Sport Management Review* 5(2): 99–128.

Wakefield, K. and Blodgett, J. (1994) 'The importance of servicescapes in leisure service settings', *Journal of Services Marketing* 8(3): 66–76.

Wamwara-Mbugua, L.W. and Cornwell, T.B. (2009) 'Visitor motivation to attending international festivals', *Event Management* 13(4): 277–86.

Wann, D.L. (1995) 'Preliminary motivation of the sport fan motivation scale', *Journal of Sport & Social Issues* 19: 377–96.

——(1996) 'Seasonal changes in spectators' identification and involvement with and evaluations of college basketball and football teams', *The Psychological Record* 46(1): 201–16.

Wann, D.L. and Branscombe, N.R. (1993) 'Sports fans: measuring degree of identification with their team', *International Journal of Sport Psychology* 24: 1–17.

Wann, D.L., Dolan, T.J., McGeorge, K.K. and Allison, J.A. (1994) 'Relationships between spectator identification and spectators' perceptions of influence, spectators' emotions, and competition outcome', *Journal of Sport and Exercise Psychology* 16(4): 347–64.

Wann, D.L., Carlson, J.D. and Schrader, M.P. (1999) 'The impact of team identification on the hostile and instrumental verbal aggression of sport spectators', *Journal of Social Behavior and Personality* 14: 279–86.

Wann, D.L., Schrader, P. and Wilson, M. (1999) 'Sport fan motivation – questionnaire validation, comparisons by sport, and relationship to athletic motivation', *Journal of Sport Behaviour* 22: 114–39.

Wann, D.L., Grieve, F.G., Zapalac, R.K. and Pease, D.G. (2008) 'Motivational profiles of sport fans of different sports', *Sport Marketing Quarterly* 17(1): 6.

Zaichkowsky, J. (1985) 'Measuring the involvement construct', *Journal of Consumer Research* 12(3): 341–52.

Zillmann, D., Bryant, J. and Sapolsky, B.S. (1979) 'The enjoyment of watching sports contests', in J.H. Goldstein (ed.) *Sports, Games, and Play: Social and Psychological Viewpoints*, Hillsdale, NJ: Lawrence Erlbaum, pp. 297–335.

12

The political analysis and political economy of events

C. Michael Hall

Introduction

Tourist events are both explicit and implicit political occasions. The image-building which accompanies such events creates a situation in which personal and institutional interests receive a high degree of visibility (Hall 2001; Jones 2001; Paul 2004; Black 2007). However, while place promotion and competitiveness is often the focus of the political analysis of events (Hall 1992, 2006; Waitt 2001, 2008; Reid 2006; Mason 2008), the spread of what constitutes 'the political' crosses over into areas such as industrial relations issues (Engels 2000), rights (Lenskyj 1996; Roche 2000, 2003; Black and van der Westhuizen 2004; Price and Dayan 2008), protest (Markwell 2002; Greene 2003; Tufts 2004; Paddison 2009), exclusion (Atkinson and Laurier 1998; MacLeod 2002) and the relationship of events to election strategies (McCarthy 2002; Whitson and Horne 2006) and international relations (van der Westhuizen 2004; Yuen 2008).

The chapter is divided into four main sections. The first two sections identify the disciplinary contexts and importance of politics and political economy, respectively, for event studies. The chapter then discusses the implications of the political analysis of events for researchers and the consequent importance of understanding the philosophical basis for research on the political dimensions of events. The fourth section examines the way in which understanding and application of the concept of power – one of the core concepts of political thought – affects the political analysis of events. The chapter then concludes by re-emphasising the inherently political nature of the study of event politics.

Politics and political analysis

In its broadest sense politics is about power: who gets what, where, how and why (Lasswell 1936). The conception of politics and the political is important because it shapes the questions that researchers do or do not consider as well as assumptions made when undertaking research (Hall 2011a). Donahue (2009) identifies seven different classes of conceptions of what constitutes politics: power-seeking conceptions, power-distributing conceptions, struggle-and-competition conceptions, collective decision-and-action conceptions, group and social order-production conceptions, authority-asserting conceptions, and shaping values and arrangements conceptions.

Some of the most widely used definitions of politics are:

- Politics is the exercise of power.
- Politics is the public allocation of things that are valued.
- Politics is the resolution of conflict.
- Politics is the competition among individuals and groups pursuing their own interests.
- Politics is the determination of who gets what, when, and how.

(Hall 2011a: 39)

All of these definitions share the central idea that the political process involves the values of actors (individuals, interest groups and public and private organisations) in a struggle for power (Danziger 2001).

The concept of power is itself grounded in broader questions as to how power is conceptualised and how it can be studied. It is an 'essentially contested' concept (Gallie 1955–6) for which there is no universal agreement as to exactly how the concept should be understood and therefore analysed. Lukes' (1974) seminal work on power conceptualised power as 'all forms of successful control by A over B – that is, of A securing B's compliance' (Lukes 1974: 17). However, Lukes (2005) stressed that the use of the concept of power is inextricably linked to a given set of value assumptions held by researchers that predetermine the range of its empirical application. Addressing the issue of power in studies of the politics of events is therefore intrinsically 'messy'. Guzzini (2001), for example, notes that any neutral definition of 'power' is elusive because power is used as an explanatory variable and there is no neutral concept of power for the dependence of theory, empirical and conceptual analyses, on meta-theoretical commitments. Morriss (1987) also notes that power is difficult to study, but nevertheless extremely important, because of its practical, moral and evaluative contexts. We are interested in power because we want to know how things are brought about. Through the assessment of power, moral responsibility for the use of power can be attributed. We are also not just interested in the judgement of individuals but in the evaluation of society. All of these issues emerge in studying events, with the connection between power and responsibility highlighting 'the importance of understanding the morality of power and the political and ethical space of what we study' (Hall 2011a: 43).

> When we see the conceptual connection between the idea of power and the idea of responsibility, we can see more clearly why those who exercise power are not eager to acknowledge the fact … to acknowledge power over others is to implicate oneself in responsibility for certain events and to put oneself in a position where justification for the limits placed on others is expected. To attribute power to another, then, is not simply to describe his or her role in some perfectly neutral sense, but is more like accusing him or her of something, which is then to be denied or justified
>
> *(Connolly 1974: 97)*

Key questions with respect to power structure research include:

1 What organisation, group or class in the social structure under study receives the most of what people seek and value (*who benefits*)?
2 Which organisation, group or class is overrepresented in key decision-making positions (*who sits*)?
3 Which organisation, group or class wins in the decisional arena (*who wins*)?

4   Who is thought to be powerful by knowledgeable observers and peers (*who has a reputation for power*)?

(Domhoff 2007)

These are questions that clearly reflect Lasswell's (1936) comment about politics noted above. Unfortunately, in event studies such questions are often never asked (Hall 2007a, 2010). As Church and Coles (2007a: 270) observed: 'Given the tourism academy contains many researchers with backgrounds in anthropology, geography and sociology it is still curious that power, a core concept in social sciences generally and more importantly very recently, has not become a more prominent issue.'

Political analysis is closely related to public policy analysis given that politics is concerned with the exercise of power and influence both in a society and in specific decisions over public policy: what officials within government decide to do or not to do about issues and problems that require government intervention. Indeed, the division between politics and public policy is arguably something related more to Anglo-American discourse, as many languages do not really distinguish between politics and policy (Hall and Jenkins 1995).

Political economy

Although the term 'political economy' was first used in the eighteenth century to refer to the economic actions of government and their contribution to national economic wellbeing, it is now used within a number of different research traditions ranging from Marxism and public choice approaches to post-structuralism (Close *et al.* 2007), although in tourism and event studies the term is more usually associated with Marxist and neo-Marxist analysis (Britton 1991; Hall 1994; Bianchi 2002, 2009; Mosedale 2011). Maier (1987: 6) provides one of the best descriptions of political economy, noting that it

> regards economic ideas and behavior not as frameworks for analysis, but as beliefs and actions that must themselves be explained. They are contingent and problematic; that is, they might have been different and they must be explained within particular political and social contexts.

A significant development in the study of urban political economy, which has paid considerable attention to the hosting of events, is the development of the field of 'cultural economy' (Scott 2001). This is a concept that is broader in scope than an association within cultural industry, as significant as these might be for hosting events (Evans 2003; Jones and Wilks-Heeg 2004; Kong 2007; Tucker 2008; Gibson *et al.* 2010). Amin and Thrift (2004: xviii) define cultural economy as the postdiscipline 'concerned with the processes of social and cultural relations that go to make up what we conventionally term the economic' (see also Amin and Thrift 2007a, 2007b; and Gibson and Kong 2005).

The recognition of culture as part of the fundamental make-up of contemporary capitalism is part of the broader 'cultural turn' in the social sciences from the 1990s on. In political economic terms this has extended some of the more traditional foci of urban political economy, and particularly the significance of urban entrepreneurialism: 'a public–private partnership focusing on investment and economic development with the speculative construction of place rather than amelioration of conditions within a particular territory as its immediate (though by no means exclusive) political and economic goal' (Harvey 1989: 8). Urban entrepreneurialism was particularly influential on some of the earlier studies of event politics (Boyle and Hughes 1994; Roche 1994; Waitt 1999; Owen 2002), especially as it reflected a recognition that 'urban politics can no longer be analyzed in isolation from the larger political and economic forces that shape the development, restructuring, and redevelopment of urban spaces and places' (Jonas and Wilson 1999: 11). The insertion of culture into urban political economy was a result not only of the increasing explicit use of culture as an economic development strategy (e.g. European Capitals of Culture or the use of museums and art galleries as economic flagships), but also the growth of postmodernism and new conceptualisations of the culture–economy relationship (e.g. gender studies, ethnic networks, postcolonialism, sexual identities, performity, everyday life, virtual space) (Ribera-Fumaz 2009).

The development of cultural political economy represents a move away from representational or materialist methodologies to develop new accounts of the dialectical articulation of both the material and the immaterial (branding, identity, image, semiotic) as co-created economic practice. According to Jessop and Sum (2001: 94) the postdisciplinary perspective of cultural political economy is

A critical, self-reflexive approach to the definition and methods of political economy and to the inevitable contextuality and historicity of its claims to knowledge. It rejects any universalistic, positivistic account of reality, denies the subject–object duality, allows for the co-constitutions of subjects and objects and eschews reductionist approaches to the discipline. However, in taking the 'cultural turn', political economy should continue to emphasize the materiality of social relations and the constraints involved in processes that also operate 'behind the backs' of the relevant agents ... 'Cultural political economy' should recognize the emergent extra-discursive features of social relations and their impact on capacities for action and transformation.

The approach has arguably been significant for at least four main lines of research that place events within the context of cultural economic processes. First, the urban morphology of economic restructuring in which events are implicated in the cultural–material production of urban space (Hall and Hodges 1997; Evans 2003; Beriatos and Gospodoni 2004; Alegi 2007; Monclús 2009). Second, the development of the 'new' and 'symbolic' economy in which events, in conjunction with the leisure and tourism sectors, are integral to postmodern economic and political urban strategies (Smith 2001; Yang and Hsing 2001; McCallum *et al.* 2005; Broudehoux 2007). Third, entrepreneurialism and ethnicity in which cultural discourses of race and ethnic difference become part of entrepreneurial place strategies (Silk 2002; Hall and Rath 2007; Gold and Gold 2008). Fourth, the role of events in the construction of place competition (Jones 2002; Malecki 2004; Turok and Bailey 2004; Hall 2006; Connelly 2007). Undoubtedly, a political economy approach is significant for understanding how events are embedded in broad processes of economic development, the decision-making processes that accompany event bids and hosting, governance and regulatory processes, and the uneven distribution of the costs and benefits of events. However, one of the remarkable aspects of the political economy of events is that nearly all of the literature occurs outside of event studies and tourism. Although concepts such as competitiveness, for example, are included in research from within event studies and tourism studies the associated discourse tends to ignore the contribution of political economy and associated critique (Carlsen and Taylor 2003; Getz 2007). It instead strongly tends to be technical-rational in scope and grounded in a business and marketing paradigm that regards 'competitiveness' as inherently good and unproblematic (Hall 2007b). Therefore, before examining the way in which a core concept of political analysis and political economy – that of power – is applied in research on the politics of events, the chapter will discuss the ontological basis of event research and its relationship to the relative lack of research on the politics of events within event studies.

The philosophical basis for research on the politics of events

Research into the political impacts of hallmark events has only received limited attention within the field that has come to be termed 'event studies' (see Chapter 2). However, the political dimension has received considerably more attention from the broader social sciences, and particularly from sociology, sports studies and geographers. Several factors can be recognised as accounting for this situation. First, in its institutional form 'event studies' has primarily been developed from within a framework of managerialism (Enteman 1993) and is geared strongly towards the interests of event associations, organisations and the event market. This has meant that the understanding of politics and political economy, or even recognition of their broader significance, is cursory at best. Arguably this issue arises in great part because of fundamental differences in ontology (Hay 2009).

Ontologically and epistemologically there is not an encouragement of critique in event studies, as the classical realist empiricism (Bhaskar 2008) that underlies much of the work that is undertaken is strongly driven by a materialist and mechanistic orientation that often serves to artificially divide facts and values in the political process. Such a situation may help explain the apparent unwillingness by many researchers and individual and institutional actors in the political process to acknowledge the significance of hallmark events at both the macro- and micro-political level. In contrast an ontological position that sees not only political processes but also the research process itself as being socially constructed is far more likely to recognise the overtly political nature of events, in terms of favouring certain interests and values over others, as well as the inherently political nature of event research and results. Such an ontological position is much stronger within political studies (Bates and Jenkins 2007) than it is within event studies as it has usually been conceived (Getz 2007). This observation is extremely important as it emphasises that not only are events political but also the research that is undertaken on them.

Reflexivity on knowledge and action (Habermas 1978) highlights the extent to which events research is politically bounded, even if sometimes researchers are unaware of it. Gupta and Ferguson (1997) suggests that research locations should be conceptualised as political locations rather than as 'spatial sites' – a position that finds substantial support amongst feminist research. For example, from a broad understanding of politics, the locations in which events occur are positionings in time and space which have specific effects and consequences, or 'politics', that need to be analysed and historicised (Lorenz-Meyer 2004). Even from a narrower conceptualisation, event research and fieldwork is something that is subject to regulation and the exercising of power within the relations between fieldworkers and subjects/informants/gatekeepers within the institution(s) both of the researcher and of the subjects of research (Hall 2011b).

The institutional context provides a second reason as to why the political dimension of events has been little studied within event studies. The institutional dimension is highly important in political analysis as researchers into the politics of events should be aware of not only the institutions that shape the manner in which events are developed and held (Boyle 1997), but also those which affect their work. Institutions play an extremely important role in determining the trajectories of research (Demeritt 2000). An institution represents a social order or pattern that has attained a certain state and which helps establish the 'rules of the game' (Hotimsky *et al.* 2006: 41). They are 'production systems, enabling structures, social programs or performance scripts' (Jepperson 1991: 145). For many event researchers the institutional context that surrounds universities, and business schools in particular, often provides a disincentive to investigate the political dimension of events. Successive series of governments in many developed countries have been supporting a research and tertiary education agenda that is increasingly focused on supposedly apolitical economic and market-oriented research deliverables (Demeritt 2000).

Analysis of the politics of events, particularly large-scale events, will usually entail study of the activities of the very government that is funding research and education. In such a context it can be extremely hard to 'bite the hand that feeds' particularly if government puts substantial emphasis on the hosting of large events and simultaneously provides funding for 'appropriate' research for which universities and individuals within them are being encouraged to bid. Simply put, there is a lack of interest in conducting research into the political dimensions of events and there is little incentive from government and the bodies that manage events to conduct such research. Indeed, as Ritchie (1984: 10) observed, 'there are undoubtedly pressures in the opposite direction'.

One way in which event research is bound up in issues of political power and interest is with respect to such matters as access to elite respondents and the opportunities to directly interview them, as opposed to the relative ease of talking directly to people who may have been affected by the hosting of events. As Cormode and Hughes (1999: 299) note, undertaking research on

> 'the powerful' presents very different methodological and ethical challenges from studying 'down'. The characteristics of those studied, the power relations between them and the researcher, and the politics of the research process differ considerably between elite and non-elite research ... When studying elites, the scholar is a supplicant.

The third major reason for the relative lack of research on the politics of events is that there are substantial methodological difficulties in conducting political studies of events because of the ideological nature and political implications of such research (Hall 1989, 2011a). Although this is partly the result of different ontologies, it points to wider differences into the acceptability of method and the ways in which political research issues are framed.

Nevertheless, research on the political dimensions of hallmark events may actually be of an extremely practical nature and of value to governments and event organisers. For example, political analysis may indicate how the impacts of events affect host communities and increase the understanding of related decision, planning and policy-making processes (Hall 1992; Adranovich et al. 2001), and improve the design of the public–private partnerships that are often involved in event organisation (Wettenhall 2003, 2005). Political research may help make event decision making more open, transparent and democratic and, perhaps most critically, may also encourage greater dialogue as to the value of hosting events and the relationships between ends and means in public policy (Felsenstein and Fleischer 2003; Macchiavelli 2003). For example, Pillay and Bass (2008) suggested that it was unlikely that poverty alleviation would constitute a significant outcome of the hosting of the 2010 FIFA World Cup in South Africa because of the manner in which urban development was being fast-tracked. The notion of event legacy, the authors argue, should therefore be expanded and a vigorous public debate should be encouraged to develop broad agreement as to what kind of legacy such events are realistically able to achieve. In political terms this may move beyond the standard events legacy discourse that is configured in terms of stadia and facilities for sporting teams, economic benefits, place branding, and employment creation (e.g. Murphy and Carmichael 1991; Walo et al. 1996; Ritchie 2000; Carlsen and Taylor 2003; Jago et al. 2003; Getz 2009), to one that is grounded in a more fundamental political debate as to who wins and who loses – and why.

Power

As noted above, power is one of the central concepts of political science and political economy. The issue of power is one that has become increasingly significant in the study of tourism and events (Adams 2006; Church and Coles 2007b; Macleod and Carrier 2010). However, much of the broader debate on power structures and how power is conceptualised has been missed in much of the tourism literature to the extent that usually the concept is presented in terms of a specific interpretation and application rather than indicating that there are a range of different interpretations, each with its own strengths and weaknesses (Church and Coles 2007a; Hall 2010). As Wolf (1999: 4) noted, power is often portrayed as if it were an independent force,

> sometime incarnated in the image of a giant monster such as Leviathan or Behemoth, or else as a machine that grows in capacity and ferocity by accumulating and generating more powers, more entities like itself. Yet it is best understood neither as an anthropomorphic force nor a giant machine but as an aspect of all relations among people.

The relational dimension is fundamental to understanding the concept of power. Power is always present in relationships between actors, whether they are individuals or institutions. Giddens (1979: 93) noted that power is always a two-way process, 'even if the power of one actor is minimal compared to another'. Such a relational understanding of power is also inherent to Lukes' (1974) seminal work on power in which power was conceptualised as 'all forms of successful control by A over B – that is, of A securing B's compliance' (Lukes 1974: 17).

To be 'political' means to be potentially changeable (Hoffmann 1988). The notion of power therefore implies counterfactuals, i.e. it could be done differently (Connolly 1974). Indeed, Lukes (1974) indicated that Bachrach and Baratz's (1962, 1970) conceptualisation of power with respect to the importance of non decision making (confining the scope of decision making so as to deliberately exclude other decision options) served to redefine what counts as a political issue in the sense that what is not done is as important as what is done, and often more so. For Guzzini (2000, 2001) this provides a constructivist dimension to the analysis of power as concept formation is part of the social construction of knowledge; and the defining and assigning of power is therefore a power or 'political' exercise in itself and hence part of the social construction of reality. Therefore, the study of power, in and of itself, runs counter to those who seek to 'depoliticise' policy and research fields and present them as 'rational' exercises in decision making and analysis (Hall 2011a). Such a perspective is also relevant to the reification in event studies of the inherent value of 'collaboration', 'partnership', 'networks' and 'stakeholder management' (Peters and Pikkemaat 2005; Gursoy and Kendall 2006; Mossberg and Getz 2006; Stokes 2007; Hede 2008), with only little consideration of the power dimensions of such social relationships and the potential exclusion of other actors and perspectives (Hall 2010, 2011a).

Lukes' (1974, 2005) identification of three different dimensions or faces of power provides a useful way to categorise power and also connects event research to broader debates on the nature of power. The first dimension of power emphasises observable, overt behaviour, conflict and decision making. In academic terms it is most associated with the work of Dahl (1961) who argued that power was intentional and active and related to several, separate, single issues and bound to the local or community context of its exercise (Lukes 2005). The emphasis by Dahl on overt preferences of interest groups served to strengthen the pluralistic conception of power that, 'since different actors and different interest groups prevail in different issue-areas, there is no overall "ruling elite"' (Lukes 2005: 5). The assumption of pluralism in decision making and its association with community interests has been extremely influential in stakeholder and community-based planning approaches to events (Tyson et al. 2005; Raj and Morpeth 2006; Hede 2008; Stokes 2008), although useful event case studies can still be developed on overt political decision making (Reid 2006).

Bachrach and Baratz (1962, 1970) identified two major weaknesses in the pluralist approach to power: that it did not provide for the exercise of power by confining the scope of political decision making; and that power had a 'second face' that was neither perceived nor understood by pluralists nor detectable by their modes of inquiry, noting that the pluralist conception of power was 'too narrowly drawn' (Bachrach 1967: 87). Critics of pluralism emphasised that power was not solely reflected in concrete observable decisions. Instead, 'the researcher must also consider the chance that some person or association could limit decision making to relatively non-controversial values, by influencing community values and political procedures and rituals, notwithstanding that there are in the community serious but latent power conflicts' (Lukes 2005: 6). The critique of pluralism is closely linked to Schattschneider's (1960) concept of the 'mobilisation of bias'. According to Schattschneider (1960: 71) 'all forms of political organization have a bias in favour of some kinds of conflict and the suppression of others because organization is the mobilization of bias. Some issues are organized into politics while others are organized out.' Such a stance led to recognition of the importance of non-decision making as a factor in tourism and events decision making (Hall and Jenkins 1995). Non-decisions are a means by which demands for change in the existing allocation of benefits in a community, or those affected by political decision making, can be kept covert, or stopped before they gain access to the relevant decision-making arena (Hall 2010); or, failing all these things, destroyed in the implementation stage of the policy process (Hall 2009).

A good example of non-decision making with respect to events is the case of the bidding process for the 2000 Summer Olympics. In the case of the Sydney bid for the 2000 Olympics the former New South Wales state premier, Nick Greiner (1994), as well as Rod McGeoch (1994), both commented on the importance of the media in creating a supportive public climate for the bid (Hall 2001). As Greiner (1994: 13) stated:

> Early in 1991, I invited senior media representatives to the premier's office, told them frankly that a bid could not succeed if the media played their normal 'knocking role' and that I was not prepared to commit the taxpayers' money unless I had their support. Both News Ltd and Fairfax subsequently went out of their way to ensure the bid received fair, perhaps even favourable, treatment. The electronic media also joined in the sense of community purpose.

Such a situation, unknown until revealed by Greiner, indicated how opposition to events can be kept out of the public agenda. However, it can also be done via law changes. For example, in the case of the 2000 Sydney Olympics the New South Wales state government passed legislation which meant that Sydney residents lost their right to initiate a court appeal under environment and planning legislation against the proposed Olympic projects. Further legislation passed under the New South Wales government's Olympic Co-ordination Authority Act allowed, somewhat ironically given the green image which was an integral part of the Games bid, all projects linked with the Games to be suspended from the usual environmental impact statements requirements (Hall 2001). Similarly, in the state of Victoria the Victorian Grand Prix Act exempted the Melbourne Formula 1 Grand Prix and its track construction from environmental impact studies, pollution and planning controls, and all agreements with the international promoters of the event from the state Freedom of Information Act (Hall 2001). As Lowes (2004: 77) noted, the Act 'effectively removed the Grand Prix event from all the usual checks and balances which ordinarily protect the public by ensuring that no single arm of government is inordinately powerful or unaccountable'. Indeed, according to a news release from the office of the then deputy premier and minister responsible for the Grand Prix, Pat

---

McNamara: 'The Grand Prix Act has been principally designed to ensure that the over 400,000 spectators who attend this event over four days won't have their fun spoiled by political protest groups' (26 October 1995, cited in Lowes 2004: 80). However, these Australian examples are not uncommon and the suspension of normal participative planning procedures, legal rights and even taxation procedures are a hallmark of large-scale events such as the Olympics, World Cup football and rugby, and Formula 1 (Hall 1996, 1998, 2001; Lowes 2002; Greene 2003; McCallum *et al.* 2005; Smith and Himmelfarb 2007; Askew 2009; Shin 2009; Guilianotti and Klauser 2010; Hall and Wilson 2011).

The deliberate mobilisation of bias and behind-the-scenes agenda setting led to the investigation of the concept of hegemony and the manufacture of consent (Hall 2010). Such voluntary consent can vary in intensity:

On one extreme, it can flow from a profound sense of obligation, from wholesale internalisation of dominant values and definitions; on the other from their very partial assimilation, from an uneasy feeling that the status quo, while shamefully iniquitous, is nevertheless the only viable form of society.

(Femia 1981: 39)

Notions of hegemony were extremely influential in the development of a third dimension of power that arises out of the role of power in shaping preferences 'through the operation of social forces and institutional practises or through individuals' decisions' (Lukes 1974: 24). According to Lukes (1974: 24), 'to assume that the absence of grievances equals genuine consensus is simply to rule out the possibility of false or manipulated consensus by definitional fiat'. Instead, 'the most effective and insidious use of power' is that 'A may exercise power over B ... by influencing, shaping or determining his very wants' (Lukes 1974: 23).

A number of authors have focused on the hegemony of urban entrepreneurial and neo-liberal discourse in the civic boosterism and growth coalitions that mark many bids for large-scale events as well as their actual hosting (Ley and Olds 1988; Boyle 1997; Schimmel 1997; Roche 2000; Paul 2004; Hall 2006), particularly with respect to the notion of place competitiveness (MacLeod 2002; Shoval 2002; Hall and Wilson 2011). Rossiter and Wood (2005) provide the example of the lead-up to the 2010 Vancouver Winter Olympic Games, arguing that the British Columbian government sought to avoid overt protest by promoting the benefits of the 2010 Winter Olympic Games for First Nations peoples, including a programme to boost 'aboriginal tourism' including the use of First Nations peoples in the Games imaging and promotion. Yet simultaneously the province denied the 'First Nations' assertions of land title and rights to self-government' and instead focused on the desire to attract investment 'within the logic of neo-liberalism' (Rossiter and Wood 2005: 365). Indeed, Paddison (2009) suggests that the new orthodoxy of neo-liberal practices within urban governance is characterised by the manufacture of consensus politics, the effect of which is to marginalise protest and dissensus. One of the main means by which this is conducted is by the use of discourse and the employment of language that seeks to persuade the populace that its policies are the only and appropriate course of action, usually via the requirement to remain 'competitive' in the light of place globalisation. As Paddison (2009: 29) observes with respect to Glasgow,

Competitive urbanism functions as a ratchet within which cities become locked into an increasingly competitive process of bidding for inwards investment. Nowhere is this more explicit than in the bidding to hold mega-events, including major sports and cultural events. Glasgow is a prime, but increasingly common, example whose record in the field within urban marketing circles is widely cited in paradigmatic terms ... The city's marketing agency is engaged in an ongoing process of bidding to host events, major conferences, tourist attractions of different types, in which precisely because other cities are engaged in it, questioning the premise on which it is based is not a political option.

Conclusions

The chapter has highlighted the role of political analysis in the study of events. It has stressed the inherently political nature of such research because of the methodological and philosophical groundings of such research but also because of the extent to which political research provides the potential to be critical of those in power or, at the very least, imply alternatives and counter-factuals. The chapter has also highlighted that much of the critical and analytical study of the politics of events has taken place outside of the immediate domain of event studies, which is regarded as being rational, managerialist and prescriptive with respect to notions of event politics and policy (indeed, the two are usually regarded as being capable of being separated from each other). Instead, critical studies of events see them as being socially constructed and deeply embedded with relations of power, institutions, interests and values in an unambiguously political process (Hall 1992, 2010, 2011a).

The chapter has also focused on the concept of power as being a cornerstone in the political analysis of events with the differing dimensions of power having implications for how the politics and operation of power in the event context is defined and studied. The study of power – as for the wider political analysis of events – is therefore theoretically contingent. Significantly, the third dimension of power emphasises the importance of the deliberate mobilisation of bias and behind-the-scenes agenda setting as part of hegemonic discourse and the manufacture of consent. Such a perspective also serves to connect the need for a better understanding of the role of the political culture of institutions and communities on event practices with greater reflexivity of the institutional context of the researcher. Arguably, in both cases a neo-liberal discourse of competitiveness and marketisation combined with a supposed lack of alternative discourse appears to prevail. Nevertheless, hegemonic discourses whether in events or in academia are never complete. Events provide conflictual and contradictory processes that simultaneously disempower localities and some individuals and yet also create new pressures for local autonomy and resistance (Gotham 2005a). When using an appropriate theoretical lens, events illustrate the contestation between different groups and interests that attempt to (re)produce them for their own ends. As authors such as Gotham (2005a, 2005b) emphasise, in the face of globalised forms of cultural production and consumption and place commodification that limit creativity and innovation, events provide opportunities to hear voices from actors who use events to sow seeds of dissent, emphasise the contradictions of converting cities and places into spectacles, create breeding grounds for reflexive action and launch radical critiques of inequality.

Further reading

Church, A. and Coles, T. (eds) (2007) *Tourism, Power and Space*, London: Routledge. (Provides good overview of approaches to power in tourism.)
Gotham, K.F. (2005) 'Theorizing urban spectacles', *City: Analysis of Urban Trends, Culture, Theory, Policy, Action* 9: 225–46. (Excellent discussion of urban theory in relation to events.)

——(2005) 'Marketing Mardi Gras: commodification, spectacle and the political economy of tourism in New Orleans', *Urban Studies* 39: 1735–56. (Very good case study of event commodification and its implications.)

Hall, C.M. (1998) 'The politics of decision making and top-down planning: Darling Harbour, Sydney', in D. Tyler, M. Robertson and Y. Guerrier (eds) *Tourism Management in Cities: Policy, Process and Practice*, Chichester: John Wiley. (Case study of top-down event-related decision making.)

——(2006) 'Urban entrepreneurship, corporate interests and sports mega-events: the thin policies of competitiveness within the hard outcomes of neoliberalism', *The Sociological Review*, 54(Issue Supplement s2): 59–70. (Relates hosting of events to urban entrepreneurialism and neoliberal discourse.)

——(ed.) (2011) *Fieldwork in Tourism: Methods, Issues and Reflections*, London: Routledge. (Provides several chapters that discuss the politics of fieldwork and research.)

Lowes, M. (2002) *Indy Dreams and Urban Nightmares: Speed Merchants, Spectacle, and the Struggle over Public Space in the World-class City*, Toronto: University of Toronto Press. (Excellent examination of the conflict between different interests in the hosting of Formula 1 and Indy Car racing.)

Lukes, S. (2005) *Power: A Radical View*, London: Palgrave Macmillan in association with the British Sociological Association, second edition. (Classic examination of the concept of power.)

Paddison, R. (2009) 'Some reflections on the limitations to public participation in the post-political city', *L'Espace Politique* 8(2009–2). Available at: http://espacepolitique.revues.org/index1393.html (very good discussion on the way in which public debate on hosting events is constrained by neoliberal discourse).

Roche, M. (2000) *Mega-events and Modernity: Olympics and Expos in the Growth of Global Culture*, London: Routledge. (One of the best discussions of the rationale behind hosting hallmark events.)

References

Adams, K.M. (2006) *Art as Politics: Re-crafting Identities, Tourism and Power in Tana Toraja, Indonesia*, Honolulu: University of Hawai'i Press.

Adranovich, G., Burbank, M.J. and Heying, C.H. (2001) 'Olympic cities: lessons learned from mega-event politics', *Journal of Public Affairs* 23: 113–31.

Alegi, P. (2007) 'The political economy of mega-stadiums and the underdevelopment of grassroots football in South Africa', *Politikon* 34: 315–31.

Amin, A. and Thrift, N. (eds) (2004) *The Blackwell Cultural Economy Reader*, Oxford: Blackwell.

——(2007a) 'On being political', *Transactions of the Institute of British Geographers NS* 32: 112–15.

——(2007b) 'Cultural-economy and cities', *Progress in Human Geography* 31: 143–61.

Askew, D. (2009) 'Sport and politics: the 2008 Beijing Olympic Games', *European Studies: A Journal of European Culture, History and Politics* 27: 103–20.

Atkinson, D. and Laurier, E. (1998) 'A sanitised city? Social exclusion at Bristol's 1996 international festival of the sea', *Geoforum* 29: 199–206.

Bachrach, P. (1967) *The Theory of Democratic Elitism: A Critique*, Boston: Little, Brown.

Bachrach, P. and Baratz, M.S. (1962) 'Two faces of power', *American Political Science Review* 56: 947–52.

——(1970) *Power and Poverty: Theory and Practice*, Oxford: Oxford University Press.

Bates, S.R. and Jenkins, L. (2007) 'Teaching and learning ontology and epistemology in political science', *Politics* 27(1): 55–63.

Beriatos, E. and Gospodoni, A. (2004) '"Glocalising" urban landscapes: Athens and the 2004 Olympics', *Cities* 21(3): 187–202.

Bhaskar, R. (2008) *A Realist Theory of Science*, Abingdon: Routledge, second edition.

Bianchi, R. (2002) 'Towards a new political economy of global tourism', in R. Sharpley and D. Telfer (eds) *Tourism and Development. Concepts and issues*. Clevedon: Channel View.

——(2009) 'The "cultural turn" in tourism studies: a radical critique', *Tourism Geographies* 11: 484–504.

Black, D. (2007) 'The symbolic politics of sport mega-events: 2010 in comparative perspective', *Politikon* 34: 261–76.

Black, R. and van der Westhuizen, J. (2004) 'The allure of global games for "semi-peripheral" polities and spaces: a research agenda', *Third World Quarterly* 25: 1195–214.

Boyle, M. (1994) 'The politics of urban entrepreneurialism in Glasgow', *Political Geography* 25: 453–70.

——(1997) 'Civic boosterism in the politics of local economic development – "institutional positions" and "strategic orientations" in the consumption of hallmark events', *Environment and Planning A* 29(11): 1975–97.

Boyle, M. and Hughes, G. (1994) 'The politics of urban entrepreneurialism in Glasgow', *Geoforum* 25(4): 453–70.

Britton, S. (1991) 'Tourism, dependency and place: towards a critical geography of tourism development', *Environment and Planning D: Society and Place* 9: 451–78.

Broudehoux, A.-M. (2007) 'Spectacular Beijing: the conspicuous construction of an Olympic metropolis', *Journal of Urban Affairs* 29: 383–99.

Carlsen, J. and Taylor, A. (2003) 'Mega-events and urban renewal: the case of the Manchester 2002 Commonwealth Games', *Event Management* 8: 15–22.

Church, A. and Coles, T. (2007a) 'Tourism and the many faces of power', in A. Church and T. Coles (eds) *Tourism, Power and Space*, London: Routledge.

——(eds) (2007b) *Tourism, Power and Space*, London: Routledge.

Close, P., Askew, D. and Xin, X. (2007) *The Beijing Olympiad: The Political Economy of a Sporting Mega-event*, Abingdon: Routledge.

Connelly, G. (2007) 'Testing governance – a research agenda for exploring urban tourism competitiveness policy: the case of Liverpool 1980–2000', *Tourism Geographies* 9: 84–114.

Connolly, W.E. (1974) *The Terms of Political Discourse*, Oxford: Martin Robertson.

Cormode, L. and Hughes, A. (1999) 'Editorial: The economic geographer as a situated researcher of elites', *Geoforum* 30: 299–300.

Dahl, R.A. (1961) *Who Governs? Democracy and Power in an American City*, New Haven: Yale University Press.

Danziger, J.N. (2001) *Understanding the Political World*, New York: Longman, fifth edition.

Demeritt, D. (2000) 'The new social contract for science: accountability, relevance, and value in US and UK science and research policy', *Antipode* 32: 308–29.

Domhoff, G.W. (2007) 'C. Wright Mills, Floyd Hunter, and 50 years of power structure research', *Michigan Sociological Review* 21: 1–54.

Donahue, T.J. (2009) 'Research note', *Conceptions of Politics* 46(1/2) (18 September). SSRN. Available at: http://ssrn.com/abstract=1151265 (accessed 1 January 2010).

Engels, B. (2000) 'City make-overs: the place marketing of Melbourne during the Kennett years, 1992–99', *Urban Policy and Research* 18: 469–94.

Enteman, W.F. (1993) *Managerialism: The Emergence of a New Ideology*, Madison: University of Wisconsin Press.

Evans, G. (2003) 'Hard-branding the cultural city – from Prado to Prada', *International Journal of Urban and Regional Research* 27: 417–40.

Felsenstein, D. and Fleischer, A. (2003) 'Local festivals and tourism promotion: the role of public assistance and visitor expenditure', *Journal of Travel Research* 41: 385–92.

Fernia, J. (1981) *Gramsci's Political Thought: Hegemony, Consciousness and the Revolutionary Process*, Oxford: Clarendon Press.

Gallie, W.B. (1955–6) 'Essentially contested concepts', *Proceedings of the Aristotelian Society* 56: 167–98.

Getz, D. (2007) *Event Studies: Theory, Research and Policy for Planned Events*, Oxford: Butterworth-Heinemann.

——(2009) 'Policy for sustainable and responsible festivals and events: institutionalization of a new paradigm', *Journal of Policy Research in Tourism, Leisure and Events* 1: 61–78.

Gibson, C. and Kong, L. (2005) 'Cultural economy: a critical review', *Progress in Human Geography* 29: 541–61.

Gibson, C., Waitt, G., Walmsley, J. and Connell, J. (2010) 'Cultural festivals and economic development in nonmetropolitan Australia', *Journal of Planning Education and Research* 29: 280–93.

Giddens, A. (1979) *Central Problems in Social Theory: Action, Structure and Contradiction in Social Analysis*, Los Angeles: University of California Press.

Gold, J.R. and Gold, M.M. (2008) 'Olympic cities: regeneration, city rebranding and changing urban agendas', *Geography Compass* 2: 300–18.

Gotham, K.F. (2005a) 'Theorizing urban spectacles', *City: Analysis of Urban Trends, Culture, Theory, Policy, Action* 9: 225–46.

——(2005b) 'Marketing Mardi Gras: commodification, spectacle and the political economy of tourism in New Orleans', *Urban Studies* 39: 1735–56.

Greene, S.J. (2003) 'Staged cities: mega-events, slum clearance, and global capital', *Yale Human Rights and Development Law Journal* 6: 161–87.

Greiner, N. (1994) 'Inside running on Olympic bid', *The Australian*, 19 September: 13.

Guilianotti, R. and Klauser, F. (2010) 'Security governance and sport mega-events: toward an interdisciplinary research agenda', *Journal of Sport and Social issues* 34: 49–61.

Gupta, A. and Ferguson, J. (1997) 'Discipline and practice: "the field" as site, method, and location in anthropology', in A. Gupta and J. Ferguson (eds) *Anthropological Locations: Boundaries and Grounds of a Field Science*, Berkeley: University of California Press.

Gursoy, D. and Kendall, K.W. (2006) 'Hosting mega events: modeling locals' support', *Annals of Tourism Research* 33: 603–23.

Guzzini, S. (2000) 'A reconstruction of constructivism in international relations', *European Journal of International Relations* 6: 147–82.

——(2001) 'The significance and roles of teaching theory in international relations', *Journal of International Relations and Development* 4(2): 98–117.

Habermas, J. (1978) *Knowledge and Human Interests*, London: Heinemann, second edition.

Hall, C.M. (1989) 'The politics of events', in G.J. Syme, B.J. Shaw, D.M. Fenton and W.S. Mueller (eds) *The Planning and Evaluation of Hallmark Events*, Aldershot: Avebury.

——(1992) *Hallmark Tourist Events*, Chichester: John Wiley.

——(1994) *The Politics of Tourism*, Chichester: John Wiley.

——(1996) 'Hallmark events and urban reimaging strategies: coercion, community and the Sydney 2000 Olympics', in L.C. Harrison and W. Husbands (eds) *Practicing Responsible Tourism: International Case Studies in Planning, Policy and Development*, New York: John Wiley.

——(1998) 'The politics of decision making and top-down planning: Darling Harbour, Sydney', in D. Tyler, M. Robertson and Y. Guerrier (eds) *Tourism Management in Cities: Policy, Process and Practice*, Chichester: John Wiley.

——(2001) 'Imaging, tourism and sports event fever: the Sydney Olympics and the need for a social charter for mega-events', in C. Gratton and I.P. Henry (eds) *Sport in the City: The Role of Sport in Economic and Social Regeneration*, London: Routledge.

——(2006) 'Urban entrepreneurship, corporate interests and sports mega-events: the thin policies of competitiveness within the hard outcomes of neoliberalism', *The Sociological Review*, 54 (Issue Supplement s2): 59–70.

——(2007a) 'Tourism, governance and the (mis-)location of power', in A. Church and T. Coles (eds) *Tourism, Power and Space*, London: Routledge.

——(2007b) 'Tourism and regional competitiveness', in J. Tribe and D. Airey (eds) *Advances in Tourism Research, Tourism Research, New Directions, Challenges and Applications*, Oxford: Elsevier.

——(2009) 'Archetypal approaches to implementation and their implications for tourism policy', *Tourism Recreation Research* 34: 235–45.

——(2010) 'Power in tourism: tourism in power', in D. Macleod and J. Carrier (eds) *Tourism, Power and Culture: Anthropological Insights*. Bristol: Channel View.

——(2011a) 'Researching the political in tourism: where knowledge meets power', in C.M. Hall (ed.) *Fieldwork in Tourism: Methods, Issues and Reflections*, London: Routledge.

——(2011b) 'Fieldwork in tourism/touring fields: where does tourism end and fieldwork begin?', in C.M. Hall (ed.) *Fieldwork in Tourism: Methods, Issues and Reflections*, London: Routledge.

Hall, C.M. and Hodges, J. (1997) 'Sharing the spirit of corporatism and cultural capital: the politics of place and identity in the Sydney 2000 Olympics', in M. Roche (ed.) *Sport, Popular Culture and Identity*, Aachen: Meyer & Meyer Verlag.

Hall, C.M. and Jenkins, J.M. (1995) *Tourism and Public Policy*, London: Routledge.

Hall, C.M. and Rath, J. (2007) 'Tourism, migration and place advantage in the global economy', in J. Rath (ed.) *Tourism, Ethic Diversity and the City*, New York: Routledge.

Hall, C.M. and Wilson, S. (2011) 'Neoliberal urban entrepreneurial agendas, Dunedin Stadium and the Rugby World Cup: or "If you don't have a stadium, you don't have a future"', in D. Dredge and J. Jenkins (eds) *Stories of Practice: Tourism Policy and Planning*, Farnham: Ashgate.

Harvey, D. (1989) 'From managerialism to entrepreneurialism: the transformation of urban governance in late capitalism', *Geografiska Annaler B* 71: 3–17.

Hay, C. (2009) 'Your ontology, my ontic speculations ... on the Importance of showing one's (ontological) working', *Political Studies* 57: 892–8.

Hede, A.-M. (2008) 'Managing special events in the new era of the triple bottom line', *Event Management* 11: 13–22.

Hoffmann, J. (1988) *State, Power and Democracy: Contentious Concepts in Practical Political Theory*, New York: St Martin's Press.

Hotimsky, S., Cobb, R. and Bond, A. (2006) 'Contracts or scripts? A critical review of the application of institutional theories to the study of environmental change', *Ecology and Society* 11(1): 41. Available at: www.ecologyandsociety.org/vol11/iss1/art41/

Jago, L., Chalip, L., Brown, G., Mules, T. and Ali, S. (2003) 'Building events into destination branding: Insights from experts', *Event Management* 8: 3–14.

Jepperson, R.L. (1991) 'Institutions, institutional effects, and institutionalism', in R.W. Powell and P.J. DiMaggio (eds) *The New Institutionalism in Organizational Analysis*, Chicago: University of Chicago Press.

Jessop, B. and Sum, N.L. (2001) 'Pre-disciplinary and post-disciplinary perspectives', *New Political Economy* 6: 89–101.

Jonas, A.G. and Wilson, D. (1999) 'The city as a growth machine: critical reflections two decades later', in A.G. Jonas and D. Wilson (eds) *The Urban Growth Machine: Critical Perspectives Two Decades Later*, Albany: State University of New York.

Jones, C. (2001) 'Mega-events and host-region impacts: determining the true worth of the 1999 Rugby World Cup', *International Journal of Tourism Research* 3: 241–51.

——(2002) 'Public cost for private gain? Recent and proposed "national" stadium developments in the UK, and commonalities with North America', *Area* 34: 160–70.

Jones, P. and Wilks-Heeg, S. (2004) 'Capitalising culture: Liverpool 2008', *Local Economy* 19: 341–60.

Kong, L. (2007) 'Cultural icons and urban development in Asia: economic imperative, national identity, and global city status', *Political Geography* 26: 383–404.

Lasswell, H.D. (1936) *Politics: Who Gets, What, When, How?* New York: McGraw-Hill.

Lenskyj, H.J. (1996) 'When winners are losers: Toronto and Sydney bids for the Summer Olympics', *Journal of Sport and Social Issues* 20: 392–410.

Ley, D. and Olds, K. (1988) 'Landscape as spectacle: world's fairs and the culture of heroic consumption', *Environment and Planning D: Society and Space* 6(2): 191–212.

Lorenz-Meyer, D. (2004) 'Addressing the politics of location: strategies in feminist epistemology and their relevance to research undertaken from a feminist perspective', in S. Strbánová, I.H. Stamhuis and K. Mojsejová (eds) *Women Scholars and Institutions*, Volume 13b, Prague: Research Centre for History of Sciences and Humanities. Available at: cec-wys.org (accessed 10 January 2010).

Lowes, M. (2002) *Indy Dreams and Urban Nightmares: Speed Merchants, Spectacle, and the Struggle over Public Space in the World-class City*, Toronto: University of Toronto Press.

——(2004) 'Neoliberal power politics and the controversial siting of the Australian Grand Prix motorsport event in an urban park', *Society and Leisure* 27(1): 69–88.

Lukes, S. (1974) *Power: A Radical View*, London: Macmillan.

——(2005) *Power: A Radical View*, London: Palgrave Macmillan in association with the British Sociological Association, second edition.

McCallum, K., Spencer, A. and Wyly, E. (2005) 'The city as an image-creation machine: a critical analysis of Vancouver's Olympic bid', *Association of Pacific Coast Geographers Yearbook* 67: 24–46.

McCarthy, J. (2002) 'Entertainment-led regeneration: the case of Detroit', *Cities* 19: 105–11.

Macchiavelli, A. (2003) 'Report on workshop III: Sport as a public good? What is the role of the state in the development of sports and tourism?', *Tourism Review* 58(4): 39–40.

McGeoch, R. with Korporal, G. (1994) *The Bid: How Australia Won the 2000 Games*, Sydney: William Heinemann.

Macleod, D. and Carrier, J. (eds) (2010) *Tourism, Power and Culture: Anthropological Insights*, Bristol: Channel View Publications.

MacLeod, G. (2002) 'From urban entrepreneurialism to a "revanchist city"? On the spatial injustices of Glasgow's renaissance', *Antipode* 34: 602–24.

Maier, C.S. (1987). *In Search of Stability: Explorations in Historical Political Economy*, Cambridge: Cambridge University Press.

Malecki, E.J. (2004) 'Jockeying for position: what it means and why it matters to regional development policy when places compete', *Regional Studies* 38: 1101–20.

Markwell, K. (2002) 'Mardi Gras tourism and the construction of Sydney as an international gay and lesbian city', *GLQ: A Journal of Lesbian and Gay Studies* 8(1–2): 81–99.

Mason, D. (2008) 'Urban regimes and sport in North American cities: seeking status through franchises, events and facilities', *International Journal of Sport Management and Marketing* 3(3): 221–41.

Monclús, F.J. (2009) *International Exhibitions and Urbanism: The Zaragoza Expo 2008 project*, Farnham: Ashgate.

Morriss, P. (1987) *Power: A Philosophical Analysis*, Manchester: Manchester University Press.

Mosedale, J. (ed.) (2011) *Political Economy of Tourism: A Critical Perspective*, London: Routledge.

Mossberg, L. and Getz, D. (2006) 'Stakeholder influences on the ownership and management of festival brands', *Scandinavian Journal of Hospitality and Tourism* 6: 308–26.

Murphy, P.E. and Carmichael, B. (1991) 'Assessing the tourism benefits of an open access sports tournament: the 1989 BC Winter Games', *Journal of Travel Research* 29(3): 32–6.

Owen, K.A. (2002) 'The Sydney 2000 Olympics and urban entrepreneurialism: Local variations in urban governance', *Australian Geographical Studies* 40: 323–36.

Paddison, R. (2009) 'Some reflections on the limitations to public participation in the post-political city', *L'Espace Politique* 8(2009–2). Available at: http://espacepolitique.revues.org/index1393.html (accessed 25 December 2010).

Paul, D.E. (2004) 'World cities as hegemonic projects: the politics of global imagineering in Montreal', *Political Geography* 23: 571–96.

Peters, M. and Pikkemaat, B. (2005) 'The management of city events: the case of "Bergsilvester" in Innsbruck, Austria', *Event Management* 9: 147–53.

Pillay, U. and Bass, O. (2008) 'Mega-events as a response to poverty reduction: the 2010 FIFA World Cup and its urban development implications', *Urban Forum* 19: 329–46.

Price, M.E. and Dayan, D. (eds) (2008) *Owning the Olympics: Narratives of the New China*, Ann Arbor: University of Michigan Press.

Raj, R. and Morpeth, N. (2006) 'Local community structures in events and festivals: opportunities for destination marketing or communities "caring for place"?', *Tourism Today* 6: 82–95.

Reid, G. (2006) 'The politics of city imaging: a case study of the MTV Europe Music Awards Edinburgh 03', *Event Management* 10: 35–46.

Ribera-Fumaz, R. (2009) 'From urban political economy to cultural political economy: rethinking culture and economy in and beyond the urban', *Progress in Human Geography* 33: 447–65.

Ritchie, J.R.B. (1984) 'Assessing the impact of hallmark events: conceptual and research issues', *Journal of Travel Research* 23(1): 2–11.

——(2000) 'Turning 16 days into 16 years through Olympic legacies', *Event Management* 6(3): 155–65.

Roche, M. (1994) 'Mega-events and urban policy', *Annals of Tourism Research* 21: 1–19.

——(2000) *Mega-events and Modernity: Olympics and Expos in the Growth of Global Culture*, London: Routledge.

——(2003) 'Mega-events, time and modernity. On time structures in global society', *Time and Society* 12: 99–126.

Rossiter, D. and Wood, P. (2005) 'Fantastic topographies: neo-liberal responses to Aboriginal land claims in British Columbia', *The Canadian Geographer* 49(4): 352–66.

Sadd, D. (2009) 'What is event-led regeneration? Are we confusing terminology or will London 2012 be the first Games to truly benefit the local existing population?', *Event Management* 13(4): 265–75.

Schattschneider, E. (1960) *Semi-sovereign People: A Realist's View of Democracy in America*, New York: Holt, Rinehart and Wilson.

Schimmel, K.S. (1997) 'The edifice complex: reliance on new sports stadiums to solve urban problems', *Sporting Traditions* 14: 146–55.

Scott, A.J. (2001). *The Cultural Economy of Cities*, London: Sage.

Shin, H.B. (2009) 'Life in the shadow of mega-events: Beijing Summer Olympiad and its impact on housing', *Journal of Asian Public Policy* 2(2): 122–41.

Shoval, N. (2002) 'A new phase in the competition for the Olympic Gold: the London and New York bids for the 2012 Games', *Journal of Urban Affairs* 24: 583–99.

Silk, M. (2002) '"Bangsa Malaysia": global sport, the city and the mediated refurbishment of local identities', *Media, Culture and Society* 2: 775–94.

Smith, A. (2001) 'Sporting a new image? Sport-based regeneration strategies as a means of enhancing the image of the city tourist destination', in C. Gratton and I.P. Henry (eds), *Sport in the City: The Role of Sport in Economic and Social Regeneration*, London: Routledge.

Smith, J. and Himmelfarb, K.M.G. (2007) 'Restructuring Beijing's Social Space: observations on the Olympic Games in 2008', *Eurasian Geography and Economics* 48: 543–54.

Stokes, R. (2007) 'Relationships and networks for shaping events tourism: an Australian study', *Event Management* 10: 145–58.

——(2008) 'Tourism strategy making: insights to the events tourism domain', *Tourism Management* 29: 252–62.

Tucker, M. (2008) 'The cultural production of cities: rhetoric or reality? Lessons from Glasgow', *Journal of Retail and Leisure Property* 7: 21–33.

Tufts, S. (2004) 'Building the "competitive city": Labour and Toronto's bid to host the Olympic games', *Geoforum* 35: 47–58.

Turok, I. and Bailey, N. (2004) 'Twin track cities? Competitiveness and cohesion in Glasgow and Edinburgh', *Progress in Planning* 62: 135–204.

Tyson, B., Hayle, C., Truly, D., Jordan, L.A. and Thame, M. (2005). 'West Indies World Cup Cricket: hallmark events as catalysts for community tourism development', *Journal of Sport Tourism* 10: 323–34.

Van der Westhuizen, J. (2004) 'Marketing Malaysia as a model modern Muslim state: the significance of the 16th Commonwealth Games', *Third World Quarterly* 25(7): 1277–91.

Waitt, G. (1999) 'Playing games with Sydney: marketing Sydney for the 2000 Olympics', *Urban Studies* 36: 1055–77.

——(2001) 'The Olympic spirit and civic boosterism: the Sydney 2000 Olympics', *Tourism Geographies* 3: 349–278.

——(2008) 'Urban festivals: geographies of hype, helplessness and hope', *Geography Compass* 2(2): 513–37.

Walo, M., Bull., A. and Breen, H. (1996) 'Achieving economic benefits at local events: a case study of a local sports event', *Festival Management and Event Tourism* 4(3–4): 95–106.

Wettenhall, R. (2003) 'The rhetoric and reality of public–private partnerships', *Public Organization Review* 3(1): 77–107.

——(2005) 'The public–private interface: surveying the history', in G.A. Hodge and C. Greve (eds) *The Challenge of Public–Private Partnerships: Learning from International Experience*, Cheltenham: Edward Elgar.

Whitson, D. and Horne, J. (2006) 'Underestimated costs and overestimated benefits? Comparing the outcomes of sports mega-events in Canada and Japan', *The Sociological Review* 54(Issue Supplement s2): 71–89.

Wolf, E.R. (1999) *Envisioning Power: Ideologies of Dominance and Crisis*, Berkeley: University of California Press.

Yang, M.-C. and Hsing, W.-C. (2001) 'Kinmen: governing the culture industry city in the changing global context', *Cities* 18: 77–85.

Yuen, B. (2008) 'Sport and urban development in Singapore', *Cities* 25: 29–36.

13

Managing uncertainty

(Re)conceptualising aspects of operations for events

Julia Tum[1]

Introduction

Even though the events management literature has grown in recent years, significant research gaps remain. Indeed, while academics have made considerable inroads into understanding the sociological, cultural and economic role and consequences of events and festivals, there has been much less progress on researching their effective management. Scholarly output to date on events management – as opposed to events studies (Getz 2007) – has tended to consolidate knowledge and disseminate it in the form of textbooks (see for example Yeoman *et al.* 2004; Tum *et al.* 2006; Bowdin *et al.* 2011). It is no less valuable for this but, as the field matures, it is appropriate that more effort is made to research aspects of management relating to events. This chapter seeks to make a modest contribution to this process by shifting academic attention towards some of the operational issues that are relevant to those engaged in the practice of events management.

Producing events precipitates a number of managerial challenges. Their often peripatetic or transient nature stimulates, for example, the need for particular kinds of approaches to the management of employees (including the high incidences of temporary or voluntary staff; Shone and Parry 2004), to crowd control (Still and Draper 2010), to ticketing (Smith 2007), to risk and stakeholder management (Leopkey and Parent 2009) as well as reflection on a range of consumer and marketing issues (Bowen and Daniels 2005; Tkaczynski and Rundle-Thiele 2011). Silvers *et al.* (2006) have attempted to encapsulate these dimensions of management by developing an event management body of knowledge (EMBOK). EMBOK contains a range of domains, values, phases and processes that enable the effective development of event managers and event management. If such an approach is to flourish, it requires ongoing research to enhance understanding within each category of effective management practices so that training and development may be appropriately informed.

This chapter aims to create a means of responding to one of the central challenges of events management, namely uncertainty. It introduces a matrix as a possible framework to help managers deal with the inherently uncertain environment within which they operate. More specifically, the matrix takes into account eight characteristics, four of which are traditionally offered as being the main *differences* between manufacturing and service management (Shostack 1977; Walker 1995; Kandampully 2002; Stevenson 2005; Chase *et al.* 2006; Heizer and Render

2006), and incorporates a further four which are argued to be particularly relevant to the management of events. Though its potential application is illustrated here via the case of le Tour de France, further empirical research is required before the value of the framework can be confirmed. Such work is underway but will be reported elsewhere at a later date.

Managing uncertainty: a matrix approach

Correa *et al.* (2007) devised a radar representation that allowed for simultaneous presentation of different characteristics they believed to be pertinent to service management. They proposed a framework that could assess the kinds of management processes and flexibility which could be provided alongside a range of tools used by operations managers in developing, planning, organising or controlling the production and delivery of services. Their framework took the four traditional sets of characteristics (intangibility, inseparability, heterogeneity and perishability) and combined them with stockability, intensity of interaction, simultaneousness of consumption and ease of performance assessment. Their framework is an applied way that can improve operations management and embraces how businesses compete and operate today.

The events matrix proposed in this chapter follows the principles advanced by Correa *et al.* (2007) but amends it to include eight characteristics which are seen as being peculiar to an event. As Figure 13.1 shows, it has four lines which cross to create a matrix with eight points.

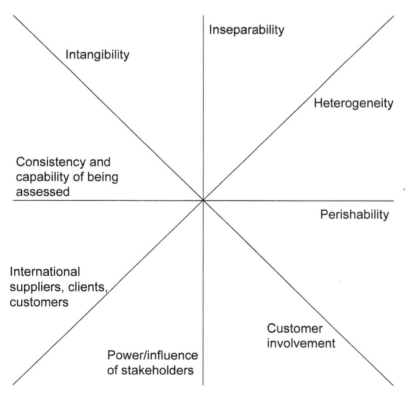

Figure 13.1 A matrix as a possible framework to help managers deal with the inherently uncertain environment within which they operate

Table 13.1 The impact of phenomena and record of interventions taken

Phenomenon	Position on axis	Intervention	Changed place on axis
Intangibility	Low	An awareness of pre-event litter	Increasing tangibility
Inseparability	Low	Can be achieved and checked after the event	Low, no change
Heterogeneity	Low	Discussion with stakeholders	Lower
Perishability	High	Well-planned and good logistical system	
Customer involvement	Low	Provide more waste bins, opportunities to sort; increase public awareness of need to control litter. Cyclists to discard waste packaging only where there are crowds	Medium
Power/influence of stakeholders	High	Keep involved and satisfied. Clarify expectations. Reduce packaging from caravan gifts	Medium
International suppliers, clients, customers	Medium	Be fully aware of all cultural differences	Low
Consistency and capability of being assessed	Medium	Devise and share common agreement	High

Along each of the lines, the degree of impact of each phenomenon can be plotted and the appropriate management intervention can be noted (see Table 13.1). The notion of heterogeneity is crucial to service operations since all events require a high level of staffing, i.e. are delivered by people to people. People's performance can fluctuate every day and so the level of consistency that can be counted upon is not a certainty (Knisely 1979). This matrix itself is heterogeneous and can be manipulated and used by event managers and interpreted for different events with a myriad of different micro-operations in order to determine the most appropriate set of controls or changes that should take place.

What follows is an explanation and justification of each dimension of the matrix. The discussion is structured to reflect the operational needs of managers. This should not be taken to imply that there is no need to test the framework for effectiveness. As has been noted, such testing will be undertaken soon as part of an ongoing events management research project.

Dimension 1: The degree of intangibility of the service

Intangibility of a service can be described as something that cannot be touched even though its results can be identified (Slack *et al.* 2010). Shone and Parry (2004) describe attending a wedding as being more or less intangible. It is possible to experience the activities, participate, enjoy and remember, but there are few tangible things that are possible to touch, other than perhaps a piece of wedding cake, photographs and video. However, intangible dimensions are usually the core aspects within a service: what some might term the actual process, the deed and the act (Gilmore 2003). Indeed, most services, and this applies especially clearly to events, are performances (Kandampully 2002) that are experienced and go out of existence the moment they have been consumed. The managerial difficulty of intangibility is acute when trying to promote an event which is, by its very nature, intangible. The event manager can use more branding and merchandising and try to *fix* the event in people's minds and consciousness. Service intangibility reduces clients' ability to assess the quality of an event and reduces the ability of the manager to establish quality and service standards and to communicate what is required to the staff who will deliver the service. These gaps in delivering service to achieve customer satisfaction are more than amply demonstrated in Parasuraman *et al.*'s (1985) work on SERVQUAL and the subsequent numerous papers analysing their findings (Cronin and Taylor 1994; McDougall and Levesque 2000; Ladhari 2009). SERVQUAL is a useful tool for measuring and managing service quality and is an instrument that can be adapted by managers for a specific industry or specific study context; the SERVQUAL scale consists of twenty-two items representing five dimensions, namely: reliability, which considers the ability to perform the promised service dependably and accurately; responsiveness, which is the willingness to help customers and provide prompt service; assurance that customers will receive the knowledge and courtesy of employees and their ability to inspire trust and confidence; empathy, demonstrating a caring, individualised attention to customers; and finally tangibility, which, as has been said above, is the appearance of physical facilities, equipment, personnel and communication materials.

Tangibility or intangibility can be plotted on one of the lines in the matrix. Where any aspect of an event is tangible, it can more easily have set standards or expectations which can be measured and evaluated. It is desirable for event managers and customers to be able to predict and measure the output of different aspects of an event. For example, the range of menu choices at a wedding breakfast, the temperature at which they are served, the time taken to clear the dining area and to set up a dance floor are clearly tangible and measurable aspects and would, therefore, appear higher up the scale. It is less tangible to ascertain whether all guests have had a good time. Perhaps that could be measured by the number of guests who continue to stay at the event or how many are willing to recommend the venue to future couples.

Dimension 2: The inseparability of production from consumption

It is widely recognised that the simultaneous production and consumption of an event necessitates the use of techniques to limit potentially negative influences. Carlzon (1987) and Normann (1984) refer to the quality experienced by customers as the 'moment of truth', i.e. the moment when the service is first experienced by the customer. It is understood that once an event is produced and delivered, it is at that very moment being consumed. The moment that a sound system bursts into life at a major musical festival is the same moment that the crowds of people hear the music and acoustics. The elements of production, delivery and consumption are inseparable. This makes advance checking and evaluation of the service not possible, since as the event unfolds it is being consumed. Not only that, but its quality is being judged and evaluated at the same time. Inseparability forces customers and service personnel into intimate contact with both the process of production and the process of delivery (Kandampully 2002).

The relevant axis on the matrix does not try to distinguish between inseparability and separability, but more importantly it is crucial to assess whether its influence on the event is potentially high or low. Where an aspect of inseparability does have a high influence on the event, e.g. the audio equipment at the formal opening of a new town square which is to be dedicated to a visiting dignitary, it is crucial that the audio equipment works. Controls, therefore, need to be put into place so that even the unexpected is expected and scenarios are planned and rehearsed to prevent failures.

Dimension 3: The notion of heterogeneity

Kandampully (2002) draws a distinction between heterogeneity at various levels: quality of service varying between one service organisation and another; quality of service varying from one service performer and another; quality of service varying for the same performer on different occasions. These three distinctions can be applied easily to the event sector. Managers, therefore, need to facilitate consistency within each event and the service being offered, and to streamline procedures and systems to reduce variability (Gilmore 2003). It is argued here that elements of an event can be standardised. Technology may be used, for example, to standardise aspects such as the on-line bookings or arrival registrations; audio tapes for visitors to historic places of interest; plasma screens so that everyone attending an open-air opera can have a good view of the principal characters. To eliminate heterogeneity is not always a desirable outcome for events, of course, because consumers may well reject too much standardisation.

The axis can be used to plot those aspects of an event that can be standardised (these would appear higher up the scale) and those that are more difficult (lower down the scale). For example, where it is possible to introduce technology that will create standardisation and reduce heterogeneity, e.g. pre-registration for a conference, this can be plotted higher up the scale. Contact numbers can be included for those who still wish to query via a 'real person' and that would appear lower down the scale, unless set questions and responses can be given to staff and so reduce the level of inconsistencies. Where variations cannot be reduced they should be plotted lower down the scale, but as far as possible standard methods and practices should be introduced. Thus, an event manager would be looking for many of the micro-operations having a point of low heterogeneity and high standardisation.

Dimension 4: The notion of perishability

Gilmore (2003) argues that a core feature of services is perishability. In manufacturing it is possible to create a product dependent on the demand for that product (Slack *et al.* 2010). The purchase of relevant raw materials and the cost of staff to create the product are all dependent on that request. But an outdoor operatic concert cannot begin to perform until the customers arrive (Slack *et al.* 2010). The problem with perishability (Kandampully 2002) is not an inability to offer the service as required at all, but to offer it when it is required by the customer. Hence, this is essentially an inability to store services and offer them when required. Because services cannot be stored, the event manager should focus on how to manage the demand, and not the supply (Kandampully 2002).

The challenge of perishability is that there is often a mismatch between supply and demand. Elements of an event will perish and not get sold or consumed before the end. The matrix offers an opportunity to consider how those elements can be moved along the scale towards having a lower perishability rating. In events, this might involve reducing the amount of time taken to set up a conference room for an unknown number of delegates or, if the number were capable of being predicted, then wastage could be reduced. Perishability does not pose a problem when demand is predictable (Kandampully 2002) and staffing levels can be pre-arranged. To move higher up the axis, the event manager would need to create a steady and controllable demand and understand what causes random variations.

Dimension 5: The degree of customer involvement

Customers are often involved with the production of an event. Customers become part of the service staff when they serve themselves to food from the buffet table at a conference; audiences will hopefully laugh and join in at a comedy night; customers queue patiently at rides at theme parks. The degree of customer involvement can influence event complexity and reduce the amount of control exerted by event managers. Correa *et al.* (2007) point out that greater customisation requires a greater degree of interaction in order to ascertain clearly what the customer requires. Interaction between customers and staff also requires staff that can readily engage with the customers and anticipate, interpret and respond to their needs. Getz (2007) refers to Herzberg's (1966) classification of 'dissatisfiers' which undermine visitors' experiences, while others are 'satisfiers' which provide benefits. The 'dissatisfiers' must be provided to expected levels of quality but in themselves do not delight or provide satisfaction.

A balance needs to be drawn to determine where high customer involvement is desirable and where the need for control is paramount. The manager needs to analyse each of the micro-operations to register that balance. Where it is in the customers' interest, e.g. to produce an atmosphere at a major sporting or musical event, then the activity for the event will be placed in the high customer involvement segment of the matrix. Where it can be minimised, it gives back control to the manager.

Dimension 6: The power and influence of stakeholders

Several commentators have noted the importance of stakeholder involvement in events and the implications for management (Leopkey and Parent 2009). Johnson *et al.* (2008) present stakeholders as being able to be plotted on to a matrix utilising axes of power, influence and interest. Getz (2007) offers a different set of categories, which are not mutually exclusive, to show that some stakeholders can have multiple roles. For example, local councils can be both facilitators and regulators for a major outdoor event, suppliers can often become sponsors, and the audience can become positively and negatively influenced by an event. Johnson *et al.* (2008) argue persuasively that stakeholders will have varying degrees of influence dependent upon their power, and this can be both positive and limiting for the manager.

Satisfaction levels of all stakeholders may not provide the full picture. Getz (2007) explains there are varied experiences, expectations and desires from the different stakeholders. In-depth research of stakeholders can reveal how memorable the event was, its value to the customer, how it matched their expectations and if it conformed to their pre-event ideals. Evidently, event managers must pay specific and close attention to all of their stakeholders, identifying who should be courted and given all of the information and facilities they need and who should be respected and offered access to the planning and organisation of the event. By managing the different groups intelligently, stakeholders can be considered as allies and groups to be worked alongside. The event manager can record on to the axis all of the different stakeholders for each event and consider what action can be taken to limit this impact. For example, at an outdoor carnival with fireworks, the manager should engage the help and advice of the Health and Safety Executive. Similarly the power of a major supplier can be reduced if there are other suppliers with similar products who could be approached. The impact of a major buyer could be reduced by finding other potential customers, instead of having a heavy reliance on one.

Dimension 7: Emphasis and involvement and use of international suppliers, clients and staff

It is important to consider the impact of globalisation on events. An important trend facing an event manager is the globalisation of services, including events or aspects of events supply. Pagell *et al.* (2005) argue that it is not just a requirement to be aware of differences between countries and regions but that it is also necessary to understand the impact of national cultures on the management of staff, customers and on the operation itself. This impact can be perceptible at operational level and can be created by the culture of the operatives working at an event in one country which has been devised and set up by another country, or by a client who comes from another country, or using different materials, equipment and suppliers imported from other countries (Thompson 2001). Managers in different countries may pursue different approaches and yet share common factors like language, religion, customs, beliefs and ethnic heritage, and so the differences may or may not be so marked. Pagell *et al.* (2005) argue that countries may differ on one element of culture but not on all. It can be argued that the UK is closer to the US on many points of culture than its closer neighbours in Europe. Similarly, Hong Kong is not necessarily the same as China and Taiwan (Pagell *et al.* 2005)

All of the suppliers and customers who are attending the event can be plotted on to the matrix to show the degree of involvement of different groups. At this juncture it would be necessary to spend some time in establishing the different cultures, laws and traditions that should be taken into account with the planning and management of the event. This is an area often overlooked, yet by detailed consideration of the possible impact that different cultures will have, it could avoid problems at a later date.

Dimension 8: The importance of consistency and of each event being capable of being assessed and reviewed

There is evidence to suggest that each event must be capable of being assessed and reviewed and there are degrees to which this can be undertaken easily or with added complications (Shone and Parry 2004; Tum *et al.* 2006). Indeed, as Getz (2007) points out, it is important for event managers to establish an overall process for collecting information and to become a learning organisation. An event should be capable of being reviewed and evaluated not only at the end, but also while it is being planned and delivered. Silver (2004) and Shone and Parry (2004) stress the importance of setting out objectives when planning an event and to determine what is to be evaluated, why and how. These objectives should also review the planning process and all of the major decisions taken.

The axis can be used to plot at the highest point those aspects that are capable of being assessed and reviewed. For example, this could be regarding numbers of attendees, the effectiveness of the event in achieving its tangible goals and the efficiency in the manner that this is to be achieved. An example would be the most effective use of staff and resources. Aspects which would be plotted towards the lower end of the axis would be those that are least capable of being assessed and more worthy of attention by the event manager, particularly if they are of importance should aspects go wrong. Getz (2007) refers to these incidents as those capable of being corrected through 'process evaluation' with a view to being corrected and while the event is running.

Applying the matrix: the case of le Tour de France

The following case is designed to illustrate how the approach advocated in this chapter might be operationalised at an event. It is not a research case study (Yin 2009). An empirical assessment of the utility of what has been conceptualised in this chapter will be undertaken at a later date. All data for the case are taken from www.letour.fr/2011/TDF/COURSE/us/caravane_publicitaire.html (accessed 24 October 2010).

Le Tour de France was established in 1903 and has gained in popularity since then. In 1930, Henri Desgrange, Race Director, offered the opportunity to all sponsors to promote their goods and services on travelling floats ahead of the cyclists. By calling on France's major brands to take part in a publicity caravan, Henri Desgrange was able to offset the

---

increasing costs of le Tour and it created a unique spectacle, transforming the nature of the event. It continued to grow to the extent that it now has more than 160 sponsors and more than 600 participants, and it takes at least one hour to pass by a standing spectator in any town or village or on mountain passes of the Alps or Pyrenees. Each year the spectacle draws 12 to 15 million spectators who line the route. Thirty-nine per cent of the spectators who cram the roadside come first and foremost to see the sponsored caravan, to marvel at the inventiveness of the floats and to receive the free gifts. The event might be described as a parade of multi-shaped and multi-coloured decorated vehicles 'advertising their wares' and giving away gifts (16 million each year). These aspects are an integral part of the event and go hand in hand with the race that they precede. It is estimated that the investment cost is €200,000 to €500,000 for each advertiser.

One of the issues facing the event manager is how to return the roadside, after the event has passed through, to its former clean and rubbish-free state. Figure 13.1 shows each axis treated separately and this analysis can be enhanced by involving each event manager and team of stakeholders. The following summarise the considerations that would apply when using the matrix.

Intangibility of the service

The need to have a rubbish-free area at the end of the day can clearly be measured and seen. So the intangibility is quite low. The ability to achieve it involves a great deal of work and logistics of vehicles coming after the riders and collecting rubbish and removing road blocks as quickly as the highways agencies can permit it. The need for a balance between hurried collection of waste and the continuing enjoyment of the parties is an intangible concern and should be discussed with the operators before the event, and to decide on numbers of staff required.

Inseparability of production from consumption

The actual collection of rubbish could be considered as occurring at the exact moment it is collected, but since this *follows* an event it could be considered as being able to be separated. It is, therefore, capable of being achieved and checked for completeness and success without detriment to the event itself, although a partial clearance would be unsatisfactory and might attract fines, as well as a bad reputation.

Heterogeneity

The event will have appeal to different spectators, although all will recognise a complete removal of rubbish as being achieved or not. A question could be raised about how the rubbish is collected and the need for sorting into its different components, e.g. glass, recyclable material, aluminium. This would need to be discussed with the stakeholders, but in this scenario an agreement could be reached.

Perishability

There is high perishability of the work associated with the collection of rubbish. If it is not completed on time, the roadside will be left untidy for some length of time. It has to be a very well-planned effort, with teams fully clear and knowledgeable about their roles and when they are needed to collect, what equipment and vehicles are needed, and the type and amount of rubbish that will be encountered.

Customer involvement

The level of customer involvement is currently low. There a few roadside bins, but this could be much improved. The organisers of the race could go ahead of the caravan on the day, leaving out empty plastic bags for the spectators themselves to fill. This would be more successful if little sorting of the rubbish was required. Or different coloured bags could be left at the wayside for glass and aluminium. The amount of waste could also be controlled by working alongside the sponsors so that material thrown from the sponsorship floats could be more environmentally friendly and create less waste.

Power and influence of stakeholders

To successfully plot this accurately on the axis, a thorough analysis of the stakeholders would have to be undertaken. This could be accomplished by using Johnson *et al.*'s (2008) power and influence matrix. Once the power has been predicted, the major stakeholders could be plotted on to the matrix according to their power and influence. The axis should then be studied by the management team and each stakeholder analysed to see if by intervention the influence of a stakeholder could be made more advantageous to the operation. In this case, the local communities through which le Tour passes would be considered. Not all of them will be involved with le Tour and some may not gain anything from its presence in the region. They will be dissatisfied with litter left after the race. Since the local community could effectively campaign against le Tour coming through that area in the future, it would be advantageous to keep the local community involved and happy with the clean-up operation.

Emphasis and involvement and use of international suppliers, clients and staff

In order to accurately plot this, an analysis of all of the major suppliers and clients is necessary, annotated with their country of origin, cultural differences and any legal issues which may arise from different interpretations of laws and/or their implementation. For the clean-up operation this may be limited, so the impact would be relatively low.

Consistency and capability of being assessed and reviewed

A shared appreciation of what is meant as being 'free of rubbish' must be agreed at the start between the operatives and the managers. The time scale for the clean-up should also be agreed. Given clear details, it is easier to assess and review the outcomes.

Each of these solutions should be annotated on to the matrix or recorded in an adjacent table, such as the one illustrated by Table 13.1.

Concluding comments

This chapter has argued that insufficient academic attention has been paid to aspects of operations management associated with events. In an attempt to redress this lack of research, it has suggested a framework to help managers deal systematically with elements of uncertainty that are inherently part of events management.

The value of the matrix is that it offers event managers a new perspective on planning, managing and controlling the production of an event. It has been shown that small changes in each of the phenomena discussed can have far-reaching consequences for the successful delivery of an event. A sensitivity to the potential impact of these changes is a key part of the matrix. The application of the matrix to le Tour de France illustrated how the management team and relevant stakeholders might use and benefit from using this technique.

The matrix approach proposed here remains untested but forms part of an ongoing research project being undertaken by the author. Such testing will enable confirmation, refinement or rejection of its utility for events managers. Whatever the conclusion of the forthcoming empirical research, the case for greater academic energy being expended on understanding more about the operational management at events will remain.

Note

1 I am grateful to Rhodri Thomas for his comments on an earlier draft of this chapter.

References

Bamford, D.R. and Forrester, P.L. (2003) 'Managing planned and emergent change within an operations management environment', *International Journal of Operations and Production Management* 23(5): 546–64.

Bowdin, G.A.J., Allen, J., O'Toole, W., Harris, R. and McDonnell, I. (2011) *Events Management*, Oxford: Butterworth-Heinemann, Elsevier, third edition.

Bowen, H.E. and Daniels, M.J. (2005) 'Does the music matter? Motivations for attending a music festival', *Event Management* 9: 155–64.

Carlzon, J. (1987) *Moments of Truth*, Massachusetts: Ballinger.

Chase, R., Jacobs, R. and Aquilano, N. (2006) *Operations Management for Competitive Advantage*, New York: Irwin/McGraw-Hill, eleventh edition.

Correa, H.L., Ellram, L.M., Scavarda, A.J. and Cooper, M.C. (2007) 'An operations management view of the services and goods offering mix', *International Journal of Operations and Production Management* 27(5): 444–63.

Coughlan, P. and Coghlan, D. (2002) 'Action research for operations management', *International Journal of Operations and Production Management* 22(2): 220–40.

Cronin, Jr, J.J. and Taylor, S.A. (1994) *The Journal of Marketing* 58 (1, January): 125–31.

Getz, D. (2007) *Events Studies: Theory, Research and Policy for Planned Events*, Oxford: Butterworth-Heinemann.

Getz, D., Andersson, T. and Carlsen, J. (2010) 'Festival management studies: developing a framework and priorities for comparative and cross-cultural research.' *International Journal of Event and Festival Management* 1(1): 29–59.

Gilmore, A. (2003) *Services, Marketing and Management*, London: Sage.

Heizer, J. and Render, B. (2006) *Operations Management*, New Jersey: Pearson Prentice-Hall, eighth edition.

Johnson, G., Scholes, K. and Whittington, R. (2008) *Exploring Corporate Strategy*, Harlow: Pearson Education, eighth edition.

Kandampully, J. (2002) *Services Management. The New Paradigm in Hospitality*, Australia: Pearson Education.

Knisely, G. (1979) 'Greater marketing emphasis by Holiday Inns breaks mould', *Advertising Age*, 15 January: 47–51.

Ladhari, R. (2009) 'A review of twenty years of SERVQUAL research', *International Journal of Quality and Service Sciences* 1(2): 172–98.

Leopkey, B. and Parent, M.M. (2009) 'Risk management strategies by stakeholders in Canadian major sporting events', *Event Management* 13: 153–70.

McDougall, G.H.G. and Levesque, T. (2000) 'Customer satisfaction with services: putting perceived value into the equation', *Journal of Services Marketing* 14(5): 392–410.

Normann, R. (1984) *Service Management: Strategy and Leadership in Service Business*, New York: John Wiley, third edition.

Pagell, M., Katz, J.P. and Sheu, C., (2005) 'The importance of national culture in operations management research', *International Journal of Operations and Production Management* 25(4): 371–94.

Parasuraman, A., Zeithaml, V.A. and Berry, L.L. (1985) 'A conceptual model of service quality and its implications for future research', *Journal of Marketing* 49 (Fall): 41–50.

Ruffini, F.A.J., Boer, H. and van Riemsdijk, M.J. (2000) 'Organisation design in operations management', *International Journal of Operations and Production Management* 20(7): 860–79.

Shone, A. and Parry, B. (2004) *Successful Event Management: A Practical Handbook*, London: Thompson.

Shostack, G.L. (1977) 'Breaking free from product marketing', *Journal of Marketing* 41(2): 73–80.

Silvers, J.R. (2004) *Professional Event Co-ordination*, New Jersey: Wiley.

Silvers, J.R., Bowdin, G.A.J., O'Toole, W.J. and Nelson, K.B. (2006) 'Towards an international event management body of knowledge (EMBOK),' *Event Management* 9: 185–98.

Slack, N., Chambers, S. and Johnston, R. (2010) *Operations Management*, Harlow: Financial Times Prentice Hall, sixth edition.

Smith, K.A. (2007) 'The distribution of events tickets', *Event Management* 10: 185–96.

Stevenson, W. (2005) *Operations Management*, New York: Irwin/McGraw-Hill, eighth edition.

Still, K., and Draper, P. (2010) *Crowd Dynamics Event Planner, Reference Guide*. Available at: www.crowddynamics.com/products/event-planner.php

Taylor, A. and Taylor, M. (2009). 'Operations management research: themes, trends and potential future directions.' *International Journal of Operations and Production Management* 29(12): 1316–40.

Thompson, J.L. (2001) *Understanding Corporate Strategy*, London: Thomson Learning.

Tkaczynski, A. and Rundle-Thiele, S.R. (2011) 'Event segmentation: a review and research agenda', *Tourism Management* 32: 426–34.

Tum, J., Norton, P. and Wright, N. (2006) *Operations Management in the Events Industry*, Oxford: Butterworth-Heinemann.

Walker, J.L. (1995) 'Service encounter satisfaction; conceptualised', *Journal of Services Marketing* 9(1): 5–14.

Yeoman, I., Robertson, M., Ali-Knight, J., Drummond, S. and McMahon-Beattie, U. (2004) *Festival and Events Management: An International Arts and Culture Perspective*, Oxford: Butterworth-Heinemann.

Yin, R.K. (2009) *Case Study Research: Design and Methods*, Los Angeles: Sage, fourth edition.

Section 3
Policy, planning and management

Section 4
Policy Information and Management

14

The private sector and events

Robyn Stokes

Introduction

This chapter profiles the multiple contributions of the private sector to event planning and policy making, funding, management and marketing. Event stakeholders from the commercial world are diverse and range from corporate leaders and entrepreneurs to small to medium-sized businesses whose services make up the numerous links in the event supply chain.

At the *macro-level*, the vision and resources of corporate leaders impacts on both national and local portfolios of events. Sponsorship resources from the private sector and philanthropic contributions of business leaders provide a significant proportion of the funds needed to grow arts, sports and business events. Apart from the political and strategic leverage of corporate leaders and the provision of dollars through sponsorship and philanthropy, the private sector also brings entrepreneurial vision to the design and creation of events. Event organisers and promoters who are involved in staging, producing and marketing events make up a highly specialised industry globally that is gaining increased professionalism and credibility.

At the *micro-level*, a complex network of businesses provide *event-specific* services (e.g. planners, promoters, venue owners/managers, entertainers, merchandise and licensing firms) while many others provide *event-support* services (travel and transport, tourist attractions, accommodation, retail and professional services). In effect, the private sector is both a recipient of revenue from events as well as the provider of direct and in-kind sponsorship.

Another growing avenue of private sector concern and engagement with events relates to their impacts on local and global communities and contributions that can be made by businesses to social, environmental and economic sustainability. Increasingly, a significant role must also be played by business leaders and operators in ensuring the responsible management and continuity of events.

Private sector engagement with events

Ownership of events does impact on the extent and ways in which the private sector is involved in their planning and staging (Andersson and Getz 2009). Medium- to large-scale public events (e.g. national competitions, the Commonwealth Games, World Cup Soccer and the Olympic Games for which governments often serve as underwriters) and profit-oriented festivals and events run by venues, firms or investors as commercial initiatives (e.g. rock concerts and blockbuster theatre productions) may seek more private sector services and generate higher revenues. While not-for-profit events may be influenced by business leaders who engage with them for philanthropic reasons, business opportunities do tend to be fewer where market expansion or growth of the event is not a primary goal. However, the private sector has a collective interest in the economic impacts generated by events of all types and a commercial interest in the business opportunities to be achieved through engaging with one or more events.

As towns, cities and nations rely increasingly on place marketing to promote economic growth, the stature of events (business, sports and arts-related) as vehicles to re-image and position destinations for investment or tourism has grown (AT Kearney 2005; Hall 2006). There are now many illustrations of event staging for the purpose of place branding to attract new and repeat tourists, to expand current industries and businesses and create new ones. Cities are under constant pressure to show positive economic development and 'mega-event strategies' bring the potential for new funding sources. Among the myriad of events globally that are sought after are FIFA's World Cup Soccer event, the Olympic and Commonwealth Games, government meetings, e.g. the Commonwealth Heads of Government meeting (CHOGM), and business events like World Expo. However, the injection of funds into local hallmark events and well-known cultural and artistic festivals, e.g. Carnival in Rio and the Edinburgh Festival in Scotland, also serves to maintain a strong brand presence for their host cities.

The 2010 FIFA World Cup in Cape Town was a major place-imaging initiative for South Africa. In order to generate long-term business legacies (in addition to sport and community benefits) at least R14 billion in public sector investment was spent on infrastructure and more than double that amount was invested by the private sector (www.capetown.gov.za). Industry development was facilitated through sector-specific interventions to showcase local products and services and to establish contacts for long-term business. However, opportunities provided by events such as the World Cup for small to medium enterprises (SMEs) can be variable. With 95 per cent of all tourism businesses in South Africa in the SME category, concern was expressed in the lead-up to the Cup that around 85 per cent of these businesses could provide services to the event, but at least half of them needed support to properly leverage the opportunities (Correia and van Lill 2010). Hence, benefits from events can accrue somewhat unevenly across the private sector and serve a fairly narrow range of interests. Equitable representation of the private sector can be particularly challenging in developing economies where the quality, quantity and reliability of products and services can be less predictable.

Aside from immediate tourism industry benefits (related to travel, accommodation and visits to attractions), the infrastructure improvements and upgrades associated with special events are key activities that directly engage the private sector. The bid by Australia's Gold Coast for the 2018 Commonwealth Games was prompted in part by the upgrades anticipated for sports facilities, road and transport infrastructure and new high-density housing and offices along the coastal strip (Queensland Events 2010). While the forecast cost of the bid was in the vicinity of $11m ($Aust. without staging costs), both the community and private sector operators were expected to benefit from these infrastructure projects. The staging of major and mega events also leads to greater success in attracting other events. The IOC session to select the host for the Olympic Games illustrates this snowball effect. In 2005, this event brought over 100 voting members of the IOC, some 1,500 journalists and 500 other visitors to Singapore. Beyond the $19 million generated in tourism receipts, this was an event where hoteliers, media, logistics and programme providers each shared in the benefits (Yuen 2008). In turn, the event brought new interest among international sports federations in holding world and regional championships in Singapore. Again, expanded business for companies in the events, tourism, construction, retail, entertainment and service sectors was expected.

Although government policies and decisions to support major or mega events absorb much of the debate in popular media, the role of the private sector is far-reaching. Business leaders can play a role in strategy making, *influencing* the events agenda of a city or nation, *facilitating* the success of individual events, *leveraging* new business from events and *sustaining* events in ways that optimise positive outcomes and minimise adverse impacts. In turn, stakeholders in the commercial world can exert political and strategic influence on the size and type of events that are staged; contribute financial and in-kind support to create or bid for events and offer the products and services needed to stage and implement them.

Proactive planning to leverage business opportunities and to ensure the sustainability of flagship events is a fast-growing contribution of the business world. Many companies now see events as vehicles to cut through the media clutter and build emotional connections with their brands. This role of events in product and service marketing receives most attention in marketing communication and marketing literature. According to Crowther (2010: 228), 'the attractiveness of events for private sector organisations in competitive and often saturated markets is palpable'. However, far greater attention is given to the role of events as vehicles for destination branding (Crowther 2010) in tourism and events literature.

Commercial involvement in different event sectors

The involvement of the private sector spans events in the world of sport, education, culture and the performing arts as well as 'business' events, e.g. meetings, conferences and conventions, exhibitions and those activities aligned with incentive travel. Each sector has its own unique characteristics, which brings different requirements for private sector support and engagement. Business events can inject significant dollars into a host city or region based on longer stays and higher spending than leisure travellers. These events also disseminate new knowledge, enhance technologies and build post-event collaboration and innovation between the public and private sectors (Jago and Deery 2010). Business events are reported as producing the highest daily yield of any tourism sector (Business Events Council for Australia 2009), but there is general agreement that they also provide enduring advantages that extend beyond tourism. As Harry (cited in Jago and Deery 2010: 6) notes, 'the meetings and events industry should be thought of as part of the global knowledge economy, rather than as a branch of tourism'. Accordingly, meetings, conferences, conventions and exhibitions have become both a significant area of enterprise in their own right as well as generating additional business for the industries they represent e.g. education, ICT, agriculture, health and medicine, professional service industries and more.

In most events categories, there has been considerable interest in fostering improved linkages between events and the tourism sector. *Sports tourism* or travel to participate in a sports activity, to observe sport or visit a sports attraction has dominated discussions about the need for improved inter-sectoral partnerships since the mid-1990s. International sport has become one of the most powerful and effective vehicles for showcasing cities and nations and for creating a 'destination image' attractive to tourists (Whitson and Macintosh 1996: 279) and investors. Sport is now well established as a tourism generator. In terms of audience size, potential revenue generation and image, sports events are incomparable with other events. The destination image-making potential of sports events is further enhanced by television coverage. For example, the Football World Cup attracted a quarter of the world's population as a viewing audience in 1998 (Smith and Jenner 1998) and in 2010, FIFA estimated that a worldwide television audience of more than 700 million people watched the World Cup final held in South Africa, surpassing the 600 million viewers of the 2008 Beijing Olympics (Moodie 2010).

The *cultural tourism* phenomenon has also experienced market growth. This phenomenon embraces visitors' attendance at festivals or fairs, performing arts events and concerts as well as permanent or static arts attractions outside the events domain (Craik 2001). The audience potential of arts tourism has led to the creation of many new arts/cultural events to capitalise on this demand, bringing a new source of revenue to arts organisations. The 'blockbuster' events strategy adopted by both cities and cultural institutions in recent decades (Craik 2001) has placed a far greater emphasis on staging major shows and exhibitions in capital cities and metropolitan centres. Major musicals like *The Lion King* and *Les Miserables* have attracted significant regional tourism audiences, providing an additional secondary attraction for tourists visiting London and other world cities. While some cultural events are initially designed to be staged internationally, others have achieved sufficient stature to be toured to other regions or countries. Private sector event promoters play a primary role in organising these international tours (for example, the Edinburgh Tattoo and the Moscow State Circus). Here, public sector events agencies often forge relationships with the promoters of these events to bring them to a city when a substantial tourism impact is envisaged.

Stakeholder roles and relationships

A deeper insight to private sector engagement with events can be achieved by modelling the spectrum of commercial stakeholders and activities that feature in the world of events. Private sector stakeholders are generally defined as those corporations, businesses and individuals engaged in commerce with which an event or events interact or have interdependencies (Carroll 1993; Merrilees *et al.* 2005). This definition tends to embrace business leaders who engage with events for reasons related to commercial gain as well as successful individuals that serve as social entrepreneurs by way of philanthropic gestures. The *primary* stakeholders of events in the private sector are corporate leaders and firms, media owners and entrepreneurs to event promoters and owners and SMEs that participate in the event supply chain, e.g. local event production companies, audiovisual suppliers, caterers, entertainers and others who supply services.

Secondary stakeholders enjoying an indirect relationship with the event may include operators of accommodation places and tourist attractions, transport service providers, retailers and other local businesses that benefit from the staging of events. To fully capitalise on the legacy of events, including mega and hallmark events, the use of metrics to establish goals and measure outcomes for each key stakeholder group has been suggested (AT Kearney 2005). Accordingly, a diagrammatic representation of commercial event stakeholders and their inputs is a useful tool to classify the contributions of private sector stakeholders to events. Figure 14.1 depicts the involvement of these stakeholders in different event domains.

The extent and type of input of private sector stakeholders to an event may be related to: its ownership structure, the size and geographic reach of the event and its markets; whether the event is created within the community or acquired through a competitive bid; and, the nature of resources needed to plan and stage it. A major event that is subject to a competitive bid could well involve corporate leaders and firms in a range of activities from the event feasibility assessment through to sponsorship of the bid and an early assessment of the likely event impacts on a city or nation.

Between inception and completion, different stakeholders may be involved in the decision to bid, the bidding process, host destination imaging, the development of the event theme and programme, planning of infrastructure and facilities and the promotion and staging of the event (Catherwood and van Kirk 1992; Carlsen and Williams 1999; Getz 1999).

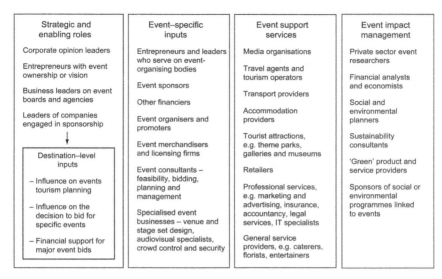

Figure 14.1 Roles and contributions of the private sector to events
Source: Developed for this chapter.

In cases where events are privately owned, governments and/or venues may be involved in a different type of negotiation to attract and host them. The Goodwill Games was an example of a major sports event that was corporate-owned, in that case by Time Warner Inc., which profited from both event ownership and contracts struck with service providers. A public–private sector partnership was forged between the Queensland state government in Australia, Time Warner Inc. and Turner Broadcasting Inc. to stage that event which was held for the last time in Brisbane in 2001 and telecast to around 100 countries.

A focused analysis of the stakeholders engaged in branding and marketing the Brisbane Goodwill Games by Merrilees *et al.* (2005) offered a clear illustration of the importance of robust inter-organisational linkages in staging a major event. Private sector players in the Goodwill Games stakeholder map were extensive and included the marketing department in Goodwill Games Inc., the sponsors, the media, travel firms, accommodation providers, ticketing agencies, merchandisers and venues. Media partners and sponsors provided the two dominant sources of funding for the games (Merrilees *et al.* 2005), but there was also extensive involvement of travel agencies and ticketing agencies. Importantly, an analysis of private sector stakeholders in events often uncovers not just working relationships but a range of connections through ownership. For example, in the case of the Goodwill Games, there was a tie-up between Ticketek as the sales and distribution agent for the Games in Australia and the Nine Network (the local television operator and event broadcaster).

The structural bonds between events (owners and promoters), media organisations, ticketing agencies and merchandisers are certainly growing in the events sector, particularly in the arena of sports. Giant media and entertainment conglomerates have emerged as a result of the continued globalisation of sports (Law *et al.* 2002). In particular, the relationship between the media and sport has been cemented by 'exclusive media coverage rights and equity ownership, both of which exert high levels of control' (Law *et al.* 2002: 281). In Asia, the heavy promotion of Western sport is underpinned by large media conglomerates like the US-based Disney and Rupert Murdoch's News Corporation that control a significant chunk of Western sports rights content through their global networks (Rowe and Gilmour 2010).

Over time, this complexity of event ownership and networks will only grow as the private sector plays an increasing role, particularly in sport. The game of rugby is a good example where the injection of private capital into the ownership of clubs in Australia has taken the game a long way from its amateur roots. The city of Melbourne's entry to the expanded Super 15 tournament in 2011 heralds the first privately owned rugby team with the Mitchell Communication Group as the largest investor (Grigg and Clout 2010). However, in looking at ownership, there is also a wide variety of small to medium events that are invented and staged by the private sector for commercial reasons. For example, BMW often creates sports events at the metropolitan and suburban levels that are self-sponsored such as the BMW Ride for Life Challenge, a corporate cycling event where BMW's loyal customers rub shoulders with professional cycling teams.

Strategic and enabling roles of the private sector

Outside of the power that private sector players can exercise through event ownership, their strategic input can also be seen at the level of city and national strategies. Today, a strong emphasis is placed on stakeholder inclusive approaches to planning and strategy development, where both public and private interests are involved. This applies in many industrial spheres, but interest in stakeholder input to events plans and event tourism strategies has grown (Gursoy and Kendall 2006; Boyko 2008; Stokes 2008). A potential influence on this contribution of business or the 'top end of town' to event strategies is the trend towards corporatism, where governments have privatised and commercialised various functions. Corporatism has prompted the joint engagement of governments and business leaders in tourism planning (Hall 1999) but also, in the events strategies of cities. Sometimes referred to as the 'hollowing out of the state' (Milward 1996) this phenomenon has continued to stimulate partnerships with the private sector (Hall 1999, 2000) in recent decades.

In line with corporatisation, many countries have progressively established event development agencies in states and provinces as quasi-government or privatised entities to attract and sustain events. These agencies have emerged in the UK, e.g. Scotland, a number of countries in Europe, Canada and Australia. The mandate of these agencies is primarily economic development, with a greater or lesser focus on tourism occurring in different locations. Some of these agencies operate as a specialised unit within a national or state government, while others have been established as corporate entities with more of an arm's length relationship to government, e.g. Victorian Major Events Corporation in Australia. The majority of these agencies also build very close ties with the business community in shaping their agenda.

In 2010, the Scottish government injected £5 million to their agency, Event Scotland (www.eventscotland.org). This initiative came close on the heels of an earlier boost in expenditure of about the same amount to celebrate the 250th anniversary of the birth of poet Robert Burns. However, the agency also shows a very proactive engagement with the private sector. Supported by the Scottish Government, Event Scotland and leading business organisations, an organisation called Business Club Scotland (Event Scotland 2010) has been established to ensure that local companies are supported, engaged and given the chance to create commercial opportunities from major events. In particular, the aims of this club (reflecting similar clubs initiated in North America and Australia) are to pave the way for improved business competitiveness and supply chain networks, facilitate procurement for major events and bring business people together to create relationships during the staging of events.

According to O'Brien (2006: 257) this 'strategic business leveraging represents a subtle, but significant paradigm shift in the international event sector'. The formulation of Business Club

Australia for Sydney Olympics 2000 did lead to national events agencies and owners and managers of events taking an increased interest in the long-term business outcomes from events (O'Brien 2006). In a similar vein, South Africa recently set up event ambassadors programmes to mobilise community and businesses around the FIFA World Cup and city officials and business leaders spearheaded a range of initiatives around the country's priority industries for growth (AT Kearney 2005; Correia and van Lill 2010).

Destination-level inputs

At a macro-level, the business leaders of a country or city often play a key role in shaping event and event tourism strategies. However, the extent to which these leaders can influence destination-level strategies for events may well depend on whether a political economy or functionalist perspective is adopted (Truly Sautter and Leisen 1999) by those planning the events agenda. A political economy perspective means that corporate and government leaders and planning bodies will largely determine the direction of events on behalf of local populations. In contrast, the functional view suggests that all interested stakeholders should contribute to the development and management of industries like tourism and events (Truly Sautter and Leisen 1999). In this collaborative approach, the competitiveness of the destination relies upon formulating a vision through a publicly driven process based on stakeholder values and consensus, rather than a private, expert-driven process based on market forces (Ritchie and Crouch 2000).

While the functionalist perspective often works well at the grassroots level where festivals and events are collectively created and staged by local residents and institutions, a political economy perspective may be more prevalent in shaping events strategies at state and city levels. In some cases, this means that outside of government planners, it is corporate leaders who have more potential for input to strategy than the wider community. For example, Stokes (2008) found a corporate government-led approach to events tourism strategy-making in various states of Australia. Politicians, government officials, private sector corporations and venue managers had the most influence in shaping directions for events tourism at the metropolitan level.

The involvement of parties outside this immediate circle, e.g. the wider community and small businesses in the tourism sector, occurred at later stages in the strategy process or on an 'as needs' basis. In effect, decisions about major events were mostly made by event development agencies of governments whose boards of directors include a range of corporate leaders. Frequently, these leaders are senior executives in tourism, finance, aviation or other sectors with a stake in the economic benefits generated. In some cities, these individuals gain influence and notoriety over some years of engagement in the tourism and events industries and through membership of the boards of tourism marketing and/or event development agencies. While the involvement of these leaders can be quite advantageous, especially where there is a clear link between their strategic input and the potential to attract resources (for an event bid and/or to assist with staging), the retention of decision-making among corporate and political leaders has some drawbacks. Reflecting on strategic planning surrounding Sheffield's staging of the World Student Games, Bramwell (1997) observed that public–private partnerships meant that decisions were often taken by individuals who were not democratically elected or accountable. In that case, the political legitimacy of the investment in the Games was affected by the lack of wider consultation with residents (Bramwell 1997: 175).

Beyond their role as board members or close associates of event development agencies, Stokes (2008) noted that the influence of the private sector in shaping destination strategies is mostly seen in soft networks such as advisory panels and professional relationships. Venue owners and managers were influential in some cases because of the need to fill seating capacity in facilities. The input of corporate leaders to events strategies was most evident where businesses were regular sponsors of events. If a firm was traditionally a key sponsor of events in the city/region, they were often consulted about major event ideas or plans. However, for the wider population of SMEs in events and tourism, tactical input by way of services to implement or run the events far exceeded their strategic inputs or influence.

Formal networks that give the private sector more opportunities for strategic influence have begun to emerge in specific sectors, e.g. business events. The Business Events Council of Australia exerted a strong influence on the National Business Events Strategy released in 2008, a comprehensive document that responds to opportunities and challenges faced in that sector, e.g. airline access and capacity, environmental sustainability, workforce skills and training and the harnessing of new technologies (Business Events Council for Australia 2009). In summary, there are informal networks and mechanisms as well as formal membership of events agencies, forums and councils that enable the private sector to contribute to the future of events in destinations.

Event-specific inputs of the private sector

At the level of individual events, private sector input ranges from *entrepreneurial vision and concept creation* through to *event organisation and delivery, promotion, sponsorship* and *service provision*. The organisation, delivery and promotion of events are often executed with the help of those who would collectively define themselves as members of the events industry. Businesses who serve the needs of events are quite tightly aligned and industry associations provide valuable frameworks to further enhance these ties and build the professionalism of those involved in planning and delivering events. For example, the International Special Events Society (ISES) and its local chapters as well as national level associations like Meetings and Events Australia (MEA) play a vital role in supporting the continued education of practitioners. In Australia, the MEA Awards recognise excellent business practice and reward those event businesses and practitioners that excel in their business and personal goals and achieve outstanding results.

Event vision and concept creation

Throughout history, there have been many instances of *individual entrepreneurs* who have lobbied for or established significant public events. The Cape Town bid for the 2004 Olympics began under the leadership of businessman Raymond Ackerman, the owner of a grocery store chain (Hiller 2000). As Hiller (2000: 450) observes, the bid was run on a corporate model in which a 'team of decision-makers promoted their ideas about bidding and primarily sought the endorsement of the city for what was still their initiative'. Similarly, the Goodwill Games, discussed earlier, was the brainchild of Ted Turner who created the international sports competition as a response to the political troubles surrounding the Olympic Games of the 1980s. Outside of sport, the multi-venue Live Aid concerts that raised some $US284 million for African famine victims were events initiated by Sir Bob Geldof and Midge Ure that ultimately became the largest television broadcasts ever, attracting around 2 billion viewers across 60 countries. These are just some examples of the stand-out contributions of private individuals in establishing events, outside of governing boards or public sector agencies.

Within the events industry, there are some fine examples of *event and concert promoters* whose entrepreneurialism has led to the staging of blockbuster events and the introduction of major talent to new markets around the world. These promoters are responsible for organising live events and concerts, contracting the artist(s) or performers, obtaining the venue, pricing the event or tour and supporting it with marketing communication. Promoters either underwrite the event themselves and/or attract sponsorship to stage the event or tour. Well-known examples of promoters are the US-based rock promoter Bill Graham, who produced concerts from the 1960s to 1990 including several Rolling Stones tours and America's Live Aid concert in JFK Stadium. His company, Bill Graham Presents, was sold and re-sold to various event companies including Clear Channel Entertainment which in time morphed into Live Nation, the largest concert production/promotion company in the world. In 2005, Live Nation merged with Ticketmaster to become Live Nation Entertainment.

Alongside this direct contribution of entrepreneurs to the events sector, *corporations or businesses* also enter into *partnerships with government* to attract or bid for major events. Where events are controlled by international sports federations or event organising bodies rather than event promoters, working partnerships are usually formed between government and business leaders in the course of bidding for major events. These event bid teams usually involve both corporate opinion leaders and sponsors, event development agencies, destination marketing organisations, community representatives, government departments and the relevant business or interest groups associated with the event.

Tight inter-organisational relationships between government, non-government bodies and the private sector are mandatory to achieve competitive and marketing advantages over other cities and nations where a pitch for the right to stage an event is required. The London 2012 bid reflected this teamwork and the importance of having international and local business partners in the bid process. The senior team of the London Organising Committee for the Olympic Games (LOCOG) led by Sebastian Coe had extensive government and corporate expertise derived from other events as well as the media, legal and financial sectors. The team formed community and business partnerships early and ten international companies, e.g. Visa, Coca-Cola, McDonald's and various UK firms such as British Airways, Thomas Cook and BP, were active partners throughout the bid.

Event planning, organisation and management

Private sector businesses providing direct input to the success of events can be found at all stages of the event planning and management cycle. First, in the planning stages, there are *event consultancies* and *financial service* firms that produce feasibility studies and bid strategies. Here, agencies work on behalf of governments and major venues to develop successful bid strategies and creative approaches to attract events. For example, the core business of Major Events International (MEI) is helping companies to win key contracts with advice on bid planning and strategy, customer contact and publicity support. These consultants write key elements of the bid and serve as external reviewers on the content of event bid documents. As Westerbeek *et al.* (2002) note, a range of factors including organisational skills, political support, infrastructure and facilities, reputation, networks, relationships and media exposure are influential in event bidding. Accordingly, a team of private and public sector specialists will usually come together to plan and deliver this early stage of activity in international event development.

Once secured, event practitioners and consultants continue to remain centre-stage in running events and many graduates of event management courses find work among the myriad of agencies employed to launch, stage and organise them. In the operational phase, it is not uncommon to find a network of highly *specialised event businesses* involved that only provide services to this sector, e.g. event planners and producers (spanning festivals, corporate and community events), venue and stage design specialists, event crowd managers, security specialists and others. Here, the student of events management can readily find many case studies of networks of private sector event specialists working together to deliver remarkable events in regional and capital cities throughout the world.

4.3 Sponsorship, merchandising and licensing

Perhaps the event-specific input of the private sector that is most widely discussed is that of *sponsorship* of the bid process and/or events themselves. Quester and Thompson (2001: 34) have defined sponsorship as 'an investment in cash or in kind, in an activity, person or event in return for access to the exploitable commercial potential' associated with that investment. Sponsorship represents a valuable investment that can be actively pursued by businesses where events are seen to be hot properties with an ability to reach the target markets that are of direct interest to the event sponsor.

Relationships between well-established major events and sponsors are commonly formalised for three- to seven-year periods, in order to cement business ties and optimise the goals of each partner. For example, FIFA has formal arrangements in place for the sponsorship of its entire soccer events programme, including the flagship FIFA World Cups, from 2007 to 2014 (www. fifa.com). In general, sponsorship is a primary funding strategy of many events, even when a government provides seed funds or underwrites the event to ensure its success and longevity. Because sponsorship represents such a significant area of commercial opportunity for the private sector, it is treated in more depth later in this chapter.

In addition to the use of events sponsorship for corporate brand building and product and service marketing, avenues for business engagement also exist in *merchandising* and *licensing products* associated with events. Clearly, more sophisticated strategies involving a range of commercial operators can be observed at mega events such as the Olympics and FIFA World Cup, but major events also provide merchandising opportunities. For major or international events, a network of businesses can be involved in event merchandising and licensing. Event licensing enables sponsors, in particular those businesses who have invested in event naming rights, to create and sell co-branded (sponsor and event) merchandise (Canalichio 2010). However, licensing brings brand benefits to a range of event stakeholders.

In addition to the merchandise manufacturer (licensee) who obtains revenue from product sales, retailers are able to reach and satisfy new markets and the event itself is able to support the sponsor and gain some revenue from the royalties earned on merchandise sales. In 2005, the Business Incentives Group (BIG) in the UK exceeded all sales forecasts with its range of giftware and commemorative items for Trafalgar 200, the event to recognise the history of the Royal Navy (The Business Incentives Group 2010). Mega-events such as FIFA World Cup and the Olympic Games, where there is global recognition of the sports event symbols on the packaging of merchandised products, result in billions of dollars in sales. With such high-profile event brands, it has been suggested that consumers are more than 50 per cent more likely to buy the products (FIFA.com, 2010). The initial release of official merchandise for the Sochi 2014 Olympics in 2010 was expected to generate around $500 million from the sale of merchandised goods, with $35 million to be made available to the local Olympic organising committee to help fund the Games (RT Business 2010).

4.4 Recent trends in event sponsorship

In a cluttered media and information environment, it is no surprise that there has been a marked shift towards investments in more targeted brand communication including event sponsorship. Just as cities and nations have recognised the power of events for brand positioning, the corporate sector has also cashed in on the marketing benefits that can accrue from an event sponsorship portfolio. Competition for the hearts and minds of consumers in an increasingly online world of marketing and information-sharing means that events frequently deliver a higher return on investment than other marketing vehicles (Crowther 2010). A special event or festival can achieve 'cut-through' by getter much closer to the market (often in emotion-charged environments where consumers are more likely to form brand relationships).

The choice of an event as a marketing medium provides businesses with an opportunity to attract attention during self-selected activities. At events, the consumer's passion and loyalty towards a sport, an artistic pursuit, a cause or business interest is running high and marketers find an environment that is ripe for the transfer of positive attitudes towards their brands. As Meenaghan (2001) has suggested, a well-managed sports event sponsorship will see a build-up in awareness and goodwill towards a sponsor's brand running in parallel with the intensity of the fans' involvement, passion and loyalty towards the sport. The key to optimising the brand image effect is the ability of the sponsor to demonstrate that their relationship with the event results in benefits to that event and, in turn, benefits those that support or attend the event. Such is the power of sponsorship as a marketing tool that AC Nielsen's 2009 Global Online Consumer Survey (Nielsen Company 2009) found brand sponsorship to have a very high level of consumer trust (64 per cent of online consumers) which has only served to increase in recent years. In some regions, such as Latin America, this trust in sponsorship is as high as 81 per cent of surveyed consumers (Nielsen Company 2009). Hence, it is no surprise that even in the aftermath of the global financial crisis, sponsorship as a marketing medium has continued to perform well. The Sponsorship Decision-Makers Survey conducted by global sponsorship specialist, IEG in 2010 found that the level of commitment to sponsorship had set a new benchmark compared with other forms of marketing communication (IEG, 2010b).

Where the personal preference of senior managers and CEO markedly influenced the event sponsorship decisions of companies in the past, an increased science and professionalism has accompanied sponsorship choices in the twenty-first century. Just as cities consider very carefully how events that are the subject of competitive bidding will align with their socio-cultural and economic goals, the private sector also considers the synergies it has with an event's purpose and its target markets (type, size and, of course, buying power). In particular, the evaluation of events as sponsorship properties is strongly affected by how well the event will increase brand loyalty, create awareness or visibility and change or reinforce a company or brand image. With a range of event properties to choose from and many proposals from event managers crossing the desks of marketing departments each month, policies and criteria for selection have become increasingly prescriptive.

Some companies are choosing to focus on a smaller number of sponsorships so that they 'do better with less'. General Motors illustrates this trend with its shift away from support for many different types of event engagements including the US Olympic Committee, the PGA Tour and PGA of America, to have just one major sponsorship platform for each brand of motor vehicle. An example is Chevy, which aligned with Major League baseball, a deliberate move by the company to get back to the grassroots of the community with marketing partnerships between Chevy dealer groups and baseball teams throughout the USA (IEG 2010a).

Alongside this goal of some companies to re-establish their connections with local-level audiences, there is also a strong trend towards sponsorships that show good corporate citizenship or social responsibility (Smith and Westerbeek 2007; Seguin et al. 2010). Such investments can span sports, the arts or any number of events linked to social causes. In the sports arena, Smith and Westerbeek (2007: 50) have identified seven unique features of sports CSR including: the ability to achieve global reach via mass media, provide immediate gratification to audiences, appeal to youth, deliver positive health impacts, aid social interaction, improve cultural understanding and integration and enhance environmental and sustainability awareness. Walters (2009) investigates this use of sports CSR in an exploration of community sports trusts or independent charitable bodies that deliver a range of community initiatives with the help of both government and corporate dollars. With some 50 football clubs from the UK's Premier League and Football Leagues having a community trust, including Manchester United (Walters 2009: 92), this is just one avenue through which the private sector will continue to align itself with event audiences in a way that is seen to be socially responsible.

Sport continues to dominate the global sponsorship market accounting for close to 90 per cent of the total value (SportBusiness 2009). The biggest spenders on sports sponsorship are the automobile industry, the banking sector, sports clothing manufacturers and telecommunications firms. Outside of this group but continuing to enjoy prominence are Pepsi Co. Inc. and Coca-Cola, which together ranked number one and two in the top US sponsors of 2009 jointly injecting some US$580 million into the American economy (IEG 2010c). Looking at the sponsor family of the world's biggest events such as FIFA World Cup Soccer, the most prominent industries for sports event sponsorship are well represented with Adidas, Visa, Coca-Cola and Hyundai Kia Motors among the major partners for the 2007–14 period, and Sony and Emirates airline also featured in this group. Emirates is a particularly good example of an airline that has used event sponsorship as an international market entry and expansion strategy in recent years.

Where sport is and continues to be the major beneficiary of sponsorship dollars, there is also a growth in private sector investment in the arts, and in some regions this is being seen in increased spending on festivals and fairs. In 2009, projected sponsorship spending on festivals and annual events of this nature totalled US$775 million, up 2.9 per cent from $753 million the previous year (IEG 2009). Interest in arts events in general has been growing, but managers of arts-based events have also had to become far more commercial and marketing savvy in their orientation to secure sponsorship and in-kind support from the private sector. In some cases, support for festivals can come from unlikely quarters. A good illustration is the provision of land for the Australian staging of the 2010 Creamfields Festival by Brisbane Airport in Queensland, Australia, where the airport management team also provided some operational support for the event to go ahead. With a long-term vision of creating an airport city with a range of aviation and non-aviation land developments, support for Creamfields was just one element in a much wider event-sponsorship agenda of Brisbane Airport Corporation. Like many private sector entities, the company's community-directed event investments range from sponsorship of small-scale suburban family days and surf lifesaving events through to support for metropolitan festivals and orchestral groups, e.g. the Brisbane Festival and the Brisbane Philharmonic Orchestra.

Contemporary issues facing events and their sponsors include the challenges of accurately forecasting the value of event properties, ensuring that sufficient promotional dollars are spent on leveraging the sponsorship (over and above the initial investment) and using appropriate systems to measure both return on investment (ROI) and return on objectives (ROO). The latter takes into account those outcomes that go beyond the marketing revenue derived by sponsors. In some cases, companies engage in event sponsorship to build corporate reputation and goodwill as well as to generate brand awareness and sales. Accordingly, the strategies to evaluate event sponsorships must be tied to different business objectives, and in this regard measurement has become far more scientific in recent decades. Supplementing their own records of retail sales and hospitality programmes for leading clients, event sponsors do seek robust reports from event managers about the event audience and their post-event sponsor awareness and behaviour.

Event support services

Critical to the health of the event sector is the network of businesses engaged in media and marketing, travel and transport, tourist attractions, accommodation, retail sales and professional services. Successful implementation of an events strategy (destination-wide or for an individual event) relies on a *critical mass of businesses working together* to provide the package of experiences necessary to attract and satisfy visitors. Often, the provision of these *event support services* is by no means singular or discrete, with major hotels serving as prime examples of businesses that at once provide the venue, the event management services (e.g. programming and processing of meeting delegates), food and beverages at the event and the supporting accommodation.

In regional towns and cities, a large annual event can become the source of revenue and employment for a diversity of businesses over time. Raj and Musgrave (2009) cite the example of the Notting Hill Carnival in the UK which generates jobs in the arts, clothing businesses, car rental, hotels and catering, tour operations, marketing and advertising and transport. For Notting Hill, the event has become 'a key resource for the development of local businesses and the local community' (Raj and Musgrave 2009: 64). In some cities, an 'event-related' industry has expanded in conjunction with a longstanding event. The Tamworth Country Music Festival in rural Australia was initiated and promoted by media and music production interests and various business interests in the town of Tamworth have been stimulated by the annual event.

Some reflection on what makes for a successful destination mix (Mill 1992) can be very useful for event planners thinking about the types of services that must be continually re-energised to support events, e.g. tourist attractions (including events), transport/access, facilities, infrastructure and hospitality. Illustrating the importance of this mix, the key recommendations underpinning Australia's 2020 National Business Events Strategy (Business Events Council for Australia 2009) include a boost in aviation access from emerging markets, more streamlined visa processes, more sustainable events, increased exhibition space, more competitive hotel accommodation and improved IT services as well as hospitality and event skills and training. While the events on offer in a city can be very attractive in themselves, those cities or countries that fail to consider the whole destination mix and the quality of event-support services generally enjoy less visitation and business benefits.

Once events are secured, local businesses also need to be ready to satisfy the specialised needs of different visitors. To capitalise on the influx of international rugby fans to New Zealand for Rugby World Cup 2011, businesses were advised to gain increased knowledge about existing and potential export partners from visiting nations, to consider extended retail trading hours to tap into visitor spending and to improve their cultural insights and language skills (New Zealand Trade and Enterprise 2010).

Supporting events of all types and sizes are those businesses that shape the brand awareness and reputation of the event through *media and marketing* activities. Media organisations may serve as sole owners or co-owners of events, as sponsors and broadcasters, and provide a vehicle for event advertising and publicity. The place marketing potential of events is widely recognised. Emerging destination Abu Dhabi is one of many countries that have developed a strategy to utilise the media profile of events to globally convey an image of a desirable destination. Although the 2009 Formula 1 Etihad Airways Abu Dhabi Grand Prix attracted only 50,000 trackside spectators, it was televised in more than 180 countries to a purported audience of around 600 million viewers (World Sport Destination Expo 2010). This relationship between events and the international media is markedly stronger for sport than other types of events.

As indicated earlier, relationships between sport and the media are tightly linked through media coverage rights and equity ownership. It has even been suggested that in many cases the control of sports events, teams and athletes has been all but lost to media distribution conglomerates (Law *et al.* 2002). An outcome of this continued increase in the power of media over particular types of sport is the struggle for peripheral events, particularly arts-based activities to attract the attention and dollar investment of broadcasters. As Law *et al.* (2002: 299) have suggested, the presence of vertical media conglomerates and the interconnectedness between elite sports and the media could potentially jeopardise the exposure of the world's sport-cultural heritage outside commoditised versions of major events. In recent years, Asia has been a prime target for powerful media and sports businesses. Rowe and Gilmour (2010: 1530) point to the influence of transnational broadcasters in Asia which tend to privilege European and American-based sports leagues and 'crowd out' domestic Asia professional sports events. In this context, it is very important for nations to consider how the meshing of media and event marketing interests impacts on the opportunities to communicate the attributes of local events. While the media is an essential partner in ensuring the success of events, there are issues to manage in terms of the balance of local and global content and a need to grow the brand reputation of artistic/cultural events alongside sport.

Within the supply chain of event service providers, another important set of businesses is those providing event *travel services*. Event travel agents typically provide domestic, outbound and inbound travel packages and bookings for event-goers travelling to and from cities and countries hosting events. Specialised travel agents and tour operators are particularly influential in maximising the geographic reach of international events. The Events Worldwide Travel Group (Events Worldwide 2010) is one such group of companies that offer these event-support services in a number of countries (Australia, Hong Kong, Singapore, Thailand, Japan and the UK). In addition to organising travel packages for individual fans and enthusiasts, the company is the official travel agent for rugby events in Dubai and Hong Kong and includes among its key clients the Victorian Rugby, BMX Australia, Triathlon Victoria and others. Event travel specialists can help with accommodation, flight, train or bus information as well as procuring event tickets. Information about package deals that also include visits to other local attractions can be particularly helpful in boosting the overall spending by tourists at the event destination. Travel agency involvement in booking a suite of services including internal charter flights, car rentals and taxi services can be time efficient for sports teams, artistic troupes and companies sending employees and/or their clients to events.

Event impact management and sustainability

As interest in the sustainability of events grows alongside worldwide concerns about environmental change and unsustainable practices, there is a role for the private sector in helping to achieve sustainability goals. These goals extend beyond ecological responsibility to the society and economy in which events are staged. From the outset, more holistic and informed assessments of event legacies are needed and here, event *researchers*, financial *analysts*, social and environmental *planners and consultants* have a role to play alongside their public sector counterparts. Clearly, there is a responsibility on the part of the business sector to facilitate gains across both established and emerging businesses and to avoid the temptation to 'rake in short-term dollars' at the expense of long-term social conditions. Olds (2010: 258) argues that: 'the dominant state and private sector goals are to bring new people, new facilities and new money to cities at a rapid pace, and this goal is rarely evaluated in an open democratic manner'. In this context, there is an apparent need for more of a functionalist perspective to be adopted in event planning (Truly Sautter and Leisen 1999) with more collaboration across public, private and community partners about long-term outcomes.

The private sector is impacted by both the positive and negative impacts of events. The business world is a clear beneficiary of the *economic* gains from events. Capital infrastructure and facilities construction and airport, rail and road network developments are areas where direct benefits are felt in advance of the event (Zimbalist 2010) in terms of business profitability as well as employment. During the event, ticket sales, broadcast rights, event management services and tourism operators generate revenues, while immediately after the event participating businesses may also feel the brand benefits derived from sponsorship and media and visitor exposure. The staging of the IOC session in Singapore in 2005 led to a reported $19 million in tourism receipts but, post-event, several sports federations also expressed interest in holding world and regional championships in Singapore (Yuen 2008). For local firms to effectively leverage the potential regeneration from events, it is vital that they are made aware of the events being staged and jointly work on initiatives to optimise the dollar outcomes. In particular, Chalip (2004) refers to a four-pronged attack to generate economic spin-offs from events that include: enticing visitor spending, lengthening visitor stays, retaining event expenditures and using the event to improve regional business relationships.

For large-scale events, it is the extended timeframe of an event such as the Olympics that provides a short-term spike in spending on hospitality and accommodation (European Tour Operators Association 2005). However, as Zimbalist (2010) observes, actual outcomes of a modest surplus or long-term debt experienced by many Olympic cities have prompted a new financial model for the Games with more private financing. Accordingly, the focus on commercial investment in major and mega events via sponsorship and direct investment has continued to intensify. Given the cost of bidding for major events, this shift in the business model for major events underlines the importance of persuading businesses upfront about the related return on investment. Bidding for major events has certainly continued unabated. Walmsley (2008: 1) notes that: 'the 2007 Dubai International Sports Conference valued the market [for international sports events] at US$50 billion worldwide, while UK Sport estimates that such events contribute £1.5 billion to the British economy each year'. In this context, the overall dollar value of commercial sponsorship in these events is likely to continue to grow. In addition, it is likely that the corporate networks that start out as event sponsorships will be translated into longer-term sponsorships of legacy projects and community programmes (AT Kearney 2005). As sponsorships designed to demonstrate the corporate social responsibility of firms increase (Seguin et al. 2010), this sponsorship of programmes and initiatives to ensure longer-term legacies of events is far more likely.

The private sector benefits from various *socio-cultural* impacts that accompany events. There is the potential for the psychological benefits, cultural interface and community pride accompanying events (Tassiopoulos and Johnson 2009) to indirectly encourage economic activity in the same way that consumer confidence generally aligns with household spending. Westerbeek et al. (2002) suggest that these psychological outcomes can provide the confidence needed for future event bids as well as a sense of 'accomplishment and empowerment'. In effect, some towns and cities have 'grown up' through their event experience, with additional retail and hospitality outlets and new urban precincts.

These social benefits are most evident when infrastructure has been well utilised after the event. This was the case in Brisbane, Australia, following the city's staging of the Commonwealth Games and World Expo, the latter being the prime driver for the refurbishment of the riverside Southbank precinct which has subsequently become a busy inner-city leisure, retail and commercial centre. However, the reverse has been true in some other locations including Athens, Greece, where the post-Olympic period has seen stadia left largely unused. As a result, London 2012 has taken deliberate steps to learn from previous events (e.g. the Olympics in Sydney and Barcelona) about how to optimise social outcomes. Sadd and Jones (2009) note that London's 2012 Olympic bid enjoyed success through its deliberate intent to rejuvenate a socially deprived area of the city. Well-planned initiatives will obviously bring both community benefits and business opportunities.

Some of the social costs of events draw attention towards the ethics and responsibilities of the private sector, in particular displacement of existing residents, reported rises in the price of real estate and local products and services. Similarly, the commodification of local culture (indigenous products and performances) and staged authenticity (Tassiopoulos and Johnson 2009) often exposes the 'underbelly' of commercial engagement with events. These are areas that demand responsible behaviour from the private sector, but also point to the need for public–private sector programmes that ensure that local communities including indigenous groups are adequately protected.

The increase in environment-directed events as well as the environmental goals of events in general has given rise to a new style of involvement of the private sector with events. Numerous events have emerged that are dedicated to environmentalism and sustainability, and the meetings and conventions sector itself has produced 'green' event guidelines, e.g. Business Events Australia's green checklist for business events (Business Events Australia 2009). In addition to the construction of energy-efficient event venues, transport networks and villages, 'green events' have created a raft of new opportunities for event sponsors and service providers. Zero-waste events with carbon-neutral initiatives and ecologically sustainable sites provide new avenues for private sector sponsorship and product supply, but must also meet the 'green' criteria established by the event to guide its choice of business partners. Recycling is commonplace and products ranging from compostable cutlery to biodiesel-fuelled generators and environmental audits have opened up supply side opportunities.

Various authors (Getz 2009; Laing and Frost 2010) have acknowledged the growth of green energy providers among the suite of event sponsors and exhibitors. However, this is a domain where additional research is still needed, in terms of how to ensure that events are operationally sustainable as well as how to responsibly market 'green' events and profile the support of the private sector (Laing and Frost 2010) in a way that is not perceived to be simply 'green washing'.

Conclusion

This chapter has outlined various levels of private sector engagement with events drawing upon the conceptual diagram of stakeholders shown as Figure 14.1. A review of the sector shows a pervasive influence of entrepreneurs, business leaders, corporations and small to medium-sized businesses on the creation and sustainability of events. At the 'top end', research shows strategic and enabling roles being played by business leaders to ensure that events that are bid for and/or supported are those that bring revenue and reputation advantages. There is also a notable contribution made by business leaders in shaping strategies for events tourism which represents a destination-level input to the sector.

At the level of individual events, many businesses provide event-specific services that assist with funding, planning, promoting and staging the event while others offer event support services such as media and marketing, travel and transport, other tourist attractions and accommodation. Finally, the chapter has looked at the current and future role played by the private sector in managing event impacts and helping to ensure the long-term sustainability of the sector. While there is already a conscientious engagement by business in sponsorships that show corporate social responsibility and environmental concern, there is still room for more innovative partnerships and planning models that involve private–public sector collaboration about events and their sustainability.

References

Andersson, T. and Getz, D. (2009) 'Festival ownership: differences between public, non-profit and private festivals in Sweden', *Scandinavian Journal of Hospitality and Tourism* 9: 249–65.

AT Kearney (2005) *Building a Legacy: Sports Megaevents Should Last a Lifetime*, Chicago, IL: AT Kearney. Available at: www.atkearney.com/index.php/Publications/building-a-legacy.html

Boyko, C. (2008) 'Are you being served? The impacts of a tourist hallmark event on the place meanings of residents', *Event Management* 11: 161–77.

Bramwell, B. (1997) 'A sport mega-event as a sustainable tourism development strategy', *Tourism Recreation Research* 22: 13–19.

Business Events Australia (2009) *Green Checklist for Business Events*. Available at: http://businessevents.australia.com/Files/GREEN_CHECK-LIST_fact_sheet.pdf

Business Events Council for Australia (2009) *National Business Events Strategy for Australia 2020*. Available at: www.businesseventscouncil.org.au/page/national_businessbrevents_strategy.html

Canalichio, P. (2010) 'Tying brand licensing into event marketing', *Licensing Brands Inc. Online Blog*. Available at: www.brandlicensingexpert.com/blog/?Tag=event%20licensing

Carlsen, J. and Williams, P. (1999) 'Events tourism and destination image in Western Australia', in T. Andersson, C. Persson, B. Sahlberg and L.-I. Strom (eds) *The Impact of Mega Events*, Ostersund, Sweden: European Tourism Research Institute.

Carroll, A. (1993) *Business and Society: Ethics and Stakeholder Management*, Cincinatti, OH: Southwestern Publishing.

Catherwood, D. and van Kirk, R. (1992) *The Complete Guide to Special Event Management*, Canada: John Wiley and Sons.

Chalip, L. (2004) 'Beyond impact: a general model for host community event leverage', in B. Ritchie and D. Adair (eds) *Sport Tourism: Interrelationships, Impacts and Issues*, Clevedon: Channel View Publications.

Correia, M. and van Lill, D. (2010) *Report on the International Colloquiem on Mega-event Sustainability*, Johannesburg, South Africa. Available at: www.tourism.gov.za/Common/Downloads/tsme/2010-mar03/Colloquiumreport.pdf

Craik, J. (2001) 'Cultural tourism', in N. Douglas, N. Douglas and R. Derrett (eds) *Special Interest Tourism*, Brisbane: John Wiley and Sons.

Crowther, P. (2010) 'Strategic application of events', *International Journal of Hospitality Management* 29: 227–35.

European Tour Operators Association (2005) *Olympic Report*, London: ETOA. Available at: www.etoa.org/Pdf/ETOA%20Report%20Olympic.pdf

Event Scotland (2010) *Business Club Scotland: Creating Opportunities within Scotland's Events Industry*. Available at: www.eventscotland.org/scotland-the-perfect-stage/business-club-scotland/

Events Worldwide (2010) *Home Page*. Available at: http://events.com.au/default.aspx?s=contact_us (accessed 12 July 2010).

FIFA.com (2010) *Historical Development of the FIFA World Cup Licensing Programme*. Available at: www.fifa.com/aboutfifa/marketing/marketing/licensing/history.html (accessed 15 July 2010).

Getz, D. (1999) 'The impacts of mega-events on tourism: strategies for destinations', in T. Andersson, C. Persson, B. Sahlberg and L.-I. Strom (eds) *The Impact of Mega Events*. Ostersund, Sweden: European Tourism Research Institute.

——(2009) 'Policy for sustainable and responsible festivals and events: institutionalisation of a new paradigm', *Journal of Policy Research in Tourism, Leisure and Events* 1(1): 61–78.

Grigg, A. and Clout, J. (2010) 'Break down time: rugby faces a long hard fight to claw back prominence among Australia's winter codes', *Australian Financial Review Magazine*, August: 26.

Gursoy, D. and Kendall, K. (2006) 'Hosting mega events: modelling locals' support', *Annals of Tourism Research* 33: 603–23.

Hall, C.M. (1999) 'Rethinking collaboration and partnership: a public policy perspective', *Journal of Sustainable Tourism* 7: 274–89.

——(2000) *Tourism Planning: Policies, Processes and Relationships*, Harlow, UK: Prentice Hall.

——(2006) 'Urban entrepreneurship, corporate interests and sports mega events: the thin policies of competitiveness within the hard outcomes of neoliberalism', *Sociological Review* 54: 59–70.

Hiller, H. (2000) 'Mega-events, urban boosterism and growth strategies: an analysis of the objectives and legitimations of the Cape Town 2004 Olympic bid', *International Journal of Urban and Regional Research*, June: 439–58.

IEG (2009) *Arts Sponsorship Spending to Total $838 million in 2009*. Available by subscription at: www.sponsorship.com/IEGSR.aspx (accessed 15 July 2010).

——(2010a) *Inside GM's New Sponsorship Strategy*. Available by subscription at: www.sponsorship.com/IEGSR.aspx (accessed 10 August 2010).

——(2010b) *Report on IEG Performance Research Sponsorship Decision-makers Survey*. Available by subscription at: www.sponsorship.com/IEGSR.aspx (accessed 21 July 2010).

——(2010c) *Who Spent What in''09: IEG's Top Sponsors List*. Available by subscription at: www.sponsorship. com/IEGSR.aspx (accessed 15 July 2010).

Jago, L. and Deery, M. (2010) *Delivering Innovation, Knowledge and Performance: The Role of Business Events*. Available at: www.businesseventscouncil.org.au/files/ Business_Events_Innovation_Report_Mar10.pdf

Laing, J. and Frost, W. (2010) 'How green was my festival: exploring challenges and opportunities associated with hosting green events', *International Journal of Hospitality Management* 29: 261–7.

Law, A., Harvey, J. and Kemp, S. (2002) 'The global sports mass media oligopoly', *International Review for the Sociology of Sport* 37: 279–302.

Meenaghan, T. (2001) 'Understanding sponsorship effects', *Psychology and Marketing* 18: 95–122.

Merrilees, B., Getz, D. and O'Brien, D. (2005) 'Marketing stakeholder analysis: branding the Brisbane Goodwill Games', *European Journal of Marketing* 39: 1060–77.

Mill, R.C. (1992) *The Tourism System: An Introductory Text*, Englewood Cliffs, NJ: Prentice Hall.

Milward, H.B. (1996) 'Symposium on the hollow state: capacity, control and performance in interorganizational settings', *Journal of Public Administration Research and Theory* 6: 193–5.

Moodie, G. (2010) *Weighing the Cost and Value of World Cup Coverage*. Available at: www.bizcommunity. com/Article/196/147/49995.html (accessed 1 January 2011).

New Zealand Trade and Enterprise (2010) *Start Planning for 2011 Now*. Available at: www.nzte.govt.nz/ latest-events/rugby-world-cup-2011/pages/rugby-world-cup-2011.aspx (accessed 15 July 2010).

Nielsen Company (2009) *Global Advertising: Consumers Trust Real Friends and Virtual Strangers the Most*. Online blog. Available at: http://blog.nielsen.com/nielsenwire (accessed 16 August 2010).

O'Brien, D. (2006) 'Event business leveraging: the Sydney 2000 Olympic Games', *Annals of Tourism Research* 33: 240–61.

Olds, K. (2010) 'Urban mega-events, evictions and housing rights: the Canadian case', in J. Connell and S. Page (eds) *Event Tourism*, London: Routledge.

Queensland Events (2010) *Queensland to Support Commonwealth Games Bid for Gold Coast*. Media release. Available at: www.queenslandevents.com.au/news/?nId=200&cId=26.

Quester, P. and Thompson, B. (2001) 'Advertising and promotion leverage on arts sponsorship effectiveness', *Journal of Advertising Research,* January–February: 33–47.

Raj, R. and Musgrave, J. (2009) 'The economics of sustainable events', in R. Raj and J. Musgrave (eds) *Event Management and Sustainability*, Oxfordshire, UK: CABI International.

Ritchie, J.R.B. and Crouch, G. (2000) 'The competitive destination: a sustainability perspective', *Tourism Management* 21: 1–7.

Rowe, D. and Gilmour, C. (2010) 'Sport, media and consumption in Asia: a merchandised milieu', *American Behavioral Sciences* 53: 1530–48.

RT Business (2010) *Sochi Plans to Cash in on Merchandise Licensing*. Business news. Available at: http://rt. com/Business/2010-01-29/sochi-olympics-symbols-profit.html

Sadd, D. and Jones, I. (2009) 'Long term legacy implications for Olympic Games', in R. Raj and J. Musgrave (eds) *Event Management and Sustainability*, Oxfordshire, UK: CABI International.

Seguin, B., Parent, M. and O'Reilly, N. (2010) 'Corporate sponsorship support: a corporate social responsibility alternative to traditional events sponsorship', *International Journal of Sport Management and Marketing* 7: 202–22.

Smith, A. and Westerbeek, H. (2007) 'Sport as a vehicle for deploying corporate social responsibility', *Journal of Corporate Citizenship* 25: 43–54.

Smith, C. and Jenner, P. (1998) 'The impact of festivals and special events on tourism', *Travel and Tourism Analyst* 4: 73–91.

SportBusiness (2009) *The Sports Sponsorship Market*. Report available at: www.sportsbusiness.com (accessed 15 July 2010).

Stokes, R. (2008) 'Tourism strategy making: insights to the events tourism domain', *Tourism Management* 29: 252–62.

Tassiopoulos, D. and Johnson, D. (2009) 'Social impacts of events', in R. Raj and J. Musgrave (eds) *Event Management and Sustainability*, Oxfordshire, UK: CABI International.

The Business Incentives Group (2010) *Case Study: Trafalgar 200*. Available at: www.officialmerchandising. com/trafalgar200-casestudy.html (accessed 15 July 2010).

Truly Sautter, E. and Leisen, B. (1999) 'Managing stakeholders: a tourism planning model', *Annals of Tourism Research* 26: 312–28.

Walmsley, D. (2008) *Sports Event Bidding: A Strategic Guide for Bidders and Sports Property Owners.* Available at: www.sportsbusiness.com

Walters, G. (2009) 'Corporate social responsibility through sport', *The Journal of Corporate Citizenship,* Autumn: 81–94.

Westerbeek, H., Turner, P. and Ingerson, L. (2002) 'Key success factors in bidding for hallmark sporting events', *International Marketing Review* 19: 303–22.

Whitson, D. and Macintosh, D. (1996) 'The global circus: international sports, tourism and the marketing of cities', *Journal of Sport and Social Issues* 20: 278–95.

World Sport Destination Expo (2010) *WSDE Exhibitor Profiles: Abu Dhabi Tourism Authority.* Available at: http://www.worldsportdestinationexpo.com/press-releases/article/wsde-exhibitor-profiles-abu-dhabi-tourism-authority/ (accessed 20 July 2010).

Yuen, B. (2008) 'Sport and urban development in Singapore', *Cities* 25: 29–36.

Zimbalist, A. (2010) 'Is it worth it? Hosting the Olympic Games and other mega sporting events is an honor many countries aspire to – but why? *Finance and Development,* March: 8–11.

15

Event staging

Nicole Ferdinand and Nigel Williams

Introduction

Event managers are required to demonstrate a host of skills and attributes, simultaneously performing the roles of entrepreneur, artisan, technician, project manager and quality inspector. Nowhere is the multifaceted nature of event management better exemplified than in the area of event staging. It requires the combination of a plethora of elements, which must be creatively and competently brought together to host a successful event. This chapter seeks to provide an understanding of the various concepts of event staging, highlighting the differences in the scope and scale of the task and its implications for an event's stakeholders and key considerations. It briefly describes education and training options for careers in the area. It also highlights how event staging is practised by outlining the main considerations involved in stage selection, utilizing special effects and devising audio and/or visual systems. The chapter closes by examining how key trends such as the use of virtual and holographic technologies, increasing environmental consciousness and the popularity of cultural tourism is impacting event staging requirements.

Understanding event staging

The concept of event staging has multiple meanings and has been referred to in several ways by both academics and practitioners who have written about the subject. It can have a very narrow interpretation, such as the setting up of an entertainment stage within a venue, or it can be a more wide-ranging, inclusive construct which encompasses the consideration of political, socio-cultural, economic and environmental issues raised by the staging of events. The following highlight some of the ways in which the term 'event staging' has been used.

Stage set-up

In its smallest sense, event staging can refer to 'the organization of a venue within a much larger event' (Bowdin *et al.* 2006: 385), perhaps most typically the set-up of the stage area in an event featuring live entertainment. In this case, staging will be within the remit of specialized contractors providing services such as lighting, sound, audiovisual equipment, special effects, flooring, rigging and barricades. Although staging as it is understood in this context is a relatively small aspect of an event, it is nonetheless quite critical because of the risk and safety issues involved. The tasks involved in the constructing and setting up of stages are highly technical and potentially hazardous, and if not carried out with due care could result in fires, serious injury and even death (Silvers 2004). Additionally, because stages are required to support the weight of people, heavy equipment and other large objects, the potential risk of collapse has severe implications for not only the performers and staff on stage but for others in close proximity, particularly audience members. Stages are also very often the focal point of many events and may be the only area of the venue which is decorated or themed, so in addition to being safe, they must be attractive and durable, as they can be vital in delivering an event organizer's concept or key message (Matthews 2008).

Management of event logistics

Staging can also refer to the logistical organization of an event, which involves ensuring an event is delivered on time and within budget. Logistics in the context of an event will involve 'the distribution and flow of services and goods to the venue' (Harrison and McDonald 2004: 237). If event staging is defined in this way, it will involve a wide range of activities including location management and choice (Tum *et al.*, 2006) providing the event infrastructure and developing the event site (Silvers 2004). Event logistics involves a host of stakeholders, such as the event and host organizations and the contractors responsible for preparing the site, including decorators, equipment rental companies, producers of signage and banners, providers of waste management and recycling services, caterers, security and on-site ticketing and souvenir staff.

The key to the successful staging of events, in this case, will be largely dependent on the ability of the event organization to effectively translate the complex requirements of an event into clear guidelines and directions for all those involved (Harrison and McDonald 2004). The aim will be to ensure alignment of an event's objectives with the layout of the venue and event activities, whilst providing efficient operations and quality customer service to patrons. Key considerations will be optimizing movement, reducing congestion and maximizing the use of space (Tum *et al.* 2006).

Staging of event experiences

Morgan *et al.* (2010) have observed that the events sector, as part of the tourism and leisure industries, is one in which organizations engage in the staging of experiences for their customers. In their recently published book entitled *The Tourism and Leisure Experience: Consumer and Managerial Perspectives* they highlight the relevance of the idea of work as theatre for service-oriented businesses, such as those involved in the hosting of events. Morgan (2010) identifies the work of a number of authors dating back to the 1970s who have pioneered this particular perspective, including Csikszentmihalyi (1975), Booms and Bitner (1981), Lovelock (1981), Holbrook and Hirschmann (1982), Berry *et al.* (1985), Gronroos (1985), Grove and Fisk (1989), Grove *et al.* (1992) and Pine and Gilmore (1999).

Currently, the idea of event staging as the delivery of a theatrical performance is quite prevalent in events management literature (see Silvers 2004; Bowdin *et al.* 2006; Berridge 2007; and Getz 2007). The underlying assumption made in this concept of event staging is that memorable events are created when the disparate elements that are involved in events management are brought together into a seamless, holistic experience. For this to be achieved every inter-action that the customer has with the event must be in keeping with the event's theme. Silvers (2004: 271), highlights the need for the event manager to choreograph an event as carefully as a play or dance performance so that it takes the guest: 'through a structured progression of various sights, sounds, tastes, textures, smells, highs, lows, climaxes, diversions, and discoveries that delivers the impact and message of the event'.

Similarly, Bowdin *et al.* (2006) note the importance of a theme as a means of bringing together the various elements of staging. Berridge (2007) and Getz (2007) also highlight the importance of attendees in the making of the event experience, as their interpretation and level of involvement in the event that is staged will impact how memorable or meaningful it is to them. When events are viewed as a staged experience every interaction that attendees have with the event becomes important, including those that take place outside of the event site, such as the marketing and communications received prior to coming to the event and souvenirs purchased upon leaving.

Staging of large-scale events

Much of the literature on the staging of events is devoted to the hosting of large-scale events also known as major and mega events (see Preuss 2004; Gold and Gold 2005; and Clark 2008). Unlike smaller events, which are essentially the undertaking of the host and the event organi-zations, the staging of major and mega events are the undertaking of entire communities, cities or even countries. When the staging of events is viewed from this standpoint, the extent of the activities involved goes much further than the logistical requirements of the event or the staging of an experience for attendees. Because significant amounts of resources, often taken from public sources, are involved in the staging of large-scale events, a number of larger political, socio-cultural and environmental issues must also be addressed. Particularly crucial is the need to justify the expenditure on the event. Thus, the task staging of major and mega events extends far beyond what happens just prior to and immediately after the event.

For large-scale events such as the Olympic Games, long before a bid is even put in to stage the event, bidding delegations are required to consider their existing long-term development plans against the Olympic-related structural requirements (Preuss 2004). This is because the revenues raised from the event will not be enough to cover the considerable investment that cities have to make, not only in sporting facilities but in other facilities like public transportation and tourist accommodation. It is for this reason, as well, that the legacy of these events must also be planned. When the benefits and legacy of major and mega events are properly managed they can become a catalyst for long-term development and global reach for its host (Clark 2008). Conversely, poor legacy planning can also leave a country facing tremendous debt and saddled with sporting facilities and accommodation that go unused and fall into disrepair. The staging of events of this scale requires the involvement of a host of government officials at both national and local levels and also international bodies, giving the staging of large-scale events a distinct political dimension that other smaller, local and community events do not possess.

Event scope, stakeholders and considerations for staging events

As has been discussed, depending on whether event staging is interpreted as 'Stage Setup', 'Managing Event Logistics', 'Staging Event Experiences' or 'Staging Large-Scale Events' the scope, number of stakeholders and considerations will vary. In Figure 15.1 this has been depicted as a series of ever-increasing concentric circles.

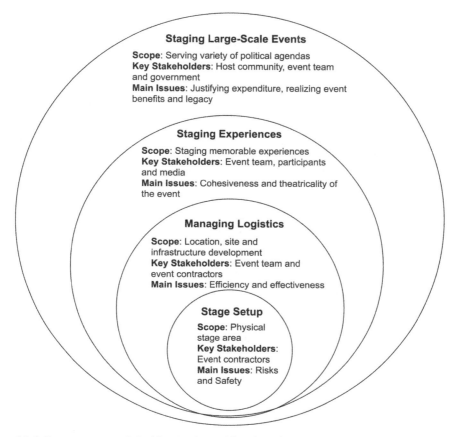

Figure 15.1 Event scope, stakeholders and considerations for staging events

The study of event staging

University courses

With the expansion of the events industry that has taken place in the last two decades, many universities have begun to offer specific degrees at both undergraduate and postgraduate levels targeting those students wishing to become professionals in this sector. These programmes are not limited to the more popular event destinations, such as the US, UK and Australia, but are dispersed throughout the world (Silvers *et al.* 2006). Many of them will have one or more modules or courses which specifically address event staging. Typically this component of the degree will deal with both the logistical and creative requirements of staging an event. Common features of many university programmes which specifically target event staging are that they are very practical and that the specific event staging module(s)/course(s) is/are used to provide real-life working experience. Liverpool John Moores University's second-year module entitled 'Planning and Staging Events', for example, offers students the opportunity to organize a live event for UK charity Barnardos (LJMU 2010). Other universities that offer courses in event staging deliver them as part of a continuing education or practitioner-based qualification. The instructor is typically an experienced professional employed in a relevant field. City University

London offers both novices and practitioners alike the chance to put on a live music event at some of London's key venues, as part of a course taught in the university's Centre for Adult Education. The course 'Staging a Live Music Event' is led by an experienced club promoter with over ten years' experience (City University London n.d.).

Other training options

As Silvers *et al.* (2006) note, options for the study of events management are not limited to universities. They highlight specifically the role of international industry associations in providing training opportunities for events management professionals and draw attention to a number of associations that offer professional certifications. The authors identify the International Special Events Society (ISES), the International Festival and Events Association (IFEA), the Meeting Professionals International (MPI), the Convention Industry Council (CIC) and the International Association of Assembly (IAA) as notable industry associations that provide professional certifications for members. These certifications are professional credentials which examine a broad body of knowledge in which event staging would be included. For instance, the Certified Special Event Professional (CSEP) qualification which is offered by ISES identifies five content areas, two of which focus in great detail on the content typically included in university modules or courses in event staging. These are highlighted in the course content outline under the headings 'Pre-production Phase' and 'Production Phase' (ISES n.d.). Specialized courses are also offered in various areas of event staging, such as lighting, sound, health and safety and stage management by private training organizations who may also be engaged in providing event staging services for clients.

Event staging in practice

In practice the job of event staging tends to refer to the more theatrical and technical aspects of event management. Organizations that offer event staging tend to be concerned with the technical requirements necessary for the entertainment aspects of an event. Typical tasks would include stage set-up and erecting of other temporary structures, such as sets, props, rigging and other technical installations. The highly technical nature of these tasks requires the use of highly trained professionals who very often have to be specially licensed. As was mentioned previously, event managers, unless they too are specifically trained and licensed, should seek the help of specialized contractors. However, event managers should nonetheless be knowledgeable about the various possibilities that stages, special effects, lighting and audiovisual systems can offer an event. Clients wanting to keep up with the latest trends or create something that is unique or has a 'wow factor' will want an event manager who is up-to-date with the latest technologies and/or knowledgeable about traditional staging practices which can be re-interpreted to achieve new and unusual events.

Staging possibilities

According to the type of entertainment featured at an event, the event manager will chose a stage that is most suitable. Stages can vary greatly in terms of size, function and the location in which they are used. The three most common stage, types are the proscenium stage, thrust stage and round stage, which are most often permanent stages such as those found in theatres and other entertainment venues. There are also a variety of temporary stages which can be manufactured in standard sizes or custom built, or mobile stages such as those found in outdoor festivals, concerts and exhibitions. If entertainment is to take place in a venue without a built stage and there is a limited budget, virtually any area the event manager designates can become a stage. However, as with other types of stages, the event manager should be mindful of the benefits and limitations of these staging areas.

Proscenium stages are traditional theatrical stages which date back to the seventeenth century (Styan 2005). With this type of stage, curtains are used to frame the activities from all sides save one, where the audience is seated. Typically the back of the stage is masked by an off-white curtain pulled taut which can be lit different colours to create various atmospheres or moods. The curtains on the left and right are generally dark coloured and are used to mask any lighting equipment suspended above the stage. These curtains also mask objects and performers before they appear on stage, making the unexpected possible. Events which feature theatrical performances such as plays, musicals and dance recitals are most suitable for these types of stages. Award ceremonies, graduations and even product launches can be given a heightened sense of drama when these types of stages are used: the entrances and exits of speakers, presenters and entertainers are made more dramatic as these persons can be hidden entirely from the audience's view until such time as they are revealed during the event's proceedings.

Thrust stages, in contrast, offer audiences a view of the stage from three sides – only the back of the stage remains hidden from view. Thrust stages, unlike proscenium stages, put the audience closer to the action on stage. Smaller events, in which a sense of intimacy is desired, such as acoustic musical performances, are best suited to these types of stages. If the 'thrust' extends far into the audience, a thrust stage can function as a fashion runway. Burlesque shows may also be done on these types of stages. However, the use of elaborate props and scenery is restricted because of audience sightlines (Ionazzi 1996).

Round or arena *stages* gather the audience in a full circle around the stage. With round stages the audience is even closer to the action than with a thrust stage, but at the same time there is no possibility of hiding or masking anything from them with draping or fake walls. Entertainment utilizing these types of stages should make use of the sense of community that is created from audience members being clearly visible to one another (Barton and McGregor, 2008). Community-based theatre and performances aimed at young children that benefit from audience participation are best suited to these types of stages. Magicians, fire-eaters, acrobats and other circus-type or novelty acts are also appropriate for these types of stages because of the nature of the entertainment they provide, simple yet highly dramatic.

Other stages, such as those that are manufactured, custom-built or mobile, offer a degree of flexibility and customizability not possible with traditional proscenium, thrust or round stages. However, it should be noted that these stages do have their disadvantages and limitations. For instance, manufactured stages come in standard sizes consisting of a series of decks (also called risers or platforms) which connect with each other to form larger surfaces and, as Matthews (2008) notes, not all manufacturers can make all the different sizes of decks through proprietary designs issues. He also points out that decks from one manufacturer are not usually compatible with decks from another manufacturer. Additionally, although custom-built stages offer several advantages, such as creating a unique one-of-a-kind design, the ability to fit into awkwardly shaped rooms and the capacity to feature unique forms of entertainment, they also necessitate the expertise of a certified structural engineer to ensure that the staging built is adequate for the loads anticipated. Mobile stages, which are designed to be self-contained and fit entirely in or as part of a towed trailer, are ideal for one-off outdoor events, but set-up and break-down can be considerably more complex and time-consuming when compared to traditional indoor stages. Environmental stages are perhaps the most flexible and cost effective of all stages, as these include 'any space designated by an agreement of the audience and performance as a theatre' (Barton and McGregor 2008: 138). In some avant-garde performances, a space may be designated as a stage without the agreement of the audience. A modern manifestation of this type of performance is the flash mob, which is described as 'an organized gathering of strangers to perform a short often surrealistic task to make an artistic or political statement' (Adams and McCrindle 2008: 58). The main problem of these types of stages is managing audience sightlines. Additionally, audiences unused to this type of entertainment may find it disconcerting and uncomfortable.

Special effects options

Special effects include a wide range of devices that are used to create atmosphere and give events their wow factor. They can be described as 'unusual and creative technological surprises timed to emphasize an event element' (Matthews 2008: 266). According to the character or budget of an event, special effects need not necessarily be elaborate or particularly expensive. Balloon drops or confetti and streamers can provide a surprising and dramatic finale for a sales meeting or team-building event. Conversely, at bigger events such as music concerts and festivals, special effects can be spectacular shows created with lasers and pyrotechnics. It is not possible for event managers to be familiar with all possible special effects options, as the list grows longer and more elaborate with each passing year. However, they should be familiar with some of the most commonly demanded types of special effects, such as those that can be achieved with fireworks and pyrotechnics, lasers and lighting and smoke, fog and haze.

Fireworks (sometimes called outdoor pyrotechnics) are most commonly used outdoors at large festivals and pubic events. They are of three types – high-level, low-level and ground-level. High-level fireworks (also known as aerial fireworks) are launched high into the air and burst to create various patterns of light, colour and sound. Low-level fireworks burst below 60 metres (200 feet) in the air (Matthews 2008), whereas ground-level fireworks remain on the ground and are often put into set pieces such as spinning wheels or used to illuminate company logos or banners. Although the terms 'pyrotechnics' and 'fireworks' are used interchangeably, the former are used indoors and the latter outdoors (Wanklin 2005). Pyrotechnics can be described as small devices that emit little smoke and create sparks, flame and other effects (Goldblatt 2004). They are most commonly used at events with indoor stages to highlight specific points of an event's programme of activities, such as the climax of an event's entertainment or to introduce a special guest.

Laser shows can be a form of entertainment in and of themselves or they can be used in a similar manner to pyrotechnics to create added drama to an event's entertainment. The beams or waves of coloured light may be set to music or formed into distinct shapes such as company logos, letters or abstract graphics. Generally, lasers used in these types of displays are of three types – low-power helium/neon (red), medium and high-power argon (green–blue), and mixed gas argon/krypton (red–yellow–green–blue). *Lighting*, although perhaps not as dramatic as lasers, can be used just as effectively to create a heightened sense of theatricality at an event. Spotlights provide narrow and controlled beams of light which can be used in a variety of ways, such as highlighting speakers and presenters on stage and following roving performers through the audience. Backlights, which have a UV light source, used on fluorescent materials can create energy and set the mood for a performance. Neon lights, which are lights made of glass tubes of neon gas, can be bent into various shapes (Matthews 2008).

Smoke, fog and haze are used to create atmospheric effects. They can be used in theatrical performances to simulate the real-life occurrence of these elements or in other types of events to create atmospheres and moods. Smoke is created by dispersing small, solid particles into the air (ESTA 1996 cited by Moody 1998). It is typically used to make coloured beams of light visible. Fog, though similar to smoke, is a different effect as it is by definition 'a cloud which touches the ground' (Moody 1998: 104); while smoke rises, fog stays low to the ground. Fog is typically created with dry ice by a machine. Haze, unlike smoke and fog, is a fine mist which is created by dispersing a vaporized oil or glycol (a type of alcohol) into the air to give an opalescent appearance (Matthews 2008).

Audio/visual systems

Specialized support equipment is required at all but the most informal of events to ensure that audio elements are presented at the required volume and clarity. This equipment is arranged into an integrated system that is configured to the demands of the event and characteristics of the venue. For events that have speech as the core component, such as business meetings and academic conferences, the focus is on accurate projection without obscuring the audience's view of the speaker. *Audio systems* are generally distributed on the perimeter of the venue, set at a moderate volume and individually adjusted for the acoustic properties of particular rooms. For events that rely on audio as entertainment, such as music, systems need to reproduce a wider range of audio types and volumes. Multiple speakers are used and need to be positioned in a manner that does not restrict views of the performance. Generally, speakers to reproduce low frequencies for bass and drums are large and placed on the floor while those for other instruments and vocals can be positioned higher. Depending on the size of the venue, performers may need an independent audio system, called a monitor, in order to hear themselves. Increasingly, *video systems* are deployed alongside audio systems at events to enhance presentations and entertainment. The selection of equipment is based on the purpose of the event. In meetings and conferences, visual elements organized using software such as PowerPoint are used for supporting presenters with primary displays positioned near the stage. Secondary displays may be utilized in areas without a direct view of the stage. For events where visuals are required to enhance a performance or venue, more complex arrangements can be deployed. Combinations of projectors and screens are used to present information, artwork, animations and video which are synchronized to other entertainment elements (Matthews 2008).

Event staging challenges in the twenty-first century

New technologies

Like other aspects of the event industry, event staging practices are changing and evolving with the development of new technology. Virtual reality is one of the more ground-breaking technologies to have been popularized in the twenty-first century. In 2006, Suzanne Vega became the first major recording artist to perform live in avatar form in the virtual world of *Second Life* (Vega 2010). In the following year, British band Red Zone became the first band to tour Second Life, with shows that included custom built animations and instruments (van Buskirk 2007). The virtual world platform, developed by the Linden Lab (Linden Research Inc. n.d.) is also host to real-life music events that are recorded and relayed into *Second Life*, in addition to events that are hybrids of virtual reality and real life (see http://secondlife.com/). *Second Life* presents opportunities for the building of fantastical, elaborate stages in surreal surroundings that would not be possible in real life. Special effects can include stages that float above the crowd and performers who can fly. The twenty-first century was also witness to the world's first 3D hologram performance, featuring the virtual band Gorillaz, staged at the 2005 MTV Music Awards in Lisbon, Portugal (Musion Systems Limited n.d.a). Holograms have since been used to bring David Beckham to Adidas' 2007 London 2012 Press Launch (Musion Systems Limited n.d.b), at the 2008 World Future

Energy Summit in the United Arab Emirates to project a life-sized image of Prince Charles to world leaders and to feature fashions at the 2009 British Fashion Awards (Musion Systems Limited n.d.c). This technology has opened up a host of possibilities for the staging of events, as the only limit to what can be viewed on an event stage will be the event manager's imagination.

Staging green events

In the last fifteen years or so there has been increasing awareness in the tourism and leisure industries regarding the need for sustainability. Recently in the events sector, large-scale music events such as Glastonbury Festival and Live Earth have been used to raise awareness about environmental issues such as the water crisis, CO_2 emissions and deforestation. Both these events have also showcased cutting-edge sustainable event staging technologies.

The Green Fields at Glastonbury possesses a solar-powered generator which collects and stores energy in over two tonnes of batteries. Its stages utilize low-voltage amplifiers and low-resistance circuits with a 'solar system' powered by a 10 kilowatt PA system. There is also a LED stage lighting rig that only uses the energy of two 100 watt household light bulbs (Glastonbury 2009).

Live Earth's 2007 concerts came closer to the ambitious goal of being carbon neutral than any large public event in history. This was achieved by combining the latest technological innovations with commonsense solutions. To reduce energy consumption stage lighting used energy-efficient discharge and LED lights. Generators that powered the stages used neat 100 per cent or blended bio-diesel. Additionally, very practical initiatives such as deciding to stage most of the concerts during the day and using stage props and signage which were either reused or donated were just as important for achieving the concert organizers' carbon-neutral goal (Live Earth LLC 2008).

Sustainability is now also a critical component of the assessment criteria for bids on mega sporting events (Laing and Frost 2010). For small event organizers, the decision to become sustainable may be one that comes about through potential cost savings, the opportunity to brand their event as sustainable or perhaps for contractual obligations that arise from clients' sustainability or environmental policies. The British Standards Institute (BSI) has led the way in terms of creating guidelines for sustainable events by launching a new standard in 2007. BS 8901 is the first specification for a sustainable event management system to have been launched, and specifies requirements for the staging of all types of events in a sustainable manner. It was updated in 2009 and has already been adopted by leading UK-based and international event organizations, and it will be used in the staging of the London 2012 Olympic and Paralympic Games (British Standards Institute 2010). There are also a number of organizations which event companies and their suppliers can join that are dedicated to promoting sustainability in the tourism and leisure industries, such as the International Tourism Partnership (see www.tourismpartnership.org), the Green Meeting Industry Council (see www.greenmeetings.info/) and EarthCheck (see www.greenglobe.org/).

Staging events at heritage sites

The potential of festivals and cultural events to simultaneously promote tourism and local cultural engagement and understanding at heritage sites continues to be recognized as an important opportunity for tourism operators (Smith *et al.* 2006). However, when events are staged at heritage sites they pose significant threats to the conservation of physical structures and rural environments (Smith *et al.* 2006). Event managers staging cultural performances, re-enactments and other events must also be careful not to desecrate these spaces by staging activities which may be considered sacrilegious. At the same time historic buildings and ruins can provide unique and culturally symbolic settings for the staging of cultural events as they come with an atmosphere of their own. Event managers and production teams working in these settings need to create innovative and interesting events which animate these spaces, whilst conserving structures and observing cultural sensitivity. Simple staging which uses minimal props, scenery and special effects whilst making the most of heritage settings is perhaps the best approach for stage management at heritage sites. Cultural entrepreneurs Banglanatak dot com demonstrate how the delicate balance of tourism, stage management, conservation and cultural sensitivity can be achieved in the following case study.

The staging of a traditional Indian folk festival – Palash Parban 2009

Tribal people of Purulia, West Bengal, in eastern India have a rich heritage of folk dance, drama and music. They are also rich in folk art and traditions which offer tremendous potential for economic development of people who lack formal education and thereby marketable skills for employment in conventional sectors. To help realize this potential, Banglanatak dot com organized festivals in rural India. In 2009, the company organized the festival at Deulghata in the Joypur Block of the Purulia district, which is six hours' journey into the forest. The area has an ancient Jain temple which dates back to the sixth to eighth centuries AD. The entire forest area is laden with palash trees and a dam beside the festival site gives it an ethereal glow.

Overall site preparation

Site preparation is started a month before the festival. A team of four to five people – the manager, two coordinators, a sound and light expert and a food expert – goes to the site. During this initial three to four days they stay at the festival site, talk with local villagers, understand their expectations from the festival and also mobilize them to take active participation. The entire area is mapped and locations are identified for events, tent arrangement, sanitation facilities, eating areas and resting.

Stage set-up

To ensure that the intimate nature of the event is maintained, a thrust stage arrangement is used. The stage is decorated and mats are placed in front of the stage for the audience to sit on. The meal area is also decorated, along with the tents and shaded areas. The village women also make several colourful traditional folk motifs in the mud walls of their houses, thereby extending the stage decoration to the entire village.

Lighting

The festival starts with an inauguration: the veteran Chau, Jhumur and Baul artists light up a camp fire. For the performances, the lighting is specifically arranged so that the ambience of a full-moon night remains intact, giving a mystical effect to the entire festival area (Figure 15.2).

Audio and video

Opportunities were also given to researchers and exponents and gurus of Chau, Jhumur, Baul/Fakiri, Patachitra and Gambhira culture to present their work. The audio system was

---

Figure 15.2 Jhumur dancers on the simple stage with basic lighting

designed to support the speeches of researchers and, later, reproduce the music of the Baul and Jhumur and the beatings of percussion instruments of the Dhamsa, Dhol and Madol. Video documentaries on the Jhumur and Patachitra were showcased at the festival using projectors and simple cloth screens.

Outcomes from the festival

The staging of Palash Parban 2009 has given the tribal people of Purulia, West Bengal, in eastern India an opportunity to earn money by providing cultural tourism experiences to visitors from nearby urban areas. In addition to economic benefits, it has served to overcome the social isolation and exclusion from which these communities have long suffered. As the festival site was decorated with light and sound, the long desolate temple structures got a new look. The villagers who passed the temples, ignoring them for years, now feel a sense of pride from them. These communities always had their own festivals but the tribal peoples never thought that they could benefit from them. With the help of Banglanatak dot com, the tribal people of Purulia have been able to use their local festival Palash Parban to promote their local temples as heritage sites. The folk artists are now regarded with greater respect by their communities and the people of Purulia are taking more pride in their culture and heritage. Furthermore by involving the local villagers and keeping the lighting, audio and visual systems simple, the rural environment was not compromised.

Acknowledgements

The authors would like to thank Mr Amitava Battacharya, Director of Banglanatak.com, for providing us with this case study. For further information on the work of Banglanatak dot com, please go to http://banglanatak.com/

Summary

Event staging can be seen as a fluid concept with the potential to include an increasing number of stakeholders and considerations depending on how it is interpreted. The responsibility of event staging can be limited to a single specialized contractor or extended to include government representatives at local and national levels. With the expansion of the events industries in the last two decades, there have been increasing opportunities for individuals to receive training in event staging at universities, industry organizations and private training institutions. In practice, event staging involves the more theatrical and technical aspects of an event. Whilst event managers may not necessarily be specifically licensed to offer the services involved in event staging, they nonetheless should be knowledgeable about stages, special effects and audio and/or visual systems and keep abreast of new trends if they are to offer their clients innovative, unique events with a wow factor. Today virtual reality and the real world collide to create spectacular entertainment, thanks to virtual reality and holographic technology. Increasing environmental awareness is changing the way many leading event organizations stage events. The British Standards Institute, along with a host of organizations dedicated to improving the sustainability of the leisure and tourism industries, offers guidelines on how more sustainable events can be produced. Cultural tourism has emerged as a sustainable tourism alternative, offering benefits for both visitors and host communities. Staging cultural events and festivals for the cultural tourism market has the potential to contribute to the quality of life of local residents by revitalizing traditional culture and heritage and increasing local leisure options. However, staging these types of events particularly at heritage sites threatens the conservation of physical structures and rural environments. Event managers operating in these locations must take care to balance tourism and stage management with conservation and cultural sensitivity.

Further reading

Camenson, B. (2003) *Opportunities in Event Planning Careers*, New York: McGraw Hill. (A guide to studying and working in event staging and other areas of event management.)

EarthCheck (n.d.) Website at: www.greenglobe.org/ (A website which provides information to travel and tourism organizations on validating their carbon claims and implementing sustainability initiatives.)

Green Meeting Industry Council (n.d.) Website at: www.greenmeetings.info/ (A website featuring the latest education, research, policy and standards aimed at improving sustainability in the meeting industry.)

International Tourism Partnership (n.d.) Website at: www.tourismpartnership.org/ (A website featuring tools and techniques, research and stories from around the world on making the hotel, travel and tourism industry more sustainable.)

Linden Research Inc. (2010) 'What is Second Life?' Available at: http://secondlife.com/whatis/ (accessed 2 August 2010). (An explanation of the 3D virtual world where users can socialize, connect and create using free voice and text chat.)

O'Toole, W. (2010) 'Event Project Management System'. Available at: www-personal.usyd.edu.au/~wotoole/epmspage1.html (accessed 2 August 2010). (A resource featuring examples of tools and techniques for managing the event staging process.)

References

Adams, A.A. and McCrindle, R. (2008) *Pandora's Box: Social and Professional Issues of the Information Age*, Chichester: John Wiley and Sons.

Balme, C.B. (1998) 'Staging the Pacific: framing authenticity in performances for tourists at the Polynesian Cultural Center', *Theatre Journal* 50(1): 53–70.

Barton, R. and McGregor, A. (2008) *Theatre in Your Life*, Boston: Wandsworth.

Berridge, G. (2007) *Events Design and Experience*, Oxford: Butterworth-Heinemann.

Berry, L., Zeithaml, V. and Parasuraman, A. (1985) 'Quality counts in services too', *Business Horizons* 28: 44–52.

Booms, B. and Bitner, M. (1981) 'Marketing strategies and organizational structures', in J. Donnelly and W. George (eds) *Marketing of Services,* Chicago: American Marketing Association, pp. 47–51.

Bowdin, G., Allen, J., O'Toole, W., Harris, R. and McDonnell, I. (2006) *Events Management,* Oxford: Butterworth-Heinemann, second edition.

British Standards Institute (2010) 'BS 8901:2009 Specification for a sustainability management system for events', British Standards Institute. Available at: http://shop.bsigroup.com/ProductDetail/? pid=000000000030196056 (accessed 2 August 2010).

Chhabra, D., Healy, R. and Sills, E. (2003) 'Staged authenticity and heritage tourism', *Annals of Tourism Research* 30(3): 702–19.

City University London (n.d.) 'Staging a live music event,' City University London. Available at: www. city.ac.uk/cae/cfa/creative_industries/music_events/staging_live_music.html (accessed 1 August 2010).

Clark, G. (2008) *Local Development Benefits from Staging Global Events,* Paris: Organisation for Economic Co-operation and Development.

Csikszentmihalyi, M. (1975) *Beyond Boredom and Anxiety,* San Francisco: Jossey-Bass.

Getz, D. (2007) *Event Studies: Theory, Research and Policy for Planned Events,* Oxford: Butterworth-Heinemann.

Glastonbury (2009) 'Our green policies'. Available at: www.glastonburyfestivals.co.uk/information/green-glastonbury/our-green-policies (accessed 2 January 2011).

Gold, J. and Gold, M. (2005) *Cities of Culture: Staging International Festivals and the Urban Agenda 1851–2000,* Hants: Ashgate.

Goldblatt, J. (2004) *Special Event Leadership for a New World,* Hoboken: John Wiley and Sons, fourth edition.

Gronroos, C. (1985) 'Internal marketing: theory and practice,' in T. Bloch, G. Upah and V. Zeithaml (eds) *Services Marketing in a Changing Environment,* Chicago: American Marketing Association, pp. 41–7.

Grove, S.J. and Fisk, R.P. (1989) 'Impression management in services marketing: a dramaturgical perspective', in R. Giacalone and P. Rosenfeld (eds) *Impression Management in the Organization,* Hillsdale: Lawrence Erlbaum, pp. 427–38.

Grove, S.J., Fisk, R.P. and Bitner, M.J. (1992) 'Dramatising the service experience: a managerial approach', in T.A. Swartz, S. Brown and D. Bowen (eds) *Advances in Services Marketing and Management,* Greenwich: JAI Press, pp. 91–121.

Harrison, L. and McDonald, F. (2004) 'Event management for the arts: a New Zealand perspective,' in I. Yeoman, M. Robertson, J. Ali-Knight, S. Drummond and U. McMahon-Beattie (eds) *Festival and Events Management: An International Arts and Culture Perspective,* Oxford: Butterworth-Heinemann, pp. 232–45.

Hecht, J. and Teresi, D. (1998) *Laser: Light of a Million Uses,* Mineola: Dover Publications.

Holbrook, M.B. and Hirschmann, E.C. (1982) 'The experiential aspects of consumption: Fantasies, feelings and fun', *Journal of Consumer Research* 9: 132–9.

Ionazzi, D.A. (1996) *The Stage Craft Handbook,* Ohio: Betterway Books.

ISES (n.d.) 'CSEP content outline'. Available at: www.ises.com/ProfessionalDevelopment/CSEP/CSEP ContentOutline/tabid/110/Default.aspx (accessed 1 August 2010).

Live Earth LLC (2008) *Life Earth Carbon Assessment and* Footprint. Available at: http://liveearth.org/docs/ Live_Earth_Carbon_Report.pdf (accessed 1 January 2011).

LJMU (2010) 'Students fundraise for Barnardos: LJMU Events Management students raised over £3500 for the charity Barnardos'. Available at: www.ljmu.ac.uk/NewsUpdate/index_101402.htm (accessed 1 August 2010).

Lovelock, C. (1981) 'Why marketing management needs to be different for services', in J. Donnelly and W. George (eds) *Marketing of Services,* Chicago: American Marketing Association, pp. 5–9.

Matthews, D. (2008) *Special Event Production: The Process,* Oxford: Butterworth-Heinemann.

Moody, J.L. (1998) *Concert Lighting: Techniques, Art, and Business,* Burlington: Focal Press Publications, second edition.

Morgan, M. (2010) 'The experience economy ten years on: where next for experience management?', in M. Morgan, P. Lugosi and J.R.B. Ritchie (eds) *The Tourism and Leisure Experience: Consumer and Managerial Perspectives,* Bristol: Channel View Publications, pp. 218–30.

Morgan, M., Lugosi, P. and Ritchie, J.R.B. (2010) 'Introduction', in M. Morgan, P. Lugosi and J.R.B. Ritchie (eds) *The Tourism and Leisure Experience: Consumer and Managerial Perspectives,* Bristol: Channel View Publications, pp. xv–xxii.

Musion Systems Limited (n.d.a) 'Gorillaz hologram: "Feel Good Inc" – live at the MTV Awards 2005'. Available at: www.musion.co.uk/Gorillaz_MTV_Awards.html (accessed 1 August 2010).

——(n.d.b) 'David Beckham hologram Adidas London 2012 press launch'. Available at: www.musion.co. uk/David_Beckham_Adidas_London_2012_Press_Launch.html (accessed 2 August 2010).

——(n.d.c) 'Prince Charles hologram World Future Energy Summit '08'. Available at: www.musion.co. uk/Prince_Charles.html (accessed 2 August 2010).

Pine, B. and Gilmore, J. (1999) *The Experience Economy: Work is Theatre and Every Business a Stage*, Boston: Harvard Business School Press.

Preuss, H. (2004) *The Economics of Staging the Olympics: A Comparison of the Games 1972 −2008*, Cheltenham: Edward Elgar.

Schechner, R. (1989) *Between Theatre and Anthropology*, Pennsylvania: University of Pennsylvania Press.

Silvers, J.R. (2004) *Professional Event Coordination*, Hoboken: John Wiley and Sons.

Silvers, J.R., Bowdin, G.A.J., O'Toole, W.J. and Nelson, K.B. (2006) 'Towards an international event management body of knowledge (EMBOK)', *Event Management* 9 (4): 185–98.

Smith, M., Carnegie, E. and Robertson, M. (2006) 'Juxtaposing the timeless and ephemeral: staging festivals and events at World Heritage Sites', in A. Leask and A. Fyall (eds) *Managing World Heritage Sites,* Oxford: Butterworth-Heinemann.

Sonder, M. (2004) *Event Entertainment and Production*, Hoboken: John Wiley and Sons.

Styan, J.L. (2005) *Drama: A Guide to the Study of Plays*, New York: Peter Lang Publishing.

Tum, J., Norton, P. and Wright, J.N. (2006) *Management of Event Operations*, Oxford: Butterworth-Heinemann.

van Buskirk, E. (2007) 'Band to tour Second Life', *Wired Online*, 7 February. Available at: www.wired. com/listening_post/2007/02/band_to_tour_se/ (accessed 1 August 2010).

Vega (2010) 'Detailed 2010 bio', *Suzanne Vega Online*. Available at: www.suzannevega.com/suzanne/ detailed-2007-bio/ (accessed 1 August 2010).

Wanklin, T. (2005) 'Organisations and organising events', in D. Tassiopoulos (ed.) *Event Management: A Professional and Developmental Approach*, Lansdowne: Juta Academic, second edition, pp. 122–46.

16

The experience of events

Chris Ryan

Introduction

As Getz (2007) notes in his review of the literature relating to event tourism, events *per se* have a long history even whilst the term 'event tourism' arguably dates only from the 1980s. Yet in the intervening decades the literature has reached a point where 'The literature on events has now grown beyond anyone's capability of reading it all, with a number of distinct specializations having emerged and gained recognition – including event tourism' (Getz 2008: 410). Yet, although Getz notes research drawn from a wide range of research paradigms including the anthropological, he also comments, 'It has been clear for some time that there has been a preoccupation with the economic costs, roles and impacts of events' (Getz 2008: 419) and this, with a post-positivistic paradigm, has tended to dominate research other than perhaps in the area of cultural and heritage tourism which also considers the significance of events in a wider cultural setting.

The purpose of this chapter is to consider how events may be experienced and what determines the depth of the experience. The author has argued that at the heart of tourism research lies observation, for which participation and immersion in various activities is a requirement. Potentially, therefore, an approach to research based on participant observation is auto-ethnographic, and the research outcomes are to be informed not simply by observation, but also reflection upon that which is observed. Reflection in turn is informed by interpretations shaped by an immersion not only in the event observed, but in a literature about the phenomenon, and possibly all researchers should, from time to time, seek to write a reflective piece freed from the constraints of statistical exercises, because only then, possibly, may they then consider the ethics of their research processes (Ryan 2005). The auto-ethnographic approach combines the self with observations of society (Reed-Danahay 1997; Wall, 2008; Noy 2009). This chapter is therefore offered in that vein, and seeks primarily to identify the variables that shape any experience of events. It does not seek to generalise, as experiences may be contextualised within places and times that each have their unique characteristics and thereby inhibit or constrain generalisation. Indeed, Ryan, Zhang and Zeng (2011) have gone so far as to suggest from an examination of meta narratives of the impacts of tourism on communities that possibly the study of tourism can only advance by comparisons of case studies, each of which, however, offers only limited lessons for other places and times. That too may be true of the study of events and the experiences they induce.

If, therefore, this chapter is to be based upon the auto-ethnographic, then I must state my own role and involvement in events. For part of my life I was the director of the Nottingham Festival Fringe and for nine years had a role in organising theatrical and other cultural events based at a college in Nottingham in the UK. I therefore had some experience of how news media operated in addition to organising and promoting events. I later came to research events as an academic, and as an academic have played other roles at events, such as being a keynote speaker at conferences or being involved on different occasions at a political level in different countries. Indeed, on my arrival in New Zealand I again became caught up in event organisation for a city council. Additionally I have, to my own wry amusement, been one of those people spied in cars accompanied by a police escort weaving their way through the overcrowded traffic of a foreign city as VIP at some political event. Hence my experiences have ranged from those of event organiser, to being a member of a crowd, to being one of the privileged 'dignitaries' of whom, I suspect, most at the event have never heard! In drawing on these experiences to comment about the nature of the experience of attending an event, I have not sought to define what an event is. That is perhaps best left to other chapters and authors; to my mind an event can be of any size, but its essential characteristic lies in the promise of something special outside of the confines of daily life, something that is promoted based on a specific theme, artist, or occurrence, and which takes place in a defined space – whether a conference venue, sports stadium or theatre. Such a definition is not meant to be too restrictive. After all, attending a theatre for a show can be treated as 'an event' for the members of the audience, and for all its uniqueness, the Olympics is but one more competition of note along with world or regional sporting championships. Events may therefore involve a bounded liminality – an idea that is further addressed below. It should also be noted by the reader that the auto-ethnographic is not without its critics, and indeed Shepherd (2011) in response to Ryan and Gu (2009) stated that such approaches and those where researchers 'construct' moments of truth are lapses into self-indulgence, and hence by implication are to be avoided. On the other hand, researchers always make choices as to modes of research. For example, positivism is itself a value judgement, and indeed the very references that academic authors chose to cite are acts of selection on their part and thus expressions of preferred paradigms of research. Certainly it is my belief that researchers should not deny their own expertise of informed observation, subject to the caveat that it is a carefully considered and reflective writing.

Emotional responses to events

Hence, as described elsewhere in this book, events can vary in size and nature, ranging from a family event such as a wedding to a mega sporting event such as the Olympics. Their antecedents are also equally varied, some being based in long-held traditions derived from pre-industrial societies based on times such as the gathering of the harvest, while others are a rediscovery or re-adaptation of older events, of which perhaps the modern Olympic movement is one such example. Many are of recent vintage, born of the need of local, regional or national governments to address economic needs, or to simply introduce some variety into their vicinities. The modern city is not simply a functional workplace but a multiple place of recreation, leisure, the creative arts and retailing, to such an extent that tourism and associated MICE need to be seen as part of a portfolio of income, image and politically inspired policies that bear upon modern urban design and planning. Hence to treat tourism in whatever form as something separate and isolated from these other considerations seems to be a denial of many of the potentialities inherent in tourism as part of a leisure–recreation–urban design nexus. Equally the experiences felt by those who attend such events can also vary. Those attending the Olympics or any major sporting event in any city may be excited by the success of an athlete with whom they can identify for any number of reasons. Such reasons can include being of the same nationality, and hence the excitement may be influenced by a sense of national pride, or of having some familiarity with the story of the athlete through national media coverage, or, at other times, there may be support for athletes of another nation because of perceptions of adversity overcome. Hence for example, the Jamaican bobsleigh team at the Calgary 1988 Winter Olympics touched many outside of Jamaica simply because of the very panache displayed by the team by not simply being there but achieving credible performances with less than state-of-the-art equipment, and their determination to finish even after crashing. Indeed, in 1994 the team went on to finish fourteenth overall, ahead of teams from Russia and the USA, thereby creating much excitement in their home country. Crowds may be moved to tears of joy, exultation, and at times despair as disaster of various kinds can occur, as illustrated perhaps most notoriously at the Munich Olympics. While sporting events can perhaps evoke a wide range of emotions in both spectators and competitors, so too can other events. At the 2010 Shanghai World Exposition attendees of different nationalities may have experienced a sense of wonder about the creativity of design on show, about the promise of new technologies, or the beauties of natural landscapes to which countries refer. For the participants a range of emotions can be experienced, from initial delight of being representatives of their respective countries to, as time passes and as, for the most part, visitors' questions remain the same, one of tiredness as the task becomes that of simply being another job. At other times an event may elicit sombre moods, as for example each year young New Zealanders and Australians reflect on the loss of past lives and the meaning of what it is to be an ANZAC nation as they commemorate the landings at Gallipoli during the First World War.

Not all events evoke emotional experiences. At the other end of the scale, while conferences, exhibitions and meetings can evoke senses of comradeship among fellow delegates through socialising, such events tend also to appeal to the cognitive, as perhaps found at academic conferences. Yet even conferences can evoke different feelings that may have little to do with the subject of debate. Conferences are times of stress. Delegates seek to complete tasks before they depart their normal place of work; they sometimes travel across different time zones that may leave them depleted of sleep. At the conference centre they may socialise, eat and drink more than they normally do, and in their hotel rooms may find themselves viewing television sets in early mornings, unable to sleep. Tired, they return to their places of work after another trip across time zones to find that yet more emails and physical mail await them in their in-trays, while colleagues have been storing requests that require their immediate attention. There has been on my part a feeling that a research topic awaits on the physical wellbeing of conference attendees!

In assessing these experiences one can therefore observe that event experiences can be rich or shallow, emotive or cognitive (or a combination of both), can be memorable or fade in the memory over time, and can be perceived as significant and a lifetime marker (does one count memories of the assassination of John F Kennedy, John Lennon or 9/11 as 'events'?). What then might be the determinants of an event's impact upon the way a person experiences an event?

Role of meaning and identification with events

The above examples begin to identify some of those variables. First, the event is perceived as having meaning for the individual. There is something about an event with which the attendee identifies – it reflects degrees of interest that at the time of the event are deemed significant. Attributed significance to the *nature* of the event, however, may be either temporary or enduring, and is to be distinguished from the significance of the *experience* as being temporary or enduring, although the two are linked. Events of little local, regional or national importance may nonetheless attain significant personal importance on the part of the attendee for any number of reasons – some are initially insignificant yet which later bear fruit, while others may engender significant emotional responses at the time. A spectator at the Olympic Games may be attending the sporting event for any number of reasons, and it cannot be assumed that the person normally identifies with that sport. They may be present because a team mate is competing, or a family member, or because their company is a sponsor, or they have received free tickets as a prize. Yet something happens that triggers an immediate response, and the intensity of that response lives in the memory for years yet to come, even though the attendee may never again be present at such a sporting event. If there is meaning for the person, then one possible source of that meaning is the shared excitement of the crowd. As social creatures, people are able to receive and communicate excitement in crowd situations. The experience of attending a football match when it is the final of a FIFA World Cup or an FA Cup Final is different from watching a match in a Sunday League at the local park. It is not simply a matter of possible differences in skill levels – at its heart it might be claimed that football is a simple game – but the difference in size of the crowd and its participation changes the experience. So the depth of experience may be primarily determined by identifying with the excitement of the crowd rather than any specific identification with the nature of the event being observed.

Enduring meaning associated with the nature of the event arises when the individual has a continuing interest with the subject matter of the event. They may play the sport, be interested in the event's subject as a hobby, work in the venue or the industry or otherwise have reasons as to why they retain a seriousness about the subject of the event. Given this, their terms of reference as to the nature of the experience may go beyond the immediacy of the crowd reaction as they are better able to make comparisons. Indeed, if present with other enthusiasts, the evocation of comparable feats with friends and colleagues adds a further dimension to the experience being engendered.

Experience is thereby associated with processes of attachment and identification with the event in question. The closer one's association with an event through interests or personal connections, the more one identifies with the desired success of the event. Identification is a two-way process, and as evidenced by the literature relating to serious leisure (Giddens, 1991) so one's own sense of being is reinforced by association with being present at, or playing an organising role in, the event. However, to play a role raises a series of other issues as to the efficacy of the role-playing and the recognition that may be gained from that role-playing.

Signification and media

Anticipation is a determinant of depth of experience and the evaluation of that experience, and the sources of anticipation are many. Today the role of the media is important. In many instances the attendee is 'informed' that an event is important by the fact that its taking place is deemed to be 'newsworthy' by the news media. The event is thereby 'signified' – and the act of signification has many consequences. It initiates sets of expectations that may be fulfilled or disappointed. Additionally, events have formats that determine what are deemed to be appropriate forms of behaviour. It has almost become a cliché that the winning actor or actress at an Oscar ceremony will babble thanks to everyone, from parents to the 'wonderful supporting cast', not to mention the director, producer and, when appropriate, a spouse. The person who is a conference delegate is, for the most part, just as skilled at being a spectator at a sporting event, a guest at a wedding or a participant in a show. Events possess formats and rubrics that determine modes of behaviour and hence the patterns of experiences that may be sought, expected and lived.

Today, when assessing the role of media in determining the significance of events, one must not only take into account the more traditional media such as newspapers, television and magazines, but also the media of the internet. Indeed, the latter may play a greater role in the post-evaluation of event experiences at a personal level. The more traditional media are subject to many pressures of a socio-political–economic nature, being dependent on a symbiotic relationship of circulation and advertising – the former justifies the use of the media by those wishing to advertise, while the revenues derived from advertising permit the medium to exist. A constant tension may therefore exist between readers' right to know, advertisers and others who control access to 'sources' of news to have their case promoted positively, and the financial needs of the medium, even while it seeks to protect an independence that provides a source of credibility for its different stakeholders. News and evaluation of events thereby tends to be formalised and filtered, although interestingly world news organisations such as the BBC and CNN seek to utilise the internet media to elicit personal comments to support their own news collecting and news worthiness through means such as the BBC's 'Have Your Say', as evidenced during the FIFA World Cup in South Africa in 2010. The boundaries between 'old' and 'new' media become blurred – but it is perhaps still possible to say that the new media through its immediacy and blogging may better provide immediate personal reactions to experiences of events. Hence an experience of an event is transmitted through other than simple word of mouth or act of being there. With my own Chinese students, some of whom were in Beijing for the 2008 Olympics but most of whom were not, there was nonetheless a transmission of a shared excitement and pride on their part in the opening and closing ceremonies – even while for many there was the recognition that such ceremonies were specifically designed to achieve that very end. Yet the same was also true of the 2010 Canadian Winter Olympics that portrayed a 'Canadian Way' just as assuredly as Beijing showcased an ancient Chinese culture. The issue is not simply that these were carefully staged events, but that these events immediately elicited wider senses of shared excitement beyond those simply present at the venue. On television one was shown people holding their cell-phones, taking photographs, sending them immediately to friends and loved ones, sending emails, text messages and tweats, so that one could from a distance watch on television and simultaneously receive and send messages to those at such an event. If part of an experience is the ability to transmit and share that experience to further make the experience more intense, then the technologies of the world wide web have brought an experience of events to more people, and more quickly.

Such 'event experience transmission' has not gone unnoticed by commercial and political interests, and there exist today more 'events' specifically staged for commercial and economic reasons than ever before, at many levels including the local. It is as if not to stage an event is to possess some deficiency. Thus my own university at Waikato in New Zealand feels obliged to stage and be involved at 'events'. The Gallagher Great Race pits the university's rowing teams against the universities of Oxford and Cambridge in some derivative of the more traditional Oxford–Cambridge boat race, and the university also seeks to be prominent in what may be the southern hemisphere's largest rural show, Fieldays, at Mystery Creek. As I watch football on television, I can sometimes catch an advertisement for a British university 'proudly' proclaiming itself to be a sponsor of a football team. Sponsors therefore also wish to derive an 'event experience'. As with traditional sponsorship the sponsor of an event wishes to be associated with some 'thing' that possesses characteristics that complements the sponsor's own aims and purposes, and thereby better promote a desirable image. Within the sponsoring organisation there thereby comes to exist a group charged with finding and exploiting such opportunities, and for them the event is a justification of their own role. Imbued with a professional sense of 'image creation', not only the event itself but the acts of sponsorship and association with an event create further product, namely 'desirability of image' and 'desirability of association'. To this end budgets are generated and justified – and once participation is achieved, then over time it becomes difficult to change the status quo and the budgets associated with it. Professional participation by such people thereby also becomes a form of event experience on their part – and it is an experience that provides not only a source of the fulfilment of professional duties but also a means of engendering relationships with people perceived as occupying positions of influence, whether university vice-chancellors, chief executive officers or politicians, local or national. Events are photo opportunities for such personnel – and such personnel experience events from a privileged position. They are often escorted to the venue, have the best seats, meet event organisers and famed participants, enjoy fine wining and dining, and may have favourable media coverage. They are 'seen', and even if not interviewed, being seen may be sufficient. The act of being 'seen', while possibly momentary on the stage itself, can be captured in photographs and continues a more enduring life on web pages, in official publicity material, in house news magazines or journals, and in the 'official' lives of organisations besides the personal life of the sponsor or celebrity. For such individuals, a portfolio of event experiences is created, and the experience of events becomes a round of handshakes, official posing for photographs, and an experience of the event removed from the participation of the members of the public, who may, however, obtain more joyful experiences of the event.

If, therefore, events have become increasingly motivated by commercial, economic and other interests, what emerges is a segmentation of events targeted at different groups within society. Such segmentation again shapes the potential experiences to be derived from events. Pop concerts aimed at a younger clientele may seek to excite crowds, yet as pop groups increasingly seem to tour for much longer in their careers (think of the Rolling Stones or AC-DC), then nostalgia also becomes a part of the experience. Dare one propose that within the arena of popular culture a Stones tour is a form of heritage tourism? At what age does a cultural phenomenon become a cultural asset? Does a theatrical event such as Abba's *Mama Mia* become, for all its catchy tunes, a complex product of freshness for a younger generation and a moment of nostalgia for older people? Certainly such tours and events are perceived as marketing opportunities, and part of the experience may be the purchase of a t-shirt or poster, whereby the experience of 'being there' is subsequently resurrected by the wearing of the t-shirt. Such a purchase is also a signifier to other cognoscenti, and hence experience and personal identity are interwoven into a continuum of time that exists after the event itself has finished.

A bounded liminality

From the discussion above, and the way in which an 'event' was envisaged in the second paragraph, one is led to a potential conceptualisation of an 'event' as something outside of 'ordinary experience'. Such an approach implies that attendance at an event is liminal in the sense used by Turner (1977, 1986, 1990), for it is possessed of a mixture of forces that Bakhtin (1981: 360) described as 'mute and opaque, never making use of conscious contrasts and oppositions … [Yet] such unconscious hybrids have been at the same time profoundly productive historically: they are pregnant with potential for new world views, with new "internal forms" for perceiving the world.' In my book *The Tourist Experience* (Ryan 2002) this conceptualisation was used for the process of holidaying, and indeed the hybridity inherent in such conditions as described by Bhabha (1994) was stated to be potentially cathartic. The *Shirley Valentine* syndrome described in that book (Ryan 2002) provides evidence of such. While major events, such as the FIFA World Cup or World Expositions, may be of significant durations of time, for many attendees the period of participation may be quite short. The writings of sociologists such as Gluckman (1965),

Bhabha (1994) and Bakhtin (1984) provide insights into the tensions that may be experienced. During sports events, the sports fan has the emotion of supporting their team, yet as a fan of a game may suppress or only grudgingly admit good play by an opponent. Support for a game is subsumed as a lesser support when compared to the support for a team, while support for a national team may momentarily mean setting aside a lack of support for a player who comes from a club not generally supported. Many events other than sporting events pose occasions of recognition of 'good form' from those not normally followed or admired by an attendee – whether in the sense of adhering to an academic theory, a marketing strategy or political policy. Organic and intentional hybridities arise from the commonality of people with differing views being together – and this may be visceral or intellectual. Even at a theatre performance where the actors are the 'active' party and those in the theatre seats the more passive spectator, one intuitively becomes aware that a responsive audience brings forth a 'better' performance. Both actor and audience come fused in a new entity that reinforces the nature of 'being there' – thereby changing the experience.

As events, sports and aesthetic, cultural performances may possess richer potential than many other events for generating more intense emotion, for they set aside the rules of normal order. The theatre production invites its audience to look at the lives and events of others in a 'dramatic' fashion, the sporting event may literally turn unruly if opposing fans clash, and even in the more formal meetings, conventions and Expos, the attendees are taken from their normal milieu into the staged managed setting of a conference centre to be subjected to lines of debate or argument designed to be a space apart from usual duties – a space that is both physically, socially and psychologically designed to generate *communitas*. In Turner's (1977, 1986, 1990) writings, *communitas* does not only relate to a sense of being with others and of organisation through rituals, but also refers to *marginality*, 'otherness' and issues of superior–inferior. In the experiences of events as described above, implicit references to these concepts exist. As noted, the t-shirt commemorating an event is a signifier to others that an event was attended – it both separates from those who did not attend, and reconfirms with those who did. Participation divides attendees and organisers from non-participants, and thereby defines the margins of membership of groups. For Turner, however, marginality is 'betwixt and between', for it is relatively unstructured – and within the rubrics of events the division between active player and spectator is permeable: in some cases cross-referencing is easier than in other circumstances.

While it may be objected that Turner's concepts derived from anthropological studies of African tribesmen ill fit many of the events sponsored within the realm of tourism, I am not alone in drawing attention to the role of the travel away from home being characterised by transformations of 'departure from', 'being away from', and 'returning to' contrasted daily life, and these transitions are marked by different rituals, such as at the check-in at the airline desk (Ryan, 2002). For example, Pritchard and Morgan (2006) have observed guest behaviours at hotels and noted how the hotel serves as a space for escapes from responsibility in many different ways, both large and small. More recently, Jaimangal-Jones *et al.* (2010) used similar arguments to denote the special spaces of events held as 'raves' within the dance music scene.

Such observations informed by Turner's and Bhabha's concepts of liminality and hybrid spaces are also often connected to Bakhtin's concept of the carnivalesque. Again, I too would share these interests (e.g. Ryan and Gu 2007; Ryan and Prendegast 2007). Bakhtin derives the concept of the carnivalesque from the Medieval 'Fool's Days' when order was inverted and the king's clown became, at least in appearance, ruler. Such inversions were condoned and constrained by church authorities in Bakhtin's studies, and are notably characterised by references not simply to the secular but to the profane and the role of bodily functions. Evidence may be found at major sporting events as evidenced not simply by the cacophony of sound of the *vuvuzela* at the FIFA World Cup games themselves but as part of the street partying in the streets of South African cities and elsewhere. As a symbol of the imposition of a black South African 'experience' on the senses and rituals of European football, possibly few things better illustrate a form of carnivalesque inversion and marginality.

An event management perspective

Such considerations are not lost on those responsible for event management. From one perspective event managers are always interested in the answers to questions such as who travels, why they travel to an event, how long they stay, what they do during that period, whether they will come again, whether they will recommend an event to friends, and how much they spend and what can be done to make them spend more in the future. Certainly, in my own past such questions were of importance even when acting as the director of a festival fringe, as venues and performers needed to be paid and budgets adhered to, even if some contracts were 'gentlemen's agreements' – that is, you get paid if we made money. The irony, of course, was that the willingness of a performer to perform actually increased the pressure on me as organiser to ensure enough revenue was generated to make as generous a payment as possible! Truly it might be said that the demand and supply side of the event tourism industry possess symbiotic interests – event promoters want their event to be successful by whichever criteria they select, attendees attend with the expectation of having a satisfactory experience, and performers seek payment. Given the range of events that exist, care must be taken not to generalise too much, but given the questions asked by event promoters, various implications arise. First, whether informally or in more structured ways, event promoters will undertake some research. Second, new initiatives will be undertaken from one year to another, thereby creating changes in event format. Events may grow, perhaps move venues or times of performance, suffer from unsuccessful initiatives or change in such a way as to no longer appeal to initial audiences but become more or less mainstream, as the case may be. In short, events may come to have their own lifecycles of origination, development, later growth stages, consolidation, stagnation and perhaps decline over time. Such periods may be short or long. Just as in tourism, where destinations may change over time and where such changes impact on land use patterns, dependency on external resources such as capital, the focus of marketing efforts and changing clientele, so too parallel changes might be identified on the part of events. Events may, in order to grow, seek wider audiences, become more commercial, seek promotion and marketing outside of their own region, attract differing types and sizes of sponsors – and just as destinations over time offer potentially different product and experiences to a changing pattern of guests, so too some events may generate similar histories. To mention briefly but one example, a music festival such as Glastonbury has gone through various organisational stages while its clientele slowly changes. The modern version of the festival commenced with the Pilton Pop, Blues and Folk Festival in September 1970 as part of the hippie ethic, and over the years has developed its own history of stories that involves floods, fights, commercialism and counter-commercialism, and as it ages so too does at least a part of its audience. Consequently today there is arguably a more heterogeneous audience than in the past, ranging from 'Glastonbury veterans' to newcomers. Each such group experiences the same acts and conditions, but each interprets these tangible features within differing networks of recall, history and comparisons, thereby creating different experiences. Marketing and ticket distribution has also changed over the years, and much pre-planning by both organisers and clientele is required today.

Given this type of development, attendee experiences become subjects of commodification for different reasons. First, event organisers may come to depend increasingly on revenue sources other than simply ticket revenues, foremost amongst which may be sponsorship. In other arenas sponsorship might involve strategies such as product placement in films. Here the sponsor seeks an congruity of identification of images between product, sponsor, medium (e.g. a given film thought to aim at a given market segment) and purchasers of cinema tickets, whereby the product lends credence to the authenticity of a story. This, it is thought, makes it a more 'real' experience for the audience, thereby linking product with cinematic experience that might carry over into other parts of a person's life. The attempt is to create product awareness and a predisposition to purchase on the part of the audience member. Musante *et al.* (1999) applied this concept to the sponsorship of sporting events, entitling the concept 'schema congruity theory'. Cornwell and Coote (2005) argue that clear evidence exists for the efficacy of these relationships, and given this it might be argued that when an event matures and grows, increased commercialisation may occur as event organisers become capable to delivering an audience, and the event becomes one whereby a managed experience becomes an aim to achieve a commercial end. However, the same processes may be found in other cases. For example, the portrayal of China through the ceremonies and television coverage of the Beijing Olympics in 2008 was found to affect not only overseas attitudes towards China but also domestic opinions (Brady 2009). From the wider perspectives of sponsorship, events and experiential marketing these and other ideas are considered by writers such as Berridge (2007), Getz (2007) and Schmitt (1999).

Conclusion

If, as Shepherd (2011) argues, research based on paradigms other than the post-positivisitic with its clearly defined processes of testing validity is to be adopted, then to avoid 'self-indulgence' the author should seek to establish some form of credibility and 'trustfulness'. In this chapter, perhaps paradoxically, the above discussion can be posed in a systematic way that permits future testing.

Consequently the above discussion might be summarised diagrammatically as shown in Figure 16.1. A simple matrix can be constructed based on two continua – the level of meaning ascribed to an event, and the duration of interest in the event. This gives rise to four cells. The top right-hand one indicates high levels of meaning and duration of interest, and thus potentially represents what Hall and Weiler (1992), drawing on concepts derived from Stebbins (1992), called 'serious leisure tourism', whereby individuals draw in part a sense of their own identities by being closely involved with such events. One example would be those who engage in American Civil War battlefield re-enactments. The top left-hand cell represents a situation where a person can get caught up with the environment and atmosphere of an event (for example, a sporting event like a football match) and while not a 'hard-core fan' may still very much enjoy the event. The bottom left-hand cell represents a position of temporary interest but of little importance, meaning that some enjoyment may be obtained but the possibility of a repeat visitation is unlikely. On the other hand, in the remaining cell, while meaning is low, there exists a longer-term interest such that, if there are no other attractions or inducements, an attendee or participant may be drawn to the event for a repeat visit.

Each of these cells has implications for wider management. It is suggested that the main pattern is represented by the diagonal arrow running from the bottom left-hand corner to the top right-hand corner. Sponsors and commercial interests may have little interest in the market segment represented in segment of the bottom left-hand corner, whereas the top right-hand corner will attract strong interest from sponsors because it opens up an opportunity for

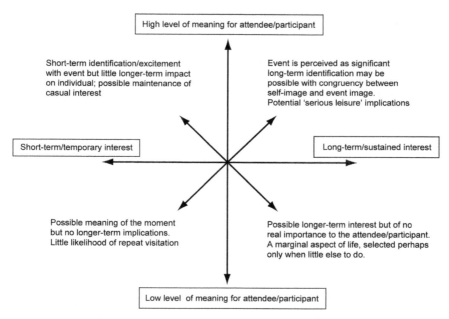

High level of meaning for attendee/participant

Short-term identification/excitement with event but little longer-term impact on individual; possible maintenance of casual interest

Event is perceived as significant long-term identification may be possible with congruency between self-image and event image. Potential 'serious leisure' implications

Short-term/temporary interest

Long-term/sustained interest

Possible meaning of the moment but no longer-term implications. Little likelihood of repeat visitation

Possible longer-term interest but of no real importance to the attendee/participant. A marginal aspect of life, selected perhaps only when little else to do.

Low level of meaning for attendee/participant

Figure 16.1 Matrix of event meaning and duration of interest

long-term relationship marketing and merchandising. The field of membership organisation conferences might occupy this cell of the matrix.

The second arrow, from the top left-hand corner to the bottom right-hand corner, also indicates a potential marketing opportunity. The top left-hand cell represents the potential for event-based merchandising such as programmes, DVDs, t-shirts and similar paraphernalia that often may come to litter a household!

Before leaving the framework proposed by Figure 16.1 there is a further observation to be made. It can be objected that the two dimensions are not wholly independent. Surely, the presence of a very high level of interest and meaning in an event is going to imply the existence of a long-term, sustainable degree of interest? However, in response to what might be argued it can be said that the framework of analysis shows an interaction between a cognitive state ('meaning') and a behavioural outcome (sustained or shortened interest) while the cells reflect actual behavioural and evaluative factors.

Additionally it has been noted that the duration of an event itself is constrained and limited. Participation in the event is temporarily liminal, and takes the person outside of their ordinary lives (just as much of tourism does). Yet, in spite of these persuasive examples of how events and attendance at events may represent liminal and carnivalesque moments, any conceptualisation must recognise the increasingly commercial nature of such events. It may be concluded that where moments of *communitas* and temporary *habitus* exist, they are increasingly constructed by commercial interests, just as in the past, according to Bakhtin, carnival was a period condoned and permitted by the Medieval Church for its own purposes. Experiences of events are thus complex phenomena, yet however constrained and manipulated by the venue, the programme and event management, events may still have that existential authenticity referred to by Wang (2000) for the attendee. Events are, as many things in tourism, moments of potentiality for change – sought for or unexpected – and significant and insignificant. What determines the eventual significance of attendance at an event, the nature of the event itself and the degree to which it is recalled by a participate in the lingering after-life of the event, is very much determined by the skills and attitudes brought to an event by each attendee and participant. Events are social occasions that elicit human interactions with a programme designed to amuse, sell, educate, create a sense of wonder, and celebrate – and the venue becomes a nexus where these may well be fused into something memorable.

References

Bakhtin, M. (1981) *The Dialogic Imagination*, trans. C. Emerson and M. Holquist, Austin: University of Texas Press.

——(1984 [1968]) *Rabelais and His World*, Bloomington: Indiana University Press.

Berridge, G. (2007) *Events Design and Experience*, Oxford: Butterworth-Heinemann.

Bhabha, H.K. (1994). *The Location of Culture*, London: Routledge.

Brady, A.-M. (2009) 'The Beijing Olympics as a campaign of mass distraction', *The China Quarterly* 197: 1–24; doi: 10.1017/S0305741009000058.

Cornwell, T.N. and Coote, L.V. (2005) 'Corporate sponsorship of a cause: the role of identification in purchase intent', *Journal of Business Research* 58: 268–76.

Getz, D. (2007) *Event Studies: Theory, Research and Policy for Planned Events*, Oxford: Butterworth-Heinemann.

Giddens, A. (1991) *Modernity and Self-identity: Self and Society in the Late Modern Age*, Stanford: Stanford University Press.

Gluckman, M. (1965) *Politics, Law and Ritual in Tribal Society*, Oxford: Basil Blackwell.

Hall, C.M., and Weiler, B. (1992) *Special Interest Tourism*, London: Belhaven Press.

Jaimangal-Jones, D., Pritchard, A. and Morgan, N. (2010) 'Going the distance: locating journey, liminality and rites of passage in dance music experiences', *Leisure Studies* 29(3): 253–68.

Musante, M., Milne, G.R. and McDonald, M.A. (1999) 'Sport sponsorship: evaluating the sport and brand image match', *International Journal of Sports Marketing Sponsorship* 1(1): 32–47.

Noy, C. (2009) 'The poetics of tourist experience: an autoethnography of a family trip to Eilat', *Journal of Tourism and Cultural Change* 5(3): 141–57.

Pritchard, A. and Morgan, N. (2006) 'Hotel Babylon? Exploring hotels as liminal sites of transition and transgression', *Tourism Management* 27(5): 762–72.

Reed-Danahay, D.E. (1997) 'Introduction', in D.E. Reed-Danahay (ed.) *Auto/Ethnography: Rewriting the Self and the Social*, Oxford and New York: Berg.

Ryan, C. (2002) *The Tourist Experience*, London: Continuum.

——(2005) 'Ethics in tourism research: objectivities and personal perspectives', in B.W. Ritchie, P. Burns and C. Palmer (eds) *Tourism Research Methods: Integrating Theory with Practice*, Wallingford: CABI Publishing, pp. 9–20.

Ryan, C. and Gu, H. (2007) 'Bodies, carnival and honey days: the example of Coney Island', in A. Pritchard, N. Morgan, I. Ateljevic and C. Harris (eds) *Tourism and Gender: Embodiment, Sensuality and Experience*, Oxford: CABI, pp. 126–37.

——(2010) 'Constructionism and culture in research: Understandings of the fourth Buddhist Festival, Wutaishan, China', *Tourism Management* 31(2):167–78.

Ryan, C. and Prendegast, D. (2007) 'Darling Harbour – site of the carnivalesque?', *Journal of Hospitality and Tourism.* 5(1):1–16.

Ryan,C., Zhang Chaozhi and Zeng Deng (2011) 'The impacts of tourism at a UNESCO heritage site in China – the need for a meta-narrative? The case of the Kaiping Diaolou', *Journal of Sustainable Tourism*, DOI: 10.1080/09669582.2010.544742.

Schmitt, B. (1999) *Experiential Marketing: How to Get Customers to Sense, Feel, Think, Act, and Relate to Your Company and Brands*, New York: The Free Press.

Shepherd, R.J. (2011) Historicity, fieldwork, and the allure of the post-modern: a reply to Ryan and Gu, *Tourism Management* 32(1):187–90.

Stebbins, R. (1992) *Amateurs, Professionals, and Serious Leisure*, Montreal and Kingston: McGill-Queen's Universities Press.

Turner, V. (1977) *The Ritual Process: Structure and Anti-structure*, Ithaca, NY: Cornell University Press, first Cornell edition.

——(1986) 'Dewy, Dilthey, and drama: an essay in the anthropology of experience', in V. Turner and E.M. Bruner (eds) *The Anthropology of Experience*, Urbana: University of Illinois Press.

——(1990) 'Are there universals of performance in myth, ritual, and drama?', in R. Schechner and W. Appel (eds) *By Means of Performance: Intercultural Studies of Theatre and Ritual*, Cambridge: Cambridge University Press.

Wall, S. (2008) 'Easier said than done: writing an autoethnography', *International Journal of Qualitative Methods* 7(1): 38–53.

Wang, N. (2000) Tourism *and Modernity: A* Sociological Analysis, Oxford: Pergamon Press.

17

Social capital in the music festival experience[1]

Linda Wilks

Introduction

Social and cultural government policies in the United Kingdom (UK) in 2010 are currently in a state of flux due to the recent change of government. Early signs are that the new government might emphasise the economic aspects of the role of culture, as well as initially focus on the Olympics within that portfolio, although there are also indications that community cohesion may feature. This paper uses in-depth interviews with participants recruited at three music festivals in the UK to examine issues of social and cultural policy. To give added focus, the theoretical tool of social capital provides a lens through which to conduct the study.

Focus on festivals

Music festivals were chosen as the context for this study for several reasons. Festivals are an expanding sector of the cultural industry, with spending on festivals up by 18 per cent in 2009 compared to the previous year, a sharper rise than any other area of live music (BBC 2010). At the time of the study, attendance at live music performances and events, including classical, jazz and opera, already formed the biggest type of arts event attended by adults in England (Aust and Vine 2007). Festivals' generally extended and geographically constrained nature gives the potential for the investigation of extended social interactions within a cultural context, a feature mentioned by Larsen and O'Reilly (2005).

There have been several studies and reports which have been useful in building knowledge of social and cultural issues in relation to festivals featuring music. Some studies focus on economic impact, whilst touching to a greater or lesser extent on social issues, and are often commissioned by festival organisers or sponsors with the aim of demonstrating benefit (Association of Festival Organisers 2004; Maughan and Bianchini 2004; AEA Consulting 2006; Long and Owen 2006; Sussex Arts Marketing 2008). A review of the literature relating to the economic and social benefits of events and festivals by Wood *et al.* (2006) concludes that social benefits are usually seen by organisers to be of secondary importance, however, despite some studies claiming that the social benefits often outweigh the economic benefits.

Social impact, rather than economic impact, as in the above studies, is the focus of a study of a Gaelic Festival by Matarasso (1996). Although this is worth noting as one of the first to attempt to assess the social impacts of festivals, it has since been heavily criticised for its poor research design (Merli 2002; Selwood 2002).

Literature reporting academic research on the social and cultural characteristics and behaviours of music festival audiences is particularly relevant to this study's aims of studying social capital in the context of music festivals. Waterman (1998a, 1998b), Quinn (2000, 2003), Jamieson (2004), Long *et al.* (2004) and Sharpe (2008) have all published studies which explore the roles of shared values and social division in the context of festivals which include music.

However, hints that social diversity may be identified at some festivals were reported by Gardner (2004), for example, who claims that people from a wide variety of educational, occupational and religious backgrounds mingle at bluegrass festivals. Willems-Braun's (1994) study of Canada's fringe festivals also warns that the attendees cannot be unproblematically categorised into social groups owing to the possibilities of multiplicities within individuals and within the festival space.

There is a general lack of recent empirical research focusing on social issues relating to festivals which could be used to explore social and cultural policy in the UK. Calls have been made for further research to discover the connection between social capital and festivals in particular (Arcodia and Whitford 2007), as this has not been attempted previously, and for further insights which might contribute to the development of cultural policy (Selwood 2006).

The cultural policy context

The use of the arts as a social tool to combat exclusion, promote community cohesion and bridge barriers between groups was a key aim of the previous UK government (Bennett and Silva 2006; Labour Party 2006). The Labour government's Department for Culture Media and Sport (DCMS) set out, in its PAT 10 Progress Report, strategies for widening participation in the arts by sectors of the community identified as having low levels of engagement (Department for Culture Media and Sport 2001). 'Cultural Partnerships' aimed to offer young people from deprived areas new opportunities to engage with the arts, for example. This PAT 10 document also set out commitments to encourage people from all ethnic backgrounds to engage fully with the arts by removing any barriers to participation.

More specific arts-related claims by the former government that the sharing of musical experiences can enable people from different cultural backgrounds to build mutual understanding are of particular relevance to this study (Department for Culture Media and Sport 2008). The Public Service Agreement (PSA) 21, released by HM Treasury in 2007, for example, linked social issues to involvement in the arts, citing studies which demonstrated that people taking part in cultural activities were more likely to know many people in their neighbourhood and more likely to trust others (HM Treasury 2007).

Interestingly, the first (informal) statement from the new Secretary of State for Culture, Olympics, Media and Sport, Jeremy Hunt, focused on the potential of culture and the creative industries' role in the UK's economic recovery (Department for Culture Media and Sport 2010b), rather than choosing to highlight culture's social value, for example. However, his first official speech, on 19 May 2010, also included a statement that 'culture and arts are for everyone, not just the lucky few' (Department for Culture Media and Sport 2010a).

Hints that community and social capital are likely to be of importance to the new government have already been made. Prime Minister David Cameron made specific mention of social capital in his launch of the 'Big Society' concept, for example, whilst Deputy Prime Minister Nick Clegg also stressed the importance of 'community' at the same event (Prime Minister's Office 2010).

Although, as highlighted above, government cultural policy is currently in a state of flux, policy-related documents prepared in partnership with or by other bodies, such as the arm's-length Arts Council England or consultancies such as Audiences London, are still available and worth noting. Key outputs include the ongoing Taking Part survey commissioned by the DCMS along with the Arts Council England and other public partner bodies to improve knowledge of audiences (Department for Culture Media and Sport 2010c) and the pilot version of CultureMap London (Audiences London 2010), which aims to bring together information about cultural provision and audiences in London. The Arts Council England is also in the process of analysing the results of a recent consultation on how to achieve its 'Great Art For Everyone' initiative (Arts Council England 2010), launched in 2006 with a publication in 2008 (Arts Council England 2008). This initiative aims to include a consideration of barriers to participation, as well as identifying opportunities and challenges for the future. Although now also moved to the web-based National Archives, the McMaster review of the arts, commissioned by the Secretary of State for Culture in 2007, provides key evidence and recommendations relating to encouraging wider and deeper engagement by audiences (McMaster 2008).

Of relevance on the wider policy-making stage and echoing the British discourse at European policy-making level, mention was made by Androulla Vassiliou, the European Commissioner for Education, Culture, Multilingualism and Youth, of the role of the creative and cultural industries in encouraging cultural diversity (European Commission 2010). Also at European level, the 2008 'European Year of Cultural Dialogue', the 'magical power' of the arts 'to connect value systems and open new spaces for encounter' was highlighted during the Brussels debate (European Commission 2008b), with arts festivals in particular being emphasised as being 'vital for promoting intercultural dialogue … offering a concentrated possibility of exchange and enrichment' (European Commission 2008a).

Although this chapter focuses on case studies situated in the UK, issues of diversity and community cohesion are of concern in countries across the world. Many of these countries also hold festivals and will find parallels in the UK experience.

Review of the theoretical literature

The theoretical concept of social capital is useful when examining issues relating to community cohesion, social inclusion and broadening participation in the arts. Social capital theorist Putnam (2000), whose views have attracted the attention of American and British politicians (Bunting, 2007), specifically suggests that the arts can bring together diverse groups and thus promote well-being by allowing the production of mutually beneficial norms of reciprocity, generalised trust and co-operation. Putnam (2000) also claims that arts events could be used to transcend social barriers: people may make new connections with others whom they perceive to have a different, though equally, rigid set of values.

Social capital is a broad term, with theorists interpreting and developing the concept in various ways. These approaches vary from a macro-scale view, which highlights the operation of social networks and their potential for indirect public good, to a micro-level focus on the individual, highlighting personal actions and potential benefits, although some coalescence between the two perspectives is apparent. Bennett *et al.* (2009) combine the two perspectives neatly by indicating that their reading of the literature concludes that friendship and social contact networks are useful considerations for social capital measurement.

Putnam emphasises the macro approach to social capital in this definition, regarding it as being related to: 'features of social organization such as networks, norms and social trust that facilitate coordination and cooperation for mutual benefit' (Putnam 1995: 67).

He sees social organisations as encouraging the growth of civic virtue, tolerance, reciprocity and trustworthiness, as well as lessening shirking and cheating and improving health. Putnam's conceptualisation of social capital has, however, attracted criticism, including for its over-emphasis on supposed positive outcomes (Mouritsen 2003); for the lack of emphasis on context which its macro scale encourages (Edwards and Foley 2001; Wallis *et al.* 2004; Koniordos 2008); and for its measurement flaws (Healey 2004).

However, as the research settings of this study provided bounded contexts and a critical perspective is employed, it was concluded that Putnam's more specific concepts of bridging social capital and bonding social capital (Putnam 2000) are useful conceptual tools. Putnam explains that bonding social capital is inward-looking, reinforcing exclusive identities and pro-moting homogeneity, whereas bridging social capital is outward-looking, promoting links between diverse individuals. Putnam suggests that many groups simultaneously bond across some social dimensions and bridge across others. He sees bonding social capital as increasing solidarity with people who are already similar, bolstering the narrower self and creating strong in-group loyalty. Bridging social capital, however, links people to others who move in different circles. These theories help when considering issues of community cohesion and bridging boundaries between groups of people.

The theoretical concepts of bridging and bonding social capital therefore directed the study towards examination of the social networks in operation at the festivals, as well as the ways in which the individuals operated within these networks.

Methodology

In order to discover the role of social capital in the music festival experience, and thus throw light on to social and cultural policy, this study uses post-festival in-depth interviews of festival attendees.

Three UK festivals were used as the case settings. These festivals were carefully selected to be aligned in terms of features such as scale and the presence of a public funding stream. In order to provide the potential to draw on the experiences of people with differing music tastes, as well as to allow for different modes of festival operation, the festivals chosen were of three types: an opera festival (OperaFest), a folk festival (FolkFest) and a festival concentrating on indie-pop music (PopFest). A data-collection screening stage using structured sampling collected basic demographic, attendance and music taste information from 219 festival attendees at the events. From the screened responses, eleven interviewees from each festival, a total of thirty-three, were selected for the hour-long follow-up in-depth interviews, with the aim of reflecting the various characteristics of the population of festival patrons from each festival.

Critical discourse analysis

Following thematic analysis of the interviews, the interview texts and observations were further analysed using critical discourse analysis (CDA) (Fairclough 2003). CDA acknowledges as sig-nificant, non-discursive material elements which exist beyond the text, but which also feature within it, such as styles of dress and the possession of culturally related artefacts. A CDA approach offers rich possibilities for the analysis of data relating to social capital within the setting of festivals and will allow conclusions to be reached relating to the context of social and cultural policies.

CDA uses the identification of the 'orders of discourse' which feature within a text as its crux. An 'order of discourse' represents the discursive facet of a particular set of social practices within a particular social order. When broken down into their constituent parts, 'orders of discourse' comprise competing and complementary 'discourses'. According to Fairclough, discourses are specific ways of representing aspects of the material, mental and social world. The analytical strength of a focus on discourses is that patterns, similarities and differences in their use, between participants and between festivals, can reveal much about the role of social capital in the festival experience. For individual speakers, the deployment of different discourses enables them to achieve different social and personal 'styles' as well as to illustrate their social relationships with other people. A CDA approach, with its emphasis on discourses and styles, as well as its critical standpoint, therefore offers rich possibilities for the analysis of data relating to social capital within the setting of festivals and will allow conclusions to be reached relating to the context of social and cultural policies.

Exploring the social landscape of the festival

Overview of the connection/detachment order of discourse

An overarching connection/detachment order of discourse was identified within the texts of this research data and may be used to examine issues of social capital in the festival experience. This order of discourse surfaces the ways in which the research participants did or did not relate to others during their festival experience, focusing particularly on talk relating to social networks and personal image. Three competing discourses comprise this order of discourse:

- The 'persistent connection' discourse relates to individuals' talk about attending the event within a close-knit group of friends, meeting up with other previously well-known contacts at the event, forging enduring connections as a result of festival meetings, as well as telling known people with common interests about the festival after the event.
- The 'temporary connection' discourse includes comments about casual conversations with strangers.
- The 'detachment' discourse includes talk on avoiding contact with other festival attendees and feeling apart from the festival community.

Examples of the three competing discourses within this order of discourse will be presented here. Interviewees' talk will be drawn on, as will the researcher's observations of social practices at the festival sites.

The persistent connection discourse

The persistent connection discourse included reference to close-knit social relationships which were already in existence before the festival, as well as enduring beyond the event, thus being a feature of the festival experience. Some of the relationship groups existed outside the festival context as well as within it, whilst others were focused on the festival, to be resurrected each year or at a range of similar festivals. Within the persistent connection discourse there was an emphasis on presenting as friendly, sociable, popular and as an insider.

Matt from FolkFest's network tended to be focused on festivals and he characterised it as having two levels of closeness.

> Matt: You have your pocket group of friends who you get up, suffer your hangover with, have your breakfast and your coffee and then you just kinda split during the day, disappear off to do your own things. Then lunchtime, there'll be a couple of phone calls, oh you

know, where are you at, ah in this pub, whatever. Go and have a beer in your lunch. Uhm and then you split again for the afternoon and you'll see them wandering around, or working, or doing something. And then you meet up in the evening and um, more beer!

Beer, phone calls, pubs and lunchtime are all non-discursive elements referred to by Matt, which help to texture this discourse and provide insight into the way these persistent connections work. As well as his close group of friends, Matt made reference to a wider set of persistent connections made through folk festivals, displaying a sociable style:

Matt: It's one massive circle of friends. I mean, everybody basically knows everybody through somebody.

Geoff from OperaFest, when talking about the friends he met up with at the festival, described a similar modus operandi. Geoff, like Matt, described the group coming together then dividing up again, then reconnecting within the festival as well as being brought together year after year to attend, positioning himself as a social lynch-pin:

Geoff: We've got other friends who come up from London and one who comes up from just outside Oxford and we all get together. We all get our seats in the same place usually so that we can sit together. We tend to go out to lunch. Everybody does their own thing [before and after the opera]. Unless we have an evening free and then we'd all get together.

There were also examples of talk from PopFest interviewees about close-knit groups, which also existed outside the festival, which can be categorised as persistent connections discourse. Alan from PopFest made use of the term 'friends' as well as establishing a style as a family man, to describe his group of fifteen or so fellow PopFest attendees, with his reference to the number of years he had known them giving credence to the closeness of their connections.

Alan: These are mainly friends that we've got to know in the local villages over the last ten or twelve years. There was probably a link through our son, I think. We do see that sort of group of people quite you know every couple of weeks. It's if you bump into people, or I play tennis with some of them. My wife knows them well and plays tennis with some of them.

OperaFest had also brought together Jill's friendship group of six people. Although they were now spread around the country, most of the group members were persistently connected through university attendance and still met up regularly, including annually at OperaFest. Jill stressed their musical links as well as their academic alignment, using a styling as a maths graduate to affirm her own musical credentials too:

Jill: Well, put it this way, friends of my husband were commiserating with him because he was going to be the only member of the group who wasn't an Oxford mathematician. So we're all keen on music.

Persistent connections made as a result of becoming closer with people from their outer network at festivals were also mentioned by some of the PopFest participants. Lucy and Madeline, styling themselves as friendly, for example, spoke of maintaining the new connections they had made from within an existing wider friendship network.

> Madeline: I met a few new people who were perhaps friends of friends. Two girls I've kept in contact with since. They'll perhaps come out with us now.
> ...
> Lucy: I actually met someone that I've seen him around but I've never really been introduced to him properly who I've become really friends with since.

The persistent connection discourse therefore features within the discourse from all three festivals, encompassing friendship groups which are already in existence. This discourse was particularly prevalent amongst the FolkFest participants. Closeness within a group of previously more distantly connected friends was engendered by attendance at the festival in some cases. What was not in evidence in the dataset, however, was evidence of new persistent connections formed between people who were completely unconnected before the festival.

The temporary connection discourse

Examples of temporary connection discourse were again identifiable in participants from across the three festivals and related to talk of fleeting, non-persistent connections made by chance rather than design. Temporary connections were usually made through chatting to adjacent audience members, during refreshment breaks, or to festival neighbours. Within the temporary connection discourse, styling was of restraint and friendliness when necessary.

The impression of chance encounters was gained from the use of phrases such as 'happen to' or 'find yourself', as illustrated by Christine, Barry and Janice of OperaFest:

> Christine: If we're at things we'll talk to people but there's no, we don't meet friends up there. It's just the people that we happen to be at the same thing with, effectively people we're sat next to.
> ...
> Barry: There was a couple, I don't know quite where they came from, but they were staying where I was and we had to come out the doors together. So we had a conversation.
> ...
> Researcher: Do you find yourself talking to people that sit next to you?
> Janice: I think you, maybe in your B&B, sometimes you do have a little bit of a chat about things.

There was no talk of keeping in touch with these temporary acquaintances, however, rather a styling of being friendly and open where necessary, but within limits, separating this discourse from that of persistent connection. PopFest interviewees, such as Mike and Alan, also spoke of chance encounters, demonstrating a style of restraint, again using the phrase 'happened to' and emphasising forced proximity, as the key to connection:

> Mike: There was just the occasional people that you happened to be sitting at the same table, sort of chat about things. But nothing more than that.
> ...
> Alan: We spoke to a few people on the campsite that were next door to us.

OperaFest interviewees, such as Lydia, for example, also referred to personal image as a vehicle of temporary connection:

> Lydia: It's quite nice to look the part. I think there's an atmosphere that does encourage you to dress up.

Evidence of the temporary connection discourse was not particularly common throughout the dataset, but most prevalent amongst OperaFest interviewees, indicating a willingness to acknowledge a connection to other festival attendees but a reluctance to take the connection further.

A general trust in fellow festival-goers and a feeling of safety at the event was also highlighted by some as an enabling factor in feeling able to make casual conversation with others.

Callum from FolkFest remarked on the feeling of trust and safety at the festival:

> Callum: You're in a private area where you've had to have a ticket to get in so everyone's like-minded. There's no-one malicious there, no-one's going to come up to you to distract you while your wallet's being pinched. Walk around drunk all day and not feel unsafe – it's great!

Several of the PopFest interviewees also mentioned the feeling of security, with Stephen and Daniel commenting on this:

> Stephen: It's not overly rowdy, not a lot of misbehaving.
>
> …
>
> Daniel: I feel safe in the crowd.

The detached discourse

Within the connected/detached order of discourse, the detached discourse includes talk about attending the festival alone, as well as talk of being different or separate from the other festival attendees in various ways. Styles within the detached discourse tend to be of a focused and intended separateness.

There were numerous examples of detached discourse amongst OperaFest attendees, indicating a styling of focused separateness. Both Barry and Keith, for example, mentioned attending 'alone', and Clive emphasised his detachment:

> Clive: I think I'm a fairly solitary person. I don't really think it's a social experience. I don't feel I'm mixing with like-minded people who I could talk to opera about.

Similarly, Roy, Sylvia and Maureen also stressed that they tended to purposely stay detached from others at the festival, but by using the pronoun 'we' styled themselves as within a private, self-sufficient married unit:

> Roy: We don't talk to a lot of other people. It's a going out together thing.

as did Sylvia:

> Sylvia: It's a private holiday for us. We might occasionally chat to somebody but we're not looking to be particularly sociable when we're there.

Detached discourse was not common amongst PopFest interviewees. Daniel, despite attending with a group of three friends, hinted at feeling detached from others and purposely distancing himself when commenting on his perception of the outlooks of the festival crowd. This comment implies a self-styling as adventurous in contrast with the other festival attendees:

> Daniel: I think other people are quite conservative.

Of the FolkFest participants, only Kath hinted at 'detachment' when reporting staying in the pub whilst the friends with whom she was spending the weekend attended events, styling herself as uninterested in festival events:

> Kath: The couple that we stay with go to a lot of events. They go to as many as they can but they'll leave us in the pub and they'll go and see someone.

The detached discourse was therefore, like the persistent connection and temporary connection discourse, in evidence in the talk of interviewees from each of the festivals, although it appeared most common amongst the talk of OperaFest attendees.

Conclusions

Focus on the role of social capital in the festival experience

As shown above, examples of the connection/detachment order of discourse were identifiable within participants' talk from across all three festivals. The use of this discourse within the talk of the interviewees tended to vary between festivals, with OperaFest talk tending to feature detached or temporary connection discourse, although persistent connection discourse was not completely absent, whilst the FolkFest and PopFest interviewees tended to display more examples of the persistent connection discourse and less temporary connection or detached discourse. The interviewees' discourse, as demonstrated above, therefore contributed to the gaining of an understanding of the role of social capital in the festival experience.

In terms of social networking with others at the festivals, social capital notions of connection and detachment come to the fore. Reflecting Putnam's (2000) bonding and bridging inter-pretation of the theory of social capital, highlighted earlier, interviewees reported that different forms of social connection emerged during the festivals. This reflects the idea that social capital takes different forms which can facilitate different types of social connection.

Many of the pop and folk festival attendees established a 'socially connected' style, demon-strated through their persistent connection discourse, which was an important part of their fes-tival experience. In doing so, they referred to the large friendship groups at the festival of which they were part. These groups had either specifically arranged to attend the festival together or had anticipated, based on previous experience, that known contacts would be there. By choosing to attend the festival, the opportunity was created, and taken, to build social capital with existing acquaintances: that is, 'bonding social capital' (Putnam 2000). Bridging social capital, where new social relationships are formed, was only rarely reported by any of the interviewees. The temporary and detached discourses examples shown above demonstrate the resistance to forming this type of social capital, despite evidence of a feeling of trust and safety. It can thus be concluded that bonding social capital played a role in the pop and folk festival experience, whereas bridging social capital did not. However, this study's findings also suggest that Putnam's concept of bonding social capital should be modified in connection with festivals.

Putnam's theory is that bonding social capital brings together people who already share social and cultural similarities. As the festival attendees were observed to be relatively homogeneous in their socio-demographic characteristics, the findings of this study suggest that bonding at festivals is only between people already known or socially connected to each other, not merely between people who share social and cultural similarities.

Attendance within large friendship groups was not reported as the norm at the opera festival. Interviewees reported a greater tendency for social detachment, punctuated by brief serendipitous social interactions. As such, it can be concluded that neither bonding nor bridging social capital played a major role in the opera festival experience.

Implications for cultural policy

Relevance to cultural and social issues

This study has shown that festivals are a useful setting for the study of key social and cultural issues and several implications for cultural policy can be identified. The former government's policies saw culture and the arts as tools to combat social exclusion, bridge barriers between groups and foster community cohesion (Labour Party 2006), as mentioned earlier. This study concludes that music festivals do not appear to perform this function.

This study found that bridging-type social interactions between people who were previously unknown to each other were not common, particularly at OperaFest. The policy-related term 'community cohesion' is also problematic. It could be interpreted as denoting cohesion within groups, rather than the across-group cohesion which is usually understood to be the aim. This study has shown that cohesion, or bonding, within groups of people who are already known to each other is promoted by festival attendance, but bridging between those who were previously unknown to each other was not generally a feature.

Festivals policy

Cultural policy at various levels has incorporated reference to festivals, including by Arts Council England (Arts Council England 2005, 2006), the Greater London Council (Nadkarni and Homfray 2009) and the Milton Keynes Council (Milton Keynes Council 2008), for example. The National Carnival Arts Strategy (Nindi 2005) also mentions festivals briefly and Arts Council England has commissioned investigations specifically relating to festivals (Long and Owen 2006). However, there is no published national strategy relating to festivals and this could be considered, having identified their increase in importance within the cultural sphere. Meanwhile, it is vital that reference to festivals is incorporated into new strategy documents as they are devised.

Finally, the festival directors themselves have the opportunity to shape the social as well as the cultural policy for the festival they are organising. This opportunity could be further enabled by support from the continued inclusion of festivals in national strategy. It is hoped that the findings of this study will provide impetus for action.

Suggestions for further research

Although this study used a rigorous qualitative methodology and a recognised theoretical framework to use the investigation of festival settings as a lens for the examination of cultural policy in the UK and beyond, it should be noted that the findings were based on data collection at only three small-scale music festivals located in England. The qualitative methods used were strong in their close focus on individuals, but did not allow the analysis of large numbers of individuals or the statistical analysis of the demographics attendees. Further research, using qualitative or quantitative approaches, set in festivals of other types, including community-based festivals, music festivals of other genres, festivals with a commercial, non-public funded position and non-arts festivals, as well as research situated on festivals beyond the UK, is recommended in order to throw light on the under-researched topic of social capital at festivals.

Note

1 An extended version of this article is available as: L. Wilks (2011) 'Bridging and bonding: social capital at music festivals', *The Journal of Policy Research in Tourism, Leisure and Events*, 3 (3).

Bibliography

AEA Consulting (2006) *Thundering Hooves: Maintaining the Global Competitive Edge of Edinburgh's Festivals*, Edinburgh: Scottish Arts Council.

Arcodia, C. and Whitford, M. (2007) 'Festival attendance and the development of social capital', *Journal of Convention and Event Tourism* 8(2): 1–18.

Arts Council England (2005) *Children, Young People and the Arts: London Regional Strategy*. Available at: www.artscouncil.org.uk/documents/publications/cypstrategy_phpfp6sGO.pdf (accessed 15 May 2009).

——(2006) *Our Agenda for the Arts in London 2006–8*. Available at: www.artscouncil.org.uk/documents/publications/phpgoLALC.pdf (accessed 15 May 2009).

——(2008) *Great Art for Everyone. Arts Council England's Plan for 2008–11*. Available at: www.artscouncil.org.uk/plan/home (accessed 25 November 2008).

——(2010) *Achieving Great Art for Everyone: Consultation Paper*. Available at: www.artscouncil.org.uk/media/consultation/NAS_ConsultationPaper_A4_12Pt.pdf (accessed 17 May 2010).

Association of Festival Organisers (2004) *The Impact of Folk Festivals*. Available at: www.folkarts-england.org/UserFiles/File/Resources/Event%20and%20Festival%20Management/AFO%20Impact%20Report%20March%202004.pdf (accessed 19 September 2008).

Audiences London (2010) *CultureMap London*. Available at: from www.culturemaplondon.org/ (accessed 17 May 2010).

Aust, R. and Vine, L. (2007) *Taking Part: The National Survey of Culture, Leisure and Sport*. Annual Report 2005/2006. Available at: www.culture.gov.uk/Reference_library/Research/taking_part_survey/surveyoutputs_may07.htm (accessed 14 May 2007).

BBC (2010) *Festivals Thrive in Concert Boom*. Available at: http://news.bbc.co.uk/1/hi/entertainment/8681763.stm (accessed 18 May 2010).

Bennett, T. and Silva, E.B. (2006) 'Introduction. Cultural capital and inequality: policy issues and contexts', *Cultural Trends* 15(2–3): 87–106.

Bennett, T., Savage, M., Silva, E.B., Warde, A., Gayo-Cal, M. and Wright, D. (2009) *Culture, Class, Distinction*, London and New York: Routledge.

Bunting, M. (2007) 'Capital ideas', *Guardian*, 18 July: 1–2.

Curtis, R.A. (2010) 'Australia's capital of jazz? The (re)creation of place, music and community at the Wangaratta Jazz Festival', *Australian Geographer* 41(1): 101–16.

Department for Culture Media and Sport (2001) *Building on PAT 10: Progress Report on Social Inclusion*. Available at: www.culture.gov.uk/PDF/social_inclusion.pdf (accessed 11 February 2009).

——(2008) *Creative Britain: New Talents for the New Economy*. Available at: www.culture.gov.uk/Reference_library/Publications/archive_2008/cepPub-new-talents.htm (accessed 25 February 2008).

——(2010a) *Arts, Heritage and Sport Funding Boost: Jeremy Hunt, Secretary of State for Culture, Olympics, Media and Sport, has Given his First Keynote Speech*. Available at: www.culture.gov.uk/news/news_stories/7067.aspx (accessed 20 May 2010).

——(2010b) *New Culture Secretary Appointed*. Available at: www.culture.gov.uk/news/news_stories/7044.aspx (accessed 17 May 2010).

——(2010c) *Taking Part: England's Survey of Culture, Sport and Leisure*. Available at: www.culture.gov.uk/what_we_do/research_and_statistics/4867.aspx (accessed 17 May 2010).

Edwards, B. and Foley, M.W. (2001) 'Much ado about social capital', *Contemporary Sociology* 30(3): 227–30.

European Commission (2008a) *Arts Festivals Join in Support for the European Year of Intercultural Dialogue.* Available at: http://europa.eu/rapid/pressReleasesAction.do?reference=IP/08/21&format=HTML& aged=0& language=EN&guiLanguage=en.

——(2008b) *The European Year of Intercultural Dialogue: The Second 'Brussels Debate' Concentrated on Cultural Exchange.* Available at: http://europa.eu/rapid/pressReleasesAction.do?reference=MEMO/08/217& format=HTML&aged=0&language=EN&guiLanguage=en.

——(2010) *Green Paper: Unlocking the Potential of Cultural and Creative Industries.* Available at: http://ec. europa.eu/culture/our-policy-development/doc2577_en.htm (accessed 25 May 2010).

Fairclough, N. (2003) *Analysing Discourse: Textual Analysis for Social Research,* Abingdon and New York: Routledge.

Gardner, R.O. (2004) 'The portable community: mobility and modernization in bluegrass festival life', *Symbolic Interaction* 27(2): 155–78.

Healey, T. (2004) 'Social capital: old hat or new insight?', *Irish Journal of Sociology* 13(1): 5–28.

HM Treasury (2007) *PSA Delivery Agreement 21: Build More Cohesive, Empowered and Active Communities.* Available at: https://financialsanctions.hm-treasury.gov.uk/d/pbr_csr07_psa21.pdf (accessed 17 May 2010).

Jamieson, K. (2004) 'Edinburgh: the festival gaze and its boundaries [2008–12]', *Space and Culture* 7(1): 64–75.

Koniordos, S.M. (2008) 'Social capital contested', *International Review of Sociology* 18(2): 317–37.

Labour Party (2006) *Culture Media and Sport.* Available at: www.labour.org.uk/culturemediaandsport04 (accessed 22 March 2006).

Larsen, G. and O'Reilly, D. (2005) 'Music festivals as sites of consumption: an exploratory study', Working Paper No. 05/05, University of Bradford. Available at: www.brad.ac.uk/acad/management/external/ pdf/workingpapers/2005/Booklet_05=05.pdf (accessed 13 November 2006).

Long, P. and Owen, E. (2006) *The Arts Festival Sector in Yorkshire: Economic, Social and Cultural Benefits, Benchmarks and Development.* Available at: www.artscouncil.org.uk/publications/publication_detail.php? rid=9&id=514 (accessed 13 March 2007).

Long, P., Robinson, M. and Picard, D. (2004) 'Festivals and tourism: links and developments', in P. Long and M. Robinson (eds) *Festivals and Tourism: Marketing, Management and Evaluation,* Doxford: The Centre for Tourism and Cultural Change, pp. 1–14.

McMaster, B. (2008) *McMaster Review: Supporting Excellence in the Arts – from Measurement to Judgement.* Available at: http://webarchive.nationalarchives.gov.uk/+/http://www.culture.gov.uk/reference_ library/publications/3577.aspx (accessed 17 May 2010).

Matarasso, F. (1996) 'Northern lights: the social impact of the Fèisean (Gaelic festivals)', *The Social Impact of the Arts.* Available at: www.comedia.org.uk/pages/pdf/downloads/northern_lights.pdf (accessed 16 March 2006).

Maughan, C. and Bianchini, F. (2004) *The Economic and Social Impact of Cultural Festivals in the East Midlands of England.* Available at: www.artscouncil.org.uk/documents/publications/phpvY0hNv.pdf (accessed 19 September 2008).

Merli, P. (2002) 'Evaluating the social impact of participation in arts activities', *International Journal of Cultural Policy* 8(1): 107–18.

Milton Keynes Council (2008) *Milton Keynes Arts Strategy 2008–13.* Available at: www.miltonkeynes.gov. uk/arts/documents/MKC_Arts_Strategy_2008–13.pdf (accessed 15 May 2009).

Mouritsen, P. (2003) 'What's the civil in civil society? Robert Putnam, Italy and the Republican tradition', *Political Studies* 51: 650–68.

Nadkarni, A. and Homfray, A. (2009) *Shaping Places in London through Culture.* Available at: http://arts council.org.uk/downloads/shapingplaces.pdf (accessed 15 May 2009).

Nindi, P. (2005) *National Carnival Arts Strategy 2005–7.* Available at: www.artscouncil.org.uk/publications/ publication_detail.php?browse=recent&id=464 (accessed 15 May 2009).

Prime Minister's Office (2010) *PM and Deputy PM's Speeches at Big Society Launch, 18th May 2010.* Available at: www.number10.gov.uk/news/speeches-and-transcripts/2010/05/pm-and-deputy-pms-speeches-at-big-society-launch-50283 (accessed 24 May 2010).

Putnam, R.D. (1995) 'Bowling alone: America's declining social capital', *Journal of Democracy* 6(1): 65–78.

——(2000) *Bowling Alone: The Collapse and Revival of American Community,* New York: Simon & Schuster.

Quinn, B. (2000) 'Whose festival? Whose place? An insight into the production of cultural meanings in arts festivals turned visitor attractions', in M. Robinson, P. Long, N. Evans, R. Sharpley and J. Swarbrooke (eds) *Expressions of Culture, Identity and Meaning in Tourism,* Doxford: The Centre for Travel and Tourism in association with Business Education Publishers, pp. 263–74.

——(2003) 'Symbols, practices and myth-making: cultural perspectives on the Wexford Festival Opera', *Tourism Geographies* 5(3): 329–49.

Selwood, S. (2002) 'Measuring culture', *Spiked-online*. Available at: www.spiked-online.com/Articles/00000006DBAF.htm

——(2006) 'A part to play? The academic contribution to the development of cultural policy in England', *International Journal of Cultural Policy* 12(1): 35–53.

Sharpe, E.K. (2008) 'Festivals and social change: intersections of pleasure and politics at a community music festival', *Leisure Sciences* 30(3): 217–34.

Sussex Arts Marketing (2008) *Festivals Mean Business III*, London: British Arts Festivals Association.

Wallis, J., Killerby, P. and Dollery, B. (2004) 'Social economics and social capital', *International Journal of Social Economics* 31(3): 239–58.

Waterman, S. (1998a) 'Carnivals for elites? The cultural politics of arts festivals', *Progress in Human Geography* 22(1): 54–74.

——(1998b) 'Place, culture and identity: summer music in Upper Galilee', *Transactions of the Institute of British Geographers* 23(2): 253–68.

Willems-Braun, B. (1994) 'Situating cultural politics: fringe festivals and the production of spaces of intersubjectivity', *Environment and Planning D: Society and Space* 12(1): 75–104.

Wood, E.H., Robinson, L.S. and Thomas, R. (2006) 'Evaluating the social impacts of community and local government events: a practical overview of research methods and measurement tools', in S. Fleming and F. Jordan (eds) *Events and Festivals: Education, Impacts and Experiences*, Eastbourne: Leisure Studies Association, pp. 81–92.

18
Designing event experiences

Graham Berridge

Introduction

The principal starting point for understanding event design is to consider this question: to what extent can planned event experiences be designed? Events form part of all our lives and they have been used to signify important aspects of our culture throughout the ages (Shone and Parry 2004; Tassiopoulos 2010) with records showing that celebratory and ceremonial events were taking place over 60,000 years ago (Matthews 2008a). The range of different event types is considerable, with at least eleven event 'genres' being identified, ranging from business to festivals to social and sports events (Bowdin *et al.* 2006). Getz (2008) prefers to identify events firstly through their function, i.e. why they are held, and lists eleven 'functions', such as premier, cause-related, spectator and participant events, and secondly through to their form, of which he suggests there are twenty-three, including festivals, parades, religious, visual exhibitions and sports. In the last decade, the significant growth in undergraduate courses in event management and subsequent study of events has tended to focus upon the praxis of events, that is the management, design and production process involved in creating planned events. As Getz (2008) argues, though, there is also need to develop theory and explore the meanings of events. He suggests that with the maturation of the study of events so there will be an increased awareness of what events are and what significance they have for society as the field of events is studied by researchers in other disciplines.

A common prefix often used before the word events is 'special', indicating that an event has some kind of uniqueness that makes it special, and by definition it is therefore not something that is normal or everyday. A popular expression used to describe the special factor contained within these events is that they have a 'wow' factor (Malouf 1999). This 'wow' often takes the form of a theme for the event, and as such there is no doubt that for certain occasions it requires knowledge of the resources needed to create such thematic settings (Matthews 2008b). Green (2010), for example, has stated that we will be debating and interpreting the meaning of the 2008 Olympic Games Opening Ceremony in Beijing for years to come, such was the complexity and depth of meaning conveyed by the elaborate design. It is within such occasions, then, that there is, as Getz (2005) notes, the opportunity for an event to provide a range of cultural, social and leisure-based experiences that go beyond those of the everyday routine experience, and it is these occasions that we call special events. Nevertheless, some events, for example business events or meetings, may not contain such special or unique moments that are memorable and could be said to be more pragmatic or prosaic in purpose. They may contain less artistic design and creative content, since any theme is likely to be less visually stimulating than in an entertainment event; nevertheless, design and creativity themselves are not intrinsically absent either, since such events are still purposefully planned occasions that have been designed and created to provide certain experiences (Vanneste 2008)

Planned event experience

Modern event management is largely about delivery of experiences; this applies irrespective of the size and type of event (Silvers 2004), and today's attendees are sophisticated consumers. Important to the understanding of the concept of events is the appreciation that such moments and occasions are a part of either a planned or unplanned process (the planning and management of an event) that is undertaken in order to produce this experience. Thus Getz (2008: 9) argues that the 'core phenomenon of event study is the planned event experience and its meanings'. The connecting factor of all the different types of planned events is that there is intent to create some kind of experience for either audiences and/or participants. This idea of creating experiences (irrespective of whether it is unique and memorable) is not only central to the practice of event management but it is also central to our way of consumption. It is argued that consumption has evolved beyond the simple purchase of products and services into the differentiated pursuit of experiences (Tofler 1972; Holbrook and Hirschmann 1982; Schmitt 1999; Jensen 1999).

Experiences result from engaging people in a personal way, and because of this their value (of the event) persists long after the work of the event stager is done (Pine and Gilmore 1999: 12–13). *Ergo*, it is of great interest to deepen our understanding of how such event experiences are designed and created. This chapter argues that the very creation of such planned event experiences should be part of a deliberate and integrated design-based process whereby each element of the event is carefully mapped out in order to produce an environment (or setting) where there is the opportunity for experiences specific to that event to be consumed, and that this includes the pre-, actual and post-event stages. Design activity, in this context, therefore ranges from initial concept of the event through to all the successive elements that are required to ultimately deliver the experience (Allen 2002; Silvers, 2004; Berridge 2007, 2009; Goldblatt 2008; Van der Wagen 2008).

Concept of experience

The concept of experience has become more widespread in the last twenty years, largely because the corporate sector has adopted experience as a tool to make its businesses more competitive, and its influence has grown in importance across the business, tourism, leisure, hospitality and event sectors as organisations operating within the sector exist to provide consumers with experiences (Pettersson and Getz 2009). Experiential marketing has and is becoming more popular in the events industry through the use of live events in marketing communications, and is replacing print media as a more appropriate way of engaging potential customers (Carmouche *et al.* 2010). There is clear evidence of a more psychographic approach to the consumer replacing the old 'four P's of marketing with 'experiential marketing' and with it the emergence of more complex approaches (Schmitt 1999; Shukla and Nuntsu 2005). As an evolution of the product/ service axis of provision, experience management has emerged as a way of retaining competitiveness in global markets (Morgan *et al.* 2010). Pine and Gilmore (1999) coined the term 'experience economy' to describe how the relationships between provider and consumer had advanced beyond price and into 'experience', where unique and memorable experiences played a key part in consumer decision-making (as opposed to simply price).

In their examination of the emergence of experiential marketing O'Sullivan and Spangler (1999) argued that such consumer offerings needed to be enhanced, infused and ultimately made to successfully connect with people. Pre-event communication forms the basis for such an experience by providing a pre-experiential excitement and anticipation. It incorporates three separate phases: need recognition, alternative search and preparation (O'Sullivan and Spangler 1999). Subsequently studies have critically examined the production and management of experiences (Jensen 1999; Schmitt 2003; Morgan 2010), the role of customers in the formation of experience (Prahalad and Ramaswamy 2004); the creation of experience as a business and innovation (Darmer and Sunbo 2008) and the evaluation and analysis of experience (Berridge 2007; Gilhepsy and Harris 2010). Within event management experience has been initially linked to the emergence of brand events where, rather than use more traditional forms of communication (i.e. advertising), companies have used the direct connection with customers that a live event can offer. Subsequently experiential events like La Dolce Vita, which promises the 'taste of Italy' for people who are not in Italy, have emerged and developed successfully. First appearing in 2006 at London's Earl's Court, the 2011 version will be at the Business Design Centre and the event offers a celebration and experience of all things Italian. Naturally enough, these brand or concept events have in turn drawn the attention of researchers and academics, who have begun to apply the framework of experience to develop a more detailed understanding of not just these but of all types of events (Morgan 2006; Berridge 2007; Getz 2008; Nelson 2009; Pikkemaat *et al.* 2009).

In explaining what an experience is Schmitt (1999) indicates they are private events, the result of stimulation prompting a response that affects the entire living being. People either collectively or individually attend or participate in an event and they are doing so on the basis that some type of experience will result. Several authors have begun to develop an understanding of what an event experience is and to widen the knowledge base of what they consist of and how they are formed by drawing upon work undertaken in leisure and tourism (Berridge 2007; Getz 2008; Pettersson and Getz 2009). Latterly Morgan *et al.* (2010) have presented a compendium of papers on the consumer and managerial perspectives of experience within a tourist and leisure context, whilst Darmer and Sundbo (2008) have reflected upon how experiences emerge out of creation and innovation on the part of a provider. However, the nature of experience is complicated. Experience is not static and is always open to the effects of people's interaction, and it is also multi-dimensional (Lee *et al.* 1994; Botterill and Crompton 1996; Hull *et al.* 1996; Li 2000) and multi-faceted (Rossman 2003; Ooi 2005) across the course of any given time period. Experiences are said to have three dimensions to them: the conative, cognitive and affective dimension (Mannell and Kleiber 1997). These represent, respectively, the behaviour and what people actually do, how they make sense of experience through awareness, judgement, etc., and lastly the feelings and emotions that they use to describe the experience. The components of experience, on which people (as consumers) base their evaluation, consists of several hedonic aspects such as satisfaction, sensation, emotion and imagery (Holbrook and Hirschmann 1982) whilst Csíkszentmihályi's research (1975, 1990) postulates that achieving optimum flow is the desirable outcome of all experiences. Considering there is great diversity of event types then the range of these experiences is also hugely varied (Getz 1997) and serves to demonstrate the complex nature of experience design.

Design and event management

Design has a large and lengthy list of definitions (see Berridge 2007) which often relate to the discipline in which that design is practised (architectural, graphic, communication, interior, product, etc., etc.). There is a numerous, almost exhaustive list of sources for explaining design (for example, Cooper 1995; Markus 2002; Potter 2002; Lipton 2002; Byars 2004; Ullrich and Eppinger 2004; Beverland 2005) and several of these approach it from the point of view of the application of artistic skill from within a discipline. What ultimately emerges, irrespective of the platform used for design, is that it is essentially seen as a 'purposeful activity' in which not only do design ideas emerge to solve a problem, but the occurrence that solves the problem is the result of the predetermined activity of designing. In this way design can be seen as a purpose, intention or plan of the mind to solve a problem. Such an idea of design can also be understood as being expansive rather than restrictive: it posits the concept of design beyond the realms of the artistic who are gifted with the appropriate level of knowledge and skill and into the realm where a planned and deliberate process is undertaken to reach a specific outcome or set of outcomes (Monroe 2006; Berridge 2009). In this view design therefore becomes an integrated aspect of any intentional or deliberate effort to solve a problem.

Within the practice of event management, 'Design is essential to an event's success because it leads to improvement of the event on every level' (Brown and James 2004: 59). Nevertheless, its use is often limited to certain aspects of the event process. A useful summary of the general consensus on design within event management is provided in a glossary of terms by Sonder, who states that design is 'the incorporation of a themed message along with audiovisual, entertainment and musical elements' (Sonder 2004: 411). This appears to immediately confine design to a limited role with no other function within an event other than when there is a theme. This is not an uncommon association, as Berridge (2007) observes, since many sources on the study of event design characterise it in relation to creativity, such as conceptualising (Goldblatt 2004), entertainment experience (Silvers 2004), staging (Allen *et al.* 2005), event design (Yeoman *et al.* 2004), ambience (Shone and Parry 2004), creativity (Sonder 2004), theming and event design (Allen *et al.* 2005), designing and decorating (Monroe 2006), props and design (Malouf 1999), co-ordinating the environment (Silvers 2004). What also emerges here is use of a wide range of terms to explain where event design is applied, and outwardly there does not appear to be a specific common language of terms that are consistently used to reference where design takes place and what it affects other than that it is creative.

But is design therefore only a feature of the lived moment of a creative theme, a feature only of that momentary setting, a setting that according to Goffman (1959) involves such things as the physical layout, furniture, décor and similar artefacts that help provide the scenery and stage props? Whilst not fully suggesting that a design agenda embraces all aspects of the planned event, Nelson (2009) in a paper discussing enhancing experience through creative design, draws upon theories of the relationship between individuals and their settings. These are contained in the theoretical frameworks of Goffman's dramaturgical perspective, Kotler's ideas on atmospherics and Bitner's components of servicescape to suggest that design does have a far more wide-reaching purpose and application than theme and decoration. Design itself does not have to be a creative act although many events clearly have a creative aspect to them (Nelson 2009). Whilst event design can be seen as the combination of form and function, aesthetics and practicality, it is more than just creating a theme or idea, and should in fact address the whole process involved in the presentation of the live event to the client (Allen 2002; Allen *et al.* 2005). An event exists to solve the problem that is presented by the rationale and concept of having the event in the first place (Watt and Stayte 1999; Allen 2002; Salem *et al.* 2004;

Bowdin *et al.* 2006). The successful solution to the problem is achieved through a purposeful approach to designing and delivering the event. Essentially this process leads to the creation of the event environment from which guest experiences' will emerge (Goldblatt 2004).

Experience design

The discussion above revolves around what design contributes towards the event experience. In separating out the design elements utilised to create enhanced experiences for attendees, design becomes a tool used in the construction of the relationship between individuals and their physical setting (Nelson 2009). In constructing this relationship the emphasis is placed on a deliberate series of actions that culminate in the lived experience (Rossman 2003). This raises the question of the extent to which experience itself is consciously designed and for whom. Is it for all stakeholders, are there prime stakeholders or is it only for the guest or participant stakeholder? The answer is that all stakeholders involved in the event will have experiences, but different ones. Such experiences will be dependent largely on each stakeholder's expectations, and this applies as much to sub-contracted suppliers of events services as it does to guests (Getz 2008). With guest experiences that are purposefully planned engagements, the role of design becomes one of harnessing and directing the skills and knowledge of individuals involved in the events planning and management towards creating experiences that engage, inspire, educate and entertain, each of which is central to the event's success.

Designing and creating such experience environments is a predictive skill based on the concept of the event. Whilst this can be a specific act or acts of creativity, it can also be a more general process designed to generate experience. By anticipating the experience, design then becomes a tool able to predict the future (Morello 2000). Pettersson and Getz (2009) contend, however, that 'experiences cannot be fully designed, as they are both personal (i.e. psychological) constructs that vary with the individual, as well as being social and cultural constructs related to influences on the individual and the (often) social nature of events' (p. 310). This may well be true since an event designer cannot possibly know all the variables and multiples of experience that a group of individuals relate and respond to. Consequently there are some events that

> adopt a more holistic approach in attempting to attract as wider audience as possible and provide experiences that can touch all of them at some point during the event whereas other events are broken down, perhaps via branding or theming, in order to appeal to particular groups of individuals.
>
> *(Berridge 2007: 193)*

Advancing this viewpoint, such approaches to experience design have been labelled 'generic experiences' and 'specific event experiences' respectively (Pettersson and Getz 2009). Some event experiences do have some shared commonalities whilst others seemingly have very little apart from the event itself. Drawing disparate people towards the event is a key aspect of pre-experience and can depend upon what factors serve as key determinants of participation, the importance of the characteristics or descriptors of the participants, the benefit being sought from the experience or something inherent in the experience itself (O'Sullivan and Spangler 1999: 75). So designing and creating an experience requires foresight of the nature of interactions between people and the relationship they have with each other and the physical environment.

An event ultimately merges customer service with design, experience creation and emotional connection and so a different model identifying what is event design is perhaps appropriate, and one that is, for example, based on a combined set of tools or principles that include atmospherics, servicescape and dramaturgy (Nelson 2009).

Perhaps there should be a distinction made between the overall concept of the event experience created 'by design', which we might even refer to as event architecture, and the creative aspects of an event that is produced by the 'application of design' tools and skills, something we might more logically call artistic or aesthetic design and creation. Design then becomes not a single-medium tool, but one that transcends several in order to create successful experiences. Within this understanding, experience design is employed at several levels whereby it is also concerned with the internal organisation, structure, culture, processes and values within an organisation that allow it to successfully create experiences and respond to both market and customer needs (Shebroff 2001).

Connecting and creating designed experiences

Experience then becomes the result of directed observation or participation in events and as such they are not self–generated but induced (Schmitt 1999). Here Schmitt is not arguing that individuals within an event setting are incapable of interacting and generating experience, but he is advocating that the event experience setting is selectively created to induce such an experience. A marketing framework for customer experience should then focus on five types, namely sense, feeling, thinking, acting and relating. By connecting with these via implementation components such as spatial environments, communications and people, experience providers are able to perceive how experience environments are created. In this way experiences can then be infused with special or novel qualities of experience that aid their marketability; they can be enhanced through either personal or individual skill of the provider which characteristically results in providers making an experience that people can immerse themselves in (O'Sullivan and Spangler 1999). Experience seeking may then rest upon the attainment of something fulfilling, unique or special; it could also be something that is educational and transformational. Equally it could be something that is socially and culturally enhancing as well as something that is challenging, participative, re-affirming or passive, and it can be something that is based on business connections and network relationships.

Whilst it can be seen that any decision to attend an event can be based on numerous factors, experience is without doubt a central driving force. Therefore the logical continuum of this viewpoint is that the experience creation must be a prime consideration when designing the event. Getz rightly argues that 'if we cannot clearly articulate what the events experience is, then how can it be planned or designed? If we do not understand what it means to people, then how can it be important?' (2008: 170).

Designing event experiences

To reiterate, at this stage, the argument is that if the core phenomenon of an event is the experience, then event design effectively becomes the platform upon which it is built. Whilst event design can help create the entire system and process of planning, managing and delivering an event, including the environment and setting, what it cannot do is guarantee how people will respond to it or whether the stimuli provided will be received in the way it was intended. This raises the question of how an event experience is designed, and what principles might be used to do this.

Discussing the anatomy of the event presents a clear argument for event design and experience to be an overarching philosophy:

> Remember that you are packaging and managing an experience. This means that you must envision that experience from start to finish, from the guests' point of view. Imagine every minute of their experience. Identify event elements that will build on previous successes,

elements that will take advantage of opportunities and strengths, and elements that will mitigate challenges, weaknesses, and threats.

(Silvers 2004: 5)

Design as an underpinning framework used in this context then addresses the whole experiencescape (O'Dell and Billing 2005) of the event and in many ways this itself can be seen as extension of Bitner's (1992) servicescape concept. Hence the design of an event should immediately be concerned with the broader or generic range of the event experience. This idea of broader experience creation, involving interpretative frameworks and physical arrangements, locates experience creation not purely as an artistic expression but as one that includes more peripheral circumstances and has a wider perspective that includes the organisational and managerial aspects of the construction of the experience (Darmer and Sunbo 2008). It emphasises the importance of the customer: 'experiences occur whenever a company intentionally uses services as the stage and goods as the props to engage the individual' (Pine and Gilmore 1999: 11). Experience then occurs through the creation of such an intentional construction that engages customers (Darmer and Sunbo 2008).

Some conceptual ideas on designing experiences have commented upon the utilisation of a theatrical and dramaturgical metaphor (Grove *et al.* 1992; Rossman 2003; Morgan *et al.* 2008; Nelson 2009). Getz (2008) argues that a model for planned event experience should have liminoid/liminality at the core, drawing directly on the work of Turner (1969), who explained the term as the detached state of being in association with ritual. Roughly translated this means the event zone becomes the special place or time out of time of a unique event experience where communitas, the shared temporary state removed from ordinary life is commonly shared. Any experiences involve:

> participation and involvement; a state of being physically, mentally, socially, spiritually or emotionally involved; a change in knowledge, skill, memory or emotion; a conscious perception of having intentionally encountered, gone to or lived through an activity or event; an effort that addresses a psychological or inner need.
>
> *(O'Sullivan and Spangler 1999: 23)*

Any attempt to design an experience should be based on knowledge of how guests participate and become involved. In order for something to be created that can justifiably be called an experience they further explain that five key parameters of experience must be addressed by the experience provider (or creator):

1 The stages of the experience – events or feelings that occur prior, during, and after the experience.
2 The actual experience – factors or variables within the experience that influence participation and shape outcomes.
3 The needs being addressed through the experience – the inner or psychic needs that give rise to the need or desire to participate in an experience.
4 The role of the participant and other people involved in the experience – the impact that the personal qualities, behaviour and expectations of both the participant and other people involved within the experience play in the overall outcome.
5 The role and relationship with the provider of the experience – the ability and willingness of the provider to customise, control and coordinate aspects of the experience.

(O'Sullivan and Spangler 1999: 23)

Another conceptual approach to designing experiences is the notion of the 'experience realm' (Pine and Gilmore 1999). Framing their model within four dimensions of experience involvement – passive, active, immersion or absorption – an experience will be sought and received as being either one of or a combination of educational, escapist, aesthetic or entertaining. They contend that 'staging experiences is not about entertaining customers; it's about engaging them. An experience may engage guests on any number of dimensions' (Pine and Gilmore 1999: 30). The experience realm offers a framework for experience design where purposeful decisions are made to engage guests (or stakeholders) depending upon which dimensions of the realm are pre-eminent.

Example 1: The Silent Disco

The Silent Disco is a variant on the club disco event. There is no grandiose theme or spectacular entertainment production, no fabulous backdrop or decoration, but the event experience rests firmly on an integrated approach. The concept is to subvert the classic 'disco' to allow guests to experience a more personal music interface but in public, where interactions with other clubbers rests not necessarily on collective listening and participation but on a segmented quasi-individualistic encounter. The disco has no audible public sound system; instead, guests are given their own personal audio cans that have a track selector console in them. This gives the wearer the chance to personally choose, usually from between one to five channels each playing a different music type (e.g. R'n'B, House, Latin, Urban and Indie). The system is not dissimilar to one found on long-haul flights. With up to two or three hundred people choosing music tracks this creates a maelstrom of uncoordinated and unstructured movement as people dance and respond to different tracks and different beats. Unlike the usual disco that thrives on an atmosphere generated by a collective soundscape, the Silent Disco thrives on the absurdity of no sound and the peculiarity of unconnected rhythm. One of the oddest aspects of this is the fact that guests can talk to each other in perfect silence or, as has been observed, listen to other people singing or humming along to a particular track. This is unlike most club discos, which have booming PA systems making conversation often difficult.

In explaining what is needed to design experiences Rossman (2003) advocates that those engaged in producing them need to understand the phenomena they are dealing with, a point echoed by Getz, as discussed previously. Drawing upon the work of Irving Goffman's theory on symbolic interaction (1959), and the subsequent research and advocacy of Blumer (1969) and Denzin (1978) Rossman proposed that experience designers needed to adopt a methodological tool whereby six key elements that make up any planned occurrence are understood and applied by the experience designer. These are: interacting people, physical setting, objects, rules, relationships, animation. Rossman asserts that in order to fully understand and apply the model we must first recognise the three points that need to be developed. These are the nature of objects, how meaning is derived, and how interaction unfolds and permits the ongoing interpretation of meaning. During the course of designing the experience any single element may constantly change as a result of participants' interaction, as they interpret for themselves the meaning of the elements they encounter, and so the nature of the experience itself may constantly change. The value of using SI theory is the recognition that any reality is constructed and that it enables us to explore the different levels and types of interactions that take place in any given environment (Berridge 2007).

Creative design tools

The relationship of design to creativity is a significant one and it is usually regarded as the innovative and inventive aspect of the event; thus it is hardly surprising to see design and creativity linked.

In terms of tools or principles of design there are some key considerations that the aesthetic creation part of an event can address. Many of these conform to accepted models of the principles of design and creativity and there is a useful summary of these in practice in Berridge (2007, 2010a). They include, though, an awareness of the basic principles of design and aesthetics (Allen 2002; Monroe 2006; Goldblatt 2008), the characteristics and techniques of creativity (Matthews 2008a) and the elements that event décor should address (Malouf 1999). Van der Wagen (2008) suggests that there are only certain elements of an event that can be designed, namely theme, layout, décor, technical requirements, staging, entertainment and catering.

Getz (2008) advocates that there are four general categories of event design elements – setting, theme and programme design, services and consumables. These headings include a whole range of features of an event such as layout and décor, activities, theme, stimulation, gastronomy and so forth, suggesting that the role of design is integral to the event's success.

General process design

Although this also seems to suggest that design has a restricted role, there is a very important expanded range for design to be applied that includes signage, crowd management, servicescape, staff, volunteers and hidden management systems. In contrast to other uses of design, this approach suggests that non–creative design does exist and would perhaps be seen to be part of the planning and management processes of event management. There is process design evident in space planning, seating arrangements, queuing systems, registration management, technology, programmes and marketing, amongst many others. To illustrate the point, a significant amount of research has focused on the impact of events (Ritchie and Smith 1991; Spilling 2000; Emery 2002; Hall 2004; Bowdin *et al.* 2006; Getz 2008; Van der Wagen 2008; Berridge and Quick 2010) and there is a clear implication that event impacts are intended (although there are also unintended impacts). The point is that intended impacts are part of a purposeful plan to generate (usually) positive and beneficial impacts to an area. As Bob (2010) illustrates, event factors such as the process of incorporating sustainability have a direct relationship to how the event is designed, whilst Singh *et al.* (2008) observe that specific indicator tools need to be designed into the process at an early stage if sustainability is going to be effectively implemented and monitored.

Example 2: Designing a registration experience

This case study draws attention to the seemingly innocuous feature of event registration, something that is rarely categorised as design-based or creative. A university holds its annual teaching conference on its main campus. The event is an opportunity for all staff to contribute to, discuss and participate in a series of lectures, seminars and workshops on a theme linked to a topic of relevance to learning, teaching and assessment practice. Registration for the event is held in the main entrance foyer. Delegates are 95 per cent pre-registered. In 2008, delegates were issued with a simple pre-laminated name badge that attached to a garment by safety pin. Eight staff not pre-registered attended the event. With no name tag prepared, they were given a sticky label with their name handwritten upon it. It became a source of amusement and comment amongst colleagues

---

about the 'second-class' status placed upon those receiving their label badges. In 2009 a company specialising in registration, OutStand, were contracted to create name badges using a mobile, on-site laminator. The Pro-Vice Chancellor of the university attended the event, and had not pre-registered, but within less than thirty seconds he had been given a fully laminated name badge with neck cord. So impressed was this person that he made a note of putting it into his 'report' on the event for the Academic Quality Office and the university's in-house weekly news e-bulletin, praising the conference team and the event. Post-conference feedback in 2008 had included several negative comments about the registration, whereas in 2009 the feedback was 100 per cent positive.

Such a use of design, as a function of previous iterations of an event where the processes of delivery have been proven, does not have to be uniquely creative; in other words, it does not have to offer any new solutions to a problem as it can use existing ones that were previously developed. Here design does not have to have the stamp of creativity to it, but nevertheless, by looking at these elements within the event that ultimately contribute to the overall experience, it becomes clear that design is a central, not peripheral, component. Marketing and communication messages require design, as do travel and transportation arrangements and welcome entrances. The physical environment that will create the atmosphere is design-led and the food and beverage provision requires a menu design as well as staff delivery and uniform. An activity within the event requires a programme design, or choreographing to deliver the requisite experience. Ultimately the event experience can be 'personalised' through tangible gifts or mementos, and finally an evaluation of the event requires an instrument to collect that data. Such a research instrument has to be designed.

Event experience analysis

If event design is the purposeful activity to create event experiences, then it is logical to argue that it can consequently provide more opportunity to understand the meaning of such experiences, not only to guests, but to all stakeholders. Research and analysis of the dimensions of leisure and tourism experiences focuses upon the phases of experience, the influence on the experience or on the criteria or outcomes of experience (Morgan 2010). Interesting tools within experience design have emerged, for example out of the digital media field, with obvious synergies for understanding event experiences. The 'experience matrix' developed by Zoels and Gabrielli (2003) argues that adopting a clear human-based strategy for event management will enable event experiences to become ever more predictable. The experience matrix suggests therefore that foresight of experience can be designed when consideration is given to the following human-centric concerns: sensory, tactile, visual, photographic, auditory impact, intellectual, emotional, functional, informative, cultural, core. The argument follows that with this matrix as a design value there is a ready-made framework for the basis for research into responses to such experience creation.

Analysis of event design, experience and meaning requires attention. Given the range of different event types discussed earlier, there is enormous scope to study the influence design and creativity have on experience and meaning, both in the totality of an overall event as well as in the specified creative components. The principle guiding such analysis should be the underpinning concepts used to create the event experience in the first place. Qualitative research into how events are experienced and understood is essential if we are to deepen our understanding of how people respond to the range of stimuli created by and within event environments. For example, the theory of semiotics has been adopted (White 2006; Berridge 2007, 2009) to help establish meanings of key elements of an event experience, namely symbols contained within an

Olympic ceremony and the images created to promote the Tour de France. There is a need to 'create knowledge' of events through inter-disciplinary approaches that discuss experience and meaning, antecedent and choices, management planning and design, patterns and processes and outcomes and impacts (Getz 2008).

In an interesting industry development to the discussion around experience and design, the term 'Meeting Architecture' (Vanneste 2008) has recently emerged in relation to meeting, incentive and event planners. The concept or 'manifesto' is being created to enhance the overall effectiveness of meetings by globally creating Meeting Architecture. The term appears to have emerged out of a growing recognition that the key feature of meetings, the designed environment and experience of delegates, has not been studied sufficiently to give meaningful evaluation of the planned outcomes, and that existing ROI methodology is not very receptive to measuring individual responses.

Example 3: Martin Vanneste and Meeting Architecture

Meetings and conferences form an integral part of the events sector. Rarely, though, is design or creativity associated with planning them, unless it is linked to food and beverage provision or room layout. Vanneste, President of the Belgian Chapter of MPI (Meetings Professional International) has developed Meeting Architecture, in which he calls for a paradigm shift for people involved in the sector. He argues that meetings are about creating experiences as much as any other event, and that to create 'an experience that would stick ... requires creative, technical and technological tools ... (and) lots of time and resources in analysing, designing and executing the meetings on the content side'. Advocating that all meetings be treated with a holistic approach where the design of the event objectives and the content to deliver them is paramount, he refers to a Meeting Support Matrix as a tool to help people organise meetings. The tool consists of a 3 x 5 table which has Learning, Networking and Motivation on the vertical axis (the action terrains) and Conceptual, Human, Artistic, Technical and Technological on the horizontal axis. Using the model is the 'starting phase in designing the meeting'. Vanneste ties the Meeting Architecture model into the increasing use of ROI, and suggests that by designing meetings content to generate outcomes will inevitably impact on the ROI, particularly at the level of participant satisfaction and learning. Interestingly, and whilst there are obvious differences, the tool has some similarities with J.R. Rossman's Designing Leisure Experiences model, which in turn is based on the theory of symbolic interaction and the work of Goffman, Blumer and Denzin respectively. Using the model enables the development of the idea and is a basis upon which to anticipate (or predict) the results of the engagement (experience) and how that can be facilitated.

Meeting Architecture, by its very name, supposes a purposefully designed meeting environment, where the experience created is conducive to delegates attaining specific outcomes. Its development should be followed with interest to see what methodology or framework emerges that will help further our knowledge of the process and meaning of designed experiences within a meetings context.

Summary: Towards a framework for designing planned event experiences?

The challenge facing anyone developing an event is largely the same: the need to create the event environment (Goldblatt, 2008) that in turn gives people the experience (or outcomes) they seek.

An event can be seen as a simulated stage-managed environment, creating authentic moments of experience within that setting for guests and participants. The debate on whether or not the event experience is authentic is explored in various tourism literature in relation to mass tourism attractions and destination development (Wang 1999; Ryan 2003: Ritzer 2004; Pearce 2005). But whilst the managed attraction environment itself may be inauthentic, and this itself is highly subjective (Uriely 2005), the experience of guests at an event is not, since all individual event experience is authentic (Silvers 2004). The ultimate success of the event depends on this ability, therefore, to follow a design-led approach that allows the creation of the environment to meet and satisfy guests' expectations.

Design should be regarded as the basis of the framework for successful event experience production. Event design is the concept of a structure for an event, the manifest expression of that concept expressed verbally and visually which leads, finally, to the execution of the concept (Monroe 2006: 4). Aligned with the need to produce the experience, design becomes an integrated, systematic series of actions that are purposeful at every stage of the event execution. Expressed in simple terms, if the event is not being designed to deliver certain experiences, such experiences are in effect being left to chance. The less chance, the more predictability there is in the experience outcome. But chance itself can be a design decision to create moments where unexpected interaction and experiences evolve. The experience outcomes of any event are undeniably influenced by the interactions of guests and participants; does the design of event experiences seek to provide appropriate environments for such to occur? Figure 18.1 offers a speculative framework by suggesting that what we call event management needs a paradigm shift in order to place event design as the central core element of practice where design awareness should resonate through every decision stage of the event planning and management process. The Event Experience Design Framework suggests that if event design underpins all initial decisions about planning and managing the event, then the planned experience becomes the core of all subsequent action, leading to final analysis that considers the true nature of the overall experience.

Once a decision has been made to hold an event, then two considerations must immediately occupy the mind: that the event is a planned experience influenced by the nature or genre of

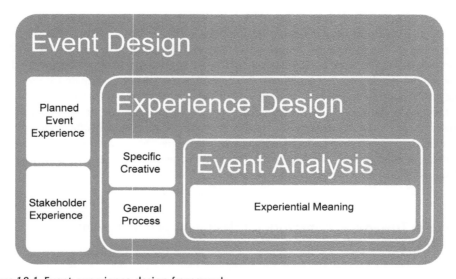

Figure 18.1 Event experience design framework

the event, and the experience of stakeholders, with an emphasis on the prime stakeholder experience. At this stage the event manager should embrace event design as a solution and objective-setting tool to ensure that the types of experience envisaged in the concept are integrated through purposeful action. Using foresight of experience design enables a focus on: (1) specific creative elements of the event and (2) general process elements of the event. At this stage all the event objectives and outcomes should be understood as a part of a deliberate plan to design an experience. Lastly, with design being so integrated, the analysis and evaluation of the meaning of the experience can be analysed and evaluated in relation to decisions taken to design each element of the event.

This is an advocacy that design should not be regarded simply as a singular component reflected only in the act of creativity and applied to the part of the event that is concerned only with décor and entertainment. Instead it should apply holistically to the very foundation upon which the event premise is built. Event experiences do not of themselves exist, they have to be designed and created from scratch. In order to create such experiences event planners, managers and designers need sets of tools to employ and equate design with overall planning and purpose as well as with theme and creativity. By understanding that design permeates all elements of the event, the nature of event experiences becomes a (potentially) predictive skill based on purposeful action.

Bibliography

Allen, J. (2002) *The Business of Event Planning*, Missisauga, ON: J.H. Wiley.

Allen, J., O'Toole, W., Mcdonnell, I. and Harris, J. (2005) *Festival and Special Event Management*, London: J.H. Wiley, third edition.

Archer, B. (1973) *The Need for Design Education*, London: Royal College of Art.

Bayley, S. (ed.) (1985) *The Conran Directory of Design*, London: Conran Octopus.

Berridge, G. (2007) *Events Design and Experience*, Oxford: Elsevier.

——(2009) 'Event pitching: the role of design and creativity', *International Journal of Hospitality Management* 29(2): 208–15.

——(2010a) 'Design management of events', in D. Tassiopoulos (ed.) *Events Management: A Developmental and Managerial Approach*, Johannesburg: Juta Publishing.

——(2010b) 'The promotion of cycling in London: the impact of the 2007 Tour de France Grand Depart on the image and provision of cycling in the capital', paper presented at the Global Events Congress IV, Leeds Metropolitan University, July.

Berridge, G. and Quick, L. (2010) 'Bidding for and securing an event', in D. Tassiopoulos (ed.) *Events Management: A Developmental and Managerial Approach,* Johannesburg: Juta Publishing.

Beverland, M.B. (2005) 'Managing the design innovation–brand marketing interface: resolving the tension between artistic creation and commercial imperatives', *Journal of Product Innovation Management* 22: 193–207.

Bitner, M.J. (1990) 'Evaluating service encounters: the effects of physical surroundings and employee responses', *Journal of Marketing* 45(2): 69–82.

——(1992) 'Servicescapes: the impact of physical surroundings on customers and employees', *Journal of Marketing* 56(2, April): 57–71.

Blumer, H. (1969) *Symbolic Interactionism*, New York: Prentice Hall.

Bob, U. (2010) 'Sustainable events design', in D. Tassiopoulos (ed.) *Events Management: A Developmental and Managerial Approach*, Johannesburg: Juta Publishing.

Botterill, T.D. and Crompton, J.L. (1996) 'Two case studies exploring the nature of the tourist's experience', *Journal of Leisure Research* 28(1): 57–82.

Bowdin, G., Allen, N., O'Toole, W., Harris, R. and McDonnell, I. (2006) *Events Management*, Oxford: Elsevier, second edition.

Brown, S. (2005) 'Event design – an Australian perspective', paper presented at Second International Event Management Body of Knowledge Global Alignment Summit, Johannesburg.

Brown, S. and James, S. (2004) 'Event design and management: ritual sacrifice', in I. Yeoman, M. Robertson, J. Ali-Knight, S. Drummond and U. McMahon-Beattie (eds) *Festival and Events Management*, Oxford: Elsevier.

Byars, M. (2004) *The Design Encyclopaedia*, New York: MOMA, second edition.

Carmouche, R., Shukla, N. and Anthonisz, A. (2010) 'Events marketing and communications strategy', in D. Tassiopoulos (ed.) *Events Management: A Developmental and Managerial Approach*, Johannesburg: Juta Publishing.

Cooper, R. (1995) *The Design Agenda: A Guide to Successful Design Management*, London: Mike Press.

Csíkszentmihályi, M. (1975) *Beyond Boredom and Anxiety*, San Francisco, CA: Jossey-Bass.

——(1990) *Flow: The Psychology of Optimal Experience*, New York: Harper Perennial.

Darmer, P. and Sunbo, J. (2008) 'Introduction to experience creation', in J. Sunbo and P. Darmer (eds) *Creating Experiences in the Experience Economy*, Cheltenham, UK: Edward Elgar.

Denzin, N.K. (1978) *The Research Act*, Boston, MA: McGraw-Hill, second edition.

Diller, Steve, Shedroff, N. and Rhea, D. (2008) *Making Meaning: How Successful Businesses Deliver Meaningful Customer Experiences*, New Jersey: New Riders Press.

Emery, P.R. (2002) 'Bidding to host a major sports event: the local organising committee perspective', *International Journal of Public Sector Management* 15: 20.

Fernandes, C. and Brysch, T. (2009) 'Animation, creativity and tourism workshop', paper presented at ATLAS Winter University 'Tourism, Leisure and Creativity' Conference, Barcelona 18 February to 1 March.

Getz, D. (1997) *Event Management and Event Tourism*, New York: Cognizant.

——(2005) *Event Management and Event Tourism*, New York: Cognizant, second revised edition.

——(2008) *Event Studies*, Oxford: Elsevier.

Gilhepsy, I. and Harris, D. (2010) 'Researching visual culture: approaches for the understanding of tourism and leisure experiences', in M.J. Morgan, P. Lugosi and J.R.B. Richie (eds) *The Tourism and Leisure Experience: Consumer and Managerial Perspectives*, Bristol: Channel View Publications

Goffman, I. (1959) *The Presentation of Self in Everyday Life*, Garden City, NY: Doubleday.

——(1967) *Interaction Ritual*, New York: Anchor Books.

Goldblatt, J.J. (2004) *Special Events: Event Leadership for a New World*, Hoboken: J.H. Wiley.

——(2008) *Special Events: The Roots and Wings of Celebration*, Hoboken: J.H. Wiley.

Green, M. (2010) *Plenary Presentation at World Events Congress IV*, Leeds: Leeds Metropolitan University, UK.

Grove, S.J., Fiske, R.P. and Bitner, M.J. (1992) 'Dramatising the service experience: a managerial approach', in T.A. Swartz, S. Brown and D. Bowen (eds) *Advances in Services Marketing and Management*, Greenwich, CT: JAI Press, pp. 91–121.

Hall, C.M. (2004) 'Sport tourism and urban regeneration', in B.W. Ritchie and D. Adair (eds) *Sport Tourism; Interrelationships, Impacts and Issues*, Clevedon, UK: Channel View Publications.

Holbrook, M.B. and Hirshmann, E.C. (1982) 'The experiential aspects of consumption: consumer fantasies, feelings and fun', *Journal of Consumer Research* 9(2): 132–40.

Hull, R.B., Michale, S.B., Walker, G.J and Roggerbuck, J.W. (1996) 'Ebb and flow of brief leisure experience', *Leisure Sciences* 18: 299–314.

Jensen, R (1999) *The Dream Society*, New York: McGraw-Hill.

Lee, Y., Dattilo, J. and Howard, D. (1994) 'The complex and dynamic nature of leisure experience and leisure services', *Journal of Leisure Research* 26(3): 195–211.

Li, Y. (2000) 'Geographical consciousness and tourism experiences', *Annals of Tourism Research* 9(4): 239–45.

Lipton, R. (2002) *Designing across Cultures*, Cincinnati, OH: HOW Design Books.

Malouf, L. (1999) *Behind the Scenes at Special Events*, Hoboken: J.H. Wiley.

Mannell, R.C. and Kleiber, D.A. (1997) *A Social Psychology of Leisure*, Pittsburgh, PA: Venture Publications.

Markus, G.H. (2002) *What is Design Today?* New York: H.N. Abrams.

Masterman, G. and Wood, E.H. (2006) *Innovative Marketing Communications for the events industry*, Oxford: Elsevier.

Matthews, D. (2008a) *Special Event Production: The Process*, Oxford: Elsevier.

——(2008b) *Special Event Production: The Resources*, Oxford: Elsevier.

Monroe, J.C. (2006) *Art of the Event: Complete Guide to Designing and Decorating Special Events*, Oxford: Wiley.

Morello, A. (2000) 'Design predicts the future when it anticipates experience', *Design Issues* 16: 35–44.

Morgan, M.J. (2006) 'Making space for experiences', *Journal of Retail and Leisure Property* 5 (4, October): 305–13.

——(2010) 'The experience economy ten years on: where next for experience management?', in M.J. Morgan, P. Lugosi and J.R.B. Richie (eds) *The Tourism and Leisure Experience: Consumer and Managerial Perspectives*, Bristol: Channel View Publications.

Morgan, M., Watson, P. and Hemmington, N. (2008) 'Drama in the dining room: Theatrical perspectives on the foodservice encounter', *Journal of Foodservice*, 19(2): 111–18.

Morgan, M.J., Lugosi, P. and Richie, J.R.B. (eds) (2010) *The Tourism and Leisure Experience: Consumer and Managerial Perspective*, Bristol: Channel View Publications.

Muller, E., Schwameder, H., Kornexl, E. and Raschner, C. (1997) *Science and Skiing*, London: E. and F.N. Spon.

Nelson, K.B. (2009) 'Enhancing the attendee's experience through creative design of the event environment: applying Goffman's dramaturgical perspective', *Journal of Convention and Event Tourism* 10: 120–33.

O'Dell, T. and Billing, P. (eds) (2005) *Experience-scapes: Tourism, Culture, and Economy*, Copenhagen: Copenhagen Business School Press.

Ooi, C. (2005) 'A theory of tourism experiences', in T. O'Dell and P. Billing (eds) *Experience-scapes: Tourism, Culture, and Economy*, Copenhagen: Copenhagen Business School Press, pp. 51–68.

O'Sullivan, E.L. and Spangler, K.J. (1999) *Experience Marketing*, State College, PA: Venture Publishing.

Pearce, P. (2005) *Tourist Behaviour: Themes and Conceptual Schemes*, Clevedon: Channel View Publications.

Pettersson, R. and Getz, D. (2009) 'Event experiences in time and space: a study of visitors to the 2007 World Alpine Ski Championships in Åre, Sweden', *Scandinavian Journal of Hospitality and Tourism* 9(2–3): 308–26.

Pikkemaat, B., Peters, M., Boksberger, P. and Secco, M. (2009) 'The staging of experiences in wine tourism', *Journal of Hospitality Marketing and Management* 18(2–3): 237–53.

Pine, J. and Gilmore, B.H. (1999) *The Experience Economy: Work is Theatre and Every Business a Stage*, Boston: Harvard Business School.

Potter, N. (2002) *What is a Designer? Things, Places, Messages*, London: Hyphen Press.

Prahalad, C.K. and Ramaswamy, V. (2004) *The Future of Competition: Co-creating Unique Value with Customers*, Boston, MA: Harvard Business School.

Ritchie, J.R.B. and Smith, B.H. (1991) 'The impact of mega event on host region awareness: a longitudinal study', *Journal of Travel Research* 30(1): 3–10.

Ritzer, G. (2004) *The McDonaldization of Society*, London: Pine Forge Press.

Rossman, J.R. (2003) *Recreation Programming: Designing Leisure Experiences*, Urbana, IL: Sagamore Publishing.

Ryan, C. (2003) *Recreational Tourism: Demand and Impacts*, Clevedon: Channel View Publications.

Salem, G., Jones, E. and Morgan, N. (2004) 'An overview of events management', in I. Yeoman, M. Robertson, J. Ali-Knight, S. Drummond and U. McMahon-Beattie (eds) *Festival and Events Management*, Oxford: Elsevier Butterworth-Heinemann.

Schmitt, B. (1999) *Experiential Marketing: How to Get Customers to Sense, Feel, Think, Act, Relate to your Company and Brands*, New York: The Free Press.

——(2003) *Customer Experience Management*, Hoboken, NJ: John Wiley and Sons.

Shebroff, Nathan (2001) *Experience Design 1*, New York: Prentice Hall.

Shone, A. and Parry, B. (2004) *Successful Event Management: A Practical Handbook*, London: Thomson.

Shukla, N. and Nuntsu, N. (2005) 'Event marketing', in D. Tassiopoulos (ed.) *Event Management*, Johannesburg: Juta Publishing, second edition.

Silvers, J.R. (2004) *Professional Event Coordination*, Hoboken: J.H. Wiley.

Singh, R.K., Murty, H.R., Gupta, S.K. and Dikshit, A.K. (2008) 'An overview of sustainability assessment methodologies', *Ecological Indicators* 9(2): 189–212.

Sonder, M. (2004) *Event Entertainment and Production*, Hoboken: J.H. Wiley.

Spilling, O. (2000) 'Beyond intermezzo? On the long term industrial impacts of mega–events – the case of Lillehammer 1994', in L. Mossberg (ed.) *Evaluation of Events: Scandinavian Experiences*, New York: Cognizant.

Tassiopoulos, D. (ed.) (2010) *Events Management: A Developmental and Managerial Approach*, Johannesburg: Juta Publishing.

Tofler, A. (1972) *Future Shock*, London: Pan Books.

Turner, V (1969) *The Ritual Process: Structure and Anti-structure*, New York: Aldine De Gruyter.

Ullrich, K.T. and Eppinger, S.T. (2004) *Product Design and Development*, Boston, MA: McGraw Hill.

Uriely, N. (2005) 'The tourist experience: conceptual developments', *Annals of Tourism Research* 31(1): 199–216.

van der Wagen, L. (2008) *Events Management for Tourism, Cultural, Business and Sporting Events*, Sydney: Pearson, third edition.

Vanneste, M. (2008) *Meeting Architecture: A Manifesto*, Poland: Meeting Support Institute.

Wang, N. (1999) 'Rethinking authenticity in tourism experience', *Annals of Tourism Research* 226(2): 349–70.

Watt, D. and Stayte, S. (1999) *Events from Start to Finish*, Reading, UK: ILAM.

White, L. (2006) 'National identity and the Sydney 2000 Olympic Games opening ceremony', in M. Robertson (ed.) *Sporting Events and Event Tourism: Impacts, Plans and Opportunities*, Eastbourne: LSA.

Yeoman, I., Robertson, M., Ali-Knight, J., Drummond, S. and McMahon-Beattie, U. (2004) *Festival and Events Management*, Oxford: Elsevier Butterworth-Heinemann.

Zoels, J.C. and Gabrielli, S. (2003) 'Creating imaginable futures: using design strategy as a foresight tool', in Interaction Design Institute Ivrea for the European Commission (ed.) *DFFN Case-study Technical Report*, Brussels: Ivrea, 10–11 December.

19

The media, marketing and events

Andrew Bradley

Introduction

During the last thirty years there have been energetic image enhancement and promotional campaigns by a number of different localities throughout the world (Pike 2008), with the enhancement and promotion of location image now being seen as a vital part of economic development strategies (Richards and Wilson 2004). In order to attract both footloose industries and highly qualified employees, locations are increasingly promoting themselves 'through the use of imaging strategies in the form of attractive slogans and marketable images as well as through development projects, events and festivals that are in line with the[ir] chosen image' (Chang 1997: 547). As Page (1995: 217) notes, 'the development of festivals and special events may make an important contribution to the image of a location' and therefore may have a significant impact upon economic development.

Media coverage of these events disseminates images of place throughout the local, national and international media, potentially reaching a far greater number and range of audiences than conventional place marketing campaigns would do (Bradley 2002; Jago *et al.* 2003). This coverage reaches a number of discrete audiences and has tangible and intangible impacts. These include potential investors whose decisions may be influenced by the images of the location that they receive through the media and the local business community who might be convinced that the economic strategies of the local authority and other bodies responsible for place marketing and development have been successful. The coverage of these events, then, is crucial in selling places to both internal and external audiences and thus, 'the perception of cities, and their mental image, [become] active components of economic success or failure' (Ashworth and Voogd 1990: 3)

The purpose of this chapter is to examine the way in which locations have invested in events and festivals with a view to generate positive images of place which can be transmitted via the media to a variety of different audiences. However, in order to do this, there is a need to examine the broader place promotion context in which this has taken place and to uncover the increasing role that events have played in this process. The chapter concludes with an analysis of the current research into the transmission of place image through the media coverage of events from the perspective both of the various audiences receiving the images and of event managers who are trying to control the images that are disseminated, based on two case studies of the media coverage of Cheltenham's (UK) various events.

Broader context: place promotion and the marketing of locations

Selling or marketing a particular geographical locality has emerged as a central part of the contemporary process of inter-urban competition for global capital (Medway and Warnaby 2008). In this competition, a location's attributes and local cultural identities are often used in the form of 'cultural capital' to project an alluring image to potential residents, investors and visitors (Gay 2009; Hankinson, 2009). The marketing of these images has been seen as a response by policy makers to adjust to the changing nature of the economic structure of Western Europe and North America (Brooker and Burgess 2008) as the economies attempt to adjust from heavy industry and manufacturing to a reliance on services or high-tech industries. This in turn has an impact upon a place's appeal to potential investors and residents. The older virtues of a central location, cheap labour and low taxes are not abandoned, but much more emphasis is placed upon quality of life issues (Youcheng and Krakover 2008).

Therefore, 'place marketing images can thus be viewed simply as exemplars of, for example, broader economic and political changes, such as the rise of enterprise culture or postmodernism' (Ward 1998: 5). Ward also notes that a common feature of place marketing strategies is investment marketing, which includes the refurbishment of cultural attractions such as museums or art galleries, the holding of business conventions and the hosting of major sporting or cultural events. Yet for larger cities, at least, such consumption-based activities were also intended to attract not only businesses themselves but also entrepreneurs and investors to live and conduct their businesses in the place being marketed. Bailey (1989: 3) views this as part of a fundamental shift in the ways that places are promoted as he believes that 'the logic that more jobs make a city better is giving way to the realisation that making a city better attracts more jobs'.

Places are now instead marketed as a great place to live, as well as a great place to do business. As firms increasingly rely on recruiting and retaining highly paid managers and with technical innovation making business less dependent on the supply of unskilled or semi-skilled workers, so must the city be seen as habitable or consumable by upscale executives and middle-class professionals. This creates an important distinction within the literature on place marketing, as it is being increasingly recognised that

> urban promotion involves the selling of a location not only for business but also as a place to live ... these images of lifestyle tend to be predominantly anchored around two things, culture and environment. The use of leisure time is considered an increasingly important aspect of the decision making process for both long-term relocation decisions and short-term (e.g. convention location decisions) business or tourist decisions.
>
> *(Hall 1998: 127)*

The increasing centrality of events to place promotion initiatives

The contemporary promotion of a location's events can be defined as one strand of local economic policy that is used to cushion the negative effects of the painful transition from an industrial to a post-industrial economy (Tsu-Hong *et al.* 2008). In this model, events are incorporated within the language of economics, with the attendant measurements applied to policy analysis: investment, leverage, employment, direct and indirect income effects, social and spatial targeting and so forth. Events are then bundled up with business services, with tourism, with the leisure industries as part of a narrow definition of urban regeneration driven by the objectives of employment creation and retention. These policies are used as part of a local response to the globalisation of capital and the political necessity to marshal all available resources to attract and to hold international investment.

In order to attract both footloose industries and highly qualified employees, places are increasingly promoting themselves 'through the use of imaging strategies in the form of attractive slogans and marketable images as well as through development projects, events and festivals that are in line with the[ir] chosen image' (Chang 1997: 547). As Page (1995: 217) notes, 'the development of festivals and special events may make an important contribution to the image of a destination'.

As such, events become a strand of place promotion, with cities vying against other cities to flaunt their ownership of top quality events, museums and galleries, fine architecture, symphony orchestras or rock musicians. Depending on the audience, a location's events are packaged and re-packaged to become an incentive for the potential investor, property developer, potential tourists or potential residents. In doing this policies relating to the holding of events have become a significant component of physical regeneration strategies in many Western European cities, where a lively, cosmopolitan cultural life is increasingly being seen as a crucial ingredient of city marketing and internationalisation strategies designed to attract mobile international capital and specialised personnel, particularly in the high-tech industrial and advanced services sectors.

Locations, however, have not all followed the same path in the way that event-based initiatives have been employed to help remodel their images and find new economic roles. One approach to make theoretical sense of this differentiation has been through the elaboration of typologies. For example, it has been suggested (Griffiths 1993) that a number of models can be identified, reflecting different political priorities and different spatial emphases. The three models that have received attention are: the promotion of civic identity, cultural industries, and city boosterism.

Events as a mechanism for promoting civic identity

In this model, events, alongside other measures, are used as key elements of a strategy aimed at revitalising public social life, reviving a sense of civic identity and shared belonging to the city, creating a more inclusive and democratic public realm, and raising expectations about what city life has to offer (Montgomery 1990; Fisher and Worpole 1991).

Events as a mechanism for developing cultural industries

The emphasis in this model is on the holding of events in order to stimulate development and growth of local cultural industries as an important form of wealth creation in its own right, and one which has significant potential for future growth (Money 1989; Wynne 1992).

Events as a means of city boosterism

Using events as an instrument of city promotion is an idea that first emerged in the USA (Whitt 1987), but has subsequently been adopted by many European cities, (Liverpool being a prominent example, O'Brien 2010). This can be thought of as a consumerist model, as its primary emphasis is upon consumption of events as a means of attracting tourists (cultural tourism), enticing business investment by projecting a better quality of life for professional and executive employees, and securing the profitability of physical renewal projects by keeping people in town after work with a view to producing synergies between office uses, shops, restaurants and cultural facilities in mixed-use developments and cultural districts (Bradley 2002).

Although it is certainly useful to be able to distinguish analytically the different ways in which events have been incorporated into broader strategies of urban regeneration, it does not mean that these models have, in practice, been mutually exclusive. Places have typically employed a combination of approaches, displaying in the process greater or lesser degrees of creativity and imagination. Among the factors that have been important in determining the particular pattern of initiatives being pursued are:

- the place's current and desired position in the regional and international hierarchy;
- the place's recent and long-term experiences of economic and industrial restructuring;
- the underlying political culture of the place;
- the political demand and priorities thrown up by the place's changing social make-up;
- the opportunities made possible by local administration and governmental structures.

In analytical terms, therefore, it can be argued that, while the delineation and categorisation of the use of events as a part of a cultural policy helps to bring into focus the variety of approaches that have been adopted, it suffers by virtue of being essentially static and descriptive and therefore the transferability between specific locations must be called into question. It has also been argued that the juxtaposition between ephemeral programmes of events and activities and other cultural animation initiatives and permanent facilities, such as concert halls, libraries, art museums, for example, is, in many ways, artificial, as ephemeral events, if coherently organised and repeated, can become permanent features of a city's cultural landscape, producing long-term benefits in terms of image, tourism and support for local cultural production (Bradley 2002).

The importance of the media coverage of locations and its implications for events

The media can play an important role in the dissemination of images of place, and as such it cannot be considered that urban managers and other parties who are concerned with the production and promotion of positive images of place with a view to either counteracting negative images or maintaining positive images can exercise complete control over the images that are produced, as the media are an external factor beyond their immediate control which can help to shape a place's image. The media also have the ability to change images of place relatively quickly through the dissemination of news stories about a particular place.

The media can be an essential component of how people construct place images and cognitive maps (Avraham and Daugherty 2009). The role of the mass media in this process is crucial: while people usually become aware of occurrences in their immediate environment from direct contact with the events, they learn about events that occur in more distant places primarily from the media. Information about a far-away place is not considered crucial to most people and thus they do not attempt to locate first-hand responses to verify what happened there (Kunczic 1997). For this reason, the 'reality' that the media transfers from distant places is conceptualised as the 'objective' or 'true' reality by those who do not live there (Avraham 2004).

The role of the media in the creation of images of place is therefore crucial as the media form part of a complex cultural process in which meanings are produced and consumed (Avraham and First 2006). Reality is constructed through shared, culturally specific, symbolic systems of visual and verbal communications, and the media play a fundamental role in the construction of this reality by selectively providing knowledge about the lives, landscapes and cultures of different social groups. Therefore the media industry can be seen to be participating in a complex cultural process through which meanings are produced and consumed (Burgess 1990).

An example of this is given by Burd (1977: 1) as he believes that 'in a very real sense ... a city becomes the image that the media projects'. Yet the images that the media project are not static and are flexible over time. However, whilst the images related to a specific place may be flexible over time myths created around a place, be they positive or negative, continue to exist for years. As such, the media image of place is becoming increasingly important to those parties responsible for managing economic development strategies as

> mayors, urban planners and policy makers are all concerned about their city's coverage patterns in the news media. These decision makers tend to accuse news people of distorting their city's images by means of news definitions that focus mainly on negative effects such as crime, violence and social problems while ignoring positive events and important developments.
>
> *(Avraham 2000: 363)*

This concern on the part of the key decision-makers demonstrates their belief that the way in which the media construct images of place and the way in which these images are consumed are key determinants in the economic fortune of specific localities.

However, whilst it is generally recognised that images of place contained in the media have the potential to act as a complement to 'traditional' place marketing schemes, there is a lack of empirical evidence to substantiate these general claims. Overall, as Avraham (2000: 363) notes,

> it is surprising that the [media] images of cities do not receive more attention, as they are important and have a considerable effect, along with other factors, on the ability of cities to change their position in the growing national and global competition for various resources. A city's position in this competition might be affected by its image because people will usually hesitate to invest in, move to, or visit cities that are covered mainly in relation to crime, poverty and social disorder. The importance of a city's portrayal in the national media stems from our belief that such images affect these groups, the general public, the decision makers on a national level and place's inhabitants

For the general public, the image of cities can affect a number of decisions, including those relating to places to re-locate to, either on a temporary basis as tourists or on a more permanent basis in relation to migrating to a new job (Judd 1995). For national policy makers, media images can affect decisions regarding revenue grants, capital and resource allocation and legislation (Walker 1997). As Hanna (1996: 633) notes, 'representations of places in the media play crucial roles in the development and definition of ... places. Nations, counties, cities and towns depend upon representations to create a sense of community among residents and to present themselves to others'. In addition, the external image of places can have an impact on the self-image of the place's inhabitants and can also shape their relations with the inhabitants of other places.

Similar sentiments are expressed by Barke and Harrop (1994: 93), in that they believe that 'inevitably, the media in all their forms play the most prominent role in the representation and reconstructions of place'. Films, television shows, novels and newspapers all contain representations of place and make it possible for governments, businesses and individuals to understand and communicate about places (Hanna 1996). However, the texts, films photographs and other forms of representation that collectively constitute the media do more than capture aspects of reality and communicate information about them, they are part of popular culture and have an important influence on both individual and societal experience in the world.

The potential of attracting media coverage for an event has been seen as one of the principal reasons why major cities have chosen to bid to host prestigious tournaments such as the

Olympic or Commonwealth Games (Essex and Chalkey 1998). However, whilst the attraction of a large television audience with the associated opportunity for a location to present its 'best face' to the cameras for a short, but intensive, period of time, is often given as one of the main reasons for gambling local taxpayers' money on developing the necessary infrastructure and associated marketing campaign in order to succeed in the bidding process, little is known as regards the effectiveness of this exposure on producing the benefits in terms of image dissemination that policy managers intend.

Perhaps the most common way that images of the events in a location are transmitted to external audiences (i.e. those who do not attend the festivities themselves) is via the media. If an event is of a sufficiently high profile to attract national and international media attention, this attention focused on the host location, even if it is only for a relatively short period of time, can have enormous publicity value and some locations will use this fact alone to justify expenditure on events (White 2008).

In a media-conscious age, it is not only the performers and their audiences that can participate in a festival, but also the millions of persons who will never buy a ticket, never personally visit the site who broaden the base of interest in the event (Bradley 2002). The focus of the media on the location of a festival can convey images of that place to a vast audience and has the potential to produce some of the positive images of place required to produce indirect economic impacts. However, the extent of coverage and the nature of media coverage of a festival can do more than convey positive images of place: it can also have an impact on the future funding of festivals in a location, as it can have impacts in relation to the popularity of the festival among the general public and the attitude of funding bodies, including business sponsors.

Current research into place images in the media and the media coverage of events

Despite the media seemingly becoming more and more integrated into everyday life in the developed world via an increasing number of television channels, radio stations, newspapers and the Internet, relatively little is understood about how the media distribute images of place, how these images are consumed, and what, if any, impact the consumption of these images has (Chalip 2005). This inattention may be, in part, due to the media's very ordinariness, with television, radio, newspapers, fiction, film and pop music being such a common part of people's everyday life that this has perhaps masked the media's importance. The media have become 'threaded into the fabric of daily life with deep taproots into the well being of popular consciousness' (Harvey 1989: 137) and therefore the institutions and practices which comprise the media have a significance that demands our attention. They are an integral part of popular culture and, as such, are an essential element in moulding individual and social experiences of the world and in shaping the relationships between people and place.

Much of the research that has been conducted into media images of place has been concerned with identifying the characteristics of individual places that are contained within media reports. This research emphasises two different dimensions to the coverage that places receive: nature and quantity (Avraham 1998).

The quantity dimension refers to the amount and visibility of the coverage that a place received in the news media. Factors examined include such details as number of reports about the place, on what page or section the articles appear, the article's size (in the press) or the length of the report (in television news) and so forth. These studies are primarily quantitative in nature and often based on counting the total amount of words used, airtime given, occurrences of certain words or phrases within text or typifying the types of images used. Whilst these studies do offer a guide to the type of coverage that places receive, the quantitative nature of enquiry removes the data from its context of both the means of production of media reports and the way in which they are received by audiences.

The nature of the coverage that places receive is often arrived at by the use of a more qualitative mode of study, with media reports being deconstructed, compared over a certain time period or by using a different variety of media. Research into the nature of place images in the media often makes reference to several individual factors (Avraham 2004):

- which subjects are most frequently covered from the place (e.g. crime, poverty, social and community events);
- the way that the place is described in reports;
- who is represented as being responsible for the events that are covered;
- who is quoted and the source of the information reported.

In this dimension, the studies examine the media images 'beyond the numbers' in that their authors are looking for stereotypes, generalisations and myths which appear in the coverage of certain places (Avraham 2004). Also important to these studies are the construction of power relations through the media reports on place, as an emphasis is placed upon those who are responsible for providing the direct quotes and other items of primary 'evidence' in order to lend additional credence and authority to the article.

Research on the media coverage of events

Media management for events-specific purposes has been defined as 'the deliberate management or manipulation of media coverage to achieve both strategic and tactical objectives for the event, its sponsors, and the host destination' (Getz and Fairley 2004: 130). The importance of gaining media coverage for events is noted in a study by Hudson *et al.* (2002) who assessed the goals of event organisers and destination marketers in North America, Australia and the United Kingdom and found that the most important overall goal (of a list provided to respondents) was to attract media coverage (Getz and Fairley 2004).

It is surprising, therefore, that the media coverage that events receive has, until very recently, been ignored by researchers. In one of the few studies dealing with the media coverage of festivals that pre-dates the turn of the century, Rolfe (1992) notes that the local press frequently printed previews but rarely reviewed actual festival performances, and that the organisers of festivals complain of the difficulty in achieving serious coverage of festival events and a tendency of the local press, in particular, to seek out trivia and scandal. For instance, the organisers of the Sidmouth Festival of International Folk Arts were dismayed when a story about an argument between a Norwegian coach driver and a traffic warden reached the front page of a local paper, while the arguably more impressive performance of the Norwegian choir went unreported. With regard to national coverage, festival organisers frequently stated that, while the national press produced lists of previews and therefore served a useful role in advertising festival events, it rarely reviewed festival performances. Frustration was expressed at the apparent reluctance of the press to leave London to attend any festival other than the larger, more prestigious ones, which receive international as well as national coverage. Some festival organisers also complained that the artistic content of their festival went unreported in favour of other aspects, while others found it regrettable that the coverage of arts events was restricted to the arts and entertainment pages.

Similar paucity of research in this area is also noted by Köhler *et al.* (2009), who note that media impacts of events have received limited attention. Besides few studies on the connection of media coverage and image enhancement (Chalip and Green 2003), the primary concerns have been quantitative media values such as the reach and frequency of destination exposure and their equivalent advertising space or time (see Table 19.1).

An analysis of the research conducted to date identifies that there has been a movement towards producing a detailed analysis of the amount and nature of the media coverage that events receive; however, what is also apparent from this is that there have been no attempts to understand the attempts that are made by those involved with the event to shape the media coverage that an event can receive. The lack of this information has implications for our subsequent understanding of the nature and content of the images produced as it removes them from the context in which they were originally produced and transmitted.

Within the literature, there is some divergence of opinion as to the extent to which an event organiser can control or influence the event images that are subsequently produced in the media. For example, Green (2003: 338) notes that 'the coverage of a city during an event does not represent a targeted message controlled by city marketers. Rather, the images and messages communicated to audiences are a haphazard collage of images gathered, selected and edited by the broadcaster.' Similarly, Getz and Fairley (2004) believe that media personnel are not necessarily interested in promoting the destination through their coverage of the event, and that television media in particular might resist incorporating the broadcast of destination imagery as part of their coverage of the event.

Table 19.1 Further reading related to the media coverage of events

Study	Content
Bradley and Hall (2006)	An analysis of the amount and nature of newspaper coverage received by four events in Cheltenham
Smith (2005)	An analysis of whether sports initiatives within a local influence the image of that place in the minds of potential visitors
Green (2003)	An analysis of the amount and nature of television coverage of a sports event in San Antonio
Reid (2006)	The reaction of local people to the media coverage of Edinburgh contained in the 2003 MTV awards
Boyko (2008)	The relationship between coverage of the 2002 Capital of Culture event in Brugge and the meanings created by local residents
Köhler *et al.* (2009)	Analysis of the newspaper and television coverage of the Bob and Skeleton World Championships in Germany in 2008
Hede (2005)	An analysis of the Australian media coverage of the 2004 Olympic Games in Athens
Ritchie *et al.* (2007)	An analysis of whether the media coverage of the Australia Day Live Concert in 2006 changed people's opinion of the city of Canberra
Garcia (2006)	An analysis of the media coverage received by the Liverpool City of Culture event
Chalip and Green (2003)	An analysis of the media coverage of the Honda Indy 300 and its ability to shape viewer perceptions of Australia's Gold Coast

Alternatively, Richards and Palmer (2010) believe that the media can be manipulated to present an event's location in a positive light and that media coverage can thus become part of the marketing strategy both for the location and for future events. However, an analysis of texts which deal with issues related to event management (Bowdin *et al.* 2006, van der Wagen 2008) only have very limited advice for potential event managers when dealing with the media, and this tends to be found within sections related to event marketing and doesn't identify different types of media and the opportunities and threats that they can provide, as it would be a mistake to believe that all media coverage of arts festivals has a positive impact. For instance, the organisers of the Notting Hill carnival have experienced considerable difficulty in attracting business sponsorship for their event as a direct consequence of what they see as inaccurate and adverse media coverage (Rolfe 1992). There are also dangers of damage being done to a host location's image to have it connected with a festival that is perceived to have failed (e.g. the Millennium Experience at the Millennium Dome, in Greenwich) or one that is beset by problems (e.g. traffic problems at the Olympics in Atlanta, 1996) or one associated with social problems (e.g. crime at the Glastonbury festival) (Bradley 2002).

The importance of media coverage of events: a case study of Cheltenham, UK

Cheltenham lies midway between Bristol and Birmingham on the edge of the Cotswold Hills in the UK. It is the second largest population centre in the county of Gloucestershire, after Gloucester. Cheltenham's relatively good accessibility also means that it serves as an extensive catchment and travel-to-work area for central and eastern Gloucestershire and the South Midlands (Bradley and Hall 2006).

Cheltenham does not engage in any premeditated conventional place marketing campaigns. Therefore, the principal way in which Cheltenham seeks to promote itself is through the perceptions of the quality of life that it can offer. A crucial part of this is the many events that take place within Cheltenham that are designed to offer a varied menu of sporting and cultural entertainment aimed to appeal to visitors of all ages and interests. These festivals have been instrumental in Cheltenham claiming itself to be the 'festival town of Britain' (Cheltenham Borough Council 2001) and the year-round series of regional, national and international festivals has sustained Cheltenham's appeal to visitors, businessmen and residents alike and compensates for the town's lack of a major historical or geographical attraction such as a river, cathedral or castle. These festivals allow Cheltenham to 'culturally punch above its weight ... [and are] a significant factor in retaining and attracting businesses to the area' (Cheltenham Borough Council 2002: 4). Moreover, one of Cheltenham Borough Council's stated aims is to develop Cheltenham's reputation as a festival and event town. Central to this aim is maintaining and protecting 'the image that the town has in offering a high quality of life ... [as] ... employers relocate to, and stay in, Cheltenham because the profile is good for business and is attractive to employees ... [and Cheltenham] ... would lose this image at its peril' (Cheltenham Borough Council 2002: 9).

Whilst Cheltenham does not engage in any conventional place marketing campaigns, the two main agencies responsible for the promotion of the town's festivals (the Festivals and Events Department of Cheltenham Borough Council and the staff at Cheltenham Racecourse) are extremely active both in the day-to-day management of Cheltenham's festivals and also in examining the opportunities in relation to the procurement of festivals from other locations and the creation of new festivals for the town.

The lack of conventional promotional campaigns, however, does not mean that Cheltenham does not face serious development issues. Mergers between existing companies and relocations from the town when coupled with the expected growth in the next decade of the local workforce have created a need to develop both a defensive policy, in order to retain and foster growth and development of the businesses that are already located there, and also policies designed to stimulate enquiries in relation to possible relocations. Central to these policies is the projection of a strong positive image of Cheltenham that acts as an encouragement to new businesses and new well-qualified employees for existing businesses, and also maintains the regular influx of tourists. Therefore, the town's festivals, and the media attention that they receive, have become a key component of Cheltenham's economic development strategies.

In an interview with a representative of Cheltenham Borough Council it was noted that,

> [Cheltenham's events] *are absolutely vital to both the economic and social development of the town. Myerscough in the late 1980s claimed that the arts was the second most important driver or influence for companies relocating out of London, after proximity to the countryside. The Bath festivals capitalise on the tourists that come to Bath, but Bath would have its visitors whether or not it has its festivals. Cheltenham needs events/festivals to give Cheltenham a profile ... If you think of what other places have done, Birmingham has improved its image through culture and events ... what would Stratford be if it didn't have what it has? Any town that is of any size is trying desperately to promote itself for direct tourism or profile to get businesses in and we can't just let go as it is a very competitive business and we have to keep investing.*
>
> *(Informant: Cheltenham Borough Council)*

Events are therefore seen as not only being an integral part of Cheltenham's image, but also as a key component of the town's economic fortunes.

> *The arts festivals have a relatively small direct impact, when you think of the numbers of people that come and spend money, whilst it is insignificant relative to the races with a real influx of people it isn't as big. The impact, I think, is much more of an indirect one, in the feel that they create.*
>
> *(Informant: Cheltenham Borough Council)*

The importance of the media coverage of Cheltenham's events is not lost upon the main bodies who are responsible for producing the town's festivals.

> *The festival committee do a very good job of getting festival coverage in the media and ... 99 per cent of the time it is positive coverage in the media and it is all part of the strategy in putting these festivals on and getting the media coverage and getting positive media coverage. This is not just about advertising, but also the wider issue of showing that there are all these things happening in Cheltenham and what a good place it is.*
>
> *(Informant: Cheltenham Borough Council)*

The relationship between event managers and the media

Whilst the use of events as a place promotional tool with a view to generating positive images of place through the media coverage they receive is widely accepted (Pike 2008) and there is now a burgeoning literature which examines the media images of event locations that are portrayed in the media (Green 2003; Smith 2005), the ways in which event organisers have tried to use the media in order to maximise the potential for positive media coverage of both their events and the broader geographical location have been largely ignored. 'It cannot be assumed that the host destination will be positively featured in media coverage of events' (Getz and Fairley 2004: 130) and therefore it is somewhat surprising that the actions of event organisers have received so little attention as they provide highly important contextual material that helps us to understand the media images of events that are subsequently produced.

The only article that has examined these issues looked at the relationships with the media of five different events in Australia (Getz and Fairley 2004), but this only examined who was responsible for liaising with the media in each event and didn't examine how the event organiser can attempt to manipulate the media to try to generate the most favourable media coverage possible. In order to address this empirical lacuna in depth, interviews were conducted with the principal organisers of Cheltenham's festivals to examine the extent to which they attempt to influence the media coverage that their festivals subsequently receive.

Influencing the media coverage of events: the relationships between event organisers and the media in Cheltenham

The results of the interviews conducted with those responsible for managing and promoting Cheltenham's events demonstrate that the fostering of the relationships with media outlets starts long before the scheduled start of the event and the lengths to which event organisers are prepared to go to in order to generate positive relationships with media personnel.

> We organise it so there is a story every week for the festival from the 1st of January. We believe in treating the media well, we like to get close to them, we take them all away, put them up in nice places, see how good they are at getting up early after spending all night in the casinos and generally getting close to them.
>
> *(Informant: Cheltenham Racecourse)*

It also became apparent that, having generated positive working relationships with the press, there was almost an expectation that they may be more compliant with the wishes of event organisers.

> You cannot risk the media picking up their own impression, you have to give them their lines, tell them this is what so and so says. Look after the press, look after the photographers, get them to point their cameras in the right direction and with any luck they will show what you want them to show.
>
> *(Informant: Cheltenham Racecourse)*

One of the principal ways in which media outlets were given 'their lines' was through the distribution of official press releases from event organisers. A belief was expressed by event organisers that 'journalists are notoriously lazy and they will pick up the sense of something from very, very few people that create that sense' (Informant: Cheltenham Festivals). An analysis of thirty-six press releases issued in relation to Cheltenham's Festivals of Music and Literature demonstrated that each of them appeared in the United Kingdom's broadsheet press with less than 1 per cent of the total content (measured by the number of words changed, deleted or edited) being different from the press release issued by the event organisers.

Event organisers are also creative in thinking of ways of generating media coverage of their events and will look to exploit relationships with famous people in order to obtain media coverage of their event.

> We were looking to revamp our junior membership and I hadn't actually found a vehicle to do it. We wanted it to be run by young people for young people and one of the staff here knew Zara [Phillips] socially so we got her in. We launched that and that got unbelievable coverage and immediately the phones were red hot with the sort of people you would die to have writing articles wanting to write articles. Certainly all the tabloids, and most of the broadsheets, but also TV and radio. We had them all waiting patiently in line, and we decided how we wanted to release and manage that. They allowed us to control it and allowed us to verify and agree draft copy.
>
> *(Informant: Cheltenham Racecourse)*

Also, where opportunities for media coverage weren't readily apparent to event organisers they were of the opinion that it was possible to manufacture 'news' in order to keep information about their event in the media.

> [several] years ago we had Michael Berkeley write a new piece especially for the festival ... who, for the media, conveniently lost [the transcript of] his opera and then found it. That created a good story.
>
> *(Informant: Cheltenham Borough Council)*

Similarly,

> It would be great if the jockeys were a bit less friendly to each other, that would be a help, a pub brawl wouldn't do anyone any real harm ... and it helps to get the stories about Cheltenham and racing to a much wider audience from those that would normally read the Racing Post or the racing pages.
>
> *(Informant: Cheltenham Racecourse)*

Summary and conclusions

The procurement and staging of high-profile events is becoming a central facet of place marketing strategies (Baker 2007) that are designed to counter the changing industrial and economic base in Western Europe and North America (Baker 2008). The centrality of events to the urban marketing process may relate to their ability to disseminate images of place through the local, national and international media reaching a far greater and far broader audience than conventional place marketing campaigns would do. As a result of this, urban managers are paying increasing attention to the way that locations for which they are responsible are being portrayed in the media. The images of events that are transmitted are believed to act as a mechanism to help in the production of rejuvenated images of place and counter the negative images associated with a declining manufacturing sector. Therefore, events can help to bring a competitive edge to a location and are becoming increasingly important complementary factors in the competition between places to attract footloose industries, entrepreneurs, tourists and residents.

Data generated by interviewing those responsible for managing Cheltenham's events indicates that they had established a working relationship with members of the national media. This relationship allowed those responsible for the promotion and management of Cheltenham's events to feel that they are able to exercise a degree of control over the content and style of the media reports that were subsequently produced. The nature and extent of this relationship and its potential for manipulating the images of place that are contained within the media, however, remains largely unexplored and there is a need for this topic to be investigated further. This relationship has further significance when the importance of the media for the construction of images of place, as identified by this chapter, are considered.

References

Ashworth, G.J. and Voogd, H. (1990) *Selling the City*, London: Belhaven Press.

Avraham, E. (1998) 'Media and the social construction of reality: the coverage of settlements in marginal areas in national newspapers', unpublished PhD thesis, Hebrew University, Jerusalem.

——(2000) 'Cities and their news media images', *Cities* 17(5): 343–70.

——(2004) 'Media strategies for improving an unfavourable city image', *Cities* 21(6): 471–9.

Avraham, E. and Daugherty, D. (2009) '"We're known for oil. But we also have watercolors, acrylics and pastels": media strategies for marketing small cities and towns in Texas', *Cities* 26: 331–8.

Avraham, E. and First, A. (2006) 'Media, power and space: ways of constructing the periphery as the "other"', *Social and Cultural Geography* 7(1): 71–86.

Bailey, J.T. (1989) *Marketing Cities in the 1980s and Beyond*, Chicago: American Economic Development Council.

Baker, B. (2007) *Destination Branding for Small Cities*, London: Creative Leap Books.

Baker, M. (2008) 'Critical success factors in destination marketing', *Tourism and Hospitality Research* 8(2): 79–97.

Barke, M. and Harrop, K. (1994) 'Selling the industrial town: identity image and illusion', in J.R. Gold and S.V. Ward (eds) *Place Promotion: The Use of Publicity and Marketing to Sell Towns and Regions*, Chichester: John Wiley, pp. 93–114.

Bowdin, G.A.J., Allen, J., O'Toole, W., Harris, R. and McDonnell, I. (2006) *Events Management*, Oxford: Elsevier, second edition.

Boyko, C.T. (2008) 'Are you being served? The impacts of a tourist hallmark event on the place meanings of residents', *Event Management* 11: 161–77.

Bradley, A. (2002) 'Media representations of cultural and sports festivals, the marketing of place image and local economic development: the case of Cheltenham, England', unpublished PhD thesis, University of Gloucestershire.

Bradley, A. and Hall, T. (2006) 'The festival phenomenon: festivals, events and the promotion of small urban areas', in D. Bell and M. Jayne (eds) *Small Cities: Urban Experience Beyond the Metropolis*, London: Routledge.

Bradley, A., Hall, T. and Harrison, M. (2002) 'Selling cities: promoting new images for meetings tourism', *Cities: The International Journal of Urban Policy and Planning* 19(1): 61–70.

Brooker, E. and Burgess, J. (2008) 'Marketing destination Niagara effectively through the tourism life cycle', *International Journal of Contemporary Hospitality Management* 20(3): 278–92.

Burd, G. (1977) 'The selling of the sunbelt: civic boosterism in the media', in D.C. Perry and A.J. Watkins, *The Rise of the Sunbelt Cities*, London: Sage, pp. 129–49.

Burgess, J. (1990) 'The production and consumption of environmental meanings in the mass media: a research agenda for the 1990s', *Transactions of the Institute of British Geographers* 15: 139–61.

Chalip, L. (2005) 'Marketing, media and place promotion', in J. Higham (ed.) *Sport Tourism Destinations: Issues, Opportunities and Analysis*, Oxford, Elsevier, pp. 162–76.

Chalip, L. and Green, B.C. (2003) 'Effects of sport event media on destination image and intention to visit', *Journal of Sport Management* 17: 214–34.

Chang, T.C. (1997) 'From "instant Asia" to "multifaceted jewel": urban imaging strategies and tourism development in Singapore', *Urban Geography* 18(6): 542–62.

Cheltenham Borough Council (2001) *Cheltenham: A Splendid Regency Town*. Available at: www.cheltenham. gov.uk/libraries/templates/cheltenham.asp?FolderID=4 (accessed 1 August 2001).

——(2002) *Draft Cultural Strategy*, Cheltenham: Cheltenham Borough Council.

Essex, S. and Chalkey, B. (1998) 'Olympic Games: catalyst of urban change', *Leisure Studies* 7: 187–206.

Fisher, M. and Worpole, K. (eds) (1991) *City Centres, City Cultures*, Manchester: Centre for Local Economic Strategies.

Garcia, B. (2006) *A Retrospective Study: UK National Press Coverage on Liverpool Before, During and After Bidding for European Capital of Culture Status*. Available at: www.liv.ac.uk/impacts08/Papers/Impacts08%28 Dec06%29Press_analysis-96-03-051.pdf (accessed 16 July 2010).

Gay, N.M. (2009) 'New logo part of plan to position St. Lucia as a major player', *Travel Weekly* 68(7): 72.

Getz, D. and Fairley, S. (2004) 'Media management at sport events for destination promotion: case studies and concepts', *Event Management* 8: 127–39.

Green, B.C. (2003) 'Marketing the host city: analyzing exposure generated by a sport event', *International Journal of Sports Marketing and Sponsorship*, December/January: 335–53.

Griffiths, R. (1993) 'The politics of cultural policy in urban regeneration strategies', *Policy and Politics* 13(1): 39–46.

Hall, T. (1998) *Urban Geography*, London: Routledge.

Hankinson, G. (2009) 'Managing destination brands: establishing a theoretical foundation', *Journal of Marketing Management* 25(1/2): 97–115.

Hanna, S.P. (1996) 'Is it Roselyn or is it Cicely? Representations and the ambiguity of place', *Urban Geography* 17(6): 633–49.

Harvey, D. (1984) 'On the history and present condition of geography: an historical materialist manifesto', *The Professional Geographer* 36: 1–10.

——(1989) 'From managerialism to entrepreneurialism: the transformation of urban governance in late capitalism', *Geofragiska Annaler* 71(B): 3–17.

Hede, A. (2005) 'Sports-events, tourism and destination marketing strategies: an Australian case study of Athens 2004 and its media telecast', *Journal of Sport and Tourism* 10(3): 187– 200.

Hudson, S., Getz, D., Miller, G.A. and Brown, G. (2002) 'The future role of sporting events: evaluating the impacts on tourism', Proceedings of the Leisure Futures Conference, Innsbruck, Austria.

Jago, L., Chalip, L., Brown, G., Mules, T. and Ali, S. (2003) 'Building events into destination branding: insights from experts', *Event Management* 8: 3–14.

Judd, D.R. (1995) 'Promoting tourism in US cities', *Tourism Management* 16: 175–87.

Köhler, J., Drengner, J. and Geier, R. (2009) 'The significance of media effects within impact analysis of major sports events: the case of the Bob and Skeleton World Championships 2008', Proceedings of the 17th EASM Conference.

Kunczic, M. (1997) *Images of Nations and International Public Relations*, New York: Lawrence Erlbaum.

Medway, D. and Warnaby, G. (2008) 'Alternative perspectives on marketing and the place brand', *European Journal of Marketing* 42(5/6): 641–53.

Money, R. (1989) 'Making an industry of culture', *Local Work* 10: 1–4.

Montgomery, J. (1990) 'Cities and the art of cultural planning', *Planning Practice and Research* 5(3): 17–24.

O'Brien, D. (2010) "No cultural policy to speak of' – Liverpool 2008', *Journal of Policy Research in Tourism, Leisure and Events* 2(2, July): 113–28.

Page, S. (1995) *Urban Tourism*, London: Routledge.

Pike, S. (2008) *Destination Marketing: An Integrated Marketing Communications Approach*, Oxford: Butterworth-Heinemann.

Reid, G. (2006) 'The politics of city imaging: a case study of the MTV Europe music awards Edinburgh 03', *Event Management* 10: 35–46.

Richards, G. and Palmer, R. (2010) *Eventful Cities: Cultural Management and Urban Revitalisation*, Oxford: Elsevier.

Richards, G. and Wilson, J. (2004) 'The impact of cultural events on city image: Rotterdam, Cultural Capital of Europe 2001', *Urban Studies* 41(10): 1931–51.

Ritchie, B.W., Sanders, D. and Mules, T. (2007) 'Televised events: shaping destination images and perceptions of capital cities from the couch', *International Journal of Event Management Research* 3(2): 12–23.

Rolfe, H. (1992) *Arts Festivals in the UK*, London: Policy Studies Institute.

Smith, A. (2005) 'Re-imaging the city: the value of sports initiatives', *Annals of Tourism Research* 32(1): 217–36.

Tsu-Hong, Y., Da Gama, G. and Rajamohan, S. (2008) 'Perceived image of India by US business travellers', *Marketing Management Journal* 18(1): 121–31.

van der Wagen, L. (2008) *Event Management: For Tourism, Cultural, Business and Sporting Events*, Harlow, UK: Pearson.

Walker, D. (1997) *Public Relations in Local Government: Strategic Approaches to Better Communication*, London: Pitman.

Ward, S.V. (1998) *Selling Places: The Marketing and Promotion of Towns and Cities 1850–2000*, London: E. and F.N. Spon.

White, L. (2008) 'Indigenous Australia and the Sydney 2000 Olympic Games: mediated messages of respect and reconciliation', in J. Ali-Knight, M. Robertson, A. Fyall and A. Ladkin (eds) *International Perspectives of Festivals and Events: Paradigms of Analysis*, London: Elsevier, pp. 97–106.

Whitt, J.A. (1987) 'Mozart in the metropolis: the arts coalition and the urban growth machine', *Urban Affairs Quarterly* 23(1): 15–36.

Wynne, D. (1992) 'Urban regeneration and the arts', in D. Wynne (ed.) *The Culture Industry: The Arts in Urban Regeneration*, Aldershot: Avebury, pp. 84–95.

Youcheng, W. and Krakover, S. (2008) 'Destination marketing: competition, cooperation or coopetition?', *International Journal of Contemporary Hospitality Management* 20(2): 126–41.

20

Staffing for successful events

Having the right skills in the right place at the right time

Clare Hanlon and Leo Jago

Introduction

There is now wide recognition that successful events can have very positive economic, social and cultural benefits for a host region. As staff play such an important role in the operationalization of events, for an event to be successful it is essential that there be sufficient numbers of the right staff at the right place and right time in order to deliver a high-quality event experience. The fact that events are short-term in duration and are staged infrequently adds a level of complexity to the recruitment and training of staff that is not prevalent in most other sectors. Staffing for events is a complex management operation in that it often involves both paid and volunteer staff who provide a range of complementary services. Adding to this complexity is the fact that paid staff can be full-time, part-time or casual, and services can also be provided by a wide range of external contractors.

This chapter examines the relevance of conventional human resource management strategies to the field of events, and assesses the staffing needs of events throughout the event life cycle as there are different needs and constraints across the various stages of the 'pulsating' event cycle (Hanlon and Jago 2009). As staffing needs and constraints can vary depending on whether the event is single pulse or repeat pulse, both types of events are considered.

Conventional human resource management strategies

Human resource management (HRM) strategies in generic business organizations are usually founded upon a platform of stability. In these organizations, staff numbers tend to operate within a fairly tight band and roles are generally well defined as are power and communication channels. The fact that most conventional organizations are stable in terms of their general operations means that there is the opportunity to gradually modify and improve systems over time, with each change being made based on an assessment of what has gone before. Huselid (1995) identified that the most important HRM strategies were selective hiring, performance-based reward systems focused on organizational strategy, and sophisticated training and performance management systems. Although computer technology has helped managers operationalize these strategies, the strategies themselves have changed little over the years. Taylor *et al.* (2008) provide a summation of recent research on 'good' HRM strategies covering selection, training, performance management and reward systems, and show that the strategies have not changed substantially in recent years.

Research has shown that organizational context is a vital component and different strategies work best in different environments. The adoption of HRM strategies and the level of formality within the human resource system are influenced by a complex array of cultural, economic, demographic and organizational factors (Taylor and McGraw 2006), in addition to the organizational size, social conditions and the personalities of staff concerned (Tyson 2006). Nikandrou and Papalexandris (2007) examined strategic HRM practices that distinguish top-performing firms from others. Results showed that successful companies had increased HR involvement in strategic decisions, formalized HR practices, built organizational capability through training and development activities, devolved HR activities to line managers, and emphasized internal labour market opportunities.

The question then arises as to how and when to adopt HRM strategies into an organization with a complex array of factors, such as those associated with an event. In particular, organizations that are established for the purpose of single pulse events have a limited existence and have neither established HRM practices nor an organizational history.

The following sections overview the organizational context in which events operate. The special cyclic nature of events will underpin the discussion of the staffing needs of events for both single and repeat pulse events.

The pulsating event cycle

Toffler (1990) introduced the concept of pulsating organizations that expand and contract over their life cycle. Given the cyclic nature of events, Toffler's concept of 'pulsation' is most apt in describing the manner in which an event operates. Pulsating organizations can be divided into two types. The first is a repeat pulse organization that 'expands and contracts in a regular rhythm', which occurs around a periodic cycle, such as the annual Chelsea Flower Show or the Edinburgh Military Tattoo. The second is an event that grows, declines and then is dismantled; it is a one-off event that is not repeated in the same location. These organizations are known as 'single pulse', and examples include concerts such as the Billion Hands (2008) and the Hope for Haiti (2010). It also includes events such as the Olympic Games that are not repeated as far as a single destination is concerned. Whilst these two categories of pulsating event organizations have much in common, each category demonstrates a range of distinct characteristics. The manner in which staffing for events has to be organized and managed is a dimension of event management that must be closely aligned to the pulsating nature of events, as will be shown in this chapter.

Hanlon (2003) further developed the pulsating concept and related it to major sporting event organizations (MSEOs), which operate around an event cycle. Generally, they operate with a small core of staff and have to expand quickly and substantially in the lead-up to an event. Hanlon (2003) found that regular pulsating events, such as the Australian Open Tennis Championship (AOTC) operate in four stages, namely pre-event, during the event, post-event and throughout the remainder of the year. The staffing requirements can vary substantially in each of these stages. In the case of the AOTC, the core staff of 108 who are employed in permanent positions expands to a workforce of over 1,500 for the two-week event each year and then shrinks back to its core staff number (Tennis Australia 2007). This massive increase in staff numbers required during different stages of the event cycle highlights the unique nature of events and the fact that HRM practices that are so successful in conventional organizations may not apply to event organizations.

From an HRM perspective, combining the pulsating nature of an event with the event cycle produces staff challenges. The pulsating workforce dynamic can present a daunting landscape for human resource managers. One example is from Hanlon and Stewart's (2006: 83) research, where human resource managers from major sport events referred to the management of their event staff as an 'explosion'. When staffing numbers dramatically increase in the lead-up to an event, managers felt that they literally 'lose control'. One manager stated that he managed thirty staff for three months and then, within only a few days, staff numbers 'explode' to 3,000 on-site staff, which did not include the players and media, who also had to be considered in the mix. This study highlighted the fact that a pulsating event cycle produces unique staffing requirements that result in the need to modify conventional HRM strategies in order to suit an event setting.

Event characteristics

Van der Wagen (2007) identified a number of characteristics of events that differentiated them from other activities. These characteristics include:

- Events are generally short in duration.
- Some events are place-dependent.
- Many events depend heavily on volunteers to work alongside paid employees.
- Events and their management cannot be seen or managed in isolation as they regularly form a central focus within the wider tourism, community and economic development agendas at community, regional or national levels.

Event researchers have identified additional event characteristics, many relating to staffing that go beyond those proposed by van der Wagen (2007), and these are listed below:

- the pulsating effect of staff movements (Toffler 1990);
- the complex structure and multi-skill requirements of staff (Challadurai 1999);
- the high proportion of staff on short-term contracts (Compton and Nankervis 1998);
- the varied range of staff categories (Crawford 1991; Graham et al. 1995);
- the event cycle (Hanlon 2003).

These event-specific characteristics further highlight the fact that event organizations are quite different from conventional organizations, particularly in relation to the staffing dimension, which can pose problems in simply applying conventional HRM strategies to event organizations that are pulsating in nature. The question then arises as to what staffing strategies are required to maximize overall performance during the pulsating event cycle.

Staffing needs during the pulsating event cycle

The number of event characteristics that were highlighted by researchers in the previous section signifies that staffing needs in event organizations are different from those in generic business organizations. A number of researchers identified the need to formalize HRM strategies for both paid and volunteer event staff as they generally have quite different roles, motives and commitment. Parent (2008), for example, identified that specific HRM strategies were required for paid and volunteer staff in relation to management and roles, leadership, motivations and teamwork. In addition, common HRM strategies that frequently arose in Hanlon and Jago's (2009) research were selection and induction of staff, managing teams, and retention of staff.

In addition to the need to identify HRM strategies tailored for event management organizations, there is a need to identify the timing as to when these HRM strategies apply within an event cycle as well as to consider the differences between single and repeat pulse organizations. This section endeavours to address these needs by identifying the relevant HRM strategies that need to be incorporated into the four stages on an event cycle, namely pre-event, during an event, post-event and throughout the remainder of the year. The discussion also looks at how strategies may differ between single and repeat pulse event organizations.

Pre-event

The lead-up to an event is an intensive stage where timelines are tight, budgets are fixed and staffing becomes an important priority. Hanlon and Stewart (2006) recommended five HRM strategies to incorporate in a customized HRM framework for the purpose of an event. These strategies can be established during the pre-event stage. First is to establish an organization structure that has the flexibility to be expanded and contracted. Second is to incorporate core competencies for all positions and introduce a stringent selection process. Third is to formulate an induction process for new, permanent and returning staff in each staff category. Staff manuals and active group sessions are important components of these induction processes. Fourth is to create processes for establishing clearly defined and goal-directed teams. The final strategy is to develop retention strategies for each staff category at different stages of the event cycle.

Poor timing and implementation of a HRM strategy could indicate to staff that management is not treating the staffing component seriously, which could have negative consequences for the event's performance. For example, Parent and Seguin's (2007) research identified that the timing of when to appoint members to the event organizing committee can be a cause for concern. Their research found that when a committee member was appointed too late in the process it reflected badly on the attitude management was perceived to have towards the role that member played in the development of the event.

Each 'category' of staff needs to be managed differently. For example, volunteer staff need to be managed differently from paid staff because volunteers are more likely to leave an organization abruptly if they become dissatisfied (Taylor and McGraw 2006). Blanc (1999) explained that tasks allocated to volunteers could distance them from their primary source of motivation to volunteer for the event. Volunteers are often motivated to volunteer for an event because of their passion for the theme of the event, unlike paid staff who more often are motivated by the compensation they receive and are thus often less able to leave at short notice. As a result, managers need to be mindful of this motivation issue when determining tasks, recruiting, training and supervising volunteers (Giannoulakis et al. 2008).

The time spent to design, develop and evaluate the effectiveness of the HRM strategies during the lead-up to an event would generally be different in a single pulse event organization from a repeat pulse event organization. For example, for a one-off event that has paid and volunteer staff, the pre-event stage will often not allow for the introduction of a more formalized HRM framework, let alone one that is tailored for each staff category. Since the event will not be repeated, the formalization process is often seen to be a waste of valuable resources for no long-term benefit. For a repeat pulse organization, however, there is generally seen to be merit in introducing a more formalized HRM process as it is recognized that the benefits will be recouped over time.

In addition, management in a single pulse organization must contend with an environment that presents no organizational history or established relationships to assist the development of its workforce (Hanlon and Jago 2009). Managers in single pulse environments are unable to draw upon the corporate knowledge of an organization in the development and management of the staff, despite the complex profiles of their workforces (Hanlon 2003). They can, however, take advantage of staff who have worked in other single pulse organizational environments, in order to draw upon their knowledge gained from previous single event experience. The fact that there are many single pulse events in some destinations allows them to develop an internal labour market of event expertise within the destination that can be drawn upon by different events. This allows single pulse events to derive some of the benefits experienced by repeat pulse events without having to make the same investment.

During an event

The time taken to select and induct staff and form teams during the pre-event stage makes it vital to ensure that measures are in place to retain these staff for the duration of their event contract. This particularly applies to events that are conducted for a period lasting more than just a few days. For example, the Australian Open Tennis Championships is a two-week event. After the first week, the number of players in the tournament has decreased substantially and there are fewer spectators overall. As noted in Hanlon's (2003) research, halfway through such events there seems to be 'flatness' in the attitudes of personnel. To assist with staff 'flatness' for events that are conducted over a longer duration, motivation was frequently referred to by researchers (Giannoulakis *et al.* 2008; Parent 2008) as being an important issue to address within the event. Motivation in the form of rewarding, recognizing and empowering individuals (Taylor and McGraw 2006) was important to incorporate during an event where the environment is rapidly changing. This needs to be coupled with appropriate retention strategies during this stage of the event cycle to overcome the problem of key staff leaving during the most important period.

The pressure associated with managing staff during an event, particularly one that is conducted over more than a few days, creates demand for effective team management and teamwork practices. For example, in their research on the Sydney Organizing Committee for the Olympic Games, Halbwirth and Toohey (2001) identified the effective utilization of a formal information system to assist in the creation of a shared learning culture amongst its varied staff categories. The virtual shared workspace and information-sharing portal helped develop a sense of community amongst staff, whereby staff were encouraged to share information rather than store knowledge. This strategy improved relationships amongst staff.

Irrespective of whether it is a single or repeat pulse event, research highlights that staff need effective team management, teamwork and motivation practices. However, the need to incorporate team management and retention strategies during this stage of an event may be more intense in single compared to repeat pulse event organizations. This is largely due to the fact that staff, paid in particular, tend to be on the lookout for positions elsewhere, knowing that their involvement with the single pulse event will be coming to an end. Staff in repeat pulse event organizations often have ongoing opportunities owing to the recurring nature of the event.

Post-event

This stage is often known as the 'trough' stage (Hanlon 2003), where the excitement of the event has finished and the majority of paid and volunteer staff have departed. Team and retention strategies for staff who remain in the event organization post the event are vital (Hanlon and Jago 2004), in order to overcome the deflated attitude created after the event has concluded.

After an event, obvious differences between single and repeat pulse event organizations appear. Instead of retaining staff for the longer term, managers in single pulse event organizations need to motivate particular staff to remain for the purpose of 'closing down' an event. Holding these staff is often not easy, as the excitement of the event has passed and staff need to find other employment opportunities. Therefore, different team and retention strategies are required for the limited time that remains before the organization ceases to exist. Providing payment incentives could be one way of holding staff during this final stage. In a repeat pulse event organization, conducting a 'thank you' function after the event and performance appraisals a couple of months after the event would be more appropriate.

Throughout the remainder of the year

This stage of an event applies only to repeat pulse organizations. Hanlon's (2003) research identified that when the hype of an event had dissolved in repeat pulse organizations, the attitude, particularly amongst full-time staff, moves towards 'it's going to be the same event next year', and so is their role.

In order to prevent this attitude forming for full-time staff, repeat pulse event organizations such as the Australian Tennis Open and the Australian Formula 1 Grand Prix organize specific retention strategies such as staff appraisals and career management programmes, as well as encouraging staff to attend related national and international events (Hanlon and Jago 2004). One of the greatest HRM challenges for repeat pulse event organizations is to retain seasonal staff from one event to the next (Hanlon and Jago 2004). During this stage, managers need to motivate staff beyond the specifics and timing of their employment contract by maintaining contact with them in order to try and motivate them to return for the following event (Hanlon and Jago 2004).

The timing of staff needs

This chapter has identified the importance of incorporating the needs of event staff within each of the four stages of an event cycle in order to assist in the performance and retention of paid and volunteer staff. This chapter has also identified that, although similar, the staffing needs and strategies for single and repeat pulse event organizations vary during some stages. To illustrate what has been discussed, Table 20.1 is presented. Table 20.1 highlights that the first three stages of an event cycle are applicable to single pulse event organizations whilst all four stages of an event cycle apply to a repeat pulse event organization. The table also illustrates the different categories of staff, whereby each HRM strategy needs to cater for their different needs. For example, in the pre-event stage when establishing an effective team, consideration needs to be given to whether strategies required for full-time staff are different from those for volunteers, in order for staff to gain a sense of identity and operate at optimal levels.

The discussion in this chapter has proposed a number of approaches to the HRM of events that could be used to enhance their overall performance. The next section contains two case studies relating first to a single pulse event and second to a repeat pulse event. The first event is

Table 20.1 The life cycle of pulsating event organizations

Pulsating event organizations	*Event cycle*	*Staff category*	*Strategies to tailor according to each staff category*
Single pulse Repeat pulse	Pre-event	Full time Part time Casual Seasonal External contractors Volunteer	Establish a flexibly expanded organizational structure Incorporate core competencies and implement a stringent selection process Formulate an induction process for new and/or permanent and returning staff and implement active group sessions and on-line manuals Create and implement a process for establishing clearly defined and goal-directed teams, which gain a sense of identity and determines the team outcomes Develop retention strategies
Single pulse Repeat pulse	During the event		Ensure teams have a sense of identity Implement retention strategies
Single pulse Repeat pulse	Post-event		Ensure teams have a sense of identity Implement retention strategies
Repeat pulse	Throughout the remainder of the year		Ensure teams have a sense of identity Implement retention strategies

World Youth Day 2008, a single pulse event that was held over eleven days, whilst the second is the Australian Open Tennis Championships (AOTC), a repeat pulse event that is conducted annually over two weeks. These case studies are included to highlight the HRM strategies that have been adopted in specific cases, in order to compare expected approaches with the actual approaches that were incorporated. In doing so, gaps can be identified within stages of an event. For example, with the organization that conducted the single pulse event, there was a notable absence of post-event retention strategies for volunteers who remained working at the organization to perform tasks immediately after the event. This simple exercise shows the importance of incorporating HRM strategies within the stages of an event to ensure the timing of implementing strategies are coherent throughout an event cycle.

It could be noted that organizations that exist for the purpose of a single pulse event do not have time to formulate staffing needs around the three stages of an event. On the other hand, organizations that conduct repeat pulse events have time to reflect and continually improve practices associated with HRM to assist with staff satisfaction. This was the case with the AOTC, where a range of strategies were incorporated throughout the four stages of the event cycle.

One notable similarity that existed between both types of event organizations was the reliance on electronic communication. The enormity of casual, contract and volunteer staff numbers meant that both organizations were reliant on electronic means for recruiting and inducting, and for the repeat pulse organization such communication was important for training, development and retention. At times, similar HRM strategies that were incorporated by both organizations complement those identified in Table 20.1. For example, online induction manuals were incorporated during the pre-event stage.

World Youth Day case study

World Youth Day that involved a Papal visit to Australia in 2008 was conducted across two States in three different locations: Sydney, regional Sydney and Victoria. Fifty thousand pilgrims attended during the eleven-day event. Despite this being an event that is conducted every four years and held in different locations around the world, no post-event report is provided to the organizers of the following event. Therefore, minimal information is provided from one event to the next.

Pre-event

According to one of the managers employed two years prior to the event, there was a general lack of knowledge as to the enormity of the event, and timelines and budget were tight. As a result, 90 per cent of staff were recruited in May or June, prior to the event in July. In addition, event staff managers were dealing with religious leaders where varied considerations had to be made with limited background knowledge upon which to draw.

Online communication was the main source of communication used by the organizers to paid and volunteer staff and pilgrims. The majority of staff were volunteers. The online administration system streamlined communications that helped organize staff to work with other parishes, schools and religious organizations, both internationally and locally (Days in the dioceses: Melbourne 2008).

Both NSW and Victoria had respective websites for interested volunteers and pilgrims. Volunteer job descriptions and selection criteria were placed on the website and applications were submitted online. Centralized group induction sessions were conducted and an online resource manual was provided for volunteer staff. If volunteers were unable to attend one of the induction sessions, the online manual was the source for induction and training. Individual induction sessions were conducted for full-time staff and the online manual used for referral. A train-the-trainer programme was incorporated whereby Coordinators attended four key induction sessions and then rolled out community programmes for the purpose of the event. In addition, the Coordinators attended a training session that included information on Code of Conduct, legal matters and emergency procedures. The online manual also provided incentives for volunteers, for example why become a Coordinator and the highlights that were to be experienced (Days in the dioceses: Melbourne 2008).

During the event

In order to retain staff, full-time staff were offered financial incentives, and the majority of staff who were volunteers were retained through motivational mechanisms such as verbal recognition that occurred both independently and during meetings. Since many volunteers were retired workers and committed to the church ethos, they remained loyal to the event because of their religious beliefs (Days in the dioceses: Melbourne 2008).

Post-event

The same strategies were used as during the event.

This case study clearly highlights the characteristics of an event that were noted by researchers earlier in this chapter: for example, events depending heavily on volunteers to work alongside paid employees (Van der Wagen 2007) and the high proportion of staff on short-term contracts (Compton and Nankervis, 1998). However, one notable point that became obvious in this case study was the special features that could be associated with events. In this case, religion was the feature. The volunteers were committed to the church ethos and thus had a strong commitment to assist with the success of World Youth Day. These people were committed to what the event represented, namely a cele-bration of their religion. Consequently, implementing retention strategies for the majority of staff at World Youth Day may not have been as intense as at other events. The life cycle of a single pulse event organization was evident that incorporated strategies tailored for each staff category.

Australian Open Tennis Championship case study

The AOTC is an annual two-week event that is organized by Tennis Australia in Mel-bourne, Australia. Evidence of continued HRM improvement is noted in the Annual Reports (Tennis Australia 2007, 2009). The HRM strategies can be identified within the four stages of an event cycle.

Pre-event

The majority of staff comprise casual and contract staff and appointments begin at least eight months prior to the event, therefore e-learning involving a self-paced induction process is provided. New systems are continually incorporated to make HRM a smoother process for staff. Recently, the HRM electronic information system, called ConnX, incor-porated new functions and modules for staff such as ilearn-elearning training platform, occupational health and safety, performance development and employee information. The Australian Open Event Safety Management System is continually updated, where new safety initiatives are instigated and resources such as safety cards provided to media during the induction and training sessions.

During the event

Owing to the length of the event, team debriefs and activities are performed. Hanlon's (2003) research found that team activities were conducted after the first week of the event to further motivate staff. The reason was that many participants and crowds had departed and the atmosphere was not as intense.

Post-event

Employee communication sessions and e-mail bulletins are incorporated to assist with developing a 'one team' culture. Performance appraisals and career management programmes are conducted.

Throughout the remainder of the year

A centralized electronic application service called E-recruitment enabled Tennis Australia to reflect on its service and further improve on strategies for the following year. For example, after the conclusion of the annual tournament, further improvement that enhanced management performance, improved communication with applicants and reduced manual labour contributed to the service's success the following year. In addition, contract organizations have been employed to consult with managers and staff to establish credible remuneration packages and to establish an employee mobility policy and framework to ensure that consistent and transparent decision-making, practice and benefit provision exists.

Strategies for staff retention include monthly drinks to celebrate occasions and share information, an annual Tennis Australian Conference, health and lifestyle assessments, discounts to the gymnasium and sponsor-related resources such as Kia vehicles and Optus mobile telephones, a Fun club for internal and external social events, counselling services and weekly fruit delivery. A leadership development programme was established, which amongst other things fosters collaborate relationship building between varied management levels.

In contrast to World Youth Day, the nature of the AOTC was different; there was a notable absence of volunteers, the feature was sport and stringent strategies were incorporated to ensure staff retention. At the same time, the life cycle of a repeat pulse organization was evident that incorporated tailored strategies for each staff category. Although the AOTC relied heavily on volunteers until about a decade ago, excluding the reliance on ball kids, the use of volunteers was phased out for a variety of reasons including the need to more effectively maintain continuity and standards from year to year and for occupation health and safety issues.

Whilst the AOTC is an annual event, unlike World Youth Day, and relies on a larger percentage of paid staff, passion for tennis is an important driver for staff at the AOTC in a similar way to religious commitment being a key driver for staff and volunteers at World Youth Day.

Conclusion and future directions

This chapter has highlighted the fact that staffing for events is both different and more complex than staffing for conventional organizations. This is due to the pulsating nature of the event cycle and the massive pressure that event organizers face in having a 'successful event on the night'. For most events, there is little scope to have a 'soft launch' to test people and systems. As events are so heavily reliant on staff for their success, it is critical to ensure the right skills are in the right place at the right time.

Whilst research has helped identify the range of HRM strategies required for event staff, literature is sparse as to the most effective time to implement these strategies to maximize the benefits for staff and the event itself. The case studies used in this chapter have highlighted the fact that there are two distinct types of events, namely a single pulse event and a repeat pulse event. It has been found, however, that staffing needs for both types of events can be formulated within the three or four stages of an event cycle, depending on whether it is a single or repeat pulse event. The case studies highlighted that the length of each cycle depended on whether it was a single or repeat pulse event. For example, the majority of volunteer staff were appointed one to two months prior to World Youth Day 2008, thus intense induction sessions and electronic communication systems were utilized during the time-poor pre-event cycle, whereas the majority of casual or contract staff are appointed up to eight months prior to the AOTC and a self-paced induction process is utilized during the time-rich pre-event cycle.

The feasibility of formalizing a structured human resource plan within each stage of the event life cycle could be questioned in single pulse event organizations such as the one organizing

World Youth Day 2008, where timing is tight. However, demonstrating how the HRM strategies implemented in this case study could be placed within the respective stages of an event life cycle highlights how gaps can quickly be identified. In addition, it would ensure the timing of implementing these strategies are coherent to the event.

More work is required to fine tune the staffing needs during the pulsating event cycle, in order to maximize the overall performance of staff. In destinations where there is an event calendar offering events throughout the year, there is the opportunity to explore and exploit the benefits that can be derived from developing an internal labour market (ILM) for events within the destination. Whilst a single event may not be able to employ full-time staff where their skills can be developed over time, facilitating an ILM where staff rotate between events across the year mean that the skills needed for the sector to prosper can develop over time. The benefits of such an endeavour would apply to both single and repeat pulse events, where HRM strategies during the life cycle of an event may not be as intense because of the competencies gained by staff in similar events.

As events have become such an important element in the tourism product in many destinations, providing leisure and tourism activities for local residents and tourists alike, it is crucial that such events are delivered to a high standard. With consumers becoming increasingly discerning, an event that does not exceed expectations will quickly fail. Staff, both paid and unpaid, are crucial to the delivery of the event experience, and their ability to perform at the expected level is essential. Selecting, training and retaining staff with the requisite skills underpins the success of events and, given that the characteristics of events pose special challenges not faced by more conventional organizations, it is important that more is done to tailor HRM strategies to event staff.

Further reading

Baum, T., Deery, M., Hanlon, C., Lockstone, L. and Smith, K. (eds) (2009) *People and Work in Events and Conventions: A Research Perspective*, Oxford: CABI International. (An analysis of varied employees and their event needs.)

Hanlon, C.M. and Jago, L. (2004) 'The challenge of retaining personnel in major sport event organizations', *Event Management* 9: 39–50. (A guide to retaining varied staff categories according the four stages of an event cycle.)

Parent, M. and Seguin, B. (2007) 'Factors that led to the drowning of a world championship organizing committee: a stakeholder approach', *European Sport Management Quarterly* 7(2): 187–212. (Points to consider when dealing with and managing stakeholders.)

Taylor, T. and McGraw, P. (2006) 'Exploring human resource management practices in non-profit sport organizations', *Sport Management Review* 9(3): 229–52. (Applying conventional human resource management practices to a sport community.)

Tyson, S. (2006) *Essentials of HRM*, Oxford: Elsevier, fifth edition). (The development and contribution HRM makes to organizations.)

van der Wagen, L. (2007) *Managing the Event Workforce*, Oxford: Butterworth-Heinemann. (Event-specific HRM strategies.)

References

Blanc, X. (1999) 'Managerial problems in combining sports projects with volunteerism', paper presented at the Volunteers, Global Society, and the Olympic Movement Conference, Lausanne, 24–26 November.

Challadurai, N. (1999) *Human Resource Management in Sport and Recreation*, Champaign, IL: Human Kinetics.

Compton, R.L. and Nankervis, A.R. (1998) *Effective Recruitment and Selection Practices*, Sydney, Australia: CCN, second edition.

Crawford, R. (1991) *In the Era of Human Capital: The Emergence of Talent, Intelligence, and Knowledge and the World-wide Economic Force and What it Means to Managers and Investors*, New York: Harper Business.

Days in the dioceses: Melbourne (2008) July. Available at: www.did08.com/?id=programsresources (accessed 2 June 2010).

Giannoulakis, C., Wang, C. and Gray, D. (2008) 'Measuring volunteer motivation in mega-sporting events', *Event Management* 11: 191–200.

Graham, S., Goldblatt, J.L. and Delph, L. (1995) *The Ultimate Guide to Sport Event Management and Marketing*, Homewood, IL: Richard Irwin.

Green, B.C. and Chalip, L. (1998) 'Sport volunteers: research agenda and application', *Sport Marketing Quarterly* 7(2): 14–23.

Halbwirth, S. and Toohey, K. (2001) 'The Olympic Games and knowledge management: a case study of the Sydney organising committee of the Olympic Games', *European Sport Management Quarterly* 1(2): 91–111.

Hanlon, C.M. (2003) 'Managing the pulsating effect in major sport event organizations', PhD thesis, University of Victoria, Melbourne.

Hanlon, C.M. and Jago, L. (2004) 'The challenge of retaining personnel in major sport event organizations', *Event Management* 9: 39–50.

——(2009) 'Managing pulsating major sporting event organizations', in T. Baum, M. Deery, C. Hanlon, L. Lockstone and K. Smith (eds) *People and Work in Events and Conventions: A Research Perspective*, Oxford: CABI International, pp. 93–107.

Hanlon, C.M. and Stewart, B. (2006) 'Managing personnel in major sport event organizations: what strategies are required?', *Event Management* 10: 77–88.

Huselid, M.A. (1995) 'The impact of human resource management practices on turnover, productivity and corporate financial performance', *Academy of Management Journal* 38(3): 635–72.

Lockstone, L. and Baum, T. (2009) 'The public face of event volunteering at the 2006 Commonwealth Games: the media perspective', *Managing Leisure* 14: 38–56.

Nikandrou, I. and Papalexandris, N. (2007) 'The impact of M& A experience on strategic HRM practices and organizational effectiveness: evidence from Greek firms', Human Resource Management Journal 17 (2): 99–121.

Parent, M.M. (2008) 'Evolution and issue patterns for major-sport-event organizing committees and their stakeholders', *Journal of Sport Management* 22: 135–64.

Parent, M.M. and Seguin, B. (2007) 'Factors that led to the drowning of a world championship organizing committee: a stakeholder approach', *European Sport Management Quarterly* 7(2): 187–212.

Strigas, A.D. (2003) 'Motivational factors for student volunteers and the development of an incentive typology in sport settings', *Research Quarterly for Exercise and Sport* 74: 90.

Taylor, T. and McGraw, P. (2006) 'Exploring human resource management practices in non-profit sport organizations', *Sport Management Review* 9(3): 229–52.

Taylor, T., Doherty, A. and McGraw, P. (2008) *Managing People in Sport Organizations: A Strategic Human Resource Management Perspective*, Oxford: Elsevier.

Tennis Australia (2007) *Tennis Australia 2006/07 Annual Report*, Melbourne: Tennis Australia.

——(2009) *Tennis Australia 2008/09 Annual Report*, Melbourne: Tennis Australia.

Toffler, A. (1990) *Power Shift*, New York: Bantam Books.

Tyson, S. (2006) 'The contribution of HRM to organizational performance', in S. Tyson, *Essentials of HRM*, Oxford: Elsevier, fifth edition.

van der Wagen, L. (2007) *Managing the Event Workforce*, Oxford: Butterworth-Heinemann.

21

Volunteering and events

Katie Schlenker, Deborah Edwards and Stephen Wearing

Introduction

An event workforce comprises a range of different types of employees including paid staff, external suppliers, contractors and volunteers. Event organisers depend on volunteers who are recognised as an integral part of the workforce at local, regional, national and international events. This chapter describes how event organisations face a series of unique challenges and additional complexity when they are recruiting, training, managing, rewarding and retaining a volunteer workforce. With events increasingly depending on the volunteer worker, it has become essential to develop mechanisms of management that ensure the provision of a positive and satisfying volunteer experience, and the retention of volunteers. Drawing from extant literature on event management, this chapter focuses on the management challenges faced by event organisations in incorporating volunteer labour into their workforce and the management strategies used to overcome these challenges. The chapter begins with an introduction to volunteering and events and the episodic nature of event volunteering. There are a number of elements important to the management of event volunteers which include training and induction, motivating, rewarding and retaining volunteers. Managing these elements well can assure volunteers have a positive event experience and will encourage the volunteers continued contribution for future events. The chapter concludes with an overview of suggested areas for further research, the findings of which could enhance the volunteer experience and the contributions they can make to the success of the events sector.

Volunteering and events

Volunteers are an important part of a diverse event workforce, which can comprise a range of different types of employees including paid staff, external suppliers and contractors (Harrington *et al.* 2000; Green and Chalip 2004; Holmes 2008; Lockstone *et al.* 2010). A major challenge facing the event human resource manager relates to the 'pulsating' nature of events. 'Pulsating organisations' is a term coined by Toffler in 1990, to explain the expansion of organisations in their workforce numbers in the lead up to an event and their contraction, after the completion of the event (cited in Hanlon and Cuskelly 2002). By virtue of their 'pulsating' nature, special events organisations are different from 'generic organisations' in their structure and functioning and in particular the challenges they face in recruiting and inducting a workforce (Hanlon and Cuskelly 2002; Monga 2006). Complexity arises from the multi-stage cycle of events management (pre-, during and post-event), which is not experienced by generic organisations (Hanlon and Jago 2004). This pulsating nature of events is one reason why volunteers are required to assist in the event workforce. Volunteers represent a resource for event organisers to draw on quickly to expand the event workforce at different times throughout the event lifecycle. Not only do volunteers enable the rapid expansion of the 'pulsating' event workforce, they also represent an economically beneficial resource to event organisations (Green and Chalip 2004; Bryen and Madden 2006; Baum and Lockstone 2007). Volunteers contribute to special events by offering 'their labour, knowledge, skills and experience' for no remuneration to the event (Monga 2006: 47). In this way, the use of volunteers as part of the event workforce allows an event organisation to reduce its costs, while still delivering a quality event 'greater than its immediate financial resources would allow' (Monga 2006: 49). In fact, mega events such as the Olympic Games would not be able to run without large numbers of volunteers (Giannoulakis *et al.* 2008).

The significance of volunteers as part of the event workforce is well acknowledged and research has documented the vital contribution they make in a range of areas, from event planning right through to operational delivery (Cuskelly *et al.* 2004; Green and Chalip 2004; Bryen and Madden 2006; Baum and Lockstone 2007). Holmes and Smith (2009) refer to two types of event volunteers, core and non-core. Core volunteers usually give a substantial time and responsibility commitment to an event organisation while 'non-core' volunteers tend to fill operational roles, committing to intense work over fewer hours. It is acknowledged that 'the majority of events conducted rarely accommodate permanent long-term employment' (Ingerson 2001: 55), but rather event organisations tend to operate with a smaller number of core staff throughout the event lifecycle, supplemented with 'periodic, large scale infusions of workers' (Getz 2007: 286), who often come in the form of core and non-core volunteers.

Lynch (2000) identifies at least three different types of volunteers and their roles, with the level and complexity of their responsibility differing accordingly. He gives an account of the recruitment process for the 2000 Olympic and Paralympic Games, where approximately 50,000 volunteers were needed to make these events run successfully. 'Pioneer' volunteers are those who were involved from the beginning of the project and involved in all aspects of the organisation. 'Specialist' volunteers were those with specific skills in technology, sports, languages, media, communications and so on, while 'generalist' volunteers were involved in spectator services, transport, accreditation and logistics. Roles undertaken by volunteers in the National Folk Festival in Canberra, an annual event that attracts more than 42,000 people, highlights the depth, breadth and integral nature of volunteer involvement in the event. The roles included 'key volunteer coordinators' and their teams of 'core volunteers', working in the operational areas of 'ticket office, performer reception, festival shop, childcare, Master of Ceremonies, festival office, camping and parking, security, bar, performer transport and instrument lock-up, stall holders, garbology, and the volunteer management team … virtually every operational aspect of the event' (Hodges 1998: 22–3).

Episodic nature of event volunteering

Event volunteering is commonly referred to as 'episodic' because of the pulsating nature of events (Baum and Lockstone 2007; Holmes and Smith 2009; Lockstone *et al.* 2010). Episodic volunteering represents short-term volunteering assignments or 'discrete task-specific volunteering projects' in place of more traditional ongoing commitments to an organisation (Bryen and Madden 2006: 1).

Hustinx and Lammertyn (2004) describe episodic volunteers as having a 'distant' relationship with an organisation, characterised by their short-term and/or infrequent involvement with the organisation. In general, episodic volunteers demand a high level of flexibility and mobility and prefer functionally oriented roles (Hustinx and Lammertyn 2004). Macduff (2005) describes three main types of episodic volunteering. 'Temporary' volunteering is described as a short period of volunteering, e.g. for a few hours or one day. 'Interim' volunteering describes volunteering for a defined period of less than six months on a regular basis, e.g. volunteering for a one-month project, followed by a three-month project. The third type of episodic volunteering is 'occasional' volunteering, which describes volunteering for short periods of time at regular intervals, e.g. volunteering for an event.

A further classification of volunteer involvement in relation to occasional volunteering is volunteer 'bounce-back' (Bryen and Madden 2006). This term describes volunteers who 'return or re-engage with a single organisation in a series of episodic relationships' (Lockstone *et al.* 2010: 112). This is evidenced when volunteers who return each year to volunteer their time, skills and/or knowledge at a recurring event (Bryen and Madden 2006; Holmes *et al.* 2010). Such episodic volunteering suggests 'a regular temporal occurrence but with an ongoing connection to the event', thus increasing the complexity of the relationship between the volunteer and the event organisation (Holmes *et al.* 2010: 258). The episodic nature of events, the diverse range of personnel required, the rapid expansion and contraction of staff and a reliance on the use of temporary work teams results in a high level of operational complexity (Hanlon and Stewart 2006). The dependency of events on volunteers means that encouraging, managing, sustaining and rewarding them is critical to the success of an event.

Management of event volunteers

Much of the research and improved understanding of event volunteers is drawn from the generic volunteer and more recently sport event literature with the latter arising from studies focusing on major and mega sport events. This is not problematic as issues related to encouraging, managing, sustaining and rewarding volunteers are similar across all sectors that utilise volunteers and in which volunteers act as both hosts and guests (Edwards and Graham 2006; Baum and Lockstone 2007; Holmes and Edwards 2008). The event literature has taken a managerialist approach suggesting that emphasis be placed on the recruitment, management, work performance and rewarding volunteers (Chappelet 2000; Coyne and Coyne 2001; Ralston *et al.* 2005; Chanavat and Ferrand 2010). Such an approach is not surprising given the demanding environment of episodic events. Although each of these tasks is dealt with separately the elements within them overlap. For example, rewarding volunteers is closely linked with their reasons for volunteering (Edwards 2005) and it is necessary to identify the reasons that motivate individuals to become volunteers, to assist managers to make appropriate recruiting decisions (Bang, Alexandris and Ross 2009).

Recruitment, training and induction

Recruiting volunteers requires different strategies depending on the size of the event. Chappelet (2000) argues that it is not too difficult to recruit volunteers for a mega event as there are many individuals who are keen to be a part of a major event, particularly one in which the reputation of the event is high (Coyne and Coyne 2001), mega sporting events often receive more applications than they are able to accommodate (Baum and Lockstone 2007). However, through when significant numbers of volunteers and various skills are required to host mega events multiple strategies are required to reach this wide audience (Smith and Fox

2007), including utilising volunteer resource centres (Smith and Lockstone 2009), identifying organisations likely to contain potential volunteers ('sourcing') (Lechat 2006; Bang, Alexandris and Ross 2009) and involving well-known figures as ambassadors for the event (Lechat 2006).

Local community events are often managed and staged solely by volunteers (Getz 1991; Small *et al.* 2005). It is most common for these events to recruit from their local communities by word of mouth, the local paper, special interest groups or a local volunteer resource centre (Smith and Lockstone 2009). However, the need to ensure a suitable supply of people to stage the event often results in event organisers over-recruiting volunteers as a strategy to ensure successful outcomes (Monga 2006; Holmes and Smith 2009). This over-recruitment can typically lead to higher training and induction costs, as well as an under-utilisation of the pool of volunteers. Poor management can exacerbate this problem further, particularly if volunteers are mismatched to tasks. Finding the balance between recruiting the right number of volunteers and volunteer satisfaction marks the uniqueness of the relationship as compared to generic employee–employer relationships, with much of the coercive or remunerative influence over volunteers missing.

The event literature argues that recruitment should be followed by an induction process, stating that induction is an extremely important element of preparedness for all events (Hanlon and Cuskelly 2002; Hanlon and Jago 2004). Induction can inculcate staff into cultural norms such as multicultural awareness and respect, organisational culture, management practices and a sense of community spirit and engagement (Presbury and Edwards 2010). This is necessary as event organisers will need to ensure their volunteers are aware of the role they will play in the event, along with a recognition of their importance to the success of the event (Chappelet 2000). In a review of the induction processes of the Australian Formula 1 Grand Prix and the Australian Open Tennis, Hanlon and Cuskelly (2002) found that induction was necessary not just for new managers but for all management categories (including volunteers) in the organisations prior to any event.

Training is seen as a vital element for assisting volunteers to realise best practice work standards (Holmes and Smith 2009). For example, volunteer training in risk minimisation or emergency procedures can increase knowledge and improve control measures in the management of emergency situations as evidenced in European outdoor music festivals (Earl *et al.* 2004).

Training plans that incorporate 'test runs' can provide excellent 'rehearsal' opportunities for volunteers prior to the actual event. For example it is estimated that 10,000 volunteers for the Sydney Olympics had the opportunity to practise and fine-tune their skills on one of the forty world-class sporting events that were scheduled to take place before the Olympic Games (Lynch 2000). The Sydney Olympic Games also provided the opportunity for approximately 5,000 'student' (TAFE or university) volunteers to gain recognition for practical work as part of their courses (Lynch 2000). This allowed for 'value-adding' to the event, as a professional service, as well as benefitting students who gained accredited training and valuable work experience.

Managing, motivating, rewarding and retaining volunteers

In the event context the usual control relationship, typical to the employment association is replaced by a different set of power relationships between the volunteer and the volunteer organisation (Monga 2006). Baldamus (1961, cited in Monga 2006) notes that in a typical employment relationship the employee is connected to the employer by a wage–work bargain. This is different from the bargain struck between volunteering parties, which involves other elements and offerings designed to provide volunteer satisfaction. Recognising and appreciating volunteer contributions, seeking volunteer evaluations and keeping volunteers happy are integral to the successful retention of volunteers (Hodges 1998). Too much emphasis on extrinsic rewards reduces the importance of intrinsically rewarding motives such as enjoying the roles and social interactions volunteers experience while contributing to a greater social good, and as such can be counterproductive (Cuskelly *et al.* 2004). Volunteer satisfaction in its own right can be regarded as a non-wage form of remuneration and reward (Edwards 2005; Monga 2006).

Bang, Won and Kim (2009) believe that volunteers are more likely to be committed to and continue with their involvement if they perceive a fair balance between the efforts they exert and the rewards they receive from their voluntary contribution. Reinforcing motivations and creating meaningful experiences can be achieved by matching volunteers to particular tasks, and by appealing to such factors as interpersonal contacts (e.g. building social webs), love of sport (encouraging engagement in events) and personal growth indicators (sense of accomplishment, ownership and providing recognition) (Bang, Won and Kim 2009; Clary *et al.* 1992; Farrell *et al.* 1998). Extrinsic rewards such as pins or t-shirts are often ranked lowest in importance. Rewards linked to more intrinsic qualities such as personal growth (letters of reference and recognition) and love of sport (branded apparel and equipment) play an important role in volunteer motivation and satisfaction (Bang, Alexandris and Ross 2009). Feedback from managers, feeling appreciated, the quality of food available to volunteers, meeting event heroes, wanting to help and the event being connected with hobbies and interests are factors that have been found to impact on maintaining commitment (Elstad 2003). Conversely, studies found that individuals who volunteer primarily for material rewards, such as tickets, t-shirts or to improve their status, are less committed to continuing their involvement (Elstad 2003; Slaughter and Home 2004; Bryen and Madden 2006; Giannoulakis *et al.* 2008).

Volunteer motivation, satisfaction and retention represent challenges facing event organisations of all sizes, from mega sporting events to small-scale community festivals. Lessons to be learnt from the case study below suggest that understanding volunteer motivations and appropriately rewarding volunteers is key to engaging, satisfying and retaining a volunteer workforce, whatever the size of the event.

Small (2007) studied two community music festivals, that have strong links to the local communities in which they took place, to understand the social impacts that festivals have on their communities: Hadley Music Festival* in Western Australia, Australia and the Rockford Music Festival* in Victoria, Australia. Hadley Music Festival* has been running since 1993 and the Rockford Music Festival has been running since 1997.

When the study was conducted, Blues at Bridgetown maintained and encouraged its community focus, overseen by a majority voluntary organising committee made up of members of the local community. The festival could not be staged without the assistance of a dedicated group of volunteers, service clubs and community voluntary organisations who contribute time, skills and service in a range of operational areas. During the course of the festival a contingent of anywhere between 250 and 300 volunteers are utilised, drawn mostly from the local community. While the majority of these volunteers are on the ground over the festival weekend, many undertake volunteer work in the lead up to or following the festival. For their efforts, volunteers receive a 'volunteer pack', consisting of a t-shirt and a ticket to the festival. These packs are distributed the night before the festival begins, at a volunteer barbecue hosted by the organising committee. The volunteers then get together after the festival for another barbecue, allowing them to celebrate their efforts.

The Rockford Music Festival* at the time of investigation operated under three tiers of management starting with a Board of Management, followed by the Executive Management team, and supported by a large volunteer contingent. The festival draws on approximately sixty volunteer team leaders who coordinate operational areas such as customer service, infrastructure, the artistic division, security and control functions. Working within these areas are approximately 450 volunteers who contribute their time over the festival weekend and are critical to delivering a successful festival. Of the volunteers, approximately 300 are individual members from the local community, with the remaining 150 volunteers coming from various local community organisations such as the local fire brigade, Coast Guard, Lions Club, the Scouts and several local schools. Volunteers receive a t-shirt and a free ticket to the festival in return for their efforts. Also, on the final night of the festival, the volunteers are invited, along with the festival organisers and other VIPs, to the 'wind-up party', to celebrate the weekend's efforts and achievements, and as a thank you to the volunteers.

Volunteer motivation, satisfaction and retention represent a unique challenge for both event organisations. Event organisations at each festival recognise the importance of understanding volunteer motivations, to assist them to deliver satisfying and meaningful experiences for their volunteers. It was found that volunteers for both Hadley Music Festival* and the Rockford Music Festival* were motivated by a range of intrinsically rewarding motives such as enjoying the event entertainment, social interactions experienced and the meeting of new people. Volunteering also provided them with strong feelings of community identity, togetherness and pride. This is because volunteers see their contribution as not only assisting the event, but also in contributing to other community outcomes such as community cohesion, image and development. Although volunteers received extrinsic rewards, such as festival tickets and t-shirts, it was the individual benefits gained and the benefits volunteers saw themselves making to their communities that were considered most important. It is this intrinsic satisfaction that sees volunteers returning each year ('bouncing-back') to contribute their time to these festivals.

The implication for event organisations is that to ensure volunteer engagement, satisfaction and bounce-back, it is important that these benefits can continue to be experienced by volunteers. In fact, some benefits are experienced simply by volunteering, and may not require any action or initiatives to be put in place by event organisations. Through appropriately rewarding volunteers, event organisations will be well placed to engage, satisfy and retain their volunteer workforce.

References

Small, K. (2007) 'Understanding the social impacts of festivals on communities', unpublished doctoral dissertation, University of Western Sydney, Australia.

Note: *Name changed to protect anonymity

The pitfalls associated with an organisation's inability to retain volunteers can lead organisations to over-recruit to make up for perceived or lack of dependability on the volunteer. This can lead to increased costs in all aspects of the recruitment, training and rewards process for volunteers and as previously discussed a strong possibility of under-utilisation and dissatisfaction of volunteers as a result of an oversupply of personnel (Cuskelly *et al.* 2004). More recently it has been suggested that government or public policy can assist organisations to recruit and retain volunteers by reducing the costs incurred by the volunteers themselves (Downward and Ralston 2006). Such support may include tax incentives and concessions to student loans for young people who volunteer.

Regardless of the policy environment, management has the responsibility to balance appropriate workloads, provide feedback and recognition, and allow space for volunteer participation in the organisational development of goals and strategies. Social activities that foster team development, orientations and debriefings that are enjoyable and innovative, and the provision of appropriate rewards that recognise volunteer contributions, are all integral to ensuring both volunteer satisfaction and event success (Hodges 1998; Bang, Alexandris and Ross 2009).

The discussion thus far highlights the complexity of engaging and retaining event volunteers (Ralston *et al.* 2005; Monga 2006). A way of dealing with this complexity may be in using flexible practices. Lockstone *et al.* (2010) suggest that by allowing for flexible volunteering opportunities such as flexible hours or short-term commitments, event organisers may find benefits by way of increased volunteer participation rates and higher levels of volunteer satisfaction.

Hanlon and Stewart (2006: 85) suggest that the future practice of managing personnel in major sport events will be fashioned by the increasing event complexity and broadening personnel requirements. As a result, a tailored and integrated approach to assist this growing complexity of event management is an essential step in ensuring that human resource practices will be effective. Monga (2006: 50) warns against applying generic human resource management frameworks based on a conception of a homogenised volunteer rather than recognising the complexity that arises from volunteer motivations (Fisher and Cole 1993; Noble & Rogers 1998; Macleod and Hogarth 1999). Monga (2006: 59) further states that volunteers do not act through any one particular motive but for multiple reasons and managers should understand the motives people have for volunteering for an event. Events volunteering, for some, satisfies the desire to do something that is altruistic or it can also appeal to the egoistic nature of individuals. For example, such volunteering can be 'mostly about me' benefits (Edwards 2005), where the volunteer is concerned about their self-interest rather than outcomes for others. The responsibility lies with event managers to first understand and then provide for satisfaction of volunteer motivations which can then lead to volunteer retention or 'bounce-back' (Bryen and Madden 2006).

It is recognised that volunteers should be appropriately acknowledged and 'nurtured' after an event, encouraging 'evaluation and perpetuation' of their skills base for future events (Chanavat and Ferrand 2010: 264). As such, major event volunteers who have worked on previous events can be regarded as 'pools' of job-ready volunteers, needing little training and able to provide quality services, whether for other events or for tourism-based services (Lockstone *et al.* 2010; Ralston *et al.* 2005).

Further research and conclusions

This chapter has provided a review of volunteering for events and the importance of volunteers in the organisation and management of events. It points to the contribution that volunteers make to the event workforce and how the provision by event organisers of a positive event experience is essential. This chapter is based on the existing literature, and current thinking on the management of volunteers across all areas of the event human resource management process, including recruitment, training and induction, motivation, rewards and retention, and provides the platform for the future management of volunteers at events.

A review of the literature has identified a number of areas for future research. Small community events remain an under-researched area in relation to volunteers. Understanding volunteer retention, particularly for smaller events, by comparing committed volunteers to those who leave their volunteering roles could potentially enhance knowledge of what motivates and generates volunteer continuance commitment and dependability, as well as influence recruitment and retention processes for organisers of these events.

Longitudinal studies would enhance understanding of volunteers' life choices and the consequences of gaining skills, training and experiences as a result of their volunteering. The findings could be used to enhance government policy. Especially beneficial would be longitudinal studies on the impact of socially excluded, isolated or disadvantaged members of a given community, especially in terms of skills gained and future employment opportunities, as well as the differences between regular and episodic volunteers in tourism and events contexts (Holmes and Smith 2009; Holmes *et al.* 2010).

Further, replication and testing of previous studies would also be useful. For example, research into the link between volunteer satisfaction and flexibility options for volunteers, together with associated constructs such as commitment and performance, could enhance volunteer contributions (Lockstone *et al.* 2010). An area requiring theoretical development is the causal processes behind volunteer motives. This would fit well within a human resource management framework of obtaining suitable personnel who would be dependable for the jobs assigned. It may also help to explain the role culture plays in the development of volunteerism, especially when the motives and behaviour of volunteers in different countries are compared (Bang, Alexandris and Ross 2009).

This chapter has explained that event organisers need to consider the nature of volunteering in events, and the various important roles and contributions that volunteers make to events. Unique challenges are faced by event organisations in incorporating volunteer labour into their workforce. Issues around recruitment, training, managing, rewarding and retaining volunteers need to be given priority in order to assist event managers to effectively manage their volunteer workforce. Sensitive volunteer management is important in ensuring a successful event, a satisfied volunteer workforce and, therefore, one which is likely to 'bounce-back' to engage in an episodic relationship with the event organisation.

References

Australian Bureau of Statistics (2008) *Australian Social Trends, 2008* (No. 4102.0), Canberra: ABS.

Baldamus, W. (1961) *Efficiency and Effort: An Analysis of Industrial Administration*, London: Tavistock.

Bang, H., Alexandris, K. and Ross, S.D. (2009) 'Validation of the revised Volunteer Motivations Scale for International Sporting Events (VMS-ISE) at the Athens 2004 Olympic Games', *Event Management* 12: 119–31.

Bang, H., Won, D. and Kim, J. (2009) 'Motivations, commitment and intentions to continue volunteering for sporting events', *Event Management* 13: 69–81.

Baum, T. and Lockstone, L. (2007) 'Volunteers and mega sporting events: developing a research framework', *International Journal of Event Management Research* 3(1): 29–41.

Bryen, L. and Madden, K. (2006) 'Bounce-back of episodic volunteers: what makes episodic volunteers return?', *Working Paper No. CPNS 32*, Brisbane: Centre of Philanthropy and Nonprofit Studies, Queensland University of Technology.

Chanavat, N. and Ferrand, A. (2010) 'Volunteer programme in mega sport events: the case of the Olympic Winter Games, Torino 2006', *International Journal of Sport Management and Marketing* 7(3–4): 241–66.

Chappelet, J.L. (2000) 'Volunteer management at a major sports event: the case of the Olympic Winter Games', in M. de Moragas, A.B. Moreno and N. Puig (eds) *Volunteers, Global Society and the Olympic Movement*, Lausanne: Documents of the Museum, International Olympic Committee Editions, pp. 245–55.

Clary, E.G., Snyder, M. and Ridge, R. (1992) 'Volunteers' motivations: a functional strategy for the recruitment, placement, and retention of volunteers', *Nonprofit Management and Leadership* 2(4): 333–50.

Coyne, B.S. and Coyne, E.J. (2001) 'Getting, keeping and caring for unpaid volunteers for professional golf tournament events: a study of the recruitment/retention of unpaid volunteers for staging large, mass-attended, high-profile Professional Golf Association (PGA) golf tournaments', *Human Resource Development International* 4(2): 199–214.

Cuskelly, G., Auld, C., Harrington, M. and Coleman, D. (2004) 'Predicting the behavioural dependability of sport event volunteers', *Event Management* 9: 73–89.

Downward, P.M. and Ralston, R. (2006) 'The sports development potential of sports event volunteering: Insights from the XVII Manchester Commonwealth Games', *European Sport Management Quarterly* 6(4): 333–51.

Earl, C., Parker, E., Edwards, M. and Capra, M. (2004) 'Capacity building in public health and emergency management for volunteers at outdoor music festivals', *Australian Journal on Volunteering* 9(2): 19–24.

Edwards, D.C. (2005) 'It's mostly about me: reasons why volunteers contribute their time to museums and art museums', *Tourism Review International* 9(1): 21–31.

Edwards, D.C. and Graham, M. (2006) 'Museum volunteers: a discussion of challenges facing managers in the cultural and heritage sectors', *Australian Journal of Volunteering* 11(1): 19–27.

Elstad, B. (2003) 'Continuance commitment and reasons to quit: a study of volunteers at a jazz festival', *Event Management* 8: 99–108.

Farrell, J.M., Johnston, M.E. and Twynam, G.D. (1998) 'Volunteer motivation, satisfaction and management of an elite sporting competition', *Journal of Sport Management* 12(4): 288–300.

Fisher, J.C. and Cole, K. (1993) *Leadership and Management of Volunteer Programs*, San Francisco: Jossey-Bass.

Getz, D. (1991) *Festivals, Special Events and Tourism*, New York: Van Nostrand Reinhold.

——(2007) *Event Studies: Theory, Research and Policy for Planned Events*, Oxford: Butterworth-Heinemann.

Giannoulakis, C., Wang, C.-H. and Gray, M. (2008) 'Measuring volunteer motivation in mega-sporting events', *Event Management* 11:191–200.

Green, B.C. and Chalip, L. (2004) 'Paths to volunteer commitment: lessons from the Sydney Olympic Games', in R.A. Stebbins and M. Graham (eds) *Volunteering as Leisure. Leisure as Volunteering. An International Assessment*, Wallingford: CABI Publishing, pp. 49–67.

Hanlon, C. and Cuskelly, G. (2002) 'Pulsating major sport event organizations: a framework for inducting managerial personnel', *Event Management* 7: 231–43.

Hanlon, C. and Jago, L. (2004) 'The challenge of retaining personnel in major sport event organizations', *Event Management* 9: 39–49.

Hanlon, C and Stewart, B. (2006) 'Managing personnel in major sport event organizations: what strategies are required?', *Event Management* 10: 77–88.

Harrington, M., Cuskelly, G. and Auld, C. (2000) 'Career volunteering in community-intensive serious leisure: motorsport events and their dependence on volunteers/amateurs', *Loisir et Société* 23(2): 421–52.

Hodges, J. (1998) 'Volunteering and the National Folk Festival – a positive approach', *Australian Journal on Volunteering*, August: 22–4.

Holmes, K. (2008) 'Changing attitudes towards volunteering and the implications for tourist attractions', paper presented at CAUTHE Conference, 'Where the Bloody Hell Are We?', 11–14 February.

Holmes, K. and Edwards, D. (2008) 'Volunteers as hosts and guests in museums', in K.D. Lyons and S. Wearing (eds) *Journeys of Discovery in Volunteer Tourism: International Case Study Perspectives*, UK: CABI, pp. 155–65.

Holmes, K. and Smith, K. (2009) *Managing Volunteers in Tourism: Attractions, Destinations, and Events*, Oxford: Butterworth-Heinemann, Elsevier Science.

Holmes, K., Smith, K.A., Lockstone-Binney, L. and Baum, T. (2010) 'Developing the dimensions of tourism volunteering', *Leisure Sciences* 32(3): 255–69.

Hustinx, L. and Lammertyn, F. (2004) 'The cultural bases of volunteering: understanding and predicting attitudinal differences between Flemish Red Cross volunteers', *Nonprofit and Voluntary Sector Quarterly* 33 (4): 548–84.

Ingerson, L. (2001) 'Comparative economic impacts of arts and sports events', in C. Gratton and I. Henry (eds) *Sport in the City: The Role of Sport in Economic and Social Regeneration*, London: Routledge, pp. 46–59.

Lechat, B. (2006) 'Interview concerning the volunteer management of the 32nd America's Cup Valencia 2007', Valencia, 21 March, unpublished.

Lockstone, L., Smith, K. and Baum, T. (2010) 'Volunteer flexibility across the tourism sector', *Managing Leisure* 15 (January–April): 111–27.

Lynch, B. (2000) 'Volunteers 2000 – the recruitment process', *Australian Journal on Volunteering*, February: 41–3.

Macduff, N. (2005) 'Societal changes and the rise of the episodic volunteer', in J. Brudney (ed.) *ARNOVA Occasional Paper Series* 1(2): 49–61, Indianapolis: Association for Research on Nonprofit Organizations and Voluntary Action.

Macleod, F. and Hogarth, S. (1999) *Leading Today's Volunteer: Motivate and Manage Your Team*, Vancouver: Self-Counsel Press.

Monga, M. (2006) 'Measuring motivation to volunteer for special events', *Event Management* 10: 47–61.

Noble, J. and Rogers, L. (1998) *Volunteer Management: An Essential Guide*, Adelaide: Volunteering SA.

Presbury, R. and Edwards, D. (2010) 'Sustainable operations management', in J. Liburd and D. Edwards (eds) *Understanding the Sustainable Development of Tourism*, Oxford: Goodfellow.

Ralston, R., Lumsdon, L. and Downward, P. (2005) 'The third force in events tourism: volunteers at the XVII Commonwealth Games', *Journal of Sustainable Tourism* 13(5): 504–19.

Slaughter, L. and Home, R. (2004) 'Motivations of long term volunteers: human services vs events', *UNLV Journal of Hospitality, Tourism and Leisure Science* 2: 1–12.

Small, K. (2007) 'Understanding the social impacts of festivals on communities', unpublished doctoral dissertation, University of Western Sydney, Australia.

Small, K., Edwards, D. and Sheridan, L. (2005) 'A flexible framework for evaluating the socio-cultural impacts of a small festival', *International Journal of Event Management Research* 1(1): 66–77.

Smith, A. and Fox, T. (2007) 'From "event-led" to "event-themed" regeneration: the 2002 Commonwealth Games legacy programme', *Urban Studies* 44(5/6): 1125–43.

Smith, K.A. and Lockstone, L. (2009) "Involving and keeping event volunteers: management insights from cultural festivals', in T. Baum, M. Deery, C. Hanlon, L. Lockstone and K. Smith (eds) *People and Work in Events and Conventions: A Research Perspective*, Oxford: CABI, pp. 154–67.

Victorian Seniors Festival (2005) 'Communication plan'. Available at: www.docstoc.com/docs/4962580/Communication-Plan-Victorian-Seniors-Festival-Volunteer-Program-AUDIENCE-AUDIENCE (accessed 29 September 2010).

Volunteering Australia (2009) *Definitions and Principles of Volunteering*, Melbourne: Volunteering Australia.

Section 4
The impacts of events

22

A spatial extension to a framework for assessing direct economic impacts of tourist events

Timothy J. Tyrrell and Robert J. Johnston[1]

Introduction: spatial distinctions are crucial when evaluating economic impacts

Tourism events contribute to local tourism industry success and often enhance quality of life for residents. These same events draw revenues away from businesses outside the region in the short run and attract investment from outside the region in the long run (Heilbron and Gray 1993). While there is no unique formula for cooperation among tourist destinations and there are significant impediments to its success (McCarthy 2003), future regional economic development is expected to depend more on cooperation than on competition (Gordon 2009).

The common reliance on traditional economic impact analysis to promote activities and events runs counter to the critical role of regional cooperation in economic development strategies (Lombard and Morris 2010). Specifically, economic impact analysis as traditionally practised does not thoroughly consider the full spatial impacts of tourism events, promoting analyses that ignore (often negative) impacts in areas that are not the central focus of the analysis. That is, economic development costs or benefits to the larger region are overlooked. Instead, the success of an event is measured by the amount of direct expenditures (or a multiple of it) captured by a specific 'local' study region as chosen by the analyst. Little thought is given to the fact that the analysis, in doing so, implies a competitive perspective between localities; costs to a larger region are ignored in the pursuit of narrow local economic impacts. Among the many shortcomings of this spatially myopic approach is that a combination of self-interested activities by numerous localities within a broader region may lead to lesser benefits than otherwise similar activities that were better coordinated and incorporated a broader perspective towards economic impacts.

More broadly,

> the competition between local governments for economic development is generally regarded as producing both inefficiencies and inequities. Competition forces governments to increase subsidies and incentives offered to private firms, favors new firms over existing businesses, and often results in merely the relocation of investment rather than in increased levels of private sector activity.
>
> *(Goetz and Kayser 1993: 63)*

The question for local economic development is philosophical: should short-term local gain be sacrificed for longer-term regional gains? Economic impact analysis itself cannot answer this question. Nonetheless, more comprehensive analysis may provide decision-makers with information necessary to make more informed decisions. At the present, few economic impact analyses provide sufficient information to enable decision-makers to effectively balance local vs regional, or shorter- vs longer-term impacts.[2] Traditional focus on the immediate neighbourhood of a development project or event treats impacts elsewhere solely as losses or leakages from the study region. While some care is given to choosing a study region, once this accounting stance is chosen, the impact analysis will generally ignore or at least discount out-of-region impacts.[3]

Tourist impacts can stretch over considerable distances. For example, a study of Connecticut casinos found that municipal revenue and expenditure impacts varied unevenly across twenty-one municipalities because of three factors: residential locations of employees, business location of enterprises and the routes of increased traffic caused by visitor travel (Tyrrell and Johnston 2009). Tourism jobs bring income into the parts of the community where the wage-earner resides. Tourism businesses, however, are frequently located elsewhere. Visitor traffic patterns involve still other locations where tourists spend time and money before and after they reach the major attraction. All of these are relevant to broader regional impacts.

Research concerning spatial aspects of economic impacts has been chiefly concerned with overestimation of economic benefits to the host community (Long and Perdue 1990) when expenditures out of the region or not originating out of the region are inadvertently included. While this literature promotes consistency in analytical methods and perspective, it does not promote a broader understanding or analysis of the potential redistributional effects of tourism events. As stated by Getz (2008: 417), '[e]vent geography is not a well-developed theme', especially as it applies to economic impacts of tourism events.

This chapter illustrates a broadly applicable framework for a more detailed analysis of direct expenditure flows between several localities (sub-regions) as they are influenced by a short-term tourism event. The framework extends and adapts previous work (Tyrrell and Johnston 2001) which described the separation of expenditures according to whether they are related to the event site or the event activities. The extension described here gives greater emphasis to the parallel treatment of impacts on origins and destinations in the analysis of such events. Advantages of the proposed framework include an ability to encapsulate an entire set of event-related transactions as part of the balance between sub-regions within a larger region. The framework explicitly recognizes economic winners and economic losers as determined by spatial or geographical considerations. A region realizes a net expenditure gain only if an event pulls more money in than it pushes out. The value of that gain will depend on the substitutes available to each of the participants both in and out of the region.[4]

The remainder of this chapter is presented in three major parts: a discussion of conceptual issues in spatial analysis of economic impacts, the proposed spatial framework, and a case study illustrating an application of the proposed framework. We conclude with observations about the practice of tourism event impact analysis and suggestions for further extensions.

Conceptual issues in spatial analysis of event impacts

The choices of a 'single study region' and a set of simple rules for identifying legitimate expenditures can simplify the analysis of the monetary transactions but can also disguise full spatial distributions and values of tourism event impacts. Accounting for spatial impacts appropriately requires one to account for a variety of factors that are often ignored in applied economic impact analysis. As in our previous work, we suggest that the first of these factors is the distinction between the attraction of the *event site* and that of *event activities*. An additional consideration is the identification of all regions of importance to participants. It is not adequate to identify a single study region reflecting only supporter goals of increasing local revenues in the short term. By accounting for spatial expenditure patterns and identifying a realistic set of spatial alternatives to an event, an economic impact analysis can provide more relevant information for judging the contribution of an event to regional economic development goals. The various issues that must be considered in detail when seeking a more comprehensive spatial perspective on event expenditures are detailed below.

The nature of transactions associated with tourism events

Tourist spending at an event site and within the host region is generally accepted as the most important economic impact of an event. While attention to tourist spending is well deserved, its primary emphasis in the analysis of event impacts overshadows equally important impacts made by residents and impacts felt outside the region.[5] Residential spending at events is rarely recognized as a legitimate event impact since expenditures are not new to the study region. This type of spending, however, deserves more attention since it is a substitute for other spending which may have occurred, particularly when the activities of an event are more important to residents than its site. It is interesting to note that new recognition has been given to residential spending in the development of Tourism Satellite Accounts which focus on the balance of economic flows and investments in and out of a region rather than simple inward flows (OECD 2001). Similar attention given to the flows associated with tourism events would provide a more comprehensive and useful perspective on event impacts.

As noted above, traditional impact analyses recognize direct spending outside the region by residents and tourists only as a loss to the study region. Indirect spending out of the region is similarly referred to as 'leakage' in the language of input–output (I–O) analysis. Both 'losses' and 'leakage' reflect gains to outside regions. However, traditional impact analyses consider them as problems which, if solved, could benefit the study region. This 'single study region' approach ignores the possibility that economic development can be enhanced by regional cooperation.

Accounting stance: choice of study region(s)

The choice of a study region determines geographic and political distinctions between locations in and out of the study region. This distinction, frequently dictated by the event or festival organizer, will also determine the types of transactions that will need to be estimated.

> The divergence between the political regions often used for regional modeling and the functional economic areas in which economic activity actually takes place sometimes causes analysts to incorrectly specify their accounting stance, resulting in biased estimates of project impacts and project benefits and missing important spillovers between accounting regions.
>
> *(Carmichael 2002: 343)*

The definition of a relevant study region can vary depending on the group whose perceptions are considered. While tourism industry professionals often espouse a political/jurisdictional view of a tourism region, tourists may view the places they visit as destinations with little correspondence to these regions. In conceptualizing 'destinations,' Dredge (1999) found that 'boundaries of destination regions are tied to travel patterns and characteristics. Depending upon characteristics of the visit (e.g. mode or distance travelled), destination regions may be large or small and may or may not overlap' (p. 781).[6] Planners and developers may have still different views of relevant regions (cf. Ritchie and Zins 1978; Formica and Kothari 2008). Even the approach taken to asking about regional definitions can reveal differences. Raymond and Brown (2007), for example, found that a spatial attribute method of analysing perceptions (using coded sticker dots on maps) suggested different residential and tourist preferences for tourism development than traditional survey methods based on words alone. These distinctions are clearly relevant to an analysis of impacts; while industry professionals and government officials may prefer analyses grounded in familiar political/jurisdictional regions, such regions might be of little relevance when considering visitor behaviour and associated expenditures.

Despite the potential relevance of such issues, the tourism and event literature provides only general guidance about the choice of a study region. For example, Kinsey (2002) recommends that 'the "local" area should be chosen based on the project's area of interest, keeping in mind that the defined region should include any localities that are economically linked to the area in which [it] is located'. Given this lack of guidance, study areas are often determined or influenced largely by the desires of event supporters (Crompton 2006).

> While the effects of the festival (event) may be spread over some distance, local supporters may want only to show the effects of this event on the local community or even on a narrow segment of the community. In other cases, they may want to emphasize the spillover of benefits into other communities in an attempt to gain broader support.
>
> *(Davidson and Schaffer 1980: 14)*

In other words, study areas are often chosen in order to encourage outcomes desired by project supporters.

The choice of a region, however, has important consequences. 'When the geographical area of impact is changed, it changes the definition of which participants are visitors and which are locals' (Crompton 2006: 73). Ryan (1999), for example, found a convention visitor share model to be highly sensitive to regional boundary assumptions. Generalizing somewhat, when larger regions are chosen, fewer dollars will be measured flowing into the region from outside (since more participants are local residents), but fewer indirect dollars leak outside the region (since more suppliers are local businesses). When smaller regions are chosen, more dollars will be measured flowing into the region but there will also be more leakage out of the region. It is not surprising that event supporters favour choosing small study regions around the event for measuring direct expenditures and large regions for measuring multiplier effects.

Substitution and the 'without' scenario

In addition to distinguishing residents from non-residents, regional definitions impose a choice category upon the assumed behaviour of event participants: whether transactions measure expenditures internal, external, inward or outward from a study region. Since expenditure choices are assumed to reflect consumer or corporate behaviour they reflect substitutions chosen between these goods and services and alternatives available in the same or a different sub-region. When transactions are internal to a sub-region, they substitute only for other expenditures that could have been made in the sub-region and no gain is received by the sub-region. When transactions cross a boundary going outward they reflect a loss for the sub-region. When analogous transactions cross the boundary coming inward they reflect a gain. When the transactions don't involve the study region, they only impact the larger region. So the boundary chosen for the study region determines the substitute that is assumed, and whether or not a transaction reflects a gain to any sub-region.

The assumed categorization of expenditure choices imposed by the regional definition only roughly distinguishes the motives behind the actual choices made by event participants, since it does not reflect the true substitutes considered. We have previously proposed (Tyrrell and Johnston 2001) that the true substitutes might be categorized as being related to either the location of the event (its site within the host region) or the activities associated with the event (the activities that have special importance to each type of participant.) The relative importance of these motives can be used to allocate expenditures.

Johnson and Moore (1993: 281) have recognized these two types of motives in expenditure substitutions made by recreational river users in Oregon:

> For those users on multiple destination trips who would still visit [the region] without the Upper Klamath [river resources], all shuttle and guide expenditures and the proportion of the remaining expenditures devoted to the Upper Klamath would be lost in the region. While it is possible that these visitors would then spend more on other activities in the area, the assumption here is that this will not happen. Finally for those on multiple destination trips who would no longer visit, all nonlocal expenditures would be lost, while expenditures by locals would be lost only if they would substitute a different river or an activity outside the region.

However, these are assumptions, and not based on data gathered from those making the expenditures.

The immediate implication of the identification of a substitute region or activity is that there exists an identifiable 'without' scenario that might be realized if the event being studied did not occur. 'An economic impact assessment is most useful for evaluating the effects of a particular action or policy. If so, the action and assumptions about alternatives should be spelled out in presenting a with vs without scenario' (Stynes 1997: 27). The 'without' scenario depends critically on the available substitutes. In the case where a specific tourism event is the 'with' scenario, several 'without' scenarios might be possible: a similar event held in the same region, a similar event held in another region or no alternative event. In each case the appropriate economic impact measures for a region will be the differences between actual expenditures and those made under the most likely 'without' scenarios.

Site- versus event-related expenditures

The importance of event activities to visitors is well documented (Alexander 1991). Unique and hallmark events generally target planned activities to visitors' interests (Hall 1989; Getz 2008). The importance of event activities to other types of participants, however, is not well documented. Seeing and meeting famous persons associated with an event activity might, for example, be categorized as an important activity for a volunteer. As a case in point, the Newport Tennis Hall of Fame tournaments depend on volunteers who are motivated by the opportunity to see their favourite professional players (Tyrrell and Toepper 1991). Hence, event activities may not only influence spending of visitors, it may also influence the behaviour of others influenced directly or indirectly by the event.

In contrast to event activities which are given primary importance in economic impact analysis, the importance of the site is generally treated as a nuisance in the estimation of the event impacts. In some studies, for example, a respondent's expenditures are counted as having an impact only if the event was the most important reason for the trip to the event site. The rationale is that if the event is not the primary cause of the visit, then the related expenditures should not be counted as part of the event's impacts. A more comprehensive perspective, however, will provide information on all types of expenditures, while at the same time allowing one to distinguish between the primary causes of different types of expenditures (e.g. event- or site-related). This is the approach proposed here. There are many motives for participation in a tourism event. Our approach of labelling all of them as either site-related or activity-related is only a first step toward identifying comprehensive impacts. That is, it is a necessary but not sufficient step for analysing spatial impacts of an event.

In Tyrrell and Johnston (2001), we identified six basic types of event participants other than the organizing committee. Each of these groups incurs different event-related expenditures and each expenditure is motivated by different site- and activity-related attributes. These are summarized as follows:

1 Spectators may be avid followers of the event activities who are not concerned about the site or, alternatively, may be 'walk ins' who have many other reasons to be at the site (such as being with friends and family) and are largely or completely unaffected by the event activities. Both groups, however, may pay admission fees, travel and hospitality expenses, and buy gifts and souvenirs.
2 Players and competitors are usually motivated to participate because of the activities of the event, but may choose a site based on other interests. They pay entry fees and travel expenses for themselves and their entourage, and purchase equipment maintenance, repairs, and services such as docking fees and photography.
3 Volunteers and contributors to local events are usually motivated by the site attributes. However, some events require volunteers to travel long distances. These long-distance volunteers are probably motivated by activities. Volunteers have expenses similar to spectators, but it is important to value their 'in-kind' labour and contributions. Without these many events could not take place.
4 Media, umpires and other official or VIP attendees are motivated mostly by the activities of the event, but also might choose between sites of similar events. Their expenditures are similar to those of players and competitors and include travel expenses, equipment maintenance and repairs, and support services.
5 The major sponsors may be supporting local community development (site), seeking to enhance broad market image for products (event activities), or some combination of these. Expenditures include their direct contributions to the event, travel expenses, and other public relations expenses.
6 Exhibitors and vendors: vendors are frequently from the local area, taking advantage of their proximity to the site to sell merchandise or promote regional business. Exhibitors and non-local vendors seek to broaden market opportunities related to the event activities. Expenditures are similar to those of sponsors include vendor fees, public relations, exhibit construction and operation and other business and travel expenditures.

In order to determine the relative importance of the site and event activities to the different types of participants, specially designed questions must be developed for each type at each different event. Examples are provided below for a case study of the Newport–Bermuda Yacht Race.

A spatial framework for event evaluation

Short of a full multi-regional CGE model (cf. Dwyer *et al.* 2006), there is no unifying framework for evaluating the full spectrum of direct spatial impacts of a tourist event.[7] This chapter describes a movement toward that framework. The proposed framework provides a formal structure through which source and destination of expenditures, as influenced by event vs site attributes, may be incorporated when estimating event impacts. It incorporates the considerations identified below to provide more transparent and informative estimates of event impacts. The economic analysis of a tourism event begins with estimates of the numbers of participants and their expenditures. It then accounts for the origins of expenditures, the destination of impacts and motives behind the expenditures. We then further extend the model through inclusion of a broader region for analysis, consideration of the origin and destinations as sub-regions to be analysed individually, and through analysis of specific 'without' scenarios for the tourism event as related to participant motivations. The proposed framework is applicable to multiple regions that both benefit from or are harmed by the event, as related to both origins and destinations of expenditures.

As noted above, the framework begins with the foundation of Tyrrell and Johnston (2001). This original model uses a simple, traditional *one-region* accounting stance and distinguishes among: (1) source and starting point of the expenditure; (2) the destination or end-point of the expenditure; and (3) reasons for the expenditure. That framework has been applied to more than a dozen tourism events, some of which impact large geographic areas. However, all applications retain a focus only on a single geographical region – an emphasis that is relaxed below.

The framework for evaluating economic impact of a one-region event is represented by a three-dimensional table of economic flows. The first two dimensions indicate the source and destination of direct economic impacts of the tourism event. These dimensions are illustrated as impact categories in Table 22.1. Four major categories have been used: Categories (1) and (2) are expenditures made by non-residents (visitors to the study region) while (3) and (4) are expenditures made by residents. Categories (1) and (3) are expenditures made in the study region while (2) and (4) are made out of the study region. These four basic categories are used to disaggregate ultimate expenditure impacts by all economic entities, including spectators,

Table 22.1 A framework for evaluating tourism events

Origin of expenditures/ contributions	Location of purchases	Expenditures depend on		
		Site	Event	Either
Out of region	In region	(1a)	(1b)	(1)
	Out of region	(2a)	(2b)	(2)
In region	In region	(3a)	(3b)	(3)
	Out of region	(4a)	(4b)	(4)
Total	In region	(1a)+(3a)	(1b)+(3b)	(1)+(3)
	Out of region	(2a)+(4a)	(2b)+(4b)	(2)+(4)
GROSS SALES		(1a)+(3a)+ (2a)+(4a)	(1b)+(3b)+ (2b)+(4b)	(1)+(3)+ (2)+(4)
NET DIRECT SALES IMPACT (DSI)				(1b)+(3b)-(4a)
TOTAL VALUE ADDED (VA)				DSI * Value Added Multiplier
TOTAL SALES IMPACT (TSI)				DSI * Sales Multiplier

performers, government agencies and corporate sponsors. Since admission fees, vendor fees, sponsorships and monetary donations are initially paid to the organizing committee, their impacts are measured after they are spent with suppliers and event employees – that is, after they pass through the organizing committee's accounts. The result of this analysis is a calculation of the gains to the host region.

While it is important that the origin and destination of all expenditures by each type of event participant be accurately determined from surveys and event records, it is equally important to distinguish the impact of the event activities from the impact of the event site. Subcategories (a) and (b) under each of the major four categories in Table 22.1 specify whether the purchase or contribution is made because of the location of the activity (site) or purely because of the activities associated with the event. For example, subcategories of (1) (expenditures made in the region by a tourist) correspond to expenditures that would (a) or would not (b) be made in the region if the event did not take place. A variant of the following question may be used to estimate the percentage allocation between the two categories for visitors.

On a scale of 0–100, how much of your reason for being in _____ is due to this event?

One may interpret the point circled on the line to be the percentage of spectator expenditures at the site that can be attributed to the event. A related question may be asked of residents to determine if their expenditures would have been lost to the destination if it had been located elsewhere. One version of that question is:

If this event were not held here, how likely is it that you would you have travelled to a similar event nearby but out of _____?

Although such estimates are subjective, they are generally more appropriate than the standard assumption that 100 per cent of attendees' expenditures are made as a direct result of the event (e.g. Della Bitta et al. 1977; Hubbard et al. 1989; Yardley et al. 1990), and of finer detail than the alternate distinction between primary and secondary purpose visitors (e.g. Daniels et al. 2004).

Totals in subcategories denoted with the suffix 'a' reflect expenditures made because the event was held at a particular site in this region; these are site-related expenditures. These expenditures would have been made regardless of the activities at or associated with the event, either because the location of the event required specific investment (modifications or improvement by the organizing committee, for example) or because of other reasons for participants to be at this location (spectators visiting family and friends, for example). The site could be a heavily used urban location, so that the event precludes (or substitutes for) usual activities. Or it could be a remote rural site that requires clearing land for parking or installing utilities. Site selection will determine to some degree the expenditures made in the region and out of the region, regardless of the specific activities of the event.

Totals in subcategories denoted with the suffix 'b' reflect expenditures made because of the specific activities that define the event. These expenditures reflect the nature of the event; for example, related to specific operations (such as construction of stages and contracts with performers) or because of the types of participants that are attracted (regional family parties versus distant competitors). The chosen event activities will motivate expenditures that are conceptually distinct from the expenditures determined by the site location, and will react differently to changes in the event and/or site.

In the framework outlined in Table 22.1, the visitor impact of the event activities is indicated by (1b), reflecting new money coming from outside the region into the region because of the event activities. But there is also the potential to *avoid* the loss of money already in the region leaving because an alternative event out of the region is a viable substitute. Three cases are possible:

A   If a similar (substitute) event is held out of the region the 'direct sales impact' of the event is the sum of categories (1b) and (3b). This sum represents positive spending by both local residents and tourists that occurs in the region as a direct result of the event activities. If the event was held out of state, (3b) would be lost because residents would have travelled out of the region to attend. Finally, the 'net direct sales impact' is the direct sales impact minus (4a), as shown in Table 22.1, since site-dependent expenditures by residents out of the region would not have been lost to the region without the event. Because a similar event out of the region also would have attracted residential expenditures (4b), this loss could not be avoided.
B   If a similar event is held in the region then all impacts would be the same and there would be no loss to the region. There would, however, be winners and losers within the region.
C   If no similar event is held in or out of the region the 'direct sales impact' of the event is simply (1b). Since there is no viable alternative out of the region the amount (3b) would not be lost without the event. Residents would simply spend the same money locally. 'Net direct sales impact' in this case consists of direct sales impact (1b) minus both (4a) and (4b) since both the site- and activity-dependent residential expenditures out of the region are lost.

The first case (A) is considered for calculations presented in Table 22.1 since there are many out-of-region substitutes for most events. Therefore, case C is not likely. The intermediate case (B) is possible but its analysis would require a narrower scope in order to distinguish between specific events within a region. This is equivalent to establishing a smaller regional boundary with the result that the situation becomes case A. Put another way, if event or non-event substitutes exist within the region, the expenditures at the event will generally not be lost to the region if the event does not take place. They will simply be made elsewhere in the region. If there is no good substitute for the event in or out of the region, then only non-residential event activity-related expenditures will be lost without it. If event substitutes exist, but only outside the region, then non-resident site-related and all activity-related expenditures will be lost to the region if the event does not take place.

The framework outlined above assumes a single event site in a well-defined visitor destination sub-region, and therefore focuses on 'new' monies in the sub-region. It does not allow for analysis of impacts distributed across several regions nor does it account for transfers between regions. Finally, because it assumes a simple input–output structure for a single study region, it fails to address indirect regional spillovers. These assumptions and simplifications are relaxed in the following section that presents spatial extensions to the basic framework.

Spatial extension of the framework

In cases where event activities are specifically tied to multiple sites and where origins and destinations of participant expenditures are widely spread, a more explicit spatial framework is required. The 2010 Winter Olympics, for example, planned to use fifteen venues over seventeen days, attracting visitors from around the world (Tyrrell *et al.* 2004). In such spatially diverse situations the separation of site- and event-dependent expenditures becomes even more important, specifically as related to the economic values of flows between all regions which generate or receive expenditures. A three sub-region illustration of our proposal for such a framework is shown in Table 22.2.

Timothy J. Tyrrell and Robert J. Johnston

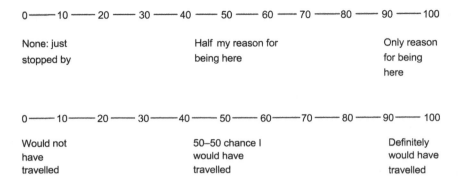

Table 22.2 identifies sites in two regions where the event takes place (primary expenditure recipients) and all other origins and destinations are grouped as 'elsewhere' (primary expenditure generators). Expenditures are tracked between each of the nine pairs of the three regions ((1) to (9)) under the 'All' column in Table 22.2 and separated according to whether they are more

Table 22.2 A spatial framework for evaluating tourism events

Origin of Expenditures	Location of Purchases	Expenditures Depend on			
		Site 1	Site 2	Event Activities	All
Region 1	Region 1	(11a)	(12a)	(1b)	(1)
	Region 2	(21a)	(22a)	(2b)	(2)
	Elsewhere	(31a)	(32a)	(3b)	(3)
Region 2	Region 1	(41a)	(42a)	(4b)	(4)
	Region 2	(51a)	(52a)	(5b)	(5)
	Elsewhere	(61a)	(62a)	(6b)	(6)
Elsewhere	Region 1	(71a)	(72a)	(7b)	(7)
	Region 2	(81a)	(82a)	(8b)	(8)
	Elsewhere	(91a)	(92a)	(9b)	(9)
Total	Region 1	(11a)+(41a)+(71a)	(12a)+(42a)+(72a)	(1b)+(4b)+(7b)	(D+(4)+(7)
	Region 2	(21a)+(51a)+(81a)	(22a)+(52a)+(82a)	(2b)+(5b)+(8b)	(2)+(5)+(8)
	Elsewhere	(31a)+(61a)+(91a)	(32a)+(62a)+(92a)	(3b)+(6b)+(9b)	(3)+(6)+(9)
GROSS SALES		$\sum_{i=1}^{9}(i1a)$	$\sum_{i=1}^{9}(i2a)$	$\sum_{i=1}^{9}(ib)$	$\sum_{i=1}^{9}(i)$

	Region 1: *DSI1*	(1b)+(4)+(7)−(21a) −(22a)−(31a)−(32a)
NET DIRECT SALES IMPACT (DSI) (Assuming Out of Region Substitute)	Region 2: *DSI2*	(2)+(5b)+(8)−(41a) −(42a)−(61a)−(62a)
	Elsewhere: *DSI3*	(3)+(6)+(9b)−(71a) −(72a)−(81a)−(82a)
	Total	$\sum_{j=1}^{3}(DSIj)$
TOTAL VALUE ADDED (VA)	Region 1	DSI1*μ1
	Region 2	DSI2*μ2
	Elsewhere	DSI3*μ3
	Total	$\sum_{j=1}^{3}DSIj*\mu j$

closely associated with the event sites or the event activities. For example, in the first row the total in (1) is separated into (11a), (12a) and (1b).

The net direct sales impact on each region includes all expenditures made in the region from outside (whether due to the event or the site), plus the expenditures made in the region by residents because of the event, minus the local expenditures out of the region due to both sites. (For example, $DSI1 = (1b)+(4)+(7)-(21a)-(22a)-(31a)-(32a)$). The expenditures made by residents in their own region because of the sites ((11a) and (12a)) are not included as gains in their own region because it is assumed that they would be made in the region regardless of the event.

When regional residents make expenditures out of the region because of the site they are received in another region. The specific choice of a site for the event by the organizers creates this flow. In the spatially complete framework we add these expenditures to the gains of the receiving region as a complement to any gains due to the event activities. Therefore (4) and (7), not just (4b) and (7b), are included in DSI1.

This framework makes the losses 'elsewhere' – or out of the two target regions – explicit. Although the impacts on any single region include both activity- and site-related expenditures, the total impact across all regions includes only activity-dependent expenditures; these are the sum of (1b) to (9b). The site-dependent expenditures cancel when summing over regions. However, the gains and losses associated with the activities of the event may not sum to zero if the event is not unique. That is, the participants would be willing to travel outside all sub-regions if the event was held elsewhere. Thus, the sum of gains reflects the loss avoided by hosting the activities in the region.

This revised framework excludes the Total Sales Impact cells that were at the bottom of the framework in Table 22.1. Sales multipliers have problems with unmeasured spillovers, study regions that do not match political boundaries for which multipliers are available, and long-term indirect effects that are difficult to hypothesize for short-term events. In contrast, cells associated with Value Added remain in the framework; this is simply a rough estimate of the contribution of the event to Gross Regional Product (wages, profits and indirect business taxes).

Newport to Bermuda Race

Founded in 1906 as the first ocean race for amateur sailors in normal boats, the Newport–Bermuda race is one of five races in the Onion Patch Series sponsored by the New York Yacht Club, the Cruising Club of America (CCA) and the Royal Bermuda Yacht Club. The 635-mile Newport–Bermuda Race is the major offshore race of the series and regarded as one of the world's most prestigious yachting events. It is raced every even-numbered year.

About 90 per cent of the yachts entered in the Newport–Bermuda Race are from ports between West Long Island and Portland, ME. On average, the race takes four days to complete. Families and friends fly down to meet the yachts and many spend the next four days on Bermuda and then return to the US by air, while replacement crews sail the yachts back to their home ports. The following section illustrates an application of the proposed framework to this event.

Methods

Data collected for the 1992 event permit an economic impact analysis to be conducted using the framework detailed above. Expenditure data was collected from interviews with the organizing committee members from both Rhode Island and Bermuda and a skipper survey. Seventy-three questionnaires were received over the period from 28 June to 20 October 1992 for a response rate of 61 per cent.

Included in the questionnaire were two questions to distinguish the importance of the event site from the event activities associated with the yacht race:

How important is the Newport–Bermuda Race to your sailing/racing season?
(Please circle a point on the line below to indicate importance to your sailing season.)

0 .... 10 ....20 ....30 ....40 ....50 ....60 ....70 ....80 ....90 100

No importance: I would have raced in another, equivalent event somewhere else.

1/2 my sailing season in one way or another depends on the Newport- Bermuda Race.

My entire sailing season is related to the Newgort- Bermuda Race.

How important to the race is the fact the start is in Newport?
(Please circle a point to indicate the importance of the Newport start.)

0 .... 10 ....20 ....30 ....40 ....50 ....60 ....70 ....80 ....90 100

No importance: I am indifferent to the starting location.

Average Importance: about 1/2 my reason for participating is that the race starts in Newport.

Extreme Importance: If this race didn't start in Newport I wouldn't race.

How important to the race is the fact the finish is in Bermuda?
(Please circle a point to indicate the importance of the Bermuda finish.)

0 .... 10 ....20 ....30 ....40 ....50 ....60 ....70 ....80 ....90 100

No importance: I am indifferent to the finishlocation.

Average Importance: about 1/2 my reason for participating is that the finish is in Bermuda.

Extreme Importance: If this race didn't finish in Bermuda, I wouldn't race.

Data

Of the 119 yachts that participated in 1992, 17.5 per cent were from New York, 17.5 per cent were from Connecticut, 15.0 per cent were from Maryland, 12.5 per cent were from Massachusetts, 6.7 per cent were from Maine and 5.8 per cent were from Rhode Island. The remaining 25.0 per cent were from fourteen states in the US plus Canada and Bermuda.

Expenditures were more than $31,000 per yacht for the ten-day event. Expenditures before the race, elsewhere than Rhode Island or Bermuda, were about $8,000 – mostly on gear, transportation and supplies. Expenditures during the average of four days in Newport totalled almost $11,000 – about two-thirds on sails, gear and equipping the yachts and the other third on lodging, meals and entertainment. Expenditures during the average six-day stay in Bermuda were approximately $13,000 per yacht, with the largest share (88 per cent) going to lodging, meals, transportation and shopping on the island.

Ninety four per cent of skippers responding to the survey indicated they were likely to return to Rhode Island over the next year or two (excluding the next Newport–Bermuda Race). Seventy five per cent indicated they were likely to return to Bermuda. On average, 58 per cent of the sailing seasons of skippers depended, in one way or another, on this race. The start in Newport was reported to be 48.2 per cent of the reason to participate and the Bermuda finish was 87.9 per cent of the reason to participate. The fact that these percentages add to 194.1 per cent (even before adding any other reasons) confirms the difficulty of separating out reasons for participating. To derive approximate allocations we normalized these results by dividing individual percentages by 194.1. The result was an assignment of 45.3 per cent of boater expenditures to the finishing site in Bermuda, 29.9 per cent to the race activities and 24.8 per cent to the starting site in Newport. There were few spectators at this event, so their impacts were not measured.

Results

The calculated impacts are shown in Table 22.3. Newport is listed as an origin and destination in the table to be consistent with the name of the event, even though the analysis used the entire state of Rhode Island as the origin location. The total (gross) economic activity directly associated with the 1992 race, including monetary and non-monetary contributions, was $6.5 million.

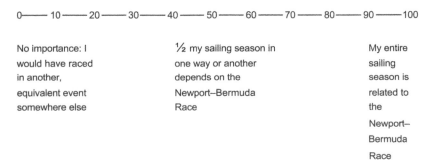

Net direct sales impacts of the 1992 race were $1.8 million in Rhode Island and $3.4 million in Bermuda. Elsewhere, there was a loss of $1 million due to the event. The total impact across all regions, assuming a substitute could be available outside the region, is $4.2 million. This total is the same as the total of expenditures due to race activities. The site-dependent expenditures cancel when adding over regions. If we had assumed that a substitute race was available within the same geographical region, the individual regional direct sales impacts would depend on the specific site locations and the total impacts of the race for the region would be zero.

If a substitute starting site for this race was available within the region, such as Marion, Massachusetts (which currently hosts such an event on alternate years to the Newport–Bermuda biennial race) the Newport–Bermuda Race would imply an avoided loss to Newport of (41a)+(71a)+(11a) = $235,000, and a cost to elsewhere of the same amount.

If no yacht racing event could produce substitutable activities, no event-related expenditures would exist without the event. Also all expenditures out of each region by residents would be lost. Thus, the net income to the region will be its only impact. For Newport, the impact of the Newport–Bermuda Race if there is no substitute is (1)+(4)+(7)-(2)-(3) = $1.7 million. Because other local expenditures would completely replace those associated with the race, so there is no impact on the region as a whole from the Newport–Bermuda if there is no substitute. The last cells in Table 22.3 show calculated value added: $1.3 million in Rhode Island, $2.4 million in Bermuda and a loss elsewhere of $0.7 million.

Table 22.3 Impacts of the 1992 newport – bermuda yacht race

Origin of Expenditures	Location of Purchases	Expenditures Depend on			
		Newport Site	Bermuda Site	Race Activities	All
Newport	Newport	$1,522	$78,570	$102,731	$182,823
	Bermuda	$8	$119,619	$144,547	$264,174
	Elsewhere	$65	$1,436	$1,933	$3,434
Bermuda	Newport	$12,661	$539	$39,268	$52,468
	Bermuda	$45,601	$48,471	$197,749	$291,821
	Elsewhere	$477	$539	$2,096	$3,112
Elsewhere	Newport	$220,719	$402,586	$1,154,767	$1,778,072
	Bermuda	$364,477	$664,820	$1,907,001	$2,936,298
	Elsewhere	$118,750	$218,207	$623,089	$960,046
Total	Newport	$234,902	$481,695	$1,296,766	$2,013,363
	Bermuda	$410,086	$832,910	$2,249,297	$3,492,293
	Elsewhere	$119,292	$220,182	$627,118	$966,592
GROSS SALES		$764,280	$1,534,787	$4,173,181	$6,472,248
NET DIRECT SALES IMPACT (DSI)				Newport	$1,812,143
(Assuming Out of Region Substitute)				Bermuda	$3,384,005
				Elsewhere	−$1,022,967
				Total	$4,173,181
TOTAL VALUE ADDED (VA)				Newport	$1,268,500
				Bermuda	$2,368,804
				Elsewhere	−$716,077
				Total	$2,921,227

Critical findings that would otherwise be overlooked

Benefits to a destination of a short-term tourism event reflect the value of new and interesting experiences to visitors. They also reflect substantial monetary transfers out of the regions where the participants originate. This transfer of costs is universally ignored by the event promoters and host communities. If interregional regional collaboration is a viable long-term strategy for regional development, tourism event impact analyses should at least acknowledge the benefits and costs of tourism events on neighbouring communities. This acknowledgement will require a more complete analysis of the causes, directions, magnitudes and substitutability of events inside and outside the host region.

The illustrated, spatially explicit approach bases the value of a tourism event on the avail-ability of substitute alternatives in and out of the region, using the separation of site-induced expenditures and activity-induced expenditures. The importance of this separation is particularly important when impacts are measured for sub-regions. For example, in the illustrated case study of the Newport–Bermuda Yacht Race, total regional impacts are found to be exactly the same with and without site effects: $4.1 million in direct sales impacts. But without site effects Newport impacts are reduced by $0.5 million, Bermuda impacts are reduced by $1.1 million, and impacts elsewhere are increased by $1.6 million. This is because travel expenditures asso-ciated purely with travel to and visiting the site are substantially those of the participants who do not reside in Newport or Bermuda.

The site versus activity separation also recognizes residential expenditures that are made because of event activities. The traditional approach excludes expenditures made by locals in or out of state whether made because of the event or the site(s). The proposed framework, in contrast, includes residential expenditures that otherwise would have followed the activities out of the region. Excluding residential expenditures at the sub-regional level has a major effect on impacts: Newport expenditures are reduced by $0.6 million, Bermuda expenditures are reduced by $1.3 million and the impacts elsewhere are increased by $1 million. However, since everyone is a resident in the larger region, an aggregate measure excluding residents is zero. (That is, excluding residents doesn't make sense at an aggregate level.)

Conclusion

Successful regional economic development requires cooperation between localities, together with information describing the gains and losses caused by economic development projects such as tourism events. Other than a few exceptions, economic analyses of tourism event impacts consider only the gains to a host region, ignoring the costs to other regions. This chapter extends a previously developed framework for analysing direct expenditures of tourism events to a multi-regional framework that accounts for both winners and losers. Accounting for the origins, destinations and reasons for event-related expenditures allows for the measurement of two important dimensions of the impact of a tourism event, reflecting the performance of the event organizer (or host committee) in two specific areas: (1) generating impacts related to event activities and (2) generating impacts related to the site at which the activity occurs. The economic impacts associated with the event activities measure the performance of the event organizer in using a site. This impact (and performance measure) is different from and should not be confused with the attractiveness of the site itself. Clearly an event organizer must recognize the qualities of the site chosen, but even a poor organizer can attract visitors to a high-quality or popular site.

The extension of this idea to multiple regions requires the consideration of where the participants originate and what and where substitute alternatives exist. At this larger regional scale, the impacts of tourism events become important to regional development officials and a much broader community of stakeholders. At this level, regional cooperation requires compromise, balance and collaboration. Tourism promotional efforts by counties and states in the US have only begun to embrace joint marketing and sales efforts. Tourism event managers have yet to adopt this idea. Within this context, the framework proposed here represents more than a simple analytical tool. It reflects a broader aspiration and vision that tourism events can be better managed to generate benefits for a larger region than a host community through improved collaboration and communication, supported by more insightful analysis of economic impacts.

The case study of the 1992 Newport–Bermuda Yacht Race demonstrates an application of the model, illustrating the flows between origins and destinations of event- and site-related expenditures between Newport, Bermuda and other places in the Northeastern US. As expected, the two host communities of Newport and Bermuda gain from the event while origins elsewhere lose. As noted above, the analysis depends critically upon the availability of a substitute event; in this case we assume an out-of-region yachting event is possible. A regional analysis of an event of this type could provide important information about sub-regional gains and losses which could be used in the development of a regional tourism plan. It is possible, for example, that locations elsewhere in the Northeast could provide support for the event in exchange for cross-marketing of other types of events. The result could be an efficient clustering of travel services between and among sub-regions.

Taken as a whole, this chapter is meant to provoke introspection among tourism researchers and analysts concerning value judgements implied by traditional approaches to economic impact analysis, and provide an initial framework within which more comprehensive analysis might be grounded. The proposed approach does not answer all questions regarding spatial and temporal considerations in event analysis, nor is it a panacea for the all too common use and abuse of economic impact analysis to support predetermined goals (Crompton 2006). It does, however, provide an analytical foundation through which analysis of tourism event impacts might be paired with broader, cooperative regional development and sustainability initiatives.

Notes

1 The authors would like to thank J.R. Brent Ritchie for helpful comments on an earlier draft of this manuscript. Any remaining errors are those of the authors alone.
2 The Multiregional CGE model described by Dwyer *et al.* (2006) is one of the exceptions. However, this model extends far beyond the methods traditionally incorporated within economic impact analysis and used for event evaluation and planning.
3 Many event impact studies have emphasized the importance of spatial impacts (Cooper 1981; Liu and Var 1983; Murphy and Carmichael 1991; Wicks and Fesenmaier 1995; Verhoven *et al.* 1998; Bohlin 2000; McHone and Rungeling 2000; Yu and Turco 2000; Thrane 2002; Lee and Crompton 2003; Prabha *et al.* 2006; Dwyer *et al.* 2006; Dai and Bao 2008). However, they have generally adopted the principle stated by Stynes that '[V]isitor spending that takes place outside the study region (whether at home or en route) is not included, nor are businesses outside the region that benefit directly or indirectly from visitor spending within the region' (Stynes 1997: 24). In fact, until recently, residential spending has been completely ignored because it does not reflect new money to the local economy.
4 The analysis of non-monetary or long-term gains for the region is not treated by this framework.
5 Several authors attribute the ills of event impact analysis to their sponsors and their political purpose (Crompton and McKay 1994; Crompton 1995).

> Economic-impact analyses have an obvious political mission. They invariably are commissioned by tourism entities and usually are driven by a desire to demonstrate their sponsors' positive contribution to the economic prosperity of the jurisdiction that subsidizes their programs or projects. The intent of a study is to position tourism in the minds of elected officials and taxpayers as being a key element in the community's economy.
>
> (Crompton 2006: 67)

and 'economic impact studies are frequently commissioned by advocates to engender support for tourism. In their enthusiasm to make the economic case as strong as possible, many such studies are methodologically flawed' (Ap and Crompton 1998: 121).
6 Finding that the World Tourism Organization provided only a fuzzy definition of a destination, Lew and McKercher (2006) defined it as 'the area containing the products and activities that could normally be consumed in a daytrip from the heart of the destination and that are normally promoted by the destination as part of its overall suite of products' (p. 405).
7 Analytical demands of a full-scale CGE model far exceed those required for traditional economic impact analysis, and are likely impractical for most types of event evaluation. The proposed framework is designed to provide a more comprehensive perspective using methods that are practical for a broader range of applications and accessible to wider audience of analysts.

References

Alexander, Phil (1991) 'Managing festivals and events', Michigan State University Cooperative Extension Service, Bulletin E-2303, April.

Ap, John and Crompton, John L. (1998) 'Developing and testing a tourism impact scale', *Journal of Travel Research* 37(2): 120–30.

Bohlin, M. (2000) 'Traveling to events', in L. Mossberg (ed.) *Evaluation of Events: Scandinavian Experiences*, New York: Cognizant, pp. 13–29.

Carmichael, Barbara (2002) 'Global competitiveness and special events in cultural tourism: the example of the Barnes Exhibit at the Art Gallery of Ontario, Toronto', *The Canadian Geographer* 46 (4): 310–24.

Cooper, C.P. (1981) 'Spatial and temporal patterns of tourist behaviour', *Regional Studies* 15(5):359–71.

Crompton, John L. (1995) 'Economic impact analysis of sports facilities and events: eleven sources of misapplication', *Journal of Sport Management* 9: 14–35.

——(2006) 'Economic impact studies: instruments for political shenanigans?', *Journal of Travel Research* 45: 67–82.

Crompton, John L. and McKay, S.L. (1994) 'Measuring the economic impact of festivals and events: some myths, misapplications and ethical dilemmas', *Festival Management and Event Tourism* 2: 33–43.

Crompton, John L., Lee, Seokho and Shuster, Thomas J. (2001) 'A guide for undertaking economic impact studies: the Springfest example', *Journal of Travel Research* 40: 79–87.

Dai, Guangquan and Bao, Jigang (2008) 'Spatial distribution of integrated impact index of mega-event – a case study of Expo '99 Kunming', *Journal of Chinese Geographical Science* 18(3): 214 Estimating income effects of a sport tourism event', *Annals of Tourism Research* 31(1): 180–99.

Davidson, L.S. and Schaffer, W.A. (1980) 'A discussion of methods employed in analyzing the impact of short-term entertainment events', *Journal of Travel Research* 28(3): 12–16.

Della Bitta, Albert J., Loudon, David L., Booth, G. Geoffrey and Weeks, Richard R. (1977) 'Estimating the economic impact of a short-term tourist event', *Journal of Travel Research* 16: 10–15.

Dredge, Dianne (1999) 'Destination, place, planning and design', *Annals of Tourism Research* 26(4): 772–91.

Dwyer, Larry, Forsyth, Peter and Spurr, Ray (2006) 'Assessing the economic impacts of events: a computable general equilibrium approach', *Journal of Travel Research* 45(1): 59–66.

Formica, Sandro and Kothari, Tanvi H. (2008) 'Strategic destination planning: analyzing the future of tourism', *Journal of Travel Research* 46: 355–67.

Getz, D. (1997) *Event Management and Event Tourism*, New York: Cognizant.

——(2008) 'Event tourism: definition, evolution, and research', *Tourism Management* 29(3): 403–28

Goetz, Edward G. and Kayser, Terrence (1993) 'Competition and cooperation in economic development: a study of the Twin Cities metropolitan area', *Economic Development Quarterly* 7(1): 63–78.

Gordon, Victoria (2009) 'Perceptions of regional economic development: can win–lose become win–win?', *Economic Development Quarterly* 23(4): 317–28.

Hall, Colin Michael (1989) 'The definition and analysis of hallmark tourist events', *GeoJournal* 19 (3): 263–8.

Heilbron, J. and Gray, C.M. (1993). *The Economics of Art and Culture: An American Perspective*, Cambridge: Cambridge University Press.

Hubbard, William, Craig, Christine, Israel, Arnon, Peeters, Christa, VanderZwaag, George and Ervin, Michael (1989) 'Volvo International' 88: economic impact study, demographic profile', University of Massachusetts Graduate Programme in Sports Management, Amherst, MA.

Johnson, Rebecca L. and Moore, Eric (1993) 'Tourism impact estimation', *Annals of Tourism Research* 20: 279–88.

Kinsey, Billy, Jr (2002) 'The economic impact of museums and cultural attractions: another benefit for the community', paper presented at the Annual Meeting of the American Association of Museums, Dallas, Texas, 14 May.

Lee, S. and Crompton, J. (2003) 'The attraction power and spending impact of three festivals in Ocean City, Maryland', *Event Management* 8(2): 109–12.

Lew, Alan and McKercher, Bob (2006) 'Modeling tourist movements', *Annals of Tourism Research* 33(2): 403–23.

Liu, J. and Var, T. (1983) 'The economic impact of tourism in Metropolitan Victoria, BC', *Journal of Travel Research* 22: 8–15.

Lombard, John R. and Morris, John C. (2010) 'Competing and cooperating across state borders in economic development: a call for "coopertition"', *State and Local Government Review* 42(1): 73–81.

Long, P. and Perdue, R. (1990) 'The economic impact of rural festivals and special events: assessing the spatial distribution of expenditures', *Journal of Travel Research* 28(4): 10–14.

McCarthy, Linda (2003) 'The good of the many outweighs the good of the one: regional cooperation instead of individual competition in the United States and Western Europe?', *Journal of Planning Education and Research* 23(2): 140–52.

McHone, W. Warren and Rungeling, Brian (2000) 'Practical issues in measuring the impact of a cultural tourist event in a major tourist destination', *Journal of Travel Research* 38: 299–302.

Murphy, P.E. and Carmichael, B.A. (1991) 'Assessing the tourism benefits of an open access sports tournament: the 1989 BC Winter Games', *Journal of Travel Research* 29: 32–6.

OECD (Organisation for Economic Co-operation and Development) (2001) 'Tourism satellite account: recommended methodological framework', Code 78 2000 01 1P1. Paris.

Prabha, P., Rolfe, J. and Sinden, J. (2006) 'A travel cost analysis of the value of special events: Gemfest in Central Queensland', *Tourism Economics* 12(3): 403–20.

Raymond, Christopher and Brown, Gregory (2007) 'A spatial method for assessing resident and visitor attitudes towards tourism growth and development', *Journal of Sustainable Tourism* 15(5): 520–40.

Ritchie, J.R. Brent and Zins, Michel (1978) 'Culture as determinant of the attractiveness of a region', *Annals of Tourism Research* V(2): 252–67.

Ryan, Chris (1999) 'The use of a spatial model to assess conference market share', *The International Journal of Tourism Research*, January/February: 49–53.

Smith, Stephen L.J. (1995) *Tourism Analysis*, Essex, UK: Longman, second edition.

Stynes, Daniel J. (1997) *Economic Impacts of Tourism: A Handbook for Tourism Professionals*, Urbana-Champaign: Illinois Bureau of Tourism, prepared by the Tourism Research Laboratory at the University of Illinois at Urbana-Champaign.

Thrane, Christer (2002) 'Jazz festival visitors and their expenditures: linking spending patterns to musical interest', *Journal of Travel Research* 40(3): 281–6.

Tyrrell, Timothy J. and Johnston, Robert J. (2001) 'A framework for assessing direct economic impacts of tourist events: distinguishing origins, destinations, and causes of expenditures', *Journal of Travel Research* 40(1, August): 94–100.

——(2009) 'An econometric analysis of the effects of tourism growth on municipal revenues and expenditures', *Tourism Economics* 15(4): 771–83.

Tyrrell, Timothy J. and McNair, Michael B. (1994) *The Economic Impact of the 1994 JVC Jazz Festival on Newport and the State of Rhode Island*, Kingston, RI: Office of Travel Tourism and Recreation, Department of Resource Economics, University of Rhode Island.

Tyrrell, Timothy J. and Sullivan, Susan (1992) *The Economic Impact of the Newport–Bermuda Race, 1992 on the State of Rhode Island and Bermuda*, Kingston, RI: Office of Travel, Tourism and Recreation, Department of Resource Economics, University of Rhode Island.

Tyrrell, Timothy J. and Toepper, L. (1991) *The Economic Impact of the 1990 Volvo/International Hall of Fame Tennis Tournament on Newport and the State of Rhode Island*, Kingston, RI: Office of Travel, Tourism and Recreation, Department of Resource Economics, University of Rhode Island.

Tyrrell, Timothy J., Williams, Peter W. and Johnston, Robert J. (2004) 'Estimating sport tourism visitor volumes: the case of Vancouver's 2010 Olympic Games', *Tourism Recreation Research* 29(1): 75–82.

Verhoven, P., Wall, D. and Cottrell, S. (1998) 'Application of desktop mapping as a marketing tool for special events planning and evaluation: a case study of the Newport News Celebration in Lights', *Festival Management and Event Tourism* 5(3): 123–30.

Wicks, B. and Fesenmaier, D. (1995) 'Market potential for special events: a midwestern case study', *Festival Management and Event Tourism* 3(1): 25–31.

Yardley, John, MacDonald, John and Clarke, Barry (1990) 'The economic impact of a small, short-term recreation event on a local economy', *Journal of Park and Recreation Administration* 8(4): 71–82.

Yu, Yingmiao and Turco, Douglas Michele (2000) 'Issues in tourism event economic impact studies: the case of the Albuquerque International Balloon Fiesta', *Current Issues in Tourism* 3(2): 138–49.

23

Socio-cultural impacts of events

Meanings, authorized transgression and social capital

Richard Sharpley and Philip R. Stone

Introduction: the impacts of events

All events have impacts (Hall 1997). More specifically, all events or, at least, planned events have a purpose or objective and, hence, intended, desired and predicted (and, on occasion, unanticipated) outcomes. These, in turn, have impacts on host communities, participants and other stakeholders who, as Getz (2007: 300) puts it, are 'impacted' by the outcomes of events. Such impacts may be positive or beneficial. Indeed, it is the expected benefits of events, whether economic, social, cultural, political or environmental, that is the principal driver underpinning the support for and increasing popularity of them at the local, national and international scale. Of course, the impacts of events may also be negative. That is, events almost inevitably incur costs or have negative consequences that, to a lesser or greater extent, serve to reduce their net benefit. Thus, a key task for event managers is to not only identify and, as far as possible, predict the impacts of events, but to manage them in such a way that benefits are optimized and negative impacts are minimized so that, 'on balance the overall impact of the event is positive' (Bowdin *et al.* 2006: 37).

It is not surprising, therefore, that the academic study of events and event management has long focused upon the impacts or consequences of events. As Quinn (2009: 487) notes, initial research agendas focused on developing knowledge and understanding of the impacts of events: 'from early on, events came overwhelmingly to be conceived as discrete entities with an ability to unidirectionally create a series of impacts, both positive and negative, on contextual environments'. What is surprising, perhaps, is that until recently a predominantly economic perspective was in evidence (Formica 1998). In other words, despite early recognition of the wide variety of impacts that might be associated with events (Ritchie 1984), much research focused specifically on their economic consequences, a trend noted by others (Hede 2007; Moscardo 2007). Undoubtedly, this reflected the importance that was, and continues to be, placed upon the role of particular events in urban, rural, regional or national (economic) development and, hence, the need to both justify and measure the returns on often significant financial investment in festivals and events as agents of development (Andranovich *et al.* 2001). In other words, despite their potential to contribute to, for example, the enhancement of a city's image (Richards and Wilson 2004) or the development of community cohesion and pride

(Waitt 2003), the success of events is often ultimately assessed according to economic criteria such as income generation, employment generation or the attraction of inward investment (Dwyer *et al.* 2000).

However, two points must immediately be made. First and quite evidently, events are not always promoted or staged for the economic benefits that they might generate, and nor can their negative consequences be measured simply in economic terms. Indeed, events may often be staged at an economic 'loss' when, for example, their costs are covered not by income from participants but by sponsorship or local government funding. In such cases, the desired benefits of the event might be overtly socio-cultural: strengthening community identity and pride (De Bres and Davis 2001), developing social capital (Arcodia and Whitford 2006), increasing local participation in community activities (Ritchie 1984), revitalizing local culture, traditions, and so on. Equally, events may be staged for political purposes (Roche 2000). Frequently, the hosting of international mega-events may be driven by the pursuit of international prestige or legitimacy whilst other events may seek to highlight specific political issues or causes, both 'Live Aid' and 'Live 8' concerts in 1985 and 2005 respectively being notable examples of the latter. Reference should also be made, of course, to the physical or environmental impacts, both positive and negative, of events. As discussed in Chapter 24, not only may events provide an environmental benefit (for example, improved infrastructure), but also there is a pressing need to manage the environmental impacts of events within a sustainability framework.

Second, the impacts of events are neither discrete nor necessarily hierarchical. That is, all events have a variety of impacts, both positive and negative, some being more immediately evident than others, some being of potentially greater significance than the intended outcomes. For example, a study by Lee and Taylor (2005) found that the sense of national pride engendered by the South Korean national team's success at the 2002 FIFA World Cup hosted by that country far outweighed the event's economic returns. Similarly, the annual London Marathon has a major economic impact in terms of the money that participants raise for charity whilst, for the runners themselves, taking part in (and, hopefully, completing) the marathon not only provides a sense of achievement but also, as Shipway and Jones (2008) reveal, is linked to social identity formation. However, the publicity surrounding the event may also have a major influence on encouraging people to take up running and, hence, on longer-term health trends.

Together, these points suggest that, in order to fully understand the potential impact of events, there is a need for more broadly focused research that explores beyond the confines of economic analysis. Indeed, there have long been calls for a more expansive approach to researching events. Moreover, it has been suggested that 'despite the growth and popularity of festivals and special events, researchers have been very slow in directing research beyond economic impacts' (Gursoy *et al.* 2004: 171), there is evidence to suggest that, in more recent years, such a broader perspective has come to be adopted. In particular, the study of events has increasingly embraced the identification, measurement and analysis of their social and cultural impacts, whilst a special issue of the journal *Event Management* in 2008 focused on events 'beyond economic impacts'. Nevertheless, this research arguably remains limited both in absolute terms and also, as Fredline and Faulkner (2000) observed over a decade ago, relative to related research focusing on the socio-cultural impacts of tourism (see also Fredline *et al.* 2003). Thus, the purpose of this chapter is to review contemporary approaches to the study of the social and cultural impacts of events and to explore ways in which our knowledge and understanding of such impacts may be enhanced. First, however, it is useful to consider what, in a generic sense, the social and cultural impacts of events 'are' and the different dimensions within which they may be considered.

Social and cultural impacts: focus and dimensions

A major challenge facing the study of events in general and of their social and cultural impacts in particular is the sheer volume and diversity of organized activities or occasions that may be described as events. Without repeating the definitional debates addressed elsewhere in this book, this volume and diversity is such that it is difficult and, perhaps, dangerous to generalize about the purpose, management and outcomes of events. Every event is a unique activity, occasion or 'happening' with unique objectives and, hence, unique outcomes and impacts. Therefore, it is unsurprising that much research into events is case study-based although, more recently, attempts have been made to develop general frameworks for assessing the social impact of events (Delamere *et al.* 2001; Fredline *et al.* 2003; Reid 2008; Small 2008).

Nevertheless, all events share a common characteristic: people. The staging of an event attracts people from elsewhere as participants or spectators; equally, it may only involve local people, again as participants and/or spectators. In either case, however, the event may have impacts on both participants and spectators and on the local (host) community more generally as well as, depending on its nature and scale, on communities further afield or not directly involved with the event. At the same time, people are also involved in events as organizers. They may be members of the local community, local leaders, representatives of particular interest groups or professional event organizers. Importantly, it is the interactions and relationships within and between these different stakeholder groups that may go some way to determining the nature and extent of the social and cultural impacts of events.

But what are these social and cultural impacts? In other words, what do we mean by the terms 'social' and 'cultural' impacts, and can they be thought of collectively as 'socio-cultural' impacts? According to Burdge and Vanclay (1996: 59), social impacts can be defined generally as 'all social and cultural consequences to human population of any public or private actions that alter the ways in which people live, work, play, relate to one another, organize to meet their needs, and generally cope as members of society'. Conversely, cultural impacts are those which 'involve changes to the norms, values, and beliefs of individuals that guide and rationalize their cognition of themselves and their society'.

Putting it another way, the social impacts of events in particular may be defined as transformations in how people live their lives or, as Wall and Mathieson (2006: 227) suggest, 'changes in the quality of life' of local communities, participants and other stakeholders that arise from the holding of an event of any kind. On the other hand, the cultural impacts of events may be thought of as transformations in the processes (values, traditions and norms) through which individuals and societies define themselves and their behaviour (see Richards 2006) although, rather confusingly, the study of the cultural impacts of tourism, with its explicit relevance to event studies, often embraces impacts on expressions or manifestations of culture, such as both material and non-material forms of culture. Thus, the distinction between 'social' and 'cultural' impacts is not always clear, the potential commoditization of a particular cultural event, for example, arguably being definable as both a social and cultural impact. However, for the purposes of this chapter, social and cultural impacts may be defined respectively as the impacts of an event on the day-to-day life of people associated directly or indirectly with that event and on the values, attitudes, beliefs and traditions that determine or guide that day-to-day life. Moreover, there is an evident relationship between the two and therefore, for the sake of simplicity, they will be considered here collectively as socio-cultural impacts.

The question then to be addressed is: how should the socio-cultural impacts of events be assessed or researched? In other words, what broad perspective (as opposed to prescriptive research frameworks) should be adopted when considering such impacts? From the preceding discussion of the meaning of the terms 'social' and 'cultural' impacts, it is evident that there are two levels or dimensions within which they may be studied. First, what are usually referred to as social impacts of events, that is, the more immediate and tangible impacts on local people, participants and others influenced directly by an event, may be considered within a simplistic, deterministic, uni-dimensional 'cause and effect' framework. That is, the hosting of events brings about a variety of immediate, identifiable and predictable social consequences which arise from interactions between local people and visitors (in a tourism context, host–guest interactions), from activities and developments related to the event and from the extent of local participation in the event. Such impacts are similar to those associated with the development of tourism more generally, such as the tangible impacts of congestion, crime and anti-social behaviour, as well as broader transformations in the form of cultural commoditization and so on. These are often balanced against the economic consequences of events and which, implicitly, may be managed.

Second, the notion of cultural impacts, or changes to an individual's or society's values, norms, beliefs, traditions and so on, suggests that a more complex relationship exists between an event and all its stakeholders, including performers/participants, visitors/spectators, organizers, and local communities, distinctions between whom may not always be evident. That is, whilst in some cases, such as sporting mega-events, each group of stakeholders is distinctive, in other cases, such as small local events, all stakeholders may be members of the local community. This, in turn, suggests that a multi-dimensional approach which not only addresses the immediate causal relationship between the event and stakeholders (the uni-dimensional perspective) but which also recognizes the complex relationships between the event and all stakeholders may provide a deeper and richer basis for exploring the social and cultural impacts of events.

This multi-dimensional process – that is, the socio-cultural transformation arising out of complex event-related social relationships – has been referred to as 'remaking worlds' (Picard and Robinson 2006) and embraces themes such as identity creation (personal, cultural, national), ritualized transgression and so on. These will be considered in more detail shortly but, by way of comparison, the next section briefly reviews contemporary approaches to the socio-cultural impacts of events within the context of the uni-dimensional perspective.

Uni-dimensional perspectives on socio-cultural impacts

As noted above, research into the impacts of events has, perhaps understandably, adopted a primarily economic focus. For example, at the 'Events Beyond 2000: Setting the Agenda' conference in 2000, all papers focusing on 'event evaluation' emphasized the importance of economic impacts (Allen *et al.* 2000). This is not to say, however, that the non-economic impacts of events have gone unrecognized. Ritchie's (1984) widely cited paper revealed the diversity of forms of impact potentially resulting from, specifically, so-called hallmark events. Indeed, most textbooks on event studies and event management include chapters that explore or describe the impacts of events under a variety of headings, typically economic, socio-cultural, political and physical/environmental. Nevertheless, much of the research into these non-economic impacts remains limited to immediate and tangible consequences of events, often following a descriptive cause-and-effect model; conversely, more in-depth or multi-dimensional studies have, until more recently, been lacking.

This limited approach to non-economic impacts, in particular within the socio-cultural context, may be explained by three factors in particular. First, the study of events is very much concerned with management issues or, more specifically, how to manage events successfully. In other words, the academic study of events is explicitly linked with the practice of event management and, thus, much research is driven by the needs of the 'events industry'; that is, how to manage and respond to the socio-cultural impacts of events in order to optimize desired (and implicitly, measurable) outcomes. As a consequence, longer-term cultural transformations have, arguably, been of less concern (Harris *et al.* 2000). Second, academic study and research in events has very much evolved from the broader study of tourism. Many 'events' researchers are active members of the tourism academic community and are, therefore, aware of the extensive body of knowledge with respect to (tourism's) socio-cultural impacts, whilst event tourism and event management are often explicitly linked (Backman *et al.* 1995; Getz 1997). Moreover, much existing impacts literature in tourism refers to events and, thus, to explore the socio-cultural impacts of events may be seen as repeating existing research. Third, and as observed in the previous section, the diversity and scope of events is such that it is difficult, if not impossible, to progress beyond research into case-specific, tangible and measurable impacts of events.

Certainly, these three factors go some way to explaining the contemporary literature on the socio-cultural impacts of events. Textbooks, for example, tend to identify and list the positive and negative socio-cultural impacts of events before proposing management responses and strategies. Typically, these are immediate, tangible impacts caused by events. Negative impacts are those which collectively and negatively impact upon the lives of local communities, such as crowding, rowdy behaviour, traffic congestion, substance abuse, crime and loss of amenity, as well as feelings of community manipulation/commoditization or exclusion (Bowdin *et al.* 2006). Conversely, positive socio-cultural impacts reflect the commonly cited social objectives of events, such as strengthening community cohesion, engendering community identity and pride, revitalizing cultural traditions or enhancing place meanings to residents.

However, as Boyko (2008: 162) suggests, 'impacts cannot be viewed in absolute terms of good and bad … [nor] … be regarded entirely in isolation from one another. Rather, the impacts on a host community are intertwined and depend on goals and values … within that community'. For this reason, perhaps, much of the extant research into the socio-cultural impacts of events addresses one of two issues: either resident/host community perceptions of the impacts of particular festivals and events (for example, Jeong and Faulkner 1996; Mihalik and Simonetta 1998; Zhou and Ap 2009), which builds on an extensive literature focusing on resident perceptions of tourism development more generally, or the development of frameworks or scales for identifying and measuring socio-cultural impacts (for example, Delamere *et al.* 2001; Fredline *et al.* 2003; Small 2008). The latter approach is of particular note inasmuch as it identifies those impacts of events that fall under the heading of socio-cultural. Delamere *et al.*'s (2001) study, for example, lists a total of twenty-one social benefits, divided into community benefits and cultural/educational benefits, and twenty-seven costs, separated into quality of life concerns and community resource concerns – a condensed version is provided in Table 23.1. It should be noted that this study focused specifically upon community festivals, where socio-cultural impacts (both positive and negative) may be more widely and keenly sensed than at other types of events. Nevertheless, it demonstrates the more immediate, tangible impacts of events but, whilst revealing the diversity of such impacts that might be experienced by the host community, the principal contribution of this research is to the effective management and planning of events. Consequently, Delamere *et al.* (2001: 22) suggest,

> as community leaders and festival organizers become more aware of the needs and priorities of the community, they can better respond to community concerns and work together to maintain an appropriate balance between the social benefits and social costs that emanate from community festivals.

Table 23.1 Socio-cultural impacts of events

Social benefits	Social costs
Community benefits	*Quality of life concerns*
Celebration of community	Increased crime/vandalism
Enhanced community identity	Unacceptable increase in vehicular/pedestrian traffic
Enhanced community image	Overcrowding
Increased community cohesion	Litter/ecological damage
increased community well-being	Reduced privacy
Improved quality of community life	Disruption to normal routines
Individual pride through participation	Unacceptable noise levels
Shared ideas amongst community	Overuse of community facilities
Cultural/educational benefits	*Community resource concerns*
Experience of new activities	Increased disagreement within community
Participants learn new things	Event is 'all work no play'
Event showcases new ideas	Excessive demand on community human resources
Development of cultural skills/talents	Highlights cultural stereotypes
Exposure to new cultural experiences	Unequal sharing of benefits of the event
Strengthening of community friendships	Weakened community identity
Lasting positive cultural impact	Excessive demand on community financial resources
Achievement of common community goals	Potential sense of failure within community

Source: adapted from Delamere *et al.* (2001).

What is not generally explored in the extant literature is the potential for longer-term cultural transformations within host communities, nor indeed amongst individuals and groups beyond the host community. In other words, although some commentators consider non-host community perceptions of events (Deccio and Baloglu 2002), the perceptions of event organizers (Gursoy *et al.* 2004) or socio-cultural impacts experienced by participants (Shipway and Jones 2008), the predominant focus of the research on the host community has tended to exclude other dimensions. Therefore, as suggested earlier in this chapter, in order to fully understand the potential socio-cultural impacts of events there is a need for a multi-dimensional approach to research which recognizes the complexity of stakeholder relationships as well as the potential for longer-term, less tangible impacts that may well fall outside the control or influence of event managers and organizers. It is to this multi-dimensional perspective that this chapter now turns.

Multi-dimensional perspectives on socio-cultural impacts

As discussed in the preceding sections, the scope and diversity of potential socio-cultural impacts of events has long been recognized, as has the need to manage such impacts. However, the consideration of impacts within a somewhat parochial events management context has, arguably, served to focus attention on tangible, manageable impacts. Conversely, relatively few attempts have been made to explore the potential for longer-term socio-cultural transformations and impacts within a broader non-management context; that is, attention has primarily been focused inwardly on the management of events themselves rather than outwards on the world in which events take place. However, as Picard and Robinson (2006: 4) argue, 'festivals, while containing worlds, also open out and spill over into "outside" worlds and their multiple dimensions can only be understood by taking into consideration the different realties of these outside worlds'. The same may be said of events more generally (festivals generally being defined as a specific manifestation of event). As significant as the management imperative might be in order to ensure that desired benefits are achieved, the socio-cultural consequences of events can only be understood fully by relating the analysis to the various 'realties' of the world beyond the social, economic, political and environmental confines of the event itself. In short, in order to identify more completely the potential extent of the socio-cultural impacts of events, a multi-dimensional approach is required.

Of course, as with the analysis of the more specific, tangible impacts, it is both difficult and inappropriate to generalize both the broader, perhaps intangible impacts and the realities of the external worlds of events. Not only are events infinitely variable in character and purpose, but also different external realities will be more or less relevant to different events. For example, and as discussed in the case study below, the impacts of explicitly gay and lesbian events, such as Sydney's Mardi Gras, on participants, spectators, local communities, host places and the meaning of the events themselves (Hughes 2006) are directly related to a dynamic cultural, political (and legal) context with respect to homosexual communities in particular and sexuality more generally. As Markwell (2002: 96) notes,

> just as places and their meanings and interpretations are constructed out of processes that reflect the dynamic, often contested power relations between the social and cultural groups occupying those places, so Mardi Gras continues to emerge from a dynamic mix of contested views and philosophical positions.

Nevertheless, most, if not all, events occur in a world that is, according to Picard and Robinson (2006: 2), characterized by 'structural change, social mobility and globalisation processes', referred to more generally by some as globalization (Held and McGrew 2000) and by others as the condition of postmodernity (Harvey 1989). However labelled (a full consideration of these alleged processes is beyond the scope of this chapter, but see Sharpley 2008), these transformations are typically manifested in or, more precisely, bring about, amongst other things, cultural dislocation, a loss of self-identity and a sense of 'placelessness' (Relph 1976) or anomie. Therefore, individuals, communities or specific social groups within contemporary societies seek meaning, authenticity and identity; this, in turn, may go some way to explaining the rapid increase in both the number of events being organized and hosted in recent years and their growing popularity amongst visitors (MacLeod 2006). For host communities, events or festivals provide an opportunity to re-assert or re-invent cultural identity where 'recognised systems of symbolic continuity are challenged by the realities of new social, economic and political environments' (Picard and Robinson 2006: 2). A widely cited example of this is the city of Glasgow which, through its 'reign' as the 1990 European City of Culture, was able to re-invent itself as a post-industrial cultural city (Garcia 2005), though innumerable other places/communities have followed a similar process at a smaller, more local scale. For visitors or tourists − tourism more generally being seen by some as a search for meaning or authenticity (MacCannell 1989; Wang 1999) − festivals and events may be perceived as offering the opportunity for authentic experiences. The extent to which they do so remains the subject of intense debate, yet the ever increasing 'supply' of events feeds a growing demand for such experiences.

The important point is that events in general, and their inherent meanings, processes and social relationships in particular, can be better understood by locating their analysis in the context of their dynamic outside worlds. In other words, the external context provides an essential multi-dimensional framework for exploring the socio-cultural impacts of events. Inevitably, different external realities will be of greater or less relevance to different kinds of events. For example, religious events, whether one-off events, regular festivals/rituals held in recognized locations (or, as Shackley (2001: 101) refers to them, 'nodal' events) or 'linear' events, such as pilgrimages, the socio-cultural impacts on participants, spectators, local communities and others must be considered within the context of understandings of different religions, the significance of the event within local culture, transformations in the significance or meanings of religion (or spirituality), particularly within postmodern, secularized cultures, and so on. Research has demonstrated, for instance, that visitors to particular sacred sites and events behave and respond differently according to their particular faith or belief (Collins-Kreiner and Kliot 2000). Similarly, the analysis of dark events, termed here *thana-events* – that is, those festivals and special events that have commemoration or display of death or the seemingly macabre as a main theme – should be considered within a broader socio-cultural context of post-conventional society (Stone and Sharpley 2008). In other words, as contemporary societies 'demand an open identity capable of conversation with people of other perspectives in a relatively egalitarian and open communicative space' (Hyun-Sook 2006: 1), thana-events may provide a temporal and spatial opportunity to collectively convey moral discourse about particular atrocities, tragedies, or customs (Stone 2009). For instance, events commemorating wars or battles must be considered within a framework of national/international politics, history, culture and a broader moral economy; the commemoration of Gallipoli, for example, is of particular cultural significance to both past and present generations of Australian and New Zealanders (Slade 2003). Consequently, each event and its socio-cultural impacts should be considered within its unique external realties.

However, it is possible to identify three potential impacts or consequences of events that, as suggested above, lend themselves to multi-dimensional analysis. This list is by no means exhaustive; nor does space permit a detailed discussion of each. Nevertheless, for the purposes of this chapter, it serves to demonstrate the breadth of the potential socio-cultural impacts of events and the benefits of a multi-dimensional approach in revealing them.

Events and place identity/meaning

Events of all kinds are being increasingly utilized or promoted as a means of enhancing the identity of places, both 'externally' and 'internally'. Externally, events potentially serve to position or market places, to distinguish them in a world where places are becoming more similar and homogenous, and allow them to compete more effectively amongst a variety of stakeholders, including investors, tourists, policy-makers and so on (Richards and Wilson 2004). The purpose is typically economic: that is, to regenerate or build the local economy through attracting inward investment, new businesses or increased tourist visitation and expenditure, though of course socio-cultural benefits may also accrue through, for example, improved infrastructure, amenities and so on. Internally, the purpose of events and festivals is often primarily socio-cultural, to celebrate or strengthen local culture and, as a consequence, to enhance a sense of identity amongst local communities. Such events may also lead to an increase in tourism and associated economic benefits – as noted above. Indeed, the growing popularity of events may be explained by increased numbers of tourists seeking authentic experiences – as well as the inevitable dis-benefits associated with the development of tourism – yet, as research has shown, festivals and events may positively enhance community identity (De Bres and Davis 2001).

Beyond these immediate impacts, however, a number of issues deserve attention with respect to the socio-cultural impacts related to place identity and meaning creation through events. As is widely considered in the literature, place or, more precisely, place meaning is dependent upon semiotic truism and the polysemic nature of space. In short, construction of place identity is not a given, but is a function of three elements, namely: the physical/objective environment; people's experiences of place; and socially constructed meanings of places (Stedman 2003). Putting it another way, an undifferentiated space only becomes a place 'when we endow it with value' (Tuan 1977: 6). This value emanates from both the social constructs of place, or shared cultural understandings of a particular place, and the conscious choices people make regarding their use of places (Manzo 2003). Therefore, there is a general need to consider the impacts of events on place identity and meaning not only from the perspective of different stakeholders (visitors, local communities, event participants, event organizers) and non-stakeholders, but also within a framework of place meaning construction, for it is likely that different stakeholders will have different cultural understanding of places and different reasons for using them. These, in turn, will reflect the realities of each stakeholder's cultural reality. For example, MacLeod (2006: 232) suggests that events can remain or become placeless as they become the focus of interactions between visitors seeking not authentic local culture but 'convivial experiences with similar people converging in the no-space spaces of festival destinations'. In other words, the place culturally becomes subordinated or irrelevant to the activities of visitors/participants and, in the extreme, becomes simply the venue for what MacLeod refers to as 'global parties'. For local communities, this may mean a loss of identity, or a transformation in identity more closely aligned with the event. For example, Glastonbury in the UK was traditionally known for its links with spiritual myth and legend, often being claimed to be the Avalon of King Arthur; nowadays, however, it is perhaps better known and more widely associated with the annual music festival and, arguably, the place is consumed as a rite of musicological passage.

Conversely, the cultural identity and meaning of places (and local communities) may come to reflect the event and, consequently, 'true' culture is replaced by 'an emphasis on the spectacular as the preferred experience of the visitor' (MacLeod 2006: 235). Yet, rather than viewing this negatively, local communities may embrace it as a basis for a reformulation of local culture. For example, though not related to a specific event, it has been argued that, in Bali, 'interaction with tourists and the tourist industry ... has become such a central component in the definition of ethnic identity ... that the very presence of masses of tourists is commonly cited by Balinese as proof of the continued authenticity of their culture' (Wood 1998: 223; also Picard 1995). In other words, Bali's culture has evolved into a tourism culture in a process that may potentially be repeated in event-specific contexts.

Events and social capital

As previously noted, commonly cited socio-cultural benefits of events relate to the development of community cohesion, the enhancement of community identity or image, the encouragement of community well-being. In some cases, this might be a primary objective of an event, particularly when it is organized and run at a local level; in other cases, it may be an expected or, indeed, unexpected by-product of an event. These impacts may also, of course, be negative. At the time of writing, for example, the controversy surrounding the readiness of the facilities for the 2010 Commonwealth Games in India may, irrespective of the eventual success of the Games, impact negatively on the image of the country and its people, both internationally and within the country itself.

Less attention, however, has been paid to the potential of events to contribute to the development of *social capital*. Arguably, this is a more fundamental and significant element in the enhancement of individual and community well-being, yet one which, according to some, is in decline as a result of the cultural and structural transformations in contemporary societies referred to above (Putnam 1995). This lack of attention may reflect the fact that social capital is a rather ambiguous concept and, as Arcodia and Whitford (2006) suggest, it is difficult if not impossible to measure. Nevertheless, the concept of social capital provides a framework for developing a deeper understanding of the socio-cultural impacts of events on communities.

However, what is social capital? Adler and Kwon (2002: 17) define it as 'the goodwill that is engendered by the fabric of social relations and that can be mobilised to facilitate action' whilst Coleman (1988: 98), a notable proponent of social capital, states that

> social capital is defined by its function. It is not a single entity but a variety of different entities, with two elements in common: they all consist of some aspect of social structures, and they facilitate certain actions of actors ... within the structure.

In other words, social capital is a resource that arises from relationships or interaction between people or groups of people – that resource being manifested in, for example, trust, mutual support and co-operation, or a collective will to work towards particular objectives – and which create value through actions that result in benefits for society. In a sense, therefore, social capital may be thought of as a form of collective or community spirit embodied in a society generally, or within specific organizations, groups or institutions, which underpins positive actions for the benefit of society.

The question then is: to what extent can an event facilitate the development of social capital? Arcodia and Whitford (2006) propose three ways in which this may occur:

- *building community resources* – such resources include: skills and knowledge, social links between community groups, networks, volunteer groups, and so on;
- *social cohesiveness* – events provide the opportunity for community members to unite, for diverse ethnic groups to share experiences and world views, and to give voice to a common social purpose;
- *celebration* – collective participation in a celebratory event may generate a sense of community spirit, togetherness and goodwill.

Evidently, not all festivals will generate social capital through all of these avenues and, as Arcodia and Whitford (2006: 15) note, 'the development of social capital will only occur in a positive social environment'; that is, negative impacts may actually diminish social capital. Nevertheless, social capital represents a potentially fruitful conceptual framework for assessing community social benefits (and costs) of events.

Events and authorized transgression

Festivals and events have long been associated with the creation of liminal times and spaces, where established social conventions may be temporarily relaxed, suspended or reversed. More specifically, festivals or carnivals have long been recognized as occasions where or when social rules and mores may be inverted, where particular activities or forms of behaviour that challenge social hegemony are indulged in and, importantly, temporarily permitted. In other words, a particular feature of festivity is that it is 'related to the idea of transgression of the boundaries and taboos that define social and symbolic everyday life spaces' (Picard and Robinson 2006: 11) and, moreover, that such transgression is, in a sense authorized. That is, the permitted organization of an event implies that the behaviour that occurs within the spatial and temporal confines of the event is also permitted or authorized.

Traditionally, such authorized transgression might have been considered a controlled social 'safety-valve' that, whilst contravening dominant social convention, did not represent a serious challenge to political or cultural authority (Humphrey 2001). Indeed, many contemporary events, from music festivals to carnivals celebrating a particular culture, may be thought of as continuing this tradition, whilst the creation of specific places, such as theme parks or particular mass tourist destinations, may be equally considered authorized locations of transgression. However, the socio-cultural impacts of events may be more significant than simply acting as a safety valve, a temporary, but controlled, 'letting one's hair down'. As post-conventional societies and cultures become more fluid and open to change, as notions of acceptable or authorized behaviour expand, the potential exists for certain events to contribute to social transformation, to dissolve the boundaries of socially acceptable behaviour and to influence social attitudes and, perhaps, even the law. Indeed, as the following case study suggests, in terms of heteronormativity and homosexual identity, authorized transgression of event space allows for the construction of social capital and subsequent privatized meaning, but within a public (festival) place. Consequently, tensions become apparent within the festival place between heterosexual hegemonism and a counter-hegemonist perspective of homosexuality.

Pride or prejudice? The case of gay parades and counter-hegemonic identity

In July 2010, the gay rights organization Stonewall hosted their annual 'Education for All' conference at the British Library in London and focused upon homophobic issues faced by young people in the UK. Subsequently, the conference declared that it was 'the new public duty which requires [oneself] to proactively consider and accommodate the needs of lesbian, gay and bisexual young people and promote equality' (Stonewall 2010). Furthermore, the new Equality Act 2010 in the UK brings together a multiplicity of legislation aimed at promoting and securing equality, including sexual preference equality. Yet, despite the increasing acceptance of homosexuality, certainly in secular societies over the past few decades or so, lesbian, gay, bisexual and transgender (LGBT) individuals still suffer from a level of prejudice, either in society in general, or the workplace in particular, not afforded to heterosexual counterparts. Indeed, throughout history, homosexuality has been viewed as not only socially deviant but also criminal under a variety of sodomy and sumptuary laws. However, since the 1969 Stonewall riots in New York a LGBT rights movement, often referred to as 'gay pride', has emerged to promote cultural goals which include, but are not limited to, challenging dominant constructions of masculinity, femininity and homophobia, and the primacy of the gendered heterosexual nuclear family, or heteronormativity (Bernstein 2002). Indeed, the LGBT rights movement uses the term 'pride' as an antonym for 'shame', which throughout history has been used to socially and religiously control and oppress homosexual activity. As part of the challenging process, gay pride as a concept suggests that LGBT individuals should be proud of their sexual orientation and gender identity. Moreover, the modern gay pride movement has resulted in Gay Pride parades – organized hyperbole spectacles of music, costumes, and general showing off – that aim to affirm the homosexual Self within broader society. Presently, Gay Pride parades as mass participant events are held in many major cities and other urban spaces across the world, including Sydney, London and San Francisco. These in turn not only help expose LGBT inequality and broader homophobia within contemporary society, but also create a valorized branded space for the creation of a homosexual identity. Thus, Gay Pride events throughout the world are carnivalesque constructions of gendered identity, allowing the temporary upsetting of the cultural order and social mores with loud laughter, bawdy songs, flamboyant costumes and lots of alcohol. As a result, Gay Pride events permit authorized 'queer places' of social acceptance for individuals, as well as mercantile returns for the host. As McCarthy (2011: 141) notes, the gay market has been defined largely through the concept of the Pink Pound and an emphasis upon hedonistic consumption where 'desire has been appropriated as a motive that is predominately sexual'.

Consequently, Gay Pride events offer the LGBT Self a semiotic and authorized opportunity to (re)affirm sexual orientation through ritually transgressing polysemic spaces. In doing so, LGBT individuals both construct and draw upon a social capital of sexual identity by attempting to create social cohesiveness within a framework of celebration and candidness. However, Gay Pride parades are also microcosms of broader tensions within society, which according to Tomsen and Markwell (2007) have resulted in a steady undercurrent of hostility, abuse and unreported violent attacks by non-gays against LGBT individuals at Gay Pride events, particularly in the aftermath of the actual parades. Moreover, the political or religious elite often voice opposition to such events. For example, the inaugural Gay Pride parade in Bratislava, Slovakia, in May 2010 attracted fierce condemnation by anti-gay demonstrators who branded event participants 'deviant' and 'perverts' (Brocklebank 2010). Furthermore, Jan Slota, who is head of the Slovak National Party – a coalition partner in Prime Minister Robert Fico's government – reportedly stated that he would attend the parade personally, 'in order to spit' (Brocklebank 2010). His corrosive comment, according to Brocklebank, drew little criticism from other leading politicians in a largely Catholic country.

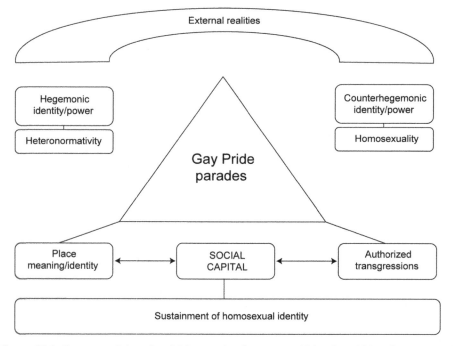

Figure 23.1 Conceptualizing Gay Pride parades: homosexual identity within a heterosexual hegemony

Of course, the dichotomy between homosexual victimhood and heterosexual aggression is complex, and cannot arbitrarity be assigned to the Gay Pride parade phenomenon. Indeed, such discussions are beyond the scope of this chapter. Nevertheless, what is apparent is the discord between those with hegemonic power, which arguably is possessed predominately by those of heteronormativity persuasion, and those with a counter-hegemonic perspective – that is, the LGBT Self. Despite legislative and educative attempts in various countries to secure and promote tolerance for homosexuals, bisexuals, and transsexuals, it is within this multi-dimensional analysis of hegemonic dissonance and the broader cultural condition of society that Gay Pride events are largely conducted. Nonetheless, despite obvious inherent tensions between those who occupy an anti-gay platform (and who may be event observers), and those who are gay or transsexual (and who are the event participants), Gay Pride parades offer participants (and even observers) a unique opportunity to construct a specific social capital. Ultimately, this in turn may help sustain homosexual identity and meaning within a dominant heterosexual hegemony (Figure 23.1).

Concluding remarks

As events by their very nature are conducted within temporal and spatial boundaries, this chapter has encapsulated fundamental socio-cultural impacts from the organization, planning and performance of such events. Indeed, the chapter sought to clarify particular impacts of events and, in doing so, has suggested that event socio-cultural consequences are firmly grounded within the broader and well-established tourism literature. As tourism may be simply defined as the *movement of people*, then events are simply the *gathering of people* that result from such a movement. Of course, any such movement and gatherings of people require multi-dimensional analyses in order to determine broader business management and social scientific issues. Thus, with regard to the latter, this chapter has suggested that events, and particularly mass participant events, have socio-cultural consequences in common. Specifically, these revolve around notions of place identity/ meaning, social capital and authorized transgressions. Indeed, by locating events and their inherent socio-cultural impacts within a paradigm of external realities, such as the example given to Gay Pride parades, then event organizers have the opportunity not only to manage the actual event, but also to understand and appreciate any event impacts and eclectic interrelationships with the cultural condition of society.

References

Adler, P. and Kwon, S. (2002) 'Social capital: prospects for a new concept', *Academy of Management Review* 27(1): 17–40.
Allen, J., Harris, R., Jago, L. and Veal, A. (eds) (2000) *Events Beyond 2000: Setting the Agenda*, Proceedings of the Conference on Event Evaluation, Research and Education, Sydney: University of Technology, Sydney, Australian Centre for Event Management.
Andranovich, G., Burbank, M. and Heying, C. (2001) 'Olympic cities: lessons learned from mega-event politics', *Journal of Urban Affairs* 23(2): 113–31.
Arcodia, C. and Whitford, M. (2006) 'Festival attendance and the development of social capital', *Journal of Convention and Event Tourism* 8(2): 1–18.
Backman, K., Backman, S., Uysal, M. and Sunshine, K. (1995) 'Event tourism: an examination of motivations and activities', *Festival Management and Event Tourism* 3(1): 15–24.
Bernstein, M. (2002) 'Identities and politics: toward a historical understanding of the lesbian and gay movement', *Social Science History* 26(3): 531–81.
Bowdin, G., Allen, J., O'Toole, W., Harris, R. and McDonnell, I. (2006) *Events Management*, Oxford: Butterworth-Heinemann, second edition.

Boyko, C. (2008) 'Are you being served? The impacts of a tourist hallmark event on place meanings for residents', *Event Management* 11(4): 161–77.

Brocklebank, C. (2010) 'Violence erupts at Slovakian Gay Pride march', *Pink News*, 24 May. Available at: www.pinknews.co.uk/2010/05/24/violence-erupts-at-slovakian-gay-pride-march/ (accessed 4 October 2010).

Burdge, R. and Vanclay, F. (1996) 'Social impact assessment: a contribution to the state of the art series', *Impact Assessment* 14: 59–86. Available at: www.hardystevenson.com/Articles/SOCIAL%20IMPACT%20ASSESSMENT%20A%20CONTRIBUTION%20TO%20THE%20STATE%20OF%20THE%20ART%20SERIES.pdf (accessed 12 September 2010).

Coleman, J. (1988) 'Social capital in the creation of human capital', *American Journal of Sociology* 94: 95–120.

Collins-Kreiner, N. and Kliot, N. (2000) 'Pilgrimage tourism in the Holy Land: the behavioural characteristics of Christian pilgrims', *Geojournal* 50: 55–67.

De Bres, K. and Davis, J. (2001) 'Celebrating group and place identity: a case study of a new regional festival', *Tourism Geographies* 3(3): 326–37.

Deccio, C. and Baloglu, S. (2002) 'Nonhost community resident reactions to the 2002 Winter Olympics: the spillover impacts', *Journal of Travel Research* 41(1): 46–56.

Delamere, T., Wankel, L. and Hinch, T. (2001) 'Development of a scale to measure resident attitudes towards the social impacts of community festivals. Part I: Item generation and purification of the measure', *Event Management* 7(1): 11–24.

Dwyer, L., Mellor, R., Mistilis, N. and Mules, T. (2000) 'Forecasting the economic impacts of events and conventions', *Event Management* 6(3): 191–204.

Formica, S. (1998) 'The development of festivals and special events studies', *Festival Management and Event Tourism* 5(3): 131–7.

Fredline, E. and Faulkner, B. (2000) 'Host community reactions: a cluster analysis', *Annals of Tourism Research* 27(3): 763–84.

Fredline, E., Jago, L. and Deery, M. (2003) 'The development of a generic scale to measure the social impacts of events', *Event Management* 8(1): 23–37.

Garcia, B. (2005) 'Deconstructing the City of Culture: the long-term cultural legacies of Glasgow 1990', *Urban Studies* 42(5 and 6): 841–68.

Getz, D. (1997) *Event Management and Event Tourism*, New York: Cognizant.

——(2007) *Event Studies: Theory, Research and Policy for Planned Events*, Oxford: Butterworth-Heinemann.

Gursoy, D., Kim, K. and Uysal, M. (2004) 'Perceived impacts of festivals and special events by organizers: an extension and validation', *Tourism Management* 25(2): 171–81.

Hall, C.M. (1997) *Hallmark Tourist Events: Impacts, Management and Planning*, Chichester: John Wiley and Sons.

Harris, R., Jago, L., Allen, J. and Huyskens, M. (2000) 'A rearview mirror and crystal ball: past, present and future perspectives on event research in Australia', in J. Allen, R. Harris, L. Jago and A. Veal (eds) *Events Beyond 2000: Setting the Agenda*, Sydney: University of Technology, Sydney, Australian Centre for Event Management, pp. 22–8.

Harvey, D. (1989) *The Condition of Postmodernity*, Oxford: Blackwell.

Hede, A. (2007) 'Managing special events in the new era of TBL', *Event Management* 11(1 and 2): 12–22.

Held, D. and McGrew, A. (2000) 'The great globalization debate: a review', in D. Held and A. McGrew (eds) *The Global Transformations Reader*, Cambridge: Polity Press.

Hughes, H. (2006) 'Gay and lesbian festivals: tourism in the change from politics to party', in D. Picard and M. Robinson (eds) *Festivals, Tourism and Social Change: Remaking Worlds*, Clevedon: Channel View Publications, pp. 238–54.

Humphrey, C. (2001) *The Politics of Carnival: Festive Misrule in Medieval England*, Manchester: Manchester University Press.

Hyun-Sook, K. (2006) 'Educating in a post-conventional society', *Religious Education*, Fall. Available at: http://findarticles.com/p/articles/mi_qa3783/is_200610/ai_n17194917?tag=artBody;col1 (accessed 4 August 2008).

Jeong, G. and Faulkner, B. (1996) 'Resident perceptions of mega-event impacts: the Taejon exposition case', *Festival Management and Event Tourism* 4(1): 3–11.

Lee, C. and Taylor, T. (2005) 'Critical reflections on the economic impact assessment of a mega-event: the case of the 2002 FIFA World Cup', *Tourism Management* 26(4): 595–603.

MacCannell, D. (1989) *The Tourist: A New Theory of the Leisure Class*, New York: Shocken Books, second edition.

McCarthy, M. (2011) 'We are family: IGLFA World Championships, London 2008', in R. Sharpley and P.R. Stone (eds) *Tourist Experience: Contemporary Perspectives*, London: Routledge, pp. 141–53.

MacLeod, N. (2006) 'The placeless festival: identity and place in the post-modern festival', in D. Picard and M. Robinson (eds) *Festivals, Tourism and Social Change: Remaking Worlds*, Clevedon: Channel View Publications, pp. 222–37.

Manzo, L. (2003) 'Beyond house and heaven: toward a revisioning of emotional relationships with places', *Journal of Environmental Psychology* 23(1): 47–61.

Markwell, K. (2002) 'Mardi Gras and the construction of Sydney as an international gay and lesbian city', *GLQ: A Journal of Lesbian and Gay Studies* 8(1 and 2): 81–99.

Mihalik, B. and Simonetta, L. (1998) 'Resident perceptions of the 1990 Summer Olympic games – Year II', *Festival Management and Event Tourism* 5(1): 9–19.

Moscardo, G. (2007) 'Analyzing the role of festivals and events in regional development', *Event Management* 11(1 and 2): 23–32.

Picard, D. and Robinson, M. (2006) 'Remaking worlds: festivals, tourism and change', in D. Picard and M. Robinson (eds) *Festivals, Tourism and Social Change: Remaking Worlds*, Clevedon: Channel View Publications, pp. 1–31.

Picard, M. (1995) 'Cultural heritage and tourist capital in Bali', in J.B. Allcock, E. Bruner and M. Lanfant (eds) *International Tourism: Identity and Change*, London: Sage, pp. 44–66.

Putnam, R. (1995) 'Bowling alone: America's declining social capital', *Journal of Democracy* 6(1): 65–78.

Quinn, B. (2009) 'Festivals, events and tourism', in T. Jamal and M. Robinson (eds) *The Sage Handbook of Tourism Studies*, London: Sage, pp. 483–503.

Reid, S. (2008) 'Identifying social consequences of rural events', *Event Management* 11(1 and 2): 89–98.

Relph, E. (1976) *Place and Placelessness*, London: Pion.

Richards, G. (ed.) (1996) *Cultural Tourism in Europe*, Wallingford: CABI.

Richards, G. and Wilson, J. (2004) 'The impact of cultural events on city image: Rotterdam, cultural capital of Europe 2001', *Urban Studies* 41(10): 1931–51.

Ritchie, B. (1984) 'Assessing impacts of hallmark events: conceptual and research issues', *Journal of Travel Research* 23(1): 2–11.

Roche, M. (2000) *Mega-Events and Modernity: Olympics and Expos in the Growth of Global Culture*, London: Routledge.

Shackley, M. (2001) *Managing Sacred Sites: Service Provision and Visitor Experience*, London: Continuum.

Sharpley, R. (2008) *Tourism, Tourists and Society*, Huntingdon: Elm Publications, fourth edition.

Shipway, R. and Jones, I. (2008) 'The great suburban Everest: an "insider's" perspective on experiences at the 2007 Flora London Marathon', *Journal of Sport and Tourism* 13(1): 61–72.

Slade, P. (2003) 'Gallipoli thanatourism: the meaning of ANZAC', *Annals of Tourism Research* 30(4): 779–94.

Small, K. (2008) 'Social dimensions of community festivals: an application of factor analysis in the development of the Social Impact Perception (SIP) Scale', *Event Management* 11(1 and 2): 45–55.

Stedman, R. (2003) 'Is it really just a social construction? The contribution of the physical environment to sense of place', *Society and Natural Resources* 16(8): 671–85.

Stone, P.R. (2009) 'Dark tourism: morality and new moral spaces', in R. Sharpley and P.R. Stone (eds) *The Darker Side of Travel: The Theory and Practice of Dark Tourism*, Bristol: Channel View Publications, pp. 56–72.

Stone, P.R. and Sharpley, R. (2008) 'Consuming dark tourism: a thanatological perspective', *Annals of Tourism Research* 35(2): 574–95.

Stonewall (2010) 5th Annual Educational for All Conference: Challenging Homophobia and Supporting Young People, British Library, London, 2 July.

Tomsen, S. and Markwell, K. (2007) *When the Glitter Settles: Safety and Hostility at and around Gay and Lesbian Public Events – Survey Report*, Newcastle: Cultural Institutions and Practices Research Centre, University of Newcastle, UK.

Tuan, Y. (1977) *Space and Place: The Perspective of Experience*, Minneapolis: University of Minnesota Press.

Waitt, G. (2003) 'Social impacts of the Sydney Olympics', *Annals of Tourism Research* 30(1): 194–215.

Wall, G. and Mathieson, A. (2006) *Tourism: Change, Impacts and Opportunities*, Harlow: Pearson Education.

Wang, N. (1999) 'Rethinking authenticity in tourism experiences', *Annals of Tourism Research* 26(2): 349–70.

Wood, R. (1998) 'Tourist ethnicity: a brief intinerary', *Ethnic and Racial Studies* 21(2): 218–41.

Zhou, Y. and Ap, J. (2009) 'Residents' perceptions towards the impacts of the Beijing 2008 Olympic Games', *Journal of Travel Research* 48(1): 78–9.

24

Event impacts and environmental sustainability

Robert Case

Introduction

This chapter will review and offer some personal insight into the historical background of the relationship between events and the environment, examine models relating to the environment, explore the concept of sustainability, review changing attitudes to the environment in the past twenty years including those in the event industry and its supporting educational infrastructure, identify and evaluate recent initiatives in the sustainable environmental management of events and suggest areas for further research. It will use a case study of the Olympics to illustrate and contextualise some of these themes.

The historical context of events and the environment

Events are designed to have impacts and impacts are intrinsic to their nature. Historically, the impacts of events have tended to be focused on cultural, social and economic outcomes. However, even in Greek and Roman times some of the outcomes were anticipated as environmental, for example the rituals effected to guarantee good harvests and harvest festivals that followed them. Examples included the Little Panathenaia,

> [a] night festival of dancing and singing, a procession, a contest for 'circular choruses' and war dances (or) the great festivals of Demeter, Athena, and Dionysis [which] had as their foundation a very much older conception of deity: the possibility that life was renewed in the spring.
>
> *(Webster 1969: 85)*

Deliberate alteration to the environment was made to create venues such as the theatre at Epidaurus and venues were designed to create different types of environment, such as the Coliseum in Rome which could be used dry or flooded to allow water-based spectacles. In Athens the festival of Adonis involved 'tiny gardens that sprang up and withered quickly on the tops of houses' (Levi 1980: 165). In addition to these deliberate impacts there were impacts that were ancillary (or 'collateral', as we might say now) but tolerated whilst some were not apprehended at all. Spivey comments on the original Olympia, oxen … were axed before a crowd, and the precincts steeped with their blood. Ash, bones, and bovine offal piled up over centuries into a huge pyramid: it must have reeked to high heaven. Could we have endured this for the sake of Olympia's pride: the great, original Olympic Games? Again, it is doubtful.

(Spivey 2004: xviii)

He goes on to note that the 'festival was noisy … (and) … hideously congested, and for hundreds of years deprived of adequate accommodation, water supply, and sanitation; not to mention marred by the standard plagues of heat, flies, and hucksters' (Spivey 2004: xviii).

Waste, therefore, was clearly an environmental impact of the former category and carbon-dioxide and resource depletion examples of the latter. It is useful, then, to distinguish between intended and unintended or collateral impacts. Both can be damaging but for many centuries the latter were unconsidered, tolerated or not understood. Despite a growing awareness of environmental fragility, green initiatives and increasing amounts of legislation, it would appear that part of the event industry still cares little about the environmental consequences of its activities, intended or otherwise. This can be seen not only in the behaviour of the industry but also in the education system. Undergraduates on event courses have expressed frustration at having to study the environmental dimension of events and even some lecturers, who should know better, have asserted that the environment is irrelevant to the study of event management. At Confex 2009, one meeting on Green Events attracted fewer than thirty attendees in an event that attracted tens of thousands. Recent initiatives such as BS 8901 and ISO 14001 (discussed later) are beginning to have an effect (although much lip service is paid to green issues for image reasons), but much remains for the industry to do to improve its environmental performance. Fortunately, the environmental dimension of events is coming under increasing academic scrutiny, although much of this remains tourism-oriented rather than focused on the plethora of events, local and national, that do not involve overnight stays by attendees.

As indicated above, not all environmental impacts are negative. Positive effects are intended and manifested at a range of scales from mega-events such as the Olympics, where the intended environmental legacy forms part of the bid, to community events that focus on cleaning up litter in local open spaces. In between are events such as the garden festivals that were held in Liverpool (1984) and South Wales (1992). These effects can be the focus of the event or a corollary of it. In either case the benefits can be significant and permanent, though little remains of the two garden festivals cited.

Environmental impacts do not exist in isolation from other types of impact – they are often intrinsically linked to each other. They may, for example, have knock-on effects on the economy, society and polity. Environmental damage can be expensive to clear up, it may upset local residents and it may embarrass politicians. Vandalism by attendees at events, for example, causes direct damage to the built or natural environment which may have to be repaired by the local council at a cost to tax payers. Meanwhile, the desecration can offend the coterminous, permanent community and they in turn can vent their frustration and irritation on their elected representatives. Similarly, positive impacts, such as clearing up litter, can increase enjoyment of open spaces, not least by making them safer, with consequent social benefits. Thus, although identification of environmental impacts is a useful analytical device, it needs always to be aware of the synergy with other impacts in a wider context.

Environmental impacts are not new, therefore, but they have changed in scale and nature. Mega-events, for example, take place on an unprecedented scale, not only in the host city but worldwide through the conduit of multi-media. The supply chains for such events are complex and the use of resources extensive. Their ecological footprints are substantial, in particular their carbon footprints. The wastes they create are more complicated, varied and difficult to process, particularly in an era of increasing environmental legislation. However, the impacts and their consequences are better understood and metrics have been established by which they can be quantified. To give an example of the scale, the 2010 World Cup can be cited. Greg McManus, managing director of the Heritage Environmental Rating Programme, suggests that

> based on existing resource consumption patterns for tourists to South Africa, the additional international tourist are expected to consume an additional 2.50 billion litres of water and 420,000 megawatts of power and create almost 23,000 tonnes of waste in just fourteen days. The duration of the mega event will be four weeks in total.
>
> *(McManus, cited in Otto and Heath 2009: 175)*

This excludes any carbon footprint which the same author calculates as 180,000 tons of CO_2 for internal travel and additional electricity generation alone during the four-week duration of the Cup. Travel to South Africa, mainly by air, needs to be added to that.

Models of the environment

It is useful to consider how events can fit within models of the environment. Models are useful, their selective, structural and suggestive nature making them helpful tools against which to test reality. Many of these derive from systems theory which emerged after 1951 (Bertalanffy 1951) and became fashionable in subjects such as geography in the 1960s. Chorley (cited in Haggett 1965) used Hall and Fagen's definition of systems as 'asset of objects together with the relationships between the objects and their attributes' (Haggett 1965: 17). An obvious example is a domestic plumbing system with water input from the mains, processes including heating and toilet flushing, and outputs such as sewage.

Blunden (1977: 110) utilised such an approach to visualise human transduction of the environment. This can be adapted to illustrate the role of events in processing environmental inputs to create a series of outputs that can either be recycled or 'dumped' to the environment, though in the latter case they may be recycled over geological time. (See Figure 24.1.)

Some writers have taken a more comprehensive view of the environmental context of human activity. James Lovelock instigated the concept of Gaia which conceptualised the entire planet as a system that had for centuries been in a state of dynamic equilibrium: that is, when changes in one part of the system occur other parts adjust to dampen down the effects of change so the degree of stability is maintained. In recent times he has taken an alarmist line with respect to global warming, arguing that the planetary system has passed a threshold and can no longer maintain a balance (Lovelock 2006).

The event industry is a significant contributor to this transformation of the planet.

The interactions of the event industry with the environment can be categorised into two types. The first concerns the use of environmental resources in delivering the event and the second the environmental outputs which can be analysed at two levels, the macro and the micro. The latter can be further broken down into short and long term. Some authorities, e.g. the International Olympic Committee (IOC), also distinguish between direct and indirect impacts, the former being the result of the event deliverers themselves, the latter the result of external organisations such as governments who improve transport infrastructure for mega-events and tourist activities outside the Games themselves.

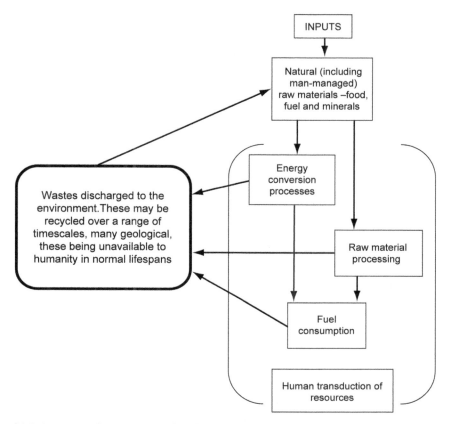

Figure 24.1 A systems theory approach to human resource use (after Blunden)

The event industry uses a very wide range of inputs in its supply chain – food, materials and energy. Many of these are limited or stock resources which have a limited lifespan. Oil is an obvious example, as many experts believe we have already passed the peak of reserves. Some of these resources can be substituted – e.g. use of other fuels – but some are more difficult to replace, e.g. germanium used in micro-electronics. Even if substitution is possible, costs of procurement may be higher. At present there is limited awareness of these issues in the events industry except at the mega-event level, the recent attraction to sustainability having rarely focused on such fundamentals.

The industry also uses the environment in a very direct way. Events take place on land, water and in the air. Temporary and permanent venues are constructed in the built and natural environment which result in temporary or permanent loss of such phenomena as biodiversity. Choice of locations needs careful consideration but selection involves social, economic and political factors as well as environmental ones – this is discussed further in the section on the Olympics. Particular events require specific environmental conditions. Sailing events need reflection on winds, tides and currents. Skiing needs reflection on probabilities of snowfall given a range of climatic variables. It is not clear whether the recent Vancouver Games considered such issues adequately.

The outputs from the event industry operate at both global and local scales. Events are designed to attract attendees and their travel to the destination involves in almost all cases the generation of carbon dioxide. The supply of materials does likewise. Although a persistent minority continues to question the nature of global warming, few contest that it is happening and the vast majority of the scientific community believes that anthropogenic inputs are a significant contributor to it. As the 2007 IPCC report notes,

> warming of the climate system is unequivocal, as is now evident from observations of increases in global average air and ocean temperatures, widespread melting of snow and ice, and rising average sea level ... most of the observed increase in globally averaged temperatures since the mid-20th century is *very likely* due to the observed increase in anthropogenic greenhouse gas concentrations.
>
> *(IPCC 2007: 5)*

Ironically, some of these effects could impact on the event industry itself, for example snow-based events in Alpine regions. It is not only global warming to which events contribute. In the past they have contributed to depletion of the ozone layer through use of refrigeration and fire protection products using CFCs (now banned by the Montreal Protocol), acid rain through carbon dioxide, sulphur and nitrogen oxide generation and riverine, lacustrine and oceanic degradation through discharges of a wide range of pollutants ranging from hydrocarbons to untreated urine from festival participants who prefer not to queue for, or walk to, the facilities provided.

At a micro or local scale some of the pollutants already cited contribute to degradation through contamination of soil, groundwater and local waterways. There is a range of other wastes, such as litter, some of which can cause fires or injury to animals if not adequately cleared up. Trampling can damage biodiversity and drainage and the erection of facilities aesthetic disruption. The built environment can also suffer through vandalism, congestion, noise and light. The IOC in its *Manual of Sport and the Environment* (IOC 2005) identifies eight issues that concern the relationship between sport and the environment. These are discussed in the case study of the Olympics. Their overview of the impacts is shown diagrammatically in Figure 24.2.

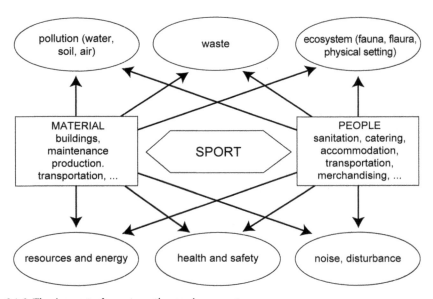

Figure 24.2 The impact of sport on the environment
Source: IOC

Sustainability

'Sustainability' has become a much used word without any clear consensus about exactly what it means or how its associated terms of 'sustainable development' and 'sustainable management' are differentiated. Often the terms are used interchangeably. Carter claims that 'sustainable development has rapidly become the dominant idea, or discourse, shaping international policy towards the environment' (Carter 2007: 208). Most writers on sustainability cite the Bruntland Report (WCED 1987) when they seek to define the term, though it has a significant antecedence. Hay (2002: 212) notes that 'O'Riordan traces "sustainable development" to a series of conferences in Africa in the mid-1960s'. Arguably it emerged from earlier strands in liberal environmental philosophy and later, specific publications such as *The Limits to Growth* and *Blueprint for Survival*, both published in 1972 (Meadows 1972; Goldsmith and Allen 1972). These books created major debates and called for urgent environmental action if catastrophe was to be avoided. Their tone, however, stimulated sceptics, to query their assumptions and an era of uncertainty ensued until the UN established the World Commission on Environment and Development in 1983. It produced its final report in 1987, published as *Our Common Future* (WCED 1987) but better known as the Bruntland Report after its chairman, a former Norwegian prime minister.

It defined sustainable development as 'development that meets the needs of the present without compromising the ability of future generations to meet their own needs' (WCED 1987: 43). It begs many questions – how can present, let alone future, needs be known or defined, and what is meant by compromise? More widely it cedes the idea of the inevitability and necessity of economic growth, an assumption not accepted by many environmentalists. Indeed, by 1992 Principle 12 of Agenda 21 notes that national environmental policies should not be used as a 'disguised restriction on international trade' (UNCED 1992, cited in Hay 2002: 213). As Hay comments in an authoritative review of the concept, it 'was apparent to most people in the environment movement that the goal of "sustainable development" had been thoroughly subverted … (and that the term) … was thought by many to be an oxymoron' (Hay 2002: 213). Hay goes on to note that for others 'the formulation was a cynical exercise to accord a fake legitimacy to full-on, business-as-usual global environmental rapine' (Hay 2002: 213). Hay notes that there are many definitions of sustainable development but ultimately they can be classified as 'weak' (like the Bruntland definition) or 'strong' like that adopted in *Caring for the Earth,* which describes it as 'improving the quality of life while living within the carrying capacity of supporting ecosystems' (WCU/UNEP/WWFN, cited in Hay 2002: 214). It would appear that the Bruntland approach has prevailed. Its catholic principles which incorporate a concern for 'human welfare and the exploitation of nature in preference to an ecocentric interest in protecting nature for its own sake' (Carter 2007: 212) are reflected in the sustainability goals of the 2012 Olympics that are discussed below. Appraisal of them may depend on beliefs as much as evidence. As Carter also notes, 'sustainable development, like beauty, is in the eye of the beholder' (Carter 2007: 212). A positive, and political, perspective on sustainable development is that it has provided a banner under which a range of protagonists of varying viewpoints can march in apparent unison.

The political context

This interest in sustainability needs to be set against a background of changing public attitudes and an increasing political awareness of environmental issues brought about by resource crises such as the supply of oil and increasing evidence of environmental degradation such as global warming.

The environmental movement can be traced back to at least the age of enlightenment and the Romantic Movement in the eighteenth and nineteenth centuries with its focus on nature – the Lakeland poets are perhaps the most egregious examples of this. In the US this was espoused by the likes of Walden and Thoreau and their concern for wilderness. As wilderness became increasingly threatened, movements began to emerge such as the Sierra Club, founded by John Muir. Pressure for preservation led to the establishment of the first national park, Yellowstone, in 1872. In the UK national intervention in preserving wilderness was somewhat later for a variety of geographical, cadastral and cultural reasons. Although the National Trust, a charity, was founded in the nineteenth century, it was not until the late 1940s that the Peak District was designated as the first National Park. This had been prompted by actions such as the mass trespass on Kinder Scout and the later Dower Report. There followed a lull in environmentalism until the 1962 publication of Rachel Carson's *The Silent Spring* (Carson 1962). In a decade when environmental catastrophes emerged such as Minimata and the *Torrey Canyon*, the protest movement grew. In the early 1970s the publication of *Blueprint for Survival* (Goldsmith 1972) and *Limits to Growth* (Meadows 1972) created a doomsday atmosphere which dissipated, to some extent, in the self-seeking 1980s. However, by the late 1980s even governments were becoming publicly concerned with the possibility of global warming and the IPCC was set up to advise governments (or as some cynics saw it, delay any action). Environmental NGOs, such as Greenpeace, were taking direct action and publicising issues such as the adverse impacts of the Olympic Games (discussed below). Changes in public attitudes were reflected not only in the actions of global NGOs but also locally, as residents increasingly protested at the impacts of mega-events (see below). As a result the IOC eventually added environmental criteria to its bidding process. Resource shortages resulting in price rises (e.g. petrol) brought home to the public the wider environmental concerns, as did the increasing coverage of extreme meteorological events. There can be few, especially in the media-dominated Western world, who can be unaware of environmental problems even if they contest their causes and fail to alter their lifestyles appropriately. It is in such a world that politicians now determine the legislative framework against which events take place and event managers and event students have to contemplate and implement new environmental strategies.

Event academe and the event industry

It has been noted above that the event industry has not been in the van of the push for sustainability. This is also true of much of the educational community who study event management. There may be some intrinsic reasons for this. First, events, of their nature, involve movement of people to venues. Where these events are local the resulting carbon and ecological footprints may be modest but where the events are large the footprints may be very large indeed, even when organisers try to be sustainable in their management (see below for discussion of 2012). Second, the number and scale of events is rising as consumerist societies become sated with products and seek experiences instead to satisfy their acquisitive natures. As James has noted, society in many countries is becoming subject to an 'affluenza' virus that 'entails placing a high value on acquiring money and possessions' (James 2007: vii). Third, many event organisers are small-scale SMEs without the resources or training to adopt good environmental practices. Event degrees are relatively recent (see Getz 2007: 1–8) and, as noted above, have not always prioritised the issues of environmental impacts or sustainability. Where they did, such an emphasis was not always popular with students. More recently many courses are now incorporating sustainability more extensively into their curricula, and this is reflected in the textbooks provided for study. Bowdin's ubiquitous

Events Management was published in 2001. It included a chapter on event impacts of which three pages are on physical and environmental impacts – this includes a brief review of the Sydney Games. However, the word 'sustainability' does not appear in the chapter headings or the index. By contrast, publicity for the revised edition, published in 2010, trumpets its focus on sustainability.

Sustainability in academe

Early academic interest in sustainability tended to be focused in subjects such as geography, ecology and environmental science (see Getz 2007). The 1970s, for example, saw the publication of titles such as *Ecology and Environmental Planning* (Edington and Edington 1977) which included a chapter/case study on the Brecon Beacons National Park and the effects of recreation. 1983 saw the publication of *Recreation and Resources* by a geographer, Alan Patmore (1983). It discussed extensively environmental issues and concepts such as carrying capacity but no section or index entry on sustainability. In 1999, Hall and Page took this further with *The Geography of Tourism and Recreation: Environment, Place and Space* (Hall and Page 1999).

Getz (2007: 50–125) identifies fourteen foundation disciplines that influenced the development of event studies but it was perhaps human geography, in particular, that helped spawn the study of tourism, leisure and heritage. It was out of such secondary subjects that many event courses emerged from the 1990s onwards. In shaping the event discipline, Getz notes that, amongst other things, human geography contributed the study of 'human-resource interactions, especially spatial and temporal patterns of human activity including impacts on the environment' (Getz 2007: 214). Given that a number of tourism academics had geographical backgrounds, it is not surprising that tourism began to generate books on sustainability. This was also driven by the increasing awareness within the industry that mass tourism was beginning to seriously damage destination environments and thus undermine the attractions that drew the tourists to them in the first place. This was abetted by the emerging cognisance of global environmental issues such as climate change and energy supplies. Numerous books began to incorporate the words 'sustainability', 'environment' or 'geography' in their titles. The following is a selection from many. The year 1994 saw the publication of *The Earth as a Holiday Resort – An Introduction to Tourism and the Environment* (Boers and Bosch 1994); 1998 saw Mowforth and Munt's *Tourism and Sustainability,* a fascinating study of how these issues applied to the Third World (Mowforth and Munt 1998); 2000 saw *The Development of Sustainable Tourism* (Aronson 2000) and *Environment and Tourism* (Holden 2000). More specialist texts with an environmental emphasis appeared, such as *Ecotourism – A Sustainable Option* in 1994 (Cater and Lowman 1994), *Ecotourism and Sustainable Development* in 1999 (Honey 1999) and *Ecotourism* in 2002 (Page and Dowling 2002). Generalist textbooks incorporated major sections on impacts and sustainability, such as *Global Tourism* (Theobold 1994) and *Tourism – A Modern Synthesis* (Page and Connell 2006). More populist texts included *The Good Tourist* (Wood and House 1991) and *Preserve or Destroy – Tourism and the Environment* (Croall 1995), whilst the youth market was targeted with Solway's *Sustainable Tourism* (Solway 2009).

Leisure saw a similar, though less extensive output. The year 1994 saw the publication of *Leisure and the Environment* (Spink 1994), which does not feature 'sustainability' in its index, and 2004 *The Geography of Sport and Leisure* (Terrell 2004) which does have a chapter on environmental impacts but none on sustainability. Where the environment was discussed in various texts, it was often with reference to examples from tourism (leaving aside the debate as to whether the study of tourism is just a subset of leisure studies). Torkildsen's attempt to produce a comprehensive guide to leisure and recreation management, first published in 1983, had no chapters on impacts or sustainability although the fourth edition had sections on public bodies such as the then Countryside Commission that listed aims that included sustainability. Interestingly, in his discussion of the leisure profession he says, 'Leisure Managers are concerned with creating opportunities for people to have satisfying leisure experiences. They must attract the public or fail' (Torkildsen 1999: 545). True, maybe, but there is no mention of environmental concern in his discussion.

Sports studies saw significant publications on the environment in the 1990s and early 2000s. In 1994 Chernushenko published *Greening Our Games: Running Sports Events and Facilities that Won't Cost the Earth* (Chernushenko 1994) and in 2001 daCosta published *International Trends of Sport and Environment – A 2001 Overview* (daCosta 2001). Other publications relating to the Olympics are cited below. In 1999 the Council of Europe published '*Mens sane in corpore sano*: a scientific review of the information available on the links between sport and the environment' (Oittinen and Tiezzi 1999). Overviews of sporting issues in general also began to feature significant sections on sport and the environment, notably M.F. Collins' contribution to *Sport and Society – A Student Introduction* (Houlihan 2003). One of its chapters discusses sustainability specifically and the word features in the overall index. It also details a number of specific environmental impacts and provides case studies to illustrate the issues. *The Geography of Sport and Leisure* (Terrell 1994) has already been noted and literature on the Olympics is noted below.

As noted above, some of the early texts on event management made little reference to the environment. Bowdin has already been cited. *Successful Event Management* (Shone and Parry 2001) has a chapter on *implications* of events and identifies social, economic, political and developmental ones. Environmental impacts gain a mention under the last heading. 'Sustainability' does not feature as a chapter section/heading or index entry. By 2007 Getz's *Event Studies* (Getz 2007) has sections on environmental impacts and outcomes as well as coverage of sustainability, particularly in a discussion of events and public policy. Related subjects such as hospitality were producing texts on sustainability. In 2009/10 two significant event books appeared. One was an academic collection of essays, *Event Management and Sustainability* (Raq and Musgrave 2009), the other a practical guide to managing events sustainably, *Sustainable Event Management* (Jones 2010). There are also forthcoming books that will take a catholic view of the relationship between events and the environment, for example *Events and the Environment* (Case, expected late 2012).

Event Management and Sustainability is a welcome contribution to the sustainability debate but even that treats the specific issue of environmental impacts only lightly in a single chapter, of which only five pages discuss principles and concepts before the presentation of a case study. There are sections in other chapters on aspects, such as supply chain management and techniques and policies, and urban regeneration is discussed in a separate chapter (but is the subject of Chapter 25 in this volume, so not enlarged on here). However, although academic journals have featured a range of articles on specific aspects of environmental impacts, it would appear that there is still considerable scope for further detailed research in this area and compilation of this into a book. It is pleasing to note that some of this research is already underway at undergraduate level. Recent undergraduate theses have included the carbon footprint of university event programmes, the introduction of sustainability policies into FIVE (Farnborough International Venue and Events; the student concerned helped shape these), public awareness of environmental issues at the Goodwood Festival of Speed and the carbon footprint of the Watercress Line. It is also of note that some event degrees have been revalidated to align them with the principles of responsible management education (PRME).

As well as books, conferences and academic papers were shaping environmental attitudes within the profession and education sector. These can be traced back to the 1980s and 1990s but have accelerated since 2000. In 2000 a conference entitled 'Events beyond 2000: Setting the Agenda' took place in Sydney (Allen 2000). Impacts featured in several papers but of particular interest were two of the keynote papers, 'A future for event management: the analysis of major trends impacting the emerging profession' by Joe Jeff Goldblatt (Goldblatt 2000) and *Developing a Research Agenda for the Event Management Field* by Donald Getz (Getz 2000). The former identified fifteen trends that would impact on the event profession over the next twenty-five years – five of these were environmental. Getz identified eight research perspectives, the first of which was environmental. Since then there have been many papers that range from the examination of impacts and sustainability at particular events to conceptual reviews. The former include the FA Cup (Collins *et al.* 2007), which includes ecological footprint analysis, the Turin Winter Olympics (Frey *et al.* 2008) and the 2000 America's Cup (Barker *et al.* 2002). The latter include the sustainability of festivals (Getz and Anderson 2008) and the impact of mega-events (Hiller 1998). Many articles look at broader impacts and wider concepts of sustainability but they do at least address the environment. Recently, there has been a plethora of papers on the sustainability and legacy of the 2012 Olympics, with no doubt more to follow. However, as noted elsewhere, despite the raised profile of the environment there is still much scope for further research.

Developments in the industry

In recent years a growing number of guides and protocols has appeared on sustainable management. Some of these are sector-specific such as the greening of the American meetings industry. Some focus on the environment, e.g. ISO 14001, whilst others take a more comprehensive approach to sustainability, e.g. BS 8901. Raq and Musgrave (2009) select six examples and identify their key principles. The guides are the *Sustainable Events Guide* (Defra 2007), *Sexi: The Sustainable Exhibition Industry Project* (MEBC 2002), *The Hannover Principles: Design for Sustainability – Expo 2000* (McDonough 1992), *BS 8901: 2007 Specification for a Sustainable Event Management System with Guidance for Use Developed* (BSI 2007), *Staging Major Sports Events: The Guide* (UK Sport 2005) and *The Sustainable Music Festival – A Strategic Guide* (Brooks *et al.* 2007). There are many others, such as those cited elsewhere in this chapter, that include the *Greenpeace Olympic Environmental Guidelines* (Greenpeace 2000), the IOC's *Manual on Sport and the Environment* (IOC 2005) and *ISO 14001*. BS 8901 is already being revised. No responsible event manager can now complain of a lack of guidelines if she/he wishes to utilise them. Neither is there a shortage of techniques or metrics. Griffin (in Raq and Musgrave 2009: 43–55), identifies indicators and tools for management, whilst in the same work Lamberti *et al.* (ibid.: 119–31) discuss methods for assessing and monitoring the performances of a sustainable event and Beer analyses the supply chain in an event context (ibid.: 160–71). Recent academic papers have looked at the roles of environmental impact analysis, environmental cost accounting and ecological and carbon footprint calculation. More general works on sustainability such as *Making Sustainability Work* (Epstein 2008) look at impact evaluation systems, impact auditing and projects for improving corporate sustainability. Such works also link the concept to other corporate issues such as corporate social responsibility and the triple bottom line. In a less academic context Meegan Jones provides a wealth of practical advice in her 2010 book, *Sustainable Event Management* (Jones 2010). She devotes chapters to marketing and communications, energy and emissions, transport (possibly the most intractable problem for the industry), water, purchasing and resource use and waste.

Future issues

It is ten years since Goldblatt looked at the future of event management. The environmental concerns he identified are as relevant now as then and considerable progress has been made on many of them. Some additional concerns might be identified.

The first is the persistent environmental scepticism that gains publicity disproportionate to the number of scientists who espouse such views. Often this publicity is funded by organisations, such as energy companies, who have an interest in maintaining the status quo. The publicity can have widespread influence. An example of this is the debate over global warming, where the majority of climate scientists and the IPCC believe that anthropological contributions are almost certainly adding to atmospheric warming but other minority views still gain much media coverage. The reluctance of some event management undergraduates to study, let alone believe in, environmental issues and sustainability has already been cited and has implications for the future. Nonetheless, it is possible to be optimistic about the increasing amount of embedding of the issues in the curriculum and the quantity of papers and books appearing on the subject, although much remains to be researched and taught.

The second is the global recession. Whilst sustainable management of resources can often yield long-term savings these do not always accrue in the short term. In a financial system that appears to reward early returns on investment, long-term approaches can be difficult to implement. Already the new coalition government in Britain appears to be softening its approach to coal-fired power stations and their environmental impacts (Guardian Online 2010) and this may set an example for others to follow.

The third is the intrinsic nature of events discussed earlier. Traditionally, events have been designed to bring people together. It is the travel involved in modern events that contributes substantially to the negative environmental impacts of them. The sheer scale of the problem is a deterrent to many. Recently, one major event company introduced a progressive sustainability policy. Energy used in the events and travel to them was excluded, however, as the apparent intractability of the problem could have undermined the implementation of more restricted policies. Transport will have to be tackled, however. Virtual experience of events is discussed elsewhere. This weakens, however, the intangible nature of the experience and thus a principal motivator for being involved in an event. Future improvements in technology may resolve some of these issues but in the meantime this is an important area for further research and innovation.

The fourth is the political process. Green issues feature in all the party manifestos but the track record of parties in power is variable. In the US, in particular, Republican presidencies have been perceived as less progressive environmentally than Democratic ones, as the Bush presidencies would indicate. However, the Democrats also equivocate, as the record on Kyoto and Copenhagen demonstrates. Whilst some environmentalists might wish that in future all organised events (whether commercial, public sector or voluntary) will require environmental approval before they can succeed, this appears unlikely at present except at the mega-event scale.

The fifth is that a reward system for sustainable event management needs consideration. This is true not only for rewards for internal initiatives in organisations but also for external rewards through the taxation and grant-awarding systems. Thus far green initiatives for industry and individuals have often been short term and isolated rather than holistic. A more integrated and comprehensive approach might improve sustainable performance.

As this chapter indicates, there has been progress over the past twenty years in the complex relationship between the event industry and the environment but there remains much to be achieved at all levels of the industry. The discussion of the Olympics that follows will illustrate some of the issues in the area of sport mega-events.

The Olympics

Introduction

The Olympic Games and their relationship to the environment make an interesting case study for a number of reasons. First, the Games have an ancient origin which makes possible analysis over a long period of time. Second, following their revival at the end of the nineteenth century, they were, until relatively recently, not perceived as particularly environmentally friendly. Third, they illustrate well the difficulty of reconciling environmental values with commercial imperatives and a variety of ethical issues. Fourth, their changing environmental credentials reflect wider changes in global society and polity, such as the Rio Summit. Finally, since the 1990s, environmental concerns have become a priority in the appraisal of bidders and the management of the Games.

History of the Olympics and the environment

Early days

The first recorded Olympic Games were held in 776 BC and continued as a four-yearly event until AD 261 at least. 'They were finally suppressed as a pagan cult in AD 391 or soon after' (Howatson and Chilvers 1993: 379). Their origin lay in a festival in honour of Zeus. Environmentally, the location of the Games at Olympia was 'on a well-watered site in a fertile region among gentle hills, a fairly unusual landscape for Greece and particularly appealing to Greek sensibility' (Howatson and Chilvers 1993: 378). Although religious in origin, this does show an early awareness of *genius loci* in the choice of sites for events. The Games had environmental impacts – stadia, congestion and ecosystem damage for example – though there is no record of these causing particular concern. Some of the impacts, such as local increases in gaseous emissions, were probably not perceived.

The modern Games

The Games were revived in 1896 in Athens and have continued at four-yearly intervals, with the exception of the war years, until the present. During that time they have expanded and, according to some criteria, become the biggest of all sporting mega-events. Their environmental impacts grew steadily and attracted increasingly adverse criticism from global NGOs at one end of the spectrum and local communities at the other. According to Lamartine daCosta, the 1992 Winter Games in Albertville were particularly problematic:

> In retrospect, the 1992 Winter Games in Albertville had a negative environmental impact in their prized host alpine region: landslides, road-building, deforestation, disruption of natural habitat, permanent facilities without post-event use, non-recyclable waste and other largely uncounted costs. As a result, the Albertville Games were the first ever to have their opening ceremony preceded by a local community's protest march on behalf of their natural surroundings and quality of life.
>
> *(daCosta 2002: 74)*

In the same year the United Nations Conference on Environment and Development met in Rio de Janeiro and developed Agenda 21, which put 'sustainable development' at the heart of the UN's global agenda. Thus both the IOC and the wider political establishment converged on the concept that the environment needed greater priority in the planning of resource use.

It is not that earlier host cities had not considered the environmental context of their Games. Tokyo 1964, in particular, had used the occasion to tackle some of Japan's growing environmental problems. In the post-war pursuit of economic recovery Japan had neglected the environmental consequences of many of its industrial projects and this culminated in the pollution disaster in Minimata, where mercury poisoning killed and maimed animals and people alike. Tokyo, as capital, had endured problems with water supply and treatment, air pollution and waste disposal and traffic congestion compounded by an underdeveloped public transport system. The most high-profile response was the development of the high-speed *shinkansen* rail network but important improvements were also made to the subway system within the city itself, such as the *Marunouchi* line, the *Haneda* monorail and a number of lines that connected suburbs with the centre. Although environmental improvement was not the only aim of these developments, they all could be argued to help reduce air pollution. However, the pre-Olympic phase also heralded a number of new expressways, many built on stilts, which have done little to improve the atmospheric or aesthetic environment of the city. New sewage treatment facilities were constructed along with drainage systems to cope with surface run-off, along with a special water channel designed to flush out the heavily polluted and stinking Sumida River. Many areas were cleaned up for the event and the main site for the Games has become Yoyogi Park. A less savoury clean-up saw 'vagrants and beggars ... removed from parts of the city where they were likely to be noticed, and sent off to institutions or other exile' (Seidensticker 1990, cited in Cybriwsky 1998: 96). Other host cities had also considered their legacies, particularly in terms of urban transport, such as Rome in 1960.

Some cities refused the Games whilst in others there was considerable conflict. Denver was awarded the 1976 Winter Games but later withdrew following fierce opposition from a variety of groups that 'saw continued development as destructive of the area's natural beauty and its lifestyle' (Burbank *et al.* 2001: 49). The Los Angeles Games saw conflict over the use of the Sepulveda Basin and both the Salt Lake City and Atlanta Games saw local opposition to the siting of particular venues. In all cases environmental issues were only part of complex political battles that involved a degree of 'nimbyism'. Burbank *et al.* identify a significant issue in Olympic politics, one of social justice:

> When plans for Olympic development encountered opposition from well-organised groups representing economically advantaged residents, such as in Sepulveda Basin, opponents had a good chance of success. On the other hand, when opposition came from residents who were predominantly poor, such as in Exposition Park, Olympic developers tended to get their way.
>
> (Burbank *et al.* 2001: 165)

It is interesting that London's Games will be located in a relatively poor part of the city – cleverly this has been presented as a positive, a piece of overdue urban regeneration.

The greening of the Olympics

The 1996 Lillehammer Games in Norway were, fortunately for the IOC, a contrast to Albertville but, as Cantelon and Letters suggest (Cantelon and Letters 2000: 305) this was more the result of local initiative than any systematic policy from the IOC. The bid had been presented by Bruntland and her association with the UN and the development of sustainable development was a benefit for the IOC. Collins also notes that there were a number of negative environmental impacts of the Games (Houlihan 2003). By the mid-1990s the IOC recognised the need to develop an environmental policy and the 1996 Games bidding process included, for the first time, sustainability as a selection criterion. The 1998 Nagano Games were the first to incorporate environmental guidelines on staging the Games.

Meanwhile, following a meeting in Paris in 1994 an IOC Commission on Sport and the Environment, was established and the following year the Olympic Charter, which hitherto had identified sport and culture as the central pillars of its mission, was amended to include the environment. This is reflected in the current charter which includes the following objective:

> To encourage and support a responsible concern for environmental issues, to promote sustainable development in sport and to require that the Olympic Games are held accordingly.
>
> *(IOC 2004: 1)*

In 1997 the IOC produced its first guidance on how to manage the Games sustainably which was updated in 2005 with the title *Manual on Sport and the Environment* (IOC 2005). It identifies eight key concepts and issues regarding sport and the environment. These are:

1 Biodiversity conservation
2 Protection of ecosystems
3 Land use and landscape
4 Pollution
5 Resources and waste management
6 Health and safety
7 Nuisances
8 Safeguard of cultural heritage.

It goes on to identify a number of environmental recommendations which include recognition of legislative frameworks at a range of scales from local to global, individual responsibilities (including communication and education), working with partners and specific management advice on the eight issues listed above. It concludes with brief sections on the IOC's history of environmental involvement and an outline of environmental requirements for the Olympic Games.

A new millennium

The first Summer Games to risk the label of 'green Games' were those in Sydney 2000. Kearins and Pavlovich (2002: 157–69) noted the importance of stakeholders in these Games, and one of those stakeholders was Greenpeace Australia. As they observed, the NGO had both 'planning and monitoring roles' and just before the Games awarded them a bronze medal for their environmental performance. Following the Games Greenpeace audited them and 'issued a positive report' (Toyne in Poynter and MacRury 2010: 233). However, this verdict requires qualification. Not all environmental organisations were as enthusiastic as Greenpeace. A coalition of five national and state groups had established a Green Games Watch 2000. Their final analysis was that the Games 'could at best be called the "half green" or "light green" Games, in that many environmental initiatives were adopted, but much more could have been achieved' (GGW 2000 cited in Kearins and Pavlovich 2000: 166). It listed the main green wins as public transport access, solar power applications, building material selection, recycling of construction waste, progressive tendering policies, energy and water conservation and wetland restoration. The main green losses it identified were 'the failure of most sponsors to go green, poor quality Olympic merchandising, environmentally destructive refrigerant selection, loss of biodiversity in some projects and failure to clean up contaminated Homebush Bay sediments in time for the games' (GGW 2000 cited in Kearins and Pavlovich 2000: 166). Kearins goes on to suggest that the 'Olympic Games are inherently unsustainable' (Kearins and Pavlovich 2000: 167) and that green event management raises a number of issues, notably the difficulty of getting all stakeholders to give equal priority to the environment when there are cost and other burdens associated with it.

Nonetheless, in September 2000 Greenpeace published the *Greenpeace Olympic Environmental Guidelines* (Greenpeace 2000). This identified nine principles:

1 Environmental sustainability
2 Precautionary principle
3 A preventative approach
4 Holistic and integrated approach
5 Specific and measurable environmental goals
6 Community, NGO and public involvement
7 Senior environmental management
8 Environmental reporting and independent monitoring
9 Public education and training

It then stipulated thirty-four guidelines covering energy consumption, transport, refrigeration and air conditioning, ozone depletion, timber use, habitat protection, air, water and soil protection, water conservation, indoor air quality, consumption of natural resources, waste avoidance and minimisation, genetically modified organisms, quality of life, cultural and historical heritage and transparency and monitoring of the guidelines.

This document makes an interesting comparison with the material presented in the IOC's *Manual on Sport and the Environment* (IOC 2005). It also reflects some new environmental concerns such as genetically modified organisms which are contested by many scientists as to whether they are environmentally harmful. This raises issues about the scientific, as opposed to the political, validity of some of the environmental concerns.

The Athens Games were audited by both Greenpeace and the WWF. The latter found that they were less 'green' than the Sydney Games. In advance of the Games they produced a report which 'evaluates the environmental wins and losses' of the Athens Olympics based on the Sydney 2000 Olympics benchmark for 'clean and green' Games. 'On a scale of 0–4, it rates the environmental component of the Athens Olympics at a very disappointing score of 0.77 (see Table 24.1). The lowest scores were given to areas such as environmental planning and evaluation, protection of fragile natural and cultural areas, waste management and water conservation, and the use of environmentally friendly construction technologies. The highest scores went to the fields of public transport, the improvement of existing infrastructure, and the promotion of environmental awareness. However, these wins may disappear when the Olympic Games come to a close' (WWF 2004).

The Beijing Olympics were noted for their great spectacle. They had been marketed, however, amongst other things, as sustainable. Greenpeace reviewed the Games in an

Table 24.1 Environmental assessment of the 2004 Athens Olympic Games, July 2004

Issue	Score
OVERALL PLANNING	
Environmental planning	0
Environmental assessment	0
NATURAL ENVIRONMENT	
Protection of natural habitats	0
URBAN ENVIRONMENT	
Protection of open spaces	0
Increase of urban green	0
Improvement of the built environment	3
TRANSPORT	
Public transport	3
CONSTRUCTIONS	
Siting of Olympic venues	0
Use of existing infrastructure	1
Use of green technologies	0
Energy	
Green energy	0
WATER	
Water saving scheme	0
WASTE	
Integrated waste management and recycling	0
PUBLIC PARTICIPATION	
Social consultation	1
Transparency	1
Public information	1
GENERAL ISSUES	
Respect to environmental legislation	0
Public awareness	4
Total score	0.77

4 – Very positive; 3 – Positive; 2 – Fair; 1 – Disappointing; 0 – Very disappointing.
Source: Adapted from WWF (2004).

extensive report, *China after the Olympics: Lessons from Beijing* (Greenpeace 2008a). A press release from Greenpeace notes that in its preparation for the Games China has 'made public transport more convenient, upgraded home heating methods, improved water treatment and, to some degree, reduced its reliance on fossil fuels' (Greenpeace 2008a). However, the report also observes that 'in many areas, Beijing failed to take the opportunity of the Olympics to adopt the world's best environmental practices, such as clean production, zero-waste policy, Forest Stewardship Council (FSC) certification, and comprehensive water conservation policies' (ibid.). Greenpeace China's campaign director, Lo Sze Ping, also noted that it is easy to 'pollute but much harder to clean up the damage. Air quality in Beijing is such an example' (ibid.). An earlier report by Greenpeace, cited on their website, noted that 'Beijing's air quality is still falling well short of international guidelines, despite desperate attempts to clean the Olympic host city's skies before the Games' (Greenpeace 2008b).

There is a danger that evaluation of the sustainability of these mega-events is being led by a self-selected number of NGOs and the IOC itself, both of whom have had input into the planning and delivery of past Games. Whilst their efforts can be condoned, it may be appropriate for more independent reviews to gain prominence. In this respect the establishment of the Commission for Sustainable London to oversee the 2012 Olympics (discussed below) would appear to be a step in the right direction even if some might challenge its composition.

The London 2012 Olympic Games

Many were surprised when London won the right to host 2012 Games with a vision 'to stage inspirational games that capture the imagination of young people around the world and leave a lasting legacy' (Toyne in Poynter and MacRury 2010: 234). Part of that lasting legacy was to regenerate the lower Lea Valley near Stratford. This was an area whose future had long been debated – many who took A-level geography may remember starting their course with a look at how the Lea Valley might be revitalised. That in itself was a reflection of changing attitudes to the environment as it was the first publication in the 1980s Schools Council Geography Project, with its distinctive approach to the relationship between humans and their environment. Urban legacy is discussed elsewhere in this book but it is important to note here that such a legacy represents a major set of environmental impacts and, if effectively implemented, a contribution to sustainable (re)development.

In October 2007, Ken Livingstone, Tessa Jowell, Sebastian Coe and Colin Moynihan put their signatures to the *London 2012 Sustainability Policy*. It opens:

> London 2012's vision is to host inspirational, safe and inclusive Olympic and Paralympic Games and leave a sustainable legacy for London and the UK. This vision and the strategic objectives for the Games are underpinned by the principles of 'sustainable development'. Drawing on these principles, the London Organising Committee of the Olympic Games and Paralympic Games (LOCOG) and the Olympic Delivery Authority (ODA), along with HM Government, Greater London Authority (GLA), British Olympic Association (BOA) and British Paralympic Association (BPA), are committed to working together to maximise the economic, social, health, environmental and sporting benefits the Games bring to London and the UK. This is encapsulated by the concept 'towards a one planet 2012', which creates a powerful identity for London 2012's sustainability programme and provides a framework for achieving sustainable Games in accordance with the London 2012 Candidature commitments and with respect to Olympic ideals.
>
> *(LOCOG 2007: 1)*

In so doing it aimed to support the following legacy targets:

- make the UK a world-leading sporting nation;
- transform the heart of east London;
- inspire a new generation of young people to take part in local volunteering, cultural and physical activity;
- make the Olympic Park a blueprint for sustainable living; and
- demonstrate the UK is a creative, inclusive and welcoming place to live in, visit and for business.

It identified five themes on which it would focus:

- climate change
- waste
- biodiversity
- inclusion
- healthy living

(LOCOG 2007: 1)

These are somewhat modish issues on which to focus which relate closely to priorities of the New Labour regime in power at the time. They also represent a very catholic vision of sustainability that extends (rightly) well beyond environmental considerations and in certain aspects is somewhat tenuous in its linkage to core sustainability concepts. Some of it is a little vague. The healthy living theme, for example, states 'We will use the Games as a springboard for inspiring people across the country to take up sport and develop active, healthy and sustainable lifestyles' (LOCOG 2007: 2). However, there is no indication as to what these sustainable lifestyles might be.

Finally, the document outlines the importance of the management of processes:

> The Olympic Board together with the Boards of Stakeholder organisations will ensure the delivery against these objectives through the following measures.
>
> - Integrating sustainability principles into the day-to-day management of LOCOG and the ODA, working closely with the Host Boroughs, the GLA Group, nations and regions, central Government, BOA, BPA, sports authorities and the International Olympic Committee.
> - Developing active partnerships with non-Governmental organisations, community groups, businesses, professional bodies and academia to help leverage the opportunities provided by the Games and to utilise the power of the Olympic brand to mobilise enthusiasm and maximise benefits.
> - Procuring goods, services and sponsorship sustainably with an emphasis on supplier diversity, fair employment and environmental attributes, as well as other social and ethical criteria as appropriate.
> - Establishing an independent assurance function to be overseen by the London Sustainable Development Commission in partnership with the national Sustainable Development Commission and equivalent regional structures.
>
> (LOCOG 2007: 2)

The Commission for a Sustainable London 2012 (CSL) was announced in January 2007 to monitor London's 2012 pledge to host the 'most sustainable Games ever' (Commission for a Sustainable London 2012 2010). The CSL reports on a quarterly basis to the Olympic Board and provides assurance over London 2012 and its stakeholders. It produces annual reports, the first of which was published in November 2007. At the time of writing (August 2010), the latest annual report relates to 2009 and was published in May 2010. A number of thematic reports have also been published including one on transport in June 2010. Nonetheless, the CSL acknowledges that 'while there will be some negative impacts, the Games presents an extraordinary opportunity to showcase sustainable development, to make the most of the social, economic, environmental and legacy opportunities' (Commission for a Sustainable London 2012 2010). In its most recent report it is generally positive but notes,

Our main area of concern lies in the wider commitments that were made during the bid or just afterwards. Broad promises have been made in official documents: 'to make the Olympic Park a blueprint for sustainable living' and 'to be a catalyst for new waste management infrastructure'. 'We are optimistic that the Games and venues will deliver against the sustainability promises in east London.' With the exception of a few worthy initiatives, there is no comprehensive plan to make this happen. Furthermore, it is not clear what definitions lie behind these expressions or who is responsible for making them happen. With just over two years to go before the 'inspirational power of the Games' moves to Rio, never to return to London, these issues need to be resolved.

(Commission for a Sustainable London 2012 2010)

It is, of course, not possible to assess the overall long-term impact of the 2012 Games until some years after the event itself. However, a number of features can be discerned even at this stage. First, it will be the outcome of an Olympic bidding process that contrasts sharply with that which prevailed before 1996. There is now an explicit examination of sustainability and environmental impacts by the IOC itself which contrasts with the locally based assessment that had prevailed before the 1990s and the unfortunate Albertville Games. The IOC now has its own environmental criteria and clear guidelines on managing environmental aspects of the Games. Second, it will follow Games that have been formally environmentally assessed, not least by NGOs such as Greenpeace and the WWF. It can learn from those experiences and incorporate new ideas, technology and processes. Third, it will involve clearly identified stakeholders. Fourth, it is well intentioned and incorporates sustainability into its aims and management. Fifth, the progress on sustainability will be formally monitored on a regular basis. Finally, it is evolving specific targets.

There are some qualifications. The concepts of sustainability are very broad. The environmental elements are sometimes tenuously linked to other aspirations. There is an element of the *ad hoc* in the way the specific sustainability targets and plans have evolved, though some might see this as a positive which reflects flexibility and a willingness to incorporate the latest innovations. Although inclusion is an aim there may be issues of social justice relating to environmental issues. A recent example is the delineation of traffic lanes which will benefit participants and organisers but inconvenience locals. The hoped-for increase in tourism will inevitably produce an enhanced carbon footprint, however 'green' the transport plans. This is an inherent weakness in the hosting of events until *Star Trek* technology can teleport us, with minimal energy input and carbon footprint, to the stadia. According to data used in LOCOG's Food Vision for the Games (LOCOG 2009) there will be 205,900 people involved in delivering the Games, including the athletes, the media and IOC officials. Additionally, up to 9 million are expected as spectators. This represents a very significant carbon footprint. Perhaps the Games should be 'virtual' in the future – TV coverage allowing all except local residents to enjoy the Games from home. A research programme on the viability of such an approach might be worthwhile, though any implementation of such ideas will require a radical change of philosophy amongst a wide range of vested interests.

Other uncertainties relate to the economic climate – will sustainability be compromised by the need for companies and organisations to minimise costs? Toyne points out that 'critics have suggested that most Olympics are expensive to run and result in debt to host nations' (Toyne in Poynter and MacRury 2010: 241) Will there be sustainable jobs for the local community or will the jobs be taken by short-term incomers and disappear shortly afterwards? Will sponsorship and large-scale corporate deals disadvantage small-scale and local producers? The organisers are aware of the dilemma. In their vision for food they state:

> while the scale of the operation requires us to leverage the experience and resources of larger service providers, London 2012 is also committed to promoting diversity within the overall supply chain by including smaller producers and caterers. This will give smaller catering organisations and suppliers an opportunity to be involved in an event far larger than they would otherwise be able to.
>
> *(LOCOG 2009)*

Later they comment on the role of sponsors: 'The Games could not take place without sponsors. They play a huge role in supporting the Games and promoting sport, way beyond the core provisions of their service or product categories' (ibid.). The primary sponsors are McDonald's, Coca-Cola and Cadbury. This is presumption indeed – is it impossible to envisage a Games without sponsors? The vision goes on to note that 'Although McDonald's will be the only branded food outlet at Games venues, they will be joined by a vast array of other outlets (from kiosks to food courts and dining rooms) that will provide unbranded food products' (ibid.). The key here is the branding and resulting public perception. Whatever the green credentials of the sponsors, how many people watching or attending will be aware of the companies' overall performance on sustainability? What might be the sustainability opportunity costs of not having awarded the contracts elsewhere? Additionally, who will ultimately judge, and by what criteria, whether a 'fair' balance will have been struck between big and small, local and transnational, sponsors and non-sponsors?

There are further questions that will need assessment. Will there be adequate investment in local communities in an era of savage cut-backs in the public sector? Will all social classes benefit equally? These issues can all impact adversely on the environment if they are not handled appropriately. Some issues are equivocal in this respect – express traffic lanes may benefit the athletes but may inconvenience local communities. Will the changes brought about in these Olympics diffuse themselves more widely through the capitalist system that prevails in the UK and globally, a system that already seems to be relaxing its environmental and sustainability criteria to accommodate urgent needs in areas such as power generation? In August, Allegra Stratton in the *Guardian* reported that 'the coalition is watering down a commitment to tough new environmental emissions standards, raising the possibility of dirty coal-fired power stations such as Kingsnorth going ahead' (Guardian Online 2010). Although overall evaluation must wait – and there are research opportunities aplenty here if that is not to be left to NGOs and the IOC itself – some environmental positives will emerge. Supply chain management will be made more explicit. Waste will be more carefully controlled. Carbon footprints will be discussed. Environmental awareness may be raised, in the short term at least. There will be urban regeneration, hopefully sustainable, and offering 'community access to local employment, education and a quality of life that promotes a healthy lifestyle' (Toyne in Poynter and MacRury 2010: 241). Further, as Toyne observes, 'if this can be achieved and sustained then it should provide a blueprint for transforming other parts of Britain' (ibid.: 241) but it is an experiment and it is contingent upon the many uncertainties identified above. It is in the long term that most doubts are focused but there is still time for society, including its academic community, to ensure a permanent green legacy.

References

Allen, J. (2000) *Events Beyond 2000: Setting the Agenda, Proceedings of Conference on Event Evaluation, Research and Education Sydney 2000*, Sydney: Australian Centre for Event Management.

Aronson, L. (2000) *The Development of Sustainable Tourism*, London: Continuum.

Barker, M. Page, S.J. and Meyer, D. (2002) 'Evaluating the impact of the 2000 America's Cup on Auckland, New Zealand', *Event Management* 7: 79–92.

Bertalanffy, L. von (1951) 'An outline of general systems theory', *British Journal of the Philosophy of Science* I: 134–65.

Blunden, J. (1977) *Section 1: Man and the Environment; Units 4–6, Parts 1 and 2*, Milton Keynes: Open University Press.

Boers, H. and Bosch, M. (1994) *The Earth as a Holiday Resort – An Introduction to Tourism and the Environment*, SME: Utrecht.

Bowdin, G., Allen, J., O'Toole, W., Harris, R. and McDonnell, I. (2001) *Events Management*, Oxford: Butterworth-Heinemann.

Brooks, S., Magnin, A. and O'Halloran, D. (2007) *The Sustainable Music Festival: A Strategic Guide*. Available at: http://archive.defra.gov.uk/sustainable/government/advice/documents/SustainableEventsGuide.pdf

BSI (2007) *Specification for a Sustainable Event Management System with Guidance for Use Developed*, London: BSI.

Burbank, J., Andranovich, G. and Heying, C. (2001) *Olympic Dreams – The Impact of Mega-Events on Local Politics*, London: Lynne Rienner.

Cantelon, H. and Letters, M. (2000) 'The making of the IOC Environmental Policy as the third dimension of the Olympic Movement', *International Review for the Sociology of Sport* 35: 294.

Carson, R. (1962) *Silent Spring*, Harmondsworth: Penguin.

Carter, N. (2007) *The Politics of the Environment: Ideas, Activism, Policy*, Cambridge: Cambridge University Press, second edition.

Case, R. (2012 expected) *Events and the Environment*, London: Routledge.

Cater, E. and Lowman, G. (eds) (1994) *Ecotourism – A Sustainable Option*, Chichester: Wiley.

Chernushenko, D. (1994) *Greening Our Games: Running Sports Events and Facilities that Won't Cost the Earth*, Ottawa: Centurion.

Collins, Andrea, Flynn, Andrew, Munday, Max and Roberts, Annette (2007) 'Assessing the environmental consequences of major sporting events: the 2003/04 FA Cup Final', *Urban Studies* 44(3): 457–76.

Collins, M.F. (2003) 'Sport and recreation and the environment', in B. Houlihan (ed.) *Sport and Society – A Student Introduction*, London: Sage, pp. 272–92.

Commission for a Sustainable London 2012 (2010) *Raising the Bar – Can London 2012 Set New Standards for Sustainability? Commission for a Sustainable London Annual Report 2009*, London: Commission for a Sustainable London.

Croall, J. (1995) *Preserve or Destroy – Tourism and the Environment*, London: Calouste Gulbenkion Foundation.

Cybriwsky, R. (1998) *Tokyo*, New York: Wiley.

daCosta, L.P. (2001) 'International trends in sport and environment – a 2001 overview', in L.P. daCosta (ed.) *Book of Abstracts: Sixth Annual Congress of the European College of Sports Science*, Cologne: ECSS.

——(2002) *Olympic Studies – Current Intellectual Crossroads*, Rio de Janeiro: Group of Research on Olympic Studies, University Gama Filho – PPGEF.

Defra (2007) *Sustainable Events Guide*. Available at: http://archive.defra.gov.uk/sustainable/government/advice/documents/SustainableEventsGuide.pdf (accessed 9 May 2011).

Edington, J.M. and Edington, A.M. (1977) *Ecology and Environmental Planning*, London: Chapman and Hall.

Epstein, M.J. (2008) *Making Sustainability Work*, Sheffield: Greenleaf Publishing.

Frey, M., Iraldo, F. and Melis, M. (2008) *The Impact of Wide-Scale Sport Events on Local Development: an Assessment of the XXth Torino Olympics through the Sustainability Report*, Working Paper No. 10, Milan: Istituto di Economia e Politica dell'Energia e dell'Ambiente.

Getz, D. (2000) 'Developing a research agenda for the event management field', in J. Allen, R. Harris, L.K. Jago and A.J. Veal (eds) *Proceedings of Conference on Event Evaluation, Research and Education*, Sydney: Australia Centre for Event Management, School of Leisure, Sport and Tourism, University of Technology, Sydney, pp. 9–20.

——(2007) *Event Studies*, Oxford: Elsevier.

Getz, D. and Anderson, T.D. (2008) 'Sustainable festivals: on becoming an institution', *Event Management* 12: 1–17.

Goldblatt, J.J. (2000) 'A future for event management: the analysis of major trends impacting the profession', in J. Allen, R. Harris, L.K. Jago and A.J. Veal (eds) *Proceedings of Conference on Event Evaluation, Research and Education*, Sydney: Australia Centre for Event Management, School of Leisure, Sport and Tourism, University of Technology, Sydney, pp. 1–8.

Goldsmith, E. and Allen, R. (1972) *Blueprint for Survival*, Harmondsworth: Penguin.

Greenpeace (2000) *Olympic Environmental Guidelines: A Guide to Sustainable Events*, Greenpeace.

——(2008a) *China after the Olympics: Lessons from Beijing*. Available at: www.greenpeace.org/china/en/press/release/beijing-olympics (accessed 19 August 2010).

——(2008b) *Making Waves*. Available at: www.greenpeace.org/international/en/news/blogs/making-waves/beijing-olmpics-h (accessed 19 August 2010).

Guardian Online (2010) 'Coal-fired power stations win reprieve', 15 August 2010 20.59 BST. Available at: www.guardian.co.uk/environment/2010/aug/15/coal-fired-power-stations-coalition (accessed 20 May 2011).

Haggett, P. (1965) *Locational Analysis in Human Geography*, London: Edward Arnold.

Hall, C.M. and Page, S. (1999) *The Geography of Tourism and Recreation*, London: Routledge.

Hay, P. (2002) *A Companion to Environmental Thought*, Edinburgh: Edinburgh University Press.

Hiller, Harry H.(1998) 'Assessing the impact of mega-events: a linkage model', *Current Issues in Tourism* 1(1): 47–57.

Holden, A. (2000) *Environment and Tourism*, London: Routledge.

Honey, M. (1999) *Ecotourism and Sustainable Development*, Washington: Island Press.

Houlihan, B. (2003) *Sport and Society – A Student Introduction*, London: Sage.

Howatson, C. and Chilvers, I. (1993) *The Concise Oxford Companion to Classical Literature*, Oxford: Oxford University Press.

IOC (2004) *Olympic Charter*, Geneva: IOC.

——(2005) *Manual of Sport*, Geneva: IOC.

IPCC (2007) 'Summary for policymakers', in S. Solomon, D. Qin, M. Manning, Z. Chen, M. Marquis, K.B. Averyt, M.Tignor and H.L. Miller (eds) *Climate Change 2007: The Physical Science Basis. Contribution of Working Group I to the Fourth Assessment Report of the Intergovernmental Panel on Climate Change*, Cambridge and New York: Cambridge University Press.

James, O. (2007) *Affluenza*, London: Vermillion.

Jones, M. (2010) *Sustainable Event Management*, London: Earthscan.

Kearins, K. and Pavlovich, K. (2002) 'The role of stakeholders on Sydney's Green Games', *Corporate Social Responsibility and Environmental Management* 9: 157–69.

Levi, P. (1980) *Atlas of the Greek World*, Oxford: Phaidon Press.

LOCOG (2007) *London 2012 Sustainability Policy*, London: LOCOG.

——(2009) *Food Vision for the 2012 Olympic and Paralympic Games*. Available at: www.london2012.com/publications/food-vision.php (accessed 20 May 2011).

Lovelock, J. (2006) *Revenge of Gaia*, Harmondsworth: Allen Lane.

McDonough, W. (1992) *The Hannover Principles: Design for Sustainability*, Charlottesville, VA: William McDonough and Partners.

Meadows, D.H., Meadows, D.L., Randers, J. and Behrens III, W.W. (1972) *The Limits to Growth: A Report for the Club of Rome's Project for the Predicament of Mankind*, New York: Universe.

MEBC (2002) *Sexi: The Sustainable Exhibition Industry Project*, Birmingham: MEBC.

Mowforth, M. and Munt, I. *(1998) Tourism and Sustainability: New Tourism in the Third World*, London: Routledge.

Oittinen, A. and Tiezi, E. (1999) 'A scientific review of information available on the link between the environment and sport', in Council of Europe (ed.) *Proceedings of the CDDS Bureau Meeting*, Strasbourg: Council of Europe, pp. 1–33.

Otto, I. and Heath, E.T.(2009) 'The potential contribution of the 2010 Soccer World Cup to climate change: an exploratory study among tourism industry stakeholders in the Tshwane Metropole of South Africa', *Journal of Sport and Tourism* 14(2): 169–91.

Page, S.J. and Connell, J. (2006) *Tourism – A Modern Synthesis*, Thomson: London, second edition.

Page, S.J. and Dowling, J. (2002) *Ecotourism*, Harlow: Prentice Hall.

Patmore, J.A. (1983) *Recreation and Resources: Leisure Patterns and Leisure Places*, Oxford: Blackwell.

Poynter, G. and MacRury, I. (2010) *Olympic Cities: 2012 and the Remaking of London*, Farnham: Ashgate.

Raj, R. and Musgrave, J. (eds) (2009) *Event Management and Sustainability*, Wallingford: CABI.

Shone, A. and Parry, B (2001) *Successful Event Management – A Practical Guide*, London: Continuum.

Solway, A. (2009) *Sustainable Tourism*, London: Hachette Children's Books.

Spink, J. (1994) *Leisure and the Environment*, Oxford: Butterworth-Heinemann.

Spivey, N. (2004) *The Ancient Olympics: A History*, Oxford: Oxford University Press.

Terrell, S. (2004) *The Geography of Sport and Leisure*, Abingdon: Hodder and Stoughton.

Theobold, W.F. (1994) *Global Tourism*, Oxford: Butterworth-Heinemann.

Torkildsen, G. (1983) *Leisure and Recreation Management*, London: E. and F.N. Spon.

——(1999) *Leisure and Recreation Management*, London: E. and F.N. Spon, fourth edition.

UK Sport (2005) *Staging Major Sports Events – The Guide*, London: UK Sport.

UNCED (United Nations Conference on Environment and Development) (1992) *Agenda 21*, New York: UNCED.

WCED (World Commission on Environment and Development) (1987) *Our Common Future*, Oxford: Oxford University Press.

WCU/UNEP/WWFN (World Conservation Union/United Nations Environment Programme/World Wide Fund for Nature) (1991) *Caring for the Earth*, Gland: WCU/UNEP/WWFN.

Webster, T.B.L. (1969) *Everyday Life in Classical Athens*, London: B.T. Batsford.

Wood, K. and House, S. (1991) *The Good Tourist*, London: Mandarin.

WWF (2004) *No Gold Medal for the Environment in the Athens Olympics*. Available at: www.wwf.org.uk/wwf_articles.cfm?unewsid=1277 (accessed 12 August 2010).

25

The role of events in urban regeneration

Michael Pacione

Introduction

Events are major elements of the cultural economy of the post-industrial city, and are viewed by many as a catalyst for urban regeneration. The impact of an event can be social, economic and environmental, short-lived or long-lasting depending on the nature of the event and the urban context in which it occurs. While some events may be one-off or small-scale with local impact (such as the gala days held in many small towns), others are large-scale mega events with potentially major impacts on the economic, social and environmental character of a host city. Examples of such periodic impact events include the Notting Hill Carnival in London, Garden Festivals, the European Capital of Culture programme, and sporting events such as football World Cups, Commonwealth Games and the Olympic Games.

Study of the nature and impact of events on urban form and function is an important field in urban–cultural geography. This chapter focuses on the link between events and urban regeneration. First we discuss the nature of urban economic change in post-war cities then examine the concepts of urban regeneration and the urban cultural economy. On the basis of this conceptual foundation we undertake a critical examination of the impact of events on urban regeneration. A case study of Glasgow is presented to embed the discussion in an urban context. Finally, a number of lessons of relevance for future event-based urban regeneration strategies are identified.

The changing urban economy

The transition from industrial capitalism to post-industrial or advanced capitalism has been depicted as a shift from a post-war Fordist paradigm to a post-Fordist regime of flexible accumulation. De-industrialisation and tertiarisation are key components of this transformation. The expansion of the service sector is apparent in cities at all levels of a national urban system from those catering for local–regional markets to others serving a global market.

The twin processes of de-industrialisation and tertiarisation are evident in London's economy that has undergone a transformation from industrial to post-industrial over the past half-century. Until the mid-1960s London was a major centre of light industrial production with one-third

of the labour force employed in manufacturing. By contrast, although the city had long functioned as a national and international financial centre, the importance of finance and business
services for overall employment was relatively small, with only about 10 per cent of London's
workforce employed in this sector in 1961. Over the intervening period the relative importance
of manufacturing industry and financial services has been reversed and London has emerged as
one of the world's three key international financial centres.

Economic tertiarisation, however, is not limited to finance, insurance and real estate (FIRE)
activities. These along with R& D and marketing constitute the producer services sector. Other
manifestations of the service economy are to be found in distributive services (transport and
communications), public services (local and national government), and consumer services
(leisure and personal services). Consumer services represent a key component of the cultural
economy of cities (which, as we shall see later, plays an important role in urban regeneration
strategies).

Urban regeneration

For many older cities the process of de-industrialisation presented a major challenge of how to
regenerate derelict former industrial land, revive a depressed urban economy and revitalise
disadvantaged communities.

In the UK from the end of the Second World War until the late 1960s urban problems
were seen largely in physical terms. The policy response to issues of housing quality and
supply, transport, and industrial restructuring focused on slum clearance and comprehensive
redevelopment strategies, and the planned decentralisation of urban population via regional
policy and New Town development. By contrast, since the 1980s urban regeneration has
focused on economic (re)growth and use of public funds to lever in market finance (ODPM
2003).

The entrepreneurial thrust of urban policy during the 1980s was underwritten by
co-operation between the government and the private sector. This approach owed much to
experience in North America's cities, where the practice of public–private partnership in urban
regeneration dates back more than half a century. Following the Second World War US city
governments, faced with growing blight in downtown areas, and attracted by federal funding
from the urban-renewal programme, joined forces with private developers in 'quasi-public'
redevelopment corporations which were able to sidestep conventional procedures for municipal
policy-making. By the 1960s these business–government partnerships had produced a range
of downtown redevelopments, including Pittsburgh's Golden Triangle, Baltimore's Charles
Centre and Minneapolis's Nicolett Mall. In the 1970s and 1980s, prompted by the problems
of deindustrialisation and fiscal distress, city governments moved beyond single-project collaboration with developers. In the context of heightened inter-city competition for private
investment, municipal governments, especially those with high-profile 'boosterish' mayors,
became entrepreneurial, providing extensive subsidies and incentives to attract developers, and
often becoming co-developers of more risky redevelopment projects. Public–private partnerships became the cornerstone of economic development strategies of virtually all US cities –
strategies that centred on the creation of a good business climate. This trend is exemplified by
the 'Rouse-ification' of downtowns across the USA. With its production of festival market-
places in, for example, Boston (Faneuil Hall), New York (South Street Seaport), Baltimore
(Harborplace), Milwaukee (Grand Avenue Mall) and St Louis (Union Station), the Rouse
Company became the leading downtown developer in the country. As Levine (1989: 24)
observed:

Rouse projects, with their distinctive architecture and innovative linkage of entertainment and retailing, have been credited with changing the image of centre cities, stimulating spin-off downtown redevelopment, and rekindling investor confidence in downtown areas – all factors that have made mayors, anxious to promote growth and claim political credit for it, line up to coax Rouse to their cities.

The distributional impact of these projects has been typically uneven, with, in most cities, redeveloped downtowns resembling 'islands of renewal in seas of decay'. Baltimore's Inner Harbor is heralded as a national model of public–private waterfront reclamation, but during the course of its redevelopment the poverty rate increased in 90 per cent of the city's non-white neighbourhoods. A principal reason for such contrasts is that downtown corporate centres based on advanced services and tourism often have only limited links with the local economy and rarely generate economic development in surrounding neighbourhoods. In addition, since the kinds of jobs created are unlikely to provide employment opportunities for urban poor and minority populations, many of the benefits of redevelopment are taken up by suburban commuters. The efficacy of relying on the 'trickle-down' effect, rather than public targeting to encourage economic development in the most distressed urban neighbourhoods, is open to question.

Property-led regeneration

Property-based development has played a prominent role in urban regeneration projects undertaken by public–private partnerships. During the 1980s property-led regeneration assumed a central place in urban policy, with the key role of the private sector demonstrated most visibly in flagship projects such as the redevelopment of Canary Wharf in London's Docklands or the transformation of Baltimore's waterfront. However, property development alone is an insufficient basis for urban economic regeneration. Although property development and rehabilitation can improve a residential environment and construction projects can provide scope for employment, a property-led approach fails to consider crucial issues including the development of human resources, such as education and training, which have long-term effects on people's incomes and employment prospects; the underlying competitiveness of local production; and necessary investment in infrastructure, such as transport and communications.

Nowhere has the impact of property-led urban redevelopment been more evident than in the global cities of London and New York, where, during the 1980s in particular, the growth of the financial services industry and the concomitant expansion of office space interacted to engineer a major restructuring of urban space. By the end of the 1980s London was witnessing the largest office-building boom in its history as a result of the Conservative government's opening up of a once highly regulated property-development arena to speculative ventures. Much of the new development appeared in the traditional heart of the City, which sought to protect itself from a leakage of financial-sector activity to European rivals such as Frankfurt and Paris, as well as to the emerging Docklands, with its flagship development at Canary Wharf. In recent decades the cultural economy has been viewed as a key component of, and catalyst for, such post-industrial urban regeneration.

The cultural economy and urban regeneration

Cultural production embraces activities such as printing and publishing, film production, radio, television and theatre, libraries, museums and art galleries. High fashion, tourism and sports-related activities are also included in some definitions of the cultural industries (or creative industries) sector (Mort 1996; Power and Scott 2004). Such activities cut across the conventional production–consumption divide, blur the distinction between the functions of cities as centres of production and consumption, and illuminate the post-industrial/postmodern concept of flexible specialisation. Los Angeles represents the largest cultural-industries economy in North America, if not the world. In Britain the co-incidence of production and consumption activity in 'consumption spaces' is seen in the regeneration of favoured areas such as Sheffield's cultural industries quarter, with the emphasis on media production, and Nottingham's lace-market quarter, with its focus on fashion, design and media industries. The development of cultural-industries quarters in contemporary cities has also involved the redevelopment of past urban landscapes as heritage areas as in the Gastown district of Vancouver, Albert Dock in Liverpool and the Merchant City in Glasgow. As urban places compete within the global economy for limited investment funds, their success often depends on the conscious and deliberate manipulation of culture in an effort to enhance their image and appeal.

Post-industrial cities across the globe have sought to employ leisure and culture-based strategies to regenerate declining central areas, as is evident in Pittsburgh (Holcomb 1993), Brisbane (Stimson and Taylor 1999), Barcelona (Jensen-Butler *et al.* 1997) and Dublin (McCarthy 1998). In many US cities cultural activities, often delivered by public–private partnerships, have been central to growth strategies (Whitt 1987), predicated on attracting the professional workforce needed to sustain a post-industrial economy, footloose companies seeking a pleasant work–life environment, and tourists. The traditional location of cultural facilities and events in the urban core or on the edge of the city centre has a direct impact for regeneration of brownfield sites. In the US sports events have been of considerable importance in urban regeneration of a large number of cities. Hosting a major league sports team can enhance a city's image – consider Green Bay without the Packers pro football team – and attract inward investment and visitors. Since professional sports franchises are privately owned, competition between cities to attract and retain a team can be fierce – between 1982 and 1995 the Raiders football team moved from Oakland to Los Angeles then back to Oakland. To gain the kudos of hosting a pro team cities often provide a subsidised low-rent publicly built stadium. Hosting a winning team can project a city image of success and, as in the case of the 2010 Superbowl champions, New Orleans, of urban recovery and regeneration. In North America, the policy of subsidising stadiums has been closely linked with policies to revitalise the city centre and prevent decentralisation. In Baltimore an old stadium in a middle suburb was replaced by a modern structure adjacent to the downtown, boosting expenditure in the central city (Hamilton and Kahn 1997), while the Toronto Skydome is a tourist attraction in its own right.

UK cities have followed the trend for leisure and cultural-based regeneration (Miles and Paddison 2005) with culture acknowledged explicitly as a significant part of successful regeneration in the post-industrial city (Evans 2001; Aitcheson and Pritchard 2007). During the 1980s and 1990s several British cities adopted culture-led regeneration policies including Bristol (Griffith *et al.* 1999), Coventry (Comedia Consultants 1989), Dundee (McCarthy and Lloyd 1999), Newcastle-Gateshead, Sheffield (Bianchini 1991), Edinburgh, where the International Festivals are acknowledged to be the largest arts festivals in the world (Pattison 2006), and, as we shall see later, Glasgow. Since the late 1990s the Department for Culture Media and Sport has endeavoured to place culture at the heart of regeneration, maintaining that the cultural element can be the driving force for urban regeneration (DCMS 2004), while the Core Cities Group has also advocated a 'cultural-city-led' approach to urban regeneration (Comedia Consultants 2003). This trend has been reflected in a change in focus for cultural policy. With the move to use cultural expenditure as a catalyst for urban regeneration, rather than an end in itself, a new commodified cultural policy was born that expected tangible returns on investments in the form of profits, jobs and physical regeneration (Garcia 2004).

Culture-led strategies for urban regeneration may be classified as two forms. In cultural production models of regeneration investment is geared towards developing cultural or creative industries and spaces, such as Manchester's Northern Quarter. In cultural consumption models city authorities seek to develop a culturally vibrant image that, along with other elements of quality of life such as a clean and safe environment and aesthetic architecture, can attract mobile middle-class workers and tourists (Bianchini 1993). A key component in creating this image is investment in iconic cultural infrastructure (the 'Bilbao Guggenheim effect') (Plaza 2000), and hosting cultural or sporting events. Major events are seen as a particularly effective catalyst for urban regeneration because they are able to combine tourism and urban planning strategies (Roche 1994). If done successfully event hosting can disseminate a positive city image to potential investors and visitors.

Rhetoric or reality?

A core question is whether the policy can deliver beyond the rhetoric of culture-led regeneration. Consider, for example, the rhetoric of the UK government's culture-led regeneration policy:

> Culture is a source of prosperity and cosmopolitanism in the process of international urban competitiveness through hosting international events and centres of excellence, inspiring creativity and innovation, driving high growth business sectors such as creative industries, commercial, leisure and tourism, and increasing profile and name recognition … Culture is a means of spreading the benefits of prosperity to all citizens through its capacity to engender social and human capital, improve life skills and transform the organisational capacity to handle and respond to change.
>
> *(Comedia Consultants 2003)*

The evidence base to support these ambitious claims is incomplete (Jones and Wilks-Heeg 2004). For some 'measuring the social, economic and environmental impacts attributed to the cultural element in area regeneration is problematic and the evidence is seldom robust' (Evans 2005: 977). Miles (2005: 889) suggests that 'a small number of successful case studies tends to be advanced as evidence that a cultural turn in policies for urban renewal can deliver re-vitalisation or post-industrial cities'. These cases often centre on a new flagship cultural institution, such as the Tate Modern in London or Guggenheim Museum in Bilbao. Others have questioned what they refer to as a 'just add culture and stir' approach to urban regeneration (Gibson and Stevenson 2004: 1); while Lim (1993: 594) considered that there was 'a need to sort out the hype from the substance in claims made for culture-led regeneration'. Clearly the impact of cultural projects that feature in regeneration schemes needs to be assessed more rigorously to determine which type of cultural intervention and where best serves the regeneration objectives. An important question is: can policies and strategies that are successful in one city be used with equal success elsewhere? Table 25.1 presents a set of criteria that may be used to gauge culture's potential contribution to urban regeneration. Notwithstanding the absence of a definitive assessment of the impact of culture-led regeneration, cities across the globe have adopted such a strategy as they compete within the post-industrial global economy. A central element of many such schemes is hosting a major event.

Table 25.1 Evidence of culture's contribution to regeneration

Physical regeneration	Economic regeneration	Social regeneration
Re-use of redundant buildings	Inward investment	Positive change in residents' perceptions of the city
Increased public use of space	Increased property values and rents	Displacing crime and anti-social behaviour
Reduced vandalism and increased sense of safety	Corporate support of the local culture sector	Increase in volunteering and organisational capacity
Cultural facilities and workspace in mixed-use developments	Higher visitor spending from cultural activities	A clearer understanding of individual and shared ideas and needs
Reduced environmental impacts such as traffic, pollution and health problems	Job creation and new enterprises	Increased appreciation of the value of cultural projects
Environmental improvements through public art and architecture	Employer attraction to and retention in the city	Higher educational attainment
Employment of artists on design and construction teams	Graduate retention in the city	Greater individual confidence and aspiration levels
Incorporation of cultural aspects into local development plans	A more diverse workforce	
Accessibility using public transport	Creative industries quarters	
	Public–private–voluntary sector partnerships	

Source: Adapted from Evans (2005).

Event-based urban regeneration

A great variety of types of event has been employed in pursuit of culture-led regeneration. The term 'special event' is used to describe themed events that are one-off or occur infrequently outside the normal programme of activities (Getz 1991). Special events are of finite length and, even when periodic, are unique. They vary from those that occur annually in the same location (e.g. the Cannes Film Festival) to others that are peripatetic (e.g. the Commonwealth Games). A special event may be a one-off celebration (e.g. a bi-centennial) or can be linked to an existing visitor attraction as in a special exhibition in an art gallery or museum. The term 'hallmark event' is used to describe an event held to enhance the visibility and profitability of a tourist destination (Getz 1997) and is usually a recurring event which is, or aspires to be, a distinguishing feature of the city (e.g. the Edinburgh Festival). A mega event is one distinguished by high levels of tourism, media coverage, prestige and economic impact on the host city. Barcelona is an example of a city using a mega event of the 1992 Olympic Games to transform its image from one of industrial decline, political unrest and urban decay to one founded on fashion, culture and sport. Special events can range from a village gala day to the Olympic Games. Most are of short duration, lasting only a few days or weeks, while others, such as Expos or Garden Festivals, may last up to a year.

US cities have a long history of using showcase special events to attract residents, investors and visitors (Pagano and Bowman 1995). One of the attractions of special events is that they can be used by cities with few other quality visitor attractions, and can be a significant part of the tourism-generating strategy for 'second-tier cities'. Special events are also often used to regenerate decayed downtown areas or to strengthen the role of the city centre. Many city councils have a special events unit (e.g. the Chicago Mayor's Office of Special Events) to organise activities, often in partnership with private sector activities such as retailing. As Law (2002: 142) observes, 'while these events are primarily aimed at bringing people from the suburbs back downtown, they are also an added attraction to tourists, creating an impression of vitality'. The 'big ticket' special events are international, with the greatest of all being the Olympic Games.

The Olympic Games and urban regeneration

The strength of the link between the Olympic Games and urban regeneration has varied over the modern period. Up to the Melbourne Games of 1956 the regenerative impact of the Olympic Games was limited to some landmark buildings. Since 1960 in Rome, (the first Olympics to be televised), the event has been used as a catalyst for large-scale urban regeneration. In Tokyo 1964 major urban redevelopment and infrastructure improvement projects were carried through due to the Olympic stimulus. The Moscow Games of 1980 left a legacy of improved sports facilities, communications infrastructure, and an Olympic Village now occupied by 14,500 Muscovites (Gordon 1983). The link between the event and urban regeneration legacy was broken in the 1984 Los Angeles Games which, instead, provided a model of entrepreneurialism that produced the first profitable Olympics in modern times. As in Atlanta 1996, the Olympic Games were viewed as a vehicle for promoting consumption-oriented urban development. The connection between event and regeneration was re-established in the Seoul Games of 1988 that involved slum clearance, improved leisure and recreation facilities, a modernised urban road system, and middle-class housing developments. On the other hand, the Seoul Games attracted criticism for the rapidity of plans to prepare the city, with between 1983 and 1988 clearance of 100 sites and nearly 5,000 dwellings.

The Barcelona Olympic Games of 1992, discussed below, were arguably the most successful in terms of their regeneration legacy and provided an example for subsequent event-based regeneration strategies. The Sydney 2000 Olympic Games embraced the regeneration agenda and were designed on sustainable principles to provide environmental legacies as well as making an economic profit. Thus, much of the development was on brownfield land and involved renovation of inner-city housing stock and use of old industrial sites for high-density infill developments that included the main stadium and Olympic Village. Athens 2004 and Beijing 2008 both used the stimulus of the Olympic Games to fast-track urban regeneration projects. In Beijing the Chinese government undertook a massive regeneration strategy that displaced 1.5 million residents in order to produce the modern infrastructure expected of a host city, and to demonstrate the country's economic credentials. Not all cities can host the Olympic Games, of course. At the European scale a major prestigious event is the European Capital of Culture programme.

European Capitals of Culture

The European Capital of Culture (ECOC) programme was instituted in 1985 to include a cultural dimension in European policy alongside technology, economy and commerce. In 1999 the programme attained the status of a Community Action and since 2007 has been part of the EU's Culture Programme (2007–13) that aims to express 'unity within cultural diversity'. However, the ECOC event has been used by different cities in different ways that, since Glasgow

Table 25.2 Main objectives of European Capitals of Culture, 1992–2004

Objectives	European Capitals of Culture
Improve cultural infrastructures or services	Thessaloniki 1997; Bologna 2000; Rotterdam 2001; Genoa 2004
Develop social cohesion or participation in culture	Porto 2001; Graz 2003; Lille 2004
Place the city on the European map	Copenhagen 1996; Stockholm 1998; Prague 2000; Krakow 2000
Promote the city as a cultural tourist destination	Weimer 1999; Bologna 2000; Santiago 2000
Foster long-term cultural development	Copenhagen 1996; Stockholm 1998; Brussels 2000; Helsinki 2000
Demonstrate the city's importance as a cultural centre nationally (1) and internationally (2)	(1) Weimer 1999; Prague 2000; Reykjavik 2000; Bergen 2000; Krakow 2000 (2) Weimar 1999; Avignon 2000; Krakow 2000; Bergen 2000
Enhance the city's image in general (1) and specifically from an industrial city to a post-industrial cultural city (2)	(1) Helsinki 2000; Porto 2001; Salamanca 2002; Bruges 2002; Lille 2004 (2) Bologna 2000; Rotterdam 2001; Graz 2003; Genoa 2004*

Source: Adapted from Palmer-Rae Associates (2004).
Notes: * although outwith this survey period, we may note also the two UK cities of Glasgow 1990 and Liverpool 2008.

1990, have shifted from the original aims to focus more on urban regeneration. Table 25.2 indicates the main objectives of the European Capitals of Culture between 1995 and 2004.

Gauging the legacy of an event such as the ECOC is difficult, not least because the conceptualisation of legacy lacks a strong understanding. Nevertheless, given the high levels of investment, especially from the public sector, the issue of legacy and long-term impact is critical. In a survey of ECOC 1995–2004, Palmer-Rae Associates (2004: 146) found that

> respondents in most cities were able to point to impressive cultural projects, buildings or organisations that either continued to exist beyond the cultural year, or had a long term impact. About half established funds or organisations continued pursuing their aim. However, in many cities there was a sense that the full potential of the event had not been realised. A number of respondents regretted that the ECOC had not been part of a sustainable strategy for their city. ECOC have had important short term impacts, and a number of long term benefits; however the huge levels of investment and activity they generated rarely seem to have been matched by long term development in the city.

In practice two types of legacy are possible. 'Hard' legacies that offer tangible and measurable evidence of what has been achieved, include buildings and infrastructure (e.g. the renovation of former naval yards in Copenhagen), jobs and tourists, but also ongoing events (e.g. the international film festival in Bergen). 'Soft' legacies, that are often intangible and difficult to measure, include image enhancement, increased civic pride and the experience gained by those involved in the event. It is, of course, difficult to isolate the effect of a particular event from the effects of other ongoing regeneration initiatives. Another difficulty in gauging legacy is the time scale, with some projects only bringing results long after the event. In Thessaloniki, for example, the infrastructure projects were not completed during the cultural year, causing problems and adverse media reactions, but six years later they provided new public facilities and regeneration

Table 25.3 Some reasons for hosting special events

To offer a high-quality cultural or sporting experience
To involve the community in a civic celebration
To encourage participation in the arts and sports
To promote civic pride
To attract visitors and put the city on the tourist map
To attract people outside the main season
To attract media attention, create a favourable image and contest negative stereotypes
To attract inward investment
To enhance existing visitor attractions
To encourage repeat visits
To develop a niche market
To emulate the success of other places
To lever government grants for sports, arts and culture
To aid urban regeneration

Sources: Getz 1991; Hall 1992; Law 2002.

of the port area. On the other hand, some soft legacy events may continue in the short term but face major financial problems over the longer term as municipalities and funding bodies face growing demands on their budgets. In some cities, including Glasgow 1990, cuts to the cultural budget following the culture year inevitably lead to closure of facilities. Even such problems, however, can represent a legacy if they generate debate on the financing of cultural activities.

Fundamentally, in order to achieve a sustainable long-term legacy it is essential to plan in advance not just for the event but for the years to follow. This might include detailed financial plans in bid documents for ongoing support for events and venues, giving consideration to the management of new facilities beyond the culture year, and, a key factor in sustainable legacy, ensuring 'ownership' by the local population.

As the present discussion demonstrates, events, and especially mega events, can have a major physical and economic impact on a city, and consequently in recent years the strategy has been used as a catalyst for urban regeneration by a growing number of cities (de Lange 1998). Table 25.3 illustrates some common reasons for hosting special events.

The impact of event-led urban regeneration

Hosting large-scale peripatetic sporting events is seen as a major trigger for urban regeneration (Smith 2007). The gold medal sporting event is the global spectacle of the Olympic Games. Hosting the Olympics can bestow international recognition, give the populace of the host city and nation a psychological boost, and provide an opportunity for business investment and real estate development. Over the past twenty years competition to host the Olympic Games has been fierce, recent successful cities being Barcelona, Atlanta, Sydney, Athens, Beijing and London (Gold and Gold 2007). The Winter Olympics perform a similar role (Essex and Chalkley 2004).

Events normally take place in flagship venues. These structures, usually performing a leisure–cultural function, are also attractions in their own right (Figure 25.1). They can act as marketing tools for the city as well as central elements in an urban regeneration project, as in the case of the City of Manchester stadium built for the 2002 Commonwealth Games. These large projects aim to create multiplier effects through employment in the construction, retail, leisure and entertainment sectors, and may become magnets for further investment in housing,

Figure 25.1 The Bird's Nest Olympic Stadium in Beijing
Source: Author

retail and office developments (Bell and Jayne 2003). But such benefits are not guaranteed, as demonstrated by high-profile failures such as the 1976 Montreal Olympics (Whitson 2004) that resulted in a heavy debt burden for the city, and events such as the 1992 Seville Expo that was not integrated successfully with the rest of the city, producing only limited regeneration bene-fits. Sheffield's hosting of the 1991 World Student Games was subsidised by Sheffield City Council and facilitated regeneration of the Don Valley but left the city in financial crisis (Foley 1991). Other problematic issues in seeking to use mega events as a regeneration tool include the fact that even successful events have often had limited legacy benefits for the wider community, and increased visitor numbers experienced during the event are not guaranteed in the longer term. Furthermore, in the bidding period for an event uncertainty may produce planning blight and obstruct private investment, while a failed bid can prove to be costly. Table 25.4 illustrates the main impacts of a special event, not all of which are positive.

The most obvious legacy of event-led regeneration is the new facilities and venues often located on brownfield land. However, this is not always the case. Much of the infrastructure for the 1992 Olympic Games in Atlanta comprised temporary constructions (Rutheiser 1996). This highlights the problem facing host cities of having to balance goals of providing a lasting phy-sical legacy and ensuring that public money is not wasted on unnecessary new venues, as in the case of the 1998 Commonwealth Games in Malaysia (Silk 2002). If a long-lasting legacy is to be achieved events need to be seen not as one-off occasions but must be embedded within a wider regeneration strategy from the outset. This integrated approach was employed by Barcelona, where the Olympic Games event was used as a stimulus to bring to fruition urban development projects that had been in planning for over twenty-five years. The Olympic event (as with the build-up to London 2012), provided a finite deadline for completion of long-standing plans to develop urban transport infrastructure; housing, office and commercial developments;

Table 25.4 Types of impact of hallmark events

Impact	Positive	Negative
Economic	Increased revenues and employment	Price increases for locals, real estate speculation
Tourism/commercial	Enhanced image of the city as a locus for tourism and investment	Damaged image as a result of inadequate facilities or practices
Physical	Improvement of infrastructure and construction of new facilities	Overcrowding, environmental damage
Socio-cultural	Increase in local participation in types of activity associated with the event, strengthening of local values and traditions	Commercialisation of activities that may be of a private nature, modification of the event to suit tourism
Psychological	Increased local pride and community spirit, increased awareness of non-local views	Defensive attitudes in host city, possible hostility between hosts and visitors
Political	Enhanced international recognition of the political values of the local government	Exploitation of local population to satisfy the political ambitions of an elite

Source: Adapted from Ritchie (1984).

telecommunications; and hotel facilities. The fact that more was invested in these four forms of development than on new event venues ensured that the 1996 Olympic Games left a physical infrastructure legacy that provided a basis for Barcelona's subsequent economic regeneration.

In creating a sustainable legacy it is necessary to focus not only on the physical dimension but also on economic and social regeneration in the form of skills training for local people that can equip them for post-event employment. Although the 2000 Sydney Olympic Games involved more than 60,000 volunteers, many were sports enthusiasts who did not require job skills training. By contrast, in order to target benefits to the less skilled the Manchester Commonwealth Games included an initiative to ensure that most participants came from disadvantaged groups (Jones and Stokes 2003). In an evaluation of the Manchester 'Legacy Programme' Smith and Fox (2007: 1140) considered that it 'surpasses the plans and achievements of the vast majority of previous examples of event regeneration'. Even in Manchester, however, there was 'a conspicuous failure to involve local communities in the planning and implementation of projects' (Smith and Fox 2007: 1140). One explanation may relate to the relatively short time frame for event planning, leading to developments being fast-tracked past local communities, as was the case in the Sydney Olympics (Owen 2007). Another explanation, exemplified by the Atlanta Olympics, is the division of responsibility between private sector event management companies focused on logistics and marketing, and urban planning authorities with responsibility for regeneration and legacy aspects.

As Table 25.4 suggests, the impact of events is not always positive. Regeneration will almost inevitably lead to social and economic disruption to impacted communities. In extreme cases people may be forced from their homes to accommodate event facilities. In Brisbane significant numbers of residential relocations were required for the 1988 Expo event (Hall 1997). Also, while Barcelona's regeneration strategy is widely applauded it too involved removal of several hundred small businesses that had traditionally benefited from low rents, a concern that has been echoed by Raco (2004) in relation to the London Olympics. Some critics of event-led regeneration go further to portray mega events as part of the revanchist city in which sanitisation of the city is undertaken through removal of homeless people from prominent locations. In

Atlanta, construction of Centennial Park for the 1996 Olympic Games dislodged over 1,000 homeless (Whitelegg 2000). Clearly some relocation is unavoidable given the scale of mega events and the nature of much brownfield land, but protecting the interests of the powerless and disadvantaged must be part of a sustainable event legacy. The Co-Chair of the delivery organisation for the Atlanta Olympics may well have been correct to state that the Atlanta Games were a business, not a welfare programme, but in the interim growing emphasis on principles of sustainable urban development (Pacione 2007) has focused greater attention on the long-term social and economic legacy of events.

Calculating the costs and benefits of events is far from straightforward. Although some evidence is available on the economic benefits of sports events, many of the broader benefits to a local community remain under-researched. Gratton *et al.* (2005) in a review of a number of major sporting events concluded that a sport strategy based around events can provide an economic benefit to cities. However, they also point out that whether such benefits justify the expenditure involved is more difficult to answer. When money for sporting infrastructure investment is provided by the local taxpayer, as in the World Student Games in Sheffield, the question arises of whether other projects might have provided better returns to the local community. When the investment comes primarily from outside the local community, as in the Manchester Commonwealth Games,

> it is an unequivocal benefit to the local community in economic terms, but may not be the best use of the funds from a national perspective. At this point, we simply do not have adequate evidence to make judgements of this type.
>
> *(Gratton* et al. *2005: 998)*

Most of the evidence available relates to the economic impact during and immediately after the event. There is also need for research into the longer-term urban regeneration benefits of events. In this vein, Smith (2007) concludes that unless the event is embedded within a set of related strategies to encompass post-event outcomes for the local area it should only be regarded as a city promotion tool rather than as an instrument for genuine urban regeneration.

The 'Glasgow model'

We can illustrate the foregoing arguments with reference to the experience of the city of Glasgow that has been used as a model for culture-led event-based urban regeneration for other cities, including the successful bid by Liverpool to be European Capital of Culture in 2008. Glasgow was the first city to see the European Capital of Culture designation as a catalyst to accelerate urban regeneration. While this approach may have been out of synch with the philosophy of the previous European cultural capitals of Athens (1985), Florence (1986), Amsterdam (1987), West Berlin (1988) and Paris (1989), it was consistent with earlier city strategies to use culture and the arts to promote a post-industrial future. As Table 25.5 shows, the strategy of Glasgow's bid to become European Capital of Culture was clearly promotional and heralded the need for the city to direct attention to international markets. Culture was to be used as a strand of economic planning directly through the attraction of tourists to major events and indirectly through supporting an image that could bring inward investment. This culture-led event-based regeneration strategy had been in place for a decade prior to the European Capital of Culture initiative. Since 1980 Glasgow District Council had pursued a range of initiatives designed to regenerate the city's economic base. A key document was the McKinsey Report of 1983

Table 25.5 Principle objectives of Glasgow's bid to be ECOC 1990

To maintain the momentum already generated by the city marketing and image reconstruction
To provide a corporate marketing platform for the city's artistic activities
To utilise and build upon existing organisational experience and co-operative effort in the city
To stimulate increased awareness, participation and cultural developments in the city

Source: Adapted from Glasgow District Council (1987).

that recommended the city seek to maximise the potential of the city centre by following the entrepreneurial model developed in US cities such as Baltimore and Denver (McKinsey and Company 1983). Central to these efforts was an attempt to rehabilitate the negative image of the city which was seen to be a disincentive for both potential investors and tourists (Pacione 1982). Early attempts to portray a new Glasgow included stone cleaning and floodlighting of the city's Victorian heritage buildings, the annual Mayfest arts festival which began in 1982, and the opening of the Burrell Collection in 1983. A major catalyst for successful renewal of the city's image was the 'Glasgow's Miles Better' campaign which ran from 1983 to 1990. Prior to the GMB campaign the city attracted 700,000 visitors per year but by the time of the Glasgow Garden Festival in 1988 this had risen to 2.2 million, with four out of five visitors finding the city to be a 'very interesting and enjoyable place' (Myerscough 1988: 3). The Garden Festival was succeeded in 1990 by the city's designation as European City of Culture, which focused further international attention on the positive attributes of Glasgow.

The organisation of the Year of Culture did not meet with universal approval within the city, however. Heated debate occurred over the role and merits of indigenous working-class culture which some considered to have been ignored in favour of an imported high culture of opera and ballet (McLay 1988; Mooney 2004). According to this point of view Year of Culture events should reflect on questions of morality and be a vehicle for the expression of dissent in the tradition of Clydeside socialism. They wrote of the Glasgow experienced by disadvantaged citizens, seeking to provide them with a critical voice, and complained that the Year of Culture had more to do with 'power politics' than culture

It is impossible to deny that the Year of Culture was an economically driven image-building event, but in view of the limited success of the city's earlier stereotyped image (Pacione 1982; Damer 1990) in attracting inward investment and visitors this was perhaps inevitable. It is also incontrovertible that the benefits of the city's cultural renaissance and image re-packaging did not trickle down to the disadvantaged residents in the deprived estates. However, the fact that urban image re-building has not challenged the structural causes of the socio-spatial divisions that exist within Glasgow does not invalidate use of culture-led event-based strategies in order to enhance the city's external image, bring economic benefits and enhance civic pride (Paddison 1993; Garcia 2005). Any event-based strategy must be evaluated in terms of its stated objectives, which in the case of Glasgow 1990 were aimed primarily at economic growth and regeneration of a declining industrial city. In these terms the Glasgow 1990 event must be judged a success. The European Capital of Culture year should also be seen as one element in a consistent culture-led event-based strategy that has subsequently led to the city hosting a number of other major national and international showcase events including the City of Architecture and Design 1999, the Champions League Final 2002, UEFA Cup Final 2007 and the successful bid to host the 2014 Commonwealth Games.

Conclusion – some lessons for culture-led event-based regeneration

In response to the processes of de-industrialisation and tertiarisation, cities across the world have turned to culture-led event-based urban regeneration strategies as they attempt to manage the transition from an industrial past to a post-industrial future. As this discussion has revealed, a culture-led event-based strategy is by no means a panacea for the ills of urban society. Positive benefits of culture-led event-based regeneration can include environmental improvements through physical redevelopment of decayed land, improved urban infrastructure, provision of modern cultural facilities, promotion of heritage and culture, enhanced city image and civic pride, a broadened local skills base, increased inward investment and an expanded visitor economy. On the down side, culture-led event-based regeneration can lead to overcrowding and price increases for local populations, exploitation of the local population to satisfy the preferences and/or political ambitions of an elite, the inequitable distribution of the costs and benefits of the event, residential displacement and gentrification, and limited trickle-down of benefits to disadvantaged areas of the city. This critical analysis allows us to distil a number of 'lessons' for future successful use of culture-led event-based urban regeneration strategies:

- It is essential to plan ahead, not just for the event but for the legacy years to follow.
- The event must be part of a broader and longer-established policy for urban regeneration in the city.
- The event must be profitable and assist regeneration activity already in progress.
- The event must be city-based and facilitate developments in other sectors such as tourism.
- The city and citizens must benefit.
- It is necessary to develop a shared ownership, effective organisational and management structures, and common understanding of goals between event organisers, urban planners and local communities.
- It is important to avoid marginalisation of local culture through selective narratives that favour elite groups.
- Cities should seek to initiate their own events rooted in their own particular cultural traditions.
- Whilst any single event must produce its own benefits, there can be additional urban regeneration benefits from a cumulative use of events over a period of time.
- Cities should not attempt to bid for every event since it is expensive.
- Finally, a major challenge is to produce a coherent plan for an event strategy to provide a legacy that contributes to the city's economic, social, cultural and environmental regeneration, and to ensure that the costs and benefits of events are distributed equitably throughout the city.

Further reading

Balsas, C. (2004) 'City centre regeneration in the context of the 2001 ECOC', *Local Economy* 19(4): 396–410. (Case study of Porto as ECOC.)

Falkner, B., Chalip, L., Brown, G., Jago, L., March, R. and Woodside, A. (2001) 'Monitoring the tourism impacts of the Sydney 2000 Olympics', *Event Management* 6(4): 231–46. (Impact analysis of a mega event.)

Gratton, C. and Henry, I. (2001) *Sport in the City*, London: Routledge. (Examines the role of sport in urban economic and social regeneration.)

Jones, M. and Stokes, T. (2003) 'The Commonwealth Games and urban regeneration', *Managing Leisure* 8: 198–211. (Study of effect of training initiatives on disadvantaged groups.)

Lee, P. (2002) 'The economic and social justification for publicly financed stadia', *European Planning Studies* 10(7): 861–73. (Critique of the case for Vancouver's BC Place Stadium.)

Mangan, J. (2008) 'Prologue: guarantees of global goodwill', *International Journal of the History of Sport* 25(14): 1869–83. (Evaluates post-Olympic legacies.)

Matheson, C. (2010) 'Legacy planning, regeneration and events', *Local Economy* 25(1): 10–23. (Review of legacy planning for the 2014 Commonwealth Games.)

Munoz, E. (2006) 'Olympic urbanism and Olympic Games', *Sociological Review* 54: 175–87. (Review of planning strategies in host cities.)

Pacione, M. (2009) *Urban Geography: A Global Perspective*, London: Routledge, third edition. (Provides an overview of processes of contemporary urban change and urban regeneration.)

Smith, A. (2005) 'Conceptualising image change', *Tourism Geographies* 2(4): 398–423. (Explores the Olympic-led re-imaging of Barcelona.)

References

Aitcheson, C. and Pritchard, A. (2007) (eds) *Festivals and Events*, Eastbourne: Leisure Studies Association.

Bell, D. and Jayne, M. (2003) 'Design-led urban renaissance', *Local Economy* 18: 121–34.

Bianchini, F. (1991) 'Urban renaissance? The arts and urban regeneration', in S. MacGregor and B. Pimlot (eds) *Tackling the Inner Cities*, Oxford: Clarendon Press, pp. 215–50.

——(1993) 'Remaking European cities', in F. Bianchini and M. Parkinson (eds) *Cultural Policy and Urban Regeneration: The West European Experience*, Manchester: Manchester University Press, pp. 1–20.

Comedia Consultants (1989) *Developing a Cultural Industries Strategy for Coventry*, Coventry: Coventry City Council.

——(2003) *Releasing the Cultural Potential of our Core Cities*. Available at: www.corcities.com/coreDEV/comedia/com_cult.html

Damer, S. (1990) *Glasgow: Going for a Song*, London: Lawrence and Wishart.

DCMS (2004) *The Contribution of Culture to Regeneration in the UK: A Review of the Evidence*, London: Comedia.

De Lange, P. (1998) *The Games Cities Play*, Pretoria: Sigma Press.

Essex, S. and Chalkley, B. (2004) 'Mega sporting events in urban and regional policy', *Planning Perspectives* 19: 201–32.

Evans, G. (2001) *Cultural Planning: An Urban Renaissance*, London: Routledge.

——(2005) 'Measure for measure: evaluating the evidence for culture's contribution to regeneration', *Urban Studies* 42(5/6): 959–83.

Foley, P. (1991) 'The impact of the World Student Games in Sheffield', *Environment and Planning C* 9: 65–78.

Garcia, B. (2004) 'Cultural policy and urban regeneration in Western European cities', *Local Economy* 19 (4): 312–26.

——(2005) 'Deconstructing the City of Culture', *Urban Studies* 42(5/6): 841–68.

Getz, D. (1991) *Festivals, Special Events and Tourism*, New York: Van Nostrand.

——(1997) *Event Management and Event Tourism*, New York: Cognizant.

Gibson, L. and Stevenson, D. (2004) 'Urban space and the uses of culture', *International Journal of Cultural Policy* 10(1): 1–4.

Glasgow District Council (1987) *European City of Culture 1990: City of Glasgow District Council Submission for the UK Nomination*, Glasgow: Glasgow District Council.

Gold, J. and Gold, M. (2007) (eds) *Olympic Cities*, London: Routledge.

Gordon, B. (1983) *Olympic Architecture*, New York: John Wiley and Sons.

Gratton, C., Shibli, S. and Coleman, R. (2005) 'Sport and economic regeneration in cities', *Urban Studies* 42(5/6): 985–99.

Griffith, R., Bassett, K. and Smith, A. (1999) 'Cultural policy and the cultural economy in Bristol', *Local Economy* 14: 257–64.

Hall, C. (1992) *Hallmark Tourism Events*, London: Belhaven Press.

——(1997) 'Mega-events and their legacies', in P. Murphy (ed.) *Quality Management in Urban Tourism*, Chichester: John Wiley and Sons, pp. 75–87.

Hamilton, B. and Kahn, P. (1997) 'Baltimore's Camden Yards ballparks', in R. Noll and A. Zimbalist (eds) *Sports, Jobs and Taxes*, Washington, DC: Brookings Institution Press, pp. 245–81.

Holcomb, B. (1993) 'Revisioning place', in G. Kerns and C. Philo (eds) *Selling Places*, Oxford: Pergamon, pp. 133–43.

Jensen-Butler, C., Stackar, A. and van Weesep, J. (eds) (1997) *European Cities in Competition*, Aldershot: Avebury.

Jones, M. and Stokes, T. (2003) 'The Commonwealth Games and urban regeneration', *Managing Leisure* 8: 198–211.

Jones, P. and Wilks-Heeg, S. (2004) 'Capitalising culture: Liverpool 2008', *Local Economy* 19(4): 341–60.

Law, C. (2002) *Urban Tourism*, London: Continuum.

Levine, M. (1989) 'The politics of partnership', in G. Squires (ed.) *Unequal Partnerships*, New Brunswick: Rutgers University Press, pp. 12–34.

Lim, H. (1993) 'Cultural strategies for revitalising the city', *Regional Studies* 27: 589–95.

McCarthy, J. (1998) 'Dublin's Temple Bar', *European Planning Studies* 9: 437–58.

McCarthy, J. and Lloyd, G. (1999) 'Discovering culture-led regeneration in Dundee', *Local Economy* 14: 264–8.

McKinsey and Company (1983) *The Potential of Glasgow City Centre*, Glasgow: Scottish Development Agency.

McLay, F. (1988) (ed.) *Workers' City*, Glasgow: Clydeside Press.

Miles, M. (2005) 'Interruptions: testing the rhetoric of culturally-led urban development', *Urban Studies* 42(5/6): 889–911.

Miles, S. and Paddison, R. (2005) 'Introduction – the rise and rise of culture-led urban regeneration', *Urban Studies* 42(5/6): 833–40.

Mooney, G. (2004) 'Cultural policy as urban transformation?', *Local Economy* 19(4): 327–40.

Mort, F. (1996) *Cultures of Consumption*, London: Routledge.

Myerscough, J. (1988) *The Economic Importance of the Arts in Glasgow*, London: Policy Studies Institute.

ODPM (2003) *Sustainable Communities: Building for the Future*, London: HMSO.

Owen, K. (2007) 'The Sydney Olympics and urban entrepreneurialism', *Australian Geographical Studies* 40(3): 323–36.

Pacione, M. (1982) 'Space preferences, locational decisions and the dispersal of civil servants from London', *Environment and Planning A* 14(3): 332–3.

——(2007) 'Sustainable urban development in the United Kingdom: rhetoric or reality?', *Geography* 92(3): 246–63.

Paddison, R. (1993) 'City marketing, image reconstruction and urban regeneration', *Urban Studies* 30(2): 339–50.

Pagano, M. and Bowman, A. (1995) *Cityscapes and Capital*, Baltimore: Johns Hopkins University Press.

Palmer-Rae Associates (2004) *European Cities and Capitals of Culture*, Brussels: Palmer-Rae Associates.

Pattison, H (2006) 'Urban regeneration through the arts: a case study of the Edinburgh Festivals', in S. Fleming and F. Jordan (eds) *Events and Festivals*, Eastbourne: Leisure Studies Association, pp. 71–9.

Plaza, B. (2000) 'Evaluating the influence of a large cultural artefact in the attraction of tourism', *Urban Affairs Review* 36: 264–74.

Power, D. and Scott, A. (2004) *Cultural Industries and the Production of Culture*, London: Routledge.

Raco, M. (2004) 'Whose gold rush?', in A. Vigor, M. Mean, and C. Tims (eds) *After the Gold Rush: A Sustainable Olympics for London*, London: IPPR/Demos, pp. 31–50.

Ritchie, B. (1984) 'Assessing the impact of hallmark events', *Journal of Travel Research* 23: 2–11.

Roche, M. (1994) *Mega-Events Modernity*, London: Routledge.

Rutheiser, C. (1996) *Imagineering Atlanta*, New York: Verso.

Silk, M. (2002) 'Bangsa Malaysia' *Media, Culture and Society* 24: 775–94.

Smith, A. (2007) 'Large scale events and sustainable urban regeneration', *Journal of Urban Regeneration and Renewal* 1: 178–90.

Smith, A. and Fox, T. (2007) 'From event-led to event-themed regeneration', *Urban Studies*, 44(5/6): 1125–43.

Stimson, R. and Taylor, S. (1999) 'City profile – Brisbane', *Cities* 16: 285–96.

Whitelegg, J. (2000) 'Going for gold', *International Journal of Urban and Regional Research* 24: 801–17.

Whitson, D. (2004) 'Bringing the world to Canada', *Third World Quarterly* 25: 1215–32.

Whitt, J. (1987) 'Mozart in the metropolis: the Arts Coalition and the urban growth machine', *Urban Affairs Quarterly* 23: 15–36.

26

Faces, spaces and places

Social and cultural impacts of street festivals in cosmopolitan cities

Stephen J. Shaw

Introduction

Around the world, in the public spaces of cities that are gateways to immigration, festivals are created or re-created by people whose cultural practices seem 'exotic' to the majority population. Some street festivals attract large audiences. A few of them grow into major international events that raise the profile, not only of the neighbourhood where they take place, but also of the city as a culturally diverse and vibrant place to be. In areas known to outsiders as Chinatown, Little Italy, Punjabi Village and so on, processions and other rituals, performances of music and dance, together with more quotidian events such as street markets, delight urban 'tourists' who 'discover' inner-city and inner-suburban areas that they might otherwise avoid or even fear. Intentionally or not, the event appeals to the visitors' taste for agreeable Otherness. The spectacle may also attract publicity and media attention that influences wider public perceptions of ethnic minorities, as well as the spaces and places where the events are staged.

Street festivals may draw in visitors who are substantially more affluent than co-ethnic and other local residents. Decoration of the public realm that enhances the festive ambience, and continues well beyond a particular event, may stimulate lucrative custom for the owners of cafés, take-away food outlets, market stallholders and other traders. Banners, illuminations and street decorations such as the neon chilli peppers for Diwali, 'festival of light', in a West London suburb (Figure 26.1) are displayed conspicuously to enhance the carnivalesque atmosphere: 'festivalization' of the street to keep the party going. More permanent features such as ornamental arches proclaim entry to a place that is promoted as an 'ethnic cultural quarter'. Signage and façades for restaurants, bars and souvenir shops are designed to attract customers from the majority population and tourists from further afield; public art differentiates and designates particular spaces for leisure and tourism consumption.

The following section examines the somewhat polarized interpretations of the social and cultural dimensions of interaction between the spectacle and the spectators in ethnic minority neighbourhoods that are represented as 'cosmopolitan'. The author argues that there has been a marked tendency, especially in the literature of leisure and tourism studies, to over-generalize this relationship. The work of Arjun Appadurai (1997, 2001, 2003) on globalization and the production of 'translocalities' provides a more insightful conceptual framework that

Figure 26.1 Diwali illuminations are good for business in Southall, West London

addresses full square the apparent contradictions between cultural homogenization on the one hand and cultural heterogeneity on the other. The second section adapts and applies Appadurai's thesis to the development of 'eventscapes' and their ramifications for culture and society in cosmopolitan cities. Examples are drawn from North America, Australasia, Asia, and Europe.

Over the past twenty years or so, agencies of urban governance in the UK have intervened supportively with the expectation that this will stimulate wealth creation and employment for ethnic minorities, and on improvements to the street environment for locals and visitors alike. Less tangible benefits for 'togetherness', 'understanding' and 'creativity' may also be anticipated for the community whose identity is being celebrated and for the city as a whole. In the case of Brick Lane in London's East End, the 'Banglatown' place brand was used to promote two annual street festivals. The crowd-pulling success of the events programme encouraged the local authority to propose the permanent transformation of Brick Lane into a festival mall, but the unexpected ferocity of opposition to the scheme highlights some important issues for events-led regeneration and its impact on culture and society.

Cosmopolitanism: trading on difference or open-minded engagement?

Nicola MacLeod (2006: 232) has commented on the rising phenomenon of 'placeless' festivals and 'world parties'. Some neighbourhood festivals initiated by ethnic minorities have become major celebrations for the majority population in the events calendar of large cities. Notable examples include the New Year celebrations of Overseas Chinese communities throughout North America, the Pacific Rim and Europe. Some events 'outgrow' the streets where they originated, and their relocation may signify that their ownership has also widened. Evans and Foord (2006: 77–8) comment on the removal of Toronto's Caribana Festival from the inner city to an island on Lake Ontario in the early 1990s, and on similar proposals to move its UK counterpart to London's Hyde Park in 2005 (cf. Smith 2009: 223–7; Ferdinand and Williams, Chapter 15 in this volume). The popularity of such events may confirm the cosmopolitan character of the metropolis. But how is the term 'cosmopolitan' to be interpreted?

In their study of ethnically diverse neighbourhoods in Montreal, Germain and Radice (2006: 113) observe that few authors have related the concept of cosmopolitanism explicitly to urban places and spaces, but amongst them there are two distinct camps:

> Crudely, there are the *cynics* who see it as an elitist ideology that strategically co-opts 'cultural' difference in order to sell experiences to urban consumers; and the *idealists* who still believe in its Enlightenment-inspired progressive potential to unite citizens and/or political movements and institutions across national and other boundaries.

With respect to the first school of thought, there is a well-established social critique that markers of difference extracted from other cultures – such as street festivals and other events associated with immigrant communities – are increasingly de-contextualized, transformed and homogenized to create objects of consumption. Szerszynski and Urry (2002: 461–2) note the influential critique by Marx and Engels (1952 [1848]: 46–7) of the systematic appropriation of marketable features of other cultures: 'the bourgeoisie has through its exploitation of the world market given a *cosmopolitan* character to production and consumption ... The individual creations of individual nations become common property.' If it is accepted that power is distributed unequally, a contemporary observer may conclude that astute capitalists continue to select, adapt and commercialize elements of Otherness that are valued by the privileged elite, and that the socio-cultural impact is demonstrated in the appropriation, not only of street festivals, but also of the street itself.

This more cynical interpretation has been made with particular reference to 'Disneyfied Latin Quarters' in North American cities. Critics characterize the process as top-down homogenization. Global competition impels cities to create 'cosmopolitan' spaces in which to entertain the desirable target market of affluent, footloose cosmopolites. In *Variations on a Theme Park*, Sorkin (1992: 1) identifies the prototypes of the emerging 'placeless' world city that include the 'phoney historic festivity of a Rouse marketplace' (ibid.: 4) where non-scripted events are strictly prohibited. Judd (1999: 36) describes Greektown in Baltimore: 'a two-block-square renovated district' that envelops the traveller 'so that he/she only moves inside secured, protected and normalized environments'. He concedes the possibility that these *may* 'help foster community solidarity and spirit', such as St Patrick's Day parades. Nevertheless, he concludes that tourist bubbles are 'more likely to contribute to racial, ethnic, and class tensions than an impulse toward local community' (ibid.: 52–3; cf. Zukin 1995; Bell and Jayne 2004; Binnie *et al.* 2006; Jayne 2006). More recently, Hannigan (2007) has highlighted the sophisticated 'controlled edge' that satisfies the desire of young professionals for a visibly gritty street panorama without the danger: a safe adventure in neo-bohemia.

In sharp contrast, the second 'camp' (Germain and Radice 2006: 113) adopts an optimistic perspective from which cosmopolitan street festivals are seen to foster open-minded interaction. Hannerz (1996: 103) defines cosmopolitanism as a 'willingness to engage with the Other' that encourages individuals to 'develop abilities to make their way in other cultures, building upon active listening, observation and reflection'. The 'creative city' model proposed by Landry and Bianchini (1995: 28) welcomes opportunities for people with diverse cultures and lifestyles to interact productively, casually and without friction (Shaw 2007a: 189). This argument for *inter*culturalism, developed further by Wood and Landry (2008), resonates with Beck's (2002) egalitarian construct of a spontaneous clash of cultures that encourages 'creative reflexivity': an urbanity which allows creative intermediaries and merchants to move with relative ease, and negotiate between different 'worlds'. Likewise, Sandercock (2003, 2006) uses Salmon Rushdie's (1992) metaphor of the 'mongrel city', an evolving hybridity that will lead to the desirable normative outcome of a tolerant and inclusive cosmopolis.

Bloomfield and Bianchini (2004: 88–9) comment that some festivals, carnivals and community events can be seen *both* as cultural expressions of specific ethnic minorities *and* as civic celebrations belonging to the whole city. Berlin's annual Karnivale der Kulturen (carnival of cultures) has participants from many minority cultural organizations, and by the early 2000s it was attracting over half a million Berliners, but its performances of music and dance are presented on different stages according to national or ethnic 'origins', e.g. African, Latin American, Asian, Turkish, Indian. So, 'while it succeeds in creating a multicultural public space, it does not recognize the full inter-culturality of the event, by denying the cultural mixes that are a unique product of Berlin' (ibid.: 90). According to Bloomfield and Bianchini (ibid.: 89), Rotterdam's Caribbean Carnival is closer to their normative model as it is presented more explicitly as an inter-cultural event that has evolved and interacted with contemporary Dutch culture. Some argue that an international outlook combined with day-to-day interaction stimulates artistic innovation. Such 'globalization from below' produces grassroots fusions such as 'British Bhangra' music (Henry *et al.* 2002).

The polarized interpretations of 'trading on difference' versus 'open-minded engagement' only underline the ambiguities of cosmopolitanism. The dichotomy sheds little light on the complex processes through which particular spaces are festivalized, or the subtleties of their social and cultural impacts. The two prognoses are clearly very different, but both envisage universal and unilinear trajectories, the former towards commodification of the 'same difference', the latter towards creativity and plurality of outcomes. As Appadurai (1997: 32) emphasizes, the 'central problem of today's global interactions is the tension between cultural homogenization and cultural heterogenization'. Theorists are only beginning to grasp an 'overlapping *disjunctive* order'. As an alternative to the grand narrative, he proposes an 'elementary framework' (ibid.: 33) to conceptualize and explore such disjunctures using the suffix '-*scape*' to convey the idea that they are gazed upon from diverse perspectives. These landscapes are the building blocks of *imagined* worlds, the multiple worlds that are constituted by many actors and audiences. As Taylor (2000: 28) observes, Appadurai refuses the temptation to interpret the 'dynamic interaction of global culture, local conditions and migrant peoples in terms of some one-dimensional or reductionist model'. Rather, his thesis reveals a complex set of '-scapes' that enables cultures to slip and slide over spatial borders and between the boundaries of economics, politics and societies (Adey 2010: 188).[1]

The term *ethnoscape* describes the 'landscape of persons who constitute the shifting world in which we live: tourists, immigrants, refugees, exiles, guest workers, and other moving groups and individuals' (Appadurai 1997: 33). For these people on the move, the warp of relative stabilities – communities and networks, including kinship, friendship, work and leisure – are 'everywhere shot through with the woof of human motion, as more persons and groups deal with the realities of having to move, or the fantasies of wanting to move' (ibid.: 33–4; cf. Shaw *et al.* 2004; Shaw and Karmowska 2006). Later, Appadurai (2003: 339) expanded the argument to situate ethnoscapes in local and global space, and suggested the need to investigate more closely how such 'translocalities' are formed. Examples that 'require serious attention' include: tourist sites and free trade areas, border zones, refugee camps, migrant hostels and neighbourhoods of guest workers:

> what little we do know suggests many such locations create complex conditions for the production and reproduction of locality, in which ties of marriage, work, business and leisure weave together various circulating populations with various kinds of 'locals' to create localities that belong in one sense to particular nation-states but are, from another point of view, what we might call *translocalities*.

Street festivals are notable meeting grounds where the cultural spectacle and spectators interact. In common with other translocalities, such landscapes are truly fluid and irregular; each is shaped by its context: a set of circumstances and influences in a particular place, at a particular time. The following section adapts and develops Appadurai's framework. The term 'translocal eventscapes' is used in this chapter to examine the creation of a particular form of ethnoscape: cultural spectacles of immigrant communities, (re-)created in spaces and places to which the majority population and other publics have access.

Social and cultural impacts of translocal eventscapes

As yet, little attention has been given in the literature to the development of translocal eventscapes, or to their social and cultural impact. Historical evidence suggests that middle-class bohemians among the White Anglo Saxon Protestant (WASP) majority of North American cities in the second half of the nineteenth century were attracted to the more exotic, and in some cases erotic, pleasures of low-income non-WASP districts, especially late-night drinking, dining, gambling, music and dancing. However, such practices were decidedly counter-cultural, at least until the mid-twentieth century. Disapproval of others may well have added to the *frisson* of going 'slumming' or 'rubbernecking' (Cocks 2001; Gilbert and Hancock 2006). As Lin (1998) observes, Chinatowns, Jewish and African-American ghettos, and Mexican barrios were more commonly regarded as lowlife districts in an unstable inner-city zone of transition. Such places were thought to harbour disease and criminal gangs; their very names reflect their marginal status to the majority population, e.g. Sonora, 'Dogtown', and Calle de los Negros, 'Nigger Alley', in Los Angeles.

Anderson (1995) considers the shift as the economy picked up in the mid-1930s, towards greater official acceptance of the idea that White visitors of mainly British descent should seek entertainment in Vancouver's Chinatown. Her jeweller's eye analysis of racial discourse expressed in city council records, press coverage and other documents, highlights the impact of the city's Golden Jubilee celebrations that marked a turn from the dominant narrative that hitherto had characterized it as an unwholesome place of gambling and opium dens. As their contribution to this landmark event, merchants funded an elaborate Chinese village that was opened by the mayor on 17 July 1936, and described in the official guidebook (Yip 1936: 6) as 'most artistically and becomingly decorated' with lanterns and 'hundreds of Oriental splendours'. The *Province* newspaper reported on the 'gay parade' that symbolized 'customs and traditions that were old when the oldest firs on the coast were seedlings'; thousands watched the procession, including 'a weird Chinese ceremony [in which] the spirit of the ancient warrior was invoked to aid the carnival' (cited in Anderson 1995: 156). The *Sun* asked why Vancouver's Chinatown could not be made a permanent tourist attraction, following the examples of New York and San Francisco: 'Even without the pagodas and palaces and bazaar of the Chinese village, Chinatown has a rare fascination ... Perhaps the present exhibit will remind us that our Chinatown is worth exploiting as a tourist attraction year in and year out' (13 July 1936, quoted in Anderson 1995: 158).

By the 1950s, the eventscapes of Vancouver's Chinatown were indeed becoming mainstream attractions. Nevertheless, the reimaging of Chinese and other ethnic minority neighbourhoods was far from complete and, like its counterparts fringing downtowns across North America, its existence was threatened by wholesale demolition to make way for motorways and other modernization; cf. Guan (2002) on Philadelphia. In the United States, as the Civil Rights and urban social movements gathered more broad-based support, the bulldozers were resisted, albeit with varying success in the 1960s and 1970s. And, by the 1976 Bicentennial, 'ethnic heritage recovery' included renovation of historic cityscapes and enactment of festivals that highlighted the valuable contribution of immigrant communities to the American metropolis, e.g. Little Tokyo in Los Angeles (Pearlstone 1990; Shaw 2007b). Thus, by the 1980s and 1990s, a greater emphasis on multicultural policies and practices by agencies of urban governance in many North American cities encouraged revalorization and restoration of enclaves within particular neighbourhoods where non-WASP communities had settled in former times.

By the 1990s, many members of the 'original' immigrant communities had long dispersed, especially where the main wave of immigration had been in the first half of the twentieth century or earlier. Furthermore, other communities had arrived and settled, in some cases in the very same districts. Many street festivals staged in such historic 'ethnic' neighbourhoods, self-consciously evoke ancient traditions from far-away places. Nevertheless, like the Chinese village parade, they have been re-created in comparatively recent times. The intended outcomes of such events may include one or more of the following:

(a) to capitalize on wealth creation and employment for ethnic minorities where an exotic spectacle attracts high-spending visitors, and stimulates investment in neglected street environments;

(b) to connect and reunite members of a diasporic population, who participate in symbolic eventscapes that feature on the community's calendar;

(c) to bring together people with different ethnic and cultural identities, a catalyst to improve mutual understanding and to stimulate creative interculturalism.

The subjectivity and plurality of Appadurai's 'overlapping disjunctive order' allows the possibility that elements of (a), (b) and (c) may coexist as the intended outcomes of festivalization. Organizers or 'producers' of eventscapes may have mixed motives or multiple objectives; 'consumers' may gaze upon the spectacle from different cultural viewpoints. In some cases these may be compatible. However, in other contexts significant tensions may arise. The balance between different aspirations may vary between different neighbourhoods within the same city; the rationale for a particular event may change over time.

Realization of outcome (a) is illustrated in many of the street festivals held in Toronto's inner-city and inner-suburban 'neighbourhoods': areas associated with immigration and settlement by particular minority groups. Sponsors include the boards of Business Improvement Districts (BIDs), not-for-profit agencies that are empowered to promote their localities with special purpose funds raised from additional local taxes that are levied on commercial property (Shaw 2007b). Where restaurateurs and bar owners are strongly represented on their boards, it is understandable that ethnic and cultural identities are linked with food and drink, e.g. Taste of the Danforth celebrates Greek cuisine. Toronto's Greektown is further embellished by Greek as well as English street signs, and a small square that is beautified with a statue of Alexander the Great (cf. Hackworth, and Rekers 2005). Likewise, the Corso Italia BID has an Italian food and wine festival, Italianate streetlights, banners and floral displays. In both cases, the 'original' residential population is declining. Nevertheless, the streets have continuing significance to Canadians of Greek and Italian origin, and their bars are popular venues to watch sporting events on TV when their national teams are playing, a theme that concurs with outcome (b). See Figure 26.2.

The rejuvenation of Montreal's *quartier chinois* in the early 2000s was guided by a formal plan for Chinatown, formulated by a panel on which residents, faith and community organizations, as well as traders, were represented (Shaw 2007a). A comprehensive set of proposals was negotiated with Ville de Montréal, and most of the panel's recommendations were incorporated in the Downtown Master Plan, the official plan that has guided land use and development. A key achievement was the creation of Sun-Yat-Sen Park on a vacant lot in the early 2000s. On summer weekends this provides an important meeting area for Chinese Canadians from across the Province of Quebec and further afield, who celebrate religious and cultural ceremonies, and gather for family occasions such as weddings. These people are the primary users of the public space, but spectacle attracts non-Chinese spectators who observe the rituals, and dine

Figure 26.2 Chinese Canadians are the primary users of the Sun-Yat-Sen Park in Montreal's historic Chinatown

in nearby cafés and restaurants (Figure 26.2). Thus, elements of (a), (b) and (c) are combined with relative ease and little friction.

Strategic reimaging of ethnic cultural quarters as eventscapes is evident in many gateway cities outside North America. Like Toronto, a large proportion of Sydney's population was of British descent until the closing decades of the twentieth century. Collins and Kunz (2007: 206) note that since the 1960s, Sydney's suburban precincts have diversified with a Little Vietnam, Little Turkey and so on, and 'ethnic enterprises, clustered together … formally or informally adopt the symbolism, style and iconography of that group in their public spaces' (ibid.: 207). Their survey of traders confirmed that 'ethnic' place-descriptors were important to their marketing strategies. Vietnamese restaurants opposed the idea of a more neutral 'Asian' branding, and Turkish traders wanted a more visible 'Turkish feel' for their precinct. In contrast to this commercially driven transformation, the Singapore government has intervened to support the refurbishment and revitalization of historic districts that were established under British colonial rule for non-British communities. Henderson (2008) explains that the rationale for this state assistance explicitly combined the anticipated benefits of tourism (a) with policies to promote multicultural even-handedness, a high-profile project to renovate Chinatown, Little India and Kampong Glam, and represent their respective street festivals (b) and (c).

Elsewhere in the Pacific Rim, a street in Osaka has been reimaged as 'Korea Town' to enhance its appeal to Japanese shoppers. Hester (2002: 182–3) notes that initially this project was highly controversial and that its promoters encountered opposition. Nevertheless, it was implemented with support from state funding that was justified in three ways: first, to rejuvenate a thoroughfare that was showing signs of retail decline, second to create a cosmopolitan retail offering, and third to demonstrate a new civic ideology of 'international co-operation' and 'living together with cultural difference': a rationale that, like Singapore's official multiculturalism, fits closely with the more altruistic outcome (c). Hester observed (ibid.: 186) that the street has been turned into a kind of proscenium arch for festivals and other events:

> These most often involve the alternating display of 'traditional national arts' … of Korea and Japan, such as Korean *p'ungmul* percussion/dance performances and Japanese *wadaiko* drumming, which work to summarize the 'cultural' differences between Koreans and Japanese, while at the same time dramatizing mutual respect for such difference in the spirit of 'living together'.

Current patterns of migration within Europe are strongly influenced by liberalization of cross-border movement of people between Member States of the European Union. The cultures that are represented through translocal eventscapes have been shaped in the post-war, postcolonial nevertheless, by national immigration policies and the unique circumstances of particular gateway cities. Berlin's Karnivale der Kulturen, introduced above, is a notable example. The large number of people originating from Turkey and the former Yugoslavia who settled in the Kreuzberg district of the German capital were originally invited as 'guest workers' to fill labour shortages when the city was physically divided in the Cold War of the 1960s. National policies to address labour shortages through immigration from former colonies likewise encouraged large-scale immigration to former hubs of empire in Spain, Portugal, the Netherlands and Belgium, France and the United Kingdom. The following case study of the deeply contested festivalization and branding of events in one street in London's East End as 'Bangla-town' illustrates the multiple benefits that may be anticipated, as well as the unanticipated tensions that may arise.

The festivalization of 'Banglatown' in London's East End

Brick Lane, busy thoroughfare of Spitalfields in London's East End, has been an important commercial and social hub for successive waves of immigrants, including Huguenot refugees from France in the late 1600s, and Jews from Russia and Poland in the late 1800s. Since the 1970s, it has accommodated many new immigrants from Bangladesh, one of the UK's poorest communities. Initially, many found work in the textile trade, but its steep decline exacerbated unemployment. Unfortunately, Brick Lane became the scene of violent intimidation by race-hate groups. Somewhat against the odds, in the early 1990s its cafés acquired a certain 'shabby chic' and some began to welcome an increasing trade from 'bohemian' customers from the majority population, especially artists and designers, and a few adventurous tourists. To cater for this demand, Asian entrepreneurs converted run-down buildings into restaurants, bars and nightclubs. From the mid-1990s the London Borough of Tower Hamlets (LBTH) gave its active support to this rising visitor economy, and government funding through the 'Cityside Partnership' 1997–2002 gave it a further boost (Shaw 2008, 2010). This secured £1 million for 'Raising the Profile' (LB Tower Hamlets 1996), and through Cityside's Town Management Group two major initiatives were launched in 1998:

1 two new street festivals, one an explicitly multicultural Brick Lane Festival (autumn), the other to celebrate Bengali New Year, Baishakhi Mela (spring);
2 promotion of these and other events and local cuisine using the place-brand 'Banglatown', e.g. through advertising on public transport.

Eade (2006) observes that the aims of both events reflect the Left-libertarian ideology of an influential group of LBTH councillors. Brick Lane Festival promoted Bangladeshi cuisine that was offered by the streets expanding restaurant trade to a multicultural audience, but the festivities also featured 'Asian drumming bands, Caribbean DJs, the London School of Samba and lots of mad Brazilians' (ibid.: 68, extract from flyer). The positive impacts (a) and (c) were explicit features of its rationale. By 2001, the Mela was attracting around 60,000 visitors from diverse cultures (Cityside 2002: 8). The ethos of the Bengali New Year celebrations also fits with (b): the 'joyful mingling of a nation, united beyond the boundaries of social difference, also stretched implicitly across national borders to embrace a transnational Bangladeshi community across the globe'. Despite the benign intent and the care taken by its organizers not to disturb prayers at the Great Mosque on Brick Lane, the staging of Baishakhi Mela offended some individuals who championed the moral regeneration of Bangladeshi youth. Eade's interview with the Imam of the East London Mosque (ibid.: 61) revealed the cleric's objections to a secular festival that led young Muslims astray with its eclectic hedonism.

Promotion of Banglatown was also controversial. Identification of the place with one ethnic minority may deny the existence of others, past or present. Initially, the *Evening Standard* newspaper ran a critical campaign against the 'renaming' of Brick Lane, an inappropriate branding which downplayed the significance of Spitalfields and its long history of immigration and settlement. Andrew Bramidge, Director of Cityside, mused that five years later the place-brand seemed unproblematic, but at the time such criticism was unhelpful (interview with author, 7 October 2002):

> The *Evening Standard* ran what I thought was quite a scurrilous campaign against Banglatown. They had all sorts of ridiculous stories about taxi drivers getting lost … It

was just ludicrous, they were just using that to mock the whole concept. It's interesting now that papers like the *Evening Standard* and *Time Out* use the term just as a matter of fact now. There doesn't seem to be any connotations to it any more.

Relaxation of land use zoning to allow conversion of retail units to restaurants in the middle section of Brick Lane brought objections from people who, with some justification, feared the loss of local convenience shops that this would bring. There was also opposition from Spitalfields residents who anticipated a rise in antisocial behaviour by late-night customers. Undeterred, in 2000 LBTH and Cityside proposed a scheme to redesign Brick Lane and transform it into a fully pedestrianized festival mall. The plan was supported by a group of restaurateurs who envisaged new opportunities for *al fresco* dining. Understandably, other firms opposed the exclusion of goods vehicles for collection/delivery of stock and parking. Many residents objected to any further expansion of the party zone or late-night extension of licences. After a heated public meeting at which these varied criticisms were voiced, the scheme was hastily withdrawn. Following two years of consultation with a wide range of local stakeholders, the revised scheme was designed to create a much more inclusive street environment for locals as well as visitors. The revised street design was implemented in stages 2002–6; the southern section is shown in Figure 26.3).

Urban designer Richard Simon oversaw this wider public engagement and the more sensitive festivalization that it informed. Solutions that included traffic calming, pavement widening and public art brought benefits for its diverse local users as well as visitors. In an interview with author (9 June 2008), Richard Simon reflected on the consultations and

Figure 26.3 Public engagement informed more socially and culturally sensitive festivalization of London's Banglatown

participants' fears of the adverse social and cultural impact that the previous scheme might have produced:

> There were definite concerns that … it would become a sort of Bengali ghetto. Furthermore, the Bengali community is tending to migrate away from Brick Lane to other places … So people weren't necessarily saying this is the heart of the Bengali community in London … We felt that you could create a Banglatown identity without the obvious use of permanent features such as brightly coloured paving and highways. You could do it through more subtle means like gateway markers and public art, which can, if the area changes over a period of time, be changed. And we felt that this was a more long-term sustainable view.

Closer examination of how and why this street was transformed from the mid-1990s reveals problematic negotiation between the agencies of urban governance and a wide range of local stakeholders. Ironically, despite well-meaning intentions to create a spirit of 'togetherness', the proposals proved highly contentious. By the mid-2000s, however, the Brick Lane Festival could be presented as a showcase for multiculturalism (Shaw 2008: 199). In 2004, it was warmly endorsed by the prime minister[2] as 'a truly inclusive Britain that takes pride in its diversity'.

Conclusion

The discussion above highlights the global influence of the North American 'Chinatown model': associations of merchants initiate and continue to influence the construction of a spectacular setting for street festivals that attract members of the majority population and tourists, as well as co-ethnic customers. It can be argued that permanent festivalization has helped overcome the prejudices and anxieties of others. Areas of the city that were portrayed in the dominant discourses of news media and urban authorities as squalid, unhealthy and unwholesome have been reimaged as spaces of leisure and tourism consumption. Although the signs and symbols are very different, commercial thoroughfares of other immigrant communities such as southern Europeans in Canada, Koreans in Japan, and Bangladeshis in the UK are similarly communicated through elements of a theatrical convention. Passing through an ornamental arch, visitors suspend their disbelief. In doing so, they enter a liminal and libidinal half-world, very different from 'their' city, where visual cues reinforced by unfamiliar sounds and smells provided the backdrop to festivals and other events.

A sceptical reading is that appealing features of the other cultures continue to be taken out of context and commodified to the commercial advantage of traders. In time, the stage set becomes more permanent: elaborate street furniture, signage, sculptures and other public art, a nightscape of neon signs. As with the landscape of beach resorts in exotic locations, scripted performances are presented as entertaining diversions that 'animate' the scene. Local people doing regular activities, such as shopping in local markets or attending places of worship, are cast as 'extras' to be photographed or captured on video. Successful formula are copied and adapted across the world, a 'racialized construct tuned to multicultural consumerism' (Jacobs 1996: 100). Ironically, places of difference become bland and homogenized extensions of 'cosmopolitan' non-places experienced by international travellers (cf. Richards and Wilson 2006; Auge 2008). Such formulaic reproduction denies the spontaneity, creativity and evolving hybridity advocated by Sandercock (2003, 2006) and by Wood and Landry (2008). Nevertheless, the opposition of 'trading on difference' versus 'open-minded engagement' is too simplistic and limiting.

The phenomenon of festivalization cannot be explained by grand narratives of convergence. Indeed, the examples discussed above suggest a marked *divergence* of outcomes. Many foreground the role of ethnic minority entrepreneurs as key drivers of change, but they also underline the importance of local context: negotiation with other interest groups; the spaces and places where events take place; and the stick and carrot of urban governance that shapes the transformation. The construct of 'translocal eventscapes' derived from Appadurai's thesis (1997, 2001, 2003) admits the possibility that production and consumption of the spectacle has a range of consequences, some of which are hard to predict. In some cases, a range of desirable outcomes are compatible: wealth creation, employment and environmental benefits for ethnic minorities; re-uniting a scattered community; bringing together different communities. However, in other contexts they may conflict with one another, and significant tensions may arise. Further, the balance may change over time as a result of local challenge and accommodation of different needs, a scenario that was amply demonstrated in the evolving translocal eventscape of Brick Lane.

At the turn of the twenty-first century, the commercially driven festivalization of Banglatown in London's East End seemed well positioned to emulate its more established Chinese counterpart in the West End. Some important lessons can be drawn from the unintended consequences of this transformation. To summarize:

(a) Where festivalization is driven by an emerging visitor economy, insensitivity to the lifeworlds and cultural values of local residents and organizations may disrupt everyday routines, marginalize and in some cases offend members of the 'host community'.
(b) Particular sensitivities may arise if the eventscape is branded with a single ethnic identity, and the existence of other communities (past or present) is ignored; in time, the brand may lose credibility as the local population changes.
(c) Without the valuable input of local users, the reconstruction of public spaces to accommodate visitors of the majority population and tourists in a disadvantaged ethnic minority neighbourhood may alienate and displace the very people and organizations that are supposed to benefit most from events-led regeneration.

Notes

1 *Technoscapes* (Appadurai 1997: 34) are landscapes and fluid configurations of technology; *financescapes* (ibid.: 34–5), the volatile flows of money around the world; *mediascapes* (ibid.: 35–6), the landscapes of information and far-reaching global distribution of data; and the term *ideoscape* (ibid.: 36–7) refers to the ideologies of states and the counter-ideologies of global movements, including those derived from the Enlightenment worldview embraced in the more altruistic construct of cosmopolitanism above.
2 Quotation from the introduction to Brick Lane Festival (2004) *Official Guide*, n.p.

References

Adey, P. (2010) *Mobility*, London and New York: Routledge.
Anderson, K. (1995) *Vancouver's Chinatown: Racial Discourse in Canada, 1875–1980*, Montreal and Kingston: McGill-Queen's University Press.
Appadurai, A. (1997) *Modernity at Large: Cultural Dimensions of Globalisation*, Minneapolis: University of Minnesota Press.
——(ed.) (2001) *Globalization*, Durham and London: Duke University Press.
——(2003) 'Sovereignty without territoriality: notes for a postnational geography', in S.M. Low and D. Lawrence-Zuniga (eds) *The Anthropology of Space and Place: Locating Culture*, Oxford: Blackwell, pp. 337–50.
Auge, M. (2008) *Non Places: An introduction to Supermodernity*, London: Verso.
Beck, U. (2002) 'The cosmopolitan society and its enemies', *Theory, Culture and Society* 19(1–2): 17–44.
Bell, D. and Jayne, M. (2004) *City of Quarters: Urban Villages in the Contemporary City*, Aldershot: Ashgate.

Binnie, J., Holloway, J., Millington, S. and Young, C. (eds) (2006) *Cosmopolitan Urbanism*, London and New York: Routledge.

Bloomfield, J. and Bianchini, F. (2004) *Planning for the Intercultural City*, Stroud: Comedia.

Cityside (2002) *SRB3 Final Report*, London: Cityside Regeneration.

Cocks, S. (2001) *Doing the Town: The Rise of Urban Tourism in the United States*, Berkeley: University of California Press.

Collins, J. and Kunz, P. (2007) 'Ethnic entrepreneurs, ethnic precincts and tourism: the case of Sydney, Australia', in G. Richards and J. Wilson (eds) *Tourism, Creativity and Development*, London and New York: Routledge, pp. 201–14.

Eade, J. (2006) 'Class and ethnicity in a globalising city: Bangladeshis and contested urban space in London's "East End"', in G. Arvaston and T. Butler (eds) *Multicultures and Cities*, Copenhagen: Museum Tusculanum Press, University of Copenhagen, pp. 57–69.

Evans, G. and Foord, J. (2006) 'Rich mix cities: from multicultural experience to cosmopolitan engagement', in G. Arvaston and T. Butler (eds) *Multicultures and Cities*, Copenhagen: Museum Tusculanum Press, University of Copenhagen, pp. 71–84.

Germain, A. and Radice, M. (2006) 'Cosmopolitanism by default: public sociability in Montreal', in J. Binnie, J. Holloway, S. Millington and C. Young (eds) *Cosmopolitan Urbanism,* London and New York: Routledge, pp. 112–29.

Gilbert, D. and Hancock, C. (2006) 'New York City and the transatlantic imagination, French and English tourism and the spectacle of the modern metropolis, 1893–1939', *Journal of Urban History* 33: 77–107.

Guan, J. (2002) 'Ethnic consciousness arises on facing spatial threats to Philadelphia's Chinatown', in A. Erdentug and F. Colombijn (eds) *Urban Ethnic Encounters: The Spatial Consequences*, London and New York: Routledge, pp. 126–41.

Hackworth, J. and Rekers, J. (2005) 'Ethnic packaging and gentrification: the case of four neighbourhoods in Toronto', *Urban Affairs Review* 41(2): 211–66.

Hannerz, U. (1996) *Transnational Connections: Culture, People, Places*, London: Routledge.

Hannigan, J. (2007) 'From fantasy city to creative city', in G. Richards and J. Wilson (eds) *Tourism, Creativity and Development*, London and New York: Routledge, pp. 48–56.

Henderson, J. (2008) 'Managing urban ethnic heritage: Little India in Singapore', *International Journal of Heritage Studies* 14(4, July): 332–46.

Henry, N., McEwan, C. and Pollard, J.S. (2002) 'Globalisation from below: Birmingham – postcolonial workshop of the world?', *Area* 34(2): 117–27.

Hester, J. (2002) 'Repackaging difference: the Korean "theming" of a shopping street in Osaka, Japan', in A. Erdentug and F. Colombijn (eds) *Urban Ethnic Encounters: The Spatial Consequences*, London and New York: Routledge, pp. 177–91.

Jacobs, J.M. (1996) *Edge of Empire: Postcolonialism and the City*, London and New York: Routledge.

Jayne, M. (2006) *Cities and Consumption*, London and New York: Routledge.

Judd, D. (1999) 'Constructing the tourist bubble', in D. Judd and S. Fainstein (eds) *The Tourist City*, New Haven and London: Yale University Press, pp. 35–53.

Landry, C. and Bianchini, F. (1995) *The Creative City*, London: Demos, in association with Comedia.

LB Tower Hamlets (1996) 'Eastside Challenge Fund Submission' (NB the name was changed to 'Cityside').

Lin, J. (1998) 'Globalization and the revalorizing of ethnic places in immigration gateway cities', *Urban Affairs Review* 34(2): 313–39.

Low, S.M. and Lawrence-Zuniga, D. (2003) *The Anthropology of Space and Place: Locating Culture*, Oxford: Blackwell.

MacLeod, N.E. (2006) 'The placeless festival: identity and place in the post-modern festival', in D. Picrad and M. Robinson (eds) *Festivals, Tourism and Social Change: Remaking Worlds*, Clevedon: Channel View, pp. 222–37.

Marx, K. and Engels, F. (1952) [1848] *The Manifesto of the Communist Party*, Moscow: Foreign Languages.

Pearlstone, Z. (1990) *Ethnic Los Angeles*, Los Angeles, CA: Hillcrest.

Richards, G. and Wilson, J. (2006) 'Developing creativity in tourist experiences: a solution to the serial reproduction of culture?', *Tourism Management* 27: 1209–23.

Rushdie, S. (1992) *Imaginary Homelands*, London: Granta Books.

Sandercock, L. (2003) *Cosmopolis II: Mongrel Cities in the 21st Century*, London and New York: Continuum.

——(2006) 'Cosmopolitan urbanism: a love song to our mongrel cities', in J. Binnie, J. Holloway, S. Millington and C. Young (eds) *Cosmopolitan Urbanism*, London and New York: Routledge, pp. 37–52.

Shaw, S. (2007a) 'Cosmopolitanism and ethnic cultural quarters', in G. Richards and J. Wilson (eds) *Tourism, Creativity and Development*, London and New York: Routledge.

——(2007b) 'Inner city ethnoscapes as cultural attractions: micro-place marketing in Canada', in M. Smith (ed.) *Tourism, Culture and Regeneration*, Wallingford: CABI.

——(2008) 'Hosting a sustainable visitor economy: messages from London's Banglatown', *Journal of Urban Regeneration and Renewal* 1(3, December/January): 275–85.

——(2010) 'Marketing ethnoscapes as spaces of consumption: "Banglatown – London's Curry Capital"', *Journal of Town and City Management* (in press).

Shaw, S. and Karmowska, J. (2006) 'The multicultural heritage of European cities and its re-presentation through regeneration programmes', in G. Arvaston and T. Butler (eds) *Multicultures and Cities*, Copenhagen: Museum Tusculanum Press, University of Copenhagen, pp. 41–56.

Shaw, S., Bagwell, S. and Karmowska, J. (2004) 'Ethnoscapes as spectacle: re-imaging multicultural districts as new destinations for leisure and tourism consumption', *Urban Studies* 41(10): 1983–2000.

Smith, M. (2009) *Issues in Cultural Tourism Studies*, London and New York: Routledge.

Sorkin, M. (1992) (ed.) *Variations on a Theme Park: The New American City and the End of Public Space*, New York: Hill and Wang.

Szerszynski, B. and Urry, J. (2002) 'Cultures of cosmopolitanism', *Sociological Review* 50(4): 461–81.

Taylor, I. (2000) 'European ethnoscapes and urban redevelopment: the return of Little Italy in 21st century Manchester', *City* 4(1): 27–42.

Wood, P. and Landry, C. (2008) *The Intercultural City: Planning for Diversity Advantage*, London: Earthscan.

Yip, Q. (1936) 'Vancouver's Chinatown, an official guide to the Jubilee celebrations', quoted in K. Anderson, *Vancouver's Chinatown: Racial Discourse in Canada, 1875–1980*, Montreal and Kingston: McGill-Queen's University Press.

Zukin, S. (1995) *The Cultures of Cities*, Oxford: Blackwell.

27

Events, cities and the night-time economy

Graeme Evans

Introduction

Evening entertainment and night-time activities have long featured in tourism destinations as an essential element in what has been coined the 'experience economy' of events, live performance and social gatherings around clubs, bars, restaurants and other venues. These invariably cater primarily for tourists during the peak season. Cities and urban tourism, on the other hand, offer a range of late-night activities all year round for a mix of residents, day visitors and tourists alike. These range from the traditional 'night life' of theatre, cinema and other cultural venues to bar and catering outlets often located on and around routes that are designed for public movement and circulation such as shopping streets, entertainment zones and squares – for example, Leicester Square, London, and Times Square, New York. These areas are often well lit and represent what Hannigan (2007) calls 'controlled edge', but they essentially provide a backdrop to consumption and visitor activity, window shopping and soaking up the night-life atmosphere. Another familiar image of historic towns and cities is illuminated heritage sites and buildings – from cathedrals, churches to fountains and monuments. Events that bring the outdoor public realm together with cultural and heritage venues at night are, however, a more recent development (Evans 2010). These seek, explicitly or not, to extend the night-time economy of cities in a more festive environment, opening up traditional as well as more off-beat areas and venues to locals and visitors alike. These late- and light-night events are the subject of this chapter.

A particular example of this phenomenon are Nuit Blanche or Light Night festivals which have multiplied in European and North American cities and further afield over the past ten years. Their origins vary, but light/all-night events have been associated with religious and cultural festivals, predominantly held in the early autumn. Earlier light-night events are identified with St Petersburg's White Nights cultural festival, held over several weeks, and Berlin's Lange Nacht or Long Night of Museums, with museums staying open until 2 a.m. twice a year. Since Paris inaugurated the Nuit Blanche in 2002, a movement of such festivals has developed and gained momentum. The majority of subsequent events reference Paris and use the Nuit Blanche brand, and in several cases French cultural organisations are active in funding, sponsorship and event promotion. The latest addition to the Nuit Blanche brand is New York, which held its first 'bringtolightnyc' festival in October 2010. Other capital cities (e. g. Copenhagen, Dublin, London) also use the late-night opportunity to promote area-based cultural festivals and contemporary art events.

Features of these 'white night' events are illuminations on buildings and light installations, including fireworks displays, late-night opening of museums and galleries and in some cases performing arts venues, parks and gardens, sports facilities, and live events in major squares, stadia and waterfront sites. Public transport – normally free/low cost – is extended into the early hours along festival routes and to venues, with additional bus and tube/tram services to cope with the extra demand. This festival event is also increasingly a vehicle for new artists and award schemes, including biennales, and in some cases children and young people's events and participation, as well as community and local area development. The events are normally free, although in some cases a combined ticket is purchased for a series of museums or galleries.

Night-time economy

All of these events, however, seek to exploit and rediscover the evening and late-night economy and respond to concerns over safety and crowding out of visitor activity by 'mono-use' of city centre spaces associated with extended alcoholic drinking in bars/clubs and associated anti-social behaviour, in an attempt to 'reclaim the night'. As Hobbs *et al.* (2000) observed:

> Young drinkers now 'own' many town and city centres at night. When such ownership is established, these areas become even more attractive to young people seeking a permissive leisure environment free from the supervision or censure of the older citizens with whom they share these spaces at other times.

The growth of the late-night economy and activity is now an established feature of many cities, fuelled by liberalisation of licensing and trading hours. In the UK for example, the Night-Time Economy (NTE) represents an important element of the tourism and hospitality sector. It is estimated that NTE activity contributed £66 billion to the UK economy in 2009, employing 1.3 million people (10 per cent of all employment, 8 per cent of all firms). In London, NTE activity made up of core (pubs, bars, restaurants, clubs, theatres) and non-core activities (accommodation, taxis, food and drink supplies, and relevant public services) turned over £10 billion in 22,000 firms, a 17 per cent increase on 2006. The growth of late-night festivals and provision of hospitality and transport has therefore extended the visitor economy and calendar that was otherwise limited to specific zones and activity (e.g. cinema, private/member clubs) and tourist seasons. This phenomenon also represents the import of a more European continental lifestyle (Bianchini 1995). associated with southern European and other cities with warmer climates, where 'late-night' activity has long been normalised – manifested through café culture, relaxed licensing regulations and a more mature attitude towards open-air activity and mixed-use (buildings, streets, users), with the associated infrastructure to facilitate this, e.g. transport, cleansing, lighting. How far this city lifestyle can transfer to other countries is problematic, however, given the experience in the UK:

> most European cities have very inclusive evening economy where people of all ages participate in a range of activities. In contrast the evening activities of British cities are not so compatible with the inclusive ideals of the urban renaissance. They centre around young people and alcohol, leading to associated problems of crime and disorder, noise and nuisance.
>
> *(ODPM, 2003: 3)*

Nonetheless, the acceptance of, and economic opportunities arising from, the Night-Time Economy are therefore compelling, with the benefits to local authorities wider than just the commercial returns and income to incumbent businesses. Local authorities in the UK also link a vibrant night-life with attraction to residents and investors, as well as the gains in employment, tourist spending and economies of scale (Roberts and Gornostaeva 2007: 140). These benefits include:

1   Improvement in vitality of the area (and reduced crime/fear of crime)
2   Increased number of jobs
3   Attraction/expansion of leisure venues (cinemas, theatres, gyms, cyber-cafés, events)
4   Greater number of tourists
5   New residents moving into the area
6   Inward investment in other businesses.

The Greater London Authority (GLA) study of the Leisure Economy (2003), for example, found that on average each ward had gained twenty bar jobs between 1995 and 2000 (an increase of 12 per cent) and restaurant jobs increased by 28 per cent, presenting one of London's 'best sources of employment growth'. Attendance at *non*-alcohol based venues also recorded an increase of 25 per cent. In a survey of four London authorities (Camden, Lambeth, Newham, Southwark) the responsibility for events varied – from Parks, Leisure, and Performance to Policy and Projects departments (Pugh and Wood 2004). In Southwark (Bankside cultural quarter), the coordination of events between Leisure and Communications departments was seen to promote objectives of city positioning by the borough, which has been undergoing major regeneration and image improvement, and where: 'events do support wider social outcomes such as economic regeneration and social inclusion' (Southwark Council 2002: 4). The strategic planning of events was seen to be advantageous in meeting Council objectives in Newham (the main London 2012 Olympic borough) as: 'a place where people want to live and visit, to put Newham on the map, and to work in partnership to add diversity and value' (Pugh and Wood 2004: 67). In all boroughs, an increase in events activity and their significance was observed. In some cases larger events had displaced smaller ones, and the policy goal was of achieving financial self-sustainability. On the other hand, the need for events for children and families was stressed. Events activity and planning was generally allied with Leisure and particularly Cultural Strategies. A general trend is the geographic spread and redistribution of cultural and associated tourism activity to outer London and less developed destination areas, which has long been a policy goal of tourism and planning bodies of major cities (Evans 2000; Maitland 2010), and one aspect of late-night events and trails. These help create new visitor destinations as well as new experiences in central and existing venues (Evans and pmpgenesis 2010) – which are seen, literally, in a new light.

Nuit Blanche brand

The adoption of a wider late-night economy in 'northern' cities has in many respects transformed the landscape of their visitor and city centre economies, management and land use (e.g. retail, hospitality, urban design) and it is within this context that late-night festivals and events have evolved. In some cases these have developed from existing festivals – religious, cultural, seasonal – or, more often, have been the result of new festivals created from scratch as part of city branding and promotional initiatives (Evans 2003). Nuit Blanche and all-night events have therefore joined an international network of 'serial events' such as city marathons and biennales – of which over 125 are held in cities worldwide today.

Whilst late-night opening of museums and light-night events and festivals have been established since the 1990s, notably in Berlin (Late-Night Museums) and St Petersburg (White Night – although not an all-night event), the Nuit Blanche originated in 2002 with Paris where Christophe Girard, Deputy Mayor, first proposed this event, one year after taking office, and the concept has been quickly adopted and emulated in other cities (Table 27.1). In 2006, five capital cities (Paris, Rome, Riga, Brussels and Madrid) organised an exchange programme for artists, each welcoming an artist or theatre company from each of the capital cities that were part of the European Nuit Bianche network. The following year, Bucharest joined these six cities to formulate a shared artistic project based on the creation of a 'lounge' area in the heart of each Nuit Blanche. Bucharest joined the wider European network and held its first event on 22 September 2008 (Jiwa *et al.* 2009). In many cases there has been a rapid build-up of activity, scope and attendances at these events in only a few years, as they move from local (special interests, artists, area/business improvement), regional/city, to international appeal and status.

This evolution of Nuit Blanche events has therefore spawned a European network with common aims (below), and this reflects their cooperative nature, for instance the 'twinning' of Paris and Rome, European Museum Nights (above), and networks of national events across several cities, for example in Ireland: Dublin–Cork, Limerick, Waterford, Galway; France: Paris–Amiens, Brison, Metz; Italy: Rome–Specchia, Genoa; and the UK Light Nights cities of Belfast, Birmingham, Bournemouth, Leeds, Liverpool, Nottingham, Sheffield, Stoke and Kirkaldy and Perth in Scotland. A European Charter has been developed to promote and coordinate the Nuit Blanche brand and event, indicating the global scope of this European project which has spread to Canada (Montreal, Toronto, Halifax), the USA (Atlanta, Chicago, Santa Monica/Los Angeles, New York) as well as Peru (Lima), Israel (Tel Aviv) and Malta (Valetta), with Nuit Blanche events now held in over 120 cities:

1   Nuit Blanche is a free cultural event that is open to all, held annually at the end of summer or the beginning of autumn – and which goes on all night.
2   Nuit Blanche gives pride of place to contemporary creativity in all its forms: visual art, projections, installations, music, stage and street performers, circus and fairground arts.
3   Nuit Blanche presents all the different aspects of public space: places that are usually closed or abandoned, outlying areas, prestigious locations or places that form part of the city's cultural heritage, revisited in an unusual way by the artists.
4   Nuit Blanche enables cities organising the event to reflect together upon current developments for urban nights, to implement suitable services and means of organisation (city economy, signs, lighting, security, services).
5   Nuit Blanche provides a perfect opportunity to promote 'soft' forms of mobility: encouraging cycle paths, the use of trams, public transport, river shuttles.
6   Nuit Blanche fosters exchanges between city centres and peripheral areas.
7   The Nuit Blanche Europe partner cities have decided that a joint artistic project will be carried out each year, with the aim of developing exchanges between the cities and between European artists and audiences

Late-night cultural festivals have also evolved independently of the Nuit Blanche brand and network, notably in Dublin (below) and Copenhagen. Here, local cultural development agencies rather than city/mayors organise the event, albeit with city council funding and infrastructure support. In the UK, which so far has not created a Nuit Blanche branded event, the Association of Town Centre Managers (ATCM) coordinate a Light Nights network which does emulate the Nuit Blanche, although lacking the all-night programme of events and extended opening. The

Table 27.1 Late-night/light-night events and festivals

City	Event/festival	Year established	Timing and duration	Area	Organiser/promoter	Annual visitors (000s)
Atlanta, USA	Le Flash	2008	Early October 7p.m. to 2 a.m.	Open air/ street/park, galleries, pubs, clubs SW of downtown CBD, historic 'landmark' area	Artists Group and curators, Atlanta Cultural Affairs Dept	—
Barcelona, Spain	Nit Blanca	2008	Early July 6 p.m. to 5 a.m., museums until 2 a.m.	Montjuic Olympic Stadium and adjoining museums and gardens	Municipality of Barcelona	Main venue 15k
Berlin, Germany	Long Night of Museums; Festival of Lights	1997 2005	Twice a year: summer and winter; 2 weeks in October	Whole city area of 400km² along 5 city routes; 60 buildings and sites across the city	Kulturprojekte Berlin, City of Berlin, museums; Zander & Partner	150k 1 million
Brussels, Belgium	Nuit Blanche	2001	Early October 1 of 3 day Arts Festival 11 p.m. to 4 a.m.	Central zone, venues all over the city	City Council Cultural Services	—
Chicago, USA	Looptopia	2007	Early May 5 p.m. to 7 a.m.	Mixed-use district and central business BID area	Chicago Loop Alliance	100k
Copenhagen, Denmark	Culture Night	1995	Mid-October 5 p.m. to 2 a.m., museums until midnight	7 boroughs – Norrebro, Vestervro, Christianshavn, Osterbro, City, Orestadt Frederiksberg	Copenhagen Night of Culture Association	60k–75k
Dublin, Ireland	Culture Night	2006	Mid-September 5 p.m. to 11 p.m., bars until 2 a.m.	6 quarters – Heuston/ Museum, Historic, Temple Bar, North and South Georgian, Trinity/Docklands	Temple Bar Cultural Trust	100k
Lisbon, Portugal	Luzboa	2004	2 weeks, biannually	Castle (light show), 4 points on central route, waterfront	Lisbon Municipal Council	—
London, UK	Lates Museums at Night	2007 2009	May and October May 6 p.m. to 12 p.m.	Museums/galleries, routes, riverside. Museums (London, other cities)	Greater London Authority MLA, Culture24	—

Table 27.1 (continued)

City	Event/festival	Year established	Timing and duration	Area	Organiser/promoter	Annual visitors (000s)
Lyon, France	Fête des Lumières	1989	3 to 4 days around 8 December to 2 a.m.	Streets and parks in central area	City of Lyon	1 to 4 million over 4 days
Madrid, Spain	*La noche en blanco*	2006	Mid-September 9 p.m. to 7 a.m.	4 areas – centre, southern and northern rim and university rim	City Council	100k
Montreal, Canada	Nuit Blanche Montreal en Lumière	2003	February, 1 night during the 10-day festival to 5.30 a.m.	City centre, Old Port, Plateau Mont Royal, Pole Mainsonneuve, Pole Parc Jean-Drapeau	Hydro Quebec	275k
New York, USA	Nuit Blanche	2010	Early October 7 p.m. to 7 a.m.	Greenpoint Brooklyn – industrial waterfront	City of New York	—
Paris, France	Nuit Blanche; Nuit de Musées	2002 2007	Early October 2 a.m. to 7 a.m.	Central Paris served by Métro routes	City of Paris	2 million
Rome, Italy	Notte Bianca Romana	2005	August 8 p.m. to 8 a.m.	7-8 zones from centre to the periphery	Municipality of Rome, Chamber of Commerce	1–2 million
Toronto, Canada	Nuit Blanche	2006	Early October 12 hours sunset to sunrise	3 zones City Hall, Yong-Dundas Square, Financial District, Liberty Village BIA	Toronto Metro Council	1 million
UK cities –Belfast, Birmingham, Leeds, Nottingham, Perth, Liverpool, Sheffield, Kirkaldy	Light Night UK	2008	Mid-September/early October 10 p.m. to 12 p.m.	Central area, venues, town squares, waterfronts	City Councils, Association of Town Centre Managers	Leeds 47k B'ham 240k Newham 45k

reluctance of regional cities to go the full 'all-nighter' also reflects disquiet with the negative social effects and local culture – political and community (Thomas and Bromley 2000). UK Light Nights events thus seek:

- To create a feeling of community spirit; engender an awareness that the city is united and that there is a sentiment that everyone has something in common.
- To bring social causes to people's attention and to encourage donations towards a charity fund with publicised beneficiaries.
- To allow people to experience different forms of art and entertainment and to experience things that they would not normally.
- To promote the work of voluntary organisations.
- To create an awareness of what the city has to offer to residents and visitors alike

(ATCM 2009)

Following light-night events in Birmingham, Leeds and Nottingham in 2008, several more cities in 2009 offered their residents and visitors the opportunity to experience their city from a fresh perspective. The sentiment of reclaiming the night in these city centres is strong, as is the commercial potential:

> Light Night gives the general population the chance to 'take back' the city from the demographic group that normally occupies the city in the evening and at night. Because there are different ways for local, national and international companies to get involved there are strong, varied opportunities to attract advertising, sponsorship and also media attention to the city.
>
> *(ATCM 2009)*

Liverpool, at the finale of its 2008 European Capital of Culture programme, signed off with an evening event. An estimated 60,000 people congregated at the Pier Head, as well as at the Albert Dock and Wirral bank, for a celebration that included sing-alongs, firework displays, street artists on illuminated bikes and light projections on to famous refurbished buildings. This 'Light Night' celebration also kick-started similar events held in cities in England and Scotland, with extended opening of venues, including the centrepiece new retail centre, Liverpool One. From the perspective of the City Centre Manager:

> the careful management and promotion of Liverpool City Centre at night is essential to the well-being of its people. Liverpool realized some time ago that we needed a diverse mix of people and activities in an exciting and increasingly safe after-dark environment. Delivering this is crucial to our reputation with visitors and residents, businesses and investors.
>
> *(Cockburn, in Bevan and Turnham 2010: 2)*

The Nuit Blanche concept and brand has to date been a successful vehicle to develop a unique cultural event for city promotion and achieving local economic, cultural and community objectives. The following section profiles comparable Light/Late-Night events – both stand-alone and as part of wider festivals. These are listed in Table 27.1 in alphabetical order.

Nuit Blanche impacts

Total attendances at these events range from the smaller 40,000 to 100,000, and large-scale events attracting from 1 million (Berlin, Lisbon, Lyon, Toronto) to 2 million (Paris, Rome). Their scale has developed rapidly on an annual basis. Paris first attracted 500,000 in 2002 and now attracts 2 million; 40,000 visited Dublin's first all-night Culture Festival in 2006 and over 100,000 in 2008; Rome saw 1 million in 2005 and receives 2 million today; Toronto attracted 425,000 in 2006 and over 1 million in 2008. This expansion reflects the growing number of events, venues and geographic area covered, but also the success in marketing and generation of excitement around what has become a 'must see' event.[1] Where visitor surveys have been undertaken, satisfaction with the quality of these events was high – Rome 90 per cent (42 per cent 'Excellent', 48 per cent 'Good'; Cherubini and Iasevoli 2006; Armenia *et al.* 2008) and Dublin 94 per cent (65 per cent 'Very satisfied' and 29 per cent 'Somewhat satisfied'; Tourism Research Centre 2007; PCC 2008). Nearly half the visitors to this event participated in two or more activities and nearly 80 per cent travelled by foot or public transport. Visitors to these late-night events are primarily local/city residents, 'domestic' (whether staying overnight or not) with a growing international tourist group. The latter could be overseas visitors temporarily resident in the city, with capital cities hosting a mix of students, expat workers and other non-leisure tourists at any one time. So whilst Dublin's Culture Festival attracts 150,000 visitors, 75 per cent of these are from Ireland but the remainder are from Europe and the USA (PCC 2008). Likewise, 94 per cent of Rome's Notte Bianca is attended by Italians, but in 2004 this meant that 120,000 participants were from other countries. A similar number of tourists came to Toronto's Nuit Blanche for the 2008 festival, whilst during Berlin's two-week Festival of Lights in 2009, 300,000 overnight stays were recorded. Several events therefore form part of longer cultural festivals, running the whole weekend, for three or four days and even up to ten days. Others focus on the one late-night event of extended opening hours and transport servicing linked routes across the city and specific cultural and historic quarters.

Dublin Culture Night

Dublin Culture Night first took place in 2006 as an initiative of the Temple Bar Cultural Trust, in association with the Council of National Cultural Institutions and the Department of Arts, Sport and Tourism, to provide a new and imaginative route for people of all ages to connect with the arts and cultural life of the city. For one night in mid–late September each year the city's museums, galleries, churches, historic houses, artists' studios and cultural centres open their doors late for a night of 'entertainment, discovery and adventure' – from a handful of participating venues in 2006, over 120 venues participated in 2009. Talks, tours, performances and events are laid on from the early evening to late into the night, with public transport – rail/light rail and buses operating late services. An art competition is run as part of the festival, sponsored by the Luas tram company with the winner's artwork displayed by poster on the side of their vehicles and website.

The scope and coverage of the event has expanded year on year, starting with 40,000 visitors in 2006 and rising to over 150,000 participating in 2009. The geographic area of the festival originated in the Temple Bar regeneration zone (Montgomery 1995) of cultural and entertainment venues and now takes places in six city quarters (Figure 27.1), including historic, museum, university and docklands areas. The late-night city festival has also spread to twenty other cities and towns in Ireland – from Cork to Wicklow.

The main reasons given for attending the event were: 'Late opening hours' (38 per cent), 'Curiosity' (35 per cent), 'Free entry' (31 per cent), 'Visiting new attractions' (26 per

---

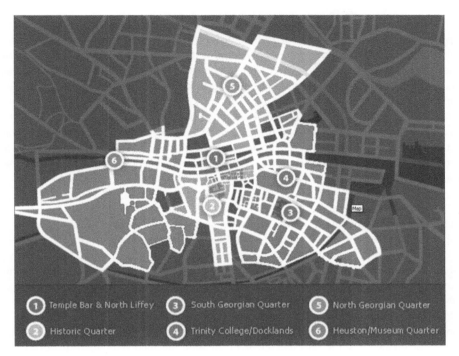

Figure 27.1 Dublin Culture Night quarters

cent). (See Table 27.2.) This confirms the 'USP' of late-night events and the rationale for participating venues in attracting new visitor groups. Over 40 per cent of participants did not normally visit cultural attractions in the city. Reasons given for this ('barriers') ranked 'Lack of time' (50 per cent) highest, followed by 'Lack of awareness' (17 per cent) and

Table 27.2 Survey of visitors to the Dublin Culture Night, 2008

Age range	*18–24 15%*	*25–34 34%*	*35–44 17%*	*45–54 18%*	*55+ 16%*	
Gender	Female 54%	Male 46%				
Country of residence	Ireland 75% (of which 82% from Dublin)	14% Europe	4% USA	2% Other	Europe: Spain 5%, England 4%, France, Germany, Italy and Poland 2% each	
Accommodation	At home 76%	In hotel 16%	With family/ friends 8%			
Group size	One 14%	Two 49% (32% couple)	Three 14%	Four 14%	Five 3%	Six+ 6%
No. of venues visited (average 4)	Two 24%	Three 21%,	Four 17%	One 11%	Five 11%	Six+ 17%
Cultural quarters visited	Two 37%	One 28%	Three 18%	Four 8%	Five 2%	Six 5%

Source: Tourism Research Centre 2007; PCC 2008 .

'Unattractive opening hours' (7 per cent). The late-night event therefore provides a useful opportunity to those with limited daytime access. Marketing and publicity of the event relies on word of mouth and prior knowledge, with radio/TV and internet coverage the most cited (32 per cent and 24 per cent respectively), but also posters/leaflets (22 per cent, down from 27 per cent in 2007) and tourist office (14 per cent – the Temple Bar Trust operates its own visitor centre).

Nearly 90 per cent of visitors surveyed in 2008 said that they would attend the following year's event, but this was down from 97 per cent in 2007, signifying a possible attendance 'decay' from regular/local visitors. As with other late-night events, growth in attendance is seen in non-local visitors as these festivals become established 'must see' tourist events.

Late/light nights tend to fall on a Saturday evening/Sunday morning in September or early October. This timing sometimes coincides with cultural or religious festivals (e.g. Barcelona – Grec), but this is also a post-summer/pre-winter event opportunity, after the peak holiday and 'closed city' summer season. In some cities the event therefore seeks to spread tourism – domestic and overseas – into a lower-demand season, including hotel occupation and venue attendance.

Information on the cost and revenues associated with these events is limited. In part this is due to their free/open nature and difficultly in counting attendances – these are estimated from transport, police and venue counts, as well as hits on event websites. Some are part of longer festivals and budgets for the all-night element are not specified, e.g. Festival des Lumières, Lyon – four days, €1.8m expenditure; Montréal en Lumière – ten days, C$6.75m. Several cities operate volunteer programmes to provide support services such as in guides, safety and clean-up. Others have been developed by groups of artists and local organisations such as galleries. Larger events combine city, cultural and commercial partners, including in Canada headline sponsors such as Scotiabank Nuit Blanche, Toronto and Hydro-Quebec High Lights Festival, Montreal.

The large-scale all-night event in Rome has a budget of €3.5m of which the city funds 48 per cent, chambers of commerce 39 per cent and sponsors 13 per cent (Severino 2005). Lyon's Light Night receives 40 per cent of its budget from sponsors. The estimated revenues generated in Rome are calculated at €30m in business/added value, plus hotel income, and with €1.12m received in transport revenue (€1 ticket). It is estimated that visitors spend on average €25. Toronto's 2008 Nuit Blanche was estimated to have produced an economic multiplier effect of C$16.7m (direct, indirect and induced), with C$18m in direct spending and C$7.6m in extra tax revenues received. The regional government provides a grant of C$300,000 for this event with the city providing C$737,000 in cash plus staff resources (six full-time equivalent per year) and C$2.2m generated in cash and kind from sponsors in 2009 (Metro Toronto 2009).

An important feature and rationale for these events is their arts and cultural focus, using the showcase opportunity and night-time atmosphere to present a range of contemporary art exhibitions, installations and media in both traditional and unlikely settings. In some cases arts groups lead the event (Atlanta) and, even here and in Lisbon, the collaboration with French institutes such as cultural services, embassy or consulate maintains the global Nuit Blanche link back to Paris and the Nuit Blanche charter: 'All Nuit Blanche projects must critically engage with the Nuit Blanche mandate to bring forward contemporary art while addressing public space and its relationship to the City' (Metro Toronto 2009: 2). Other late-night events specifically target business improvement and regeneration areas such as in Atlanta, Chicago and Brussels, which directly engages local neighbourhoods and young people with collaborating artists and amateur arts competitions (as in Dublin). Significantly, Brussels, like Copenhagen, Genoa (Figure 27.2)

Figure 27.2 Museums Night, Genoa

and Lisbon, originated its late-night festival with Expo and European City of Culture events, and these cities have therefore sought to maintain the momentum and new cultural spaces opened up by these one-off celebrations.

Museum nights

In London, cultural venues already operate extended opening times on one or more nights of the week, some daily (e.g. Barbican 11 a.m. to 8 p.m.) including the British Library and Museum (8–8.30 p.m.), Hayward, National/Portrait and Whitechapel Galleries (9 p.m.), Royal Academy, Victoria and Albert (V&A) Museum and Tate Modern (10 p.m.). On the first Thursday of each month over 100 museums and galleries in the East End stay open until 9 p.m. (www.first-thursdays.co.uk). Over fifty venues are listed as having late-night licences for drinking (i.e. after 11 p.m.) and/or music. Some cinemas have traditionally shown late-night films, for instance a midnight movie night with films and talks by experts.

In May 2009, museums in the UK joined with French museums in holding a late-night opening weekend. Paris started its Nuit des Musées in 2007 with the Museums of Modern Art, Bourdelle, Victor Hugo's House and several others opening from 6 p.m. to midnight, with talks, installations such as deckchairs in galleries, writing and drawing workshops. Since 2006 the Secretary General of the Council of Europe (which celebrated its 60th anniversary in May 2009), has promoted the Museums Open Night which takes place concurrently in the signatory countries of the European Cultural Convention, including the UK. The initiative promotes Europe/European cultures and provides the opportunity to attract a wider public, particularly young people.

Over the weekend of 15–17 May 2009 Museums at Night was held in the UK, promoted by the Museums, Libraries & Archives (MLA) Council and organised by Culture24 (www.culture24.org.uk) with museums and heritage attractions opening until midnight: 'For us it was a really successful way of promoting the [National] Gallery to new audiences and those who cannot normally visit during the day' (Culture24: 2009), where a talk by the Velvet Underground's John Cale and a late opening of the popular Picasso exhibition attracted more than 300: 'the noticeable arrival of a more fresh-faced bunch than museums normally welcome was a particular trend. Generally we noticed a much younger crowd were in throughout the night' (ibid.). In some cases museums stayed open throughout the night, e.g. Tate Modern from 5 p.m. to 5 p.m. the next day, whilst more than 120 people visited Florence Nightingale House in London 'after dark'.

Berlin's established biannual Long Night of Museums, for instance, adopts a thematic approach – in January 2009 Worldviews, and in August 20 Years After the Wall. Over 100 venues participate, including major government offices, public readings and concerts. Opening from 6 p.m. to 2 a.m., they achieve an attendance of between 30,000 and 40,000, with a single ticket entry to all participating venues. The ticket includes free travel on shuttle buses between 3 p.m. and 5 a.m. Three zones of public transport are free, but only for getting to the event and departing from the event. The event is organised by the Berliner Museum Association in cooperation with the Berlin City Council's Kultur Projekte. Promotional and web information is available in English as well as in German, with the target audience both local and international.

London Lates

London plays host to a growing number of cultural and special events, making up a year-round calendar of festivals. These range from established cultural events, such as Notting Hill Carnival (August bank holiday), Diwali Festival of Lights (October) and major international arts festivals (dance, drama, film, music, etc.) based in central venues, to numerous local and community festivals. Events focusing on the built environment include Open House, which was first held in 1992 over a weekend in September. This features routes, trails and tours, including event sites, installations and access to architects' studios – over 600 buildings and free events. These include a London Night Hike where up to 2,000 people walk a 20-mile route through the capital past lit buildings and landmarks. Open House carried out research amongst 3,000 members of the visiting public in 2008, and found that:

- 70 per cent were surprised by the architecture they saw;
- 66 per cent said that Open House London made them think differently about London;
- 24 per cent found out more about sustainable/green design through the event.
  Visiting buildings was cited as the most informative and enjoyable way of finding out more about architecture.

The success of these 'open' events led in 2007 to the Greater London Authority (GLA) launching its Lates festival, with leaflets, website, calendar of events and a media partnership with the free London newspaper. A Lates e-bulletin is circulated to over 4,000 subscribers. This late-night festival of after-hours art and culture was developed by GLA's Cultural Campaigns team with the following objectives:

1 demonstrating how the cultural sector contributes significantly to London's late-night economy.
2 encouraging London's world-class organisations to work together to present audiences with an integrated and unified offer;
3 encouraging and developing audiences in the 20–35 age range by providing them with extended opening hours and encouraging this audience to regard these venues as places to meet, socialise and think;
4 ensuring that Lates events imaginatively re-vision this content for the 20–35-year-old target audience;
5 using Lates as a flagship project to stimulate the cultural sector into providing more late openings and 'late-night activity'.

Venue partners in the Lates programme included the Barbican Arts Complex, BFI Imax, British Museum, International Contemporary Art (ICA), Museum of London, National Gallery, National Portrait Gallery, South Bank Centre, Tate Britain and Modern, V& A Museum and the Royal Academy of Art. Museums and galleries were specifically identified as they wished to build their late-night attendances.

An evaluation of the Lates launch in May 2007 and subsequent events in October 2007 and June 2008 – where sixty-eight events were held, including twelve 'highlight events' – found that most partner organisations had achieved their most successful late-night events in terms of audiences:

- The British Museum reported a 100 per cent uplift in audiences compared to their May light-night events in 2006 and their biggest turn-out for a late-night event, with 6,600 people in 2007.
- The V& A had over 4,500 people attend their surrealist ball.
- The Hayward Gallery achieved over 3,000 attendees at their Saturday-night event for the artist Anthony Gormley, 50 per cent higher than the following Sunday (normally their best day).
- The National Portrait Gallery's Fashionista Friday was their second busiest Friday ever.
- Over the 25–28 May weekend, 90,000 visitors came to the Tate Modern and Tate Britain.
- In 2008 over 120,000 people attended, with many events sold out.
- 95 per cent of respondents felt the event they had attended met or exceeded their expectations.
- 88 per cent of respondents said that they would return to the venue as a result of attending a Lates event there.

- Over 50 per cent of respondents said that the Lates festival had improved their perception of London's late-night offer; 25 per cent reported that as a result of Lates visit they spent more than they normally would.
- Across the whole sample this represented an uplift of £24 extra spend per head.
- For the twelve highlight events this had a consequent economic benefit of £2.6m.

The feasibility of London hosting a Nuit Blanche-style festival has been considered by the city, as part of a light-night event of illuminated tours and walks (Evans and pmpgenesis 2010). London is already an established entertainment city with a late-night economy, although this is not coordinated in terms of visitor target groups or city promotion. Late-night museum and Lates events have tested this concept towards what may be more focused and branded light-night festivals, but this is unlikely to be considered before the London 2012 Summer Olympics, after which such an event may fill the vacuum from 2013 and perhaps kick-start an annual festival as other cities have done after hosting a mega-event. It is also unlikely that London will adopt the Nuit Blanche brand since this is associated with Paris and emulator cities, and London's global 'world city' status and politics may require a more unique brand. Ultimately it will depend on local and geo-political considerations, as well as the promotional advantages that would benefit from an already internationally branded event, with non-Francophone cities such as New York and Toronto adopting the Nuit Blanche event, but in their own fashion.

These initiatives by major national cultural institutions, which already dominate the cultural tourism and visitor economy of the capital city, do however demonstrate a desire to extend and in some respects redistribute the visitor flow. With many major venues experiencing peak visiting and overcrowding, particularly of tourists, between 11 a.m. and 2 p.m., the opportunity has been taken to relieve this by later opening, and to offer a different experience to regular as well as first-time visitors. The critical mass of venues and routes between these is a unique offer that cities provide and one that has enabled the late-night festival to flourish and grow, year on year.

Conclusion

The adoption of late-night city festivals and events forms the latest move in rediscovering city centres that had been previously in decline or dominated by exclusionary and increasingly anti-social behaviour and mono-cultural use of streets and venues. This has been an opportunity taken up by old as well as new world and re-emergent national capitals (Maitland, 2010). Reclaiming the night has also provided an alternative and supplementary experience to the traditional night life of entertainment – theatre, cinema, restaurant – zones, that cater for a narrow range of visitors and audiences. Cultural and heritage venue visits, once confined to daytime, have been able to extend into the later evening and, with special events such as Museum Nights and Nuit Blanche, through the night. This diversification and temporal shift has benefited underdeveloped visitor areas and established cultural institutions who have attracted a younger audience and provided different kinds of experience. The use of lighting on and around buildings and light installations – a long tradition in some cities such as Paris and Barcelona, as well as seaside attractions, notably Blackpool Illuminations in the UK and Christmas lights on main shopping streets – has created a backdrop for a range of formal and informal activities which are enjoyed by locals and visitors alike.

Nuit Blanche and other late-night festivals therefore engage both citizen and tourist, although starting out as primarily local and city events for residents, they have developed in size and scope and unsurprisingly develop into larger-scale events that feature on city event and tourist calendars (as with cultural-touristic events such as Carnival Mas' in Notting Hill, London and Caribana, Toronto). Crucially this reoccupation of the city at night provides a corollary to the deleterious effects of late-night drinking, but rather than replacing this with another mono-consumption based activity, a more open and fluid event has emerged that reflects the city culture, cityscape and social life in each case (and, often, their more authentic festival roots), but under a universal 'brand' that provides validation and recognition to newcomers to the city. This is therefore a global trend and strategy that capital cities have best been able to exploit and which other cities are emulating, albeit at a smaller scale. Late-night events, in focusing on the cultural, social and spatial elements of cities that are traditionally out of the reach of locals and visitors and where well planned and managed, perhaps represent an example of sustainable events which, in Getz's view, 'are not just those that can endure indefinitely, they are also events that fulfill important social, cultural, economic and environmental roles that people value. In this way, they can become institutions that are permanently supported in a community or nation' (Getz 2009: 70).

Note

1 Getz (2007) refers to 'must see' mega-events as attracting over a million people, which some Nuit Blanche do attract; others, however, are smaller. Arguably light/late-night events and festivals are not mega-events since they do not require the development of additional venues or facilities, but build organically on existing venues, spaces and routes.

References

Armenia, S., Fiorani, G. and Meneguzzo, M. (2008) 'Analysis of economic impacts and evolution of the Italian cultural event "La Notte Bianca Romana": a system dynamic approach', paper presented at the International Conference of the System Dynamic Society, Rome.

Art in the Open (2009) *Light London: Inspiring Creative Approaches*, London: Open House.

ATCM (2009) *Light Night Network*. Available at: www.lightnight.co.uk

Bevan, T. and Turnham, A. (2010) *Night Mix News*, Summer. Available at: www.tbr.co.uk

Bianchini, F. (1995) 'Night cultures, night economies', Planning, Practice and Research 10(2): 121–6.

Cherubini, S. and Iasevoli, G. (2006) 'Stakeholders' event evaluation: Notte Bianca case study', paper presented at the Marketing Trends in Europe Conference, Venice, 20–21 June. Available at: www.escp-eap.net/conferences/marketing/2006_cp/Materiali/Paper/It/Cherubini_Iasevoli.pdf

Copenhagen Night of Culture Association (2008) *Kukltur Natten*. Available at: www.kulturnatten.dk

Culture24 (2009) *5th Edition of the European Night of Museums*. Available at: www.culture24.org.uk

Evans, G.L. (2000) 'Planning for urban tourism: a critique of borough development plans and tourism policy in London', *International Journal of Tourism Research* 2(4): 1–20.

——(2003) 'Hard branding the culture city – from Prado to Prada', *International Journal of Urban and Regional Research* 27(2): 417–40.

——(2010) 'New events in historic venues: a case of London', *Rivista di Scienze del Turismo* 2: 149–66.

Evans, G.L and pmpgenesis (2010) *Nuit Blanche London – Feasibility Study for the London Development Agency*, London: LDA.

Getz, D. (2007) *Event Studies: Theory, Research and Policy for Planned Events*, Oxford: Elsevier.

——(2009) 'Policy for sustainable and responsible festivals and events: institutionalization of a new paradigm', *Journal of Policy Research in Tourism, Leisure and Events* 1(1): 61–78.

GLA Economics (2003) *Spending Time: London's Leisure Economy*, London: Greater London Authority.

Hannigan, J. (2007) 'A neo-Bohemian Rapsody: cultural vibrancy and controlled edge as urban development tools in the new creative economy', in T.A. Gibson and M. Lowes (eds) *Urban Communication: Production, Text, Context*, New York: Rowman & Littlefield, pp. 61–81.

Hobbs, D., Lister, S., Hadfield, P., Winlow, S. and Hall, S. (2000) 'Receiving shadows: governance and liminality in the night-time economy', *British Journal of Sociology* 51(4): 701–17.

Jiwa, S., Coca-Stefanik, A., Blackwell, M. and Rahman, T. (2009) 'Light night: an "enlightening" place marketing experience', *Journal of Place Management and Development* 2(2): 154–66.

Maitland, R. (2010) 'Tourism and changing representation in Europe's historic capitals', *Rivista Scienze del Turismo* 2: 103–20.

Metro Toronto (2009) *Nuit Blanche Toronto October 3 2009 – Information and Requests for a Non-Objection Letter for the Alcohol and Gaming Commission of Ontario*, Toronto: Metro Toronto.

Montgomery, J. (1995) 'The story of Temple Bar: creating Dublin's cultural quarter', *Planning, Practice and Research* 10(2): 135–71.

ODPM (2003) *Sustainable Communities: Building for the Future*, London: Office for the Deputy Prime Minister.

PCC (2008) 'Dublin's Culture Night '08 attendees survey', Public Communications Centre, Dublin, September.

Pugh, C. and Wood, E. (2004) 'The strategic use of events within local government: a study of London Borough Councils', *Event Management* 9: 61–71.

Roberts, M. and Gornostaeva, G. (2007) 'The night-time economy and sustainable town centres: dilemmas for local government', *Journal of Sustainable Development and Planning* 2(2): 134–52.

Severino, F. (2005) '"The biggest event of the world": "a Notte Bianca" in Rome', 8th International Conference on Arts and Cultural Management, Montreal, July.

Southwark Council (2002) *Best Value, Review of the Events Service*, London: Southwark Leisure.

Thomas, C.J. and Bromley, R.D.F. (2000) 'City-centre revitalisation: problems of fragmentation and fear in the evening and night-time city', *Urban Studies* 37(8): 1403–29.

Tourism Research Centre (2007) *Dublin Culture Night 2007 Final Report*, Dublin: Temple Bar Cultural Trust.

28

Safety, security and event management

A case study of the London 2012 Olympics and the private security industry

Allison Wylde and Stephen J. Page

Introduction

Events have been heralded as an important tool capable of both promoting cities and reinforcing place-promotion strategies. In particular, events that are primarily designed to attract new visitor groups and high-profile media coverage, especially major sporting occasions such as the Olympic Games, are much coveted by destinations. The Olympic Games (both summer and winter) have long been seen as an international category of mega events designed to attract distinct visitor groups, as Chapter 4 by Weed and Chapter 7 by Gammon in this book have demonstrated. Yet the real scale of events at an individual country level and the activity associated with leisure and business travel often remains a neglected area, poorly understood in terms of its scale and volume. A study by the Business Visits and Events Partnership (2010) identified the different sectors comprising the events industry in the UK. It was estimated to have an economic impact of £36 billion and employed 530,000 full-time equivalent staff in 25,000 businesses across the sector (excluding the staging of one-off mega events such as the Olympic Games and Commonwealth Games). This illustrates not only the scale of the events industry but underlines the arguments that this sector is often a hidden element of the leisure and tourism infrastructure of countries which have active event sectors spanning a wide range of niches.

An industry that encompasses significant numbers of people, be they employees, spectators, participants or those in the media, inevitably creates and poses different degrees of risk to those involved. Consequently, the challenge for organisations responsible for staging an event (see Chapter 15 by Ferdinand and Williams in this book) is to ensure that they are staged in a manner whereby the well-being of the attendees is cared for in a responsible and safe manner. The concept has an even greater significance if one acknowledges the association by Emery (2010) that the events sector is often beset by a myriad of management problems including ticketing, crowd, legal, financial, weather and political problems. This means events are often subject to significant risk assessment in relation to the budgetary issues, legal issues (e.g. regulation) and health and safety matters. The Health and Safety Executive (1999) describe five distinct stages where risk assessment can be assessed for events: the build-up stage; the load-in stage; the show; the load-out stage and breakdown stage, where each of these stages poses different types of risk to participants and requires responses to managing safety. The concern with risk assessment is because any of the problems analysed by Emery (2010) may affect safety and security. These problems can impact upon the safety and security of the attendee, especially where the well-known problems such as overcrowding and surges could occur (see Abbott and Geddie 2000) that have led to high-profile accidents and deaths, such as the 2010 Duisbury Love Parade in Germany where nineteen people were killed and 340 were injured, with overcrowding in a tunnel that had only one entry and exit point. Therefore, developing an innovative approach as one tool to address management problems that impinge upon safety and security is a crucial issue to understand in order to reduce risk. Such innovation can have an important spin-off in impacting upon measures which affect safety and security of visitors at events. Therefore, the notion of well-being, developed by Pizam et al. (1997) and Walker and Page (2003), has an important place in the management of events and visitors, although this aspect of event management remains largely neglected in research studies. In relation to visitor well-being, research is underpinned by the concept of tourist safety and security.

This chapter commences with a review of the literature on safety and security issues associated with events, and then examines the importance of innovation in safety and security measures with reference to the London Olympic Games to be staged in 2012. It is evident that successful events are increasingly associated with security. For example, the London 2012 Olympic and Paralympics Games security preparations had, by late 2010, spent more than £95 million of an estimated £600–800 million total budget on such measures (http://news.bbc.co.uk/1/hi/business/8507768.stm) to ensure appropriate measures are in place for the event. This chapter primarily adopts a case study approach (see, for example, Yin (2009) and Miles and Huberman (1994) for more detail on the application of the case study method in management research) to derive evidence and generalisations in relation to one specific theme that has been overlooked in event research – innovation in private security firms as they engage with the London 2012 Olympic and Paralympic Games. The contribution of this chapter is to explore the interconnections between events and management processes for the safety and security of participants. In particular, this chapter examines the management of safety and security at mega events through private security firms. This forms an intriguing area of study: the management of the public good within a private sector framework, which within the event literature has not been studied. More specifically, this research engages with the event and wider social science and management literatures by presenting a new perspective, that engaging with mega events may be a driver of innovation for firms, studied in this case through the example of security firms.

We argue that there is a need to understand and characterise the security industry since it is an emerging, complex counter-cyclical and innovative industry (UKTI/DSO 2010) and its analysis is long overdue. Further, most research to date has looked at private security through the lens of the criminologist or political scientist, often limited to an issues-based approach focused on the so-called 'surveillance society' or 'police state' (see, for example, Fussey et al. (2011) and discussion below of the literature on the surveillance society) or through the functional management approach of the security and risk manager or event organiser. In contrast, the approach taken here is an empirical evidence-based study which aims to characterise innovation in the security industry. In addition, there is both a structural and policy dimension to security which needs to be incorporated in the discussion so that we can fully understand security as a public good 'without which societies cannot prosper; such benefits are intangible and not easy to measure' (Sempere 2010), a problem that also affects research on tourist well-being and its failure to fully develop since the innovative studies of Page and Meyer (1996) and Walker and Page (2003). We posit that the idea of a public good is thus nuanced; the private security sector is engaged in profit-making like other firms but at the same time is delivering a public good; this discussion is beyond the scope of this chapter but we will return to it in the conclusion as an area for future work. However, prior to examining the private security sector it is pertinent to review the literature on tourist safety and security since it provides the conceptual basis for understanding event attendee safety and well-being issues, given that attendees are short-term temporary visitors to a location: the tourism literature offers the best strategic fit with this research area and, in fact, much of the literature in this area has been developed and generated by tourism researchers.

Tourist safety and security: understanding the scope and concepts

According to Pizam and Mansfeld (2006: 22) 'tourist security incidents' include 'acts of violence or threats such as crime, terrorism, wars, civil and political unrest' which is directed against the tourism sector and tourists. Indeed as Page and Connell (2009) show, many destinations have now recognised how important visitor safety is and have created tourist police forces to both protect the individual and control crime. The research by Barker *et al.* (2002, 2003) and Barker and Page (2002), which focused on Auckland's hosting of the America's Cup, reinforced the need for safety where Operation Marlin created a police presence at the America's Cup Village in anticipation of additional criminal activity during a special event. This has important implications also for the destination in which the event is located as the attendees are likely to be staying in accommodation or visiting other attractions or facilities within the destination, so the increased volume of visitors poses two interconnected issues: first, the increased volume of visitors raises issues of personal safety in a number of domains, as Figure 28.1 shows. Second, the event raises the opportunities for crime against the visitor, though there is a debate within the tourism literature as to whether events in themselves lead to increased levels of crime in destinations. Tourist safety and crime are important components of the visitor experience at a destination and also at events (see Chapter 16 by Ryan on the visitor experience and Chapter 18 by Berridge on

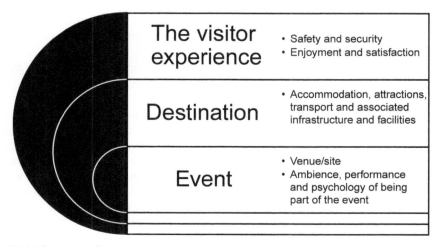

Figure 28.1 The event–destination–visitor experience nexus

the design of events and the experience). In addition, the management of large numbers of people at specific sites or venues poses issues associated with crowd management, which has developed as a specialist area of event management practice. However, when elements of that process fail the consequences can be catastrophic. Examples of failures in management systems follow a similar approach to the analysis of tourist accidents and safety research, whereby a domino effect occurs when a failure in one part of the chain of events contributes to accident-forming environments (see Page and Meyer 1996 and Bentley and Page 2008 for further detail). In this respect, the concepts used, and tools of analysis to reduce accidents and injuries in tourism, have a direct application to events, though the principle difference is one of scale where crowd management is an ever present challenge. Attention now turns to the research literature on safety and security.

Research agendas: safety, security and events

Much of the research literature on events and issues of attendee safety have been published in textbooks (e.g. Tarlow 2002; Silvers 2007) and within journal articles in the tourism field, along with a number of specialist articles in the event journals and wider management literature. The crossover into the event area suggests that existing knowledge is focused around three specific themes:

- Safety as a management process within event management, largely structured around operations management (such as practical 'how to' safety manuals and two principal texts such as Tarlow (2002) and Silvers (2007) and the Health and Safety Executive (1999) handbook). One notable area of research has been crowd management, particularly the problem of crowd surges and confinement of large numbers in a limited space that can lead to crushes and injuries (see Fruin 1993 at: www.gkstill.com/Fruin.html). Simple safety management models that examine the dynamics of these crowd-related problems have suggested that these problems can be triggered by a wide range of factors. These factors have been described by Fruin (1993) as a function of: the force of the crowd; the information available to the crowd to trigger a reaction; the space involved and time/duration of the incident. These are factors which closely relate to established accident- and injury-causation models (Page and Meyer 1996).
- Destination management and visitor safety and security (including the growing significance of tourist police at a macro level and the range of studies published in Pizam and Mansfeld 2006 and Botterill and Jones 2010) along with the long-established use of private security firms at event venues.
- The visitor experience (as discussed in Chapters 16 and 18 in this book by Ryan and Berridge) with the focus on the individual during the event experience.

This discussion poses an immediate challenge in terms of how to conceptualise the safety–security nexus at events across the divergent disciplinary areas that span criminology, sociology and geography as reviewed by Barker (2000), as well as management. The challenge in theorising is how these different components are integrated to improve understanding. According to Anderson (2010: 228), issues of security and safety are based on the notion of being protected in time and space. This means that the individual has to have confidence in being protected and is free from fear or anxiety (see Figure 28.2) and involves a cluster of feelings such as confidence in one's safety and feeling safe. For events, such concepts also have a distinct spatial dimension whereby the spaces occupied by events need to be places characterised by safety and security so that distinct geographies of insecurity do not develop. Studies by Crompton and McKay (1997)

Figure 28.2 Red alert: the ArcelorMlttal Orbit, designer, Anish Kapoor – a representation of the complex and recycled scaffolding of security

Source: London 2012

and Crompton (2003) highlight the importance of safety as one of the motives associated with event attendance, which was also reaffirmed in other studies such as Kim's (2004) examination of the FIFA World Cup.

Where issues of fear and threats exist, particularly underlying states of alert associated with terrorism, this can cause a sense of increased anxiety, especially where travel is required to access an event location in a busy urban environment. However, a study undertaken after the 9/11 attacks by Taylor and Toohey (2006), examining the 2003 Rugby World Cup, found that increased security measures did not adversely affect the experience of the event. Ultimately, the analysis of event safety and security issues are associated with the interconnections between the three perspectives identified in terms of the operations management process and safety management, the destination and visitor experience. But attempts to map out a more conceptual and theoretical agenda to understand these issues in the tourism field (which have an important application to the event literature) by Pizam and Mansfeld (2006), as summarised in Figure 28.3, indicate that there are three perspectives that need to be incorporated into any theorising of the tourism–safety nexus: the nature of security-related incidents that affect tourists (and event attendees); the impact of these upon the tourism or event industry; and the impact on tourism or event stakeholders.

From a safety and security perspective, the presence of large numbers of visitors at events may establish an environment that epitomises the concentration of people (residents, event attendees

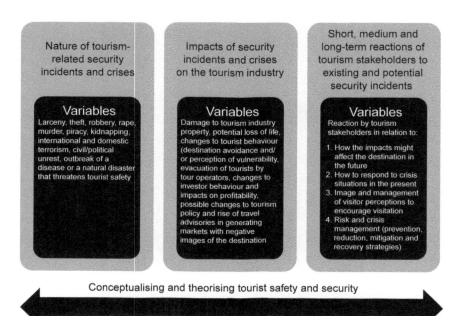

Nature of tourism-related security incidents and crises	Impacts of security incidents and crises on the tourism industry	Short, medium and long-term reactions of tourism stakeholders to existing and potential security incidents
Variables Larceny, theft, robbery, rape, murder, piracy, kidnapping, international and domestic terrorism, civil/political unrest, outbreak of a disease or a natural disaster that threatens tourist safety	**Variables** Damage to tourism industry property, potential loss of life, changes to tourist behaviour (destination avoidance and/or perception of vulnerability, evacuation of tourists by tour operators, changes to investor behaviour and impacts on profitability, possible changes to tourism policy and rise of travel advisories in generating markets with negative images of the destination	**Variables** Reaction by tourism stakeholders in relation to: 1. How the impacts might affect the destination in the future 2. How to respond to crisis situations in the present 3. Image and management of visitor perceptions to encourage visitation 4. Risk and crisis management (prevention, reduction, mitigation and recovery strategies)

Conceptualising and theorising tourist safety and security

Figure 28.3 Conceptualising tourism safety and security: the three domains and illustrations of associated variables
Source: Developed from Pizam and Mansfeld (2006).

and tourists) with opportunities for crime. Such outcomes have become major planning and security consideration within destinations that host major events, which we will return to later in the chapter. Yet as Barker and Page (2002) observed, there is also a notable lack of research on visitor behaviour at urban destinations during special events. This lack of understanding also applies to visitor perceptions of personal safety during special events. Research on tourist perceptions of safety at destinations during their travel exist (e.g. Demos 1992; Pinhey and Iverson 1994), but few studies report the impacts of visitors' perceptions and experiences of crime and personal safety during special events. This is not surprising given the political economy of events and media reporting to seek to promote a positive image of the event and destination. Such concerns tend to be downplayed and are not attractive areas for research studies by the public sector. A new interesting development emerging from the travel medicine literature on the safety issues associated with infectious diseases spreading at major events such as rock festivals (e.g. Botelho-Nevers *et al.* 2010) and the Hajj (Ebrahim *et al.* 2009; Haworth *et al.* 2010; Khan *et al.* 2010), which has certainly not been a mainstream area of concern for events and destinations prior to the 2008 influenza pandemic. In fact, such concern has not been expressed in relation to the hosting of mega events and the spread of disease since the 1918 influenza pandemic when public meetings were cancelled as a means of trying to stop the spread of the virus through human-to-human contact in crowded areas (Barry 2005). This was a feature which was considered as a contingency in the 2009 influenza pandemic in some countries if the virus escalated the scale of deaths and disruption, and highlights one area of risk assessment that emerged as a response to a major health crisis (Page *et al.* 2006).

Where purpose-built event facilities have been provided for the staging and hosting of events as part of urban regeneration strategies, implicit in the urban design is the need to improve visitor safety, from the situation discussed by Page and Connell (2010) in relation to the use of the street as a leisure resource (which can accommodate events). An improvement in physical safety is often initiated as a result of these developments, since improved lighting and clean and well-maintained surroundings are commonly associated with safety within urban environments (Barker 2000) as well as the positive contribution towards improving visitor perceptions of safety and personal security. In assessing the impacts, Barker and Page (2002) highlighted that perceptions of safety can affect a person's behaviour, including the likelihood of going out at certain times of the day, participation in activities and the overall satisfaction with an event and destination. According to Barker (2000), safety during the daytime was perceived among tourists to be very safe, although this perception declined, as expected, at night, particularly among domestic tourists and women based on research undertaken in New Zealand. Consequently as events are not necessarily staged at times of the day which are correlated with the perceived safest times (e.g. daylight and daytime as opposed to night-time), then staging events in areas which are perceived as safe is key to maximising participation by all social groups and visitor types.

In addition to the factors affecting perceptions of safety, the social changes that occur during events can thereby affect visitors' perceptions of personal safety and their likelihood of attending an event. As Barker and Page (2002) suggested, perceptions of crime and safety are influenced by a person's conditioning to safety, the image portrayed of a destination, and the way in which the media influence perceptions of risk that can affect tourism visitation and restrict behaviour based on the nature and level of reporting of crime. In this sense, perceptions of safety provide visitors with subjective reality. Yet there is evidence from Koskela and Pain (2000) that there are inherent problems in designing out fear from the urban environment where events may be staged, given the extent to which fear of crime pervades city spaces. Cybriwsky (1999) recognised the trend associated with the growth in the surveillance of public spaces to address such security concerns associated with public perceptions of insecurity. Whilst this may improve security, it also has an implicit shift of public activity to private spaces, such as shopping malls, and attempts to modify social behaviour in recreational spaces, particularly those where events are staged. This is a feature which Giddens (1990: 20) recognised, whereby 'surveillance is a means of levering the modern social world away from traditional modes of social activity'. The rise of surveillance has been a consequence of urban environments seeking to address growing concerns over citizens' (let alone visitors') concerns of safety and security along with more theoretical explanations of how these changes have come about (Henry 2009). According to Henry (2009: 95), 'surveillance' can be defined as the organised monitoring of the activities of actors in order to produce personal data. One of the hallmarks of the growing surveillance of post-modern cities is the rise of CCTV to address issues of security and safety and, as Henry (2009: 97) suggests,

> CCTV has been often cited as an example of the creeping pervasiveness of panoptic logics and disciplinary power into the spaces of everyday life. Here, urban geographers in particular have traced the explosive rise in the use of these electronic technologies as tools of urban ordering. Notwithstanding the disquiet of geographers, CCTV systems are now a ubiquitous, indeed banal, feature of urban public places, private workplaces, shops, and increasingly rural spaces. In understanding the implications of CCTV on public spaces, geographers have argued that CCTV itself is only one manifestation of broader processes of (re)ordering. In particular the deployment of CCTV systems has occurred in contexts marked by concerns over the existence of city spaces (especially inner city spaces) as economic spaces. In promising improved security CCTV has been touted as a necessary adjunct to the economic revitalisation of urban spaces.

437

For event organisers, CCTV may be a useful tool in at least increasing perceptions of safety for event participants. As a significant amount of CCTV is located in urban environments, an element of surveillance is likely to impact upon places where events are hosted, which may result in an increased sense of security, and a potential deterrent to those engaging in criminal activities. However, CCTV is seen by critics as a worrying feature and has recently been criticised as failing to deter crime while not addressing the underlying causes and symptoms of perceptions of insecurity. Accordingly, its effect is perhaps somewhat arguable.

Events have an important impact on the resident population of the destination hosting the event. As Barker and Page (2002) argued, a number of studies have examined the perceived impact of crime on the community (e.g. Pizam 1978; Rothman 1978; Snaith and Haley 1994; Lankford 1996) and some studies have indicated that this has expanded through the rise of a visitor population, which will expand temporarily with an event. As Barker and Page (2002: 274) suggested,

> research on residents' perceptions of crime and safety in the presence of tourism have found that residents often perceived a decline in the level of safety as a result of an influx of tourists (Pizam 1978; Rothman 1978). There is also research on community behaviour and reaction to increased tourism activity (e.g. Brown and Giles 1994; Dogan 1989).

It is interesting that within Tourism Studies a growing recognition of these impacts has spawned studies that examine residents' perceptions of special events on the host community (e.g. Ritchie and Lyons 1990; Soutar and McLeod 1993). Barker and Page (2002) found that in urban areas, safety and security issues are significant because tourists and tourist areas possess a range of characteristics that make them vulnerable to crime (Chesney-Lind and Lind 1986). There is also evidence that such safety issues also affect rural areas (see Park and Stokowski 2008) where tourism is a growing sector of the economy, as well as in African national parks (George 2010). These have particular salience for Event Studies because the research show that where event attendees are tourists, tourists have a statistically higher chance of being victims of crime than residents (e.g. Fujii and Mak 1980; de Albuquerque and McElroy 1999; Jackson and Schmierer 1996). However, as Barker and Page (2002) suggest, such claims are more likely to be specific to destinations in which these studies were conducted than as an all-encompassing relationship.

One of the particular features of event areas located in cities is that they often have an enclave nature which can contribute to the spatial concentration of tourists and criminal opportunities (Schiebler et al. 1996), although they also have the capacity to create visitor-friendly environments that are more effectively policed. As Barker and Page (2002) concur, such areas that are conducive to crime are consistent with what Ryan and Kinder (1996) termed a 'crimogenic place'. Consequently, Barker and Page (2002) suggest that the impact of crime can be compounded during special events where the destination's carrying capacity may be reached or exceeded and the impacts can be event-specific, which means they are difficult to anticipate when hosting events. Indeed, evidence suggests that if the site is over-secured attackers may change tactics, or move to softer, less-secured targets or a different event, or choose a different time to strike (see Smith et al. 2003). Consequently, in terms of event management, this agile responsiveness by would-be attackers or criminals means that it becomes more critical to ensure that the risk-management strategy is fit for purpose. Therefore, with these issues in mind, attention now turns to the London Olympics and safety and security matters, since London's status as a world city makes it an obvious target for criminal activity. Given London's long history of terrorist attacks, safety and security are a high-profile issue for the 2012 Games, for the teams competing as well as the expected international audience.

Security and 2012

As a starting point, policy responses and the security situation on the ground are discussed as a backdrop to the case studies. In the UK, as in many countries, security is increasingly delivered by a combination of both public and private agencies and more recently through public–private partnerships. A degree of tension exists between the sectors and this will be explored briefly. It is pertinent to start by briefly examining the structural conditions that brought the change from public to private and to partnership security in the late twentieth century. This shift was largely as a result of privatisation in response to increased levels of terrorist activities and organised crime, globalisation and demilitarisation (Gill 2006). Sociologists such as Ulrich Beck and Anthony Giddens identified concerns about globalisation in the 1990s, which they suggested resulted in feelings of uncertainty and insecurity in post-modern societies; one outcome they called the risk society (Beck 1992; Giddens 1999). Almost at the same time in the early 1990s, the cold war ended and many former armies were demobilised, including the army in Afghanistan. Former President of Pakistan General Pervez Musharraf commented on the significance of these events in Afghanistan, and said there was 'no rehabilitation of 25,000–30,000 armed Mujahedeen [they] were not resettled; they are now Al-Qaida' (Wylde and Khawaja 2010). Many commentators suggest that subsequent actions by Al-Qaida or Jihadist terrorists have their roots in this period (Cooley 2002). What is significant for us to recognise is the shift in tactics of the terrorist attackers, the focus is no longer on government but on economic privately owned and softer targets, in particular in crowded places or public spaces, such as Times Square in New York or nightclubs in London, or in sites of mass transit such as in Moscow Airport, Glasgow Airport or on the Madrid and London's Metro Underground, all of which experienced serious attacks or foiled attacks. It is also notable that although some attacks may be unsuccessful or are foiled and deemed to be geographically remote, there are still economic impacts: typically a short-term fall in value in stock market prices followed by a recovery (see, for example, OECD 2002; Saxton 2002; Mullins and Garvey 2010).

Returning to focus on the situation of private security in the UK, some have suggested that national security and corporate security have traditionally had different motives, with 'national security focused on protecting a country's population while corporate security was focused on the bottom line' (Stapley *et al.* cited in Gill 2006: 36). At the time of privatisation, police concerns over possible job losses as well as criticisms against private firms in particular over accountability, motives and capabilities (Wakefield 2003; Gill 2006). This situation has recently moved towards one of partnership. For example, the City of London Police found there was a lack of coordinated responses to emergency incidents by security teams in multi-tenanted buildings to emergency incidents and that this was compounded by the dense and transient populations in offices in the City of London (COLP 2010).

To overcome this, Project Griffin was established in 2004 by the City of London and London Metropolitan Police, to bring together the 'Police, local authorities, private sector security industry, the emergency services and other agencies to coordinate efforts by working together to deter, disrupt and support pro-active operations regarding terrorist/extremist activity within the local area' (www.cityoflondon.police.uk/CityPolice/Departments/CT/Project-Griffin/). The project has now been adopted by airports and police forces in areas around the UK, as well as abroad in Canada and Australia. These recent developments highlight a shift to mutual trust and genuine partnership working; the private sector will be the largest delivery agent for the 2012 Games (R-15)[1] and the importance of this is considered next.

At a policy level, the UK Home Office, Office for Security and Counter-Terrorism's counter-terrorism office is responsible for strategy. The current strategy CONTEST, devised in

2003, is under review by the coalition government and due to report in spring 2011. CON-TEST considers that 'the most significant security threat to the people of the UK today [is] from international terrorism' and aims to 'reduce the risk to the UK and its interests overseas, so that people can go about their lives freely and with confidence' (Home Office 2010a). CON-TEST is based on four interlinked strategies:

- Pursue – to stop terrorist attacks.
- Prevent – to stop people from becoming terrorists or supporting violent extremism.
- Protect – to strengthen our protection against terrorist attack.
- Prepare – where an attack cannot be stopped, to mitigate its impact.

The Security and Counter-Terrorism, Olympic and Paralympics Security Directorate (OSD) is responsible for the Olympic security strategy and for monitoring its actions and budgets. The OSD Security Strategy aims to protect the 2012 Games from all types of risk, including terrorism, to ensure a 'safe and secure Games', stating that the UK has a track record of 'successfully hosting major events safely and securely'; 'one of the reasons that the UK won the Olympic bid in the first place' (Home Office 2010a). An important note is the focus on 'protecting the Games', since the Games are not simply staged at one venue but geographically dispersed across different venues and locations. For the UK, this is a particular challenge as many of the major events or celebrations held or sporting events have not been of this scale (apart from the Manchester Commonwealth Games) so this poses a security challenge that goes beyond London. In light of home-grown criminal–terrorist gangs, and actions such as the London 7/7, the CONTEST focus on 'international terrorism' is redefined by the London 2012 Olympic and Paralympics Safety and Security Strategic Risk Assessment (Home Office 2010b). In this freely available and unclassified strategy, key threats are identified as: terrorism; serious and organised crime; domestic extremism; public disorder; and natural events. It is important to recognise the separation between terrorism and domestic extremism, where terrorism is focused on attacks on crowded places, mass transport and non-conventional attacks possibly through the chemical, biological, radiological and nuclear (CBRN) weapons or materials and domestic extremism encompasses a wide range of single-issue groups or individuals (Home Office 2010b). Domestic extremism is 'most commonly associated with "single-issue" protests, such as animal rights, environmentalism, anti-globalisation or anti-GM crops. Crime and public disorder linked to extreme left- or right-wing political campaigns is also considered domestic extremism.' Tactics range from 'public disorder offences, malicious letters and e-mails, blackmail, product contamination, damage to property and occasionally the use of improvised explosive devices and associating closely with legitimate campaigners' (www.netcu.org.uk). The specifics of the strategy build on CONTEST: Protect; Prepare; Identify and Disrupt; Command, Control, Plan and Resource; and Engage. It is important at this juncture to note the new additional strands that include responses. For our discussions, we note that enforcement of these actions will often be undertaken by the private sector partners, as mentioned for the 2012 Games, since the private sector will control most of the resources (R-15).

One respondent in the survey of private security firms suggested there is too much 'information in the public domain, the time-lapse footage and photos of the construction of the Olympic Stadium is a case in point', see Figure 28.4 (R-29): a possible new tension in terms of degree of transparency. One key point to note is that the threat landscape is evolving rapidly and risks may be exacerbated by modern technology, for example cyber-crime, identity theft and the social networks Twitter and Facebook. Recent events in London, the US and Australia, facilitated by social networks, resulted in civil disorder and arrests, the case of student protests in the UK in 2010 and the cancellations of concerts and injury in the US and Australia in 2010. One example is of pop idol Justin Bieber who was forced to cancel concerts as fans arrived rapidly and in large numbers as a result of real-time coordination through using social networks. In one case at a shopping mall in Long Island, a shop was swamped with fans who had mistakenly been informed that Bieber was present. In an interesting twist, Bieber's manager was arrested because he failed, when ordered by police to 'tweet to say the event was cancelled' (see, for example, Kaufman 2010). This is a new development in terms of both the shift in risk and in action from a public body (the police) to a private individual (Bieber's manager). No evidence can be found at present for the use of the social networks by authorities or through a third party to control the movements or fans or visitors, which we will return to in the conclusion. The next section focuses on private security firms and the London Games, highlighting the size and structure of the industry.

Private security firms and the London 2012 Games

To investigate the relationship between private security firms and the 2012 Games, key themes from case studies are highlighted next. These are based on primary research undertaken in London during 2009–11 through in-depth interviews, of between sixty and ninety minutes, with thirty-two senior managers of security firms and chief security officers (some were interviewed more than once) of large companies, part of a larger set of interviews with security companies involved with the 2012 Games. The findings also draw on secondary published and electronic text sources including company annual reports, websites and trade body industry information websites.

The security industry and events

A key comment made several times was that the 'security industry is not well defined' (R-4, R-9, R-29), surprisingly similar to the situation for mega events as discussed in the early chapters in this book, where typologies do not adequately accommodate the diversity of event experiences.

As a start to understand the economic significance of the industry and its global scale is illustrated by forecasts that the 'global outlay on Homeland Security will reach $295 billion by 2018, current estimates of the total global security market are around £243 billion' (Info4security 2010). This compares with 2008 when estimates were of £177 billion, of which the UK market was worth £7.4 billion (Key Note 2009). The key trend in the global security industry is one of market concentration, and the UK is no exception to this with six large companies accounting for almost 50 per cent of the UK business; many smaller companies are under pressure from such competition and several specialist security firms have recently been bought by large companies (Key Note 2010).

The UK Trade and Investment, Defence and Security Organisation was launched in 2010 and aims to capitalise and promote the UK security industry globally (Info4security 2010). The UK has expertise in managing events and in particular managing the security aspect of world sports events, for example the Beijing 2008 Olympic and Paralympics Games, the 2010 FIFA World Cup South Africa and London 2012. The expertise across the event and sports sectors includes services and products and the manufacturing of specialist screening, biometrics and electronics equipment; see Figure 28.2 for details (Key Note 2010). Therefore, as the UK has a global position in the event safety and security industry, its analysis is particularly pertinent as the following case study shows.

Case study analysis: security firms and the 2012 Olympics

Key examples presented from the interviews are used to illustrate innovations. Different types (technological and non-technological innovations) were found in different industry sectors – uncovering these may provide evidence of the effects of working on events for security firms. Different types of technology and non-technology innovations are explored next. Technological innovations include new products and patents; these were found in the ICT and high-technology (high-tech) security sectors; examples included crisis-reporting applications (Apps) for BlackBerry devices, risk and continuity assessment software and new biometric technologies. In a specific example, as a result of experience gained through working on previous Olympic Games and FIFA World Cup projects, a firm was able to develop a new crowd safety technology system for the FIFA World Cup 2010 in South Africa; this example involved a strategic partnership with a specialist manufacturer (Info4security 2011). Many other non-technology innovations were also identified; the next section focuses on these innovations.

The first example concerns innovations in business operations: We agreed to be different from the rest, [we established] the 42–48-hour roster, [which] pre-dated the legislation. We believed there was a gap in the market … we're proud to be the only company' (R14). This firm, a manned guarding firm, developed a new approach, a 42–48-hour working week for staff, as compared with the 60-hour working week used by the majority of companies. Although this initially appeared more expensive than the competition, clients were assured of the benefits which included knowledge that the service was in line with proposed EU legislation, the Working Time Directive was subsequently adopted (European Parliament 2003). This way of working, although financially risky, is arguably, an example of a service innovation. Additionally, by being ahead of the competition, this innovation resulted in the firm regularly winning new business, including a significant manned-guarding contract with the 2012 Games.

Another important area for innovation is through individuals acquiring and sharing knowledge, as the following examples show. In the first example, former colleagues share knowledge: 'I"ll pick up the phone and ask What"s the situation out there"?' (R-4). This is an example of access to high-level information which may not readily be available in the public domain. The second example concerns knowledge practices between the firms and clients 'They tell us quite a bit … we sit down and talk about it … we get chatting … [they tell me] we're trying to…' (R-1). Arguably, sharing confidential information gives the firm a timely opportunity and advantage which could result in wining new business.

Two further examples reveal information used during procurement. '[We] have to prioritise … [I"ve] been around the block … [and] use benchmarks SLAs [service level agreements] and KPIs [key performance indicators], if the service is good there is no need to change' (R-9). In this example, an on-the-job problem-solving type innovation, results in the procurement process being adjusted. Many firms are locked into automatic re-tender/procurement processes; this agile response brings the firm a cost-saving advantage. Another example concerning knowledge is through using an original idea: 'I saw something a bit different, the [government] office had one contract with thirteen sub–projects, I took a different view … there was confusion in the control room.' 'I looked at it as it was, then … made it better' (R-16). This example, one of several, from this respondent reveals an innovation which, in this instance, resulted in the firm acquiring new business.

Finally, an example based on the crisis room is presented. The crisis room is specific to the security and emergency sector. When a crisis or major incident event occurs, experts drawn from a range of business security, risk and continuity sectors together with the emergency services are brought together to work through crisis and continuity plans. Examples of a combination of high levels of problem-solving were found.

> I got the incoming call at 8:48, London Transport were in full evac [evacuation] mode, I went to the CEO ... I had complete support of the board ... it took xx minutes, [the response time (xx not shown here) was logged] until I gave the call for us to evac [during 7/7, the London terrorist attack].
>
> *(R-22)*

> We've got offices globally and strategies for each country and good working relationships with each team...
>
> *(R-9)*

> I was on the ground in eight hours going through our... [after terrorist attack on an aircraft].
>
> *(R-29)*

These examples all demonstrate high levels of fast original problem-solving which arguably may lead to innovations. In addition, the presence of team-working and close interactions between different sectors, working through a set of complex problems under extreme time pressures, lends further opportunities for knowledge exchange, learning and arguably more innovation.

Implications for event management

Preliminary evidence from the interviews indicated examples of high-technology product and ICT innovation as well as other types of innovation, including new organisational and business forms and, importantly, original approaches and on-the-job problem-solving, and the creation of one-off solutions for problems (NESTA 2007). The findings also demonstrate the access to real-time information and knowledge which may not be in the public domain or that may be difficult to find. Information transfer was frictionless and backed up by cultural norms which eased communication: 'we speak the same language' (R-4). In the crisis situation, innovation was detected, individuals learned on the job and came up with new solutions, possibly, because the 'unthinkable' had happened (Bessant and Tidd 2007: 233). Studies by Brück *et al.* (2010) found positive and significant impacts on business creation as a result of terrorist attacks. To summarise, it is suggested here that the elevated and changing risk environment associated with mega events, together with their requirements for new and rapid solutions, may play a key role as a driver of innovation.

To summarise, these findings illustrate dimensions of innovation demonstrating what Thrift (2000) calls issues of speed and time pressures faced by managers. Finally, limitations and possible future directions are presented. Limitations in the research are acknowledged; thirty-two interviews cannot give a complete picture so additional studies are underway to broaden the depth and breadth of understanding, along with a large-scale questionnaire which will be used to triangulate and build validity. Therefore whilst this analysis is still at an exploratory stage, it does highlight the fast-moving nature of the

Figure 28.4 The London 2012 Olympic Stadium

security sector and the challenges it faces with respect to mega events, especially in terms of global terrorism. In relation to the framework we present earlier in the paper (Figure 28.4), it is evident that the safety and security sectors has been neglected in the analysis of key stakeholders impacting upon the changes occurring in event management, especially the technological application of solutions to address issues such as terrorism.

A number of future directions for future research can be identified. First, the question of what constitutes safety and security was raised; no clear definition exists in the literature on event management as the safety area blurs with the security dimensions. Although this study revealed some indications of innovation in the security industry and some possible effects of mega events, these two areas require further investigation.

Finally, there appears to be an increase in the number and complexity of crisis events: 9/11 in the USA in 2001; 7/7 in the UK in 2005; 26/11 in Mumbai, India, 2008; volcanic ash across NE Europe in 2010; the floods in Queensland, Australia; a lone right wing extremist in Norway; and the London street-mob riots; all during 2011. At the same time there is the increase in the numbers of global and regional sporting and mega events. What is clear is the important role of innovations in meeting the new demands of this complicated and rapidly changing future environment and it may be that understanding how innovations are created in the event sector, this example looked at security firms, can be extended and applied to other sectors to help build resilience.

Conclusion

This chapter has only provided a generic treatment of the safety and security issues facing the event sector and those who attend events. It is evident that there is considerable research to be undertaken to expand our knowledge and horizons of the safety–security nexus in mega events, with the evidence of growing challenges to the staging of such events in a safe and secure manner. As much of the research evidence is predominantly located within tourism in relation to visitor safety and management science in relation to safety as a process to be applied to events, a greater synthesis of these perspectives is required over and above 'how to' manuals. Emery's (2010) analysis of events and the management problems associated with staging is sufficient justification for strengthening research knowledge in this area so that it is disseminated more fully into events management education and to the events industry. At a destination level, there is a greater need for a more holistic understanding of the footprint of event visitors so that the wider safety and security concerns can be understood in a holistic and meaningful manner as opposed to being segmented into specific areas such as safety, security or health and safety concerns at venues. There is a greater need to understand the event period within the destination, and the analogy from supply-chain analysis is to look at the supply of event-related services and facilities and to understand the visitor's interaction with them when designing a safety and security strategy.

One project of several currently underway is focused on the emergence of standards and governance in the security industry; the first author (director of the Security Industry Observatory) is co-chair of the American Society for Industrial Security (ASIS) Committee on the Standard for Physical Asset Protection, which will be adopted by the American National Standards Institute, and a committee member of the new British Standards Institute (BSI) standard for Societal Security in the UK. Involvement with these committees gives an industry perspective and understanding of some of the complex issues faced by senior individuals, not least the increased risks of litigation: as one respondent said, staff coming to work 'expect to be safe' (R-22). Visitors also attend events and expect to be safe and secure, and the burden of responsibility is now on the private sector; if an incident occurs and the company or agent is found negligent, litigation, corporate manslaughter and irreparable damage to brand reputation result. The question is raised: are event managers, venue owners or agents adequately advised, prepared or insured? The modern event space is a complex and transient web of contractual agreements and the issue of where final responsibility rests is made even more difficult to interpret.

There is certainly a greater need to link the disparate fields of safety management and crowd management with research on tourism and crime alongside the accident and injury literature for events and to consider the way in which the growing networked society can be developed as an important strand of future research. Social networking has emerged as an important area that requires both theorising and understanding. It is only belatedly being understood within tourism (see Page 2011) and its integration into event-related research is certainly overdue, especially in relation to creating safe environments for events. Questions posed include: how can networks be used for communicating basic and critical information, and to update Smith *et al.* (2003) on electronic guardians? As mentioned earlier, in light of attackers' ability to change venue, time and strategy, how can event organisers respond to this? Can social networks be used defensively? Can they help create fit-for-purpose threat assessments and crisis management strategies? In times of crisis, can social networks communicate with, for example, visitors or customers – the volcanic ash incident across the northern hemisphere in early 2010 is a case in point? Or can social networks be used as an alternative – as we have all experienced 'network not available'?

Acknowledgements

The pilot study for this research was funded by the London Development Agency Secondment into Knowledge Programme (2007–8). Subsequent funding was through the Higher Education Innovation Fund (HEIF4 2008–11), and London Metropolitan University established the Security Industry Observatory; Allison Wylde is the Director.

Notes

1 R refers to the respondent interviewed and discussed in the case study which follows of private security firms and the 2012 London Olympic and Paralympic Games. The names and details of the respondents are anonymised for reasons of confidentiality.

References

Abbott, J. and Geddie, M. (2000) 'Event and venue management: minimising liability through effective crowd management techniques', *Event Management* 6(4): 259–70.

Anderson, B. (2010) 'Security and the future: anticipating the event of terror', *Geoforum* 41: 227–35.

Andranovich, G., Burbank, M.J. and Heying, C.H. (2001) 'Olympic cities: lessons learned from mega event politics', *Journal of Urban Affairs* 23(2): 113–31.

Barker, M. (2000) 'An empirical investigation of tourist crime in New Zealand: perceptions, victimisation and future implications', unpublished PhD thesis, Centre for Tourism, University of Otago, Dunedin, New Zealand.

Barker, M. and Page, S.J. (2002) 'Visitor safety in urban environments', *Cities: The International Journal of Urban Policy and Planning* 19(4): 273–82

Barker, M., Page, S.J. and Meyer, D.H. (2002) 'Modelling the tourism–crime nexus', *Annals of Tourism Research* 29(3): 762–82.

——(2003) 'Tourist safety and the urban environment', in J. Wilks and S.J. Page (eds) *Managing Tourist Health and Safety*, Oxford: Elsevier, pp. 197–214.

Barry, J. (2005) *The Great Influenza: The Epic Story of the Deadliest Plague in History*, London: Penguin.

BBC News (2010) 'London 2012 Olympics may pay more in security costs', 10 February 2010. Available at: http://news.bbc.co.uk/1/hi/business/8507768.stm (accessed 12 January 2011).

Beck, U. (1992) *Risk Society: Towards a New Modernity*, New Delhi: Sage.

Bentley, T. and Page, S.J. (2008) 'A decade of injury monitoring in the New Zealand adventure tourism sector: a summary risk analysis', *Tourism Management* 29(5): 857–69.

Bessant, J. and Tidd, J. (2007) *Innovation and Entrepreneurship*, Chichester: John Wiley and Sons.

Botelho-Nevers, E., Gautret, P. Benarous, L. Charrel, R. Felkai, P. and Parola, P. (2010) 'Travel-related influenza A/H1N1 infection at a rock festival in Hungary: one virus may hide another one', *Journal of Travel Medicine* 17(3): 197–8.

Botterill, D. and Jones, T. (eds) (2010) *Tourism and Crime: Key Themes*, Oxford: Goodfellow Publishers.

Brown, G. and Giles, R. (1994) 'Coping with tourism: an examination of resident responses to the social impact of tourism', in A.V. Seaton (ed.) *Tourism: The State of the Art*, Chichester: John Wiley and Sons, pp. 755–64.

Brück, T., Llussá, F. and Tavares, J. (2010) 'Perceptions, expectations, and entrepreneurship: the role of extreme events', CEPR Discussion Papers 8098, CEPR.

Business Visits and Events Partnership (2010) *Britain for Events: A Report on the Size and Value of Britain's Events Industry, its Characteristics, Trends, Opportunities and Key Issues*, London: Business Visits and Events Partnership.

Chesney-Lind, M. and Lind, I.Y. (1986) 'Visitors as victims: crimes against tourists in Hawaii', *Annals of Tourism Research* 13: 167–91.

COLP (2010) *Project Griffin*, City of London Police Force. Available at: www.cityoflondon.police.uk/CityPolice/Departments/CT/ProjectGriffin/ (accessed 25 January 2011).

Cooley, J.K. (2002) *Unholy Wars: Afghanistan, America and International Terrorism*, New York: Pluto Press.

Crompton, J. (2003) 'Adapting Hertzberg: a conceptualisation of hygiene and motivator attributes on perception of event quality', *Journal of Travel Research* 41(3): 305–10.

Crompton, J. and McKay, S. (1997) 'Motives of visitors attending festival events', *Annals of Tourism Research* 24(2): 435–9.

Cybriwsky, R. (1999) 'Changing patterns of urban public space: observations and assessments from the Tokyo and New York metropolitan areas', *Cities: The International Journal of Urban Policy and Planning* 4: 223–31.

DCMS (2010) *Plans for the Legacy from the 2012 Olympic and Paralympic Games*, December 2010, Department for Culture Media and Sport. Available at: www.culture.gov.uk/images/publications/201210_Legacy_Publication.pdf (accessed 17 January 2011).

de Albuquerque, K. and McElroy, J. (1999) 'Tourism and crime in the Caribbean', *Annals of Tourism Research* 26(4): 968–84.

Demos, E. (1992) 'Concern for safety: a potential problem in the tourist industry', *Journal of Travel and Tourism Marketing* 1(1): 81–8.

Dogan, H.Z. (1989) 'Forms of adjustment: socio-cultural impacts of tourism', *Annals of Tourism Research* 16: 216–36.

Ebrahim, S.H., Memish, Z.A., Uyeki, T.M., Khoja, T.A.M., Marano, N. and McNabb, S.J.N. (2009) 'Pandemic H1N1 and the 2009 Hajj', *Science* 326(5955): 938–40.

Emery, P. (2010) 'Past, present, future major sport event management practice: the professional perspective', *Sport Management Review* 13: 158–70.

European Parliament (2003) 'Directive 2003/88/EC of the European Parliament and of the Council of 4 November 2003 concerning certain aspects of the organisation of working time', European Parliament.

Fruin, J. (1993) 'The causes and prevention of crowd disasters'. Available at: www.gkstill.com/Fruin.html (accessed 28 January 2011).

Fujii, E.T. and Mak, J. (1980) 'Tourism and crime: implications for regional development policy', *Regional Studies* 14: 27–36.

Fussey, P., Coaffee, J., Armstrong, G. and Hobbs, D. (2011) *Securing and Sustaining the Olympic City: Reconfiguring London for 2012 and Beyond*, London: Routledge.

George, R. (2010) 'Visitor perceptions of crime-safety and attitudes towards risk: the case of Table Mountain National Park, Cape Town', *Tourism Management* 31(6): 806–15.

Giddens, A. (1990) 'Modernity and utopia', *New Statesman and Society*, 2 November: 20–2.

——(1999) *Runaway World: How Globalization is Reshaping Our Lives*, London: Profile.

Gill, M. (eds) (2006) *The Handbook of Security*, Hampshire: Palgrave Macmillan.

Hall, C.M. (1989) 'The definition and analysis of hallmark tourist events', *GeoJournal* 19(3): 263–8.

Haworth, E., Rashid, H. and Booy, R. (2010) 'Prevention of pandemic influenza after mass gatherings – learning from Hajj', *Journal of the Royal Society of Medicine* 103(3): 79–80.

Health and Safety Executive (1999) *The Event Safety Guide: A Guide to Health, Safety and Welfare at Music and Similar Events*, London: Health and Safety Executive.

Henry, M. (2009) 'Surveillance', in R. Kitchin and N. Thrift (eds) *International Encyclopedia of Human Geography*, Oxford: Elsevier, pp. 95–9.

Home Office (2010a) *The UK Counter-Terrorism Strategy, CONTEST*. Available at: www.homeoffice.gov.uk/counter-terrorism/uk-counter-terrorism-strat/ (accessed 25 January 2011).

——(2010b) *London 2012 Olympic and Paralympic Safety and Security Strategic Risk Assessment (OSSSRA)*. Summary available at: www.homeoffice.gov.uk/publications/counter-terrorism/olympics/osssra-summary?view=Binary (accessed 25 January 2011).

Info4security (2010) *UK TIDSO Launches Marketing Strategy for Security Sector*, 7 April. SMT Online. Available at: www.info4security.com/story.asp?sectioncode=10& storycode = 4124543 (accessed 17 January 2011).

——(2011) *IP Video's the Right Match for Royal Bafokeng Stadium*, 20 January. Available at: www.info4security.com/story.asp?sectioncode=12& storycode = 4126584 (accessed 28 January 2011).

Internet Movie DataBase (2009) *Justin Bieber Fans Cause Stampede*, 21 November, 1.40 p.m., PST. Available at: www.imdb.com/news/ni1217693/ (accessed 25 January 2011).

Jackson, M.S. and Schmierer, C.L. (1996) 'Tourism and crime: more crime but less reporting', *Tourism and Hospitality Research: Australian and International Perspectives*, Australian Tourism and Hospitality Research Conference, Lismore, Australia: Southern Cross University, Lismore, pp. 549–59.

Jago, L.K. and Shaw, R.N. (1998) 'Special events: a conceptual and definitional framework', *Festival Management and Event Tourism* 5(1/2): 21–32.

Kaufman, G. (2010) *Justin Bieber Concert Cancelled In Australia Due to Crowd Stampede*, 26 April, 9.32 a.m. EDT. Available at: www.mtv.com/news/articles/1637748/justin-bieber-concert-canceled-australia-due-crowd-stampede.jhtml (accessed 26 January 2011).

Key Note (2008) *Business Ratio: The Security Industry*, London: Key Note.

——(2009) *Security Industry Market Review, Keynote Market-Intelligence Reports*, Teddington, UK: Key Note, June.

——(2010) *Market Forecasts: IT, Telecommunications and Security Market Focus*, London: Key Note, fifth edition.

Khan, K., Memish, Z.A., Chabbra, A., Liauw, J., Hu Wei, Janes, D.A., Sears, J., Arino, J., Macdonald, M., Calderon, F., Raposo, P., Heidebrecht, C., Wang Jun, Chan, A., Brownstein, J. and Gardam, M. (2010) 'Global public health implications of a mass gathering in Mecca, Saudi Arabia during the midst of an influenza pandemic', *Journal of Travel Medicine* 17(2): 75–81.

Kim, S. (2004) 'Why travel to the FIFA World Cup: effect of motives, background, interest and constraints', *Tourism Management* 25(6): 695–707.

Koskela, H. and Pain, R. (2000) 'Revisiting fear and place: women's fear of attack and the built environment', *Geoforum* 31: 269–80.

Lankford, S.V. (1996) 'Crime and tourism: a study of perceptions in the Pacific Northwest', in A. Pizam and Y. Mansfeld (eds) *Tourism, Crime and International Security Issues*, Chichester: John Wiley, pp. 51–8.

Markusen, A.R. (1999) 'National contexts and the emergence of second-tier cities', in Ann R. Markusen, Yong-Sook Lee and Sean DiGiovanna (eds) *Second-Tier Cities: Rapid Growth Beyond the Metropolis*, Minneapolis: University of Minnesota Press, pp. 65–94.

Miles, M.B and Huberman, A.M. (1994) *Qualitative Data Analysis, An Expanded Sourcebook*, London: Sage, second edition.

Mullins, M. and Garvey, J. (2010) *Radical Islamic Terrorism in the Middle East and its Direct Costs on Western Financial Markets Economics of Security Working Paper 35*, Berlin: Economics of Security. Available at: www.economics-of-security.eu/sites/default/files/WP35_Radical%20Islamic%20Terrorism%20and%20Financial%20Markets.pdf (accessed 27 January 2011).

NESTA (2007) 'Hidden innovation: how innovation happens in six "low innovation" sectors', NESTA Research Report, June, NESTA.

OECD (2002) *OECD Economic Outlook 71*. Available at: www.oecd.org/dataoecd/11/60/1935314.pdf (accessed 27 January 2011).

Page, S.J. (2011) *Tourism Management*, Elsevier: Oxford, fourth edition.

Page, S.J. and Connell, J. (2009) *Tourism: A Modern Synthesis*, London: Cengage Learning, third edition.

——(2010) *Leisure: An Introduction*, Harlow: Pearson.

Page, S.J. and Meyer, D. (1996) 'Tourist accidents: an exploratory analysis', *Annals of Tourism Research* 23 (3): 666–90.

Page, S.J., Yeoman, I., Munro, C., Connell, J. and Walker, L. (2006) 'A case study of best practice – VisitScotland's prepared response to an influenza pandemic', *Tourism Management* 27(3): 361–93.

Park, M. and Stokowski, P. (2008) 'Social disruption theory and crime in rural communities: comparisons across three levels of tourism growth', *Tourism Management* 30(6): 905–15.

Pinhey, T.K. and Iverson, T.J. (1994) 'Safety concerns of Japanese visitors to Guam', *Journal of Travel and Tourism Marketing* 3(2): 87–94.

Pizam, A. (1978) 'Tourism's impacts: the social costs to the destination community as perceived by its residents', *Journal of Travel Research* 16(4, Spring): 8–12.

Pizam, A. and Mansfeld, Y. (eds) (2006) 'Towards a theory of tourism security', in A. Pizam and Y. Mansfeld (eds) *Tourism, Security and Safety*, Oxford: Elsevier, pp. 1–27.

Pizam, A., Tarlow, P.E. and Bloom, J. (1997) 'Making tourists feel safe: whose responsibility is it?', *Journal of Travel Research* 36(1): 23–8.

Reuters (2008) *Doctors Plotted 'Wholesale Murder' in UK: Prosecutor*. Available at: http://uk.reuters.com/article/idUKTRE49848C20081009 (accessed 27 January 2011).

Ritchie, J.R. (1984) 'Assessing the impact of hallmark events: conceptual and research issues', *Journal of Travel Research* 23(1): 2–11.

Ritchie, J.R. and Lyons, M. (1990) 'Olympulse VI: a post-event assessment of resident reaction to the XV Olympic Winter Games', *Journal of Travel Research* 28(3): 14–23.

Robson, S. and Haigh, G. (2008) 'First findings from the UK Innovation Survey 2007', *Economic and Labour Market Review* 2 (4, April), Department for Innovation, Universities and Skills. Available at: www.bis.gov.uk/assets/biscore/corporate/migratedd/publications/e/elmr_apr08_robson.pdf (accessed 19 January 2011).

Roche, M. (2000) *Mega-events and Modernity: Olympics and Expos in the Growth of Global Culture*, London: Routledge.

Rothman, R.A. (1978) 'Residents and transients: community reaction to seasonal visitors', *Journal of Travel Research* 16 (Winter): 8–13.

Ryan, C. and Kinder, R. (1996) 'The deviant tourist and the crimogenic place – the case of the tourist and the New Zealand prostitute', in A. Pizam and Y. Mansfeld (eds) *Tourism, Crime and International Security Issues*, Chichester: John Wiley and Sons, pp. 23–36.

Sada, G.M. (2010) 'EXPO 2015: an impact analysis on international trade', Liuc Papers no. 232, Serie Economia e Impresa 62, March.

Saxton, J. (2002) *The Economic Costs of Terrorism*, Joint Economic Study. Available at: www.house.gov/jec/terrorism/costs.pdf (accessed 27 January 2011).

Schiebler, S.A., Crotts, J.C. and Hollinger, R.C. (1996) 'Florida tourists' vulnerability to crime', in A. Pizam and Y. Mansfeld (eds) *Tourism, Crime and International Security Issues*, Chichester: John Wiley and Sons, pp. 37–50.

Sempere, C. (2010) 'The European security industry: a research agenda', February (revised August), Economics of Security Working Paper 29.

Silvers, J. (2007) *Risk Management for Meetings and Events*, Oxford: Elsevier.

Sliverman, D. (2009) *Interpreting Qualitative Data, Methods for Analysing Talk, Text and Interaction*, London: Sage, third edition.

Smith, R.G., Wolanin, N. and Worthington, G. (2003) 'e-crime solutions and crime displacement', Australian Institute of Criminology, Trends and Issues in Crime and Crime Justice 243. Available at: www.aic.gov.au/documents/9/D/0/%7B9D0C112B-E0B5-48EE-99D2-2E82D406A6FB%7Dti243.pdf (accessed 28 January 2011).

Snaith, T. and Haley, A.J. (1994) 'Tourism's impact on host lifestyle realities', in A.V. Seaton (ed.) *Tourism: The State of the Art*, Chichester: John Wiley and Sons, pp. 826–35.

Soutar, G.N. and McLeod, B. (1993) 'Residents' perceptions on the impact of the America's Cup', *Annals of Tourism Research* 20(3): 571–82.

Stapley, C., Grillot, S. and Shaw, S. (2006) 'The study of national security values versus the study of corporate security: what can they learn from each other?', in G. Martin (ed.) *The Handbook of Security*, Aldershot: Palgrave Macmillan.

Tarlow, P. (2002) *Event Risk Management and Safety*, New York: John Wiley and Sons.

Taylor, T, and Toohey, K. (2006) 'Impacts of terrorism-related safety and security measures at a major sports event', *Event Management* 9(4): 199–209.

The Economist (2005) *After the Bombs: How Four Suicide Attacks by British Citizens Have Changed Britain*, 14 July. Available at: www.economist.com/node/4174726 (accessed 26 January 2011).

The Economist Online (2011) *Death in Domodedovo*, 24 January, 16.44. Available at: www.economist.com/blogs/easternapproaches/2011/01/terror_moscow (accessed 26 January 2011).

The Guardian (2010) *Al-Qaida May Have Lost Some Gloss, but It Has Not Been Beaten*. Available at: www.guardian.co.uk/world/2010/dec/14/al-qaida-security-review-borger (accessed 27 January 2011).

Thrift, N. (2000) 'Performing cultures in the new economy', *Annals of the Association of American Geographers* 4: 674–92.

Travis, A.S. and Croize, J.C. (1987) 'The role and impact of mega-events and attractions on tourism development in Europe', paper presented at the 37th AIEST Congress (Association Internationale d'Experts Scientifiques du Turisme), Calgary.

UKTI/ DSO (2010) 'The UK Trade & Investment Defence & Security Organisation (UKTI DSO) support for companies through a range of services', *UKTI/DSO Website*, available at: www.ukti.gov.uk/defencesecurity/security/uktidsooverseasmarketingguides.html (accessed 11 May 2011).

Wakefield, A. (2003) *Selling Security: The Private Policing of Public Space*, Abingdon: Willan Publishing.

Walker, L. and Page, S.J. (2003) 'Risks, rights and responsibilities in tourist well-being: who should manage visitor well-being at destinations?', in J. Wilks and S.J. Page (eds) *Managing Tourist Health and Safety*, Oxford: Elsevier, pp. 215–36.

Wylde, A. and Khawaja, A.K. (2010) 'On leadership in Afghanistan', presentation by former President General Pervez Musharraf, at the House of Lords, Whitehall, London, Tuesday 23 February, ASIS Newsletter, Spring. Available at: www.asis.org.uk/newsletters/ASIS%20Spring%202010.pdf (accessed 26 January 2011).

Yin, R. (2009) *Case Study Research, Design and Methods*, London: Sage, fourth edition.

29

Quantitative and qualitative research tools in events

Richard Shipway, Leo Jago and Marg Deery

Introduction

This chapter explores some of the research tools associated with qualitative and quantitative research. The chapter argues that both approaches can be used by researchers; the choice is dictated by the aim of research and the data to be collected. The strained relationship between qualitative and quantitative research, it is argued, is a thing of the past, and it is widely accepted in the academic community that the two approaches are complementary, providing different perspectives on the key research issues. The chapter will suggest that the two approaches can be used to provide answers and interpretations to the same questions. Indeed, in a single project, a mixed-methods approach is increasingly being adopted, whereby the researcher gathers both qualitative and quantitative data. This is referred to as the third paradigm and it is used by researchers to provide a more comprehensive assessment of a research issue than can be provided by a single research approach. Nevertheless, there is a bias in the literature on events and festivals towards quantitative research that this chapter hopes to redress, by encouraging the adoption of qualitative research, where appropriate.

At the centre of any quantitative–qualitative discussion is the philosophical debate that many qualitative researchers operate under different epistemological assumptions from quantitative researchers. Whilst there may be intense and fundamental disagreement about both philosophical assumptions and the nature of data being collected, this chapter will explore many of these issues and suggest that social science research, especially in the domain of events and festivals, is richer for the wide variety of views and methods that the debate generates.

In the context of quantitative methods in the area of events and festival research, this chapter will explore the use of questionnaires and debate some of the key issues related to problems of sampling, scales and the extent to which various dimensions can be measured. The focus will then move to an examination of qualitative methods of enquiry, and illustrate, through published research, two qualitative tools: interviewing and participant observation. Finally, the chapter will address the challenges and opportunities represented by the adoption of the mixed-methods approach.

Quantitative research methods

Robson (2008: 19) argues that 'quantitative methods have dominated tourism research for many years, so it should come as no surprise that they are prominent in event industry research'. This is true, although as indicated in the Introduction, there is a growing movement away from a purely quantitative approach to a more mixed-methods framework of research design. When discussing quantitative research, it is important to understand why this approach has been so widely adopted, what comprises quantitative research and when should it be used as the preferred approach.

In event and festival research, a quantitative approach is generally adopted in order to assess, if not understand, the motives, attitudes, satisfaction, behaviour (including expenditure) and future intentions of event and festival attendees. This approach is associated with post-positivism as discussed by, for example, Creswell *et al.* (2003). Quantitative research has also been used to assess the impact of events and festivals on the local community. These data are generally obtained via a survey of a sample of the appropriate population or in some cases a census using a carefully designed questionnaire. Although the questionnaire is the key 'tool of the trade' for quantitative researchers, the design and administration process adopted in its application needs to be very carefully considered as inadequate processes put into question the results obtained.

Questionnaire design

Without doubt, the design of the questionnaire is fundamental to the success of the quantitative research; if the questionnaire does not ask the relevant questions in relation to the overall objective of the study or if the questions are not clear to respondents, then the data obtained will be flawed. As a starting point in the design of the questionnaire, it must be clear what data are needed in order to address the overall objectives of the study. In questionnaire design, there is often a temptation to add questions that would be 'nice to know' but are not fundamental to the study at hand. Falling to this temptation leads to questionnaires that are too long, thereby impinging on respondents' time and generally resulting in lower response rates (Dillman *et al.* 2009). As many questionnaires used to collect data in the events and festivals area require that the data be collected during the event, it is even more important that the questionnaire is not too long as completing this task is taking the respondent away from enjoying the event and festival experience.

Ensuring that the questionnaire has the required validity and reliability is important to obtaining data that will address the overall research objectives with the appropriate confidence. As there is an art in ensuring the validity and reliability of questionnaires, as described Zikmund (2003) among others, it is best to use established questions and scales whenever possible. In event and festivals research, there are studies that do not attempt to substantiate the questions and scales that have been used to show that they are measuring the 'right thing' in a 'replicable' fashion. In order to address this issue, it is important that quantitative researchers become more familiar with questionnaire design via recognised research methods texts prior to designing questionnaires in order to enhance the credibility of the data obtained.

Choosing appropriate scales for respondents to answer the various questions is an important decision that is often overlooked in the design of a questionnaire. To decide on appropriate answers, options or scales for the various parts of the questionnaire requires a clear under-standing of the overall research objective and the data analytical techniques that will best address this objective (Christian *et al.* 2008). Often, discrete answer options are provided on questionnaires when it would be more appropriate to provide continuous Likert scales so that a more comprehensive range of statistical techniques can be employed to analyse the data. Dichotomous 'yes–no' answer options are often far too blunt for respondents to provide their true opinions/attitudes and thus valuable information is lost. In collecting data from attendees at an event or festival about their satisfaction with the event, it is much better to ask 'How satisfied were you?' with the event, using a five-, seven- or ten-point scale, than it is to simply ask 'Were you satisfied or not?' with a 'yes or no' answer option. In summary of this point, therefore, it is generally much better to use a continuous scale than it is to use a scale in which there are just discrete answer options. Clearly, this does not apply to all areas such as demographic questions, where most questions will require discrete answer selections.

For ease of data entry and analysis, it is often easier to ensure that the questionnaire is largely comprised of closed questions – that is, questions for which there are specific answer options. That said, however, there is often great merit in also providing respondents with an opportunity to explain their responses in an open format. The data thus obtained helps one understand the reasons for a particular view. For example, asking an event or festival attendee about their overall level of satisfaction identifies how satisfied s/he was with the experience, but not why this was the case. There is often value in having a supplementary question that asks the respondent the main reasons for this level of satisfaction. The open answers obtained can be invaluable for helping the organiser modify aspects of the event or festival in the subsequent year to further enhance overall satisfaction.

Pilot test

Although all good research methods texts stress the importance of pilot testing a questionnaire before it is administered to the target group, general perusal of the questionnaires used in event and festival research would indicate that this important stage is often skipped or at least not done very well. One can often find formatting errors both in expression and layout as well as questions that are not easily interpretable by respondents (Fredline *et al.* 2003). These outcomes greatly reduce the value of the data obtained.

In undertaking a pilot study, it is important that participants in the pilot are those for whom the final questionnaire will be targeted. When a questionnaire is pilot tested, it is often tested by colleagues who are familiar with the research process and would not easily identify comprehension problems that someone outside the process may have with the questionnaire. To pilot test a questionnaire for use in data collection from event and festival attendees, it is essential that representatives of the target audience be identified and engaged in the test.

Once presentation and comprehension issues have been addressed in the pilot study, the data collected should be analysed in a preliminary fashion to ensure that the data obtained will help address the overall research objectives. This pilot test analysis may identify the need to modify the scales used in various questions.

Questionnaire administration

There are a variety of methods that can be used to administer a questionnaire and each of these has various advantages and disadvantages that must be considered in each situation. This section identifies the key methods and presents some of the items that need to be taken into consideration in selecting the most appropriate one, particularly in relation to event and festival research. It is important to recognise that, over recent years, response rates in most studies have fallen substantially (Dillman *et al.* 2009) as the community has been 'bombarded' with an ever increasing number of surveys and the community as a whole is tending to become jaded. It is critical, therefore, to consider the cost per completed questionnaire, not just the cost of administering the questionnaire when deciding which method is most suitable for a particular study.

The most common method that has been used in event and festival research is the distribution of self-complete questionnaires to attendees at an event. Attendees are generally either asked to complete them during the event and returned to an identified collection point or they are given the questionnaire and asked to complete it once they return home and to mail it back using an enclosed stamped self-addressed envelope. Whilst this approach is relatively low in cost as it simply requires staff to distribute a questionnaire, it has the problem of often only achieving very low response rates even with the addition of incentives (Baruch and Holtom 2008). In event and festival research, a low response rate is even more serious than for many other areas of study, as once the festival or event has been staged it is not possible to administer the questionnaire again or to continue the distribution of questionnaires, as it is for many other areas. In 2001, a questionnaire was distributed to attendees at a cultural festival in regional Victoria in Australia. The questionnaire included a return-post envelope and a request for the completed questionnaire to be returned within seven days of the event concluding. Not a single questionnaire was returned, which was disastrous in that no follow-up was possible as the event was not ticketed and there were no details of who had attended. This highlights the problems of using self-complete questionnaires at events and festivals.

Another means of administering questionnaires that is gaining in popularity, although it involves a higher cost than the aforementioned approach, is the use of intercept interviewers to collect data on the spot. At events and festivals, this means that a number of interviewers are required to intercept attendees and ask them the questions and note their responses. A key advantage of this approach is that one can monitor the response rate that is being achieved in real time and additional interviewers or more extended interviewer shifts can be arranged if the response rate is not as high as intended. Using this approach, the interviewer can also assist respondents if they do not understand some of the questions, although it is important that interviewers do not influence respondents in the answers that they provide. There are also some disadvantages with this approach. First, the fact that respondents must give up their time during the event to answer the questionnaire can detract from their overall experience at the event. Also, some questions may require respondents to have participated in the full event experience prior to them being able to answer with any reliability. For example, an attendee may have just arrived at the event and will not be able to comment in a meaningful fashion about their satisfaction with the event as s/he will not have truly experienced the event. In a similar fashion, it is difficult to ask an attendee about their expenditure at the event when much of the expenditure may not yet have occurred.

A variation on the intercept interview approach outlined above is for intercept interviewers to collect telephone numbers or email addresses from attendees at the event or festival and advise them that they will be contacted in the week or so after the event. The questionnaire can then be administered to the attendees who agree to this request, either via telephone or email, depending on what is agreed. The advantages of this approach are that it is less intrusive on the event experience, questions can be answered more accurately after the event, and people having indicated that they will participate in the survey after the event has concluded are more likely to do so.

A newer questionnaire administration method that is gaining in popularity is the use of online research panels from which a sample of respondents can be selected to complete an online questionnaire. Whilst this approach does not have application to specific events and festivals, it does have relevance to studies where one may be seeking to obtain information relating attitudes, motives, satisfaction and behaviour to events and festivals in general. An advantage of this approach is that these online research panels are now so large that it is possible to select respondents who conform to quite tightly defined demographic and behavioural characteristics.

Whilst they can be quite expensive to use, the cost per completed questionnaire is often relatively low compared to other techniques and the data can be collected within a matter of days.

Sampling

In some cases, it is possible to collect data from all members of a particular population rather than simply from a sample of the population, and this is termed a census. Clearly, it is generally only viable to consider a census when the relevant population is relatively small and easily accessible. In the events and festivals area, a census approach could be a viable option to collect data from the competitors in a sporting event. Here the total number of competitors is often relatively small and the group is generally easily accessible through the event organiser.

Given that it is not feasible for economic and operational reasons to adopt a census approach for most studies, data must be collected from a sample of the relevant population. In quantitative research, the usual intention is to draw conclusions about the attitudes, motives, behaviour and the like about the total relevant population based on the findings related to a sample of that population (Neuman 2006). It is critical, therefore, that the sample be as random as possible and large enough in size so that the variations in the total relevant population are reflected in the sample. Although it is very difficult to obtain a sample that is truly random, there are techniques that can be used to enhance the randomness of the sample. In surveying at an event, a method that requires the interviewer to approach every 'nth' person past a particular point is much more effective than simply allowing interviewers to approach attendees of their choice, as they will generally tend to approach those with whom they most closely identify.

One of the main sampling errors that one finds in event and festival research relates to the days on which surveying is done. There are quite a number of events and festivals that are staged over four to seven days, only two of which are weekend days, but because the weekend days tend to have the largest crowds surveying often only occurs over the weekend. As a generalisation, one tends to have more attendees from out of town on the weekend days than during the week, so surveying on the weekend only will tend to over-represent respondents from outside the region. When the results of the survey are scaled up to the total population of the event, the findings will be skewed. This is particularly a problem in estimating the new expenditure for the region due to event attendance, as sampling at the weekend will tend to over-state the proportion of the population coming from outside the region and thus inflate the new expenditure figure. It is crucial, therefore, that sampling takes place on each day of the event in proportion to the total attendance on that day.

For some event and festival studies, there may be the need to understand the attitudes or behaviour of specific groups within the total relevant population and a random sample may not capture sufficient numbers of particular groups to enable analysis to occur. In such situations, there may be a need for a stratified sample where specific numbers of respondents are required from different groups (Zikmund, 2003). An example of this could be to set targets for the number of respondents obtained from outside the region so that an understanding of this group can be obtained (Jago and Dwyer 2006).

Relevant total population

As indicated earlier, most quantitative research in the event and festival field seeks to identify or explain behaviour of the total relevant population based on the findings from the sample. For expenditure estimates that are now so important for events and festivals, one needs to have an accurate estimate of the total relevant population in order to ramp up the findings from the sample. Jago and Dwyer (2006) provide a full discussion of these issues. For example, if the analysis of the sample shows that the average event attendee spent $50 during their time at the event, one needs to multiply this by the total number of attendees at the event in order to estimate the total impact. Whilst this is a fairly simple exercise for ticketed events, many events are not ticketed or are only partially ticketed so estimates of the total number of attendees are required. For some events, there are turnstiles that are used at the event even if there are not tickets and turnstile counts are often used. However, this can grossly overstate the number of attendees if a given person can enter the site on multiple occasions. For example, at a four-day event, an attendee might go each day and thus, according to the turnstile count, would be classed as four attendees. Thus, it is crucial to distinguish between attendees and attendances. Estimating the total number of attendees at an event or festival is a very difficult task and many techniques have been adopted, including tag and recapture, aerial photography, hotel bookings and the like. See Raybould et al. (2000) for discussion of these approaches.

A case study of evaluating the social impacts of events on communities

The information provided to date has related to the use of quantitative methods for understanding event attendee motivation, satisfaction and potentially to understand the economic impact that these events have on the region and the state. Another important area of event research that uses quantitative methods is that of the social impacts of events on communities. The following information details the processes used in such research. A review of the literature reveals that there are four main assessment techniques which have been employed in the evaluation of social impacts of events.

Host community perceptions This is by far the most common method and measures impacts through host community perceptions (see, for example, Ap and Crompton 1998; Fredline and Faulkner 2001). In this type of study, a sample of local residents is asked to report their perceptions of specific impacts of events on their quality of life via a questionnaire. The questionnaire methodology allows the inclusion of a large number of impacts (within reason) and therefore these studies typically adopt the broader definition of 'social' impacts.

Contingent Valuation Another method which has been occasionally employed is the use of Contingent Valuation (CV) and related techniques such as Choice Modelling (CM). These techniques attempt to assign monetary values to social impacts by asking residents how much they are willing to pay to ensure or avoid some aspects of event development (see, for example, Lindberg and Johnson 1997; Lindberg et al. 2001; Raybould and Lazarow 2009). A quasi-experimental design is used in this type of research and thus there are limits on the number of variables (impacts) and levels of those impacts, which can be manipulated. For this reason, a narrow definition of social impacts is typically adopted, and even then, only a few impacts can be tested at one time.

Social Impacts Assessment The final method, which has parallels with a technique developed in urban planning, is the method referred to as SIA (Social Impact Assessment). It has generally been used in assessing proposed tourism developments but has application to the staging of events and, as such, is undertaken prior to the event occurring. However, there are a small number of examples in the literature where this technique has adopted a post-development evaluation perspective. Researchers have identified key indicators of social impact and described the changes that can be attributed to the tourism activity. For example, Hall et al. (1995) documented some of the social impacts of the

1987 America's Cup in Fremantle, Western Australia, including increases in crime and prostitution. This technique attempts to objectively measure (or anticipate) the impacts of the event, as opposed to the subjective techniques above which rely on residents' perceptions of impact.

Other objective measures There are a range of other objective measures, such as traffic counts, changes in the price of goods and services in the region, increased crime against property and person, which can be used to assess the impact of events on a community.

Questionnaire design

The instrument design, including the scale used, is crucial in eliciting the relevant data required to answer the research question. Take, for instance, the work by Fredline and Faulkner (2000) which examines the perceptions of residents of two sporting events on the Gold Coast in Australia. Fredline's method is adopted in later studies (see, for example, Fredline *et al.* 2003; Tovar and Lockwood 2008) where respondents were asked whether a particular impact had increased, decreased, had not changed or the respondents did not know. If the respondent considered the impact had either decreased or increased, s/hey was then asked, on a seven-point Likert scale ranging from −3 to +3 what effect this had on their personal quality of life and on the community as a whole (Figure 29.1).

Fredline and Faulkner (2000) argue that the use of the more complex scaling approach using both positive and negative answers elicits higher-quality data. Small (2007) uses a similar scale, but this time from −5 to +5. Kim and Petrick (2005) and others, such as Gursoy and Kendall (2006) and Zhou and Ap (2008), have used more traditional Likert scales to collect data on residents' perceptions of the impacts of events.

Sampling frame

A key issue relates to defining the relevant population and then, in turn, determining a sample frame and sample size that is appropriate. Equally important is to ensure that the sample is chosen randomly. With regard to event research, the population could be the community, the attendees, participants, sponsors, suppliers and a range of other stakeholders. Again, taking the example of the examination of the social impacts of events on a community, the issue of the population and sampling is a complex one, as Fredline *et al.* (2003: 28), state with regard to the case studies presented from their research.

The population of interest in each of the case studies was defined as the permanent

1a. Because of the event, noise levels in and around the Grand Prix have....	Decreased	1b. How has this affected your personal quality of life?	-3 -2 -1 0 +1 +2 +3
	Increased		
	No change (go to 2a	1c. How has this affected the community as a whole?	-3 -2 -1 0 +1 +2 +3
	Don't know (go to 2a		

Figure 29.1 Example of questions used in Fredline (2000)

local population of the urban areas in which the events take place. However, finding a sampling frame that accurately represents this population is difficult. The two obvious choices are the telephone directory and electoral rolls, but each of these has their dis-advantages. A third option, mentioned by these authors, focuses on purchasing a data-base. Finding an appropriate database for community studies is fraught with issues of privacy and accuracy. Such databases can be expensive if purchased through a third party, and the opportunity to take this path is becoming less common as privacy laws in various countries prohibit the use of these.

Sampling methods

Issues surrounding the sampling method will depend on the population. If, for example, the population is the community, a stratified sampling method may be appropriate. Research by Fredline and Faulkner (2001), Jurowski and Gursoy (2004), Haley et al. (2005) and Sharma et al. (2008), for example, would suggest that those residents closest to an event or tourist activity will have different attitudes to the event from those living further away from the event, and so a sample based on distance from the event may be appropriate. In studies examining attendees' motivations for attendance and satisfaction with the event, the most common method of sampling is through convenience or random sampling.

Data collection

The use of a survey technique leads to data collection through intercept interviews, phone interviews, mail-out self-complete questionnaires or, more recently, online questionnaire completion. Phone interviews, for example, are costly, although the data can be entered at the same time as the interview is being conducted, reducing the cost of one aspect of the research design. There is also the problem of respondent fatigue with this method and a growing antagonism towards what would possibly be viewed as telemarketing by the respondent. While mail-out surveys can also be costly, there is the advantage of possibly targeting a large number of potential respondents. The difficulty here is in obtaining a reliable database to enable the mail-out. There is also the problem of response rate as recent experience indicates that response rates generally and for self-complete questionnaires from community residents in particular are very low.

Analytical techniques

Much of the research using quantitative methods now uses multivariate analysis to obtain an understanding of perceptions, motivations, groups or clusters of these or spending patterns. Work by Delamere (2001) uses exploratory factor analysis in his instrument development as does Small (2007) in her Social Impact Perception scale (SIP) to compare perceptions of events in two Australian communities. Pickernell et al. (2007) use comparison of means and correlations to determine the level of social capital that events can build. Kim and Petrick (2005) employ factor analysis, ANOVA and t-tests to determine the impacts of the events in their study, while Fredline and Faulkner (2001) and, more recently, Zhou and Ap (2008) use cluster analysis to understand the differences in perceptions of the various communities within their sample. While the use of structural equation modelling is common in the study of tourism impacts, this technique is employed less often in event research, with Gursoy et al. (2004) being an exception to this.

Having explored some of the quantitative research tools that can be used in an event and festival context, the attention of the second half of this chapter will now switch to an examination of the potential to use qualitative research methods at events and festivals.

The use of qualitative research at events and festivals

Event and festival researchers are confronted with a host of approaches when starting their research, the choice of which is a reflection of the subjectivity, culture and preferences of the researcher as well as the topic under study (Brewer 2000). It is not the purpose of the second section of this chapter to repeat the well-documented distinctions between qualitative and quantitative research, but to introduce the reader to some of the methods associated with the qualitative approach. The three most common qualitative research methods are participant observation, in-depth interviews and focus groups. Each method is particularly suited for obtaining a specific type of data. Participant observation is appropriate for collecting data on naturally occurring behaviours in their usual contexts; in-depth interviews are appropriate for collecting data on individuals' life histories, experiences and perspectives, especially when sensitive issues and topics are being explored; and focus groups are appropriate in extracting data on the cultural norms of a group and to generate broad overviews of issues of concern to the cultural groups represented. Whilst there are various qualitative methods, this chapter will explore the two primary qualitative methods of enquiry: participant observation, including an exploration of ethnography, and the interview method, which if used properly can enhance the understanding of various aspects of events and festivals. Examples and scenarios are included, along with an explanation of some appropriate research techniques and approaches to be adopted.

A review of existing events management publications (Holloway *et al.* 2010) reveals a dominance of quantitative research and a paucity of academic studies using the qualitative approach to investigate event experiences. Qualitative research should not be seen as antithetical to quantitative research, as they complement each other and answer different research questions (Holloway 2008). It is suggested that academic legitimacy for the events subject area can only be established if diversity is evident in data collection and analysis methods (Getz 2008). It is also argued by Getz that it will become increasingly necessary to 'custom design' highly targeted event experiences, which must be based on greater knowledge of the event experience in all its dimensions. This section of the chapter will now highlight how using the twin methods of participant observation and interviewing offers an unparalleled insight into the social world of the event participant.

Participant observation

Participant observation is the act of looking at the setting and people in detail and over time, systematically studying what goes on and noting and reporting it. Event researchers as participant observers look at people and events in their natural settings. Participant observation is an inductive approach that has origins in anthropology and sociology and from the early periods of fieldwork, when researchers such as Malinowski (1922) and Mead (1935) became part of the culture they studied, and examined the actions and interactions of people 'in the field'. In relation to events generally, the experiences and social, cultural and personal meanings attached by participants represents an area that until recently has received limited scholarly coverage: exceptions include studies by Getz *et al.* (2001), Morgan (2006), Frost *et al.* (2008), Morgan and Wright (2008), Shipway and Jones (2008) and Stone (2008).

Prolonged engagement and involvement is one significant characteristic of participant observation, which is needed to learn about the event setting and people being studied. Whilst observation is considered less disruptive and more unobtrusive than interviews, participant observation does not just involve watching, but also listening and talking to the people being studied. Participant observation can be conducted in open and closed event settings. An open setting will be public and highly visible, such as within the crowd at a carnival, while in closed settings, access is difficult; backstage at a comedy festival could be considered as a closed setting. The participant-observer enters the setting without intending to limit the observations to particular people or situations and adopts an unstructured approach. Certain ideas might emerge in the early stages, but usually observation would progress from being unstructured to the more detailed and focused, until specific actions become the main interest of the researcher. Researchers can then observe social processes as they happen and develop, and situations can be analysed. Holloway (2008) notes that observers can examine events and ongoing actions; however, they cannot explore past events and the thoughts of participants, which is only possible in interviews. There are various types of observer involvement in the field. These are the complete participant; the participant as observer; the observer as participant; and the complete observer (Holloway and Wheeler 2010), and these sometimes overlap and the boundaries are often blurred.

When participant observation is successful, it will uncover interesting patterns and developments that are grounded in the real world of the event participants' daily lives. It is Holloway (2008) who highlights that the task of both exploration and discovery is, after all, the aim of qualitative research.

The observation of a variety of contexts within an event setting is important. Spradley (1980) states that all participant observation takes place in social situations, and provides a framework in order to guide researchers. In Box 29.1, Spradley's framework for participant observation is applied to the festival context. Using the annual Rio de Janeiro Carnaval as a point of illustration allows the reader to grasp the applicability of the technique for the study of events and festivals.

Box 29.1 Participating in the Rio de Janeiro Carnaval

Rio de Janeiro Carnaval

Space: The Festival location, e.g. *the Rio de Janeiro Carnaval.*

Actor: The person in the Festival setting, e.g. *the performers, the security personnel, the police officers, the spectators.*

Activity: The behaviour and actions of those in attendance.

Object: The items located in the setting, e.g. *costumes, musical instruments.*

Act: The single action, e.g. *policing the festival, dancing, music.*

Events: What is happening (in the period post, during and pre)? e.g. *the context and importance of cultural festivals in Brazil, or proposed event impacts and legacies.*

Time: Time frame and sequencing, e.g. *media build-up (traditional press and online), planning and organisation activities leading up to the main days of the Carnaval, post-event activities such as clean-up operations.*

Goal: What participants are aiming to achieve, e.g. *(depending on actor role) raising awareness, minimising disruption, fun and enjoyment, profiling Rio as a tourist destination.*

Feeling: The emotions of participants, e.g. *accessible through observation on the days; the press in the build-up to the Carnaval; and the atmosphere at the Festival.*

Source: Adapted from Spradley (1980: 78)

The framework in Box 29.1 could be used as a template for the study of any event or festival. Through using an inductive approach to research, the focus of observation will inevitably change in response to the data generated as the research proceeds. In other words, the qualitative researcher has to be flexible and responsive to the conditions of the research setting – in this case, the Rio de Janeiro Carnaval.

Spradley (1980) suggests that observers take three main steps: they use *descriptive*, *focused* and finally *selective* observation. Descriptive observation incorporates general ideas that the observer has in mind, and everything taking place in the situation becomes a source of data and should be recorded, including smells, colours or appearances of people in the chosen setting. Description involves all five senses (Holloway and Wheeler 2010). As time progresses, certain important aspects or areas of the setting should become more obvious, and the researcher will be able to focus on these. Finally, the observation will then become highly selective. To aid data collection, we suggest that event researchers utilise the observation guidelines provided by LeCompte and Preissle (1993). These guidelines, detailed below in Box 29.2, will be particularly useful when starting the field research, when feelings of being overwhelmed by the task ahead existed:

The collection of papers by Morgan *et al.* (2010), which look to understand the consumer experience, to research the experience and to explore the management of the tourism and leisure experience, is recommended reading for all events researchers with an interest in examining experience management from within an events or festival setting. To illustrate the usefulness of the data collection techniques outlined above, there now follows a more specific exploration of ethnography as a qualitative method of enquiry, highlighting its applicability and relevance within the domain of events studies. This incorporates an empirical case study, grounded within the context of a sport event setting, utilising the twin qualitative approaches of interviewing and participant observation which form the foundation of this chapter's exploration of qualitative tools in events research.

Box 29.2 Observational guidelines for events and festivals

1 The 'who' questions
Who, and how many people, were present in the event or festival setting or taking part in activities and events? What were their characteristics and roles within the environment?

2 The 'what' questions
What is happening in the setting? What are the actions and rules of behaviour of those present? What are the variations in the behaviour observed?

3 The 'where' questions
Where do interactions between event attendees take place? Where are they located in the physical space of the setting?

4 The 'when' questions
When do conversations and interactions take place? What is the timing of the activities or actions, and do discussions and interactions take place at different times?

5 The 'why' questions
Why do attendees in the setting act the way they do? Why are there variations in behaviour?

Event ethnography

Ethnography is a qualitative research approach where, through participant observation, the researcher is immersed in the day-to-day lives of the people, or conducts one-on-one interviews with members of the group. Ethnography is defined as the description and interpretation of a culture or social group; its aim is to understand social reality by focusing on ordinary, everyday behaviour, and to provide an in-depth study of a culture (Holloway *et al.* 2010). The utility of ethnography as a qualitative research approach in the field of events is clear: permitting both observations and interviews with key informants, a full picture of the event experience can be captured by the researcher, who by assuming the role of participant gains a privileged access to the subculture created by participants. The case study below highlights the importance of exploring the social and emotional world of the event participant. By giving primacy to the data and focusing on the emic perspective, ethnographic approaches are useful for context-sensitive research because it can explore the nature and meanings of events for the participants who experience and are involved in them.

On the run: an ethnography of distance running events

The aim of this study was to develop a deeper understanding of the experiences of distance runners. An ethnographic research design was adopted to understand the nature of the social world of distance runners through interviews and observations which were thematically analysed. The sample comprised twenty-five international informants, and data was collected over a twenty-four-month period. The chosen distance running locations ranged from local running clubs to major sporting events such as the Flora London Marathon, UK; both Sydney's 'City to Surf 14 km' and the Gold Coast Half Marathon in Australia; the

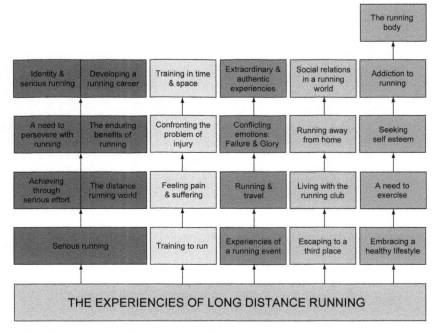

Figure 29.2 The event experiences of long distance runners
Source: Adapted from Shipway (2010).

BUPA Great North Run in Newcastle, UK; the Athens Classic Marathon in Greece; and the Cyprus International Four-day Challenge. In addition to these running events, data collection continued on a weekly basis from within the environment of the running club.

The key theme emerging from the data was the strength of identification that participants had with the activity of distance running. This theme was linked to the search for a running identity amongst participants, exploring how meaning was created through engagement with the distance running social world. In doing so, the study also explored the enduring benefits of the activity and the high levels of effort, perseverance and commitment displayed. The emerging themes are illustrated in Figure 29.2, leading to the development of a framework for understanding the experiences of distance runners.

A number of other themes emerged that were seen as consequences of this sense of identification. These included the central role of training and preparing to run, and how this contributed towards participants' sense of running identity. This theme included feelings of pain and suffering, confronting problems of injury, and the role of time and space within the participants' training regimes. The extraordinary and authentic experiences at distance running events were a dominant theme incorporating the conflicting emotions of failure and glory, and the importance of travel within the distance running social world. Feelings of escape and an exploration of the role distance running fulfilled as a 'third place' outside of the home and work environment were explored, incorporating ideas linked to social relations within the distance running social world. Similarly, the desire to embrace a healthy lifestyle was a central concept, exploring themes linked to seeking self-esteem through participation, negative aspects associated with exercise addiction, and the role of the 'running body'.

This ethnographic study, with data collected primarily within the event context, provided a series of linked themes exploring the culture of distance running, and in doing so developed a deeper understanding of the participants' running experiences, contributing towards the body of knowledge on the unique social world of the distance

Figure 29.3 Active sport event research
Source: Author (2007).

runner. Figure 29.3 features the researcher (far right) participating in the event, immersed within the culture being studied, as an active event sport tourist. The findings from both the International Running Challenge in Cyprus and the 2007 Flora London Marathon have been published in the *International Journal of Tourism Research* and the *Journal of Sport and Tourism* (Shipway and Jones 2007; 2008).

This case study, set within the environment of a series of international sport events, highlights the value of ethnography in describing and understanding cultures which could be replicated within any event setting: ethnography alone permits the study of the culture created by participants at an event or festival. Applying ethnographic methods – especially observation – will help events researchers to contextualise behaviours, beliefs and feelings, and identify the cultural influences on the individuals and groups they study. In addition to participant observation, interviews are possibly the best way to access event attendees' experiences, allowing them to express themselves in their own words and at their own pace (Brewer 2000). This technique will now be examined, and selected examples of their use within event and festival research contexts will also be highlighted.

The interview

Gratton and Jones (2009: 140) suggest that the simplest way to find out information from someone is to simply ask them! This is the underlying principle of the research interview, and in its most basic form the interviewer is trying to gain the perspectives, feelings and perceptions from the participant(s) and/or their description of the phenomenon under study (Holloway 2008). The depth and richness of qualitative data are a function of the ability to sensitively explore topics of importance with informants (Mason 2002). Qualitative interviews will vary in their degree of structure, ranging from the unstructured to the structured interview. Qualitative researchers would normally employ the unstructured or semi-structured interview. The one-to-one interview is the most common method by which qualitative data is collected in events research. In contrast to the questionnaire approach, explored in the first part of this chapter, which collects highly structured data and is often completed without the presence of the researcher, the researcher is a key element of the interview process. Their skills, attributes and interviewing technique are all an integral part of the ability to use this method to obtain 'rich' qualitative data.

There are both advantages and disadvantages to the interview method. Participants can talk about their own experiences and in their own words, elaborating on areas of interest and importance, and there is an opportunity for unexpected data to emerge, which might not have been readily apparent. Importantly, the researcher must be careful to avoid interviewer bias and avoid influencing the study either positively or negatively, depending on various external factors. Holloway (2008) also suggests that the interview can be affected by both lack of rapport and over-rapport between interviewer and informant.

Unstructured interviews draw on the social interaction between members and the interviewer to gather information. Members can let their thoughts wander, and although structuring and ordering of the questions are not utilised, there is an element of controlled communication relating to the interests of the interviewer (Edwards and Skinner 2009). As such, it is important in the unstructured interview to ask questions that are open-ended, to get interviewees talking about a broad topic area, whilst remembering that the informant guides the content (Spradley 1979). Unstructured interviews are useful when little is known about the area of study or perhaps during a preliminary study to test what the responses might be to a particular issue. Even

---

Box 29.3 Unstructured interview questions and aide memoires

'Tell me about your experience at the Woodford Folk Festival (Queensland, Australia)'

Aide memoire

- Explore feelings when entering the festival village/site.
- Interaction amongst the crowd throughout the duration of the Woodford Festival.
- Thoughts on the artists and presenters/programme/workshops at the Festival.

---

unstructured interviews are usually supported by an *aide memoire*, an agenda or a list of topics that will be covered, as illustrated in Box 29.3.

This form of unstructured interviewing allows flexibility and lets the researcher follow the interests and thoughts of the informant; and whilst it generates the richest data, it also has the highest level of material of no particular use, or what Holloway (2008) calls the 'dross rate'. There is also a danger with this type of interview that much of the data will lack focus. Another disadvantage of unstructured interviews is that the researcher is vulnerable to the interpretations and subjective insights of the informant.

A semi-structured interview has a more specific research agenda and is more focused; however, the informants still describe the situation in their own time and words. It is possible for the researcher to ensure through a tighter structure of semi-structured interviews that s/he collects important information, while still allowing informants to express their own thoughts and feelings. A semi-structured interview will allow for more guidance and direction from the researcher. It is suggested that researchers working within the domain of event studies develop an appropriate interview guide. The researcher can then develop questions and decide which issues to pursue. When compiling a list of questions for semi-structured interviews, it is important to bear in mind that the researcher will not wish to lead the participant, but on the other hand it is necessary to prepare enough questions in case the conversation dries up. The order of the questions will depend on the answers of each individual, and will therefore not be the same for each participant. The interview is likely to become more centred through progressive focusing, and it is important to not control the answers but to be guided by the informants' ideas and thoughts (Holloway and Wheeler 2010). We would suggest questions of short to medium length with the use of prompts, similar to those provided in Box 29.4: hypothetical examples from the San Fermin Festival in Spain.

Box 29.4 Interview questions and prompts

Pamplona Bull Run: San Fermin Festival, Spain

Tell me about the time when you participated in the Running of the Bulls in Pamplona.

- How did you feel prior to the Bull Run?
- Tell me about the actual Running of the Bulls, and the route taken.
- How did you feel when you saw the bulls approaching you?
- What happened after the event?
- How did your friends and family react to your participation?

And so on.

Box 29.5 Experience, feeling and knowledge questions.

Experience questions

- Could you tell me about your experience of the Hermanus Whale Festival?
- Tell me about your experience of the Albuquerque International Balloon Fiesta.

Feeling questions

- How did you feel when you arrived at the Melbourne International Arts Festival?
- What did you feel when the first act came on stage at Isle of Wight Music Festival?

Knowledge questions

- What services are available at the Notting Hill Carnival?
- How did you cope with spending four days at the Festival?

When asking questions, interviewers can use a variety of techniques. Patton (1990) highlights certain types of questions, for example *experience*, *feeling* and *knowledge* questions, examples of which are provided in Box 29.5.

Spradley (1979) also recommends the use of grand-tour or experience questions in the opening interview, followed by focused mini-tour or example questions, depending on the interviewee's response. This means often beginning with a broad question within the topic area, such as 'Tell me about the Sydney Gay and Lesbian Mardi Gras' or 'What is your experience of New Orleans Mardi Gras?' Grand-tour questions are broader, while mini-tour questions are more specific. A hypothetical example of a grand-tour question could be 'Can you describe a typical day at the Brighton Arts Festival?' to an event organiser, or 'How do you see your role at the Brighton Arts Festival?' to an event volunteer. In contrast, a mini-tour question could be 'What were your expectations of Festival de Cannes (Cannes Film Festival)?' to a festival attendee, or 'Can you describe what happens when you have a problem with one of the performing artists?' to an event manager of a cultural festival.

Whilst examples of qualitative interviews within an events context are relatively limited, some good examples have been located within existing literature. Stone (2008) provides one example of the applicability of semi-structured interviews when exploring the British pop music festival phenomenon, with findings obtained from festival-goers and current and former pop festival organisers in the UK. Waitt and Duffy (2010) provide another good example of the application of qualitative research, using interviews to probe how participants listen at a classical musical festival in Australia, and describing *how* festival attendees listened and offering insights to how they conceived of themselves in and through time and place. In contrast, through the use of semi-structured interviews with organisers, sponsors, artists, media and producers, Garcia (2001) explored the Sydney 2000 Olympic Arts Festivals and identified the circumstances affecting the relationship between cultural and sporting programmes. Garcia's semi-structured interview data encouraged marketers to explore the incorporation of cultural events and activities to foster the appeal of events to market segments that might not otherwise be reached.

In the sport event context, Hanlon and Stewart (2006) used semi-structured interviews with managers from two event organisers, the Australian Tennis Open and the Australian Grand

Prix Corporation, to explore the management processes of two major sport events, and to examine the extent to which tailored or sport-specific management practices for personnel were incorporated by each of the sport event managers. Similarly, Smith (2005) used semi-structured interviews to examine the effects of initiatives adopted by three English cities to explore the value of sport as a re-imaging theme for the contemporary city destination, and through this chosen method highlighted both the advantageous qualities and significant problems associated with place marketing. Smith's interviews were able to explore more detailed images of the cities and the attitudes and meanings generated by associating sport with a city. A semi-structured interview approach was also used by Brown (2002) in interviews with people who used Olympic sponsorship to achieve a diverse range of their commercial objectives at the Sydney 2000 Games. This included the Director of Marketing for the Sydney Organising Committee of the Olympic Games (SOCOG) and people responsible for managing the sponsorship programmes for some of the major Olympic sponsors.

In summary, the qualitative research interview will depend largely on the participants whose ideas, thoughts and feelings the researcher will try to explore, obtaining the insider's perspective. Because of its flexibility, researchers have freedom to prompt for more information, and participants are able to explore their own thoughts and exert more control over the interview as their ideas have priority. However, the collection and analysis of interview data is time-consuming. Events students, who are very enthusiastic during the early data-gathering process, only realise when involved in transcribing and analysing how much time they need for the work (Holloway and Wheeler 2010). This chapter suggests that the strength of qualitative research, be it participant observation, interviews or any other form of qualitative method of enquiry, is the ability to lift the veil on certain aspects of a chosen event or festival and to make visible unknown cultural phenomena (Edwards and Skinner 2009).

Conclusion

In events studies research, using more than one method to study the same phenomenon has the potential to strengthen the validity of the results. For example, a design might begin with a qualitative element such as an interview, which could alert the researcher to issues that should be explored in a survey of participants, which could then be followed by semi-structured interviews to clarify some of the research findings. A mixed-methods approach could also lead events researchers to expand or modify the research design and/or the data-collection methods (Edwards and Skinner 2009).

Despite the need to embrace new paradigms in event studies, there has been limited progress to date. The need to understand the underlying experiences, feelings and emotions related to event behaviour has been acknowledged in recent years, and as a consequence qualitative research is taking on increasing importance within events studies, and should no longer be viewed as 'inferior' to quantitative research. This chapter strongly supports both quantitative and qualitative approaches, and acknowledges that there is not a 'best research approach', but rather that the approach most effective for the resolution of a given problem depends on a number of variables, not least the nature of the problem itself, as also advocated by Edwards and Skinner (2009) or Gratton and Jones (2009). Thus, the approach will clearly be dictated by the research question.

Through the use of qualitative examples, this chapter has also sought to illustrate their appropriateness to finding answers to particular event-based research questions, and to open up the variety of possibilities for the development of new events management knowledge through the application of qualitative approaches – approaches which enhance and enrich the current events literature. In summary, this chapter calls for further qualitative studies that would to some extent serve to redress the predominance of quantitative-based studies through a more balanced overview of emerging research and methods (Holloway *et al.* 2010), and provide a diverse and significant contribution to knowledge in festival and events research.

Further reading

Fredline, E. and Faulkner, B. (2001) 'Residents' reactions to the staging of major motorsport events within their communities: a cluster analysis', *Event Management* 7(2): 103–14. (Identifying the perceptions held by residents in two cities of the impacts of a motor race staged within their community.)

Fredline, L., Jago, L. and Deery, M. (2003) 'The development of a generic scale to measure the social impacts of events', *Event Management. An International Journal* 8(1): 23–37. (Explaining the processes involved in developing a scale to be used in assessing the social impacts of three different events.)

Holloway, I., Brown, L. and Shipway, R. (2010) 'Meaning not measurement: using ethnography to bring a deeper understanding to the participant experience of festivals and events', *International Journal of Event and Festival Management* 1(1): 74–85. (This article highlights the need for more qualitative research within the existing events literature.)

Shipway, R. and Jones, I. (2007) 'Running away from home: understanding visitor experiences in sport tourism', *International Journal of Tourism Research* 9: 373–83. (Exploring the social world of a group of distance runners participating in the Cyprus International Four-day Challenge event.)

——(2008) 'The great suburban Everest: an "insider's" perspective on experiences at the 2007 Flora London Marathon', *Journal of Sport and Tourism* 13(1): 61–77. (Using ethnographic research tools, this study explores the event experiences of participants at the London Marathon, UK.)

References

Ap, J. and Crompton, J. (1998) 'Developing and testing a tourism impact scale', *Journal of Travel Research* 37 (2): 120–30.

Baruch, Y and Holtom, B. (2008) 'Survey response rate levels and trends in organizational research', *Human Relations* 61(8): 1139–60.

Brewer, J. (2000) *Ethnography*, Buckingham: Open University Press.

Brown, G. (2002) 'Taking the pulse of Olympic sponsorship', *Event Management* 7: 187–96.

Christian, L., Dillman, D. and Smyth, J. (2008) 'The effects of mode and format on answers to scalar questions', in J. Lepkowski, C. Tucker and J. Brick (eds) *Telephone and Web Surveys: Advances in Telephone Survey Methodology*, New York: Wiley.

Creswell, J.W. and Plano Clark, V.L. (2007) *Designing and Conducting Mixed Methods Research*, Thousand Oaks, CA: Sage.

Creswell, J.W., Plano Clark, V.L., Guttmann, M.L. and Hanson, E.E. (2003) 'Advanced mixed methods research design', in A.Tashakkori and C. Teddlie (eds) *Handbook of Mixed Methods in Social and Behavioral Research*, Thousand Oaks, CA: Sage, pp. 209–40.

Delamere, T.A. (2001) 'Development of a scale to measure residents' attitudes toward the social impacts of community festivals. Part 2: Verification of the scale', *Event Management* 7(1): 25–38.

Dillman, D., Phelps, G., Tortora, R., Swift, K., Kohrell, J., Berck, J. and Messer, B. (2009) 'Response rate and measurement differences in mixed-mode surveys using mail, telephone, interactive voice response (IVR) and the Internet', *Social Science Research* 38(1): 1–18.

Edwards, A. and Skinner, J. (2009) *Qualitative Research in Sport Management*, Oxford: Elsevier Butterworth-Heinemann.

Fredline, E. and Faulkner, B. (2000) 'Host community reactions: a cluster analysis', *Annals of Tourism Research* 27(3): 763–84.

——(2001) 'Residents' reactions to the staging of major motorsport events within their communities: a cluster analysis', *Event Management* 7(2): 103–14.

Fredline, L., Jago, L. and Deery, M. (2003) 'The development of a generic scale to measure the social impacts of events', *Event Management. An International Journal* 8(1): 23–37.

Frost, W., Wheeler, F. and Harvey, M. (2008) 'Commemorative events: sacrifice, identity and dissonance', in J. Ali-Knight, M. Robertson, A. Fyall and A. Ladkin (eds) *International Perspectives on Festivals and Events* (Advances in Tourism Research Series), Oxford: Elsevier Butterworth-Heinemann.

Garcia, B. (2001) 'Enhancing sport marketing through cultural and arts programs: lessons from the Sydney 2000 Olympic arts festivals', *Sport Management Review* 4(2): 193–219.

Getz, D. (2008) 'Event tourism: definition, evolution, and research', *Tourism Management* 29(3): 403–28.

Getz, D., O'Neill, M. and Carlsen, J. (2001) 'Service quality evaluation at events through service mapping', *Journal of Travel Research* 39(4): 380–90.

Gratton, C. and Jones, I. (2009) *Research Methods for Sports Studies*, London: Routledge, second edition.

Gursoy, D. and Kendall, K. (2006) 'Hosting mega events: modelling locals' support', *Annals of Tourism Research* 33(6): 603–23.

Gursoy, D., Kim, K. and Uysal, M. (2004) 'Perceived impacts of festivals and special events by organizers: an extension and validation', *Tourism Management* 27(5): 957–67.

Haley, A.J., Snaith, T. and Miller, G. (2005) 'The social impacts of tourism: a case study of Bath, UK', *Annals of Tourism Research* 32(3): 647–68.

Hall, C., Selwood, J. and McKewon, E. (1995) 'Hedonists, ladies and larrikins: crime, prostitution and the 1987 America's Cup', *Visions in Leisure and Business* 14(3): 28–51.

Hanlon, C. and Stewart, B. (2006) 'Managing personnel in major sport event organizations: what strategies are required?', *Event Management* 10: 77–88.

Holloway, I. (2008) *A–Z of Qualitative Research in Healthcare and Nursing*, Oxford: Blackwell.

Holloway, I. and Wheeler, S. (2010) *Qualitative Research in Nursing and Healthcare*, Oxford: Wiley-Blackwell, third edition.

Holloway, I., Brown, L. and Shipway, R. (2010) 'Meaning not measurement: using ethnography to bring a deeper understanding to the participant experience of festivals and events', *International Journal of Event and Festival Management* 1(1): 74–85.

Jago, L. and Dwyer, L. (2006) *Economic Evaluation of Special Events: A Practitioners Guide*, Altona: Common Ground.

Jurowski, C. and Gursoy, D. (2004) 'Distance effects on residents' attitudes toward tourism', *Annals of Tourism Research* 31(2): 296–312.

Kim, S. and Petrick, J. (2005) 'Resident perceptions on the 2002 FIFA World Cup: the case of Seoul as a host city', *Tourism Management* 26: 25–38.

LeCompte, M.D. and Preissle, J. with Tesch, R. (1993) *Ethnography and Qualitative Design in Educational Research*, Chicago: Academic Press, second edition.

Lindberg, K. and Johnson, R. (1997) 'The economic values of tourism's social impacts', *Annals of Tourism Research* 24(1): 90–116.

Lindberg, K., Andersson, T. and Dellaert, B. (2001) 'Tourism development: assessing social gains and losses', *Annals of Tourism Research* 28(4): 1010–30.

Malinowski, B. (1922) *Argonauts of the Western Pacific: An Account of Native Enterprise and Adventure in the Archipelagos of Melanesian New Guinea*, New York: Dutton.

Mason, J. (2002) *Qualitative Researching*, London: Sage, second edition.

Mead, M. (1935) *Sex and Temperament in Three Primitive Societies*, New York: HarperCollins.

Morgan, M., (2006) 'Making space for experiences', *Journal of Retail and Leisure Property* 5(4): 305–13.

Morgan, M. and Wright, R. (2008) 'Elite sports tours: special events with special challenges', in J. Ali-Knight, M. Robertson, A. Fyall and A. Ladkin (eds) *International Perspectives on Festivals and Events: Advances in Tourism Research Series*, Oxford: Elsevier Butterworth-Heinemann.

Morgan, M., Lugosi, P. and Ritchie, J.R.B. (2010) *The Tourism and Leisure Experience: Consumer and Managerial Perspectives*, Bristol: Channel View Publications.

Neuman, W. (2006) *Basics of Social Research: Qualitative and Quantitative Approaches*, New York: Allyn & Bacon.

Patton, M. (1990) *Qualitative Evaluation and Research Methods*, Newbury Park: Sage, second edition.

Pickernell, D., O'Sullivan, D., Senyard, J. and Keast, R. (2007) 'Social capital and network building for enterprise in rural areas: can festivals and events contribute?', in *Proceedings of the 30th Institute for Small Business and Entrepreneurship Conference*, Glasgow, Scotland: ISBE, pp. 1–18.

Ralston, R., Downward, P. and Lumsden, L. (2004) 'The expectations of volunteers prior to the XVII Commonwealth Games, 2002: a qualitative study', *Event Management* 9: 13–26.

Raybould, M. and Lazarow, N. (2009) *Social and Economic Values of Beach Recreation on the Gold Coast*, Gold Coast, Australia: STCRC.

Raybould, M., Mules, T., Fredline, L. and Tomljenovic, R. (2000) 'Counting the herd. Using aerial photography to estimate attendance at open events', *Event Management* 6(1): 25–32.

Robson, L. (2008) 'Event Management Body of Knowledge (EMBOK): the future of event industry research', *Event Management* 12: 19–25.

Seidman, I. (2006) *Interviewing as Qualitative Research: A Guide for Researchers in Education and the Social Sciences*, Williston: Teachers College Press, third edition.

Sharma, B., Dyer, P., Carter, J. and Gursoy, D. (2008) 'Exploring residents' perceptions of the social impacts of tourism on the Sunshine Coast, Australia', *International Journal of Hospitality and Tourism Administration* 9(3): 288–311.

Shipway, R. (2010) 'On the run: an ethnography of long distance running', unpublished PhD thesis, Bournemouth University, UK.

Shipway, R. and Jones, I. (2007) 'Running away from home: understanding visitor experiences in sport tourism', *International Journal of Tourism Research* 9: 373–83.

——(2008) 'The great suburban Everest: an "insider's" perspective on experiences at the 2007 Flora London Marathon', *Journal of Sport and Tourism* 13(1): 61–77.

Small, K. (2007) 'Social dimensions of community festivals: an application of factor analysis in the development of the Social Impact Perception (SIP) scale', *Event Management* 11(1): 45–55.

Smith, A. (2005) 'Reimaging the city: the value of sport initiatives', *Annals of Tourism Research* 32(1): 217–36.

Spradley, J.P. (1979) *The Ethnographic Interview*, Orlando: Holt, Rinehart and Winston.

——(1980) *Participant Observation*, New York: Holt, Rinehart and Winston.

Stone, C. (2008) 'The British pop music festival phenomenon', in J. Ali-Knight, M. Robertson, A. Fyall and A. Ladkin (eds) *International Perspectives on Festivals and Events: Advances in Tourism Research Series*, Oxford: Elsevier Butterworth-Heinemann.

Tovar, C. and Lockwood, M. (2008) 'Social impacts of tourism: an Australian regional case study', *International Journal of Tourism Research* 10: 365–78.

Waitt, G. and Duffy, M. (2010) 'Listening and tourism studies', *Annals of Tourism Research* 37(2): 457–77.

Zhou, Y. and Ap, J. (2008) 'Residents' perceptions towards the 2008 Beijing Olympic Games', *Journal of Tourism Research* 48(1): 78–91.

Zikmund, W. (2003) *Essentials of Marketing Research*, New York: Thompson South-Western.

Section 5
Future research directions for events

30

Events management education

Paul Barron and Anna Leask

Introduction

This chapter considers the development of events management education and the close association that this has with the development of academic research in the events management sector. The chapter starts with an introduction to the sector and the emergence of the area as a field of study, discussing how this was prompted initially by industry needs, with academic institutions developing relevant programmes to meet these needs, whilst underpinning this development with academic research; it then moves to outline the development, content and relevance of programme provision internationally; then concludes with suggestions relating to the future direction of events management education.

This chapter focuses on event management education at higher education level. Whilst it is recognised that event education is increasingly being offered by colleges of further education, it is argued that the origins, growth and development of event management education have occurred primarily at university level. There are a number of parallels that might be drawn between the origins and development of tourism as an academic discipline and the more recent development of event management: for example, the origins and close link with hospitality operations, a desire to professionalise the industry and an increasing recognition of the economic importance of the discipline. However, as this chapter will argue, event management education has also developed as a consequence of industry demands, a recognition, and the increasing prominence of the importance major events and, most importantly, unprecedented student demand. In addition, event management has provided extensive research opportunities for academic staff whose original interest and expertise was perhaps in other disciplines and allowed for the emergence of an academic discipline on which new academics can base their careers.

The emergence of events management education

The events industry

There has been much discussion regarding the nature and developing maturity of the events industry. For example, Finkel (2008) and Goldblatt (2000) have identified the potential growth and associated maturity of the industry with Finkel (2008: 4) stating that event management can now be seen 'as a legitimate and widely recognised profession'. However, perhaps taking cognisance of the recent emergence of the industry, Getz (2000; 2002) stated that 'as an academic field of study and career path it is quite new and immature' and Silvers *et al.* (2006) appear to agree with this notion of immaturity. Formica (1998), Harris *et al.* (2001) and Berridge (2007) conclude that the study of events is an emerging field within education, while Arcodia and Robb (2000) considered events management as an emerging industry. When discussing public sector events Getz (2002) and Berridge (2007) felt that there was an increasing need for a skilled workforce to become involved with those levels of government involved with the funding, administration and running of events. However, Getz (2002) suggested that the development of government-funded event-specific research centres was evidence of this penetration. Berridge (2007) highlighted the work of People 1st (the sector skills council for hospitality, tourism and leisure) in bringing the education requirements of the sector to government level. Berridge (2007: 56) further noted that People 1st worked with AEME (Association for Events Management Education) to 'help to understand the scope and size of the events industry'. Schmander in Allen *et al.* (2008) considered events as a dynamic industry and suggested that the growth of the industry, its economic importance and its global impact signified a need to understand the industry, arguing that, from this need, associations such as the International Festival and Events Association (IFEA) were set up.

Getz and Wicks (1994) reported that the birth of events associations evolved through the requirement of events professionals to gain accreditation within an industry that was increasingly demanding a more professional approach from managers and staff. They highlight the growth in membership of these organisations, noting that IFEA had over 1,300 members in 1993. It is argued that the creation of the European chapter of the IFEA provided evidence of the requirement for training and education within the profession (Getz and Wicks 1994). Other key researchers such as Harris and Jago (1999) and Hawkins and Goldblatt (1995) concur, noting that these associations have played an important role in setting the agenda for education and training.

The concept of event industry associations as a driver for the development of recognised programmes has been discussed more recently by Silvers *et al.* (2006) who found that event management associations have been concerned with creating accreditation programmes to ensure that current professionals are properly developed and trained in order to cope with, and respond to, the ever changing landscape of the events industry. Consequently, it might be suggested that the development of recognised event management associations, and the consequent demand for education and provision of accreditation, had a direct influence on the development of event management programmes within higher education.

In addition to, and in conjunction with, the development of event industry associations was a growing interest in event management within the academic community. As early as the mid-1990s Hawkins and Goldblatt (1995) and Formica (1998) suggested that there was a developing body of research emerging within the higher education sector that was focusing on the event industry. Getz (2000) examined the initiatives that governments were undertaking regarding the development of events education and found examples of research that was being commissioned in an attempt to further understand the event industry and its needs. Later, Getz (2008a) and Finkel (2008) considered that this research had been, and continued to be, viewed as a catalyst towards the creation of an event specific field of education.

The emergence of event management as a field of study

Whilst the history of events stretches for several millennia, the evolution of event management as a field of study wishing to gain respect in the business and academic worlds can trace its roots to the development of associations where like-minded event operators and academics came together as a means of more fully understanding the nuances of the management of events. The recognition of event management as a growing area also resulted in a call for the creation of a properly defined field of event studies that related to core competences in the area (Hawkins and Goldblatt 1995; Harris and Jago 1999; and Getz 2000). Indeed (Getz 2000: 20) considered that 'it is important to recognise event management as a distinct field of study, even though much of its theory and knowledge comes from other fields and disciplines'.

As previously seen with the development of hospitality and tourism as fields of study and the provision of higher education programmes, the need to underpin the courses with robust research is essential in ensuring the needs of both industry and education are met. In the events field this can be evidenced in the commitment of universities to event management research centres, PhD studentships, the appointment of events specialist academic staff and participation in the wider academic community of associations such as AEME, conferences and journal development.

The development of events management education (EME)

It is generally agreed that initial provision of event management as an area of study was provided by George Washington University (Getz and Wicks 1994; Hawkins and Goldblatt 1995; Formica 1998; Allen et al. 2008; Bowdin et al. 2008). Discussion centring around event management as a profession that could be studied first emerged in the academic press in the early 1990s with the publication of Getz and Wicks's (1994) article that argued for the existence of opportunities for the development of the discipline. Hawkins and Goldblatt (1995), and later Formica (1998), predicted that major growth in the events management field was imminent and that educators should consider the provision of event management education at further and higher education levels. The past decade has seen an unprecedented growth in the number of event management programmes and subsequent academic staff and writers of scholarly articles who have researched and discussed the area of events management and event education. The interest in this area has been mirrored by significant demand for event management education and has consequently emerged as a new academic field of study (Royal and Jago 1998; Silvers et al. 2006; Berridge 2007; Allen et al. 2008; Getz 2008a; Lockstone et al. 2008; Robinson et al. 2008; Getz et al. 2010). Berridge's (2007: 59) study suggested that the number of event management programmes in the UK had increased significantly in recent years from a small offering to over 200. Examining both the UK and Australian higher education sectors, Lockstone et al. (2008: 2) commented on the growth of events management education and noted that the discipline was becoming a topic of interest within the research community and that there was 'a growing body of literature in the area'.

The recognition of events management as an emerging profession has been discussed by McDonald and McDonald (2000), and a number of commentators have suggested a recently emerging career path in the area (for example, Shone and Parry 2004; Bowdin et al. 2008). Harris (2004: 103) also discussed the concept of event management as a '"new" industry and a "new" occupation'. The events industry has been described as an emerging and vibrant business sector and it is considered that tertiary education in the area has, and will continue to, develop as the industry matures (Arcodia and Robb 2000). Finkel (2008) and Allen et al. (2008) further suggest that the field is now well established within both the UK and Australia.

Australia is seen by many as an important participant in the event management industry and provider of event management education. Allen et al. (2008), Harris et al. (2001) and Perry, Foley and Rumpf (1996) all examined events in the recent past in Australia, specifically identifying the Sydney Olympic Games in 2000 as being a key driver for the growth in research. All these commentators credit the Games as a stimulus for research, with Allen *et al.* (2008) consequently suggesting that Australia is leading the field within events studies. The extent of the development of event management education in Australia was highlighted by Harris and Jago (1999) who identified that, even before the turn of the century, out of twenty-nine Australian universities, some seventeen were offering at least a course within a degree programme relating to events management and events management education. Additionally, Getz (2008b) opined that, from an Australian context, events in the recent past have assisted in demand for and creation of an industry in Australia and assisted in the creation of its position as a global leader in events management. Allen *et al.* (2008: 11) stated, however, that 'there is ample anecdotal evidence that to suggest that the growth of events is a worldwide phenomenon'. Getz (2000; 2002; 2008) and Getz and Wicks (1994) identify a variety of different areas where events management has traditionally been studied. It is concluded that whilst event management is a relatively new field of study, various elements of event management have been taught as part of other programmes. These include programmes focused on sport management, tourism and/or hospitality management, anthropology, geography and economics.

It might be suggested that since the mid-1990s the UK has emerged as a key provider of events management education. Researchers from UK institutions have also been active in the area and event management has developed into a rage of specialist sectors. For example Bowdin *et al.* (2008) considered the UK as leading the field of festivals and events listing the Edinburgh Festival, the 2002 Manchester Commonwealth Games and the organisation of the opening and closing ceremonies of the Athens 2004 Olympics as key events.

In other destinations, the provision of event management higher education programmes appears to be either non-existent or in the very early stages of development. Taking Dubai as an example from the Middle East region, a search of the Commission for Academic Accreditation (CAA) website identifies no event management programmes in any of the sixty-nine accredited universities and colleges. Indeed, only the Emirates Academy of Hospitality Management, with seven (mainly hospitality) programmes and the European International College with one programme in Destination and Leisure Management, offer programmes that might be categorised in the wider tourism area (CAA 2010). Whilst hospitality and tourism education is well established in certain locations in the Far East (for example, Hong Kong and Singapore) the provision of event management education is limited and programmes are only recently being developed and offered, often in conjunction with Western university partners (see for example the Master of Marketing and Event Management offered by Hong Kong University and Edinburgh Napier University). The situation in Africa appears similar to that in the Middle East and Far East. Whilst a number of short courses and certificates in event management are available, little or no opportunities to study event management to bachelor or master's level exist at the time of writing.

Key drivers in the growth of and demand for event management education

Previous sections have highlighted that Getz (2008a), Shone and Parry (2004), Schmader in Allen *et al.* (2008), Harris *et al.* (2001), Royal and Jago (1998) and Finkel (2008) have followed and considered the growth and development of the events industry. It has been suggested that traditionally the event industry was managed by, and relied both on the local community and on particular individuals who often volunteered to ensure events occurred. The recent maturing of the industry has resulted in a growing need for a more professional approach and, increasingly, with it comes a call for skilled individuals to take on management roles within events to ensure the success and longevity of the event. This maturing is highlighted by Finkel (2008: 4), who considered that 'event organisation is no longer considered a pastime; rather it is a viable career option'. The growing professionalism of the industry was discussed by Perry *et al.* (1996) and Finkel (2008), who suggested that the potential for mistakes at events can be disastrous for the event and for its long-term future and suggested that, with this in mind, there is a need for qualified professionals within the industry. Harris (2004) and Hawkins and Goldblatt (1995) also identified the need for more qualified professionals within this growth industry. Bowdin *et al.* (2008), Allen *et al.* (2008), Getz (2008a), Finkel (2008) and Shone and Parry (2004) considered the growing nature and importance of finance, budgets and sponsorship within the industry as being key drivers towards the requirement of properly trained professionals within the events industry. Bowdin *et al.* (2008: 26) considered that 'education and training in the events and festivals sector has arisen to meet specific needs' such as those relating to budgetary requirements and funding. Finkel (2008) further suggested that funding within events requires careful management and that the expectations of stakeholders and funding agencies need to be met. This brings a subsequent requirement for properly trained professionals within the industry.

In a manner similar to the view of the Sydney Olympic Games, Berridge (2007) and Shipway (2008) both consider the 2012 Olympics in London to be a further catalyst for education and research in the industry. It has been suggested that sporting events such as the Olympics can create a high political profile which in turn will encourage government investment in industry and education to ensure the success of the event (Berridge 2007) and government-funded organisations such as Podium have been created specifically to encourage links between higher education and the London Olympics (Podium 2010). Perry, *et al.* (1996) and Allen *et al.* (2008) opine that the Sydney Olympics had a similar effect on the provision of education and creation of opportunities for research within Australia, and Harris *et al.* (2001) suggested that large-scale events in Australia have acted as a catalyst for event education within the country. It has been argued, however, that the increasing level of research, education and consequent professionalism has resulted in higher expectations from the global audiences that mega sporting events attract. Indeed, it has been suggested that the potential loss of face should a high-profile event not go to plan should also be seen as a driver for education, training and research (Getz 2008a), identifying sporting events as key drivers within the education and training of professionals.

Harris and Jago (1999) stated that a noticeable trend for mainstream tourism conferences to dedicate part of their proceedings to the discussion of events management provided an indication of the growing importance in the area and acted as a driver for the development of event management education. The initial inclusion of event management in mainstream tourism conferences evolved into event-specific conferences in Adelaide as early as 1996 and in Sydney and Hobart in 1999. Whilst it might be suggested that the quality of papers presented at conferences (event management or otherwise) is variable, the evolution of event-specific conferences is another milestone in the development of the discipline. Indeed, it is now considered that events education and research conferences have become prominent features in the academic landscape and this, in turn, demonstrates a continued and growing interest in the industry (King 2008). Harris *et al.* (2001) and Getz (2002) indicate the growing importance of event management as a discipline within the educational community via the growth of events conferences and highlight the 'Events Beyond 2000' conference in Sydney as a prominent research conference that consolidated the connection between education and research.

It is also clear that education has become a prominent part of the industry from the creation in 2005 of a specific events education symposium within the 'Event Management Research Conference', held at the University of Technology, Sydney. Berridge (2007) suggests it is the 'phenomenon' of events and the way in which they have infiltrated our consciousness and imaginations that makes them so popular today. Getz (2008a), Berridge (2007), Goldblatt (2000) and Roche (2000) identify the celebrations and many events that took place around the time of the millennium as a driver in industry and subsequently a driver for education.

It can be seen that the provision of event management education was originally prompted by a growing desire for more professionalism from the industry and recognition of the importance of events from not only an economic but also an image perspective. The need for higher education establishments to develop and diversify their course provision in line with such industry needs has driven growth in both provision and demand for event management education.

Provision of events management education

Links between the event management education and industry

The event industry, too, has been instrumental in the development of event management education. Jackson *et al.* (2008: 6) undertook a study that determined the skills that employers are increasingly demanding from event management graduates. These included the ability to:

> Analyse and evaluate the concepts and defining characteristics of event as an area of academic and applied study; demonstrate a range of professional event planning and management knowledge and skills; recognise and value the centrality of the attendee and/or client and meet and respond to their needs and expectations; utilise, and understand the impact of, rationales, sources and assumptions embedded in policy, planning and delivery mechanisms in an events context.

Discussion and research on the provision of placements/internships within courses relating to event management has been widely covered within events management education research (see McDonald and McDonald 2000; Moscardo and Norris 2004; Burley 2005; Williamson 2005; Beaven and Wright 2006; Berridge 2007; Solent *et al.* 2007; Beer 2008; Lockstone *et al.* 2008; Robinson *et al.* 2008). A common theme evident from the above studies is the benefit to the student that accrues from the opportunity to work within the event industry. This, it is argued, is an excellent method of introducing students to the reality of their chosen field and provides a range of hitherto unknown career opportunities. The suggestion that this type of experienced-based learning can be better than classroom-based learning is noted by Beer (2008) and Robinson *et al.* (2008), who also identify the similar benefits to students through the use of industry professionals in lectures as a way of increasing interest and learning potential amongst students.

Williamson (2005), Robinson *et al.* (2008) and McDonald and McDonald (2000) considered the beneficial and rewarding nature of some form of industrial placement within an event management programme and found that students felt positive regarding industrial placements. Furthermore Solent *et al.* (2007) highlight the potential for placements to assist students in realising their own career ambitions and Robinson *et al.* (2008) suggest that placements assist in ensuring accurate perceptions of available career paths for graduates. Burley (2005), Berridge (2007), Lockstone *et al.* (2008) and Robinson *et al.* (2008) found that, within the context of the event industry, placements within industry can enhance a student's employability. Berridge (2007) and Burley (2005) also highlight that employers are more inclined to employ graduates who have spent time in industry as part of their degree programme.

There are, however, some well-documented drawbacks to facilitating and running these types of placements in programmes such as hospitality management or event management (see, for example, Barron and Maxwell [1993] for a discussion on the effects of work experience programmes on the career aspirations of hospitality students). Beer (2008) and Moscardo and Norris (2004) both suggest that the organising, administration and supervision of such industry placements is resource-intensive and stressful to both staff and students. The quality of such placements has also been brought into question. Whilst there is a general feeling that placements are beneficial to the educator, the student and the industry partner, it has been suggested that this type of experience is not suited to all students and some can become frustrated by the work and as a result do not engage appropriately (Moscardo and Norris 2004; Beer 2008). There is also some concern regarding the level of work students are often required to undertake whilst on placement and that there was an unrealistic level of expectation (from students) regarding the amount of administration and often mundane organising that is a key element to working as a manager in the events industry.

As events education continues to mature and develop it is important to ensure that key competencies remain within the discipline (Silvers *et al.* 2006). It is also clear from the literature that an element of experiential learning is required as a core element of event management programmes, as it is suggested that employers are seeking graduates with industry experience. A key task for educators is to protect this practical exposure to the industry and encourage students to undertake work in industry, be it through a placement, internship or university-run event, or in a voluntary capacity.

The content of event management programmes

Fidgeon (2010) produced an overview of the development of tourism as a discipline and it is suggested that many parallels might be drawn and lessons learned when considering the development of event management: for example, the development of an individual identity, the struggle to be taken seriously as an academic discipline and the balance between developing vocational skills whist achieving academic standards (Fidgeon 2010). It might be suggested that the experience of the tourism subject area be echoed in the development of event management. Indeed, in 1999, Harris and Jago, whilst examining the emergence of event management education in higher education, suggested that event management was being offered as an elective within five main degree areas. These were programmes whose main focus was in tourism, hospitality, sport, management (or business) and human resource management. Similarly, Getz (2002: 20) also considered that there was the potential for event studies provision within the fields of tourism, hospitality and sport management degrees. Getz (2002) proposed the opportunity for event management to evolve into a degree award in its own right and developed a model that detailed the major components that event management degrees might contain. It was considered that this model was a 'conceptual framework for defining interrelated fields of event studies and event management' (Getz 2002: 17). The model suggested that in addition to the requirement of a foundation in management functions (such as finance and human resource management), a degree in event management would include a grounding in event studies and event management. In addition, subjects addressing the various types of events, event setting and the impacts of events should also be included. See Figure 30.1.

As a means of determining the important skills and knowledge that future event managers should possess, Silvers *et al.* (2006) gathered international data and produced a framework that presents event management from a practical, project management perspective. This Events Management Body of Knowledge (EMBOK) as determined by Silvers *et al.* (2006) categorises the content of event management programmes into five domains which are administration, design, marketing, operations and risk (see Table 30.1). Each of these domains is broken down into component parts and Table 30.1 gives an indication of the areas under each domain that

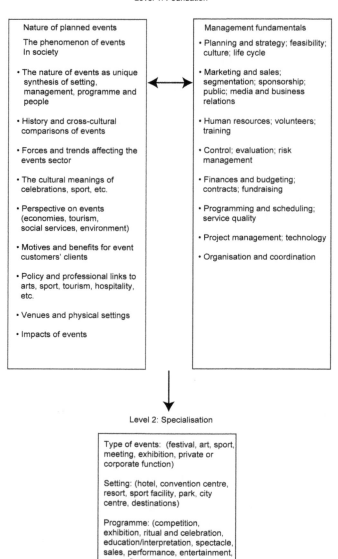

Level 1: Foundation

Nature of planned events

The phenomenon of events
In society

• The nature of events as unique synthesis of setting, management, programme and people

• History and cross-cultural comparisons of events

• Forces and trends affecting the events sector

• The cultural meanings of celebrations, sport, etc.

• Perspective on events (economies, tourism, social services, environment)

• Motives and benefits for event customers' clients

• Policy and professional links to arts, sport, tourism, hospitality, etc.

• Venues and physical settings

• Impacts of events

Management fundamentals

• Planning and strategy; feasibility; culture; life cycle

• Marketing and sales; segmentation; sponsorship; public; media and business relations

• Human resources; volunteers; training

• Control; evaluation; risk management

• Finances and budgeting; contracts; fundraising

• Programming and scheduling; service quality

• Project management; technology

• Organisation and coordination

Level 2: Specialisation

Type of events: (festival, art, sport, meeting, exhibition, private or corporate function)

Setting: (hotel, convention centre, resort, sport facility, park, city centre, destinations)

Programme: (competition, exhibition, ritual and celebration, education/interpretation, spectacle, sales, performance, entertainment, games/humour)

Target market: (participants vs spectators; socio-economic segments)

Figure 30.1 Major components of event management education

Table 30.1 EMBOK knowledge domains and classes

Administration	Design	Marketing	Operations	Risk
Financial	Catering	Marketing plan	Attendees	Compliance
Human resources	Content	Materials	Communications	Emergency
information	Entertainment	Merchandise	Infrastructure	Health and safety
Procurement	Environment	Promotion	Logistics	Insurance
Stakeholders	Production	Public relations	Participants	Legal and ethics
Systems	Programme	Sales	Site	Decision analysis
Time	Theme	Sponsorship	Technical	Security

Source: Adapted from Silvers *et al.* 2006: 194

might be addressed in an event management programme. For example, administration includes areas such as finance, human resources, procurement, etc. Whilst there is an understanding and recognition of the use of the EMBOK as providing an overview of the important elements of event management, it has, however, been criticised as not focusing sufficiently on the management function (for example, categorising finance as an administrative element) and thus placing event management in an operational, rather than managerial, sphere. However, whilst the EMBOK's rather vocational approach has been criticised by academics, it presents a distillation of information from a number of international sources (for example, Royal and Jago 1998; Getz, 2002; Nelson 2004) regarding the skills required in order to effectively organise, administer conduct and evaluate an event and consequently, it is a useful framework on which to develop academic programmes.

Growth in programme provision

Both the supply of, and the demand for, event management programmes has witnessed unprecedented growth in recent years. In 2008, King reported on a change in student preferences from traditional tourism and hospitality programmes towards a focus on the study of events management and related topics. This trend was further highlighted by Silvers *et al.* (2006); Berridge (2007); Getz (2008a); Jackson *et al.* (2008); Lockstone *et al.* (2008) and Robinson *et al.* (2008) who had, through a variety of research projects in the UK, Australia and the United States, noted a significant growth in the demand for events-related courses. Indeed, when discussing student demand for this discipline, erstwhile measured researchers adopt rather emotive, but possibly realistic, language; for example, Getz (2008b: 411) goes so far as to suggest this discipline as a 'hot growth area' within education provision. Jackson *et al.* (2008) suggested a rise in demand for higher education event programmes of over 70 per cent in three years in the UK. Further evidence of the rapid increase in demand for such programmes was found by Berridge (2007) who, in session 2004–5, identified an 80 per cent increase in event management students – with some programmes experiencing a doubling of the cohort. In Australia, Robinson *et al.* (2008) found a 300 per cent increase (albeit from a small base) of students on a specific events studies programme.

Several reasons for this growth have been proposed that explain the increase in the interest in the event industry and event management education. Getz (2002: 6) suggested that the industry is generally attractive to students through perceived accessibility and increased profile. Robinson *et al.* (2008) considered that the events industry represented a 'more cosmopolitan and marketable' industry within the more traditional fields of tourism, hospitality and leisure. From the perspective of further and higher education facilities, the need to develop relevant and innovative course provision is met in the development of popular courses that fit well with existing course provision.

Examples of provision in the UK and Australia

The above discussion clearly identifies an increase in the demand for, and supply of, event management education, especially at higher education level. The authors examined a number of governmental and individual sources in both the UK and Australia as a means of attempting to identify the number, level and scope of event management provision within the higher education sector. Table 30.2 gives an overview of the extent of such provision as at September 2010. What is obvious from the data is the proliferation and consequent quantity of event management in both the UK and Australia. It can be seen that currently sixty-four UK universities are offering 369 undergraduate programmes in event management and twenty-seven universities offer some eighty-three master's level qualifications in the area. Event education in Australia, too, appears well catered for with seventeen universities offering sixty-four event management programmes at undergraduate level and eight offering master's programmes.

Focusing on the UK provision, Table 30.3 presents an overview of the programmes within which event management has a greater or lesser presence. It can be seen that while event management is developing as a field of study in its own right, and that the highest number of

Table 30.2 Number of universities and courses available in events management within the UK and Australia

	United Kingdom	Australia
Number of universities with event mgt at undergraduate level	64	17
Number of undergraduate event mgt programmes of study	369	64
Number of universities with event mgt at postgraduate level	27	8
Number of postgraduate event mgt programmes of study	83	22

Sources: Variety of sources, for example the University and Colleges Admissions Service (UCAS).

Table 30.3 Event management and its specialisations within UK undergraduate courses

Undergraduate subjects available for 2010	Number of programmes
Event Management inc. International Event Management, International Event and Festival Management, and Event and Festival Management	54
Event Management (EM) with Tourism	23
EM with Sport/Sports Management	21
EM with Hospitality	11
EM with Marketing, Public Relations and Advertising	22
EM with the Arts including Music, performance, film studies, etc.	40
EM with Media including Journalism, media studies, digital media and internet, etc.	19
EM with Business	16
EM with/or Conference Management	5
EM with Law	3
EM with Finance including Economics and accounting	8
EM with Human Resources	5
EM with Languages	23
EM with Information Technology	9
EM with another specialism	32

Sources: Variety of sources, for example the University and Colleges Admissions Service (UCAS).

programmes have event management as the focus, many other programme areas have utilised the popularity of the event management area and developed new programmes in conjunction with existing offerings. These joint programmes link event management either to a closely related area (for example, hospitality or sports management); to a business studies-related area (for example, business management or human resources); or indeed to an area that can be quite separate in focus (for example, languages or information technology). What is evident, however, is the quantity and breadth of event management offering at undergraduate level in the UK.

Debates and directions for events management education

Current debates in event management education

It has been suggested that employers are increasingly requiring and expecting tertiary qualifications specifically in event management when recruiting and selecting managers. Research by Jackson et al. (2008) highlighted that one of the barriers to the future performance of the sector was identified as the lack of event managers with a full profile not only of general management skills, but also of skills and knowledge of the event management field. Suggestions regarding the core competencies required within the field of events management (Silvers et al. 2006) have been previously highlighted (Table 30.1). However, Getz (2002) and Lockstone et al. (2008) have criticised the lack of a core discipline within event management education and Getz (2002) suggested that events studies had reached a critical level where there is a definite requirement for a core element within each module within a programme to be related directly to events management. In addition, certain essential areas, such as risk management, have been identified as lacking in many event management undergraduate programmes (Lockstone et al. 2008).

Lockstone et al. (2008), Beaven and Wright (2006) and Robinson et al. (2008) have all identified an underlying issue for students of event management programmes which appears to stem from the students' unrealistic perceptions of the reality of working lives in the event industry and, further, the management level of employment they are likely to enjoy upon graduation. In their 2008 study, Robinson et al. (2008: 15) found that, amongst participants, there was an 'element of dissatisfaction when informed of career path options' within the events industry and suggested that this is potentially due to 'unrealistic expectations of career opportunities throughout their degree programme and, indeed, prior to commencing university'. This finding is corroborated by studies that have found a discrepancy in levels of pay that graduates expect to achieve and actual levels of remuneration common in the industry, with levels expected much higher than reality (Hamm and Robertson 2010). It was also found that there appeared a trend amongst event management students to stick to their own beliefs and perceptions of potential career paths and pay scales, despite information to the contrary from university staff and industry professionals.

The final criticism that is directed toward event management programmes in general stems from the almost unprecedented growth of such programmes and contends that the industry may not be able to accommodate the number of graduates of management programmes who are currently, and continuously, emerging into the workforce (Lockstone et al. 2008). In addition to graduates' unrealistic expectations of working life in the industry, employers too have concerns regarding the level of key skills that graduates possess and concerns have been raised regarding low levels of written and verbal communication skills amongst graduates (Beaven and Wright 2006).

Harris (2004) and Getz (2000) highlighted an industry with a relative level of immaturity, and there is potentially an issue regarding a lack of professionalism within the events management industry. The discrepancy between graduate expectations and the reality with regards to employment in industry is highlighted by Lockstone *et al.* (2008), Beaven and Wright (2006) and Robinson *et al.* (2008) and it is argued that this disparity needs to be addressed as a means of ensuring graduates have an appropriate idea of what to expect of future careers in the industry. The concept of a moral question regarding the imbalance between employment in what is still a fledgling industry and the provision of management programmes by tertiary educators wishing to take advantage of the popularity of event management programmes has been raised (Barron 2008), and connected to this argument are suggestions by Lockstone *et al.* (2008) that highlight the real danger that there may be too many graduates emerging into the profession and that there is a real need to track event management graduates to determine career destinations and trajectories. This point is further enforced by Hamm and Robertson (2010: 7), who state that there is a troubling issue of lack of job opportunities for events graduates in the events industry, and highlight a study published by mice.net magazine in 2009 that suggests that 62 per cent of respondents felt their biggest challenge was a lack of available opportunities within the sector.

Current debates in events management research

A number of researchers (see, for example, Formica 1998; Getz 2002; Allen *et al.* 2008; Bowdin *et al.* 2008) have suggested that current research into event management has focused on common themes such as the economic, environmental and socio/cultural impacts of events, and management alongside sport and marketing studies. Getz (2000) considers this a fragmented approach and suggests that there is a need to bring all groupings together to discuss an appropriate research strategy for the industry.

In a similar vein, Formica (1998) and Getz (2000, 2002) discussed the lack of a global agenda concerning event management and consider that efforts should be made to concentrate events research and studies to areas and regions where events are most prominent. It is further highlighted that future research should encompass the global community, as historically there has been a concentration on the European and Asian areas rather than in the United States. Such a Western-centric strategy, it is argued, will consolidate the concept of events as a worldwide phenomenon and, in turn, should encourage the bridging of academic knowledge within the events industry.

Getz (2000) considered that there is a major challenge involved in engaging practitioners with current research. He highlights the work of the IFEA and states that this organisation has incorporated a research symposium into its annual conference; however, he laments that it is still very difficult to engage practitioners in the research process and understand the value of studies that are increasingly reported in the academic press.

Future directions for event management education

Getz (2002: 16) stated that 'the search for disciplinary status leads to research journals publishing higher quality papers, new textbooks and academic tomes, higher degrees, new teaching materials and programmes, Master's and Doctoral dissertations on the subject, and perhaps new schools or departments being created', and suggests that within education there needs to be a firm basis of understanding the core elements of 'event studies'. Getz (2008b: 3) identifies that there may never be a proper specialisation within universities regarding events students; however, he states that 'the evolution of leisure, tourism and other closely related fields suggest that it will'. He further suggests that there 'has to be a critical mass of degree programmes in place, conferences, students and scholars doing research and publishing articles, and perhaps even academic organisations dedicated to the subject before legitimacy can be achieved for a new field' (Getz, 2008b: 2). Getz *et al.* (2010) further identify that there is a requirement to fully understand events management and the 'social constructs' behind it to ensure that it continues to be an area of academic growth in the future.

Another indicator of the stage of development of a field of study is the creation of journals specifically related to the events and festival management field alongside the conference and convention industry. Getz (2002; Getz *et al.* 2010) and Formica (1998) both identify the creation of subject specific journals within the field as a sign of a distinct 'body of knowledge' and the consequent emergence of a 'distinct field of study' (Getz 2002: 14). Prior to the emergence of these academic journals (for example, *The International Journal of Event and Festival Management* in 2010), researchers published their work in more mainstream tourism and hospitality journals. Whilst there might be some debate regarding the overall quality of research in this area, there can be no argument regarding the quality of some of the research recently published. Indeed, a rudimentary search of the *Tourism Management* website states that five out of the twenty most downloaded articles focus on event management.

Conclusion

A key feature of the development of event education has been the unprecedented growth of the sector. Many higher education institutions, especially in English-speaking destination countries, have been developing and are now offering some element of event management education at both undergraduate and postgraduate levels. Whilst a number of researchers have suggested negative consequences of such rapid growth, it might be argued that the evolution and development in this sector represents one of the major success stories in the wider tourism education provision. Consequently, it is argued that event management education will be a permanent feature of the higher education offering and there will be continued development event management programmes in regions where provision is currently limited or non-existent. However, it is also suggested that event management education in countries such as the UK, and Australia will achieve a point where there is an oversupply of such programmes and universities will inevitably experience a plateauing of demand leading to a rationalisation of supply.

However, this chapter has identified that, in order for the sector to continue its development, a number of key areas require concentration. With regard to cooperation between educators and industry, Jackson *et al.* (2008), Schmader (in Allen *et al.* 2008) and Harris (2004) have highlighted the requirement for unity throughout the industry, and identify a need for industry and academics to work together to create more meaningful research and educational programmes which benefit not only the industry but also the growing population of academics and students alike. Getz (2000) points out that academics are prone to producing theory and that there is a need to ensure that findings from the ever increasing amount of research are communicated in terms that practitioners can understand and relate to. Industry, too, has to play its part by becoming involved in the research process and more fully recognising the value of research (Harris *et al.* 2001). The gap between industry and academia requires to be addressed, through not only an adjustment of the research orientation by academics, but also a willingness to implement the results of industry-specific research by practitioners.

A vital element regarding the future development of event management education is the already identified potential mismatch between the number of event management graduates and the number of appropriate jobs available. This chapter has suggested that, in addition to research examining elements of the event industry, extensive studies regarding the career paths of event management graduates are essential. The popularity of event management programmes shows no sign of abating; indeed, anecdotal evidence would indicate an increase in the number of applications to such programmes. Regardless of the financial benefits that might accrue to an educational institution that takes advantage of the popularity of these programmes, educators have a moral responsibility to ensure that they are not producing graduates who possess industry-specific skills that will never be used.

One key opportunity within the events management sector is seen in the key role of these event graduates once they are employed within the sector. These graduates have the opportunity not only to develop the professional standing of event management, but also to recognise and develop the value of event management programmes within the workplace environment. It is argued that the increasing number of event management graduates will, in turn, lead to the maturation of the professional nature and management of events through the combined resources and knowledge of academics and practitioners.

References

Abraham, D. (2008) 'Holding world class sporting events at a HEI – expanding the curriculum experience in event management', *LINK 20. The Hospitality, Leisure, Sport and Tourism Network*: 19–20.

Allen, J., O'Toole, W., Harris, R. and McDonnell, I. (eds) (2008) *Festival and Special Events Management*, Milton, Queensland: John Wiley and Sons.

Arcodia, C. and Barker, T. (2003) *The Employability Prospects of Graduates in Event Management: Using Data from Job Advertisements*. Available at: http://espace.library.uq.edu.au/eseru/uq:10174/ca_th_jobads.pdf (accessed 12 July 2010).

Arcodia, C. and Robb, A. (2000) 'A future for event management: a taxonomy of event management terms', in L.K. Jago and A.J. Veal (eds) *Events Beyond 2000: Setting the Agenda. Proceedings of the Conference on Events Evaluation, Research and Education*, Sydney: University of Technology, pp. 154–60

Barron, P.E. (2008) 'Education and talent management: implications for the hospitality industry', *International Journal of Contemporary Hospitality Management* 20(7): 730–42.

Barron, P.E. and Maxwell, G.A. (1993) 'Hospitality management students' image of the hospitality industry', *International Journal of Contemporary Hospitality Management* 5(5): 5–8.

Beaven, Z. and Wright, R. (2006) 'Experience! Experience! Experience! Employer attitudes toward and events management graduate employability', *International Journal of Event Management Research* 2(1): 17–24.

Beer, S. (2008) 'Running a practical event unit: dirty learning', *LINK 20. The Hospitality, Leisure, Sport and Tourism Network*: 7–9.

Berridge, G. (2007) *Events Design and Experience*, Oxford. Butterworth-Heinemann.

——(2008) 'Using emotional intelligence to inspire learners: study using the experiences of the 2005 Tour de France', *LINK 20. The Hospitality, Leisure, Sport and Tourism Network*: 40–1.

Bowdin, G. (2008) 'Events management undergraduate education in the UK', *LINK 20. The Hospitality, Leisure, Sport and Tourism Network*: 43–4.

Bowdin, G., Allen, J., O'Toole, W., Harris, R. and McDonnell, I. (2008) *Events Management*, Oxford: Butterworth-Heinemann, second edition.

Brittain, I. (2008) 'The Paralympic Games, disability sport and the curriculum', *LINK 20. The Hospitality, Leisure, Sport and Tourism Network*: 16–18.

Burley, P. (2005) 'Experiential learning produces capable event management graduates', in *The Impacts of Events, Event Management Research Conference*, Sydney: UTS/ACEM, pp. 622–33.

CAA (Commission for Academic Accreditation) (2010). Website at: https://www.caa.ae/caa/DesktopModules/InstPrograms.aspx (accessed 5 December 2010).

Fidgeon, P.R. (2010) 'Tourism education and curriculum design: a time for consolidation and review?', *Tourism Management* 31(6): 699–723.

Finkel, R. (2008) 'Two paths diverge in a field: the increasing professionalism of festival and events management', *LINK 20. The Hospitality, Leisure, Sport and Tourism Network*: 4–5.

Formica, S. (1998) 'The development of festivals and special events studies', *Festival Management and Event Tourism* 5: 131–7.

Getz, D. (2000) 'Developing a research agenda for the events management field', in L.K. Jago and A.J. Veal (eds) *Events Beyond 2000: Setting the Agenda. Proceedings of the Conference on Events Evaluation, Research and Education*, Sydney: University of Technology, pp. 10–21.

——(2002) 'Event studies and event management: on becoming an academic discipline', *Journal of Hospitality and Tourism Management* 9(1): 12–23.

——(2008a) 'Event tourism: definition, evolution and research', *Tourism Management* 29: 403–28.

——(2008b) 'Event studies: definition, scope and development', *LINK 20. The Hospitality, Leisure, Sport and Tourism Network*: 2–3.

Getz, D. and Wicks, B. (1994) 'Professionalism and certification for festivals and event practitioners: trends and issues', *Festival Management and Event Tourism* 2: 103–9.

Getz, D., Andersson, T. and Carlsen, J. (2010) 'Festival management studies: developing a framework and priorities for comparative and cross-cultural research', *International Journal of Event and Festival Management* 1(1): 29–59.

Going to Uni (n.d.) Website at: www.goingtouni.gov.au/CourseFinderAdvancedSearch.htm?RefineSearch= true&award=undergraduate& courseType=both& courseName=Events+Management+ (accessed 3 August 2010).

Goldblatt, J. (2000) 'A future for event management: the analysis of major trends impacting the emerging profession', in L. Jago and A. Veal (eds) *Events beyond 2000: Setting the Agenda: Proceedings of the Conference on Events Evaluation, Research and Education*, Sydney: Australian Centre for Event Management, pp. 2–9.

Hamm, S. and Robertson, I. (2010) 'Preferences for deep-surface learning: a vocational education case study using a multimedia assessment activity', *Australasian Journal of Educational Technology* 26(7): 951–65.

Harris, R. and Jago, L. (1999) 'Event education and training in Australia: the current state of play', *Australian Journal of Hospitality Management* 6(1): 45–51.

Harris, R., Jago, L., Allen, J. and Huyskens, M. (2001) 'Towards an Australian event research agenda: first steps', *Event Management* 6: 213–21.

Harris, V. (2004) 'Event management: a new profession?', *Event Management* 9: 103–9.

Hawkins, D. and Goldblatt, J. (1995) 'Event management implications for tourism education', *Tourism Recreation Research* 20(2): 42–5. Available at: www.embok.org/ (accessed 1 July 2010).

Jackson, C., Beeston, S. and Alice, D. (2008) 'Event management skills', *LINK 20. The Hospitality, Leisure, Sport and Tourism Network*: 5–7.

King, B. (2008) *Tourism and Hospitality Education in Australia: Past, Present and Future*. Available at: www.polyu.edu.hk/htm/iast/bienniall11/conf_paper_king.pdf (accessed 12 July 2011).

Lockstone, L., Junek, O. and Mair, J. (2008) 'Experiential learning in event management education: do industry placements in degree courses complement jobs available in the events industry?', paper presented at CAUTHE Conference, 'Where the Bloody Hell Are We?', 11–14 February.

McDonald, D. and McDonald, T. (2000) 'Festival and event management: an experiential approach to curriculum design', *Event Management* 6: 5–13.

Moscardo, G. and Norris, A. (2004) 'Bridging the academic practitioners gap in conference and events management: running events with students', *Journal of Convention and Event Tourism* 6(3): 47–62.

Nelson, K. (2004) 'Sociological theories of career choice: a study of workers in the special events industry', doctoral dissertation, University of Nevada Las Vegas.

Perry, M., Foley, P. and Rumpf, P. (1996) 'Events management: an emerging challenge in Australian higher education', *Festival Management and Event Tourism* 4: 85–93.

Podium (2010) *The Further and Higher Education Unit for the 2010 Olympic Games*. Available at: www.podium.ac.uk/ (accessed 5 December 2010).

Prospects (n.d.) Website at: www.prospects.ac.uk/search_courses_results?keyword=events%20management% 20& filter = location/50/51& filter = institution/3767& delfilter = institution/3767 (accessed 20 July 2010).

Robinson, R., Barron, P. and Solnet, D. (2008) 'Innovative approaches to event management education in career development: a study of student experiences', *Journal of Hospitality, Leisure, Sport and Tourism Education* 7(1): 4–17.

Roche, M. (2000) *Mega Event and Modernity: Olympics and Expos in the Growth of Global Culture*, London: Routledge.

Royal, C. and Jago, L. (1998) 'Special event accreditation: the practitioner's perspective', *Festival Management and Event Tourism* 5: 221–30.

Schmader, S. (2008) 'The power of celebration – the globalisation and impact of the festivals and events industry', in J. Allen, W. O'Toole, R. Harris and I. McDonnell (eds) *Festival and Special Events Management*, Milton, Queensland: John Wiley and Sons.

Shipway, R. (2008) 'Using sporting and cultural event to optimise the educational power of Olympic Sport', *LINK 20. The Hospitality, Leisure, Sport and Tourism Network*: 11–14.

Shone, A. and Parry, B. (2004) *Successful Event Management*, London: Cengage Learning EMEA, second edition.

Silvers, J., Bowdin, G., O'Toole, W. and Nelson, K. (2006) 'Towards an international event management body of knowledge (EMBOK)', *Event Management* 9: 185–98.

Solent, D., Robinson, R. and Cooper, C. (2007) 'An industry partnerships approach to tourism education', *Journal of Hospitality, Leisure, Sport and Tourism Education* 6(1): 66–70.

UCAS (n.d.) Website at: www.ucas.ac.uk/ (accessed 6 July 2010).

Williamson, P. (2005) 'Event management students' reflections on their placement year: an examination of their "critical experiences"', in *The Impacts of Events, Event Management Research Conference*, Sydney: UTS/ACEM, pp. 605–21.

31

Festivals and events, government and spatial governance

Martin Robertson and Kenneth Wardrop

Introduction

This article seeks to clarify some of the current uncertainties of what politics means in a rapidly changing society. More importantly it investigates the position and role of organised events for the institutions of government. It does so with reference to two case studies – Stirling and Edinburgh, Scotland.

The authors suggest that politics and participation in politics remains a fundamental measure of the health of civil society. They also claim that an ongoing recognition of the depth of civil involvement affects the actions of government in how it chooses to initiate, support or not support festival and events in any given location. In stating this the authors propose that the changing nature of political participation, the confirmatory role played by increasing levels of social capital in our society and the predominance of national spatial development frameworks have together irrevocably altered the political environment in which events and festivals must prosper.

Six broad areas of policy intervention are identified in the first of three models employed to represent the spatial domain of politics and policy relating to events. A case study analysis of the cities of Edinburgh and the city of Stirling, Scotland, is undertaken to review the role and function of events and festival provision within the modern political setting.

With reference to the spatial domain, two further models represent the dynamic nature of networks and their proximity to spatial development objectives. These are elicited from the case study and the supporting literature. The second of these two models displays the rising importance of local spatial plans which are independent to those of the national plan.

Other than in Edinburgh, the strategic significance of festivals and other events is unclear with most local plans. The authors conclude that in the towns and cities of Scotland, festivals and events will nonetheless have an increasingly strategic function which will straddle an increasingly diverse range of government objectives. The authors warn that political ambitions and the imponderable risks faced in providing events can endanger many of these.

Politics, events and being human – a précis

Hall and Rusher (2004: 220) outline the way events and politics are intrinsically connected when they say:

Decisions affecting the hosting of events; the nature of government involvement in events; the structure of agencies responsible for event bidding, development, management, marketing and promotion; and the involvement of communities in events all emerge from a political process.

Further, events exist in a social and economic context where political theories enable understanding of what something means within this expansive and complicated environment, i.e. they provide a framework for understanding. They also provide an aid in deciding what events could be or should do in that context. This is very important in a context where events have to be facilitated or fully supported by the public sector.

Extrapolated from centuries of philosophical discussion, politics is viewed by some as weighty, impenetrable or of little relevance to ordinary life. Indeed, in academic and mass literature there is a suggestion that people are more interested in life than politics, or, more contentiously, that we now live in what Boggs (2001) calls a culture of 'antipolitics'. More particularly, it is said that the rise of wealth and the increasing number of resources available to the people of developed western countries has distracted them from political interest (van Deth 2000; Rucht 2006; van Oorschot *et al.* 2006).

A basic tenet exists: the more a person owns or has the potential to access, the more are the distractions from political engagement and political involvement. This view is addressed further with regard to the relation between here political involvement and an accumulation of social capital. It is important that, the reader is first made aware of the belief of the authors that those people who state they have no interest in politics may be mistaken in what they understand as politics, and that people are more polictical, not less.

Principally there are very few people who don't have their own views about an issue that affects them. Moreover, it has always been the case that what we do has arisen from the democratic process, a process emerging from centuries of philosophical engagement – and the institutional arrangements that have grown around or with this engagement. Politics is an ongoing process of philosophical discovery by humankind. The institutions which serve its purpose have arisen from these philosophies and are, therefore, human. The most explicit point of overlap between the institutions of politics and political theory are people. Without serving people politics would not exist. The decisions, actions and authority of government are necessarily the consequence of politics. As such we should consider that politics arise from human interaction; our action as citizens.

The address given by Pericles, General of the city of Athens, to the citizens of Athens at the annual state funeral for those who had died in the ongoing Peloponnesian war is a frequently cited reference to the superior value of engagement with politics as an indication of citizenship in a full and civil life:

> An Athenian citizen does not neglect the state because he takes care of his own household; and even those of us who are engaged in business have a fair idea of politics. We alone regard a man who takes no interest in public affairs, not as harmless, but as a useless character; and if few of us are originators, we are all sound judges of policy.
>
> *(Pericles, 495–429 BC; in Sabine and Thorson 1973: 28)*

However, with time the nature of political participation has changed and it is certainly very different now from in the times of Pericles. For the concision, the definition of participation (in civil and politically aware life) taken here is that it 'means taking part in a collective endeavour which usually requires some sort of activity from several or all of those involved' (Rucht 2006: 111).

Importantly, participation can be perceived in a variety of ways. The theory and application of policy relating to social capacity is important in understanding and explaining this variety.

Social capital and political engagement

The concept of *social capital* recognises that social relationships can be used to realise personal targets and that family and community networks which operate with high levels of trust and sense of reciprocity in their dealings are likely to enjoy exponential levels of success. Putman (2000) recognises participation, involvement and association as dynamics in the formation of social capital (Johnston and Percy-Smith 2003). The UK government recognises these associations as multifaceted forms of social engagement and development that together support heightened civic engagement.

The UK government 2003 guide to social capital (Hall 2010) recognises three levels of social capital association: *bonding* (with people who are similar); *bridging* (linking to different types of people) and *linking* (connections of people through different relations or hierarchies of power). Within this association, it is suggested that four areas of citizen participation are used to account for the extent of social capital in any locality. These include: the view of the locality (by members of the locality); the number and depth of involvement with a social network; the degree to which a person is a participating civilian, i.e. taking action in relation to both political and social issues; and, the degree to which there is trust between people and their legal position.

Importantly, as Woolcock and Narayan (2000: 243) recognise, 'social capital does not exist in a political vacuum' and does suppose a higher level of civic engagement by the population. With this level of civic engagement it is assumed that there will be a corresponding higher engagement with politics, i.e. that the intellectual engagement with civil society increases knowledge and civic interaction and, concomitantly, political involvement. Conversely some have proposed that, rather than stimulating political involvement, the rise in social capital has actually hastened the death of political interest. Moreover, they argue that the growth of individuality and individual consumption has brought with it increased autonomy and greater external interests, and a lowering in political interest and increase in the range of diversions.

In response, van Deth's (2000) findings indicate that, while an increase in the quantity of resources available to people has been matched with a large decline in political party membership, most indicators in Western Europe also show a rise in political involvement, albeit with a lower level of its saliency, i.e. there is an increased interest in political issues but a lowering in the significance of politics for the individual when related to other factors in his or her life.

Results from the large longitudinal cross-national survey of human values, the European Values Survey (EVS) and the World Value survey (WVS), record a very marked reduction in political party membership and membership of related associations from 1990 to 2000 (Rucht 2006). So again there is evidence to support a view that increased social capital in a period of increased wealth and cultural growth do reduce the significance of politics. Yet throughout Europe there has been an increasing involvement in other forms of issue activity (van Deth and Elff 2004; Rucht 2006). Importantly, the diverse range of interests and the large number of people involved in these activities (protest or otherwise) can be recorded as evidence of an increasing diversity of political views and needs.

Moreover, with reference to the World Value Survey (1995–2000) and data derived from eighty-five societies, Welzel and Klingemann (2008) conclude that this substantive form of political involvement is a positive confirmation of an effective congruence of democracy. Therefore social capital may, in the western world at least, be seen as a series of actions which while lowering the saliency or knowledge of politics has, conversely, increased levels of subjective political interest and activity. It may be concluded thus that it is not true to say that people are not actively involved, or that they are uninterested in politics.

Third way politics and spatial policy

The 1980s brought with them a neo-liberal approach to governance, an emphasis on policy convergence and an application of corporate structures to public agencies (Burns 2004; Harrison 2006). This was often referred to as 'third way politics' during the 1990s. Two political leaders of that decade, Tony Blair, prime minister of Great Britain, and Bill Clinton, president of the United States, are synonymous with its application in the western world. In the UK context this process of third way political integration saw the national government continue to create a regulatory policy framework, whilst devolving the powers of integration and application to regional and local government agencies.

The decentralisation of national government and application of corporate cultures to regional and local government encouraged networking as an organisational construct. Indeed the networking of public and private sector companies, sector associations, organisations and group interests has a well-established history for tourism (Burns 2004; Dredge 2006). With it, reference to models of corporate efficiency and output-based performance measurability have evolved.

The public sector, private sector and social networks and clusters that have formed in the last decade as result of this evolution serve to validate the potential of this governance model, to facilitate innovation and enhance competitive capacity. With this success, and being managed within a framework of tourism development, this governance framework is also viewed as an appropriate base for the development of festivals and events (Mackellar 2006; Misener and Mason 2006; Stokes 2006). The characteristics of this governance model are marked by a sequence of early involvement and support, followed by a process of integration and self-regulation to make possible future withdrawal or near withdrawal of government intervention.

However, whilst networks rely upon collaboration and the ability to work in a way which transcends organisational boundaries (Dredge 2006), the special, developing and often complex nature of public events – which include their short-term nature, the intrusion that they make on public and community space, their irregularity and the associated physical and financial risks they impart – makes them particularly hard to manage. This is most particularly the case in those locations which have a smaller draw of cultural and tourism resources or which lack the appropriate organisational structure to develop the capacity to manage them. As Dredge and Whitford (2010) suggest, there is a more complex involvement by government with the event sector. In this the involvement of government is mediated by many other factors.

In the current climate of economic uncertainties, socio-demographic shifts and an increasingly shared global culture, Europe (as elsewhere) is full of competing destinations. The entrepreneurial style of planning required by cities (Robertson and Guerrier 1998; Robertson and Wardrop 2004), in particular, exemplifies this. The need to enhance predominantly urban areas to become more competitive has required the application of a great many spatial themes, e.g. 'learning regions, knowledge communities, industrial districts, compact cities, liveable cities, creative cities, multicultural cities, fair cities' (Albrechts 2010: 75). With this has come 'new' spatial planning and spatial policy. There do not seek to repeat the comprehensive and centralised spatial planning patterns of the 1960s and 1970s but, rather, to become a process that is 'transformative and integrative' (Albrechts 2010: 79). As Hall (2003: 267) states, these policies are about economic, social and environmental objectives for a designated location, and, importantly, about ensuring 'institutional capacities to facilitate this intervention'. Led by the public sector but dependent on networks, the purpose is to create special places where there are interrelations between activities and other arising networks (Healey 2004; Albrechts 2010). Spatial policy thus aligns itself to the creation or the re-imaging and brand construction of *place*. Festivals, sport events and cultural activities are very important elements in that process (Paiola 2008), as are business events (Jago and Deery 2010). Festivals, sports, events and culture are therefore not only adding to the social capital index of a location – working at a *bonding* and *bridging* capacity – but also contribute to spatial development.

Why is the government interested in events?

Tourism has long held strategic economic and social importance for Scotland and it is supported by the government for this reason (Macleod and Todnem 2007; Page 2007). Over time, government have become more aware of the benefits and impacts of events – from the tourism development perspective, and have become rapidly more involved in their creation, funding and management (Ali-Knight and Robertson 2004; Bowdin *et al.* 2006). Correspondingly, in Scotland government involvement with events – at national, regional and local levels, and via agencies – has grown exponentially over the last ten years. Figure 31.1 has been developed from the case study analysis and the literature which covers events, festivals and government policy (IFACCA 2008; Robertson *et al.* 2009; Whitford 2009). The diagram is indicative of the great range of purpose that events can play for governments. The authors acknowledge that there are many subcategories that could be applied in addition to those detailed.

It should also be acknowledged that the relationship, purpose and process of intervention in event strategies or programmes take different forms, dependent on the level at which government power is exerted, i.e. local, regional or national. There are many more studies of regional

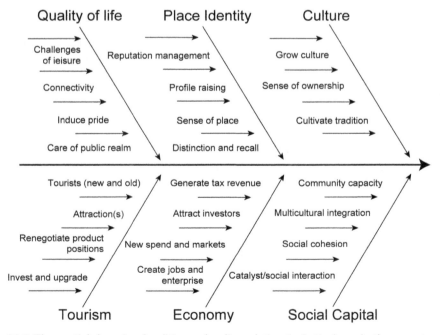

Figure 31.1 The spatial domain of politics and policy relating to festivals and other events

or national government intervention with large events than there are studies of events and event strategies instigated at a local government level. For this reason the case studies here look predominantly at local intervention. As we have seen, however, the national context is of paramount importance in the spatial planning context and we will look at this first.

National interest

Events can be used to correspond with a great number of regional and national strategy priorities and their related policy objectives. For Scotland this includes the four key aims of the National Planning Framework, with the summary titles of 'Wealthier and Fairer', 'Greener', 'Healthier' and 'Smarter'(Scottish Executive 2009). In 2004 the first National Planning Framework for Scotland was offered as 'Guidance for the spatial development of Scotland to 2025' (Scottish Executive 2004) and was a response to the European Spatial Development frameworks that emerged in the European Union at that time (Roberts 2002).

In 2009 the National Planning Framework 2 (NPF2) was formed to guide the long-term spatial development of Scotland's towns, cities and rural areas and to encourage and fund related strategies until 2030. Within this framework, emphasis is given to Scotland's sense of 'place' in a modern knowledge economy. Similarly, emphasis is also given to the need to attract creative people by developing 'a stimulating environment, amenities for a wide range of lifestyles' and a recognition that 'successful places have strong, positive identities' (Scottish Executive 2009). Further, the plan states that 'a distinctive identity, building on local traditions and developing local speciality products can help to strengthen the sense of pride and community' and that 'the presence of centres of academic excellence and well-developed social and cultural facilities are essential parts of the package' (Scottish Executive 2009).

An important influence on the 2009 document is the Scottish Executive's 2008 document *Place Race: The Role of Place in Attracting and Retaining Talent in Scottish Cities* (DEMOS/Scottish Enterprise 2008). Produced by DEMOS, the UK-based political and power 'think tank' (www.demos.co.uk), this document offers a metric for gauging regional place competitiveness which is based on the measurements of *reputation, opportunities, values* and *assets* (ROVA). Within the document festivals (mentioned thirty-one times) and events (mentioned twenty-four times) are identified by their capacity to provide prestige, both for the destination and tourism-related employment, and the combined importance this has in the ROVA competitiveness metric.

Events are identified repeatedly as having a key function as capacity-building exercises which relate both to the spatial plan objectives outlined (above) and to the development of social capital for Scotland. It is not possible within this work to cover all of the events that have matches with – and serve the purpose of – capacity building for the above-named NPF2 aims. However, one case study that can be highlighted is *Homecoming Scotland* which ran in 2009 and included more than 400 events and is reported to have attracted 95,000 visitors and generated £53.7m in additional tourism revenue (Scottish Executive 2010).

The organisation EventScotland grew out of the Scottish government's *Major Events Strategy* (2003–15) with the purpose of delivering a viable portfolio of major events and making Scotland one of world's best event destinations by 2015. EventScotland's objectives are to attract events of national and international standing and economic, cultural and environmental benefits are anticipated from these.

Event Scotland had an instrumental role in the *Homecoming Scotland* event and its actions coexist with those of NPF2. Similarly, the national tourist board, VisitScotland, has an active role in the promotion and support of events where they fit into the objectives of the organisation. They have had an active role in the *Homecoming Scotland* events.

Local interest

The responsibility for events within local government varies between department or departments or a subsection of a department. Examination of the placement of event faculties within the local government structure 'will reveal that events can be, and are, underpinned by economic, socio-cultural or environmental motives' (Dredge and Whitford 2010: 9), i.e. that there can be great variation between localities and the purpose of anticipated outcomes that drive them. While Richards and Palmer (2010) state that events can be motivated by cause, often political, in the context of events and the involvement of UK governments, it is rarely the case the programming of events is overtly political. It is the case, however, that programming is likely to be related to policy, and again this relates to NPF2 which gives spatial perspectives that are particular to each broadly defined area of Scotland, i.e. Central Belt, East Coast, Highlands and Islands, Ayrshire and the South-West and the South of Scotland. The case studies here look at the cities of Edinburgh and Stirling.

Edinburgh, like all other cities in Scotland, is defined in NPF2 as a key economic driver for the country. Edinburgh and Glasgow are also recognised as major tourism and leisure gateways for Scotland. Events and festivals have a prominent place in the social and economic fabric of the city (Carlsen *et al.* 2007) and this clearly makes a difference to the significance and potential role that they can play. The city and rural fringes of Stirling are recognised as offering important attractive areas for development with strategically important transport links. Parts of Stirling are also recognised as requiring urban regeneration.

A 2009 investigatory spatial planning document for Stirling, the *Stirling City Vision* report (Stirling Council and Architecture and Design Scotland 2009), was one document referred to in their development process of a new local development plan (LDP). The report makes extensive reference to the central focus of 'Place making' and 'Place economics' (place, economy, culture, community) as drivers for new LDPs. Events are mentioned in respect of their capacity to shape local identity and the additional possibility of using cultural events to shape new public spaces as well as new spatial and cultural elements for the city. Moreover a series of community events, conferences and a festival relating to food and culture are discussed in the document. Like the national NPF2 it identifies the influencing nature of the Scottish Executive's 2008 document *Place Race: The Role of Place in Attracting and Retaining Talent in Scottish Cities* (DEMOS/Scottish Executive 2008). However, the first publication of a proposed LDP is not due until the end of 2011. As such it serves as an indication of the political direction and function of events in Stirling, but not categorical evidence of such.

The media and national and local interest

Deserving of separate mention is the importance of media coverage as one element of government interest in events. The function of the media in enhancing the image of the location is very important to national and local government agencies. The media is in the public domain and mediates between political will, policy application and public interest. Whilst not specifically an adversary of political will, the media does have an important role in disseminating and managing the issue-led political interests of the populace as well as those of external forces, e.g. potential event-goers or financial investors. The significance of the media is local, national and – for some events – international. Festivals and events have an increasingly central role in commanding media coverage and facilitating image change for destinations, as well as cultural and image identity for visitors and residents – and creating what Stokes (2006) calls the 'feel good' factor for the community.

The policy spectrum of events

Hall and Rusher (2004) refer to public policy as having three essential study purposes. These are: to elicit academic understanding; to ensure professional application; and for political purposes. In the academic sphere, the policy of events is analysed either in respect of its capacity to depict the forces which affect its direction or to assess the effect on those influenced by the policy. In the political arena policy can be viewed with regard to its success or otherwise in matching the political function (e.g. strategy) from which it emerged. In each of these study purposes, policy can always be seen as either directly determined or indirectly influenced by the political system in which the event environment is framed. Figure 31.1 is therefore indicative of what has been identified as six broad areas of policy intervention relating to events. These are 'economics', 'tourism', ' place identity', 'quality of life', 'social capital' and 'culture', the latter representing 'cultural development'. Reference to these intervention areas have all been looked at in the previous sections. These are also points of reference for the two case studies related within this work.

Case studies – the government, political and policy environment for Edinburgh and Stirling, Scotland

The national government perspective

On 25 May 2010, the Scottish government announced that the 2009 'Year of Home-coming' created £53.7m in additional tourism revenue and was 22 per cent over the £44m target originally set for the year. This included 95,000 additional visitors, and £154m of positive global media coverage. At the same time it was announced that there would be a repeat of the event in 2014, a year which will see the hosting of the Commonwealth Games in Glasgow, the Ryder Cup at Gleneagles (the World Cup of golf) and the 700th anniversary of the Battle of Bannockburn (King Robert the Bruce's finest hour in Scotland's Wars of Independence). In addition to the announcement about the year of homecoming in 2014, the Scottish government also announced a series of themed years in the run-up to 2014, starting in 2010/11 with a celebration of Scotland's food and drink, to be followed with a focus in 2011 on Active Scotland, Culture and Creativity in 2012 and, in 2013, Natural Scotland. The 2009 Year of Homecoming included 400 arts and tourism events held in celebration of the 250th anniversary of Scotland's national bard, Robert Burns.

The Scottish government's enthusiasm for themed years such as Homecoming and their continued investment in the twin organisations of VisitScotland and EventScotland are indicative of the continued recognition of events as significant drivers of the visitor economy and as part of the country's marketing arsenal. It is encouraging to see that Homecoming 2009 generated £154m of positive global media coverage. Of course, given the fact that there is a minority Scottish Nationalist Party government in power, some (less than generous) commentators have questioned the motives behind the Homecoming theme. However, the popularity of the Homecoming brand with international visitors and amongst the Scottish Diaspora, along with the benefits of having a major marketing push running in a year when the impacts of the world economic crisis and recession hit, should surely quieten such critics. The appeal of Robert Burns and Scotland's history and heritage are strong selling points and were rightly capitalised upon.

The local (capital city) government perspective – Edinburgh

In Edinburgh the value of events as a marketing tool and part of the visitor product that make a compelling reason to visit the Scottish capital is well understood by local politicians. The economic impact assessment of Edinburgh's major festivals undertaken from 2004 to 2005 created irrefutable evidence of the economic benefits that accrued to the city from the festivals it hosted. This showed that festivals attracted 3.1m attendees, 1.4m trips to the city and an output of £170m, £40m of which was new income for the city (City of Edinburgh Council 2005).

The assessment also demonstrated that the festivals supported 3,200 FTE jobs in a year in Edinburgh. To put the return on investment into context, it is estimated that the city spends circa £35m per annum on direct and indirect support for tourism (including support of the festivals, total public funding support being £3m for the festivals in 2005). This economic impact assessment is now being revisited, some five years later, and will undoubtedly show even greater economic impacts and employment created. In 2010 the Edinburgh Fringe Festival was in its 64th year, selling close to 2 million tickets. The annual impact on the city is the equivalent of a Commonwealth Games event every year.

The international media interest in events such as Edinburgh's Hogmanay and the Royal Edinburgh Military Tattoo are vitally important in the year-on-year profiling Edinburgh gives to a global audience. The promotional benefits have also been well recognised by successive political administrations in Edinburgh and the city recognises that it holds the crown as 'the World's Festival City', with many competitors snapping at its heels. As a result of the *Thundering Hooves* report (Scottish Arts Council 2006) it was understood by those with an interest in the festivals within the city that Edinburgh could not be complacent about the need to take action to protect its competitive advantage. The creation of the new organisation Festivals Edinburgh by the festivals, the City Council and the Scottish government was in recognition of the dangers of complacency. Led by Director Faith Liddell, Festivals Edinburgh has brought together representatives of the twelve major festivals. They recognise the mutuality of their situation and the collaborative benefits that can accrue in marketing, product innovation, content control and maximisation, and data acquisition (on audience, for example). The organisation works with the support of the City of Edinburgh Council, EventScotland and VisitScotland and, in addition to the mutually supportive work mentioned, also works on ensuring good practice, sustainable and professional development.

For Edinburgh's politicians and policy makers, the context for continued support of events and festivals is both the importance of a vibrant cultural life as a driver of the economy (especially in an economy such as Edinburgh's which is based on its intellectual capital and knowledge workers) and in supporting tourism and, of course, culture and creative endeavour. The city promotion body, Destination Edinburgh Marketing Alliance (DEMA) (which came in to being on 1 April 2009), has at its heart the city's first Destination Promotion Strategy and the city's cultural offer agendas of 'visit, invest, live, work and study'.

DEMA's thesis is that the attractiveness of the city for inward investment and talent capitalises on the brand equity of the city as a visitor destination. Attending or participating in festivals and events (cultural and sporting) are cited by approximately 20 per cent of visitors to the city as a primary reason for their visit (City of Edinburgh Council 2011), while festivals such as Edinburgh's Hogmanay and the Royal Edinburgh Military Tattoo in particular have high levels of interest to international visitors.

Although the International Festival has existed since 1949, Edinburgh's real focus on events was the result of a tourism review undertaken in the 1980s. The Edinburgh tourism review was undertaken jointly by the national government economic and tourism development agencies, local government and representatives of industry. This review identified that Edinburgh was a sleeping giant in terms of the full realisation of its tourism potential. At this time there was significant investment in the tourism infrastructure taking place, such as improvements to interpretation at Edinburgh Castle (the Castle), the building of the National Museum of Scotland extension, the Festival Theatre development, the Edinburgh International Convention Centre expansion of the airport, and the new Scandic Crown Hotel on the Royal Mile. It was a natural extension of this product development to invest in the development of the existing festivals and encouraging of new events.

Events have been seen as a way to showcase the distinct cultural offerings of the city and the nation, and to engender civic pride. Investment in events such as Edinburgh's Hogmanay Street Party and the Tall Ships Race are seen as a mechanism to re-profile the city, raise awareness and attract visitors. The city has had an events unit within the city council for over a decade. The re-establishment of the Scottish Parliament in 1999 also heightened the civic nature of events in the city as it re-established its former capital city status.

The city has well-established protocols and procedures in place for the assessment and management of events and a developed infrastructure of skills and resources to facilitate events of all types. The city is also a natural stage for events with its iconic backdrops of the Castle and the UNESCO World Heritage site of the historic old town. This cohabitation of the old and the new comes with a number of pressures but, ultimately, is very good for the city (Smith *et al.* 2006). The MTV Europe Music Awards in 2003 is also a good example of how protocol and procedures were applied and how this event was used to raise and reposition Edinburgh's profile globally. Here too, politicians were quick to grasp the profiling opportunities for the city, and the opportunity to further advance the positioning of Edinburgh as a contemporary cultural capital city to a younger 'Generation Y' audience.

The local (small city) government perspective – Stirling

In Stirling in the mid 1980s there was an awakening and understanding of the under-developed tourism assets that it possessed, most particularly in the physical forms of Stirling Castle, the Old Town, the National Wallace Monument and the site of the battlefield at Bannockburn. The recognition of these sites of historic significance was matched with a heightened awareness of the centrality of Stirling in the story of Scotland. The launch of the Stirling Futureworld strategic plan (a tourism-led economic regeneration project for Stirling's Old Town) as a platform to raise the profile of the town was a significant boost for the changing needs of Stirling. The plan included a mix of physical regeneration, tourism infrastructure, management, promotion and animation through events. In the 1980s Stirling held a vibrant two-week summer festival immediately before the Edinburgh Summer Festivals. Other high-profile events included 'A Day for Scotland' (an outdoor rock concert supported by the Scottish Trade Union Council), the Battle of Stirling Bridge 700th anniversary celebrations in 1997, Stirling's Hogmanay Concert, Stirling Castle concerts and regular mediaeval markets.

From 1988, a new project, the Stirling Initiative, was established to take forward the regeneration and tourism development plans identified by the council in the Futureworld project. The Stirling Initiative was led by the national government agencies (and consequently attracted more central government resources) so the local political agenda of raising profile and engagement could be seen to have worked. A focused attempt was made to change the dominant profile of visitors as day trippers to Stirling and to encourage overnight stays. This was to enhance economic impacts and encourage new job creation and an increase in accommodation stock. This final impact was realised as a particularly vital element of the ongoing strategy.

The regeneration plans for the Old Town and Castle progressed through the 1980s and 1990s with significant investment taking place at Stirling Castle, (the Chapel Royal, the Great Hall restoration and Royal Kitchens recreation), and projects such as the Old Town Jail, Stirling Highland Hotel, the Tolbooth and Stirling youth hostel all being advanced. These projects were greatly assisted by significant funding support from European Union Structural Funds, which secured the refurbishment of the National Wallace Monument. Coincidentally – and very much to the benefit of Stirling – the making of the blockbuster film *Braveheart*, starring Mel Gibson as William Wallace (one of Scotland's greatest folk heroes), stimulated an international recognition hitherto unknown. So while the National Wallace Monument received circa 40,000 visitors per annum in the early 1990s, after the refurbishment and the release of the film visitor figures rose to over 200,000 per annum.

While new events emerged and were supported in the years following conferral of city status by Queen Elizabeth II in 2002, events remained an under-developed component of growth for Stirling (Page and Hall 2002; Connell and Page 2005). The 24th World Medical and Health Games (WMHTG) in the summer of 2003 is a noticeable exception in a portfolio of mainly small events. Composed of twenty-two different sporting events in venues throughout Stirling, and attracting health professionals from around the world, the economic evaluation of the WMHTG event (commissioned by Stirling Council) claimed a potential impact of £2.4 million (Connell and Page 2005). In their own analysis, Connell and Page (2005) argued that a more comprehensive evaluation of the spatial impacts of the event was required.

In the build-up of a new framework for economic development, the 2004 document *Making Stirling Work* (Stirling Council 2004), five service delivery themes were announced. These are 'working for enterprise', 'learning for work', 'work for everyone', 'making the place work' and 'working together'. Within the 'making the place work' theme, events are recognised as fulfilling two clear service delivery objectives: first, making the city larger, and second, making the city more attractive. A promotion campaign entitled 'Stirling – Scotland's Heart' was initiated in 2007. With the subheading 'proud to be part of Scotland's heart', this offered a clear statement of both national spatial and national historical positioning. While events and festivals are listed in the related website (www.viststirling. org) their non-prominent positioning for the user of the website can be viewed as indication of the limited strategic importance they have held.

The Shaping Stirling strategic plan 2008–12 mentions in its first strategic topic, 'Making tourism a place with a vibrant economy that is open for business', highlighting that a growth in the key sectors of tourism and culture would be an important local outcome. As this is one of five topic areas set to formulate a single outcome agreement to set out actions for the development of Stirling in compliance (and in response to) the aims and outcomes of the Scottish government, this announcement is an important one. However, no direct reference is made to festivals and events. Similarly, the Stirling Tourism Action (Destination Stirling) for 2008–12 stipulates the need to promote Stirling's compact historic city and the surrounding countryside; to increase footfall in the historic and retail areas of the city; to improve the visitor experience; and to improve and promote the identities of the towns and villages surrounding the city. Again, however, no direct reference to events is made.

In the same year (2008) a four-year cultural development plan, 'Enjoy Life in Stirling', was discussed. One of the aims stated within the plan was the building of the cultural capacity of the city, wherein the cultural plan would encourage the capture of ideas (from citizens) and also encourage the participation of citizens, to improve the cultural programmes offered throughout the wider Stirling region and to encourage people's learning and capacity to try new things. Central to the outcomes of the plan were the venues: the Albert Halls, the Tolbooth, the Smith Art Gallery, the Museum and the MacRobert Arts Centre. In website descriptions each makes reference to being an arts venue, a performance space and a festival venue. As an example of its role as a festival venue, the Mac-Robert Arts Centre worked with (and was funded by) the Scottish Arts Council in hosting mFest, a festival held specifically for people in the 12–17-year-old age range. While very important in the provision of events, the limitations of the space each venue offers does not conform to the more open public space normally anticipated for festivals. The emergent cultural development plan, 'Get Involved – Enjoying Life in Stirling', launched in February 2010, offers one explanation of why this is the case.

Stirling Council states that it wants to 'take forward its vision to make Stirling the cultural heart of Scotland where artists and creative and cultural activities are encouraged, valued and accessible to everyone'. Principally, the intention is to raise the citizens' awareness, pride and engagement in Stirling's culture, a process of increasing the cultural capacity of the city.

A series of workshops and consultations in 2009, concluding in the paper *City Vision* (Stirling Council and Architecture and Design Scotland 2009), looks at developing the vision for the city – and the spatial action required to make Stirling a world city. The three spatial concepts addressed in the paper are 'enhancing the strategic relationships to enhance Stirling as a node in the knowledge activity'; 'cross cutting spatial structures to strengthen the urban form of Stirling and pull the city together' and (looking at) 'city functions in terms of urban character, economy and sustainability'. The importance of ensuring capacity for a mixed use of the urban fabric of the city is repeatedly stated. This encapsulates an ongoing frustration in there being failure to regenerate the city extensively and, significantly, to create an events hub in the city and to redesign the Old Town as a conduit for wider event-related development.

In reviewing the role of events in Stirling, it is clear that there have been clear limitations of cross-sector collaboration. There has been a historical and counter-productive reliance on public sector support to push local tourism development (Connell and Page 2005). It is for this reason that both local government support and references made to events and festivals in local development plans are limited.

However, more recent and ongoing support of business education events in Stirling is a very positive move towards increasing the city's capacity to form collaborations. The importance of business events in the portfolio of Scotland's sixth city is to be applauded. Nonetheless Edinburgh benefits from the support of industry-wide 'Ambassadors' to encourage market for the business event sector at both a national and international level, while Stirling has, as yet, neither the support nor the extensive infrastructure that is required.

Development is therefore dependent on the spatial resources available. In the provision of business events these resources are physical and professional (skills and financial collaboration). In the provision of cultural events dependency is determined by the physical, the professional and by the cultural and social capacity (determined by the residents) of the city.

Large events held in Stirling, such as the Homecoming Finale celebration (in 2009), the Stirling's St Andrew's Day celebration (held annually) and the Commonwealth Games Handover events held in October 2010, rely upon national intervention (with VisitScotland and EventScotland) and regional agreement (with Scottish Enterprise Forth Valley), and are part of the national spatial strategy. The current government and local council are led by the Scottish National Party (SNP) and, as such, this augers well for the realisation of the ambitions of the city to celebrate the 700th anniversary of the Battle of Bannockburn in 2014 as part of the next Scottish government-designated 'Year of Homecoming'. It will be interesting to observe the degree to which the city can synthesise its own spatial objectives with those of the Scottish government in the running of the event.

As formative conclusion to these case studies, the political support for tourism development and events in both Stirling and Edinburgh can be characterised as: a recognition of the economic and employment benefits that can accrue from tourism, the role of events in creating *place identity* and raising the profile of a destination (and through this platform also the profile of politicians). Moreover, through the presentation of local cultural assets and characteristics it has been possible to engender or encourage civic pride amongst local people, most events being equally accessible to residents and visitors alike. This broadens the cultural offering, which is very important for places that seek to attract inward investment and talent. Judging by the experience in Scotland, this applies equally at a local and national level. Challenges remain at ensuring community engagement (the social capacity of the residents), and the cross-industry sector and cross-institutional collaboration required for this. The political agenda is central in facilitating responses to these challenges.

The political agenda

The national spatial development framework has been important and beneficial for Edinburgh. However, the City of Edinburgh Council has also been keen to highlight the important and defining dynamics that being a capital city brings but which are not accounted for in NFP2. In responding to the framework with its submission of evidence to the Scottish Executive in 2007, the City of Edinburgh Council highlights the importance of being a capital city in respect of the following: national economic affect; cultural development; as being a gateway city; in national decision making; and as being an ambassador for Scotland. Tellingly, the importance and ensuing cost of events and/or festivals is made in all but one of the sections of the evidence submitted.

In the presentation and discussion of a conceptual framework of event public policy Whitford (2009) puts forward an illuminating analysis of the multifarious nature of both interest and factors of strength in determining the policy and physical outcome of events and festivals, particularly with reference to affecting positive regional development. While the focus of Whitford's work is on southeast Queensland, Australia, and the iterative research design and content analysis methodology applied in the investigation of policy documentation relating to events has not been repeated here, the three areas of development investigated and proposed, i.e. policy pathway, policy community and the event development paradigm, have each influenced the model (Figure 31.2) put forward here to explain the political environment (the agenda) for events in Scotland.

In Figure 31.2 spatial planning is identified as the event development paradigm at a national level. Quality of life, culture and place identity each have significance for the wider community (national and local) while tourism, economy and social capital may be seen as having a more classic strategic fit with the public sector (national and local). Policy, networking (and clusters) and spatial planning serve to bridge and link these elements. The inner circle shown in Figure 31.2 represents the local political and policy environment for events. Here networks and policy are clearly influenced by national spatial policy.

Figure 31.3 offers a view (arising from the case study analysis and literature) of an increase in the independence of the political agenda for events and festivals in the local (largely urban) context. While national spatial planning influences the formation of both policy and the nature and

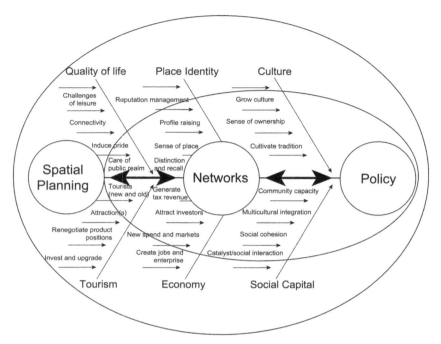

Figure 31.2 The spatial domain of politics and policy relating to events: national (outer) and local (inner)

(Edinburgh)

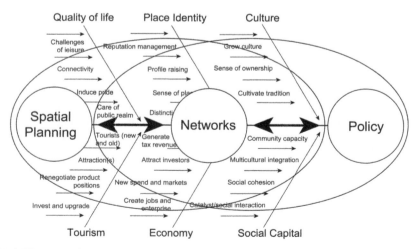

Figure 31.3 The emerging spatial domain of politics and policy relating to events: local (Edinburgh)

range of activities supported by networks, the increasing participation and extent of issues felt to be important by the wider community has augmented an extensive impact on the actions followed by networks. Importantly, the two rings in Figure 31.3 serve to illustrate the increasing independence of city spatial planning from that of the national, and its effect on local policy and the environment in which event strategies emerge. Though not covered in any depth here, the 'capital city' status of Edinburgh, its history of event provision and the extensive development of public, private and NGO networks which support this may have given an uncommon level of success in event hosting. Nevertheless, the *Stirling City Vision* (Stirling Council and Architecture and Design Scotland 2009) exercise indicates a clear willingness to do likewise.

A view of the future

The importance of networks and an awareness of the cross-sectoral nature of partnerships for events in spatial development have been voiced in a number of texts on the subject. The importance of these relationships in ensuring innovation, financial viability and overall sustainability is also stated (Getz and Andersson 2008; Hede and Stokes 2009). Equally, however, despite this significance, festival managers have been slow to involve themselves in partnership activity with destination managers (Stokes 2006; Carlsen *et al.* 2010). The actions of Edinburgh have however been noticeably more favourable to joint endeavours and have served to encourage festival and event directors to engage in this collaboration. This has been aided by the support that the NPF2 gives directly and indirectly to capacity building, and the conscious efforts by the City of Edinburgh to play an important role in the formation of networks which are innovative, both in the range of partnerships formed and in the extent of their application. The organisation Festivals Edinburgh – and its multi-membership composition – is one important example of that. In Stirling the role of events has still to be rolled out fully. The NPF2 does not give priority to events in this area, but the visioning work (2009) makes ongoing reference to events and their role in increasing community and spatial capacity.

With reflection on the case studies, event-led tourism regeneration strategies have better potential for success where events are part of a well-developed and rounded product infrastructure and marketing mix. Both the history of the city, the spatial planning to which it aligns and the local agency collaboration have played well for Edinburgh.

The value of additional spend from visitors to events would not have been fully realised if a developed infrastructure of accommodation, restaurants, retail, visitor attractions and transport infrastructure were not in place. The need for a long-term view of investment in events for a destination is clearly vital. A short-term view of events and their utility as a 'quick fix' in terms of raising a destination's profile is less likely to induce success. For Edinburgh, festivals and events require long-term and ongoing support (Robertson and Wardrop 2004; Carlsen *et al.* 2007) to manage its multiple spatial requirements.

Long-term agendas, however, are often challenges for politicians who are generally looking for immediate results. It takes time for events to develop a 'buzz', to become established in the minds of consumers, and to develop a following. There is often much trial and error in getting the format and character of an event right – until it becomes established as part of a region or country's annual event calendar. Of course, some events backed by significant media partners and corporate sponsors can enable a one-off event to be an instant success in attracting audience or customers. This type of event offers impetus for narrating new ideas and sense of place for locals and visitors. However, the transforming potential of events does not stop there.

Outdoor events are often very vulnerable to the weather, and despite the best planning and infrastructure being in place can perform differently from one year to the next. For this reason, politicians need to be aware of this in judging impacts and committing to ongoing support. The worsening winters in Scotland may have affected Edinburgh's Winter Festival and New Year celebrations, and the cancellation of the 2004 and 2007 Hogmanay street celebrations have been a great concern for Edinburgh and, for smaller cities (such as Stirling), such occurrences could be disastrous.

The spatial planning frameworks associated with Scotland's national development do include festivals and events. Historically – and certainly in Edinburgh and Stirling – festivals and events have been attached to and have grown with the government agencies associated with tourism development. The ongoing costs and development required for – and the risks associated with – festival and event programming will continue to test the governance models associated with current local government structures.

As withdrawing support from the extensive financial costs of event development is not possible, more strategic alliances will be formed and more value from the events sought. Some of this rising cost will be dispersed as festival and event programmes gain strategic associations outside of tourism, e.g. in community development, education, economic capacity generation and arts development (Carlsen *et al.* 2007) etc. It is also likely that we will see festivals and other events in many other political fora.

References

Albrechts, L. (2010) 'Strategic planning and regional governance in Europe – recent trends and policy responses', in J. Xu and A.G.O. Yeh (eds) *Governance and Planning of Mega-City Regions: An International Comparative Perspective*, Hoboken: Routledge, pp. 75–97.

Ali-Knight, J. and Robertson, M. (2004) 'Introduction to arts, culture and leisure', in I. Yeoman, M. Robertson, J. Ali-Knight, S. Drummond and U. McMahon-Beattie (eds) *Festival and Events Management: An International Arts and Culture Perspective*, Oxford: Butterworth-Heinemann, pp. 3–13.

Boggs, C. (2001) *The End of Politics: Corporate Power and the Decline of the Public Sphere*, New York: Guilford Press.

Bowdin, G., Allen, J., O'Toole, W., Harris, R. and McDonnell, I. (2006) *Events Management*, Oxford: Butterworth-Heinemann, second edition.

Burns, P.M. (2004) 'Tourism planning: a third way?', *Annals of Tourism Research* 31(1): 24–43.

Carlsen, J., Ali-Knight, J. and Robertson, M. (2007) 'Access: a research agenda for Edinburgh festivals', *Event Management* 11(1–2): 3–11.

Carlsen, J., Andersson, T., Ali-Knight, J., Jaeger, K. and Taylor, R. (2010) 'Festival management innovation and failure', *International Journal of Event and Festival Management* 1(2): 120–31.

City of Edinburgh Council (2005) *Edinburgh's Festivals – Playing an Essential Role in Economy, Country and Culture. Edinburgh's Year Round Festivals 2004–5 – Economic Study*, Edinburgh: City of Edinburgh Council.

——(2011) *Edinburgh Visitor Survey – October 2009 to September 2010 Final Analysis* (prepared by Lynn Jones Ltd). Available at: www.edinburgh.gov.uk/downloads/file/4104/edinburgh_visitor_survey_2009-10 (accessed 1 March 2011).

Connell, J. and Page, S.J. (2005) 'Evaluating the economic and spatial effects of an event: the case of the World Medical and Health Games', *Tourism Geographies: An International Journal of Tourism Space, Place and Environment* 7(1): 63–85.

DEMOS/Scottish Enterprise (2008) *Place Race: The Role of Place in Attracting and Retaining Talent in Scottish Cities*. Available at www.scottish-enterprise.com (accessed 20 May 2010).

Dredge, D. (2006) 'Policy networks and the local organisation of tourism', *Tourism Management* 27(2): 269–80.

Dredge, D. and Whitford, M. (2010) 'Policy for sustainable and responsible festivals and events: institutionalisation of a new paradigm – a response', *Journal of Policy Research in Tourism, Leisure and Events* 2(1): 1–13.

Getz, D. and Andersson, T. (2008) 'Sustainable festivals: on becoming an institution', *Event Management* 12(1): 1–17.

Hall, C. (2010) *Social Capital – Introductory User Guide*, Newport: Office for National Statistics.

Hall, C.M. and Rusher, K. (2004) 'Politics, public policy and the destination', in I.Yeoman, M. Robertson, J. Ali-Knight, S. Drummond and U. McMahon-Beattie (eds) *Festival and Events Management: An International Arts and Culture Perspective*, Oxford: Elsevier Butterworth-Heinemann, pp. 217–31.

Hall, S. (2003) 'The "third way" revisited: "New" Labour, spatial policy and the national strategy for neighbourhood renewal', *Planning Practice and Research* 18(4): 265–77.

Harrison, P. (2006) Integrated development plans and Third Way politics', in U. Pillay, R. Tomlinson and J. du Toit (eds) *Democracy and Delivery – Urban Policy in South Africa*, Cape Town: HSRC Press, pp. 186–207.

Healey, P. (2004) 'The treatment of space and place in the new strategic spatial planning in Europe', *International Journal of Urban and Regional Research* 28(1): 45–67.

Hede, A.-M. and Stokes, R. (2009) 'Network analysis of tourism events: an approach to improve marketing practices for sustainable tourism', *Journal of Travel and Tourism Marketing* 26(7): 656–69.

IFACCA (2008) *Festival Jungle – Policy Desert? Festival Policies of Public Authorities in Europe*. Available at: www.ifacca.org/publications (accessed 25 November 2008).

Jago, L. and Deery, M. (2010) *Delivering Innovation, Knowledge and Performance: The Role of Business Events*. Available at: http://businesseventscouncil.org.au (accessed 12 June 2010).

Johnston, G. and Percy-Smith, J. (2003) 'In search of social capital', *Policy and Politics* 31(3): 321–34.

Mackellar, J. (2006) 'Conventions, festivals, and tourism: exploring the network that binds', *Journal of Convention and Event Tourism* 8(2): 45–56.

Macleod, C. and Todnem, B.R. (2007) 'Performance, conformance and change: towards a sustainable tourism strategy for Scotland', *Sustainable Development* 15(6): 329–42.

Misener, L. and Mason, D.S. (2006) 'Creating community networks: can sporting events offer meaningful sources of social capital?', *Managing Leisure* 11(1): 39–56.

Page, S.J. (2007) *Tourism Management: Managing for Change*, Oxford: Elsevier, second edition.

Page, S.J. and Hall, C.M. (2002) *Managing Urban Tourism*, Harlow: Prentice Hall.

Paiola, M. (2008) 'Cultural events as potential drivers of urban regeneration: an empirical illustration', *Industry and Innovation* 15(5): 513–29.

Putman, R. (2000) *Bowling Alone: The Collapse and Revival of American Community*, New York: Simon and Schuster.

Richards, G. and Palmer, R. (2010) *Eventful Cities: Cultural Management and Urban Revitalisation*, London: Butterworth-Heinneman.

Roberts, P. (2002) 'The Scottish strategic and spatial context for sustainable development', *Sustainable Development* 10(3): 131–9.

Robertson, M. and Guerrier, Y. (1998) 'Events as entrepreneurial displays: Seville, Barcelona and Madrid', in D. Tyler, Y. Guerrier and M. Robertson (eds) *Managing Tourism in Cities: Policy, Process, and Practice*, Chichester: John Wiley and Sons, pp. 215–28.

Robertson, M. and Wardrop, K. (2004) 'Events and the destination dynamic: Edinburgh festivals, entrepreneurship and strategic marketing', in I. Yeoman, M. Robertson, J. Ali-Knight, S. Drummond and U. McMahon-Beattie (eds) *Festival and Events Management: An International Arts and Culture Perspective*, Oxford: Butterworth-Heinemann, pp. 115–29.

Robertson, M., Rogers, P. and Leask, A. (2009) 'Progressing socio-cultural impact evaluation for festivals', *Journal of Policy Research in Tourism, Leisure and Events* 1(2): 156–69.

Rucht, D. (2006) 'Political participation in Europe', in R. Sakwa and A. Stevens (eds) *Contemporary Europe*, Houndmills: Palgrave Macmillan, pp. 110–37.

Sabine, G. and Thorson, T. (1973) *A History of Political Theory*, Hinsdale: Dryden Press, fourth edition.

Scottish Arts Council (2006) *Thundering Hooves: Maintaining the Global Competitive Edge of Edinburgh's Festival*. Edinburgh: Scottish Arts Council.

Scottish Executive (2004) *National Planning Framework for Scotland*, Edinburgh: Scottish Executive.

——(2009) *National Planning Framework 2*, Edinburgh: Scottish Executive.

——(2010) *Analysis Report of Homecoming Scotland 2009 – Diaspora Events*, Edinburgh: Scottish Executive, Culture and External Affairs Directorate, Promotion of Scotland and Tourism Division.

Smith, M., Carnegie, E. and Robertson, M. (2006) 'Juxtaposing the timeless and the ephemeral: staging festivals and events at World Heritage Sites', in A. Leask and A. Fyall (eds) *Managing World Heritage Sites*, Oxford: Butterworth-Heinemann.

Stirling Council (2004) *Making Stirling Work. The Stirling Economy: A Framework for Action – October 2004*, Stirling: Stirling Council. Available at: www.stirling.gov.uk (accessed 10 June 2010).

Stirling Council and Architecture and Design Scotland (2009) *Stirling City Vision – Report on the Place Visioning Process Summer 2009*, Stirling: Stirling Council.

Stokes, R. (2006) 'Network-based strategy making for events tourism', *European Journal of Marketing* 40(5/6): 682–95.

van Deth, J.W. (2000) 'Interesting but irrelevant: social capital and the saliency of politics in Western Europe', *European Journal of Political Research* 37(2): 115–47.

van Deth, J.W. and Elff, M. (2004) 'Politicisation, economic development and political interest in Europe', *European Journal of Political Research* 43(3): 477–508.

van Oorschot, W., Arts, W. and Gelissen, J. (2006) 'Social capital in Europe', *Acta Sociologica* 49(2): 149.

Welzel, C. and Klingemann, H.-D. (2008) 'Evidencing and explaining democratic congruence: the perspective of substantive democracy', *World Values Research* 1(3): 59–93. Available at: www.worldvaluessurvey.org (accessed 24 October 2010).

Whitford, M. (2009) 'A framework for the development of event public policy: facilitating regional development', *Tourism Management* 30(5): 674–82.

Woolcock, M. and Narayan, D. (2000) 'Social capital: implications for development theory, research, and policy', *The World Bank Research Observer* 15(2): 225.

32

A futurist's view on the future of events

Ian Yeoman, Martin Robertson and Karen Smith

Introduction: the challenges of today's events industry

Events are significant in today's society. They have links to religion, to culture, to sport, to community, to commerce, and to political, policy and microeconomic and macroeconomic influence or objectives. Events are becoming ever more important as they are seen to reap a great many of the elements that a society (served by a government) requires for its development. As society has moved from a manufacturing to an experience economy over the last fifty years, the role of events has become an important element of the experience economy. At the same time, with the arrival of the experience economy and the decline of manufacturing in many places, political leaders have become champions of sporting and cultural events in their nation, city or community. It seems that countries all want mega sporting events such as the Olympic Games or FIFA World Cup or cultural events such as food and wine festivals as a means to attract tourists to a region (Yeoman 2008).

Events are often stated in terms relating to improvement of the quality of life for the populace; or of offering economic and social benefits; or of creating new business networks and opportunities; or profile raising, and in supporting other civic needs (Richards and Palmer 2010). Events are significant in today's society, but will they be significant in the future? Are we at a tipping point of over-supply which will see a rapid decline in events in a future society, triggered by the present global financial crisis and national debt? Who will be the future event tourist, given the emergence of the rising middle classes of China and the impact of demographic change in a Western society? How will social media and technology shape the consumption of live events in the future? These are interesting questions and the purpose of this chapter is to consider these questions of what might happen, how it may occur and what change could occur as a result.

This chapter uses the example of New Zealand to explore two scenarios of what events may look like in 2050 as the result of ten factors – or drivers – that will shape the future. The potential of event tourism has been recognised by the New Zealand government (Gnoth and Anwar 2000), and the *New Zealand Tourism Strategy 2015* identified the potential for events to growing year-round and regional demand. The benefits of events are identified at national, regional and local/city level. For example, in Christchurch the city council states that the liveliness and dynamism of the city is enhanced by their selection of festivals and events which increase the well-being of the city, attract economic benefit, promote business activity and employment, and position the city as a leader in events (Richards and Palmer 2010).

The scenarios developed here focus on the Rugby World Cup and a rural food, wine and music festival. While New Zealand hosts a diversity of events (Ryan *et al.* 1998), sports dominate New Zealand's event portfolio and Wright (2007: 348) notes that 'sports events are clearly seen as one of the most feasible, cost-effective and potentially lucrative avenues for sustainable development' for New Zealand. Examples include the 2000 and 2003 America's Cup Regattas, the 2005 Lions Tour and the 2010 International Rowing Championships. Forecasts by Deloitte Sports Business Group (Hall 2009) put the direct economic impact of New Zealand hosting the 2011 Rugby World Cup at NZ$1.25 billion, with at least 70,000 extra tourists expected to come to New Zealand for the event. While sport, particularly rugby, is part of the New Zealand psychology, cultural festivals are also important. In rural areas wine, food and music festivals have diversified the tourist image and introduced a more sophisticated demonstration of rural lifestyles and values (Higham and Ritchie 2001). Wine festivals have attracted tourists to rural areas, and enhanced their image as both a destination and quality wine-producing regions (Hoffman *et al.* 2001).

Why study the future?

The future is the indefinite time period after the present (Hastings *et al.* 1908). Whether it's less than a millisecond away or a billion years, its arrival is considered inevitable owing to the existence of time and the laws of physics. Because of the nature of the reality and the unavoidability of the future, everything that currently exists and will exist are temporary and will come to an end. The future and the concept eternity have been major subjects of philosophy, religion, and science, and defining them non-controversially has consistently eluded the greatest of minds. Future studies, or futurology, is the science, art and practice of postulating possible futures or, more basically, the study of the future seeks to understand what is likely to continue, what is likely to change and what is novel. Part of the discipline thus seeks a systematic and pattern-based understanding of past and present, and to determine the likelihood of future events and trends.

Future studies

Futures studies as a discontinuity with the past has its roots in *futurism* where the Italian writer Filippo Marinetti and colleagues launched his *Futurist Manifesto* on 20 February 1909, expressing a passionate loathing for everything old, especially political and artistic positions. The futurism movement was an artistic and social movement that originated in Italy in the early twentieth century. This was largely an Italian phenomenon with parallel movements in Russia, England and elsewhere. The futurists practised every medium of art, including painting, sculpture, graphic design, film and even gastronomy (Yeoman 2011). Martinetti's quotation 'we want no part of it, the past … we are the young and strong futurists' (Apollonio 1973) projects an image where futurists are admired for speed, youth, the car, the aeroplane and technological triumph of humanity over nature. Here, futurism repudiates the cult of the past and all imitation, praises originality and advocates daring. However, this boldness and daring, according to Apollonio (2009), was dismissed by art critics as useless, rebellious and not in good taste in the world of art. Apollonio comments that futurism is portrayed in films such as *Star Trek*, *Logan's Run* and *Soylent Green*. As such, Bergman *et al.* (2010) suggest futurism has resonation today, because to make predications about the future of technologies a discontinuity within the realm of *science fiction* is required in order to make a quantum leap (Yeoman 2011). This is about finding half-truths and using imagination to gaze into the future. Science fiction is a genre of fiction dealing with the impact of imagined innovations in science or technology, often in a futuristic setting. The settings for science fiction are often contrary to known reality, but the majority of science fiction relies on a considerable degree of suspension of disbelief provided by potential scientific explanations to various fictional elements. The stories may depict new or speculative scientific principles, such as time travel or psionics, or new technology, such as nanotechnology, faster-than-light travel or robots.

The futurist

As one can only live in the future, the study of the future is extremely important. Futures studies is an interdisciplinary field crossing a number of ontologies, epistemologies and methodologies found in art and science. If futures studies is a multi-disciplinary subject, an ontology is fluid, without boundaries and constructed around local realities. That ontology depends on the person creating the dialogue about the future, so future studies depends on the futurist (a so-called expert in future studies). Futurists understand the change, can see beyond the horizon. They have the ability to layer patterns of trends and to draw conclusions in order to make predictions. This is the world of subjectivity in which the mind of the futurist is an interpretation device. Futurists deal with multiple types of knowledge and could be described as jacks of all trades rather than experts in one particular field.

A futurist is a person who pieces together knowledge as a set of cognitive patterns which represents a pattern of the future and illustrates answers in a picture frame of sense. Futurists help us make sense of the world. Futurists live in a world of emergent construction that changes as data emerges from the different tools, techniques and approaches to elicitation (Weinstein and Weinstein 1991). They often deploy triangulation of methodologies in order to capture and understand the world around them. Futurists never present objectivity but a range of alternatives of subjectivity. The research they are involved in presumes interpretation, which Schwandt (1994) labels 'constructivist interpretation' (Schwandt 1994). This is an ontology that is predominantly local and specific in which the creation of knowledge is grounded in practice. This epistemology views knowledge in a subjective and transactional manner as merely suggesting directions along which to look, rather than providing descriptions of what to see (Blumer 1954).

The role of scenario planning

What are scenarios and scenario planning? There is no single, universal definition of either. For example, Michael Porter (2004: 63) talks about scenarios as an 'internally consistent view of what the future might turn out to be', whereas Schwandt (1994: 118) describes 'scenario planning as a tool for ordering one's perception about alternative future environments'. Hence, scenario planning is one methodology applied within the field of futures studies. Other methodologies include delphi, environmental scanning, future proofing and trends extrapolation. The purpose of this chapter is not to cover these methods; if readers want to know more a good website for reference is www.bis.gov.uk/Foresight.

The history of scenario planning lies in two worlds (Lindgren and Bandhold 2009). The first was future studies, where scenario analysis became an important method for generating futures thinking and scenarios became an effective presentation format. The second was strategy, where strategists and managers since the 1970s have searched for new and more relevant tools to work with complex issues. Modern scenario planning is attributed to Herman Kahn (van der Heijden *et al.* 2002) and the RAND Corporation. Kahn developed a technique called 'future-now' thinking. He adopted the term 'scenario' when Hollywood decreed the term outdated and switched to the label 'screenplay'. The scenarios he developed were part of military strategy research conducted at RAND for the US government, and he coined the term 'thinking the unthinkable'.

Walton (2008) places scenario planning in the paradigm constructivist interpretation based on the underpinning criteria of emergent construction, development of alternatives, internalisation, localism and plausibility. However, Walton's arguments are undermined by the notion of plausibility in which he argues that any scenario should be possible, credible and relevant. Fahey and Randall (1998: 9) also use the argument as:

> Plausible evidence should indicate that the projected narrative could take place (it is possible), demonstrate how it could take place (it is credible) and illustrate its implications for the organisations (it is relevant).

However, the notion of plausibility is in conflict with Bergman *et al.*'s (2010) spectrum of futures as plausibility places boundaries on one's thinking and rejects the typology of science fiction and utopia. By the very nature of futures studies, especially in the realm of technology, the use of science fiction is purposeful given the pace of change in technology futures, i.e., Ray Kurzweil's (2005) concept of technological singularity, where the pace of change is extremely rapid and exponential so that by 2050 the processing power of the computers overtakes the human brain, therefore changing the dimensions of humanity.

In the 1970s companies like Shell International (Yeoman and McMahon-Beattie 2005) adopted scenarios as part of their strategy repertoire. Shell is widely acclaimed as the 'the most famous scenario planning company'. Pierre Wack, Arie de Gues and Kees van der Heijden (van der Heijden *et al.* 2002) are famous scenario planners of this company and era. Their ability to foresee possible futures and to act quickly has been credited as the primary reason behind Shell's success during the Yom Kippur war. More recently, in a world in which uncertainty, insecurity and turbulence are evident (Yeoman and McMahon-Beattie 2005), scenario planning has received a renewed interest. The focus of scenario planning today is around 'scenario thinking', in which mental models of the future are shifted. De Gues (1997) and van der Heijden *et al.* (2002) make considerable use of Kolb's learning loop in their explanation of how learning takes place for individuals and groups during scenario planning. The learning loop describes the strategy development process in its integration of experience, sense-making and action into one holistic phenomenon. Hence, scenario planning becomes a means of thinking and learning about the future. But learning is ineffective in isolation. Eden and Ackermann (1998) contend that learning must happen in parallel with stakeholders in order to action change. It is stakeholders, whether in business or public policy, that have the power to create change. Van de Hiejden *et al.* (2002) note that there is no point in creating scenarios if you cannot action change. Hence, scenario planning is both a social and political process as well as a mechanical task process of scenario construction.

Scenarios and drivers

Using New Zealand as a case study, we consider two scenarios. First, *Martinborough Fest 2050*, which portrays the future of wine and food tourism as a cultural event. Second, *Jonah Lomu VIII wins again* is a story of the All Blacks winning the Rugby World Cup in 2050 based upon players that have been genetically bred and worldwide audience participation. One scenario considers sport and the other cultural events. The year 2050 is used as a point in time to demonstrate significant change in society rather than incremental change. We have set out to reshape your thinking and demonstrate difference.

Each scenario has been constructed using five driving forces that are an analysis of the peak of an iceberg or observable events and are significantly different. They are a recognition and combination of a number of trends and patterns that are structured through relationships that represent the forces of change that will drive the future. These drivers have been selected based upon the authors' current projects in scenario planning (www.tourism2050.com), publications (Yeoman 2008, 2011) and subject expertise.

Scenario 1: Martinborough Fest 2050

Hua Mulan is a 25-year-old from Shanghai, and has just completed an MA on the History of Interactive Technology – she has a passion for IT. The right designer brand is important to her and she owns all the latest gadgets. She is particularly proud of her new interactive Generation IV contact lenses that at a twitch give her access to the internet.

However, life is not all about technology. She has a passion for food, wine and music, reflecting the status given to wine – rather than spirits – in China in 2050. New Zealand's cultural capital captures these interests and Hua is travelling to the Martinborough wine region of New Zealand for the annual festival. She wants to be in the real place to learn about the great Martinborough wines which are seen as the elite of all wines.

Hua has booked a hypersonic flight, which means Shanghai to Wellington only takes an hour. However, environmental taxes no longer make such flights affordable to the ordinary tourist, only China's elite. She booked her accommodation on the net, looking at the hotel through virtual tour. She just would not book any accommodation that does not offer a virtual tour. Given the conspicuous designer side of her personality, she is staying in an extreme luxury boutique lodge in the centre of the vines. She loves Martinborough, tasting the wines, learning from the wine masters about Pinor Noir and listening to the very best of New Zealand's musical talent like Slim Freddy Top.

She is looking forward to meeting up with like-minded people who share her passions. She will be meeting, in person, friends who she knows only through technology, such as her blogs in the group www.chinawines.com. Hua's augmented reality contact lenses help her find out so much about her surroundings and other people. Generation IV facial recognition capability allows her to know everything about everyone she meets, from their wine preferences and marital status to financial worth.

Hau really enjoys the trip, the rural surrounds of Martinborough offering a pleasant escape from the urban metropolis of Shanghai.

Key drivers: Martinborough Fest 2050

Driver 1: The desire for authentic experiences

As the experience economy matures, it evolves into authenticity because consumers search for real experiences rather than 'products' which are manufactured (Pine 2004). There is a growing desire to find experiences and products that are original and real, not contaminated by being fake or impure. This trend away from impurity, the virtual, the spun, the manufactured and the mass-produced in a world seemingly full of falseness needs further explanation. Wilmott and Nelson (2003) have identified the complexity of consumerism, with consumers seeking new meaning. This is consistent with Maslow's motivational hierarchy where the movement to self-actualisation is a search for a deeper meaning and finding a sense of worth beyond material possessions. It is a fulfilment of self which moves beyond goods and services and on to experiences. At one level it results in increased spending on holidays, eating out, the theatre and so on. But it also includes special experiences such as white-water rafting or spending a weekend at a health spa.

Driver 2: The future of luxury: wine, food and music as the cultural capital experience

The cultural capital of consumers represents the 'stock' of their knowledge, attitudes, skills, education and tastes. Bourdieu (1993), regarded cultural capital as taking three forms: embodied (long-lasting dispositions of mind and body which must be constantly maintained and updated), objectified (the goods and services chosen by different consumers) and institutionalised (a measure of the qualifications bestowed on individuals by academic institutions). As consumers become more affluent, they differentiate themselves less by their material trappings and more by their use of cultural and social knowledge and individual identity. Increasingly, it is not what you own but what you do and who you know. As affluence grows, so also do cultural and social knowledge, and people's expectations (and the way in which these inform consumption) become more important considerations. The cultural capital of events is how communities and tourists talk about their experience of festivals and sporting occasions and their participation in them, hence the cultural consumption of festivals. As Yeoman (2008) points out, the cultural capitalism of consumerism changes definitions of luxury into a more fluid concept which combines materialism, aspiration and time. These concepts become the blurred meaning of luxury based upon an experience economy where tourists seek novelty and new experiences.

Driver 3: The environment and scarcity of resources

What if the future was a scarcity of resources, in which food and water supply are limited because of climate change and the oil runs dry? How will we cope (Yeoman 2011)? Agriculture is highly sensitive to climate variability and weather extremes, such as droughts, floods and severe storms. The forces that shape our climate are also critical to farm productivity. Human activity has already changed atmospheric characteristics such as temperature, rainfall, levels of carbon dioxide and ground-level ozone. The scientific community expects such trends to continue. While food production may benefit from a warmer climate, the increased potential for droughts, floods and heat waves will pose challenges for farmers, therefore making many parts of the world suffer food shortages, facilitated by a booming world population. However, at the same time some countries will be the beneficiaries of climate change with a more temperate climate compared to many parts of the world.

Peak oil is the point in time when the maximum rate of global petroleum extraction is reached, after which the rate of production enters terminal decline (Roberts 2005). Optimistic estimations of peak production forecast the global decline will begin by 2020 or later, and assume major investments in alternatives will occur before a crisis without requiring major changes in the lifestyle of heavily oil-consuming nations (Yeoman 2011). So, in the future does this mean international travel – highly dependent on oil supply – is only for the elite in society?

Driver 4: China's emerging middle classes

The rising economy in China will lift hundreds of millions of households out of poverty. Increasing numbers of rural Chinese will migrate to the cities to seek higher paying jobs. These working consumers, once the country's poorest, will steadily climb the income ladder, creating a massive new middle class. Forecasts by consultants McKinsey (Farrel *et al.* 2006) predict these urban households will make up one of the largest consumer markets in the world. Rapid economic growth will continue to transform the impoverished but largely egalitarian society of China's past into one with distinct income classes. This evolution is already widening the gap between rich and poor, and tackling the resulting social and economic tension has become a focus of government policy. McKinsey's projections indicate, however, that China will avoid the 'barbell economy' that plagues much of the developing world and which results in large numbers of poor, a small group of the very wealthy, and only a few in the middle. Even as the absolute difference between the richest and poorest continues to widen, incomes will increase across all urban segments. This emerging solid middle-class society will be the basis for China's outbound tourism to destinations such as New Zealand.

Driver 5: Augmented reality and the information economy

Speaking in 2005, renowned futurologist Graham Whitehead said 'consumers will see as much change in technology in the next ten years as they have in the previous 150 years' (Whitehead 2005) so the future is exponential growth. Augmented reality (AR) is a term for a live direct or indirect view of a physical real-world environment whose elements are *augmented* by computer-generated sensory input, such as sound or graphics. As a result, the technology functions by enhancing one's current perception of reality. On the spectrum between virtual reality, which creates immersive, computer-generated environments, and the real world, augmented reality is closer to the real world. Augmented reality adds graphics, sounds, haptic feedback and smell to the natural world as it exists. Both video games and cell phones are driving the development of augmented reality. Everyone from tourists to soldiers to someone looking for the closest subway stop can now benefit from the ability to place computer-generated graphics in their field of vision. Augmented reality is changing the way we view the world, or at least the way its users see the world. With augmented-reality displays, which will eventually look much like a normal pair of glasses, informative graphics will appear in your field of view, and audio will coincide with whatever you see. These enhancements will be refreshed continually to reflect the movements of your head. Similar devices and applications already exist, for example on smartphones, and a contact lens with simple built-in electronics is already within reach, being developed in a research project at the University of Washington called 'A Twinkle in the Eye' (Yeoman 2011).

Scenario 2: Jonah Lomu VIII wins again

Michael Nolan is a 69-year-old managing director of a development company from Melbourne. Michael is an avid sports fan, in particular Rugby Union, and often travels the world with like-minded male friends in the pursuit of this sporting glory. Michael is in New Zealand to watch the Rugby World Cup game between the All Blacks and Australia at the BigMac Stadium. He and his three friends are guests of one of his main suppliers and arrive in Auckland two days before the match to attend the associated Business Expo. His supplier is one of the many international and local sponsors. Corporate sponsorship of the games is critical in 2050 as governments can no longer afford to justify the economics of major sporting events, given global fiscal deficits.

Michael is staying at the Stadium Hotel, where his rooms overlook the rugby pitch just like an executive box. The stadium seating features the latest innovations in technologies and comfort, including built-in video screens at every seat for ordering food and drink, and vibration services designed to get the crowd on its feet. In 2050 many mega events have problems attracting supporters because the virtual experience is often so much better, therefore stadiums have to try and create authentic experience supported by innovate use of technologies. If Michael misses a bit of the game, he simply rewinds the play on his personal video screen and selects different camera angles. Michael can send video clips of the game to friends instantly. The national coaches ask the crowd which substitutes to use and fans can offer the manager advice on tactics using the interactive voting system.

Players have built-in RDIF chips which help the coach make predictions about players' positions, endurance and tactics. In 2050, rugby players are elite athletes whose performance is controlled by nutrition, science and genetic engineering. The development of youth players starts with designer babies at www.surrogancy-rugby-mothers.com; Jonah Lomu VIII is the most popular choice. All referees are now expert robots who never make a wrong decision. They are supported by an array of embedded technologies around the pitch, from radio frequency chips which know when the ball is outside play and global positioning systems which identify when a player is off-side. Nanotechnology medicines are incorporated into players' shirts to allow for the healing of minor scrapes.

To Australian Michael's disappointment, the All Blacks win 54–42, with Jonah Lomu VIII being named man of the match. Michael and his friends return to the Stadium Hotel, accompanied by a number of the hotel's Stepford Mistress robots.

Key Drivers: Jonah Lomu VIII wins again

Driver 1: The economic and political power of events

Sport is a key part of global business, including sports magazines, sports channels, sports medicine, professional sportsmen and women, and people going to the gym just to exercise. According to the World Economic Forum (Elliott 2009) sport represents between 2 and 3.7 per cent of world GDP, making sport one the most important industries in the world. Hosting mega sports events is highly contested and prized, not least because of the potential positive impacts on the destination. Sport event audiences are global, with the three most attended and watched sports events being the Olympic Games, the FIFA Football World Cup and the IRB Rugby World Cup (Deloitte and Touche LLP 2008; Yeoman 2008).

However, the rush by many nations to host sporting events has led to their undoing. Take the example of Greece, where some commentators point to the 2004 Olympic Games as a catalyst to the country's later economic problems (Gatopoulos 2010). The 2004 Athens Olympics cost nearly double its initial budget. In 2010, more than half of Athens' Olympic sites are barely used or empty, although the Games did bring a new metro system, a new airport, and a tram and light railway network. However, given the looming fiscal deficits in many countries, arguments about the economic benefits of mega events will wane (Yeoman 2011).

Driver 2: The insperience experience and urban tribes

According to Trendwatching (2008) futurists have always been talking about homes of the future, whether it is butlers as Robbie the Robot or talking fridges. So this isn't a new trend. However, the insperience economy is a representation of a consumer society which is dominated by experiences and consumers' desire to bring top-level experiences into their domestic domain. The key aspects of this driver include the consumers' desire to turn their homes into highly connected, comfortable places fully equipped to entertain others, as represented by Ethan Watters (2003) in his book *Urban Tribes*, where friends are the new families. This is extremely important for spectator sports – like rugby, where (predominately) men gather like tribes for the sporting occasions.

Driver 3: The future of prostitution

Given the nature of mega sporting events like the Rugby World Cup, which is mainly a middle-class male sporting occasion, when you have large gatherings of men, prostitution and sex follow. Davies (1937: 744) in the *American Sociological Review* poses the conundrum of prostitution: 'Why is it that a practice so thoroughly disapproved, so widely outlawed in western civilization, can yet flourish so universally?' But given the problems with sexually transmitted diseases and human trafficking, is the future sex with robots? David Levy (2007) suggests in his book *Love+Sex with Robots* that by 2050 technological advancement will allow humans to have sex with androids, something akin to the *Stepford Wife* concept of a woman with a perfect body who can perform great sex with a man.

Driver 4: Ethics and generic engineering

James Watson, the co-discoverer of the structure of DNA and author of *The Double Helix*, tells the story of the amazing molecule since its discovery fifty years ago, following modern genetics from his own Nobel prize-winning work in the fifties to Dolly the sheep, designer babies and genetically modified foods. So, could we nurture youth for the future through technology? Are the prospects for designer sports players possible? Dr Andy Miah (2004) discusses such a prospect in his book *Genetically Modified Athletes*. Genetic engineering is the technique used where functioning genes are inserted into cells to correct a genetic error or introduce a new function. Applications include genetic pre-selection: using the information of a person's genotype to conclude suitability for sport at either the embryonic stage or the infantile stage. Prospective winners could be chosen on their predisposition for athlete capabilities, i.e. designer babies. The University of Idaho has already used gene therapy in the cloning of racehorses (Galli *et al.* 2003), including opening up an opportunity to verify the reproducibility of traits such as character and sporting performance. If a Los Angeles fertility clinic in 2009 offered parents the choice of their children's sex, hair and eye colour (Keim 2009), does this mean sports clubs will start the apprentice scheme in the science lab? Presently, it is only society's ethics that are stopping this.

Driver 5: I, Robot

Futurist Ray Kurzweil (2005) has used Moore's law (which describes the relentless exponential improvement in digital technology with uncanny accuracy) to calculate that computers will have the same processing power as human brains by the year 2030, whereas research by Yeoman (2011) predicts Japan and South Korea are preparing for the human–robot co-existence society. Regulators are assuming that robots will be capable of adapting to complex, unstructured environments and interacting with humans to assist with the performance of daily life tasks. Unlike heavily regulated industrial robots that toil in isolated settings, next generation robots will have relative autonomy. Web-based semantic translation tools such as Google translator are already used freely in our everyday lives. At the next level, research by Lyon *et al.* (2009)

demonstrates how artificial intelligence software will allow robots to hold meaningful con-versations with humans, making decisions and offering real advice in an infinite number of languages. Such is the advance in language acquisition technology using neural organisation theory. Yeoman (2011) highlights how call centres can use language acquisition programming to replace call centre operatives; experiments show that real people couldn't tell the difference between the 'real person' and 'the computer' on many occasions. So, 2050, who will be com-peting for that gold medal? Will it be something akin to *I, Robot*, leading to the end of the human sports person as we know it?

The significant questions about the future

In order to consider the significance of the scenarios and drivers from a futures perspective, a number of significant questions are propositioned and answers pondered in this section. They include the future significance of events, how events will be funded, the importance of cultural capital, the implications of China's new creative class, and how science and technology will shape future events. These questions are what the authors consider to be the key issues pertaining to the future of events.

Will events still be significant in the future?

In both scenarios, the significance of events relates to the importance of the experience economy in the tourist consumption. Events have links to religion, to culture, to sport, to community, to commerce, and to political, policy and microeconomic and macroeconomic influence or objectives. If the future is an experience economy governments will continue to champion and promote events and put them at the centre of their tourism policies. Festivals, and other events, continue to have the capacity to work as part of a 'glue that bring people together through social cohesion, with joint plans and agreed strategic goals' (Derret 2009: 109).

Why is credibility, image and a desire for new authenticity important for the future?

In the second scenario, Michael Nolan's visit is based upon New Zealand as the home of rugby. Rugby is the image and authenticity of New Zealand, signalling that credibility, image and the desire for authenticity is important for the future (Yeoman 2011). As the literature suggests, festival and events have become a normal route to gaining credibility, status and improved trade, a process of identity building (Getz 2008). Festivals and events have been recorded as actions by host cities and other destinations to display their entrepreneurial virtues (Robertson and Guerrier 1998; Quinn 2005) and in narrating or engineering place image and place brand (Chalip and Green 2001; Jago *et al.* 2003; Boo and Busser 2006). With this, there is also discussion about the nature of image generation through events, suggesting both positive and negative outcomes. For example a post-apartheid South Africa has engaged with major and mega sports to mix economic drivers with tones of socio-political reconciliation (Cornelissen and Swart 2006).

Of particular interest here is the notion that events may be seen as responsible for broad-casting and transcribing a new hybrid authenticity. Roche (2000) viewed the growth of mega events as a key element in normalising a global narrative, i.e. moving national social expecta-tions to a shared global stage. With this shared stage are new opportunities of cross-fertilisation, or of splicing logistical and cultural consumption. In China the 2008 Olympic Games spliced authentic storytelling with a narrative of rapid change (stadia, hotels, retailing boulevards and emporium) and modern strength and conspicuous consumption (Broudehoux 2007; Zhang and Zhao 2009; Hubbert 2010). Viewed through the architecture of Beijing in particular (Hubbert 2010) but also in the other cities of China, festivals are responding to a perceived need in the larger boundaries of Asia to communicate image change (Kotler *et al.* 2002). The Olympic Games in Beijing, and other sporting events before and since, display all the attributes of political arbitration. No longer the bastion of West versus East confrontation, their role is now of global exchange, barter and – at times – partnership (Xu 2006). Events are important in producing a new global local experience, both comforting and contrasting for the visitor. This can be seen in the New Asia of Singapore, a city that has aspired to have a cultural profile comparable to Hong Kong, Glasgow, Melbourne, London and New York (Peterson 2009).

As the All Blacks have put a face on New Zealand (Rein and Shields 2007) so too the emerging countries of the world find that events aid their narrative of brand place. Within the increasing fluidity of travel media, festival and events offer a more effective contribution to brand equity than the far slower (and more costly) development of the built environment and aid affirmation of the unique promise and assurance of quality a destination needs (Blain *et al.* 2005). Event brand equity then becomes a tool to manage inconsistencies (e.g. economic strife, terrorism or climate change) and ensure a positive brand experience, supporting the drivers.

How will events be funded in the future?

Festivalisation has two meanings. The first is indicative of a sector that has grown rapidly and which there may be oversupply, and the second is where the growth of events indicates an innate socialisation effect (Richards and Palmer 2010) and festivals are rooted in the real life of people (Quinn 2005). In each case there is indication that events and festivals may become a 'norm' and less representative of what makes an event unique (despite this being a defining factor of events and festivals in the literature). Clearly in a competitive market events and festivals, with an increased level of minimum standards and within a competitive environment, there is more at risk for organisers. Here lies their dilemma. Accentuate the new and risk market rejection, compete with all others with costly improvement – and risk bankruptcy. Tie this with the fear of taking legal risks, as the litigious nature of society progresses, and it becomes clear that the potential for similarity in the design and performance of events grows.

In the *Jonah Lomu VIII wins again* scenario, the New Zealand government can't afford to host the Rugby World Cup. Why? New Zealand sovereign debt to GDP ratio is presently 8–9 per cent, but the government's Treasury department is forecasting the ratio to increase to between 106 and 223 per cent by 2050, which is unsustainable and would lead to foreclosure (New Zealand Treasury 2009). New Zealand's exchange rate would likely collapse under these circumstances and refinancing could even result in a loss of sovereignty. The New Zealand Treasury's position is that radical restructuring is preferred over incrementalism, given the demographic shifts that will occur, chronically low levels of productivity and distance-related threats (from our geographic position) in a future world of energy constraint.

So, at what cost can countries fund the future of events? The escalation of visitors and locals seeking unique event experiences comes at a price. The increasing competition between events themselves to ensure visitor numbers and between the states and countries to host the best event requires even more spectacular events. As the cost of these are driven higher, so too local councils look to federal and national governments to support their acquisition of event management companies with the prestige to manage them. While event production franchises offering 'off the shelf' experiences find some success in the business events market and for home entertainment, in the earlier years of event production their failure to adapt to the needs of more sophisticated markets means that the cost of public events does not diminish. As such, festivals and events require an increasing number of partnership funding arrangements. Linking industry sectors, arts foundations, councils, local and national tourism agencies, institutes of education (from the public and private sector) and community groups, the mapping of positive outcomes for each of the stakeholders becomes ever more demanding. Some of the pressure is, however, facilitated by simulated experience and new opportunities to evaluate visitor satisfaction.

Why is cultural capital a significant driving force of destination choice in the future?

The *Martinborough Fest 2050* scenario highlights the importance of cultural capital in the experience economy; as the urbanisation of society increases, the desire for escapism will continue to grow. As Yeoman (2008) points out, the growing affluence of the world's populations has had a profound impact on out-of-home expenditure. The tourist of the future is much more cultured, is well travelled, is searching for new experiences and wants to experience local culture. Food is a significant part of a tourist's experience of the destination, driven by the growing trend of authenticity, the rise of the experience economy and the need for a high-quality experience. Food is one of the primary drivers of destinations' choice in countries such as France and Italy and increasingly important in destinations such as Scotland, China and New Zealand. It is as if culture has moved out of the museum and is a living experience, with food and wine at the centre.

From a cultural capital perspective, the literature has dwelt on the significance of events in terms of image, which is increasingly being viewed as part of cultural collateral. Richards and Palmer (2010: 2) go as far as to state that cities either 'develop to meet the challenges created by the pace of global change, or they resist the impulse of transformation and stagnate', arguing that 'cultural capital' has become a defining factor for cities. A profile of events is, they claim, one vital display and source of that cultural capital. Festivals in particular, but cultural events in general, mobilise cultural symbols and cultural discourse in ways that are more open than elsewhere.

A new mobility of culture is being observed in society and events give consumers time to observe social expression, change and the desire for 'otherness' and escape (Picard and Robinson 2006) and with this, of course, the unique experiences. In their analysis of event-goers to four South Island events in New Zealand, Nicholson and Pearce (2000) concluded that the event-goers were not easily profiled and that they differed from event to event. They opined that in the absence of a definable event-goer it was the unique nature of each event that attracted the event type. Events offer an opportunity to create experiences for the visitor which are distinct from other experiences they are likely to have (Hall 1992; Getz 1997). The importance of experiences has increased over time and there is increasing evidence to suggest that events provide a particular type of environment that in post-modern society imparts group and individual identity.

Events and travel are increasingly the domain of the elite who can afford the finances and time to travel. They are driven by the desire for authenticity and the ability to experience destinations and events in person. Michael Nolan's access to the Rugby World Cup is as a guest of a business partner, and the majority of tickets to sporting mega events are distributed through sponsors, who have become the main funder of such events. Sports events and business events now act in parallel and by 2050 the sport event tourist is typically also a business event tourist. The business opportunities are why governments still invest in hosting sports events.

The wider population can still experience events and festivals but either at home through interactive technology – where many argue there is a better experience than at the game – or through generic franchises of international brand events. Instead of travelling, Hua could experience *The Great Wine Festival@Shanghai* simultaneously with thousands of event-goers around the globe. But for those who can afford it, being there – and sharing the experience through social networks – demonstrates wealth and social status. Hua represents the emergent Chinese middle class who have the purchasing power to access such festival experiences.

In *Martinborough Fest 2050*, Hua Mulan is a blogger. As the consumer and consumer experience becomes more significant, so too does the need to voice and share opinion. The travel blog, as diary and interactive communication tool, possesses great market significance. The credibility of word-of-mouth reporting begins to surpass official promotion and media. As such the social networks reconfigure the production of creative experience and its consumption. Attendance and reportage from destinations and the events and festivals they host becomes increasingly important. Location-specific mobile phone social network platforms (currently led by *Foursquare* and *Facebook Places*) will support the experience. However, no longer is the blog an untracked entity: the blogosphere (Carson 2008) will increasingly be shared by business and destination organisations. Attendance at festival and events and opportunities for blogging will be encouraged and utilised by these organisations, aware of the cultural and business value of doing so. Importantly the blog is a global phenomena and Asia is – and will continue to be – a 'powerhouse in blogging production' (Katz and Lai 2009: 97). As China's new creative elite become great exponents of blogging, so businesses servicing the cultural sector ensure that they can be part of this.

Will the future tourists from China be the new creative class?

Why is Hua Mulan in *Martinborough Fest 2050* a symbol of the future event-goer? In a world in which influences are becoming greater and in which there is convergence between cultures it is also the case that competition is magnified. 'Globalization, digitization, the rise of the "knowledge worker", the boom in intellectual property, changes in leisure consumption' (Tepper 2002: 159) and social networks, and the desire by cities and states to have a knowledge-rich economy have made the pursuit of creativity vital. Events and festivals are increasingly important narrations of that creativity and of a related knowledge (whether it be culture, art, business or science), each drawing and attracting new audiences and often targeted at follow-on investment. With this festivals and events have also become competing war cries between cities, states/regions and countries. Thus events and festivals are fuelled more and more by the comparative analysis of other places and the needs to surpass, with bigger names or better performance – or attempting to outwit with new and the brave.

With the growth of social networking and the democratisation of experience that prevails, a consequence of this means that the increase in festival- and event-goers from China will be palpable. The consumption of events will be a socially significant attribute of the lifestyle enjoyed by the creative class in this country. Moreover, the festival-goer from China will be savvy and aware when they come to destinations like New Zealand. The experience will be disseminated in real time, with an awareness drawn from the network of word-of-mouth reports available and the supported narratives in the blogosphere.

Hua Mulan is an international tourist, and international tourism and events have a significant relationship. As a form of special interest tourism events and festivals have a design capacity unlike most other tourism forms. They offer the potential for synergy of travel, interest and event and the opportunity for the visitor to have a fully constructed experience (Yuan *et al.* 2005). As such the Martinborough festival will take advantage of the fact that the event taps into a convergence of cultural needs.

How will science and technology shape the use future of events?

In Scenario 2, Michael Nolan can live life through the screen in a world in which virtual and real experiences have become blurred. The future for business events rotates strongly around the need for personalisation, whereby technology will facilitate the real-time capture of activities as they happen and so allow the management of future experiences by individuals. Similarly these will give opportunities for those who, because of their remoteness or lack of free time, can experience the event as it happens through video streaming and fine downloads (appropriate for mobile phone technology). The findings of the study 'Convention 2020', funded by ICCA, IMEX and Fast Future (Talwar *et al.* 2010), reports that networking before, during and after the event is seen as vital. These will be available as both video streams and downloads appropriate for use on mobile phones. Clearly these are likely to be required for the creative elite in their pursuit of unique leisure experiences (in New Zealand as elsewhere). However, unlike the business events customer, as the consumers of non-business events are also likely to require advanced immersion and experiential platforms, the cumbersome and limited opportunity allowed by mobile phones is likely to ensure that real culture cache is secured only when evidenced by attendance at the event or through advanced immersion and experiential platforms. The blending of virtual and physical experiences will, as stated earlier, allow event organisers to more readily fit into the needs of the funding organisations.

This blurred world of virtual reality and real experiences is a major threat to the future of events, as Yeoman (2011) observes; in 2050, will all the stadiums be empty because the experience is better in your living room, driven by the insperience economy and demography trends? High-definition television (HDTV) and its digital format is turning watching TV into a high-quality real experience, surpassing the stadium event itself with the development of digi-boxes in which the viewer can rewind, replay, focus on specific angles, skip adverts, watch multiple channels simultaneously and, when watching events such as rugby, choose which camera to view the matches.

The *Jonah Lomu* scenario suggests the leaping of ethical hurdles and the advent of engineered sports players. However, while sports players are still human, robots and other technology have been accepted as referees and in other aspects of sport. Sporting prowess is based on access to cutting-edge technology, with investment in technology more important than training. But will this also apply to creative performance, with genetically engineered singers who sound, look and act to a optimum standard each and every time? The *Martinborough Fest* scenario suggests not; rather, the authentic is still valued and the opportunity to experience music live remains a core element of the experience economy.

As Yeoman (2008) notes, the insperience economy is a representation of a consumer society which is dominated by experiences and consumers' desire to bring top-level experiences into their domestic domain. The key aspects of this trend include the consumers' desire to turn their homes into highly connected, comfortable places fully equipped to entertain others. In Scenario 2, Michael Nolan's friends are his urban tribe (Watters 2003). This aspect is extremely important for rugby, which is predominately a male spectator sport in which men gather like tribes for the sporting occasions.

And finally ... would men have sex with a robot?

Would you pay to have sex with a robot? Even if it was akin to something from *Stepford Wives* (Yeoman 2011)? Is this the future of sex tourism in a futurist world? A revolution of humanoid social robots (or androids) is quietly taking place in our society, as autonomous, interactive and human-like entities of various sizes and shapes are leaving research laboratories in large numbers, making their way into the world of our everyday lives. Automated teller machines (ATMs), vending machines and automated telephone response systems are standing in for human attendants to serve real people; online search agents, game bots and chat programs are working for and playing with human users; and robotic dolls and pets are cuddling up with children and talking to the elderly. This is the rise of a synthetic social world where human individuals and humanoid social robots co-mingle calls for a new conceptualisation of society. The traditional view of society as consisting of only human individuals needs to be revised. For one thing, the boundary between humans and human artefacts is no longer inviolable through the increasing technological prostheticisation of human bodies. Technologies are becoming an integral part of the human condition. Furthermore, robotic replacement of human individuals in the processes of social interaction and communication creates a human–machine nexus that is indispensable to the operation of everyday life. Society comprised not only human individuals as delimited by their biological bodies, but also technological extensions of individuals, including their robotic surrogates. In *Terminator 3*, the android terminator manifests itself simultaneously as young naked flesh but also as a declining and aging self-depreciating actor, being chased by the next-level-up android, which happens to be young, blonde and a female killing machine. Her ability to totally reconfigure her body, at a moment's notice, embues her with an unusual allure. Sex tourism and mega events go hand in hand (Yeoman 2008), so maybe prostitution will be regulated where sex workers are androids who are clean of sexually transmitted diseases, not smuggled in from all corners of the world and forced into slavery. This way authorities will have direct control over android sex workers, controlling prices, hours of operations and sexual services. Android prostitutes will offer glamour model-like features and provide an awesome service for men – and women.

Conclusions

At a time when the event sector is growing and when festivalisation will be accepted in the vocabulary as a symbol of normalised leisure experience and may be used as a rebuff of something that is not special, the future experiences of event-goers may find increasing discourse as dual physical and social network experience. *Jonah Lomu VIII* and the Stepford Mistresses may be both a real and a simulated experience, each offered in different combinations depending on the knowledge wealth of the locality or the viewer(s) that is experiencing it. The cost of being in the real audience may be restrictive to many, but continue to be a sweetener for important clients or part of an employee's bonus package. The takeaway simulated experience s/he can take home or to their hotel room are far more real than that which the non-attendees can consume. S/he has – for the most part – only minor editing capacity for the game (or sexual experience). The time-poor executives can savour the experience when they wish, the hologram images surrounding them to the level they wish. The real-time viewer has a time limit on their experience, and less control. The upgrade capacity for both continues to motivate each. Michael's friends look forward to another event next week. Hua's time in New Zealand is one of many trips. She travels to many destinations, comparing the wine and comparing the people. New Zealand is nice, but small; a weekend break. Trips to impoverished Europe (a place likely to improve, they consider) are much cheaper – and worth four or five days – but dangerous. They don't dare turn off the face recognition software there. As part of the high-spending and highly communicative young professionals of China there is panache in telling people that you went to France.

Hua Mulan's trip to *Martinborough Fest 2050* raises a number of similar issues about application of technology in the events' experience. The more technology and virtual experiences we have in society, the greater the desire for real experiences increases. This is what tourism is. Tourism is not about a game on your X-Box but a real living encounter with people. Unless humanity fundamentally shifts, the experience economy will continue. The cultural capital and authenticity of *Martinborough Fest 2050* is what is core to the scenario. How Hua Mulan blogs about the festival is important. This is a symbol of the changing nature of branding and marketing. The scenario also raises key questions about the future funding of events. Many countries will simply not be able to bid on mega events such as FIFA World Cups or the Olympic Games. Are we about to enter an era of a turn of fortunes when tourism is only for the elite and upper classes of society? A reversal to Victorian times where there was clear distinction in society of the have and have nots?

Scenario planning as a component of the strategic planning of events continues to develop as an important tool for event managers. The intangible nature of the product, frequent reliance on good weather and the ongoing safety and legal implications of having a large body of people at any event has always required a 'worst-case' scenario overview (more commonly referred to as *contingency planning*). In an increasingly busy environment where the portfolio of events held at a destination is expanding and the competition between each of these rises exponentially, and the number of stakeholder needs increase, it is not uncommon for event management companies to include responses to various scenarios as part of a bid proposal. For government agencies and many regular sponsors, evidence of this is a basic issue of *competence* (Allen *et al.* 2008). However, these scenarios have only recently grown beyond what Allen *et al.* (2008) describe as the *screening process* for events, where, in turn, the market, the operational management skills (inclusive of those required to manage risk) and finances are each screened for strengths and weaknesses before deciding on the event. Table-top scenario exercises can now be an anticipated part of a bid proposal in which creativity, destination knowledge and stakeholder collaborations between public and private sector funders are a norm in developing an innovative event. As this chapter has indicated, the rapid nature of change in the environment in which events are run requires a more extensive and sophisticated application of the scenario models. In addition, economic dislocation in the northern hemisphere, shifting demand patterns in the southern hemisphere, technological innovation around the world and ongoing political, secular and cultural tension offers further reason to ensure as inclusive and as strong a strategic plan for events as is possible. In the bid process and as an ongoing market and managerial skill development and awareness factor, the use of scenario models will increase.

What is the future? There are so many other drivers, wild cards and projections we haven't mentioned in this chapter. At a macro level, as world tourism moves eastwards, as the merging middle classes of India and China acquire wealth the world distribution of events follows this pattern. As populations age, what is the correlation between wealth and demography? How does this change the relationship between the variables of wealth and time, as today's baby boomers have both and as a consequence drive the rise of volunteerism in society. Then there is climate change. The further desertification of the Mediterranean significantly changes outdoor events in popular tourism destinations in Spain and Italy. California, one of the world's most famous food and wine destinations, will by 2050 be radically different through lack of fresh water which impacts on agricultural production. Then there is oil. Imagine a world without it or a world in which it is so expensive that only the upper classes of society could afford intercontinental travel. The pace of change in technology is changing our consumption of entertainment, whether it is mobile video on demand or 3D TV. The possibilities are endless. But this is one of the purposes of this chapter. Not to present a picture of the final future, but to make you think about the future based upon extending the present into the future (a casual link to the future) or pure science fiction (an interpretation of possible future).

For those who are interested in the future, the authors recommend the World Futures Society (www.wfs.org) and its accessible magazine, *The Futurist*.

References

Allen, J., McDonnell, I., O'Toole, W. and Harris, R. (2008). *Festival and Special Event Management*, Milton, Australia: John Wiley and Sons, fourth edition.

Apollonio, U. (Editor) (1973) *Futurist Manifestos* (R. Brain *et al.*, Trano.). London: Thames and Hudson.

Bergman, A., Karlsson, J.C. and Axelsson, J. (2010) 'Truth claims and explanatory claims. An ontological typology of future studies', *Futures* 42(8): 857–65.

Blain, C., Levy, S. and Ritchie, J. (2005) 'Destination branding: insights and practices from destination management organizations', *Journal of Travel Research* 43(4): 328–38.

Blumer, H. (1954) 'What is wrong with social theory?', *American Sociological Review* 19: 3–10.

Boo, S. and Busser, J.A. (2006) 'Impact analysis of a tourism festival on tourists' destination images', *Event Management* 9(4): 223–37.

Bourdieu, P. (1993) *Sociology in Question*, (R. Nice, Trans.) London: Sage.

Broudehoux, A.M. (2007) 'Spectacular Beijing: the conspicuous construction of an Olympic metropolis', *Journal of Urban Affairs* 29(4): 383–99.

Carson, D. (2008) 'The "blogosphere" as a market research tool for tourism destinations: a case study of Australia's Northern Territory', *Journal of Vacation Marketing* 14(2): 111–19.

Chalip, L. and Green, B.C. (2001) 'Event marketing and destination image', paper presented at the American Marketing Association, Chicago.

Cornelissen, S. and Swart, K. (2006) 'The 2010 Football World Cup as a political construct: the challenge of making good on an African promise', in J. Horne and W. Manzenreiter (eds) *Sports Mega-Events: Social Scientific Analyses of a Global Phenomenon*, Norwich: Blackwell, pp. 108–23.

Davies, K. (1937) 'The sociology of prostitution', *American Sociological Review* 2(5): 744–55.

De Gues, A. (1997) *The Living Company*, Boston: Harvard University Press.

Deloitte and Touche LLP (2008) *Potential Economic Impact of the Rugby World Cup on a Host Nation*, Dublin: The International Rugby Board.

Derret, R. (2009) 'How festivals nurture resilience in regional communities', in J. Ali-Knight, M. Robertson, A. Fyall and A. Ladkin (eds) *International Perspectives of Festivals and Events – Paradigms of Analysis*, Oxford: Elsevier, pp. 107–24.

Eden, C. and Ackermann, F. (1998) *Making Strategy: The Journey of Strategy Management*, London: Sage.

Elliott, M. (2009) *Sport: An Untapped Asset*, World Economic Forum. Available at: www.weforum.org/en/knowledge/Events/2009/AnnualMeeting/KN_SESS_SUMM_27356?url=/en/knowledge/Events/2009/AnnualMeeting/KN_SESS_SUMM_27356 (accessed 7 June 2009).

Fahey, L. and Randall, R. (1998) 'What is scenario learning?', in L. Fahey and R. Randall (eds) *Learning from the Future: Foresight Scenarios*, New York: John Wiley and Sons inc, pp. 3–27.

Farrel, D., Gersch, U. and Stephenson, E. (2006). *The Value of China's Emerging Middle Classes*. Available at: www.mckinseyquarterly.com/Economic_Studies/Productivity_Performance/The_value_of_Chinas_emerging_middle_class_1798 (accessed 27 September 2007).

Galli, C., Lagutina, I., Crotti, G., Colleoni, S., Turini, P., Ponderato, N., Duchi, R. and Giovanna, L (2003) 'Pregnancy: a cloned horse born to its dam twin', *Nature* 424(635). Available at: www.nature.com/nature/journal/v424/n6949/full/424635a.html (accessed 7 June 2010).

Gatopoulos, D. (2010) *Did 2004 Olympics Spark Greek Financial Crisis?* Available at: http://news.yahoo.com/s/ap/20100603/ap_on_sp_ol/oly_athens_financial_crisis (accessed 3 June 2010).

Getz, D. (1997) *Event Management and Event Tourism*, New York: Cognizant.

——(2008) 'Event tourism: definition, evolution, and research', *Tourism Management* 29(3): 403–28.

Gnoth, J. and Anwar, S.A. (2000) 'New Zealand bets on event tourism', *Cornell Hotel and Restaurant Administration Quarterly* 41: 72–83.

Hall, C.M. (1992) *Hallmark Tourist Events: Impacts, Management, and Planning*, London: Belhaven.

Hall, K. (2009) 'World Cup a $1.25 boost', *Dominion Post*. Available at: www.stuff.co.nz/business/industries/2271271/World-Cup-a-1-25b-boo-s-t (accessed 7 June 2009).

Hastings, J., Selbie, J.A. and Gray, L.H. (1908) *Encyclopædia of Religion and Ethics*, Edinburgh: T. & T. Clark, pp. 335–7.

Higham, J.E.S. and Ritchie, B. (2001) 'The evolution of festivals and other events in rural southern New Zealand', *Event Management* 7: 39–49.

Hoffman, D., Beverland, M. and Rasmussen, M. (2001) 'The evolution of wine events in Australia and New Zealand: a proposed model', *International Journal of Wine Marketing* 13(1): 54–71.

Hubbert, J. (2010) 'Spectacular productions: community and commodity in the Beijing Olympics', *City and Society* 22(1): 119–42.

Jago, L., Chalip, L., Brown, G., Mules, T. and Ali, S. (2003) 'Building events into destination branding: insights from experts', *Event Management* 8(1): 3–14.

Katz, J. and Lai, C.-H. (2009) 'News blogging in cross-cultural contexts: a report on the struggle for voice', *Knowledge, Technology and Policy* 22(2): 95–107.

Keim, B. (2009) 'Designer babies: a right to choose', *Wired*. Available at: www.wired.com/wiredscience/2009/03/designerdebate (accessed 7 June 2010).

Kotler, P., Hamlin, M., Rein, I. and Haider, D. (2002) *Marketing Asian Places: Attracting Investment, Industry, and Tourism to Cities, States, and Nations*, Singapore: John Wiley and Sons.

Kurzweil, R. (2005) *The Singularity is Near*, New York: Penguin Books.

Levy, D (2007) *Love + Sex with Robots: The Evolution of Human-Robot Relationships*, New York: Harper Perennial.

Lindgren, M. and Bandhold, H. (2009) *Scenario Planning: The Link Between Future and Strategy*, Basingstoke: Palgrave Macmillan.

Lyon, C., Sato, Y., Saunders, J. and Nehaniv, C.L. (2009) 'What is needed for a robot to acquire grammar? Some underlying primitive mechanisms for the synthesis of linguistic ability', Working Paper. Available at: citeseerx.ist.psu.edu/viewdoc/download?doi (accessed 28 March 2010).

Miah, A (2004) *Genetically Modified Athletes*, London: Routledge.

New Zealand Tourism Strategy 2015 (2007) *New Zealand Tourism Strategy 2015*, Wellington: Ministry of Tourism, Tourism New Zealand, Tourism Industry Association New Zealand.

New Zealand Treasury (2009) *Challenges and Choices: New Zealand's Long Term Fiscal Statement*. Available at: www.treasury.govt.nz/government/longterm/fiscalposition/2009 (accessed 10 March 2010).

Nicholson, R. and Pearce, D.G. (2000) 'Who goes to events: a comparative analysis of the profile characteristics of visitors to four South Island events in New Zealand', *Journal of Vacation Marketing* 6(3): 236–53.

Peterson, W. (2009) 'The Singapore Arts Festival at thirty: going global, glocal, grobal', *Asian Theatre Journal*, 26(1), 111–34.

Picard, D. and Robinson, M. (2006) 'Remaking worlds: festivals, tourism and change', in D. Picard and M. Robinson (eds) *Festivals, Tourism and Social Change: Remaking Worlds*, Clevedon: Channel View Books, pp. 1–31.

Pine, J. (2004) *The Authentic Experience*, Montreal: Travel and Tourism Research Association.

Porter, M.E. (2004) *Competitive Advantage*, New York: Free Press.

Quinn, B. (2005) 'Arts festivals and the city', *Urban Studies* 42(5): 927–43.

Rein, I. and Shields, B. (2007) 'Place branding sports: strategies for differentiating emerging, transitional, negatively viewed and newly industrialised nations', *Place, Branding and Public Diplomacy* 3(1): 73–85.

Richards, G. and Palmer, R. (2010) *Eventful Cities: Cultural Management and Urban Revitalisation*, London: Butterworth-Heinneman.

Roberts, P. (2005) *The End of Oil: The Decline of the Petroleum Economy and the Rise of a New Energy*, New York: Bloomsbury.

Robertson, M. and Guerrier, Y. (1998) 'Events as entrepreneurial displays: Seville, Barcelona and Madrid', in D. Tyler, Y. Guerrier and M. Robertson (eds) *Managing Tourism in Cities: Policy, Process, and Practice*, Chichester: John Wiley and Sons, pp. 215–28.

Roche, M. (2000) *Mega-Events and Modernity: Olympics and Expos in the Growth of Global Culture*, London: Routledge.

Ryan, C., Smee, A., Murphy, S. and Getz, D. (1998) 'New Zealand events: a temporal and regional analysis', *Festival Management and Event Tourism* 5(1/2): 71–84.

Schwandt, T.A. (1994) 'Constructivist, interpretivist approaches to human inquiry', in N. Denzin and Y. Lincoln (eds) *Handbook of Qualitative Research*, London: Sage, pp. 118–37.

Talwar, R., Hancock, T., Yeomans, G. and Padgett, P. (2010) *Convention 2020 – The Future of Exhibitions, Meetings and Events*. Available at: http://Fastfuture.com (accessed 12 May, 2011).

Tepper, S.J. (2002) 'Creative assets and the changing economy', *Journal of Arts Management Law and Society* 32(2): 159–68.

Trendwatching (2008) *Trendwatching Yearly Report 2008*. Available at: www.trendwaching.com (accessed 23 May 2008).

van der Heijden, K., Bradfield, R., Burt, G., Cairns, G. and Wright, G. (2002) *The Sixth Sense: Accelerating Organisation Learning with Scenarios*, Chichester: Wiley.

Walton, J. (2008) 'Scanning beyond the horizon: exploring the ontological and epistemological basis for scenario planning', *Advances in Developing Human Resources* 10(2): 147–65.

Watters, E. (2003) *Urban Tribes*, New York: Bloomsbury.

Weinstein, D. and Weinstein, M.A. (1991) 'Georg Simmel: Sociological Flâneur Bricoleur', *Theory, Culture and Society* 8: 151–68.

Whitehead, G. (2005) 'Where are you going?', VisitScotland Futures Lectures, 13 September, Apex Hotel, Edinburgh.

Wilmott, M. and Nelson, W. (2003) *Complicated Lives: Sophisticated consumers, Intricate Lifestyles and Simple Solutions*, Chichester: John Wiley and Sons Ltd.

Wright, R.K. (2007) 'Planning for the great unknown: the challenge of promoting spectator-driven sports event tourism', *International Journal of Tourism Research* 9: 345–59.

Xu, X. (2006) 'Modernizing China in the Olympic spotlight', in J. Horne and W. Manzenreiter (eds) *Sports Mega-Events – Social Scientific Analyses of a Global Phenomenon*, Oxford: Blackwell, pp. 90–107.

Yeoman, I. (2008) *Tomorrow's Tourist – scenario and trends*, Oxford: Elsevier.

——(2011) *2050: Tomorrow's Tourism*, Bristol: Channel View.

Yeoman, I. and McMahon-Beattie, U. (2005) 'Developing a scenario planning process using a blank piece of paper', *Tourism and Hospitality Research* 5(3): 273–85.

Yuan, J.J., Cai, L.A., Morrison, A.M. and Linton, S. (2005) 'An analysis of wine festival attendees' motivations: a synergy of wine, travel and special events?', *Journal of Vacation Marketing* 11(1): 41–58.

Zhang, L. and Zhao, S.X. (2009) 'City branding and the Olympic effect: a case study of Beijing', *Cities* 26 (5): 245–54.

33

Retrospect and prospect

Stephen J. Page and Joanne Connell

Since the 1960s, our understanding of events has developed as different social science disciplines have expanded their interest in new phenomena such as events. One of the drivers of its growth and development is the considerable increase in disposable income in many households in the developed and developing worlds. However, gains in affluence have to be weighed up against greater time pressures for much of the working population, which has led to a demand for structured, high-quality experiences, such as events. In this respect, the experiences that events can offer to modern money-rich time-poor leisure consumers are a reflection of wider post-modern leisure and tourism production and consumption.

One of the consequences of this demand, alongside the recognition of positive impacts that events can yield for the economy and other aspects of social and political interest, has been the development of government strategies and funding, as many of the chapters in this book have shown. As the discussion of the introduction indicated, this has also been accompanied by the rise of a growing corporate recognition of the commercial power of events and the expansion of event management companies. One indication of the scale and significance of this growth is reflected in the UK exhibition/events industry which is worth £9.3 billion per annum. Alongside this has been a growth in the voluntary/community events sector with a corresponding public sector involvement reflected in the creation of national event strategies, as well as more destination-specific strategies that have identified and developed event portfolios and a requirement for an increase in public sector funding. One of the key functions that the public sector has taken up is the coordination of event services. However, as some of the chapters in this book have demonstrated, there has sometimes been an overstatement of economic arguments but seemingly less recognition of the importance of social and environmental outcomes.

As this book has shown, the categorisation of events and attempts to delineate the scope and extent of what is an event (and, likewise, what is not) remains an area of considerable debate. One element of this discussion derives from the sociological dimension where holidays and trips are deemed to be 'events' in social and psychological terms, even though an event in this context does not fit within the conventional terminology of a staged activity with an infrastructure and of temporary occurrence. This is one example of how the terminology we currently use may be expanding and developing across the social sciences to the point where there is a need for greater integration of these disparate and yet interconnected perspectives in the future. What is apparent from this book is that the chapters have encouraged a greater multidisciplinary debate among scholars in the field of Event Studies to review many of the past, present and future research agendas and discourse on specific themes. As the introduction indicated, the intention of this book was never to provide a checklist textbook format to review every topic which a student might possibly cover in a degree. To the contrary, the book has dispensed with such an approach and commissioned essays that review specific themes in detail to extend our knowledge of the subject, as opposed to simply synthesising much of the conventional wisdom. In this respect, the book achieves its stated aim to review many of the fast-changing themes in Event Studies and to provide a greater degree of intellectual leadership for an emerging subject area that is still in the classic growth stages of the product lifecycle and enjoying major success as more and more people sample the delights of the product.

This rapid growth has posed many important questions for the subject in relation to a number of key themes and questions, including:

- What is the subject's identity after many years of profound growth?
- What are the main drivers of the research activity and how can the status of its research efforts be better elevated to the standing of many of its parent subjects?
- How can significant practitioner impact and influence be better translated into academic recognition and development?
- What are the major research topics and questions for the future?

These are major questions which this conclusion will seek to address, to provoke a greater debate amongst the academy to raise the status of the subject.

What is the identity of Events Studies in the new millennium and its research impact?

It is interesting to reflect back on the comparatively niched and specialised nature of event research in the 1970s and 1980s, marked in the 1990s by the foundation of the journal *Event Management* and the formative influence of many of the key scholars contributing to this volume (e.g. Ritchie, Getz, Jago, Hall) who have had a considerable impact on the development of the subject. Yet as the subject has expanded in educational terms, it is perhaps a fair assessment that the majority of institutions offering the subject are primarily teaching-oriented, where research assumes a lower priority. This is not intended as a criticism but is reminiscent of the situation in which Tourism Studies found itself during the 1980s (not least in the UK) where its rapid expansion required a vast amount of effort and curriculum development, resource production and systems to deliver emerging subjects to large numbers of students, as Fidgeon (2010) highlighted in the case of the UK. The situation was not dissimilar in many other countries, as key players in the subject areas of Tourism, Sport, Leisure and Recreation will attest. This initial expansionary phase of a popular and high-volume student recruitment area naturally saw research activity limited to key individuals, established research centres and clusters of researchers.

Event Studies has now moved out of that rapid expansionary phase in some institutions and research activity is now becoming a hallmark of some programmes, especially as postgraduate education has now developed. Perhaps controversially, one could argue that master's programmes should be underpinned by higher-level research activity in the subject so that they offer a true staircasing of educational programmes, from certificate to PhD, that have staff appropriately qualified and active in the academy. However, Event Studies has still some way to go until it can achieve this laudable objective, which has impacted upon its image as a subject:

many PhD-qualified staff are not from the events field (mainly as it is still a relatively new area) and the numbers of events PhDs are limited. Many staff in the academy are still pursuing their own higher degrees or have entered from an industry setting, drawing many parallels with the situation in Tourism in the 1980s, where the expansion of higher education drew upon staff with master's degrees (sometimes with only bachelor degrees) and many registered for doctorates. This does impact upon the image of the subject area vis-à-vis the more traditional subjects, where a doctorate plus publications is the entry level requirement and non-PhD-qualified staff are the exception rather than the rule.

This development cycle for new subject areas follows a typical pattern mirrored in many subjects since the vast expansion of higher education globally in the 1960s, including many in the business and marketing areas. Yet there are also very good arguments for having non-PhD-qualified staff teaching and researching events if they bring invaluable industry perspectives, experience and credibility to the programme, given that many graduates will work in this area and need these skills to develop fulfilling careers. It is perhaps even more critical than in the parent subjects from where Event Studies have grown, where their academic maturity has now seen the development of world-class research output and corresponding academic journals of repute. A recent journal-ranking event held at the University of Bournemouth in April 2010 highlighted the issue of what type of identity and position the subject held in the UK academy of researchers: an active researcher pointed out that while Tourism as a subject has a range of well-rated journals in which to publish, the event subject does not have this identity and position – there are no rated journals on the UK Association of Business School list. The consequence, as some researchers suggested, is that one needs to publish in non-event journals to 'get rated'. Of course, this is somewhat counterproductive to the longer-term development of the subject and its academic reputation, particularly if researchers do not have an identifiable community of specialist journals. We enter a chicken and egg situation where the journals will not get rated as they do not attract the top-rated researchers seeking high citations and prominence, therefore compounding the problem that the journals do not get highly rated. Herein lies the identity issue facing the development of Event Studies, as many of the research efforts are being published across a wide range of journals. A recent article by Getz (2007) exemplifies this dilemma: it is a review of the subject area and has been one of the top downloads for the journal *Tourism Management* and yet it is not published in a mainstream event journal.

While critics of this argument point to the growing sophistication of the literature-searching software to enable quicker and simplified acquisition of research studies, this does not solve the problem of identity facing the subject. The research effort is being dissipated as it is scattered across the social sciences from management-focused journals through to more esoteric social science outlets as epitomised by the seminal review by Connell and Page (2010). One response has been the formation of new journals (e.g. the International Journal of Event and Festival Management launched in 2010) to try and raise the profile and to develop a journal which is research-oriented and able to get a higher rating, but this is a lengthy process and the evidence of the niche Tourism journal the *Journal of Sustainable Tourism* on the ABS list epitomises the problem: the journal is well respected by its peers since its establishment in the early 1990s but it receives the lowest rating as a niche, compared to longer-established and more generic journals. Some critics have pointed to Event Studies as a niche within a niche (i.e. it has evolved from a niche subject that took off in the 1980s and has now evolved as a new niche). Evidence from the database *LeisureTourism* in November found that 4.5 per cent of the 107,000 articles listed in its abstracts database had the term 'events' listed, which might support the specialist nature of the subject in relation to its parent subjects of Tourism, Leisure and Sport. What the subject needs is a mainstream academic publisher with a global impact and high usage through the electronic platforms now in use, with a major drive forward to commission the best scholarship in the field to map out and set the research agenda that receives international acclaim.

Arguably, the need for this Handbook confirms the absence of this major impact to date (with some exceptions, such as Getz's 2007 article) and with a number of smaller, less visible and highly rated journals, the more career-oriented and impact-driven academics are targeting the higher-rated journals outside of the immediate event subject, where such contributions are accommodated. While there are some parallels with the situation in the subject areas of Tourism and Sport in the 1980s, what is now different is the greater attention to research-rating exercises that are differentiating between what the academy and rating bodies agree as high-quality and lower-quality journals. This is certainly a major impediment to the subject developing an international research identity alongside its parent subject areas, and in part reflects the failure of the publishers with the existing journals to make the necessary investment in time and effort to get the journals rated and to get them higher up the ladder of academic acceptance.

Practitioner research and elevating its impact

A review of the nature of event research published by the academy across the last twenty years is characterised by a great diversity of research perspectives. One consequence of this diversity is the substantial contribution made by researchers in terms of practitioner research to event evaluation, policy formulation and analysis and event development. However, it is important to acknowledge the wider context in which research has developed in Event Studies, primarily emerging as a teaching-based subject in colleges and universities with a focus on skills development and training for industry and often incorporating professional accreditation. It has retained this essential role for practitioners but has successfully expanded its scope, position and remit from one primarily oriented at a practitioner market. Through the development of academic research and creation of knowledge via publications, especially research journals and textbooks, the subject has melded academic and practitioner interests effectively given the applied nature of research and its contribution to knowledge transfer. This relatively strong relationship is a hallmark of the research activity that has a greater industry reach for many of the reasons already outlined and by its highly practical nature (i.e. events are occurrences that are a temporary phenomenon) and as such require consistent monitoring, evaluation and review to ensure they are appropriate to their target audiences, meet the objectives they set out to fulfil and meet with the sponsor and customers' needs.

Consequently, industry-focused research has a large role to play in the development of Event Studies as a subject and may sometimes filter through to academic publications with a strong intellectual rationale and conceptual framework, and sometimes without this. As researchers with experience of a number of these projects, it is apparent to us that clients are less interested in the intellectual background to the project and more interested in the results and implications for solving a problem or for future event development and investment needs. This illustrates the problem of working with policy-makers and organisations that do not necessarily employ staff with a detailed background or understanding of events as phenomena. Clients often put restrictions on the nature of the research data generated and how it can be used, and so high-quality research never sees the light of day. Where such practitioner research is publishable, it offers unique insights that many academic studies will never be able to shed on real issues and the intricacies of why decisions are made and the rationale for hosting events and for specific outcomes. The challenge for the academy is to develop lasting and mutual industry relationships where the sharing of research data and outcomes can be published, but there is always a concern about the implications for competing destinations gaining competitive advantage from the data.

A useful rule of thumb is that data is embargoed for a set period of time and then publishable once the advantage has been seized by the client. It is evident that even commercial research companies are mining the academic research in this area as it can offer many useful insights, case studies and examples of best practice, a purpose for which, in an age of industry engagement and impact for academic researchers, event research is almost tailor-made. However, it is the brave academic researcher who seeks to rest their future evaluation on a piece of practitioner research and its impact as a major output, as this is not always the view of those people assessing the research outputs who have an agenda, sometimes to diminish the quality of the subject area *per se* as well as the outputs. This is the unfortunate politics of a competitive research-funding environment where innovation and success may look too good and extend further than the assessors feel comfortable. Yet there is a need for the practitioner research to receive a much higher recognition than it currently receives and for better conversion into good-quality peer-reviewed research outputs aimed at the academy.

Research themes of the future

Whilst there is not space within a review such as this to list all the potential research directions which event research may pursue in the future, we wish to focus on three specific areas: the visitor experience and technological advances; risk management; and the sustainability agenda. Many of the other themes one might identify have been discussed in detail in many of the chapters but we now identify briefly the specific areas where greater academic research can be blended with practitioner priorities and efforts to create value in the knowledge transfer process.

In terms of technological advances, there is a growing awareness of the significance of event-staging opportunities that can develop the experiential effects which may create the 'wow factor' and provide a fulfilling event experience. With the growing academic research on the experience economy, marketing research on co-creation and value, then this is one important area for interdisciplinary research that can not only expand the notion of the visitor experience but also aid the better development of measurement tools. The different chapters in this book on event design and staging, the psychology of events and how areas have been redeveloped with an events focus clearly show the potential for further research and conceptualisation. For example, the work by Evans on the night-time economy and events is one such important area for further development, as the sensual and emotional responses to events are certainly different in a night-time setting where moods and feelings change and the senses are stimulated in a different manner. Understanding these psychological attributes of the experience in varying environments will also enable research findings and studies to feed into management systems designed to enhance the experiential elements of the event. There is also a growing importance of technology such as social networking and, as Page (2011: 206) suggests,

> A major revolution has occurred in internet use by consumers, namely the rise of Web 2.0 technology. Since around 2004, Web 2.0 has revolutionised how the second generation of web-based communities and hosted sites have evolved to allow interaction, information sharing and collaboration among users … The web technologies associated with Web 2.0 have led to the use of weblogs (commonly called blogs), where entries are displayed in reverse chronological order and where content can be added including commentary, news, images and links to other blogs, web pages and other forms of media such as music-based blogs (mp3 blogs) and audio-based 'podcasts'.

These developments are particularly important for visual stimuli and the visitor experience since they allow events to communicate with customers, and for customers to reflect upon and share their experiences with others, making this a powerful word-of-mouth marketing tool. The web also allows events to share event-related material via SMS and to offer real-time information.

An important area not dealt with in this book which has developed as a key element of event design, management and experiences is that of risk management. There is certainly scope for a greater degree of academic research with an interdisciplinary approach to examine risk management processes and plans for events and to begin a greater research effort on the way risk assessment is evaluated alongside the growing concerns about security risks, especially terrorism at major events. This is all the more important in view of the fact that such experiences depend upon a stable and safe environment for participants and spectators if events are to continue to be fuelled by economic growth and increases in leisure spending. This will not occur if the perception of attendance is shrouded in major terrorist threats and concerns. Such stability and safety is essential for events to be recognised and embedded as elements of contemporary life in a post-modern society. Academic research which works in parallel with industry developments, legislative changes and health and safety regulations, and with the less tangible aspects of audience and participant perceptions, has an important role to play as we move further into a period of instability and potential threat, as well as the growing development and use of mega-arenas for events, which despite many tragedies over time still pose a range of hazards to spectators.

The last area which is witnessing increased attention and review is the issue of the greening of events, as part of the wider sustainability debate associated with tourism and leisure activities. While we have broached the issue of sustainability and events earlier in the book, it remains a largely neglected area of research that has not really embraced the thinking of sustainability across the entire supply chain and how green events can be designed so that they are planned, organised and staged to minimise negative environmental impacts. We would not suggest that events have a deliberate impact on the environment but that impacts arise largely because organisers have not traditionally considered issues of environmental performance. Contrary to this, of course, there are some notable events where the green message is a core part of the celebration (e.g. fair trade events, green charity events, and music and community-based festivals) or where significant attention has been given to environmental impact (e.g. UNEP's first paperless meeting in 2008, the Glastonbury Music Festival and Broadway's Tony Awards) although, as part of the many thousands of events held annually across the world, such events form a small proportion. If one accepts that many events are an element of wider tourism activity, then the relative contribution to climate change and other environmental impacts must be acknowledged, managed and mitigated. It is accepted that many festival and event organisers, venues and destinations need to improve environmental performance, not only to reduce negative impacts and maximise benefits at the local level but also to assist governments in reaching carbon reduction targets, as recognised by UNEP/ICLEI in its guidelines published in 2009 for greening events. Many are actively engaged in this process already (see Roper 2006) but the future challenge is to find practical ways to reduce the associated impacts of events at both local and global scales and across the whole spectrum of events. Since the Lillehammer Winter Olympics (1994) and the emerging environmental agenda set out in Olympic bids from around the early 1990s, priorities have gradually shifted to incorporate environmental principles and technologies more widely in mega-event planning. However, we would argue that more research is required around the whole issue of legacy planning, with much greater emphasis on evaluation processes to ensure major events result in positive outcomes for the host community and local environment, i.e. leave something of future utility for an area and its people.

The wider sustainability debate now impacting on most areas of consumer activity has seen a growing focus on climate neutrality, and for the events industry this relates to reducing greenhouse gas emissions that arise from hosting an event and compensating for unavoidable emissions through purchasing carbon offsets (UNEP/ICLEI 2009). Indeed, studies that have identified the emissions and waste produced from specific events present horrifying statistics, which might make us reflect on the consumptive nature of events as an intensive human activity, and how such a phenomenon can be justified in a world of decreasing environmental resources. Academic research, working with industry bodies, has a key role to play in the use and evaluation of practical tools, such as event carbon calculators, greening guidelines, footprinting devices and offsetting schemes, and more conceptually, how (or if) such initiatives really compensate for environmental impacts at source. What is apparent is that at an industry level, the environmental footprint of events is gaining world-wide attention and momentum in terms of understanding how it can be reduced. This growing interest offers many possible avenues for greater knowledge transfer and applied research and, clearly, greening events is a developing area of practice and policy with which event researchers and managers need to engage as part of the wider political agenda.

Certainly, as more critical research indicates, the tangible and intangible benefits of events often remain surprisingly unclear, open to challenge and debate. In relation to improving the environmental performance of events, as with research in tourism and hospitality on green business-related initiatives and schemes, the equivalent research in events has considerable scope for development to assess and understand how principles are translated into operation. Innovative research that focuses specifically on the greening of events would make a welcome contribution to the academy, particularly on the themes of minimising consumption and waste, maximising local and community stakeholder benefits, procurement processes and meaningful monitoring, as well as the perceived and actual benefits of greening events. Understanding how an optimal balance of environmental-based decision-making and commercial goals might be achieved could form a fruitful area of inquiry for both academic and practitioner interests. Perhaps more crucially in an age of event planning where legacies form the bedrock of billion-pound event bids, the real benefits that events generate must be more critically evaluated to go beyond the gloss of the public relations efforts painted by well-meaning bid teams.

Final words

The publication of this Handbook arrives at an exciting point in the development of events as an academic subject, as many of the chapters herein indicate and as this concluding chapter has further emphasised. It is evident that the challenges set by creating, hosting, staging and managing the whole process of event management are complex and require significant skill, knowledge and understanding to derive benefits for economies and communities, and meet what are often multifarious objectives, aside from more obvious commercial aims. Central to this is the existence of a sound and rigorous, yet dynamic, body of knowledge that has the ability to deepen understanding of issues, concepts and problems in the events sector, particularly in a policy context where decision-making can be enhanced for the benefit of achieving wider goals through events. In an era where the links between the utility of higher education, academic research outputs and benefits to wider society, event research is arguably well placed to achieve some modest prominence as a valuable area of academic research and knowledge transfer.

References

Connell, J. and Page, S.J. (eds) (2010) *Event Tourism. Critical Concepts in Tourism*, four-volume collection, London: Routledge.

Fidgeon, P.R. (2010) 'Tourism education and curriculum design: a time for consolidation and review?', *Tourism Management* 31(6): 699–723.

Getz, D. (2007) *Event Studies: Theory, Research and Policy for Planned Events*, Oxford: Butterworth-Heinemann.

Page, S.J. (2011) *Tourism Management*, Elsevier: Oxford, fourth edition.

Roper, T. (2006) 'Producing environmentally sustainable Olympic Games and "greening" major public events', *Global Urban Development* 2(1): 1–5.

UNEP/ICLEI (2009) *Green Meeting Guide 2009*. Available at: www.iclei-europe.org/index.php?id=greening

Index

LIBRARY, UNIVERSITY OF CHESTER